THE BUILDINGS OF ENGLAND

JOINT EDITORS: NIKOLAUS PEVSNER
AND JUDY NAIRN

NORTHAMPTONSHIRE

NIKOLAUS PEVSNER

REVISED BY BRIDGET CHERRY

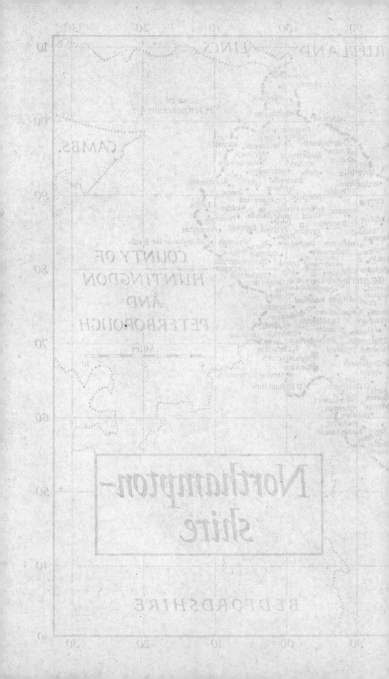

THE BUILDINGS OF ENGLAND

Northamptonshire

BY

NIKOLAUS PEVSNER

★

REVISED BY
BRIDGET CHERRY

WITH CONTRIBUTIONS
FROM SIR GYLES ISHAM
AND BRUCE BAILEY

PENGUIN BOOKS

Penguin Books Ltd, Harmondsworth, Middlesex, England
Penguin Books Inc., 7110 Ambassador Road, Baltimore, Maryland 21207, U.S.A.
Penguin Books Australia Ltd, Ringwood, Victoria, Australia

—

First published 1961
Second edition, extensively revised, 1973

—

ISBN 0 14 071022 1

—

Copyright © Nikolaus Pevsner, 1961, and
Nikolaus Pevsner and Bridget Cherry, 1973

—

Made and printed in Great Britain
by William Clowes & Sons, Limited, London, Beccles and Colchester
Photogravure plates by D. H. Greaves Ltd, Scarborough
Set in Monotype Plantin

FOR
MARGARET KASTAN

CONTENTS

9

Map References

*

The numbers printed in italic type in the margin against the place names in the gazetteer of the book indicate the position of the place in question on the index map (pages 2-3), which is divided into sections by the 10-kilometre reference lines of the National Grid. The reference given here omits the two initial letters (formerly numbers) which in a full grid reference refer to the 100-kilometre squares into which the country is divided. The first two numbers indicate the *western* boundary, and the last two the *southern* boundary, of the 10-kilometre square in which the place in question is situated. For example, Kettering (reference 8070) will be found in the 10-kilometre square bounded by grid lines 80 and 90 on the *west* and 70 and 80 on the *south*; Oundle (reference 0080) in the square bounded by grid lines 00 and 10 on the *west* and 80 and 90 on the *south*.

The map contains all those places, whether towns, villages, or isolated buildings, which are the subject of separate entries in the text.

FOREWORD TO THE FIRST EDITION

My thanks are due in the first place to Mrs Bonney (then Miss Helen Thomas), who prepared the county for me, read all that could be got hold of, arranged it with exemplary care, travelled and saw for herself, and helped me in every respect; in the second place to Mrs Ian Bailey, who was in charge of all the intricate and irritating work of organization before and after my journeys; and in the third to my wife, who drove with me through the county like an overworked taxi chauffeur without limited working hours or free Sundays. Next in the order of thanks come all those incumbents who have answered questions I had put to them and later read proofs, and all those owners of houses who put up with my visit, extended hospitality to us, and again consented to reply to intricate questions or questionnaires. Among them I must single out with special gratitude Sir Gyles Isham and Earl Spencer. To these names I hasten to add those of Mr V. Hatley of the Northampton Public Library, Mr P. I. King, the County Archivist, and Mr Bruce Bailey of the Northampton Public Library. Mr Megaw provided the entries on prehistory and Roman antiquities, Mr D. J. C. King the entries on motte-and-bailey castles, Mr Terence Miller the passages on geology in the Introduction, and Miss Sheila Gibson the drawings in the text, and I am grateful to all four of them for their work. The Ministry of Housing and Local Government (here abbreviated MHLG) have a statutory duty to draw up lists of buildings of architectural or historic interest and have again very kindly put at my disposal the lists compiled by the Chief Investigator and his staff. For the districts not covered yet by the Ministry my most valuable source of information as regards secular architecture was the National Buildings Record (NBR). Their photographer in Northamptonshire, Mr G. B. Mason, must be considered the pioneer investigator in those districts. As in all previous volumes the late H. S. Goodhart-Rendel allowed me the use of his lists of Victorian churches and Sir Thomas Kendrick the use of his lists of Victorian glass (they are marked GR and TK in the gazetteer). In connexion with prehistoric and Roman archaeology Mr Megaw would like to thank as usual the Director General, Ordnance Survey, and the Ministry of Works Inspectorate of Ancient Monuments for much useful information, as well as Mr A. L. F. Rivet for his advice on Iron Age monuments. Miss Joan Liversidge and Miss Clare I. Fell have offered much healthy criticism.

Among those who helped in more specific ways I want to record my gratitude to the Rev. P. J. M. Bryan for forgiving me, Miss H. D. Parker of the Wellingborough Public Library for information on Wellingborough, the Rev. K. F. Plummer for information on Grafton Regis, the Rev. C. E. Glynne Jones and Mr A. C. Sewter for help with the William Morris glass in the county, and Mr E. Croft-Murray for allowing me the use of the proofs of his forthcoming book on decorative painting.

The principles on which the following gazetteer is founded are the same as in the twenty-one volumes of The Buildings of England *which precede it. I have myself seen everything that I describe. Where this is not the case the information obtained by other means is placed in brackets. Information ought to be as complete as the space of the volume permits for churches prior to c. 1830 and all town houses, manor houses, and country houses of more than purely local interest. Movable furnishings are not included in secular buildings, though they are in churches. Exceptions to the latter rule are bells, hatchments, chests, chairs, plain fonts, and altar tables. Royal arms, coffin lids with foliate crosses, and brasses of post-Reformation date are mentioned occasionally, church plate of after 1830 only rarely. Village crosses are omitted where only a plain base or a stump of the shaft survives. As for churches and chapels of after 1830, I had to make a selection, and this is dictated by architectural value or by significance otherwise in the light of architectural history. The same applies to secular buildings of the C19 and C20.*

Finally, as in all previous volumes, it is necessary to end the foreword to this with an appeal to all users to draw my attention to errors and omissions.

*

The publication of this volume has been made possible by a grant from the Leverhulme Trust to cover all the necessary research work and by generous contributions from Messrs Arthur Guinness, Son & Company Ltd and Messrs ABC Television Ltd.

FOREWORD TO THE SECOND EDITION

The most dramatic change in the second edition is the result of a change of boundaries. The Soke of Peterborough is now attached to Huntingdonshire and consequently twenty-nine entries on places in this area which appeared in the first edition of Northamptonshire *were reprinted in* 1968 *in the volume on* Bedfordshire and Huntingdonshire.* *Their omission here has meant the loss of approximately sixty pages of the gazeteer and nineteen illustrations (for which others have been substituted), and because of the importance of such buildings as Peterborough Cathedral, the churches of Barnack and Castor, and Burghley House and Thorpe Hall as exemplars of their periods, has entailed some rearrangement of the Introduction.*

The other alterations are of two types. Firstly, factual errors have been corrected and new information included. Secondly, to bring the book up to date it has been necessary to record the architectural changes of the last ten years. The most notable new buildings are mentioned in the Postscript to the Introduction (p. 71). *The more depressing changes can be summarized here. First must come the ravaging of Northampton, only partly the result of the expansion of the town, for the destruction began already c.* 1960 *with the demolition of the late* C17 *Peacock Hotel, the key building of the Market Square.‡*

To a lesser extent similar changes are occurring in the smaller towns: Wellingborough has lost its C19 *Corn Exchange, Daventry a worthwhile* C17 *building in the High Street, and the* C19 *Police Station, and in both these towns and in Kettering redevelopment schemes threaten other buildings. In the country less has disappeared:*

---

* I.e. Ailsworth, Bainton, Barnack, Burghley House, Castor, Deeping Gate, Etton, Eye, Glinton, Helpston, Lolham, Longthorpe, Marholm, Maxey, Milton, Northborough, Paston, Peakirk, Peterborough, Sutton, Thorpe Hall, Ufford, Upton (near Sutton), Walcot Hall, Walton, Wansford, Werrington, Wittering, Woodcroft Castle. (Newborough, Oxney, and Thornhaugh were by mistake omitted from *Bedfordshire and Huntingdonshire*, but will appear in the second edition.)

‡ Other buildings in Northampton mentioned in the first edition and now demolished include: 21 Kingsthorpe High Street (*c.* 1700), Spencer Hotel, Horsemarket (C18), Waterloo House, Market Square (*c.* 1830), St Andrew's church (*E. F. Law*, 1841–2), Victoria Dispensary, Albion Place (*G. H. Willcox*, 1844), Royal Insurance, Parade (*E. F. Law*, 1850), St John's Station (*A. Milne*, 1872), Rheinfelden, Billing Road (*Godwin*, 1876), Masonic Hall, Princess Street (*Ingman & Shaw*, 1889), Baptist Church, Princess Street (*Dyer*, 1890).

Arthingworth Manor (C18), *Gayton House* (C18 *and* 1874), *Whittlebury Lodge* (Burn, 1865), *Collingtree Grange* (E. F. Law, 1875), *Ashby St Ledgers* N *wing* (Lutyens, 1924),* *and the remains of the C18 Fineshade Abbey are the most notable losses. But other buildings, including several of great interest, are threatened or derelict: part of Dingley Hall, Ecton Hall, Fawsley Hall, Guilsborough Grammar School,‡ Stanwick Rectory, part of Weedon barracks. The number of churches disused or threatened with redundancy has increased (All Saints Aldwinkle, Claycoton, Furtho, Holdenby, Newton-in-the-Willows, Preston Deanery). Finally the disappearance of railway stations (e.g. Thrapston) should be noted (see also p. 69 n).*

However, against this record must be set the much more satisfying one of buildings carefully restored or converted, for example at Althorp, Deene Park, Lamport, Rockingham Castle, Rushden Hall, and Stoke Park, the restoration of buildings in Oundle by Oundle School, the improvements to Daventry High Street, the preservation of the Priest's House at Easton-on-the-Hill, the work on the wall paintings in Passenham and Slapton churches, and there is much else that has been done. Two enterprising conversions deserve a special note: the transformation of a school into a youth club at Wellingborough (by the County Architect, John Goff) and the use of the redundant church at Orton as a training centre for stone-masons.

This second list testifies to an encouraging amount of local interest and enthusiasm for Northamptonshire architecture, further proved by the most generous help given by so many people in the county, which made the revision work both interesting and enjoyable. First of all I must record the very special debt which the book owes to Sir Gyles Isham and to Mr Bruce Bailey. They most generously put at my disposal vast quantities of unpublished material, and made detailed studies of many buildings specially for this book. Their names or initials in the text indicate their most important work, but I should mention here for example Sir Gyles Isham's investigations at Ashby St Ledgers, East Haddon, and Rockingham, Mr Bailey's at Deene and Upton Hall. Mr Bailey also supplied many new details about the work of E. F. Law, and about buildings in Northampton. I also want to thank especially all the owners of houses who supplied new information. I am particularly grateful

---

* An example of the now frequent removal of impractical service wings. The conversion of stables for other purposes (e.g. Delapré, Grendon, Haselbech) is another sign of the times.

‡ There are plans for converting this.

to Earl Spencer for many details about Althorp and other places. I should in addition mention the help I have received from Mr A. Révai on Stoke Park, and from Sir Michael Culme-Seymour and Commander Saunders-Watson on Rockingham Castle. I am very grateful too to Mr John Goff, the County Architect, for information on work by his department, and for numerous other details. Many people kindly contributed information on their local areas or their special interests – I am indebted to them all, in particular to Mr A. S. Ireson of the Men of the Stones, who undertook much checking in the NE part of the county, Mr James Murdoch, Miss H. Parker of Wellingborough Public Library, Mr D. Bond of Daventry Public Library, Mr Alan Cox of Abington Museum, Miss J. M. Swann of Northampton Museum, Canon C. M. Cockin and Mr J. Milton (Oundle), Mr J. Morris (Brackley), Mr T. Ireson and Mr J. M. Steane (Kettering), Canon Methuen Clarke, Canon J. L. Cartwright, and the Rev J. Gordon Cox.

Moreover, thanks are due to all the other users of the book, who have sent in for this volume (as they have for so many others) long lists of corrections and additions, especially Mr M. R. Airs, Mr Alec Clifton-Taylor, Mr H. M. Colvin, Mr J. P. Godwin, Dr A. Gomme, Mr G. Hamilton, Mr R. Hubbuck, Mr T. C. Lees, Mr J. Newman, Mr H. V. Molesworth-Roberts, Dr D. M. Palliser, and Mr J. G. Rushman. Mr Richard Marks (RM) supplied us with a definitive list of medieval stained glass in the county, Mr Paul Thompson with information on Butterfield, Mr Nicholas Taylor with information on Lutyens, Mr Brian Davison helped with the account of excavations at Sulgrave, Mr G. Spain gave us details on Victorian architecture. The Trustees of the Bedford Settled Estates kindly allowed me to quote from the correspondence of the Duchess of Marlborough (p. 78 n).

The revision of prehistoric and Roman entries was undertaken by Mr Nigel Sunter, who received much help from Mr Robert Moore of Northampton Museum. Mrs M. Mouat gave much valuable secretarial help. The map was redrawn by Miss Joan Emerson.

Finally a note on how all these alterations have been incorporated. Minor factual corrections or additions have been made without comment. For more extensive changes the source of information has been indicated. Other additions, unless they are in brackets, are the result of my own visits. I should end by putting on record that I have throughout received help and advice from Sir Nikolaus Pevsner, but that the final responsibility for the changes to the book is mine. Once again corrections and additions will be welcome.

B.C.

INTRODUCTION

To say that Northamptonshire is the county of squires and spires is not very original, but it is true all the same. Squires – that means that Northamptonshire is not only, as Camden put it, 'passing well furnish'd with noblemen's and gentlemen's houses', but that the nobility and gentry not only possess them but live in them, that many of these houses have remained in the same family for centuries, and that consequently the families belong as much to the houses as the houses to the families. The county is far enough from London to avoid developments which would make it less attractive to continue residence and near enough to London to make continued residence possible even in the twentieth century.* So much for squires; spires do not need much comment, and what architectural comment is necessary will bemade later. Spires predominate in the E of the county but are rare in the w. This is connected with the fact that the E is the stone region, the w the brick and timber region.

Northamptonshire is altogether clearly divided into regions, first geological, secondly according to the influences exerted by adjoining counties. Before the Soke of Peterborough was transferred to Huntingdonshire, Northamptonshire bordered on more counties than any other in England, nine in all (Buckinghamshire, Bedfordshire, Huntingdonshire, Cambridgeshire, Lincolnshire, Rutland, Leicestershire, Warwickshire, Oxfordshire), and it partakes of the Home Counties character, the East Anglian and Lincolnshire character, and the Midland character, without however – it must be admitted – enjoying any of the memorable scenic qualities one may connect with some of them. The traveller is not going to visit Northamptonshire for its landscape. Its beauty spots are few. There is no coast nor a

---

* It is very gratifying to see how many of the major houses are being carefully kept up. Among the families that have been in residence for centuries there are e.g. the Montagus at Boughton, the Ishams at Lamport, the Spencers at Althorp, the Comptons at Castle Ashby, the Brudenells at Deene. In other cases newcomers look after the houses equally exemplarily (e.g. at Cottesbrooke and Stoke Park). Yet other houses have been acquired by the state and are being used in different ways (Kirby, Rushton). Only a few of the great and famous houses have been demolished, and these not recently. Holdenby was pulled down in 1651, Pytchley in 1824. For recent developments *see* p. 14.

spectacular range of hills.* Northamptonshire, if sought out at
all, will be sought out for its buildings. That makes it such a
rewarding county, as far as this series of books is concerned –
rewarding, though it has no old cathedral and no big city. The
nearest cathedral town, Peterborough, is now outside the county,
and Peterborough was made a cathedral only in 1541. Northampton until recently had little more than 100,000 inhabitants. It is
a county of small towns ‡ and unforgettable villages and of
country houses from the largest to the smallest. In the houses
and the churches there is perpetual surprise and there are for
the architectural historian perpetual puzzles.§ The houses are
decidedly weaker for the early than for the later centuries. They
culminate, one is inclined to say, in the Elizabethan age, but
do not lose interest to the end of the Georgian era. The churches
on the other hand keep up an extremely high level of interest from
the Early Saxon centuries to the C14 and then begin to weaken.

But before this architectural history can be traced, a few pages
must be devoted to the soil from which building grows and to
the, on the whole less important, periods which precede the
Saxon. The rocks of Northamptonshire are comparatively young
in the GEOLOGICAL sense, lying between the Coal Measures
and Archaean strata of Warwickshire and Leicestershire to the
W, and the chalklands of East Anglia and the Thames valley to
E and S. Moreover the geological structure of Northamptonshire
is exceedingly simple: a succession of thin sheets of rock inclined
very gently to the SE, like a set of playing-cards collapsed on a
table, so that the lowest, oldest strata outcrop on the W side of
the county, and the uppermost, youngest ones on the E. Where
river-valleys have been cut down, particularly in E Northamptonshire – Nene, Ise, Tove, Ouse – the oldest formations are exposed in the river banks, and the others in succession upwards
on to the high ground. Thus at Higham Ferrers the valley floor
is cut in the Lower Jurassic Lias formation, the slope to the E
in Middle Jurassic, and finally on the top of the hill, towards the
county boundary on the road to Kimbolton, the Upper Jurassic
Oxford Clay appears. This same sequence of rock groups is laid

---

* The highest point is on the W border towards Warwickshire: 804 ft
near Arbury.

‡ Corby 49,000, Kettering 40,000, Wellingborough nearly 38,000 (1970).
But these, and Northampton as well, are now expanding rapidly. But in total
population (461,410 in 1970) Northamptonshire is still only thirtieth of the
English counties.

§ To the student the following are specially recommended as tests: Raunds
and Rushden, Rothwell and Polebrook, Tansor and Woodford.

out across the county in river-dissected strips elongated SW to NE with the oldest along the W border.

The relatively high ground (c. 500 ft) that runs from the Cherwell valley through Daventry and Naseby and the hills above Market Harborough is formed either directly or indirectly by the hard Middle Lias ironstone or Marlstone which is quarried near Banbury in Oxfordshire and forms the steep scarp of Edge Hill. Both below (Lower Lias) and above (Upper Lias), the rocks are mainly clay or clayey limestone ('cementstone') in thin bands. In the next formation above the Lias, the Northamptonshire Sand and Ironstone group, although a good deal of clay is still present, the most important unit is the brown sandy calcareous rock (a handsome dark bluish-green when freshly quarried underground) with clusters of fossil shells, which is worked in the Corby-Wellingborough orefield. In places, on the same stratal level, the ironstone is almost completely replaced by loose grey and white sands.

S of a line running across the county through Naseby to Kettering, and thence NE to Oundle, the Northamptonshire Ironstone is followed directly by clays and clayey limestones and finally by the creamy oölitic shelly and rubbly limestones of the Great Oölite group and the Cornbrash limestone. N of the line, a wedge of another limestone is interposed between the Ironstone and the Great Oölite – the Lincolnshire Limestone, which begins in Northamptonshire and stretches up eastern England as far as the Humber.

The Lincolnshire Limestone, known by a variety of local names, is perhaps the most famous of all English freestones, more famous even than Bath Stone. It has been quarried from the earliest recorded times, in the Soke of Peterborough and Northamptonshire as Barnack, Weldon, and King's Cliffe stone, in Rutland as Ketton stone, and from scores of other quarries. It is a pale-weathering buff, pink, or pale-grey limestone, full of broken sea-shells and shell-débris, sometimes oölitic and cross-bedded. It is equivalent to the Inferior Oölite of the Cotswolds. The base of the formation, in a small area between Deene in Northamptonshire and Stamford, is occupied by the Collyweston 'Slate'. This is not a true slate in the geological sense, but a thin-bedded sandy micaceous limestone that happens to split easily into slabs formerly much used for roofing. Blocks of the rock (still worked on a small scale) are quarried and then stood up on end for a winter's frost to split them. The slabs can be seen on many college roofs in Cambridge. A very similar rock, the Stonesfield Slate, is found at the base of the Great Oölite Limestone in Oxfordshire, and is to be seen on many Oxford roofs. Both rocks are very fossiliferous, Collyweston having plant remains, fish teeth, and scales, and Stonesfield, in addition, mammalian and saurian bones.

The upper valley-sides and watershed of the l. bank of the Ouse below Higham Ferrers are formed in the youngest of Northamptonshire's 'solid' rocks (i.e. not counting the glacial deposits that lie in patches all over the county) – the Upper Jurassic Oxford Clay. This clay is quarried for brickmaking on an enormous scale in Buckinghamshire, Bedfordshire, and Huntingdonshire, and especially around Peterborough, but hardly at all in Northants. It is a grey or brownish clay, with large fossil oysters which weather out and lie on the surface in arable fields. It is one of the trio of clay formations that lie below the Fens, and a traveller from the ironstone, sand, and limestone country of, say, Rockingham Forest, towards Peterborough, will easily notice the difference between landscapes based on clay and non-clay foundations.

There is thus no lack of good building material in Northamptonshire; in fact there is almost an embarrassment, and the various stones have been sent in all directions beyond the county borders. There is the warm gingerbread Marlstone in the w, from Chipping Warden and Sulgrave N by Market Harborough, and a similar stone from the ironstone areas of the centre of the county; there is the paler, rather bleached-looking stone from the Oölite formations about Brackley and Towcester; and finally there are the splendid freestones of Weldon, Glendon, Wansford, and King's Cliffe, and in the Soke of Peterborough the 'hills and holes of Barnack'. From these quarries stone was sent in Saxon times down the river to Peterborough, later to Ely, Bury, and Cambridge, and to almost every church or abbey in East Anglia.*

And now to archaeology. Although the pre-Saxon period can boast few visible sites of great interest, the county's finds range back to man's earliest occupation of the Midlands. In the PREHISTORIC period much of the county was probably covered with dense forest, and this remained so well into historical times. Rockingham Forest today stands as a poor shadow of its original self. However, the Jurassic ridge, extending from the Cotswolds along Banbury Lane to the SW and running out of the county by

* On local building stone see J. M. Steane, in *Northants Past and Present*, IV, 2, 1967–8

Stamford, links Somerset with the Yorkshire wolds, and was one natural route of major importance which declined only with the creation of the Roman road system and the making of the Fosse Way as a military boundary and route from the SW to the Humber.

In the Palaeolithic period a few pear-shaped flint hand axes in the 'Acheulian' tradition and a few flake tools from the gravels of the Nene valley set the stage for the continuing pattern of riverine settlement. All the county has to show for the intermediate hunter-fisher groups of the mesolithic are a few hundred 'microliths' or miniature flint blades, and many of the cores from which they were made, from the neighbourhood of Duston. Finds of several hundred leaf-shaped arrowheads and stone axeheads in the county indicate the presence from about 4000 B.C. of the Neolithic farming and herding communities who had made their way across from the continent. The several thousand flints found at Duston suggest that this was the site of a Neolithic settlement; at Milton Ferry a Neolithic bowl was dredged from the Nene, and at Aldwinkle a Neolithic burial has been found. Lyman's Hill, Pitsford, is the sole (though doubtful) example of a Neolithic long barrow.

A group of late Neolithic cultures, formed from the aboriginal Neolithic population and its contact with the newly arriving Beaker people, is known from the finds made in a series of shallow pits in gravel workings on the E outskirts of Peterborough. One of the main features of the culture is the coarse 'Peterborough' pottery which, with its impressed decoration, is mainly restricted to the S and E of Britain. It includes as a developed form a flat-based overhanging rimmed jar named 'Fengate'* ware, and this is the ancestor of the 'cinerary urns' of the Bronze Age.

Just before 2000 B.C. the warrior-traders from the mouth of the Rhine, named after their characteristic pottery the 'Beaker folk', whose arrival heralded the introduction of copper (which was soon followed by the use of bronze), penetrated into Northamptonshire along the Nene and its tributaries. Their overlap with the Peterborough culture is illustrated by the large number of beaker sherds found at Fengate. They went in for single burials as shown in the county by flat graves such as the 'lounger-and-stretcher' inhumation which contained a fine flint copy of a tanged metal dagger and a local British necked type of beaker found at Norton in 1862, and by the skeleton in the

---

* Fengate is in fact the name of the district of Peterborough in which the settlement is sited.

more usual crouched position found probably associated with a three-riveted bronze dagger at Corby. A second flint dagger with a quartzite axe-hammer was discovered beneath a round barrow s of Newark. Both the latter represent introductions from another Rhineland element (the corded-ware-using 'battle-axe' people). Barrow burial remained a prominent feature of the Early Bronze Age proper, which followed on the Beaker phase. In one of three barrows at Eye (Soke of Peterborough) a type of bowl with impressed decoration recalling the Peterborough tradition and termed a 'food vessel' was found, and such always indicate influence from the Yorkshire extension of the flourishing trader-chieftains of the 'Wessex' culture of about 2000 – 1500 B.C. A number of barrows are situated along the Jurassic ridge, especially in the NE; many have been destroyed by ironstone workings, particularly around Corby, Rothwell, and Desborough. The cinerary urn which developed from Fengate ware, occurs in flat grave cemeteries (six at the Corby site already mentioned and a number from Fengate) and under barrows (two at Oundle). Finds of metal are rare, but more common towards the end of the Bronze Age, largely in the form of hoards; however, these need not detain us here. By the close of the second millennium B.C. burial was in flat cremation cemeteries; one such has been discovered at Chapel Brampton.

Round about 500 B.C. new arrivals introduced the knowledge of iron working from the Hallstatt cultures of the continent into Britain. It is at this point that Fengate comes into the picture again; here, on the edge of the fenland basin (made uninhabitable due to a rise in sea level), a gravel promontory on the N bank of the Nene at its point of entry into the Fens became the site for an undefended farming settlement consisting of some thirty pits (perhaps for grain storage) spread over a wide area and overlaying the earlier Bronze Age community. Apart from such finds as saddle querns, a bronze disc-headed pin with swan's neck iron stem, 'situla'-shaped pots based on metal prototypes, and usually undecorated tall amphora forms point to an origin in the Hallstatt groups of the Low Countries. In time this latter type of pot gave place to less angular types. Bronze brooches of Hallstatt form from Castor must also be connected with this movement. A small flat-bottomed dug-out found beside the Nene at Peterborough may also belong to this period. Somewhat later, in the C4 B.C., settlers spread W to the upland zone. The construction of the Hunsbury hill-fort, overlooking the crossing of the river Nene just below Northampton, seems to have followed a simple iron-smelting group. The pottery from the fort, which begins with smooth-profiled pots of the later Fengate type, is remarkable for the fine burnished and incised bowls decorated with curvilinear geometric designs which reflect forms first introduced into southern Britain by the later La Tène immigrants from N France. In the first century B.C. a large number of rotary querns of Derbyshire or Leicestershire grit were possibly being distributed from the site for export to the corn-growing communities. The iron 'currency bars' of sword-like outlines from Hunsbury and near by, and also the quality of workmanship of the sword scabbards and mountings with their fine curvilinear and matting designs, suggest the presence and local patronage of a chieftain and his household during the first century B.C. At the S end of the county Rainsborough Camp, beside the Jurassic Way, yielded a fine C I A.D. harness fitting(?) with enamelled 'lyre' pattern. The Desborough mirror (now in the British Museum) is an outstanding example of Iron Age workmanship dating to the period immediately before the Roman conquest, with its typical Celtic adaptation of the classical palmette and lyre patterns. Near by was found a curvilinear decorated bowl. In central Northamptonshire lies the ironworkers' upland settlement of Draughton, where a little more decorated pottery similar to the Hunsbury material was found within an oval ditch and bank.*

At the beginning of the C I B.C. a new group of tribes from N France, the Belgae, overran S England. Cunobelin, son of Tasciovanus the chieftain of the Catuvellauni who had established a tribal centre near St Albans, continued a policy of aggrandisement by seizing Camulodunum (Colchester; *see Buildings of England: Essex*, p. 130) from the Trinovantes. Northamptonshire, except for the N part, was also incorporated in the territory of the Catuvellauni, probably early in the C I A.D.; evidence for Belgic settlement comes from Duston and Irchester together with burials and much later Roman material – and remains of huts have been found beneath the Roman villa at Mileoak Farm, Towcester. Very few Belgic finds have been made within the hill-forts, which seem to have fallen into disuse. Gold coins of the Catuvellauni were found at several places; some of Cunobelin at Duston, and one of the Iceni at Castor in the Soke of Peterborough. To the N lay the territory of the non-Belgic Coritani with their capital at Leicester, and it was this tribe, together with the Iceni of East Anglia, who, realizing

* The site was destroyed in building the airfield in 1943.

that the Romans of the Claudian conquest were not a relief
from the years of Belgic dominance, made an unsuccessful stand
against the legions about A.D. 47–8. The Romans drew the military
line between the Severn and the Trent, along the Fosse Way.
Imperial high-handedness and private greed led to the second,
much more serious uprising of the Iceni under Boudicca, who,
together with the Trinovantes, sacked Camulodunum in A.D. 60–
61 and cut to pieces the relieving force of the Ninth Legion sent
from their headquarters at Lindum (Lincoln). They pressed on
to raze first Verulamium and then Londinium, and were stopped
only when the governor Suetonius Paulinus, after a forced
march, defeated them at a site which may well have lain within
the Northampton region.

All this is only a preliminary to Northamptonshire's important
position under the ROMANS. After they had defeated Boudicca,
their first and most important task was the establishment of a
system of communications. Watling Street, which enters the
county on an alignment from Stony Stratford, links the posting
station of Magiovinium (Dropshort; *see Buildings of England:
Buckinghamshire*, p. 189) with the small defended settlement at
Lactodorum (Towcester). Here the road changes direction
slightly and makes for the junction at Venonae (High Cross,
Leicestershire; *see Buildings of England: Leicestershire and Rutland*, p. 120). On its way it passes another settlement at Bannaventa (Whilton Lodge). This is regarded by some as a
candidate for the birthplace of St Patrick. At the junction with
the lane to Norton a link road led SE to the extensive settlement
at Duston which succeeded that of the Belgae. From the small
Roman town of Irchester near Wellingborough a road ran due
S to Dungee Corner, Bedfordshire. Most of this route is still
clearly marked by a green lane. To the SW a link road between
Akeman Street at Alcester, Oxfordshire, and Towcester leads
from a more or less due N–S alignment commencing in Stowe
Park, Buckinghamshire (*see Buildings of England: Buckinghamshire*, p. 17). At the NE edge of the county Ermine Street forms
the main route which runs across the Nene from the walled
settlement of Durobrivae, 'the fort by the bridge' (the Castles,
Water Newton, Huntingdonshire) just on the S side of the river.
The crossing was marked by a bridge of stone and timber
recorded as late as 1715. The road then runs through the Soke
of Peterborough, swinging slightly to the NW at Barnack, and
crosses the Welland just W of Stamford. Stukely in 1776
recorded its make-up in Burghley Park. The next alignment

comes at Great Casterton, Rutland (*see Buildings of England: Leicestershire and Rutland*, p. 300). From a presumed point just N of the Nene crossing King Street ran as a W alternative to the main route, which it rejoined at Causennae (Ancaster, Lincolnshire); it was perhaps planned to connect with the Car Dyke, the major Roman waterway, which passed close by at Bourne, just over the border. The Fen road, entering the Soke E from Cambridgeshire, can just be picked up in Milton Park, though it may well have passed close to the Fengate settlement on its way from Whittlesey, Cambridgeshire. At any rate it crosses King Street at Upton, and must have continued to link up with Ermine Street. From Sutton Cross (Soke of Peterborough) on Ermine Street, just NW of a temporary fort,* a branch road is traceable through Wansford to King's Cliffe. It may have been intended to continue on to Ratae Coritanorum (Leicester). From the presumed S junction with King Street at Castor station another westerly branch road from Ermine Street led to Thrapston, crossing the Nene NE of Water Newton village; it may have extended through Ailsworth to the Fen road. Excavation at Aldwinkle revealed a Roman timber bridge showing several phases of reconstruction or renovation and probably dating back to the C1 A.D. Also passing through Thrapston, a S link between Ermine Street and the Fosse Way at Ratae is formed by a road which enters the county from the intersection at Alconbury and is clearly traceable as the traditional Gartree Road. This runs NW from just S of Corby to cross the Welland. The importance of the industrial Castor area (in the Soke of Peterborough), which must originally have caused the westward movement from the Fengate area, is underlined by a group of minor roads.

So much for communications. The major walled settlements at Irchester, Lactodorum, and Bannaventa have already been mentioned. Blacklands, Kings Sutton, seems to have been another settlement of importance near the Jurassic Way. It was probably linked southwards to Alcester and Akeman Street. At Lactodorum we have evidence of Roman occupation of the C1–2 A.D., succeeding the native settlement. The site was first fortified in the late C2.

The C1 was a time of prosperity and settlement. The simple early phases of several of the large villas such as that at Great

---

* Mention may be made here of a tile with the stamp of the Twentieth Legion, found at the settlement in the angle between Ermine Street and King Street at Lawn Wood, Bainton (Soke of Peterborough).

Weldon belong to this phase. In the s large villas, with their
attendant outbuildings and bath-houses, are at Cosgrove and
Deanshanger in the vicinity of Watling Street. The villa within
the hill-fort on Borough Hill may have been built in association
with the growing iron workings. Industries altogether deserve a
few words. The quarries at Barnack in the Soke were producing
stone for building and those at Collyweston slate for roofing
(Irchester and Apethorpe). At Kettering a large settlement was
exploiting the ironstone deposits and at Duston the amount of
metalwork also proclaims a flourishing industry. During the
C I and C2 there was a widespread pottery industry in the Nene
Valley consisting of small centres. In the C2 this became more
centralized, with Castor in the Soke the most important,
especially around the area of Normangate Field. Ecton became
the centre for the upper valleys.

Rich people certainly there were. This is proved by such fine
mosaic floors as the two squares found at Cotterstock, Glapthorn
(recorded in 1736 and 1798 respectively and found with coins of
Vespasian), and the polychrome square discovered in 1699 at
Horestone Meadow, Nether Heyford, and destroyed in 1780.
Many settlements flourished well into the C4. After domestic
buildings, those for religious purposes must be considered.
The group of rectangular, circular, and polygonal buildings
excavated in Collyweston Great Wood were most probably
shrines, dating from the C2 to the C4. At Brigstock two shrines,
one circular and one polygonal, were constructed in the C3 and
continued in use until the late C4.

The end of the Roman settlement in Northamptonshire does
not seem on the whole to have been a violent one; however villas
fell into gradual disrepair. The hoard from Nobottle contains a
large number of post-Constantinian coins, and the rampart of
Lactodorum some time in the C4 fell into the ditch, not to be
rebuilt until medieval times.

In the pre-Christian SAXON PERIOD, when Northamptonshire lay in the s of Mercia, cemeteries such as those at Marston
St Lawrence, Badby, and Norton tell of infiltration by the old
routes and some settlement along the favoured uplands. Occasional finds of fine metalwork indicate the main areas of origin:
saucer brooches from Marston make Rhineland origin probable;
a fine circular disc brooch of bronze and gold from Hardingstone
with a centre setting and fish motif and outer animal interlace
recalls the so-called 'Jutish' material from the cemetery at
Faversham, Kent. Within the burial enclosure E of Desborough

church a woman's grave contained a necklace of gold and garnets with a central cross, also of Kentish workmanship. On the other hand, the old rite of cremation survived in the burial under a barrow at Barton Seagrave found with a shield boss, glass beads, cruciform brooches, and a large amount of pottery. A second barrow, in Cow Meadow, Northampton, produced two pots and a disc brooch. However, there is nothing of structural importance to note before the construction of the great Saxon churches which represent part of the county's richest architectural heritage.

Under the Anglo-Saxons Northamptonshire belonged to Mercia. The foundation of Peterborough Abbey was due to Peada, son of King Penda. In the C9 the county was overrun by the Danes and incorporated in their territory, the Danelaw. Place-names ending in -by, such as the Ashbys or Naseby, are Danish. Northamptonshire is uncommonly rich in ANGLO-SAXON REMAINS of the first order. Brixworth must stand at 21 the beginning of any survey. As it was in all probability founded and built as early as *c.*675, it is the largest and most orderly surviving building of its date N of the Alps. It was built with much Roman brick, used in the voussoirs of arches in a technically uninformed way. It has regular N and S arcades with tall and wide openings. Some of these definitely gave into porticus, i.e. separate side-chambers, rather than aisles. The chancel was divided from the nave by tripartite arcading, just as it had been done a little earlier at Reculver in Kent and Bradwell in Essex. The E end was a polygonal apse, a Syrian form, existing however in Italy (e.g. at Ravenna) as early as the C6. This apse was surrounded, shortly after it had been built, by a sunk, tunnel-vaulted passage forming what one now calls an outer crypt. Semicircular passages below the apse, i.e. real crypts, had been built in Rome about 600 and taken over in countries N of the Alps. Outer crypts have only recently been recognized for what they are, thanks mainly to excavations in Germany after the Second World War. Carolingian Cologne e.g. possessed one; but none that we know of is as early as Brixworth. At the w end Brixworth had a two-storeyed porch comparable e.g. to the one at Monkwearmouth in the North and, like that, later converted into a w tower. There are several other important Anglo-Saxon towers in Northamptonshire. Brigstock and Brixworth have a rounded 4 projection from the w wall, the latter containing a newel staircase. Arcading with pilasters and triangle-heads ran along the exterior of the nave at Geddington. At Green's Norton is a triangular-headed Anglo-Saxon window in the E wall of the nave above the chancel arch, and there is some more minor Anglo-Saxon evidence, as there also is in other Northamptonshire churches (e.g. at Moulton, Nassington, Pattishall, Stowe-Nine-Churches, and Tansor).* One more major work of Anglo-Saxon architecture must be added: the tower at Earls Barton. Like Barnack, this is one of the most spectacular examples of the Late Saxon passion for a matchstick-like decoration of outer surfaces by lesenes or pilaster-strips and arches and triangles of the same unmoulded rectangular section. Lesenes stand on arches quite unconcerned with the structural sense of the arch and the lesene. Structural motifs are converted into pure decoration. The tower is large and broad and stands at the w end of the church. It was wider than the part which followed to the e, and it has therefore been assumed that this part was the chancel and that the tower represented the nave and not a w attachment to the nave. There is however no indication of a w porch.‡

ANGLO-SAXON SCULPTURE is as well represented in the county. The most important pieces now lie outside the county. These are the Hedda Stone at Peterborough Cathedral, which is assigned to the late c7, and belongs together stylistically with a stone at Fletton outside Peterborough, a stone at Castor, and some of the work at Breedon-on-the-Hill in Leicestershire. The fine, if small, slab with the Eagle of St John at Brixworth may be of c. 800 and makes one regret that not more is preserved. Fragments of Anglo-Saxon crosses are abundant (Brixworth, Desborough, Lutton, Mears Ashby, Moreton Pinkney, Moulton, Nassington, Northampton St Peter, Stowe-Nine-Churches), but none is of the first order.§

The NORMAN STYLE is essentially a style of clear demarcations, as is the Romanesque style everywhere in Europe – that Romanesque style of which the Norman is the English national variety. However, with the exclusion of Peterborough from Northamptonshire, the county no longer possesses a major Norman church. The county is on the whole singularly poor in MONASTIC REMAINS, too, though it should not be forgotten that the great Benedictine houses of Croyland and Thorney are only just across the border. Moreover, of the abbeys and priories

---

* Two of the most interesting churches in the area, Barnack and Wittering, lie in the Soke of Peterborough, and so are no longer in the county.

‡ Excavations have recently revealed an interesting example of ANGLO-SAXON SECULAR ARCHITECTURE: the Hall at Sulgrave.

§ Emphatically not of the first order, though curious enough to look at, is the small Saxon stone at Dallington, Northampton.

which existed in Northamptonshire hardly anything has come down to our century. A list will bear that out. The admirable book by Professor Knowles and Mr R. Neville Hadcock in the new edition of 1971, and excluding the Soke of Peterborough, counts two houses for Benedictine monks and one for nuns, two Cluniac houses for monks and one for nuns (the former including St Andrew Northampton which has totally disappeared), one Cistercian house for monks (Pipewell, which has also totally disappeared) and two for nuns, six houses of Augustinian canons (including St James Northampton and Fineshade) and one for canonesses, two Premonstratensian houses (including Sulby), two houses of the Knights Hospitallers (including Dingley), and six houses of the mendicant orders at Northampton (Dominican, Franciscan, Franciscan nuns, Carmelite, Austin, and Sack).* Of all this no more need be singled out here than the probably recognizable plan of Delapré (Cluniac nuns) outside Northampton and the C13 W front and W end of Canons Ashby (Augustinian canons).

At Peterborough‡ the abbey was founded *c.* 650. What is above ground all dates from after the fire of 1116. The chancel with its wide apse, accompanied by the side apses of the chancel aisles, which ended externally in straight walls, was built between 1118 and *c.* 1150, the nave and aisles in the second half of the C12. The style is therefore High and Late not Early Norman. The zigzag as a decorative enrichment e.g. appears from the outset. So does the motif of alternating circular and polygonal piers, a motif accepted widely only in the late C12 and early C13. Especially precocious is the use of zigzag at r. angles to the wall surface, which begins at Peterborough about 1130 or 1135 at the latest and is as a rule a sign of Late Norman date. The capitals on the other hand still have heavy scallops at first, and the arches heavy roll mouldings. The system of elevation is that almost universally adopted in Anglo-Norman major architecture: arcade, spacious gallery, clerestory with inner wall passage, flat ceiling. The ensemble is tall, forceful, and consistent.

With the exclusion from the county not only of Peterborough, but also of the spectacularly decorated church at Castor, a

---

* In addition there were the ambitious collegiate foundations of Cotterstock (1338), Irthlingborough (1388), Fotheringhay (1411), Higham Ferrers (1422), and All Saints Northampton (1460), as well as a number of hospitals.

‡ Although Peterborough Cathedral is no longer in the county, its importance, as the only surviving major medieval building in the area, and one to which reasonably precise dates can be given, is such that references to it cannot be excluded from this Introduction.

survey of NORMAN CHURCHES has to begin with the two very
impressive but exceptional examples in Northampton, Holy
Sepulchre and St Peter, the former early to late C12, the latter
of *c.* 1150–60. Holy Sepulchre, though only a parish church,
is one of the few medieval round churches of England, St Peter
is startlingly lavish (perhaps because of its proximity to the former
castle of Northampton) and exhibits a motif usual in cathedrals,
but highly unusual in parish churches: namely alternation of
supports. Morever – an equally unusual motif – there are shafts
reaching right up to the roof to support the principal beams. The
capitals are of many varieties, and there are in addition an extremely sumptuous tower arch – one of the many Norman
arches in the county which, whether tower arch, crossing arch,
or chancel arch, cannot here be enumerated – and a precious
fragment of a sculpturally quite forceful sepulchral slab. This
is mid C12, the figured tympanum at Holy Sepulchre is early
C12. Of other tympana Barton Seagrave has an ill-assembled
one, and the tympanum at Pitsford is stylistically significant in
that the figure of St George on the horse and the dragon are ready,
it seems, at any moment to tail off into ornamental interlace. But
Northamptonshire has on the whole little of Norman architectural sculpture. At Wakerley there are historiated capitals by
the workshop from Castor in the Soke of Peterborough.

Of Norman architecture there is more. St Giles Northampton
was a cruciform church, so probably was King's Cliffe, and so
was Twywell, which is to this day essentially a Norman building.
The cruciform plan can be regarded as the most usual Norman
plan, although it has in later centuries often been abolished or
disguised, either by removing the crossing and its tower or by
removing the transepts or by widening aisles until their walls
were flush with those of the transepts. Crossing towers could carry
bells. Sometimes there was a central tower without transepts, as
at Barton Seagrave. In other cases w towers were built.
St Peter Northampton and Spratton are two specially ornate
examples. The motif used for enrichment is blank arcading, as
it was also used inside the building, e.g. in the aisles at Peterborough and the chancels of Earls Barton and Kings Sutton.
Where village churches were very small, already the Norman
age replaced towers for the bells by simple bellcotes. Three
early examples survive in the Soke of Peterborough: Peakirk,
Northborough, and Werrington.*

Returning to NORMAN SCULPTURE there is more figure-

---

* Deanshanger and Sutton Bassett are somewhat later.

work to be found on FONTS. As in all English counties, fonts
were preserved more faithfully than any other objects, and
so Northamptonshire still possesses well over a dozen worthwhile Norman examples. They were the work of the masons
of the churches, as is proved by that remarkable inscription at Little Billing (Outer Northampton) which commemorates 34
Wigberthus artifex atque caementarius. As for scenes carved on
fonts, at West Haddon is the Baptism of Christ, the Nativity, 35
the Entry into Jerusalem, and Christ in Glory. Braybrooke is an
example of how absurd an arrangement of figures the Norman
carver and his clients were ready to tolerate. The font at Crick 36
rests on three kneeling figures, an Italian motif, less surprising
if one remembers the North Italian influences noticeable in the
Norman sculpture of Ely Cathedral. Many more fonts have
ornamental decoration only, ranging from simple and repetitive
intersected arcading, perhaps with an additional trail of foliage
(St James Brackley, East Haddon), or lunettes with some
stylized leaf enrichment (Paulerspury, Tiffield, Weedon Lois),
to complicated, crazily entangled patterns (Harpole).

Besides fonts it is DOORWAYS which were often preserved
and even re-erected when the rest of a wall or a church was
remodelled. We do not know the reasons for this. Was it respect
for elaborate carving? One would like to think so; for much
loving care was lavished on the jambs and arches of doorways.
Many of them of course are naive and lacking in accomplish-
ment. As a rule they belong to the later rather than the earlier
C12. Ornamental motifs are the ubiquitous zigzag, again frequently used at r. angles to the surface as well as on it. If such
zigzags meet at the angle the impression is of lozenges broken
round the angle. As far as figure-work goes the motif of the beakhead and allied motifs can be found here and there (Earls Barton,
Pitsford, Roade), though not often. Perhaps the most sumptuous 5
doorway is that of Castle Ashby, and here a late date is proved
instructively by the use side by side of the Norman motif of
zigzag and the E.E. motif of the dog-tooth.

In such cases the use of the term TRANSITIONAL is fully
justified. Northamptonshire has plenty of interesting instances
of the many ways in which the transition from Norman to E.E.
could be effected. They can be studied most profitably in the
ARCADES between nave and aisles. The hallmark of the C12 is
the circular pier with the square abacus.* At Gretton for instance

* An exception is the piers at Moulton, which are square with four demi-
shafts, a shape more frequent from *c.* 1200 onwards – *see* below.

it appears in the N arcade with scalloped capitals and round arches with roll mouldings, i.e. at the Peterborough stage.
22 The details are paralleled at Duddington. They are all still completely Norman. The Transitional can then make itself felt in a variety of ways. The keeling of shafts is one (vestry Peterborough, together with still scalloped capitals), the replacement of the scalloped by the waterleaf capital (Peterborough, W end of nave, c. 1175; Pilton waterleaf side by side with dog-tooth), and then the crocket capital (Polebrook, N arcade, also together with dog-tooth) and the stiff-leaf capital (Peterborough W transept, boss, i.e. c. 1200), the replacement of the square by the octagonal and then the circular abacus (the latter already at Holy Sepulchre Northampton and then at Grendon and Woodford), and the replacement of the round by the pointed arch (Peterborough W transept). The latter however came sometimes very late (cf. Leicestershire and Rutland). Thus the W doorways of Peterborough are still round-arched, though in a wholly E.E. ensemble, and at Barnwell Castle round-headed doorways exist of as late a date as the 1260s, perhaps because they appeared a safer, more solid form than the pointed arch. Similarly bell-openings of towers right into the late C13 often have twin pointed arches under one round arch. The details of the arches are of importance too. They develop from the unmoulded section of the Early Norman style by way of the heavy roll mouldings of Peterborough to a single-step section, slight chamfers, and finally the full double-chamfer which remained standard through the C13 and was still in use in the C14 and C15, when no special elaboration was aimed at. When the C13 wanted to be elaborate it could design the most complex mouldings with fine but strong rolls and deep hollows. Exact dating within the stages between Norman and E.E. is impossible. All that can be said is that by the arrival of the early C13 the EARLY ENGLISH STYLE was complete.

There is plenty of evidence of the C13 in the county, both major and minor. Major first of all the W front of Peterborough, complete, we can assume, by 1238. This was the outcome of much changing of minds, and if the layman's vision of the E.E. style is one of serene harmony, a glance at the Peterborough façade is enough to act as a reminder for ever of what degree of discordance the C13 in England was ready to accept. In the
8 famous W tower of Raunds, where no changes of plan need be assumed, the design is also far from harmonious, and it would be hard to suggest what made the master mason choose this rest-

less arrangement of motifs. He was obviously not satisfied with
the simple blank arcading continued from Norman precedent in
such towers as those of Brackley St James, Burton Latimer,
Caldecott, Higham Ferrers, Mears Ashby, Moreton Pinkney,
Stanwick, and Wadenhoe. He desired something livelier even at
the expense of jettisoning logic.

The tower of Raunds is crowned by a broach spire, and so
we have arrived at a first form of Northamptonshire SPIRES.*
Broaches perhaps need an explanation. They are a device to link
a square tower with an octagonal spire. The four broaches are a
more or less steep pyramid, remaining a fragment because
penetrated by the spire. Of the lower part of the spire proper
only the four cardinal sides start at once. They begin in the
middles of the sides of the pyramid. The relation of pyramid,
i.e. broaches, to spire proper can vary from very large to very
small broaches, and from a moderate steepness of the spire to
needle-thinness. At Raunds e.g. the broaches are tall, at Warmington, at Barnwell, and at Pilton they are small and low. The
variation in outline caused by the proportions of broaches to
whole spire must be studied in the field. Generally speaking the
tower with broach spire tends to have a blunt, direct, unsophisti-
cated character. Not all towers, of course, received their spires
at once. Often one can trace a development through a century
and more from the lower parts of the tower to the spire. Some
few towers were finished by saddleback roofs and have preserved
them (Cold Higham, Maidford, Rothersthorpe, Wadenhoe).

Among the parish churches of Northamptonshire the most
beautifully and unifiedly E.E. is Warmington. Polebrook is as 27 & 1
consistently E.E. but lacks unity. Hargrave is on a smaller scale.
Warmington has the very rare distinction – rare in English
parish churches – of a rib-vault over the nave, even if that vault
is made of timber, not of stone. The usual thing in England is
the open timber roof or the flat ceiling concealing the structural
timber. Of such Peterborough possesses the most precious
example in the country and one of the most precious in Europe;
for the nave ceiling here was painted with ornament and figures
about 1220. On a smaller scale C13 stone vaulting was occasionally used, e.g. in the porches at Warmington and Woodford.‡
They have blank arcading too, and this over-played motif is

* Two of the earliest are in the Soke of Peterborough: Barnack and Etton.
Barnack, of the early C13, is one of the earliest in the country. It has low
broaches with tall pinnacles, and the spire is low too.
‡ Also in the Dec style at Finedon and – with ridge ribs – Ringstead.

also to be found – admittedly an effective display – in the porch at Great Weldon, the N transept at Polebrook, and the chancels of Cogenhoe, Denford, and Newton Bromswold (Dec).

The C13 churches of Northamptonshire have naves accompanied by aisles, with one delightful exception, the extremely rare case of the unaisled, two-naved church of Hannington with its beautiful tall circular piers. The circular pier is one of the accepted C13 types, though more frequent at the beginning than the end. The C13 innovation is the quatrefoil pier, and this is used more often than can be listed. But other freer forms also occur already in the early C13, notably the alternating circular and square piers, both with demi-shafts at Rothwell,* and the piers with big keeled shafts in the diagonals and thin coupled shafts in the cardinal directions at Brafield. Rothwell, which is the largest parish church in the county, was followed by others, and so the circular pier with the demi-shafts is met at Loddington and Welford, the square pier with demi-shafts at Burton Latimer, and with the addition of fillets on the shafts in the former Infirmary of Peterborough Abbey, where the date is c. 1250–60. Another variant is the pier of four shafts and four hollows, which became standard in the Perp style, and which occurs in the tower arch at Higham Ferrers‡ and, strangely enough, set (or re-set) diagonally, at Cogenhoe. The date here is before 1281. The quatrefoil pier also appears with thin rectangular shafts in the diagonals and fillets at Brackley St James, and the extravagant multiplication of shafts – groups of three in each of the cardinal directions – at Rothersthorpe, Flore, and Great Billing (Outer Northampton) leads into the C14.

The quatrefoil was used as a blank ornamental motif too (e.g. in the tower of Raunds) and as a shape for clerestory windows (e.g. at Geddington), again leading into the C14. So far nothing has been said about windows altogether. Here again the transition from Norman to E.E. is fluid. The step from the slender round-headed to the slender pointed, or lancet, window was taken at various moments in various places. The lancet then remained the accepted shape for the major part of the C13.§ Plate tracery in the form of a quatrefoil or a trefoil or a lozenge

* Cf. the C12 incidence of the latter form at Moulton, *see* footnote on p. 31.

‡ The same motif also occurs even earlier in the N porch of Wells Cathedral.

§ Square-headed windows are not entirely absent, but very rare. Geddington is a case in point.

pierced into the spandrel below two arches, e.g. of the bell-openings in a tower, is frequent and nowhere exactly datable. Bar tracery introduced into England from France at Westminster Abbey *c.* 1245–50 appears some time *c.* 1260–70 at Peterborough in the s transept and in many places later, often in conjunction with less pure details in other windows. Already in the Peterborough transept the details are no longer quite pure, and a leaning towards variety and surprise can be felt which was going to destroy the E.E. style and establish the Dec. Of characteristic late C13 tracery forms Peterborough has much of the type with three or five stepped lancet lights under one tall two-centred arch. Y-tracery incidentally occurs as early as the first third of the century in the w porch of Peterborough, though in the county, as in all England, it was not accepted until *c.* 1275–80. Pointed-trefoiled lights, an enrichment first to be seen in the Sainte Chapelle in Paris in the mid forties and in England immediately after in the cloister of Westminster Abbey *c.* 1250–60, also entered the area quickly. The church at Longthorpe in the Soke of Peterborough where they occur can be dated as begun in 1263–4. This is a remarkably early adoption.

Northamptonshire in the C13 was certainly in close touch with events in the centre. That is shown most impressively in the w 7 tower of Higham Ferrers and its porch and sculpture. The carvers who worked on it must have come from Westminster Abbey, an offshoot of the mid-C13 lodge there, and, as so much at the Abbey is over-restored or restored away, Higham Ferrers is of great national importance for an understanding of E.E. sculpture. There is nothing else in the county to compare with it, though the exquisite carving in Purbeck marble on the plinth of the *trumeau* inside the Peterborough w porch, the equally exquisite carving of the horizontally placed figures on the capitals at Cottingham, and the larger and more summarily treated figures 29 outside the Abbot's Gate at Peterborough and the w tower of Brackley St Peter – comparable with the sculpture of Wells – would deserve to be better known than they are.

The porch which houses most of the Higham Ferrers sculpture is unusually shallow. The shallow w porch is a feature in Northamptonshire. It occurs at Raunds, Rushden, and Oundle. Ornamental sculpture of the C13 culminates in the foliage commonly called stiff-leaf. In Northamptonshire capitals there is much of the earlier type with upright leaves not venturing into too high a degree of detachment (e.g. Rothwell). Richer, of the mid C13 and specially beautiful, are the stiff-leaf capitals in the s range of the cloister at Peterborough and its portal. Another portal worth singling out is that of the w front of Canons Ashby priory church. Stiff-leaf also plays round the rare cross head with the Crucifixus at Rothersthorpe and over the surfaces of such a c13 FONT as that of Peterborough Cathedral.* Towards the end of the century foliage turns away from the conventions of stiff-leaf towards a more naturalistic and more varied interpretation of leaves. Of this Northamptonshire has no outstanding example. Where naturalistic leaves occur, they belong to the late c13.

At that time the transition from E.E. to DECORATED was complete. The motif which marks this momentous change is the ogee curve. The earliest ogee arches in England date from the years immediately after 1290 and were devised by the masons and carvers of the king's court. Northamptonshire received a share of these important pioneer pieces because it was crossed by the funeral cortège of Queen Eleanor, which in the winter of 1290–1 moved from Harby in Nottinghamshire to London and was in the next few years commemorated by a number of tall crosses, or rather polygonal pillars carrying crosses, which were erected where the sad procession had halted for the night. There
68 is one at Hardingstone just outside Northampton and another
67 at Geddington. The ogee motif is by no means prominent, but other motifs also show the change from the clarity and generous spacing of the E.E. decoration to the complexity, the crowding, and the delectable confusion of the Dec. Thus e.g. the use of the triangle instead of the octagon at Geddington is significant. It leads the eye round the pillar more easily, because there are fewer planes in the cardinal directions inviting the eye to halt. The sculptural style of the figures of the queen also, compared with that of the mid-c13 figures mentioned above, is less articulate and readier for an undulating play of surfaces or such details as the rippling hem of a mantle. In foliage the same change can be watched, though a little later. The naturalistic leaf is replaced by a more generally undulating, bossy or nobbly leaf, comparable (accidentally) with some kinds of seaweed.

It is in window tracery however that the change is most marked. By degrees what had been a harmonious and easily

* There are many other c13 fonts, with much variety of shape and decoration, but none is of outstanding quality. A special type is e.g. that of Fawsley, Great Addington, Hargrave, and Norton. They have heads sticking out from an unadorned bowl. The type is prepared in the Norman font of Wappenham and has a parallel in the font at Harlestone, where the heads project not from the bowl but from the foot.

understood combination of lancet lights with quatrefoiled or sex-foiled circles becomes a pattern of ogee curves combined into mouchettes or shapes like leaves, until one's memory refuses to retain them individually. The results are fascinating or exciting or (to some) irritating; they are never reposeful as those of the Geometrical tracery of the later C13 had been. The climax was reached about the middle of the C14. Other motifs underwent less change. Piers for instance remained very often octagonal and arches double-chamfered. A favourite arch moulding of the Dec style is the sunk quadrant. A new and eminently characteristic variation on the theme of the octagonal pier is to make its eight sides concave. This was done at Harlestone, where the church was complete in 1325, and also at Great Brington, Ravensthorpe, and Sudborough. The square pier with four demi-shafts continued (Finedon), and so did the quatrefoil pier, though the moulded capitals have now more and closer and less deeply divided mouldings. Variations were not absent in the C13; they became more frequent and fanciful in the C14. One variation is the addition of thin shafts in the diagonals (Little Addington), another that of fillets on the four shafts (with the thin diagonal shafts as well Little Brington, with spurs in the diagonals Blakesley, with filleted shafts in the diagonals Chipping Warden). The most successful variation was the introduction of a hollow between the four main shafts. This, as we have seen, had been done already in the C13. It is now found at Great Harrowden, Middleton Cheney, and Walgrave. It became, in a thinner form, one of the standard pier sections of the Perp style. The Dec, so fascinated by flowing, gliding connexions between parts instead of the crisp, determined articulation of the E.E., often chose to do without capitals. Continuous mouldings had existed in England ever since the Norman style, but only the Dec had the conviction to make a major motif of them. Thus one finds e.g. double-chamfered arches carried down to the ground in piers of the same moulding (East Farndon, Lilbourne, Marston St Lawrence, Stanford, Stoke Bruerne) or the same motif with wavy instead of straight chamfers (Charwelton), or the sunk quadrant treated in the same way (Everdon).

The dating of tracery is complicated by what can only be called English conservatism. Pre-Dec remained in use in the Dec decades. Intersected tracery e.g. occurs still *c.* 1320 etc. at Higham Ferrers. Another typical case is at Wellingborough, where the lancet lights have ogee-arched heads, but the top of the window is still a circle filled with spherical quadrangles, i.e.

another motif of *c.* 1300. Even more baffling is the chancel of Geddington. The forms are of the same stage as at Wellingborough, i.e. of *c.* 1300 except for ogee-headed lights, but an inscription which is preserved refers to the man who built the chancel and who died in 1369. So 1340 is about the earliest date one can assume. Straight-headed windows are often regarded as a sign of Late Perp date. That is not so; an E.E. example has been referred to, and the Dec style uses them in Northamptonshire certainly not rarely, and other counties also. They occur e.g. with the motif of ogee reticulation in the top parts, one of the most characteristic Dec motifs. Segmental heads are also typical (e.g. in the Soke of Peterborough, Barnack and Northborough). The variety of patterns of tracery is legion. One charming motif is that here called the four-petalled flower. It can be seen e.g. at Bozeat. Specially interesting or enjoyable
13 tracery conceits are at Milton Malsor, still C13 (a square window with a wheel of radially placed arches), at Blisworth, Brackley, Chipping Warden, and Kings Sutton. One of the most sumptuous displays of flowing tracery is the E window of Gayton.

The delight of the C14 in 'leading the eye a wanton chase' must be largely responsible for the existence and the detailing of the strainer arches at Rushden and Finedon and also between N aisle and N chapel at Easton Maudit. They are usually dated as late as *c.* 1400, but appear earlier. Their transparence and their upward-curved upper edge achieve that very surprise in unexpected vistas which guided the Dec designers in so much of what they did. The pleasure in the opening out of a vista freer and airier than they had been permitted before may have something to do with the remarkable width and openness of the new Dec aisle and Dec chancel chapel which were added at Higham Ferrers, duplicating the dimensions of the C13 nave and chancel. The date when this was done is about 1320–30.

The dating of the C14 in Northamptonshire is always a difficult task. Documented dates such as 1337 for the approximate beginning of the splendid chancel at Cotterstock are rare, and they prove no more than that e.g. reticulated tracery was used in 1320 (in the dated chancel at Harlestone) and still after 1354 (in the tower of Irthlingborough). However, even that is a warning. While the Perp style had replaced the Dec in the S transept and the chancel at Gloucester as early as the 1330s and in the chapter house of Old St Paul's in London in the same years, Dec went on in most places into the third quarter of the C14 and even beyond. It would therefore be foolhardy to assign

dates to those churches which are consistently Dec throughout
or nearly throughout. Such churches in Northamptonshire are
Finedon, where they intended to vault the chancel, Byfield, [12]
Crick, and Stanford.

One or two specially impressive or pretty motifs may be added
as an appendix, one the steeply rising transverse arches in porches
which carry the stone slates of the roof without any intermediate
timber-work (Chacombe, Corby, Middleton Cheney), the other
the foliage trails with knotty branches instead of soft stalks
(capitals Radstone, doorway Kislingbury). Neither motif can be
connected with any particular date.

The TOWERS AND SPIRES of the C14 are equally lacking in
documentation which would allow one to date them. Yet they
are the most memorable achievement of medieval parish church
architecture in the county. A county of spires – the old saying
has already been referred to. It is, like most such proverbial
sayings, not strictly true. Northamptonshire has well over 200
medieval parish churches, but no more than about 80 spires, including those which are no longer in existence, but recorded. Of
these more than three-quarters are in or near the Nene district.

There are two principal types, the broach spire and the
recessed spire rising behind a parapet. Of the broach spires
something has already been said. The recessed spire is another
possibility of combining square tower and octagonal spire. There
are yet others, and they will be described a little later. The
broach spire, as we have seen, goes back to the early C13, the
recessed spire begins a little later. Deene, of the second half of
the C13, is one of the earliest in England. A sign of this early
date is that it has broaches as well.* Aesthetically speaking, it can
safely be said that the recessed spire is the more perfect solution.
The finest spires of Northamptonshire belong to this type. It is
difficult to make a choice. Oundle must certainly be one of those [10]
selected, Kettering must be another, Higham Ferrers a third. [9]
At Kettering the tower below is sumptuously decorated with
friezes and the spire has crockets all up the edges of the spire, a
motif which occurs in other places as well, and in broach spires
as much as in recessed spires (Higham Ferrers, Islip, Kings [11]
Sutton, Naseby, Oundle, Rushden, Southwick, Wakerley).
Another decorative motif of spires, though one which has an
obvious functional reason, is lucarnes. They ventilate the spire

* So have Woodford, Denford, and Newton-in-the-Willows. An even rarer
mixture of the two types is the spire of Desborough, where the battlements
of the tower fade into the broaches.

and increase its resistance to wind, and they are used in one, two, or three tiers. They can be set in the cardinal directions exclusively or in alternating directions, and they can be large or small, shallow or deep. Tall lower or lowest lucarnes are usually early, i.e. of the C13. They may start right at the foot of a spire (Raunds, Ringstead, Hargrave) or close to the foot (Warmington, Polebrook). They may even start lower than the broaches of a broach spire (King's Cliffe), and may be taller than the broaches (Deene). Lucarnes, especially upper ones, are not without aesthetic drawbacks; for unless detailed very sensitively, they tend to come out of the smooth and sleek outlines of a spire almost like pimples or warts. The broach spire, as the more robust form, can do with them with less damage than the Dec or Perp needle spire. If Dec and Perp are here thrown together, the reason is that few spires have enough details to permit safe dating.

So a morphological survey is more advisable than a chronological. The usual transition from tower to recessed spire is by a parapet or battlements and angle pinnacles. Very occasionally a broach spire adopts the pinnacles (Brixworth, Cottingham, Piddington, Wellingborough, Wollaston). The NW tower of Peterborough Cathedral has in addition to pinnacles four spirelets closer to the spire. Higham Ferrers, Rushden, Wilby, Easton Maudit, and a few others have graceful flying buttresses to connect the spire with the pinnacles, and at Kings Sutton there is the additional combination of inner pinnacles close to the spire, so that the flying buttresses are thrown from inner to outer pinnacles.

Further enrichment of the outline is achieved where the change from square to octagon is not made between tower and spire but between the lower parts of the tower and the bell-stage. Moreover, not all towers where this was done added a spire. The prototype of the octagonal top stage was presumably the Ely Octagon of 1322 etc. The crossing of Peterborough had a wooden octagon as well, though it has long perished. It dated from almost the same years as the Ely Octagon. Examples with a stone spire are Barnack of the C13 and Helpston (both in the Soke), and Milton Malsor. To these must be added Wilby with flying buttresses between square and octagon and again from eight pinnacles to the spire, and Nassington, where the change to the octagon is awkwardly performed halfway up the bell-stage, and Stanwick, where the tower is octagonal from the ground. The finest examples without a spire are Fotheringhay, elegant and trans-

parent, and Lowick, with a profusion of pinnacles. Both are 15
Perp, and the churches will be referred to later.

The normal square-topped towers of Northamptonshire re-
quire little comment. The finest by far is that of Titchmarsh, 14
with its sixteen pinnacles worthy of Somerset. Almost as good is
Whiston, a church built in the first third of the c16. One group,
inspired by St John and St Martin Stamford, is characterized
by clasping buttresses, tall four-light (two plus two) bell-
openings, a top frieze of quatrefoils or cusped lozenges, and
usually big pinnacles (Aldwinkle All Saints, Bulwick, Easton-
on-the-Hill, Geddington, Warkton). The group is quite large,
but not all towers have all motifs. An oddity is the tower at
Ecton with its truncated pyramid roof on which stands an embattled and pinnacled recessed top stage.

In this account of towers Dec and Perp could not be separated.
The PERPENDICULAR style on its own requires indeed not
much comment in Northamptonshire. The time of greatest activity was over by the end of the c14. It had been the hundred and
fifty-odd years from *c.* 1190 to *c.* 1350 or 1360. There are some
proud Perp churches in Northamptonshire – none prouder than
Fotheringhay and Lowick – and there is of course the gorgeous 15
retrochoir of Peterborough Cathedral, which was built about
1500 and proudly fan-vaulted, but there is nothing to compare
with the c15 and early c16 in Norfolk or Suffolk or Gloucester-
shire or Somerset. Dates are now a little easier to come by. We
know that St John, the parish church of Peterborough, was rebuilt in 1402–7, that Lowick was built by members of the Greene
family who died in 1399 (nave and aisles), 1415 (chancel), and
1468 (Greene Chapel and w tower), that Fotheringhay was built
in the later c14 and c15. Of the splendid church which served a
college founded in 1411 the chancel exists no longer. The nave
with its large aisle and large clerestory windows and its flying
buttresses gives an idea of the grand conception. The interior
reminds one of the grandest in East Anglia. Dated also are the
sumptuous s porch of Oundle built *c.* 1485, the Chambre Chapel
at Aldwinkle All Saints founded in 1489, the s chapel at Blakesley
for which money was left in 1500, the Chambre Chapel at
Spratton built by 1505, the Spencer Chapel at Great Brington of
before 1522, and the church at Whiston built shortly before
1534.*

Individual motifs and elements of these Perp churches do not

---

* The N chapel at Maxey (Soke) was founded in 1367 and is thus the
earliest datable document of the Perp style in the area.

call for much analysis. Octagonal piers continue,* piers with
30 four shafts and four hollows continue (Kettering, Peterborough
St John, Weekley), at Harrington with a deep continuous wave
connecting shafts and hollows, and continuous mouldings without any capitals or abaci between piers and arches also continue.
Often the shafts towards the aisle openings have capitals but no
other members. The varieties are better seen than described
(Islip, Brampton Ash, and Great Weldon forming one group;
Stanion, Luddington, and, most complicated of all, Fotheringhay another). The strainer arches of Rushden, Finedon, and
Easton Maudit have been mentioned earlier on. Vaulted porches
were a heritage from the C13. They now have not only diagonal
ribs and ridge ribs but also tiercerons (Wellingborough etc.). The
heavily timber-framed N porch of Marston Trussell on the
Leicestershire border is unique in the county. Neither timber
nor brick entered the field of church building. Window tracery
is of the nationally accepted types without local specialities. It is
at its grandest again at Fotheringhay, but even inside Fotheringhay there is no display of decoration that could be compared with
e.g. Long Melford. A particularly rich ensemble is the monument
to John Dycson † 1445, rector of Yelvertoft, with its recess and
the window behind it, externally as well as internally.

The Dycson Monument is exceptional among Perp CHURCH
MONUMENTS of Northamptonshire. On the whole they keep
within the prosperous average of the country. There are few if
any highlights. On the subject of church monuments the most
important remark to be made is more general and includes the
post-medieval centuries. The county is uncommonly rich in
family chapels, an expression of the wealth in the county which
the growth and maintenance of country houses also attests. The
52, 53, Spencer monuments at Great Brington run from 1522 to the C19,
& 58 the Knightley monuments at Fawsley from the early C16 to the
mid C19, the Brudenells at Deene from 1531 to the C19, the
Fermors at Easton Neston from 1550 to the C19, the Caves and
their descendants at Stanford from 1558 to nearly 1900, the Mon-
63 & 64 tagus at Weekley and then Warkton from 1557 to the C19,
the Langhams at Cottesbrooke from the C17 to the early C19,
and the Northamptons at Castle Ashby from 1828 to the C20.

---

* There is even one case, Moulton, where Norman piers appeared so out
of date that they were hidden under octagonal mantles. But as the operation
was called off before it was completed, we can see exactly how it was done – a
welcome reminder of how much earlier evidence must exist encased in later
work.

In detail the earliest monuments worth attention are the ornamental mid-C12 coffin lid at St Peter Northampton, already mentioned, the series of abbots at Peterborough of the late C12 and the early C13, and then of course the beautiful cross-legged Knights of Purbeck marble at Castle Ashby, Dodford, and Stowe-Nine-Churches. They date from the late C13 to the early [48] C14. The same period was responsible for the oaken effigies of Knights and Ladies at Alderton, Ashton, Braybrooke, Cold Higham, Dodford, Gayton, Paulerspury, and Woodford. The [49] earliest brass and one of the best in England is the St Maur († 1337; for illustration see p. 257) at Higham Ferrers. Good C15 brasses are at Cotterstock, Great Harrowden, and Lowick. The brass at Newton-in-the-Willows is specially attractive.* The figures kneel below a large slender cross. Alabaster, a Derbyshire and Nottinghamshire material, was used both for incised slabs and fully carved effigies. Mr Gardner counts sixteen alabaster monuments in the county. The earliest ones are of 1365–70 (Ashton, Orlingbury, Spratton), the finest Sir Ralph Greene † 1417 at Lowick (for which the contract has been preserved), [51] Sir John Cressy at Dodford † 1444, and the Earl of Wiltshire † 1499 at Lowick. Among C14 monuments in stone the best is at [50] Warkworth (c. 1350). The monument to Archdeacon Sponne at Towcester († 1448) has a cadaver as well as an effigy, a specifically English conception and arrangement the earliest example of which is Bishop Fleming of Lincoln † 1433. Several Late Perp monuments follow the arrangement of the Dycson at Yelvertoft, i.e. use recesses with a straight top cresting. The recesses at Gayton, Harrington, and Irthlingborough, all of the first half of the C16, are of Purbeck marble or a similar grey marble. The most splendid canopied composition is however that of the tomb of Sir John Spencer † 1522 at Great Brington. The [52 & 53] painting of effigies and surround is renewed here so as to give an impression of how gay such a Perp ensemble was in its original state.‡

The absence of WALL PAINTINGS from medieval churches (and indeed houses – see below) is much to be deplored. If we had all that crowded the walls we might like some churches less, but we would understand them better. In Northamptonshire there are many churches in which the faded traces of former cycles of frescoes have been laid bare. There is hardly anywhere enough for even the most moderate enjoyment. Specially com-

* This is now at Geddington.
‡ For the angel inside the arch see below, p. 47.

⁴⁰ plete are the series of Ashby St Ledgers, Croughton, Holcot, and Slapton. Other churches with wall paintings are Burton Latimer, Great Doddington, and Raunds.

STAINED GLASS, never fading though easily broken, can take the place of wall paintings to give us an idea of the colourfulness of the medieval church. But Northamptonshire is not rich in
³⁸ stained glass. By far the most rewarding place is Stanford, where good glass from the early C14 to the C16 survives. Lowick has sixteen figures from a Dec Jesse window, Rushden good C15 glass, Thenford minor remains. At Great Weldon is a complete early C16 German window with the Adoration of the Magi.

CHURCH FURNISHINGS are on the whole not of special interest. PLATE is confined to one silver-gilt Paten of c. 1330 at Welford and one early C15 chalice at Thurning, which is however Florentine and not English. Of other METALWORK only one piece can be introduced here, the precious processional cross at Lamport of the C15. As regards furnishings of stone, there are of course plenty of FONTS, but none, except for Stanion, deserves individual mention. Generally a word may be said for the groups of fonts (not only in Northamptonshire) which are decorated with a variety of blank tracery motifs, Dec as well as Perp, as if they were copied from some mason's pattern-book of window tracery. Canons Ashby and Preston Capes have such fonts. Much more interesting is the small stone RELIQUARY of about 1300 at Brixworth. Stone REREDOSES of the C14 are preserved at Barnwell, Great Billing (Outer Northampton), Spratton, and Wilbarston – more than in most other counties. A Perp reredos is at Geddington. No PULPITS of stone need be placed on record. Perp pulpits of wood are more frequent, but again of current types. The best is that of Fotheringhay with
³⁹ its pretty rib-vaulted tester or sounding-board. At Hannington it is interesting to see that the same wood carver must have done the pulpit and the SCREEN. No Northamptonshire screens can compete with the South-West or East Anglia. Geddington may be singled out because it seems as early as the early to mid C14, Ashby St Ledgers because, with its four-light divisions and its ribbed coving, it is more sumptuous than most. Bozeat also has four-light divisions, Braybrooke also has its ribbed coving preserved. The earliest chancel STALLS are two units at Peterborough Cathedral which date from between 1233 and 1245. MISERICORDS have survived in quite a number of places, notably Great Oakley (from Pipewell Abbey), Higham Ferrers, Gayton, Great Doddington, Rothwell, and Wellingborough.

BENCHES and bench ends are frequent but not particularly interesting. King's Cliffe has bench ends and some stained glass from Fotheringhay. Benefield, Hemington, and Tansor have stalls from the demolished chancel of the same church.

The complete disappearance of the College at Fotheringhay, the almost complete disappearance of that founded by Archbishop Chichele in his native Higham Ferrers, and the scanty remains of that established in 1388 at Irthlingborough deprive us of any vision of how such late medieval DOMESTIC BUILDING for clerics was arranged and equipped. The survival of Chichele's SCHOOL of 1422 and BEDE HOUSE of 1428 is an inadequate though welcome substitute. The school is an oblong with large church windows and might just as well be a Lady Chapel, the Bede House has some of its fitments still *in situ*, and one can visualize the cubicles with their beds and cupboards and the raised chapel at the E end. The Chantry House at Towcester, established by Archdeacon Sponne in 1447, must find its place here, as must the Priest's House at Easton-on-the-Hill. At Peterborough a good deal of the domestic architecture of the abbey can be pieced together. It is a fascinating job. What survives of the Prior's Lodging, the Infirmarer's Lodging, and the so-called Hostry is all later C13 with windows with a circle or a trefoil or quatrefoil above two pointed or pointed-trefoiled lights.

We can now turn to MEDIEVAL SECULAR ARCHITECTURE. CASTLES proper are rare in the county and with two exceptions of minor interest. The chief exception is Barnwell Castle, built, it is traditionally said, c. 1266. If that is so, it represents the earliest case in England of the most monumental type of medieval castle, that of a square or oblong plan with round angle towers, a type created on Roman patterns in Italy and France c. 1230 and taken over at Caerphilly Castle c. 1267 and Harlech Castle c. 1285. Barnwell Castle precedes Caerphilly by a few years. The gatehouse of Rockingham Castle, which in its present form dates from c. 1275–80, has round towers too. It was one of the most famous castles of Northamptonshire. Of the others – Northampton and Fotheringhay – all architecturally relevant evidence has disappeared. At Fotheringhay on the other hand a curious, quite sizeable C15 house, known as the New Inn, remains. Southwick Hall is not a castle, although it has a C14 tower. This was added to a slightly earlier hall (rebuilt later). The ground floor of the tower is rib-vaulted (like the tower at Longthorpe near Peterborough). Such houses could be used in war time but were built as houses. Astwell Castle of the C15 is of a similar type.

Of the Northamptonshire MANSIONS of the Middle Ages the 69 most impressive by far is Drayton, of which part was built from 1328 onwards with a considerable enlargement in the mid C15. Later building has overlaid this C14 and C15 work with equally interesting work of a different character, but the impression of the embattled and turreted mansion of the Draytons and Greenes can still be conjured up. To this must be added the remains of c. 1320–40 at Yardley Hastings. For the C15 there is no major house, though much minor evidence,* until the Tudor Age is reached. Then, of c. 1500 and after, there are the hall range and the Back Court (c. 1530 etc.) at Apethorpe, the hall with the remarkable motif of a bow-fronted bay window at Rushton, the hall and the chamber over at Brigstock Manor House, the E range at Deene Park with its canted bay-window and roof of c. 1530, the remains of the hall with roof at Abington Abbey 71 Northampton, and the hall with splendid bay-window at Fawsley, also of c. 1530. This, the finest piece of late medieval domestic display in the county, is alas falling into decay (the roof has already been destroyed). The bay-window and the other windows have uncusped arched lights, a motif characteristic of the time of Henry VIII but continued by conservative designers and patrons into the later C16 (Great Oakley Hall 1555, Canons Ashby after 1551, hall range Deene Park after 1549, and at Rushton even after 1575). Altogether it can be observed that the Renaissance, even as a fashion, was received only with much hesitation. A house such as Canons Ashby shows no sign of it in all the work undertaken after 1551. Nor does it appear in the halls of Deene Park and Boughton House, both of the same time as Canons Ashby. At Fawsley another house, known as the Dower House, remains in the grounds. It dates from the early C16, and is partly of brick. It has the delightful twisted and decorated chimneyshafts which are so characteristic of Early Tudor architecture. Here brick makes its first appearance in this survey. It was also used at Canons Ashby and at Winwick Manor House, again after 1550. The other building material of regions poor in good stone is timber, and timber-framing therefore is also unusual in Northamptonshire. If a few examples are to be mentioned, one might refer to the Court House at Kings Sutton, and houses at Wellingborough, Braunston, and Yelver-

* In this the two circular DOVECOTES of Furtho and Upper Harlestone must be included.

toft.* Ashby St Ledgers has one timber-framed range which is a good deal more elaborate, but this comes from Ipswich and was re-erected by the first Lord Wimborne. Timber pieces of interior decoration are rare too, and no more needs a reference than the carved lintel of a fireplace at Helmdon dated 1533, the screen with various bold linenfold motifs re-erected at Cosgrove 72 Priory, also of the time of Henry VIII, and the linenfold panelling with various Late Gothic as well as Renaissance motifs re-assembled in a room at Abington Abbey Northampton.

So the RENAISSANCE has been reached. The earliest documents of the Italian style in England are the monuments to the Lady Margaret and to Henry VII in Westminster Abbey begun in 1511 and 1512. In the stained glass of King's College Chapel Cambridge Italian motifs appear in 1515–17, at Hampton Court actual Italian work in 1521. By 1530 Renaissance motifs, mostly minor and mostly Englished in a somewhat provincial way, become more abundant. What are the *incunabula* in Northamptonshire? Certainly among them is the parclose screen at Warmington which, with its ogee arches with Renaissance detail and its linenfold panels side by side with pilasters, cannot be later than the 1530s. It has unfortunately no inscribed or otherwise known dates. The earliest dates in church plate are the cup and paten of 1548 at Clopton (already with Netherlandish strapwork 37 side by side with Italian motifs), and the cup of 1553 at Great Houghton. The former of these is of secular origin, and the earliest fixed dates of Renaissance motifs have indeed to be looked for almost entirely among works of secular art and architecture. That in itself is characteristic of the changed climate of the C16. They are to be found among the houses which men built for themselves and the monuments which they set in churches to commemorate themselves.

The earliest of all Renaissance details is the Doric peplos 53 worn by the angel in the apex of the arch of the Spencer tomb at Great Brington, erected immediately after 1522. The dress is that of the angels of the tomb of Henry VII. Then come minor decorative details on other tombs, introduced by the way and without any great conviction. Such are small coarse balusters taking the place of buttress shafts to separate panel from panel on the sides of tomb-chests. They are to be found in the Brudenell monument of 1531 at Deene and the monument of

* Timber-framed houses tend to be more frequent on the w side of the county. This is also true of the use of cob (mud walls) for cottages and walls, on which see M. Seaborne in *Northants Past and Present*, III, 5, 1964.

Lord Parr, uncle of Catherine Parr, at Horton († 1546). At Deene the panels still have the blank quatrefoils of the Perp style, and there are indeed three monuments of the 1550s without a hint of the Renaissance (Weekley † 1557, Stanford † 1558, Rushton † 1559).

But it was in the mid fifties that things changed, and now for a generation Northamptonshire becomes the architecturally most important county in England. Evidence of the style of the third quarter of the C16 is more frequent and more valuable here than anywhere else. Indeed, Northamptonshire now set out on that triumphant procession of major country house building which continued without a break into the C18. It can safely be said that the history of domestic architecture in England from 1560 to 1700 could be written with Northamptonshire examples alone: with Burghley, Kirby, Rushton and Lyveden, Castle Ashby, Stoke Bruerne, Lamport Hall, Thorpe Hall, Boughton, and Easton Neston.*

The change in the 1550s to which reference has been made and which initiates ELIZABETHAN ARCHITECTURE can be illustrated by comparing Canons Ashby of after 1551, which still has the windows with arched lights as they had been current under Henry VIII, with the porch of 1558 and the gatehouse range of 1560 at Dingley, or by comparing the architecture of the Great Hall at Burghley with the fireplace in it. The porch at Dingley is the earliest piece of Renaissance architecture in Northamptonshire,‡ late if one compares with Sutton Place in Surrey or Layer Marney in Essex, both of the 1520s. The hall and fireplace at Burghley are not exactly datable but must be of c. 1560–5. Generally speaking, the first thirty years after the initial import of Italian forms by Torrigiani and the other Italians had been one of a decorative fashion more than of a new order in architecture. A sense of Italian Renaissance – or by then rather Franco-Italian Renaissance – composition appeared for the first time in England in Old Somerset House in the Strand in London, built for himself by the Lord Protector Somerset in 1547–52. Here one can also see for the first time a number of motifs which the Elizabethan style was gradually to adopt: the mullioned window without arches to the lights, the frontispiece

* Of these, Burghley and Thorpe Hall are in the Soke of Peterborough and so no longer in the county, but are too important to be excluded from this Introduction.

‡ Bridges gives the date 1555 for Great Oakley Hall, but though that date may well refer to the house with the arched lights of its windows, it can hardly refer to the porch, which looks later Elizabethan.

with superimposed orders including columns (not only pilasters), the pediment, the top balustrade. Somerset must have been personally interested in architecture, and he certainly instilled his tastes into his protégés, men such as William Cecil of Burghley, John Thynne of Longleat, William Sharington of Lacock. An example of the style of this group in the 1550s is Sharington's funeral monument in Lacock church in Wiltshire. He died in 1553. Here there are pilasters with sunk panels ornamented with close arabesque, a shell pediment, strapwork, and bulbous vase finials, but still a depressed rounded arch. At Boughton House is a fireplace which must be of before 1557 and which has the same pilasters, at Apethorpe is another dated 1562 and with again the same pilasters and strapwork in addition. Between these two dates lies the work at Dingley. This is more naive, i.e. probably of local design, and indeed starts a school which Sir John Summerson has convincingly linked with the *Thorpe* family of King's Cliffe. Yet whoever designed the porch of 1558 at Dingley was clearly aware of the innovations of the Somerset circle. The windows with a cross of mullion and transom prove this, the pediment above the upper window (though it is an incorrectly steep pediment), the bulbous vase finials, and perhaps also the shell top. The porch has moreover three superimposed orders like Somerset House, even if they are handled with less assurance. The columniation l. and r. of door and upper window is carried round the corner, a motif which we shall find again presently. The outer entrance at Dingley is dated 1560. It carries a most extraordinary inscription which refers to King Philip of Spain as the king, and thus impressively illustrates how unmolested influential Catholics still were in the early years of Elizabeth I. The doorway has a four-centred arch, and the same arches occur inside in a short cloister. The attached columns 73 of this cloister have a curiously exaggerated taper, which, however, the top floor of the frontispiece of Somerset House also had. The cresting on the other hand is still of the playful kind typical of the earliest decades of Renaissance influence in England. The fireplace at Burghley House is a very different matter, grand, simple, with a pediment as correct as those of Somerset House (and indeed the same simple geometrical ornament of a circle with four radiating spokes as is found in the façade of Somerset House) and in complete contrast to the arched lights and the double hammerbeam roof of the hall. The fireplace is a sign that William Cecil was in close touch with the most progressive trends of the moment, as indeed his preserved correspondence

with Sir Thomas Gresham demonstrates, but that, when the hall
and the great kitchen (with its tierceron-vault) were designed,
Italo-French forms were not yet *de rigueur*.

Only a few years after this work at Burghley Kirby Hall was
begun – the foundation stone was laid in 1570, and there are
76 dates 1572 and 1575 on the porch. Concurrently at Deene Park
improvements went on, documented by a fireplace dated 1571.
The splendid external showpiece, however, with the Brudenell
arms implying a date before 1572, does not seem to be *in situ*.
The fireplace is similar to that at Apethorpe, though the sunk
pilasters have instead of arabesque the simple roundels which
were a Venetian tradition taken over by the French. The frontis-
75 piece, really a large bay-window with all its lights blocked, has
fat Ionic columns, cross-windows, strapwork panels, and a trun-
74 cated ogee gable. There is in addition a porch at Deene which
must be of the same time.* This repeats the motif of columniation
(pilasters in this case) carried round the corner, a motif introduced at Dingley. The pilasters here are decorated by guilloche
and by a characteristic geometrical ornament of ovals and oblongs
connected by bands – a development really of the ornament of
the overmantel at Burghley and thus again of Somerset House.
It became highly popular in the county, and is used a little later in
the Roman Staircase at Burghley and in Sir Thomas Tresham's
78 & 79 work at Rushton and Rothwell. Kirby Hall, as against Deene,
Apethorpe, and Dingley a completely new building, fits in here,
and can serve to terminate the Early Elizabethan phase. It has
much in common with earlier Northamptonshire work, and
much also with leading earlier English work in general, but
heralds the Late Elizabethan style as well. The county motifs are
the columns and pilasters of the porch carried round the corner
and its shell top – *Thorpe* work in fact, as one can safely say here.
The nationally significant motifs are the large mullioned and
77 transomed windows and the giant pilasters. The former are an
Elizabethan development, the latter a French one (St Maur)
which did not find favour in England before the second third of
the seventeenth century. The large mullioned and transomed
windows are the most conspicuous motif of such houses as
Longleat and Burghley, and in both cases they seem to belong
to the seventies. With them the mature Elizabethan style was
established.

* At least a note must be given to the porch at Watford Court, dated 1568
and with a two-storeyed curved oriel window on a big corbel. This is
threatened with demolition (1972).

A parallel development can be shown in FUNERAL MONU-MENTS, and must be shown before the story of domestic architecture can profitably be continued. Free-standing tomb-chests with recumbent effigies represent the conservative taste. In the monuments at Weekley († 1557) and Stanford († 1558), and even the Tresham Monument at Rushton (erected 1562), there is no Renaissance detail at all yet, and the flat balusters on the Andrew Monument at Charwelton († 1564) do not essentially go beyond those of the Parr Monument at Horton of 1546 (*see* above). New types are the memorials with two kneeling figures facing one another, presented at Nether Heyford († 1556) with sumptuous foliage decoration, and the large standing memorials with no effigies at all. This type, of which a perfectly classical example had been made for Wing in Buckinghamshire as early as 1552 and one, rather more the prototype of the Northamptonshire group, for Launde in Leicestershire in 1551 (Gregory Cromwell), appears now at Stanford († 1568), Fotheringhay (1573), and Little Oakley (*c.* 1575). All these are of excellent quality. The Griffin Monument at Braybrooke of *c.* 1565–70 is different, much more exuberant and overcrowded, but also without effigies. In addition there is a group, also of a high standard, which shows kneeling figures in relief (Blatherwycke † 1575, Harrington 1588, Charwelton 1590, Thorpe Mandeville *c.* 1600).

Meanwhile what had been a matter of a few individual buildings up to 1570 developed into the broad stream of MATURE ELIZABETHAN AND JACOBEAN DOMESTIC ARCHITECTURE. While Kirby Hall rose,* William Cecil added to the old and recently still irregularly enlarged Burghley the three stupendous wings which make it the most spectacular Elizabethan courtyard house in the country. The three ranges carry dates 1577, 1585, and 1587. With its turrets and its innumerable chimneystacks, it is the most improbable apparition in the gentle landscaped grounds outside Stamford. In size and in swagger it can compete with any contemporary palace this side of the Alps. The work includes the Roman Staircase with its coffered vault, designed on the pattern of the Louvre staircase of Henri Deux, the vault of the western entrance, which is Gothic Survival (or Revival?), the fantastic frontispiece in the courtyard crowned by spiky obelisks, open arcading in the courtyard and on the S front,

---

* An exceptional feature for the period is the pair of semicircular bay-windows at Kirby, at the back (if they are original). But it should be remembered that Rushton has a purely Perp semicircular bay-window of the early C16.

and interior marvels of which we know next to nothing. Sir
Christopher Hatton, a young favourite of the Virgin Queen who
had bought Kirby Hall in 1576, also built on a prodigious scale
at Holdenby, where the completion date is probably that marked
on the garden archways, which are the only thing left of the
house. They are very similar to archways outside Kirby.* The
date at Holdenby is 1583. 1596 seems the date of completion for
Pytchley, an Isham mansion which has also disappeared and of
which only fragments survive in various places. Of Newton, a
Tresham mansion, the dovecote is all that remains. Sir Thomas
Tresham, convert to Rome and a man equally enamoured of
theology, architecture, and allegorical conceits, built the Market
78 House at Rothwell in 1578 and added to Rushton, but is princi-
79 pally remembered for the Triangular Lodge in the Rushton grounds and for Lyveden New Build, which is a Greek cross
and was never completed. The one symbolizes the Trinity, the
other the Passion. Of these conceits and of Tresham's troubled
life more is to be found on pp. 299 and 397. At Castle Ashby work
started in 1574 and went on into the c17. The Elizabethan plan
with long projecting wings and two staircase turrets attached to
them is one familiar from such mid-c16 houses as Melford Hall,
Kentwell Hall, and Rushbrooke, all three in Suffolk. Castle
81 Ashby was remodelled c. 1600–35 and then received its delightful
balustrade with lettering, a feature of French origin also to be
found at the same time e.g. at Temple Newsam outside Leeds.
A few years later still Castle Ashby received its screen across the
front, but this belongs emphatically to the style which was to
replace that of the Jacobean decades. The screen as such, however, again of French descent, had been quite a usual Elizabethan
and Jacobean motif. Kirby Hall of course has it; other examples
are among the Cambridge colleges. In Northamptonshire a late
80 and ambitious example is at Rushton, of the time (c. 1625–30)
when the Cokaynes had replaced the Treshams.

A few more Elizabethan and Jacobean houses must be referred
to in passing: Wothorpe near Burghley, another Cecil mansion,
this one small and on a compact plan similar to those of certain
North Country houses such as Barlborough and Wootton Lodge
Staffordshire, Gayton Manor, yet smaller but equally compact,
extensions at Drayton of c. 1584 including two towers, the s front
of Brockhall Hall, and the large, symmetrical, emphatically
Jacobean E front of Apethorpe with an open arcade in the

---

* Another handsome Elizabethan gatehouse is at Winwick.

centre.* Also Jacobean in style but less ambitious are Burton
Latimer Hall, Rushden Hall, the w front of Delapré, Lilford
Hall (1635, 1656), and the hall range at Ashby St Ledgers (with
additions of 1652). Lilford and Ashby St Ledgers have shaped
gables in the later work, and altogether it can be said that in more
marginal building in the county the Jacobean style was still un-
changed after 1660. An example is Coton Hall built in 1662.
Town houses of the same years are few and far between. The
fire of 1675 did not leave many houses untouched at Northampton. The only noteworthy ones are the Welsh House of 1595 and
the C17 Hazelrigg Mansion. To these may be added the Talbot
Inn of 1626 at Oundle.

Interiors of these decades and of special value are oddly rare.
The Jacobean plasterwork at Castle Ashby stands on its own in
Northamptonshire, and so does the East Staircase in the same
house with its openwork panels, a motif which, about 1630, occasionally took the place of turned balusters. The panels are still
of strapwork, though they include certain gristly details which
belong to the mid-C17 style. The West Staircase some decades 83
later has luscious openwork acanthus scrolls instead, and that
represents a different style.‡

The development from the later Elizabethan Age to the thresh-
old of the innovations of the 1630s, as the East Staircase at
Castle Ashby heralds them and the screen-front between the two
wings fully represents them, is paralleled in the development of
FUNERAL MONUMENTS between about 1580 and the 1630s.
Most of the earlier Elizabethan types remain. Very occasionally
names of sculptors are now known. Three of the Spencer monuments at Great Brington are by *Jasper Hollemans*, of Burton-on-
Trent but no doubt of Netherlandish extraction, and one monument at Steane is by *John and Matthias Christmas*. As regards
types of tombs, the free-standing tomb-chest or the tomb-chest
attached to the wall and with recumbent effigy or effigies on it is
still the most frequent (e.g. Great Brington, Sir John Spencer
† 1586; first Lord Spencer 1599; Easton Maudit † 1612).
Sometimes effigies in tombs placed against a wall now
lie, not side by side, but one behind and a little higher than

---

* Such open arcading along parts of a façade existed also at Burghley, as
we have seen, in the N range at Kirby, at Deene, and at Castle Ashby. It was
specially popular in the Jacobean decades – perhaps at Holdenby, and also
cf. e.g. Bramshill in Hampshire and Audley End in Essex.

‡ The acanthus type is also used, probably before Castle Ashby, in the
staircase of Milton Malsor Manor House.

57 the other (e.g. Stanford *c.* 1600, Easton Maudit † 1631, Steane † 1633, Maidwell 1634). Sometimes also the deceased is placed on his side propped up on his elbow in a contemplative attitude (Paulerspury † 1603, Easton Maudit † 1631). The architectural surround is most frequently an arch against the back wall with a cartouche under it, with or without flanking columns and with a top achievement (e.g. Great Brington † 1586 and erected 1599, Cottesbrooke † 1604, Stanford † 1613, and Easton Neston † 1628 with a splendid display like a peacock's tail under the back arch).

57 A great rarity is the Yelverton Monument at Easton Maudit († 1631), where the flanking columns are replaced by caryatid figures of bearded bedesmen, an echo of French *pleureurs* of the c15. Some specially ambitious monuments have four, or six, columns carrying a superstructure above the tomb-chest (Great Brington † 1599, Weekley † 1602, Easton Maudit † 1612). To this type belongs the most sumptuous c17 monument in Northamptonshire and one of the most sumptuous of its time

56 in England, that of Sir Anthony Mildmay † 1617 at Apethorpe with four life-size figures standing at the angles and a circular lantern raised above the centre. The other most frequent Elizabethan type is the kneeling figure (e.g. Marston Trussell † 1612, monument to a merchant who had died at Moscow) or the pair of kneeling figures facing one another across a prayer-desk (e.g. Rushden † 1608, Ashby St Ledgers † 1634, Kelmarsh † 1639). Occasionally yet another type is seen which had been established before, but only for clergymen and scholars: the frontally placed bust with an architectural surround or in a niche. This occurs in a monument to a rector of Barnwell who died in 1620 and again at Broughton (1631) and Clipston († 1632) in the 1630s. At the same time, or, to be more precise, in 1633, the Apreece Monument at Lutton shows three kneeling figures all placed frontally.

These were, just as in domestic architecture, altogether the years of change. The monument to Henry Montagu † 1625 at Barnwell All Saints, which consists of a tall obelisk with the small figure in a niche and many inscriptions, is a new and original conception.* So is the monument to Temperance Browne at Steane. She died in 1634, and the monument shows her in her shroud sitting up in her coffin, awakened by the last trump. The conceit is influenced no doubt by Nicholas Stone's monument to John Donne at St Paul's, which was set up in 1631, and with Nicholas Stone once more the age and style of Inigo Jones is

* Cf. the bust of a boy in front of a needle obelisk at Marholm († 1646) (Soke of Peterborough).

reached. The differences between Jacobean and classical monuments must be discussed later.

But before we can turn to Inigo Jones's own work in Northamptonshire we must cast a glance at other work in and about churches during the same period. As regards CHURCH ARCHITECTURE AFTER THE REFORMATION, there is nothing whatever to report until after the death of Elizabeth I. There were enough churches in existence, the troubled decades before the Settlement were not propitious to church building, and the Settlement itself did not lead to church building enthusiasm either. So what can be referred to between 1620 and 1639 is confined to six items, none of them major. They show an almost unquestioning adherence to the Perp style and only occasional passages in the Jacobean or the coming classical idiom. Of 1620 much or most of the disused Gothic chapel at Furtho and the larger and more ambitious chapel of Sir Thomas Crewe close to Steane Park. This has Gothic windows, some probably re-used, and Gothic pier-sections. 1621 is the date of the Mildmay Chapel at Apethorpe, where the pier towards the chancel is Perp but the plasterwork decidedly classical, that is not really Jacobean. The chancel at Passenham is dated 1626 and has Perp windows and a wagon roof. The tower of Apethorpe church with its recessed spire is also Perp and was rebuilt in 1633. The Hanbury Chapel at Kelmarsh of c. 1639 on the other hand has in its E window 16 what can only be described as Carolean tracery.

In CHURCH FURNISHINGS the situation is reversed. Here the Gothic style survives only very occasionally, and one is indeed tempted to speak of revival rather than survival, when it occurs, and most of what was commissioned was done in the Elizabethan and Jacobean style with its Netherlandish sympathies. Again little is of before the death of Queen Elizabeth. The only dated pieces are the many cups and patens of 1570 and the years immediately before and after, marking the Elizabethan Settlement in the church, and two pulpits (of 1579 and 1584) at Rothersthorpe and Newbottle, both very simple and not with the broad, blank arches on short pillars which are so familiar as an Elizabethan and Jacobean motif in church as well as house. They decorate e.g. the pulpits at Catesby and at Alderton. The latter is 41 dated 1631. The work at Passenham of c. 1626 is perhaps the most consistent that can be introduced here. The screen is contemporary with the stalls, which have to one's amazement Jacobean misericords, and the wall paintings of single figures in niches are on the Venetian Cinquecento pattern. No other painting need be mentioned, only one stained glass job (at Apethorpe, 1621, entirely Flemish-looking), and little other woodwork. By far the most interesting screen is that at Geddington which is dated 1618 and repeats the Dec tracery of the window against which it stands, even if it embroiders on it with small Jacobean motifs. Other screens are at Clipston, a specially fine piece, at Marston St Lawrence (1610) made up from a reredos, and at Apethorpe. If to these the splendid organ case at Stanford dating apparently from the C16 or the early C17, and the reredos of 1635 at Deene are added, all is listed that needs listing.

The moment has now come to turn to the great divide. *Inigo Jones* was born in 1573. He is first met in 1603 as a painter, but had then already visited Italy and there no doubt acquired the knowledge of theatrical design and the deft hand at sketching which are both his when he next appears, in 1605, as a designer and draughtsman for a court masque. He developed into the most brilliant English theatre designer of his age, on a par with the best abroad. But out of feigned architecture he moved into real architecture, and became Surveyor to the Prince of Wales in 1611 and Surveyor of the King's Works in 1613. In the same year he went to Italy again, and this time closely studied Italian architecture and especially his idol, Andrea Palladio. In his earliest works of architecture, such as the New Exchange in London of 1609, he was still essentially Jacobean, but in 1616 he designed the Queen's Villa at Greenwich as a purely Palladian work and in 1619 the Banqueting House in Whitehall for the King, equally pure and equally Palladian. In Northamptonshire two works of architecture are attributed to him, the S front or screen at Castle Ashby and the pavilions at Stoke Bruerne, the former on no better authority than that of Campbell's *Vitruvius Britannicus*, the latter on the authority of Bridges, the reliable C18 county historian who writes that Sir Francis Crane brought the design from Italy and that Inigo Jones helped him with it. This indeed is quite possible. The plan is that of Palladio's villas, i.e. a plan with a compact centre connected by quadrant wings to pavilions. Jones would have been sympathetic if Crane had made the suggestion to him to build on such a plan in England. It had not been done before, though it was just then also done in France and Holland. The date of Stoke Park is 1629–35. The centre of the house is burnt and was apparently not built to Inigo's plan. It may have been an earlier building, altered. The pavilions are characterized by giant pilasters, again a Palladio motif which about 1630–40 began to become popular

in Holland and France. The S front at Castle Ashby is charac- 81
terized by a pediment and Venetian windows, both Palladian as
well as Jonesian elements. Certain impurities need not worry
us overmuch. It is becoming more and more patent that Jones
was not as pure an architect as e.g. Gotch had surmised more
than a generation ago. The work on the N front at Kirby dating
from 1638–40 and also attributed to Inigo is less convincing.
With its Dutch, i.e. scrolly, pedimented gables, it is closer to a
more popular trend of architecture in the second third of the
C17 than to the courtly style of Inigo. An excellent example
of this more popular trend is the gateway of 1653 at Apethorpe,
another the garden temple of 1641 at Easton Neston, which
could be Jonesian if it were not for one rather wild Jacobean
intrusion.*

The situation in the mid C17 in Northamptonshire, and indeed
in England, was that Inigo Jones's battle was not won. Only few
as yet followed him, among them first and foremost his pupil
and kinsman *John Webb*. One of the best surviving works of
Webb is in the county, Lamport Hall of *c.* 1655, built at first as 86
no more than a villa, in the succession of Inigo's villa for the
Queen at Greenwich. It contains a splendid two-storeyed hall,
a staircase with the pierced acanthus panels to which reference
has already been made *à propos* the later example at Castle
Ashby, and an impressive large fireplace. Webb also designed 84
fireplaces for Drayton, and may well have designed the big fireplace at Watford Court which goes with additions dated 1657
and 1659. These have externally, however, some small and pretty
scrolls which connect them with the popular rather than the
courtly group. Mr Colvin has recently shown that this popular
version of the mid-C17 possibilities is in its most elaborate,
decidedly Mannerist form connected with *Peter Mills*, carpenter
to the City of London. Mills was responsible for the design of
Thorpe Hall (Soke of Peterborough), which dates from 1653–6.
In outline it is as compact as the houses of the Inigo circle – such
as Pratt's Coleshill or Hugh May's Eltham Lodge – but in detail
it is wilful, intricate, and undisciplined. This refers to the
decorative motifs of the façades as well as the interiors, including
incidentally another staircase with openwork acanthus panels.
The style of Thorpe Hall is reflected at Cotterstock Hall (1658)
and was reflected in a window of the now demolished Peacock
Hotel at Northampton. By an unknown architect is the staircase

* A more purely classical garden house is at Ecton. This has an oval plan,
which is noteworthy.

85 of 1666 at Althorp, one of the grandest and most classical of those years in England.

Again the CHURCH MONUMENTS tell the same story as the houses, though on their smaller scale moves tended to be quicker. Thus a tablet at Norton commemorating a death in 1624 is remarkably quiet in its decoration and not really Jacobean any longer, and the same applies to the decoration of the tomb-chest of Dorothy St John † 1630 at Stanford. The tomb-chest with the recumbent effigy remains a current type, but when it is handled by *Nicholas Stone* (Stowe-Nine-Churches 1617–20, Great Brington *c*. 1636–8), the white marble effigy becomes eloquent and elegant and belongs no longer to the tribe of the stiff, silent effigies of the Jacobean style. By Nicholas Stone also, who was trained in Holland and co-operated with Inigo Jones, is a very fine, completely simple tablet of 1640 at Blatherwycke. Such classical tablets occur in other places as well and need not be by Stone (e.g. Weekley † 1644). Worthy of Stone is the Hicklinge Monument at Green's Norton of *c*. 1620–30, where the type with two kneeling figures facing each other is rejuvenated and enriched by a baldacchino and two standing angels. *John Stone*, in the footsteps of his father at his most meta-

58 physical, appears in the monument of 1656 at Great Brington, where Sir Edward Spencer rises out of a big urn which is placed between a pillar and a column. Such curious conceits were a passing fashion of the second third of the century. A lasting effect on the other hand had the iconographical innovation of the same time which is illustrated by John Stone's monument of 1655 at Newbottle. This has two free-standing busts. The same motif can be seen at Norton, where the date of death is 1658. The free-standing bust was soon to become a favourite memorial. It must be kept separate from the bust in a niche, which we have found before, although even in this type the 1630s bring some amendment. The niche is replaced by an oval medallion (Broughton 1631; also Passenham † 1649 and Clipston † 1659),* and the bust may develop into a three-quarter length (Ashby St Ledgers 1663). As regards the free-standing bust, a type of secular origin which was going to be very popular in the C18, it occurs, placed in front of an obelisk, already in a monument of the forties at Marholm (Soke of Peterborough) († 1646), and placed in an open segmental pediment, as was also usual in the C18, in a monument of the 1660s at Clipston († 1668). But the 1660s form a border,

---

* What the 'busto' was like above an earlier tomb at Clipston, † 1636, we do not know.

the border between the style of Jones, Webb, and Mills and that of Wren, and so we must for the moment leave monuments again.*

What is often called the Wren style in domestic architecture, and really means the architecture of LATE SEVENTEENTH-CENTURY HOUSES, was not created by Sir Christopher Wren. It was used e.g. by *Hugh May* before Wren had even finally turned to architecture from science. It is probable that Hugh May was the designer of the alterations of the 1670s and 80s at Dingley.‡ This is well proportioned work, and stands for more 87 that was done externally to houses during those decades. The climax is no doubt the so-called Versailles front of Boughton 90 House built by the first Duke of Montagu after 1683, again extremely simple, but strictly regular and noble in scale and proportions. Dingley and Boughton have sashed windows, an innovation at the time. The usual windows were those of cross-type, upright, with one mullion and one transom.

A word may here be inserted on windows of the later C17 and early C18. In cottages the mullioned window of Tudor type was not given up entirely until the end of the C17.§ Examples are Old House Little Everdon of 1690, a house at Weston of 1694, Ecton Manor House also of 1694, and The Croft at Staverton of 1700. The tendency was to change over from a horizontal to a vertical shape, and that can already be noticed in the mullioned windows of the Hazelrigg Mansion at Northampton and The Sycamores at Blakesley of 1670. Upright two-light windows occur e.g. at Aynho Grammar School in 1671, Rose Manor Guilsborough in 1686, a house at Blakesley in 1689, The Firs Weedon in 1692, the Post Office at Great Billing (Outer Northampton) in 1703, and The Manor Wappenham in 1704. The cross-window replaces this type. It was used e.g. in one of the earliest houses of the classical mid-C17 type in England, Chevening in Kent, in 1638. Webb probably used it at Lamport, and so it goes on to Chipping Warden Manor House dated

---

* Of CHURCH FURNISHINGS nothing requires even a passing note except the group of FONTS of the 1660s: Culworth 1662, Rockingham 1669, and others without inscribed dates.

‡ Sir Gyles Isham's suggestion. This wing is now derelict (1972).

§ It need hardly be said that in the gazetteer no attempt is made to list all houses with mullioned windows, partly because there are far too many of them, and partly because I cannot possibly have seen all of them. Important, perhaps dated, examples may well have been overlooked. The sections of the mullions, incidentally, do not, to the best of my experience, help in dating them.

1668 and the major houses of the following decades. Boughton
e.g., except for the Versailles front, has cross-windows. So have
the stables of Lamport in 1680. They occur in fact in a village
as late as 1731 (Old). Side by side often with cross-windows
one can find in the later C17 oval windows placed vertically as
well as horizontally. Examples of the former are Guilsborough
Grammar School (1668 etc.), Old House Little Everdon (1690),
and a house at Little Houghton (1702), of the latter The Firs
Weedon (1692) and Alderton Manor House (1695).*

The typical house of the late C17 in the county, if built at one
go and not merely an addition or remodelling, however grand,
can best be exemplified by Stanford Hall of 1697–1700, just
across the Leicestershire border. This is a simple oblong block
of nine by seven bays with a hipped roof, cross-windows, and
quoins. Little is done in the way of decorative relief. On a
smaller scale the same type is represented by Finedon Vicarage
of 1688, and the core of Aynhoe, built c. 1680–2 by *Edward
Marshall*. The windows here have pediments, and the middle
window on the first floor an aedicular frame.

In complete contrast to this restraint in the exteriors is the
splendid display of decoration inside. Here it is hard to choose
what to single out, but there is the excellent plasterwork in the
89 Sessions House at Northampton of 1684–8 by *Goudge*, who
appears in the accounts for Hampton Court in the early nineties,
likewise the superb overmantels at Castle Ashby, and the staircase railing of c. 1680 in the same house with its openwork leaf
scrolls already pointed out. The grand staircases of Boughton
and Drayton (and later Burghley) on the other hand are of stone
and have wrought-iron railings, and the wrought-iron work can
be very fine indeed. By far the most splendid iron work in
Northamptonshire, however, is that of the various gates at
Drayton (1699, 1701), amply worthy of *Tijou*. The walls and
ceilings of the grand staircases of about 1700 are painted somewhat grossly by *Verrio* (a suite of state rooms and perhaps the
staircase at Harrowden Hall‡) and the other foreigners then
working in England. The Drayton staircase is probably by
Lanscroon, the Boughton staircase (and much else at Boughton)
by *Chéron*.

18 &   In CHURCH ARCHITECTURE there is only one building in the
32 class of these houses, All Saints at Northampton of 1676–80,

* But the porch at Delapré, not later than 1650, also has two blank
horizontally placed ovals.
‡ E. Croft Murray attributes these to *Lanscroon*.

designed, it seems, by *Henry Bell* of King's Lynn. It is certainly
not a provincial design. Its ancestors are Inigo Jones, whose
celebrated portico of Old St Paul's the architect borrowed, and
Christopher Wren, whose plan of St Mary-at-Hill is all but
copied. All Saints is thus externally as well as internally a church
of national importance, even if the curious tracery of the windows
introduces a provincial note. The fittings and FURNISHINGS are
equally worth while. The doorcases, the mayor's chair, and the
pulpit might be in any of the London City churches. The same
incidentally can be said of the pulpit of *c.* 1700 at Abington,
Northampton.

Far more must be said of FUNERAL MONUMENTS of *c.* 1660
to *c.* 1700. The new passion for noble display presents itself as
early as 1662 in the monument to Sir Hatton Fermor at Easton
Neston. The effigies here stand upright, alive, not dead or asleep,
and in self-conscious postures, not kneeling in prayer. In the
Palmer Monument at East Carlton († 1673) the figures also 59
stand, but they are in their shrouds and appear inside an open
black door. The conceit harks back to Stone and his Dr Donne.
The sculptor was in all probability *Joshua Marshall*. Signed
monuments become more frequent now, and bills survive more
often to identify sculptors of unsigned tombs. Standing figures
also are the centre of the monument to Sir Creswell Levinz
† 1700 at Evenley attributed to *van Ost* (*Nost*), which has lost its
architectural back-cloth, and of three Rockingham monuments.
The dates of death are 1695, 1713, and 1724. The sculptors of
the first two are *Nost* and *Palmer*. The monument to Dr Turner
† 1714 at Stowe-Nine-Churches is by *Stayner*, and here the stand- 60
ing doctor is matched by a figure of Faith, a characteristically
worldly conceit. Other types were not of course given up, and
one can for instance still see plenty of simple tablets with ornamental surrounds – in fact the cartouches of the late C17 with
their brilliantly carved garlands and cherubs' heads are among
the most enjoyable works of sculpture in the churches. The
free-standing tomb-chest with recumbent effigies also survives,
though it is becoming rare (Sir John Langham † 1671, Cottesbrooke, by *Cartwright Sen.*), and the same is true of kneeling
figures in pairs. Examples are Sir Samuel Jones † 1672 at
Courteenhall, probably by *William Stanton,** and the Earl of
Thomond (erected 1700) by *Bushnell* at Great Billing (Outer
Northampton).

---

* William and *Edward Stanton* did more work in the county, e.g. at
Lamport. For details *see* the index of artists.

This list has propelled us into the first years of the
EIGHTEENTH CENTURY, and it is to this that we must now
91 turn. At its very beginning stands Easton Neston remodelled by
Hawksmoor, completed by 1702, and with its simple cubic shape
and the even grandeur of its giant pilasters and giant columns
and crowning balustrade perhaps the finest house of its date in
England. *Wren*, Hawksmoor's master and protector, as has been
shown recently, was involved in the original design, and although
the present appearance of Easton Neston is due to Hawksmoor,
it is derived from Wren's late style, the style which influenced
Hawksmoor before he turned to more Baroque ideals. There is
no work by *Vanbrugh* in Northamptonshire, though the huge
fireplace from Pytchley Hall now at Shortwood Lodge is very
Vanbrughian, but *Thomas Archer* seems to have been responsible
93 for the wings of c. 1707–10 at Aynhoe. The door pilasters set at
an angle and similar motifs seem indeed a safe guide.* The same
development from noble grandeur to Baroque wilfulness, though
in a more playful and Continental mood, can be matched in
92 *William Talman*'s hall front at Drayton built c. 1702.‡ A
reaction against the Baroque, whether English or Continental,
set in almost at once. It acted in the name of Palladio and Inigo
Jones and was led by the third Earl of Burlington. Its earliest
works in London belong to the years between 1715 and 1720. In
Northamptonshire it appears with *Gibbs*'s Kelmarsh of c. 1727–
32, but it met with the opposition of those who believed in the
more staid Baroque which the *Smiths* of Warwick, influenced by
Buckingham House in London, had made their own. This
Baroque is characterized by an ample use of giant pilasters.
Cottesbrooke Hall of 1702–13, probably by *Francis Smith*, and
Orlingbury Hall of c. 1706–10 and later Dallington Hall near
Northampton and Bramston House, Oundle, belong to it. The
Smiths worked at Lamport Hall, keeping in their exteriors re-
markably tactfully to Webb's style. *Francis Smith* in all probabi-
lity built new fronts at Abington Abbey Northampton, and
William Smith designed Edgcote, executed by *William Jones*. Of
the leading Palladians *William Kent* himself designed Wakefield
94 Lodge, Potterspury, c. 1745, as so often very Vanbrughian outside and altogether much less Palladian than his relation to
Burlington would make one expect, and *Henry Flitcroft*, 'Burl-

* Very Archerish also is the giant open segmental pediment over the front
of Thorpe Mandeville Manor House.

‡ Woodnewton is a piece of specially wild Baroque design. It is probably
of c. 1730.

ington's Harry', designed the entrance hall of Lilford Hall.
Purely Palladian also are Astrop of after 1735, the stables at
Althorp by *Roger Morris* of before 1733 and those at Courteenhall of *c.* 1750. Of Palladian interiors the first is perhaps the
entrance hall at Althorp also probably by *Morris*, of Rococo 96
interiors the best are those at Lamport Hall of 1740, at Easton
Neston of *c.* 1740, at Cottesbrooke Hall (especially the staircase), 97
and at Upton (with stucco work of 1737 by *Artari*). Good mid- 95
C18 interiors also at Edgcote (1747–52) and Thenford. Thenford
is dated 1761–5 and is somewhat puzzling in that it has, to crown
its Palladian front, two hipped roofs side by side and a cupola
between, a 1660- rather than a 1760-looking motif. We break this
survey off just before the new and more elegant style of Robert
Adam swept the board of classical design and the Gothic Revival
began to query its validity altogether, and first look round among
secular architecture other than domestic and among ecclesiastical
architecture and decoration.

Secular architecture other than domestic should indeed have
been introduced earlier, but so far it has been enough to mention
the odd market hall or school when and how its style required.
Now the fact must be emphasized as such that such public,
charitable, and scholastic buildings grow in frequency and importance as the C16 moves into the C17 and the C17 into the C18.
A list is simple. For PUBLIC BUILDINGS it starts with Sir
Thomas Tresham's Market House at Rothwell, built by *William* 78
Grumbold c. 1578, culminates in the Sessions House at North- 88
ampton, designed perhaps by *Henry Bell* of Kings Lynn, built
in 1676–8, and provided with the masterly stucco ceilings by 89
Goudge which have already been mentioned, and ends for the
time being with the Brackley Town Hall of 1706, presented by
the first Duke of Bridgewater, and the modest Palladian Daventry Moot Hall of 1769. The list of SCHOOLS is a little longer,
and some of them are of remarkable size considering their date.
We start with the Finedon Boys' School endowed in 1595, the
Daventry Grammar School of 1600, the Wellingborough Grammar School of 1617, and the school at Burton Latimer of 1622.
The next group belongs to the mid C17. It begins with the
Cottesbrooke School and Hospital of 1651, and goes on to two
most generous and stately schools, Clipston Grammar School
and Hospital of 1667–73 and Guilsborough Grammar School
of 1668. This was for fifty boys, a remarkably large number for
a C17 foundation. In style both are still closer to the early than
the late C17. The Aynho Grammar School of 1671 has upright

two-light windows, the Courteenhall Grammar School of 1680
cross-windows and a big, open segmental pediment above the
doorway. Its arrangement of benches inside is preserved. Two
of the schools in this list were combined with HOSPITALS.
Hospitals as independent buildings were erected in 1591–3 at
Rothwell (on an interesting plan) and at Weekley in 1611. After
1675 these charitable activities came more or less to a standstill,
although a number of elementary schools were founded in the
C18.*

   CHURCH BUILDING after 1720 makes a much better show.
There is not much, but what there is has a great variety of
interest. Chronologically arranged the list of C18 churches looks
like this. Stoke Doyle 1722–5 partly by *Thomas Eayre*, Aynho
1723–5 by *E. Wing* but so much in the style of Archer that he may
well have had a hand in it, Wollaston 1737, with giant Tuscan
columns between nave and aisles, the chancel at Lamport by
W. Smith 1743, with splendid plasterwork by *J. Woolston* of
Northampton, the chancel at Warkton of shortly after 1749 with
its four niches to hold the spectacular monuments to which we
shall turn presently, the large and townish parish church of
Daventry 1752–8, by *David Hiorne*, the only larger Georgian
church in the county, with a spire and giant Tuscan columns
inside, Great Houghton of 1754 by *David Hiorne* with its good,
strong spire, the deliciously fan-vaulted chancel of Wicken by
the gentleman-architect *Thomas Prowse*, and also its nave and
aisles of 1758 with their more stately but less enjoyable tall
quatrefoil piers, and the church at East Carlton 1788, by *Wing
Jun.*, where Gothic was for the first time taken more seriously –
a foretaste of C19 Gothicism.

   The first surviving NONCONFORMIST CHAPELS in the county
are Georgian too,‡ i.e. those of the Congregationalists at Long
Buckby (1771) and Potterspury (1780) and that of the Baptists at
Thrapston (1787). There is also a Moravian Chapel of 1810 at
Culworth and a delightful Friends' Meeting House of 1819 at
Wellingborough. Many more might be mentioned, but they are
too small and too uniform to call for special listing, even in the
gazetteer.

---

* M. Seaborne: *The English School* (1971) lists the following: Ashton near
Oundle, 1705; Finedon, 1714; Lowick, 1717–25; King's Cliffe Boys' School
and Almshouses, 1749, and Girls' School, 1752–4; Ecton, 1752; Hanging
Houghton, 1775; Yelvertoft, 1792 (?); Culworth, 1795.
   ‡ Except for the Doddridge Street Congregational Chapel of 1695 at
Northampton, which is not in its original state.

Georgian CHURCH FURNISHINGS hardly fill a paragraph: some fonts (the best being at Draughton, Oundle, and Cottesbrooke), some decaying stained glass of 1732 at Apethorpe by *I. Rowell*, and two organ cases at Finedon and Towcester – that is all. The organ cases, to be sure, are both something special, the Finedon one by *Shrider*, the Towcester one French or Belgian and originally in the mansion of William Beckford's nabob father.

For CHURCH MONUMENTS on the other hand the situation is reversed, and it is evident that space is lacking to introduce and classify them all. For some the index of artists must suffice (e.g. *E. Bingham* of Peterborough, *J. Hunt* of Northampton, who made the statue of Charles II for All Saints Northampton, and was an apprentice of Gibbons, and the *Cox* family, also of Northampton). Others are anonymous and will not even be found there. We start with the coming of Baroque Classicism, that is Baroque sculpture in Palladian settings. This is what characterizes *Guelfi*'s Duchess of Richmond † 1722 at Deene and the eight monuments by *Rysbrack*. Three of these, at Edgcote, are purely architectural, two are architectural too but have a bust as well (Ecton 1732 and † 1761). Three busts are on the monument at Hardingstone, two of *c.* 1746, the third added *c.* 1759, and an excellent bust is also on the fourth monument at Edgcote (1760). Finally the early Ward Monument at Stoke Doyle has a semi-reclining figure in the C17 and early C18 tradition.* Another such semi-reclining figure is by *Hartshorne* (Thorpe Achurch † 1719). Yet more are anonymous (Lowick † 1705, Lowick † 1718). There are two *Scheemakers* in the county. One, a bust, belongs to the Isham Monument († 1737) at Lamport, whose architecture was probably designed by *Francis Smith* of Warwick. The other, at Rockingham († 1724), has standing figures, with architecture by *Delvaux*. *Roubiliac* was without doubt the most brilliant Georgian sculptor in England, and Northamptonshire is lucky in possessing two of his most spectacular monuments. They face one another in the chancel of Warkton church, and one is hard put to it to decide whether the feminine charms of the monument to Duchess Mary of 1753 or the masculine vigour of the monument to Duke John of 1752 should be valued more highly. Both compositions are completely free, and with their serpentine or zigzag movement through space eminently characteristic of the Rococo. The

* Mr Bailey suggests an attribution to *Rysbrack* for Lady Arabella Oxenden † 1734 at Rockingham.

Lynn Monument at Southwick († 1758) is not inferior to these
65 two. The sculptor of the Langton Freke Monument at Kings
Sutton († 1769) is not recorded. He was clearly influenced by
Roubiliac at his most dramatic, the Roubiliac of the Hargrave
Monument in Westminster Abbey. At Warkton, next to
Roubiliac's Duke John, is the monument to the Duchess of
64 Montagu of 1775. This was designed by *Robert Adam* and the
sculpture carved by *van Gelder*. It is the farewell to Baroque and
Rococo; for though van Gelder still composes according to
Baroque formulae, his style lacks the *brio* and the scintillating
chiselwork of Roubiliac, and Robert Adam of course provided a
setting of very refined and subdued Neo-Classicism. One excellent *John Bacon* (Ashby St Ledgers 1784), several *Nollekens*
(Whiston † 1775, Great Brington † 1783,* Whiston † 1792), and
the curious painted monuments by *Mrs Creed* at Titchmarsh
(early C18) are no more than a postscript. It is Robert Adam and
his style that we must halt at.

It has already been said that in the field of domestic decoration
it swept the board, and so, although no original work by Adam
is known in the county, the country houses of Northamptonshire
have plenty of interiors in his style. The best examples are at
Drayton and date from 1770. *Henry Holland* was responsible for
beautifully restrained interiors at Althorp (1786–90), the younger
98 *Dance* for the fine hall at Laxton Hall, and *Soane* for a series of
rooms at Aynhoe (1800–5). They are of course, with their
idiosyncratic shallow arches and vaults, a good deal removed
from the Adam style of a generation before.

In architecture proper the Adam style – broadly speaking – is
that of Eydon Hall by *James Lewis* (1789-91), of *Samuel Saxon*'s
Courteenhall of 1791–3, of the exquisite Orangery at Barton
Seagrave Hall, and of *Robert Mitchell*'s work at Cottesbrooke
Hall. This includes the lodges and gates, and other minor
structures in the grounds of houses must now be referred to. So
far such subsidiary buildings have only once been mentioned,
the summer houses at Easton Neston and Ecton, in connexion
with the Inigo Jones period. Now more must be introduced, and
work in a variety of styles: classical in the Temple, the Arches,
and the Menagerie at Horton, classical also in the Temple by
the lake at Althorp, but medievalizing in the castellated follies
round Boughton Park and the group of cottages behind a
castellated wall at Preston Capes which were an eye-catcher for
Fawsley. Most of these date from *c.* 1770, although the Hawking

* Designed by *Cipriani*.

Tower at Boughton Park was built by 1756. At about this time MEDIEVALISM made its entry into Northamptonshire. It appeared with Ecton Hall in its most engaging, if an irresponsible, form. Ecton is Gothic and was built in 1756, i.e. two years before Mr Prowse's fan-vaults in the chancel at Wicken. Gothic also are the somewhat later N front of Brockhall Hall and the exceedingly pretty Canal Bridge at Cosgrove.*

The Victorian Age is now nearly with us, and no more need prevent us from exploring its Northamptonshire aspects than two or three notes about the style of the REGENCY and after. One is connected with the FARMHOUSES built by the Duke of Grafton on his estates in the SE corner of the county. They can be seen round Abthorpe, Blakesley, Green's Norton, Paulerspury, Shutlanger, and Stoke Bruerne, and are at once recognizable by their spacious, regular, and rational planning and their plain but sound architecture. They look Regency but were, according to Mr P. I. King's unpublished research, built as late as c. 1841–3. A second note must draw attention to a similarly spacious and rationally planned enterprise, the Barracks at Weedon, begun in 1803 and comprising a tripartite group of quite stately domestic buildings and two rows of long warehouses facing one another across the canal wharf, which is shut off from the canal by a portcullis.

The third note is once again in the nature of a catalogue rather than a commentary. Its purpose is to bring the history of CHURCH MONUMENTS up to date, i.e. to carry it on from about 1800 to the verge of the Victorian style. Most of the best monuments are now signed, but by no means all of them. As for the signed pieces, here are the works of the masters. *Flaxman* first with monuments at Grafton Regis († 1808), Great Billing (Outer Northampton) († 1812), and Great Brington († 1814); *Regnart* second, a minor sculptor but one whose *chef d'œuvre* is in Northamptonshire (George Rush † 1806 at Farthinghoe); *Bacon Jun.* third, who did several monuments at Cottesbrooke including the fine free-standing vase on a pedestal (1815); *Westmacott* fourth with one monument († 1809) at Marston St Lawrence and one (c. 1820) at Grafton Underwood; *Rossi* fifth with an early monument still in the Bacon style at Canons

---

* But *Capability Brown*, while busy landscaping the vast grounds of Burghley House, built a bath house in a neo-Elizabethan derived from the Cecil mansion (or rather from Chipping Campden), and the large gate lodges of 1801 by *Legg* are neo-Elizabethan too, an anachronism, as the Elizabethan Revival is by and large an event of the 1830s and the Victorian age.

Ashby († 1797), one of curiously Victorian Quattrocento inspiration at Ecton († 1817), and a fine (attributed) Grecian monument at Canons Ashby (1818). *Chantrey* is well represented by monuments at Kelmarsh († 1807), Northampton Town Hall (from All Saints, 1817), Easton Neston (1819), Stoke Doyle († 1819), Whittlebury († 1820), and Great Brington (1833). The last empty niche in the chancel at Warkton was finally filled by a very monumental but very cold classical *machine* by *Campbell* († 1827). A monument († 1830) at Stanford is said to be by the Dutchman *Kessells*. Just within our range of dates also come three early monuments by Early Victorian sculptors, that by *Behnes* at Norton († 1825), one by *W. Pitts* at Whiston († 1835), and the two by *Baily* at Easton Neston († 1830 and 1835). By *Westmacott Jun.* is one († 1844) at Stanford. *Tenerani's* monuments at Castle Ashby on the other hand, though the earlier is of 1836, must be seen in Victorian contexts. The second is an over-life-size seated angel of white marble and dates from 1866. The combination of sentimentality with overdone size is wholly Victorian. At Castle Ashby there is also a big *Marochetti* monument († 1858), and that is Gothic and re-introduces the motif of the recumbent effigy. Finally two monuments by *John Gibson* of Rome, at Fawsley († 1856) and Stanford († 1862), the latter probably actually carved by *Mary Thornycroft*. The former is in the Georgian tradition, the latter is again a big Victorian *machine* with Gothic background and recumbent effigy. That finishes the survey of monuments. No later one need be admitted to it.

VICTORIAN ARCHITECTURE does not demand prolonged attention. Few buildings would find admittance in a national as against a county list. Of churches perhaps *Hussey's* big, serious, and prosperous churches of the 1840s (Orlingbury 1843, Braunston 1849) and perhaps the expensively High Victorian interior of Kelmarsh (1874 by *J. K. Colling*) and of Ashley (chancel, 1867 by *Scott**), of church furnishings without any doubt the superb *Morris* glass at Guilsborough (*c*. 1877), and in particular at Middleton Cheney (probably begun 1864), a church which may be called the holy of holies of Morris glass, and of secular buildings certainly *Godwin's* Town Hall of 1861-4 at Northampton, a competent essay in the Geometrical Gothic, though not yet heralding its designer's future originality, certainly *W. M. Teulon's* Overstone Park of *c*. 1860, even if only because it is so memorably self-confident in its gross display of

---

* *Scott's* very first building incidentally is in Northamptonshire, the vicarage at Wappenham of 1833.

elements of many styles, and certainly *Sir Matthew Digby Wyatt*'s Orangery and 'gloriette' at Castle Ashby. The work of the two Scots *Burn* and *Macvicar Anderson* at Lamport and Althorp is more memorable for its self-effacing respect for the past than for Victorian assertiveness. To these must be added the work of two local Northampton architects: *E. F. Law*, equally competent in Classical and Gothic, and *Matthew Holding*, a worthy follower of Pearson.

Finally a word on Victorian ESTATE HOUSING. It is prominent in a number of villages and proof of the care with which Northamptonshire land-owners looked after their tenants. Substantial and picturesque Spencer housing of *c.* 1848 is at Church Brampton, Chapel Brampton, Little Brington, and Harlestone, Grafton housing of *c.* 1850 at Potterspury, Lady Overstone's housing at Sywell of the 1860s, Pulteney housing at Ashley also of the 1860s, and so on to the remarkable Rothschild housing of 1900 etc. at Ashton.

This is TWENTIETH CENTURY, and the C20 requires no more than a postscript. *Comper*'s St Mary Wellingborough begun 33 in 1908 is probably his best church. That is all up to the twenties. And between the twenties and now? At the time of writing the most prominent structure is the M1, that is the London, 102 Birmingham, and Yorkshire Motorway, which enters the county SE of Roade and runs in a NW direction to S of Crick, where it divides into its Birmingham and Yorkshire branches. Its course was predetermined by undated reasons of geography. It is significant that it runs roughly parallel with the Romans' Watling Street, the Grand Junction Canal (built by *William Jessop*, begun 1790), and the former Midland Railway.* At or near Weedon all four meet.

The MOTORWAY is the C20 version of Watling Street. No more than 55 miles of it existed when this Introduction was written; not much compared with the German *Autobahnen* or even Italian *autostrade*, and moreover started remarkably (and very Englishly) late. However, it must be admitted that the soil of England is so closely and intimately worked and so subtly landscaped that the intrusion of the motorway was bound to be

* As for railways serving Northamptonshire in particular, the bill for the Blisworth–Northampton–Peterborough line was passed in 1843. There were many pretty neo-Tudor stations along the line of 1845 by *W. Livock*. The line was closed in 1964 and few now remain (1972). In 1960 there were still nearly fifty stations in use in Northamptonshire and the Soke of Peterborough. By 1966 they had been reduced to six.

specially violent. It was for this reason that opposition to it remained for so long. *Sir Owen Williams & Partners* were briefed in 1951, the decision to go ahead was made in 1955, and work started in 1958 and was completed in 1959 – quite an achievement, considering that e.g. more than 130 BRIDGES had to be built. They are of six standard types. The bigger ones are of mass concrete with the simplest reinforcements, and impress by a cyclopean rudeness rather than by elegance. Especially surprising are the supports between the traffic lanes in the N and S directions: a kind of elementary columns, without base and capital, but with an abacus – a curious period suggestion, not called for in this forward-looking job. Sir Owen Williams evidently wanted to impress permanence on us, and permanence is a doubtful quality in devices connected with vehicles and means of transport. Elegance, lightness, and resilience might have been preferable, an elegance achieved so spectacularly already in Swiss concrete bridges before the First World War and – with the aid of the more recent device of pre-stressing – often since in other countries. On the motorway elegance was arrived at only in the foot-bridges. Even retaining walls, revetments, etc., are of concrete blocks. The motorway has three traffic lanes in either direction, as against the two of the *Autobahnen* and the four of some American highways. The total width of the motorway is 105 ft. The centre strip is 13 ft wide and so far unlandscaped, which must be the next job to be contemplated and carried out in consultation with landscape architects.

So the Motorway is MODERN ARCHITECTURE only with reservations. Nor is there much else that would qualify for this survey,* though there is one worthwhile example of a boldly planned housing estate (King's Heath, Northampton, by *J. L. Womersley*), and there are examples of the first order of modern art and examples of interesting and important architecture of the years prior to 1930. They are The Hill, Thorpe Mandeville, by *Voysey*, a good example of his modest country-house style, actually built just before the turn of the century, *Lutyens*'s extensive additions to Ashby St Ledgers of 1904-24,‡ very impressive indeed especially in the last years, though of course emphatically pre-modern, and the houses for Mr Bassett Lowke at Northampton, one altered and decorated by *Mackintosh* in 1916, and New Ways designed by *Peter Behrens* in 1925, to

---

* The most conspicuous examples are of course the schools, and some of them are mentioned in the gazetteer.

‡ The work of 1923-4 has been demolished.

which some of Mackintosh's work in the previous house was transferred. New Ways is the earliest work in the C20 style in the whole of England, and as such deserves a Number One in the official list of protected buildings.* The somewhat cubistic late style of Mackintosh fits in surprisingly well. And the works of modern art? There are four: *Graham Sutherland*'s virtually Expressionist Crucifixion of 1946 at St Matthew Northampton, the late *Evie Hone*'s equally Expressionist stained glass at Wellingborough parish church of 1955, *John Piper* and *Patrick Reyntiens*'s moving, also Expressionist glass at Oundle School 46 Chapel of 1955–6, and *Henry Moore*'s Virgin, again at St 47 Matthew Northampton. This was commissioned in 1943 and is, apart from its noble undated beauty, historically important as the great sculptor's first step in the direction of increased concreteness for certain purposes. The placing of an image in a church was recognized by Mr Moore as such a purpose, and the name of the rector who commissioned him and Mr Sutherland must be recorded in conclusion; for he was the first patron of both for work to be made with a view to being seen in public. He is the Rev. J. W. A. Hussey, now Dean of Chichester.

POSTSCRIPT (1972)‡

Not much need be added to bring this Introduction up to date. Inevitably, it is in the larger towns that the most far-reaching changes are taking place, but it is too soon to assess the impact of the town centre redevelopments now under way at Northampton, Daventry, Kettering, and Wellingborough. (For the negative aspects of these *see* the Foreword to this Second Edition.) In two cases these redevelopments are part of major expansion schemes. Daventry is to treble its size in the next ten years. Its new housing is by the *City of Birmingham's Architect's Department*. The work of the *Northampton Development Corporation* is only just starting, with the new Eastern District of Northampton. At Corby as well (although a New Town) the centre is being brought up to date. But it is the recent housing at Corby which deserves special mention here. Kingswood, by *John Stedman* 103 (1965–72), ingenious in its compact yet humane planning, intriguing in its visual variety, is a notable example of the kind of

---

* It is in fact listed Grade II (1967).
‡ By Bridget Cherry.

low-rise housing which is now becoming increasingly popular.*
Among recent major buildings the Princess Marina Hospital at
Northampton by *Stillman & Eastwick-Field* should be mentioned. Of the many new schools one may single out St John's,
Tiffield by *James Crabtree*, and Irchester Arkwright School and
the extension to Loddington Hall, both by the County Architect's
Department, all in their different ways sympathetic to their
surroundings. This is true as well of the vestry at Weston
Favell, by *A. A. J. Marshman*, who has also built for himself an
interesting house at Horton. Finally, church furnishings, and
here the names which already appear in the Introduction have
to be repeated: excellent stained glass by *John Piper* and *Patrick
Reyntiens* at Wellingborough, and a tombstone by *Henry Moore* at
Weedon Lois.

FURTHER READING

It is customary to end these introductions with a few biblio-
graphical references. They are only too simple in the case
of Northamptonshire. The *Victoria County History* (4 vols.,
1902–37) has admirably covered so far the NE half of the county,
from a line s of Northampton to the Soke of Peterborough. The
architectural notes are by the late Sir Charles Peers and models
of their kind. In 1849 *Architectural Notes of the Archdeaconry of
Northampton* came out, and these comprise the hundreds of
Guilsborough and Nobottle Grove NW of Northampton which
the Victoria County History has not yet done. The hundreds of
Rothwell and Corby are, alas, not tackled by either. The
Ministry of Housing and Local Government's unpublished lists
of buildings of architectural and historic interest now cover the
whole county.‡ Nearly all the major country houses have at one
time or another been written up in *Country Life*. In addition
three admirable books by J. Alfred Gotch deal with them: *A
Complete Account of the Buildings erected by Sir Thomas Tresham*,
1883, *The Old Halls and Manor Houses of Northamptonshire*,
1936, and *Squires' Houses . . . of Northamptonshire*, 1939. The

* The fashion for high-rise housing has almost completely bypassed
Northamptonshire. There is an early example at Northampton, St Mary's
Court by *J. L. Womersley*, 1952. Tall office blocks are only just beginning to
appear. The new housing in the Eastern District is low-rise. The first area by
the Development Corporation (architect *Gordon Redfern*), Thorplands, under
construction in 1972, looks very promising.

‡ The Rural Districts of Brackley, Northampton, Oundle, and Thrapston
were completed after the first edition of this book was published.

ancient county histories must still be looked up, especially J. Bridges (2 vols., 1724, but published only in 1791) and G. T. Baker (2 vols., 1822–41), and in addition John Morton's *Natural History of Northamptonshire*, published in 1712, and the gazetteer in F. Whellan's *History and Gazetteer of Northamptonshire*, 1874. Among more recent guides is Juliet Smith's *Shell Guide* (1968). The learned journals to be consulted are the *Reports and Papers* of the Northampton Antiquarian Society (parts of the publications of the Associated Architectural Societies) and, more recent and more enjoyable, *Northamptonshire Past and Present*. The latter is published by the Northamptonshire Records Society, a very active and enlightened body. The following deal with particular aspects: a number of excellent books by R. M. Sergeantson on individual churches of Northampton (1897–1911); E. Sharpe, Johnson and Kersey: *The Churches of the Nene Valley*, 1880; C. A. Markham: *Church Plate of Northamptonshire*, 1894; A. Hartshorne: *Recumbent Effigies of Northamptonshire*, 1867; and Hudson and Hartshorne: *The Monumental Brasses of Northampton*, 1853. Such general books as Mill Stephenson on brasses, Aymer Vallance on screens, A. Gardner on alabaster monuments need not be referred to specially. A line must however be spared for the drawings of Northamptonshire buildings by George Clarke, a schoolmaster of Hanging Houghton who also later went to live at Scaldwell. They are kept in the Northampton Public Library and the Northamptonshire Record Office. For the prehistoric and Roman periods, the first volume of the *Victoria County History* is the only – and now much dated – summary. Recent archaeological discoveries are now usefully brought together in the *Bulletin of the Northamptonshire Archaeological Societies*. Apart from the local journals, for the Roman period the annual accounts of recent excavations of the *Journal of Roman Studies* are useful. E. T. Artis: *Durobrivae of Antonine Identified* (1828) and B. R. Hartley: 'Notes on the Roman Pottery Industry in the Nene Valley', *Peterborough Museum Soc. Occ. Pp.*, No. 2 (1960), are two valuable references for this important centre of industrial Roman Britain.

NORTHAMPTONSHIRE

*

ABINGTON see NORTHAMPTON, p. 343

ABTHORPE

ST JOHN BAPTIST. By *Ewan Christian*, 1869–71. Quite large, with a spire on its NW tower which has nothing to do with Northamptonshire. The style of the church is Geometrical to Dec. The interior is uninspired. – STAINED GLASS. E window by *Mayer* of Munich, 1873. – PLATE. Set, 1738.

Opposite the church a HOUSE of 1682 with a gable end with mullioned windows of, from bottom to top, four, three, two lights.

SCHOOL, NE end of the village. The old part is of 1642. Three bays with a central dormer. The windows are mullioned and of three–two–three lights.

FOSCOTE HOUSE, HILL FARMHOUSE, and CHARLOCK FARMHOUSE are three farms built by the Grafton estate (cf. Introduction, p. 67). They date from *c.* 1840 and are characterized by a three-bay house with widely spaced windows and a low-pitched, hipped slate roof, and in addition lower wings arranged in line with the house or at r. angles to it. The house may have a pedimental gable or a doorway with columns, a metope frieze, and a pediment.

ACHURCH see THORPE ACHURCH

ADSTONE

ALL SAINTS. Nave with bellcote and lower chancel. Early C13 s aisle of three bays. Low arcade with circular piers and octagonal abaci. Single-chamfered arches. In the nave w wall a lancet window. Heavily restored in 1843, when the chancel was added, and again in 1896 (BB). – PLATE. Cup, 1623; (Paten, of the same time, according to the Rector).

MANOR HOUSE. On the N side of the Green. Later C17. Handsome, with a recessed centre, four-light mullioned windows in two storeys, and a hipped roof. Staircase with dumb-bell balusters.

METHODIST CHAPEL. 1849, but still in the Georgian tradition, with simple arched windows. Tiny.

(OLD VICARAGE, E of the church. By *E. F. Law*, 1870. Neo-Elizabethan. SCHOOL, 1846. BB)

ALDERTON

7040

ST MARGARET. Late Perp W tower. Money was left for it in 1522 and 1528. The rest of 1848. – FONT. Octagonal, Perp. Stem and bowl in one, the stem panelled, the bowl with a frieze of leaves and small heads. – PULPIT. Dated 1631. With the usual panels with short broad blank arches and oblong panels with arabesques over. Back panel with a biblical inscription. Tester. – WEST GALLERY, incorporating Perp bench fronts or backs. – PLATE. Cup, 1570; Paten, *c.* 1650. – MONUMENT. Effigy of a cross-legged Knight. Oak. Of the early C14 (Sir William de Combemartyne † 1318 ?).

MANOR HOUSE. 1695. Symmetrical three-bay front with quoins and two horizontally oval windows above the doorway.

RINGWORK, close to the church. Obviously that of a medieval castle.

ALDWINKLE

0080

ST PETER. The oldest element is the W impost and the W pier of the N arcade. The pier is round and has a shallow capital with foliage and heads and a square abacus, i.e. belongs to the late C12. The rest of the arcade is of *c.* 1300 (quatrefoil pier, double-chamfered pointed arches), i.e. later than the S arcade which, with its round piers and round or octagonal abaci and its responds on head-corbels, is C13. C13 also the PISCINA in the N aisle on short triple shafts. Late C13 some S aisle windows (W, first S, E – i.e. Y-tracery, Y-tracery with a circle in the spandrel, two lights with a circle). Dec one other (flowing tracery) and the S porch. Dec and Perp N aisle windows, Dec chancel (see the windows, especially the tall one of three lights on the S side, and see the chancel arch on head-stops), and Dec the W tower. Ogee-arched W window with Perp tracery, triple-chamfered arch towards the nave with one chamfer on head-stops, circular windows with C19 tracery,* bell-openings with reticulation motif, spire with tall broaches carrying small pinnacles on the top and three tiers of lucarnes. Inside the

* By *Slater* (N. Taylor).

tower pretty doorway to the staircase with cusped ogee head. –
STAINED GLASS. In the s windows substantial remains of the
original early C14 glass, especially the two figures of St
Christopher and St George. – E window by *Kempe*, 1900, a
little different from his usual production. High up, to the l.
and r., a kneeling figure of a donor priest and angels, of the
C14. – MONUMENT. Mrs Davenant, 1616. Much strap
decoration; no figures.

ALL SAINTS (disused at the time of writing). The interior is
predominantly C13, the exterior C15. Of the arcades one s pier
seems earlier than the rest. All piers round with round abaci
and double-chamfered pointed arches. The chancel arch on
cone corbels with one capital with nailhead enrichment also
C13. Late C13 one chancel N window (bar tracery). Perp the
Chambre Chapel, founded by the will of Elizabeth Chambre
in 1489. Three- and four-light windows, capitals inside with
shields attached to them. Battlements, originally with corner
pinnacles. s door inserted later. The nave and aisles are
also embattled. w tower with clasping buttresses and small
decorative motifs at the corners of all set-offs (cf. St John
Stamford). Doorway with tracery panels, w window with
crocketed ogee top, tall bell-openings, two of two lights on
each side, straight-headed, with transoms, set back in rectangular frames, quatrefoil frieze above, big gargoyles, four tall
pinnacles. Some minor Dec contributions, i.e. N aisle w and E
windows, s aisle w window, s porch entrance (the porch itself
has been taken down and the entrance shifted closer to the
church). Other N aisle windows Perp. Perp vestry. – COM-
MUNION RAIL. Jacobean, with vertically symmetrical
balusters. – (STAINED GLASS. Remains of *c.* 1489 in the
Chambre Chapel and other windows. RM) – BRASS. William
Aldwyncle † 1463, a figure of *c.* 2 ft length (chancel, NE
corner).

OLD RECTORY, opposite All Saints. Dryden's birthplace.
Thatched, with C18 canted bay-window on the l. side.
(C14 walls are incorporated inside. DOE) (SW of All Saints
TAVERN COTTAGE, with a plaque with three towers and
masons' tools; also an inscription and the date 1834. BB)

BRIDGE. Of 1760, with three round arches.

Attractive, long village street, flanked by many stone houses and
fine trees.

PREHISTORIC REMAINS. At Aldwinkle is the site of a Neolithic mortuary enclosure and a 90 ft circular ditch enclosure;

two Bronze Age round barrows containing inhumations in boat-shaped coffins, both levelled by quarrying in 1963; an Iron Age ditched enclosure with a causeway and gate and containing centrally a round hut 37 ft in diameter; and a complex of Late Iron Age ditches.

ROMAN REMAINS. Evidence for a Roman timber bridge, showing several phases of reconstruction or renovation, has been found on the alignment of the Huntingdon-Leicester Roman road. The evidence suggests that the first bridge was constructed in the CI A.D.

6060

ALTHORP

The estate was bought in 1508 by John Spencer, a sheep farmer of Wormleighton in Warwickshire. He obtained leave in 1512 to create a park of 300 acres at Althorp. During alterations *c.* 1958, fragments of medieval pieces were found. They include a stiff-leaf capital, perhaps from the former church. About 1573 the house was enlarged, with a courtyard and two projecting wings. Neither the early nor the late C16 house has ever been destroyed, though no features of any eloquence belonging to them can be seen any longer. The remains of a large Tudor window and of several smaller ones were however discovered *c.* 1958 in the N wall of the Entrance Hall. The next stage in the history of the building is the making of the grand staircase in the former courtyard, for which Earl Spencer has found bills according to which work on it started in 1666. The Long Gallery was altered and panelled in 1682. Much more was done to the interior in the 1670s and 1680s. In 1688 John Evelyn called the house a palace and the state-rooms such 'as may become a great prince'. Too little of this remains, and it seems hardly worth recording that we still have three staircases with strong turned balusters. Then between 1729 and 1733 came the splendid Palladian work on the stables and the interior, by *Roger Morris*.* It is among

---

* The evidence for this attribution is in a letter from Sarah, Duchess of Marlborough to her grand-daughter the Duchess of Bedford (Bedford Office, Woburn MS H.M.C. no. 205 vol. II no. 57, undated, but ascribed to 1733), to which Earl Spencer drew our attention, and which Mrs M. Draper, the Bedford Archivist, kindly located: 'but for other debts that is yet an intire secret to me more than that my reason tells me that they must be vast, for in the first place the Duke of Marlborough I find he is disatisfy'd himself with Mr Moris's demands. . . . I found by what he did say that there is a great deal more than the stables, and some in the park, . . . whatever the ex-the most impressive at Althorp. It was begun for the fifth Earl of Sunderland, whose mother was Marlborough's daughter and who succeeded to the Marlborough title, and completed by his brother. This brother's son was created Earl Spencer. Vardy built for him Spencer House in London in 1756–65, but when repairs to the roof became necessary at Althorp in 1772, he was dead, and the job went to *Sir Robert Taylor*. In 1787–91 *Henry Holland* gave the house more or less its present appearance. Part of his work was the provision of the functionally very desirable corridors towards the forecourt. Finally, *c.* 1877, *MacVicar Anderson* made alterations inside and added the Dining Room, which projects to the E on the N side.

The house is of light grey brick, partly consisting of so-called mathematical tiles, i.e. tiles made to look like bricks, attached to the original exterior of red brick. The grey brick dates from *Holland*'s alterations. The house is two storeys in height. One approaches it from the s (or rather SE), where it has a double-stepped forecourt. The recessed centre is faced with Roche Abbey stone. It is of five bays with giant Corinthian pilasters and a pediment. The N side has nine bays and a three-bay pediment and on the ground floor three windows are distinguished by pediments. This exterior is dignified, but no more than that, and would not prepare for the glories of the interior, glories of architecture, furniture, and painting. The latter two, alas, are outside the scope of *The Buildings of England*.

Splendid ENTRANCE HALL, the noblest Georgian room in the county. Dated 1733. It rises nearly to the full height of the house and has a deep coffered coving. In the corners big cartouches with eagles and leaves. Plain panels in the middle with frames adorned with Greek key. Charming frieze below

---

pense may bee I am sure Allthrop is much the worse for it, and that all which was wanting to make that place the most agreable habitation that ever I saw was only to make sash windows in the hous, and a plain useful stable for thirty or fourty hors's at most, which is full as many as any man could keep that is not madd, when 'tis become a custom to let strangers horses goe to the inns and this might have been don in a right and usefull way for a trifle with the materials of the old stables and the stones I sent from Holdenby in your brother Robert's time, but I believe that there is now built stables for a hundred horse or near it, what can be so ridiculous as this, and to pull down the handsomest and most usefull building in the court of Allthrop, and make a very expensive building in the parks which can be of no use. . . .'

with Diana, and 'affronted' cherubs, hounds, and foxes. Grand doorway in the back wall with attached fluted Corinthian columns and an open pediment. Set into the walls – as an integral part of the decoration – large paintings of horses, grooms, hounds, etc., by *John Wootton*. In the SMALL DINING ROOM to the E a stone fireplace brought from Wormleighton *c.* 1925 and panelling of 1605 from the same house.

85   The STAIRCASE behind the hall fills the space of the former courtyard. It is of a unique monumentality for its date in England. The staircase itself is of oak and rises in the middle of the room in one straight, wide flight, with an intermediate landing, until it reaches the end wall, where for a few steps it branches l. and r. to reach two doors on each side. It then joins up with the comfortably wide gallery, or rather balcony all along the walls. This balcony dates from Holland's alterations. When in 1669 Cosimo III, the future Grand Duke of Tuscany, and Count Lorenzo Magolotti paid a visit to Althorp, Magolotti was especially taken with the staircase, which he found 'constructed with great magnificence' and described as 'dividing itself into two equal branches' and leading 'to the grand saloon from which is the passage to the chambers'. From this remark one can deduce that before Holland's balcony was added, the only access to the upper rooms on the garden side was through the door on the l. at the top of the stairs.* The balustrading of the staircase and balcony is all of wood, with dumb-bell balusters. Originally the staircase was stained the colour of walnut; in Holland's time it was painted white. The present appearance of the staircase hall owes much to *MacVicar Anderson*. He enlarged the room to the W by adding to it the small remaining part of the interior courtyard. The decoration of the coved and coffered ceiling (which formerly had plain coffering) is also his, as are the heavy brackets beneath the balcony. At the W end of the staircase hall a chimneypiece from Spencer House London, i.e. of 1758.

To the NE the SUNDERLAND ROOM. This still has Lord Sunderland's carved cornice. The two chimneypieces are from Spencer House, one by Athenian *Stuart*, the other by *Vardy*. There follows the MARLBOROUGH ROOM with two other fireplaces from Spencer House, one of them by *Scheemakers*. The LIBRARY, at r. angles to the Marlborough Room, i.e. facing W, is a tripartite apartment with screens of unfluted

* This arrangement is shown in a plan in *Vitruvius Britannicus*, Vol. II.

Ionic columns. The ceiling in the Adam style is by *MacVicar Anderson*. He also added the central double doors. The YELLOW DRAWING ROOM has a fine chimneypiece designed by *Holland* and made by *Deval* with circular, tapering, spiral-fluted shafts l. and r. and a Victorian ceiling by *Broadbent* of Leicester. By the same the ceiling in the SOUTH DRAWING ROOM. This, in Holland's alterations, was the Dining Room with an Anteroom. It has a doorcase by Athenian *Stuart* from Spencer House. Fireplace of 1802 by *Lancelot Wood*. One more room on the ground floor must be mentioned: the BLUE SITTING ROOM at the SE end of the E wing. It is a masterpiece of *Holland*'s with panels painted by *Pernotin*. It was shifted to its present position by MacVicar Anderson.*

The most interesting room on the first floor is the CHAPEL in the E wing. This was seen and commented on as too small in 1675 by John Evelyn. The later C17 balustrade with the openwork foliage comes from the Duke of Marlborough's pew at St Albans. The doorcases are from Spencer House. Plain bolection chimneypiece by *Joshua Marshall*. Armorial glass in the windows, some dated 1588, formerly in a window W of the staircase.

On the N side, the suite of five rooms made by Lord Sunderland, and later divided up, has recently been restored. The rooms have specially fine cornices. In the PATCHWORK ROOM chimneypiece by *Repton* from Harlestone. In the GREAT ROOM (previously two rooms but now one again) two fireplaces from the time of Holland. They are by *Lancelot Wood*, from elsewhere in the house. In the WEST ROOM fireplace by *P. C. Hardwick*, *c.* 1850. In the W wing, in place of the Elizabethan Long Gallery is the seven-bay gallery made for Lord Sunderland in 1682–3. This has fine, large panelling, arranged so as to fit the C17 frames of the pictures of court beauties by *van Dyck*, *Lely*, and others. Fireplace from Spencer House by Athenian *Stuart*. The frieze is a copy from that of the Lysicrates Monument.

It might well be argued that the STABLES by *Roger Morris* (*see* the footnote on p. 78) are the finest piece of architecture at Althorp. They are of ironstone with a deep Tuscan portico (two pairs of columns) – inspired without any doubt by Inigo Jones's St Paul Covent Garden and not by Palladio. Horace Walpole mentioned the 'pediments like Covent Garden

---

* And is not shown to the public.

Church, that for that purpose have good effect'. Typically English Palladian also the four corner towers or eminences, a motif familiar from Wilton and then Houghton, Holkham, Hagley, and other places. Circular and semicircular shapes among the windows – this Palladian as well as Anglo-Palladian motif. The s range has recently been restored and is to be used as a museum. Very elegant interior with Tuscan columns supporting central groin-vaults. The aisles have transverse tunnel-vaults.

To the sw *Morris*'s GARDENER'S HOUSE, small, but decidedly grand. Restored in 1971. Ashlar-faced with a 'Venetian' bay in the middle, derived directly from Palladio's Basilica at Vicenza. This bay is flanked by an arched bay on pillars l. and r. Pyramid roof with central chimney. At the back three bays and one and a half storeys. Doorway with pediment on brackets. In line with the Gardener's House to the s an ARCHWAY with quoins, a Greek frieze, and a broken pediment.

The formal GARDEN round the house and the stone pillars and ironwork to the forecourt are by *W. M. Teulon* and date from 1860–3. The gardener was *W. B. Thomas*. In the gardens to the NE, by the lake known as the ROUND OVAL, a TEMPLE of wood with portico of four Roman Doric columns and a pediment. The Temple originally stood in the garden of the Admiralty. At the other end of the Lake the DAIRY, of ironstone with a pyramid roof. This was built in 1786. Delightful interior with original *Wedgwood* tiles and dairy utensils.

Yet further NW the STANDING or FALCONRY, a curious, compact composition dated 1611 but in most of its details decidedly Vanbrughian. Oblong with a porch-like centre projection to the front and a broader projection at the back. Arched doorway; arcading on the first floor, which was originally open for watching the feats of falconry; top gable. To the l. and r. an arched window, again blank arcading on the first floor, again gables. The side elevations also have blank arcading and gables. The staircase is in the r. wing. It has stone walls and a moulded handrail partly recessed into the wall. The back with two gables and more Vanbrughian detail was added in 1901.

EAST LODGE. Of *c.* 1810, one-storeyed with raised pedimented centre. Doorways with Gibbs surrounds. An elevation exists signed by *Kirshaw*, 1818, but also an undated one by *Whiting*.* Big cast-iron gates.

* Both were builders working in Northampton in the early C19.

BRINGTON LODGES. Of c. 1730, with gatehouses.

Planting began in the PARK in the C16. There is a whole series of date stones (1576–8, 1589, 1602–3, 1625, 1798, 1800, 1901).*

APETHORPE

0090

ST LEONARD. Mostly Perp, but the S chapel of 1621. This, the Mildmay Chapel, has windows with cusped, pointed lights, but no tracery, a three-bay arcade with debased Perp, emphatically pre-Classical, piers, and above them ornate stucco work not at all Perp. Heavy cartouches with gristly rather than strapwork surrounds, fat guilloche, big cherubs' heads and draperies. The tower arch is similarly debased Perp, and the ashlar-faced tower has indeed a date 1633. Bell-openings round-arched with Y-tracery. Recessed spire. – FONT. C18 baluster with small marble bowl. – REREDOS. Of wood, with pilasters. Probably *temp.* Queen Anne. – PULPIT. Georgian with heavily moulded panels. – TOWER SCREEN. Probably of c. 1633. With sturdy balusters and moulded panels. – PAINTING. Christ walking on the Lake, by *R. S. Lauder*. – STAINED GLASS. E window. By *I. Rowell* of High Wycombe, 1732. In full decay. – S chapel E window. Interesting work of 1621, English but entirely in the Flemish C16 style. – ARMS. Arms and a silk tabard in the Mildmay Chapel, of Sir Anthony Mildmay and Sir Francis Fane. – PLATE. Set, 1635. – MONUMENTS. The huge monument to Sir Anthony Mildmay, † 1617, dominates the church. It is almost too high to fit into the S chapel built to house it. Black and white marble. Recumbent effigies on a big sarcophagus. The four life-size figures of Piety, Charity, Wisdom, and Justice stand at the angles holding open draperies which fall from a circular centre raised as a lantern. On this a seated figure, and two more seated figures at the head and foot ends of the canopy. These represent Faith, Hope, and Charity. The monument is among the best of its date in England. – Sir Richard Dalton † 1442, late C15 alabaster effigy. Above the head scene of the Coronation of the Virgin (chancel N window). – John Leigh, 1627. Tablet with broken pediment rising in two shanks outward instead of inward. On one shank a seated figure. – John Fane, infant son of Lord Burghersh, † 1816. White marble effigy of a baby with bonnet, asleep on a couch.

* Details from J. M. Steane.

STOCKS AND WHIPPING POST, W of the church.

AGENT'S HOUSE, S of the church. 1711. Five bays, two storeys, cross windows. Doorway with broad frame and pediment on brackets.

DOVECOTE, N of the Hall. Circular, with cupola. C17.

APETHORPE HALL. The house and the manor belonged to Sir Guy Wolston in 1491, and early in the C16 to his son-in-law Thomas Empson. They were bought in 1515 by Henry Keble, grocer of London. His grandson, Lord Mountjoy, sold them in 1543 to Henry VIII. In 1550 they went to Sir Walter Mildmay, and passed from his son to his grandson-in-law Sir Francis Fane in 1617. Sir Francis became Earl of Westmorland, and the estate remained in that family till 1904, when it was bought by Leonard Brassey, M.P., later Lord Brassey of Apethorpe, nephew of the first Earl Brassey, a very rich man. The house is now a school.

It is built round two courtyards, the principal one being E of the other. The house is thus an oblong. It is about 240 by 120 ft in size and very varied in appearance. The building history is complicated. It ranges from a substantial part of c. 1500 to the early C 20. The house of c. 1500 had as its core what is the core still, the Hall range between the two courts. Its façade is to the E court and has here a porch with the Hall on its l. and a canted bay-window at the l. (S) end of the Hall. There are also rooms beyond to the S and the N where half the N range belongs to the same date. The end here is the Gateway and the stair-turret to its E. The work of c. 1500 has windows with arched lights. The porch entrance has a four-centred arch, the bay-window a transom and arched lights also below it, the gateway a pretty oriel towards the court, the turret an ogee cap. The two small bay-windows in the N and S corners of the Hall range are supposed to be mid-C16 additions. The parapet, the bold curved gables, and the finials all belong to c. 1620–5, i.e. the time of Sir Francis Fane. The side of the Hall range which turns towards the Back Court, i.e. the W court, was given a new, even frontage about 1530–50. But behind this, inside the building, the back porch of the Hall is still in existence, and also the walls of several rooms including the Kitchen in the NE corner of the Back Court. This court is altogether, with the exception of the C18 Orangery on its S side, the work of c. 1530–50. Some windows still have arched lights, but most of them are simply straight-headed.

The exterior of Apethorpe Hall is most impressive from the

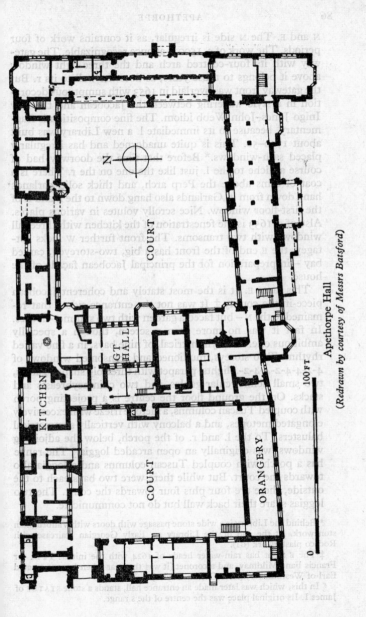

Apethorpe Hall
(Redrawn by courtesy of Messrs Batsford)

N and E. The N side is irregular, as it contains work of four periods. The work of *c.* 1500 is at once recognizable. The gateway with its four-centred arch and the three-light window above it belongs to those years, as does the wall to its r. But the gateway front was overlaid in 1653 with sumptuous decoration in a style wavering between the Jacobean and the new Inigo Jones–John Webb idiom. The fine composition is fragmentary, because to its immediate l. a new Library was built about 1740–50. This is quite unadorned and has irregularly placed sash-windows.* Before that time the doorway had of course a niche to the l. just like the one on the r. There is a coat of arms above the Perp arch, and thick solid garlands hang down from it. Garlands also hang down to the l. and r. of the first-floor window. Nice scrolly volutes in various places. Also of *c.* 1653 is the fenestration of the kitchen with three tall windows with two transoms. The front further W looks cottagey, the E end of the front has a big, two-storeyed, canted bay – in preparation for the principal Jacobean façade of the house.

This faces E. It is the most stately and coherent Jacobean piece in the county.‡ It was not the entrance side – that remained to the N – but faced a garden with two summer-houses. In fact it was no more than a screen, though a specially ambitious one. It is symmetrical, of nine bays, in a fine varied rhythm. Two storeys, mullioned and transomed windows of 4-2-4-4-2-4-4-2-4 lights, parapet with three big shaped gables, two small semicircular gables, and two chimneybreasts and stacks. On the ground floor the centre is a projecting porch with coupled Tuscan columns, a metope frieze with excessively elongated metopes, and a balcony with vertically symmetrical balusters. To the l. and r. of the porch, below the adjoining windows, was originally an open arcaded loggia.§ The range has a porch with coupled Tuscan columns and a loggia also towards the court. But while there were two bays each to the outside, there are four plus four towards the court. The two loggias share their back wall but do not communicate.

* Behind the Library is a wide stone passage with doors with Vanbrughian stonework. At the end of the Library an Early Georgian staircase with Rococo plasterwork (G I).

‡ The E front has rain-water heads of 1624 with the initials FFM for Francis Fane Mildmay, and a coronet (it was the year when he was created Earl of Westminster) (Alec Clifton-Taylor).

§ In this, which was later made an entrance hall, stands a stone STATUE of James I. Its original place was the centre of the s range.

To continue with the court, the N side, apart from the work of *c.* 1500 already referred to, has the back of the Early Georgian Library and, to the W of the gateway, remodelled windows of the same time. The S side is also of *c.* 1620–5, but was remodelled again *c.* 1740–50. It has a three-bay centre with Roman Doric columns and a pediment. Four bays to the l., three to the r. Behind this front on the ground floor is a paved passage with doorways at its E and W ends. These have heavy Gibbs surrounds. The W doorway leads to the Georgian staircase, and the room has a third such doorway in its W wall. The S façade of the range is a mixture of Jacobean and neo-Jacobean of 1904. The architect of the alterations and additions was *Sir Reginald Blomfield*. To the l. of the S façade in the S range of the Back Court is the Orangery, with an ashlar façade with parapet. This was built in 1718.

Of interiors not yet mentioned the following deserve special notice. The Great Hall has an original door of *c.* 1500 with very pretty tracery, and a roof on Early Elizabethan corbels.* The Minstrels' Gallery is of the late C17. Behind the dais end of the Hall a Jacobean staircase. The main staircase is mid C17. The most splendid Jacobean rooms lie on the first floor in the S and E ranges. In the S range (from W) first the Tapestry Room with a splendid coved ceiling with thick stucco decoration in star-shaped panels with broad frames, all very deeply modelled. The chimneypiece here is of 1562. It is, as it is dated, a historically important piece. Fireplace surround with pilasters with sunk panels and roundels (cf. Deene Park, Great Hall, pre-1572). Overmantel with inscription in a strapwork frame flanked by prettily decorated pilasters and fluted tapering pilasters. The Drawing Room, in the centre of the S range, has a chimneypiece of *c.* 1620–5. This has a relief of the Sacrifice of Isaac and standing allegorical figures to the l. and r. Coved ceiling with less fanciful stucco panels, also with broad frames. Then follows the King's Room. The ceiling is again coved, but has a large oblong centre panel with a coat of arms. Strapwork around trailing on instead of forming actual panels. Chimneypiece with Justice and Vigilance seated under a canopy with curtains pulled open. A cherub appears at the top holding a coronet. Sir Francis Fane was raised to an earldom in 1624. Termini caryatids l. and r. Pretty scene with little horsemen on the frieze above the fireplace opening. The SE corner room

* An Early Elizabethan fireplace was removed to Emmanuel College Cambridge in 1950 (Alec Clifton-Taylor). The Hall is now the chapel.

(Prince's Room) has a flat plaster ceiling, again with broad
bands. Overmantel with wide open pediment, two awkward
figures seated on it, and above the open part of the pediment
relief of a ship in full sail, again pedimented. Does the ship
refer to Prince Charles's rash journey to Spain in 1623, when
he hoped to win the Infanta? The E side is almost entirely
occupied by the Long Gallery. The plaster ceiling still has the
thin ribs of the Elizabethan style. The walls are panelled, and
the chimneypiece has a spirited standing figure of King David
in a niche. To his l. and r., on the shanks of an open pediment,
two allegorical figures. In the broad frieze above the fireplace
opening two sirens flanking an inscription and holding fat,
compact, hanging garlands. The inscription reads:

> Rare & ever to be wisht maye sound heere
> Instruments wᶜʰ fainte sprites and muses cheere
> Composing for the Body, Soule and Eare
> Which sickness, sadness and Foule Spirits feare.

ROMAN VILLA. Excavated in 1859. Its remains lie within the
park, ¼ m. SE of the Hall. The courtyard containing the main
buildings measured *c.* 230 by 240 ft. The principal block, with
hypocausts and two fine mosaics, was on the N side, with two
other wings to the E and W protruding in front of the courtyard wall and paved entrance gate; the bath block lay in the
SE corner. Collyweston slate was used for the roofs. The
pottery included both 'terra sigillata' and Castor ware, while
the coin evidence indicated that the main period of settlement
was in the C4 A.D.

BLUE FIELD FARM, ½ m. NE. With an interesting barn. Slits
in the end walls. Four posts inside, l. and r. of the cross-
cartway through.

ARBURY BANKS *see* CHIPPING WARDEN

ARBURY HILL *see* BADBY

7080

ARTHINGWORTH

ST ANDREW. The S arcade contains C12 work. One original
pier, circular with a many-scalloped capital and a square
abacus. Single-chamfered pointed arch. The second pier is
C19 but, being a piece of wall with two responds, it represents
no doubt original evidence as to the position of the W wall,

before a S aisle existed. C13 S chapel of two bays, octagonal pier, double-chamfered arches. Ashlar-faced W tower with set-back buttresses. Pairs of two-light bell-openings, rounded heads, both under one big ogee arch (cf. Desborough). The openings have transoms and cusping below them. Frieze of cusped lozenges. Battlements and square pinnacles which have lost or never had their tops. The rest mostly C19, especially the chancel interior with much foliage. This dates from 1872. What is original of external features is Perp. – PLATE. Cup and Cover Paten, 1631; Flagon, 1729; Almsdish, 1761. – MONUMENT. Mrs Jekyll † 1775. Of white and grey marble, a pretty composition. Oval medallion on an obelisk. In it an angel with a quill. Garlands hang down l. and r. of the medallion. The monument is signed by *van Gelder* (*see* Warkton).

(ARTHINGWORTH MANOR. A large part of the mid-C18 manor house was pulled down in 1967, revealing stone interior walls, which must have been part of an older manor house of the Rokebys. The manor house is being left as a shell.* The C18 STABLES E of the house have recently been converted into a house by *Kellet & Partners*. The C18 staircase from the manor house has been incorporated. GI)

ASHBY ST LEDGERS

5060

ST LEODEGARIUS. Small Dec W tower; the N chapel windows (with arches upon arches) should be early C14 too. S aisle with big Perp windows, the traceried heads occupying about half their height. Arcades of four bays with octagonal piers and double-chamfered arches. – ROOD SCREEN. Tall, with four-light divisions and mullions reaching up into the apex of the arch; ribbed coving. – PULPIT. Jacobean three-decker with C18 stairs. – BENCHES. Many; with much tracery. – Two Jacobean PEWS and C18 pews along the S and N walls facing towards the nave. Also a Musicians' Pew at the W end. – WALL PAINTINGS. One of the most complete cycles in England of the Passion of Christ, but too faded to be enjoyed. The date is *c.* 1500, but by the chancel arch there is also a Flagellation of St Margaret of *c.* 1325. There are eighteen scenes of the Passion. Upper tier, N: Entry into Jerusalem, Christ washing St Peter's feet, Last Supper, Agony in the Garden; E: Christ

See p. 517
40

---

* The house was formerly a long brick building of two storeys with two projecting wings ending in three-sided bay-windows and projecting centre bay with pedimented doorway. The interior had been altered in 1933.

before Pilate, Mocking of Christ, Crucifixion, Pietà; s: Christ carrying the Cross, Nailing to the Cross, Crucifixion. – Lower tier, N: Crucifixion, Deposition; E: Betrayal, Resurrection; s: Resurrection, the Three Maries at the Sepulchre. – In addition St Christopher, N wall. – N and s sides of doorway: Death with pick and shovel and Time with scythe (C16). – STAINED GLASS. E c. 1829, s c. 1850. – (In a s window of the nave a Bishop, c. 1470. Several windows with Catesby coats of arms, C14–C15. RM) – PLATE. Cup and Paten, 1780. – MONUMENTS. Brass to Thomas Stokes † 1416 and wife (s aisle), 13 in. figures. – Brass to Sir William Catesby † 1472? and wife (chancel floor). Only one figure in a shroud remains. – Brass to (?) George Catesby † 1505 (s aisle), kneeling figure 18 in. long. – Brian I'Anson † 1634. Two long kneeling figures, their children below (chancel N). – John Ianson, 1663. Of Alabaster. Large oval medallion with three-quarter figure. Wreath around the medallion, and garlands. – Joseph Ashley † 1738. Architectural tablet with three putto heads. – Moses Ashley † 1740. With bust in roundel. Pedimented top. Both by *Nathaniel Hedges*. – John Bentley Ashley † 1761. By *John Bacon*, 1784. A very fine standing monument. Two standing allegorical figures, amply draped, l. and r. of the inscription. Above sarcophagus in front of obelisk. On the sarcophagus stands a Roman oil-lamp. – James Ashley † 1798. Very simple, with urn in front of obelisk. All these are in the chancel. – George Henry Arnold † 1844 (N chapel). Sumptuous Gothic shrine without effigy.* – Second Lord Wimborne † 1939. By *Lutyens*. In the churchyard, s of the church. Steps down to it. The memorial is a tall tapering cross, the arms and head very little projecting. To its s an altar or sarcophagus.

ASHBY ST LEDGERS. A large mansion, the work of over three centuries, but so happily informal in its grouping that it is never overpowering. The estate had belonged to the Catesby family in the later Middle Ages and the Elizabethan period, was sold to Brian I'Anson, a London draper, in 1612, by his descendants to another London draper, Joseph Ashley, in 1703, and finally came to Ivor Guest, second Lord Wimborne, in 1903. In spite of its long architectural history it is essentially a monument of the early C20 and *Sir Edwin Lutyens*, i.e. the C20 before it developed its own style. Of the transitional phase between historicism and the modern movement Ashby St

---

* Signed by *I. Wheeler* of Reading (BB).

Ledgers is a characteristic and convincing example. Recently the house has been reduced in size by the demolition of Lutyens's N wing, and internal alterations have created more convenient living conditions for the present day. This work was done by *Jellicoe & Coleridge*, 1968–9.*

The present approach is from the W, straight along, through gatepiers, into the forecourt. The original approach was from the church, at an angle through a GATEHOUSE of stone and timber-framing. One passes then between the medieval STABLES on the W and the oblong DOVECOTE on the E, and reaches the FORECOURT. The forecourt tells the story of the house. What faces us is the Hall range, Elizabethan or Jacobean, with regularly placed three-light windows in two storeys. The lights still have four-centred arches as their heads. But on the l. the display is continued round the corner by Lutyens. There is first the imitation Jacobean gable of the Stone Hall of 1909–10, then the big bay-window added in 1938 to the first Dining Room of 1904 (now kitchen), and then, half-hiding it, the later extension of the Dining Room (1924) with its rubble masonry, unrelieved cubic shapes, and one and only window, a large canted bay-window with three transoms. To the W of this range a passage leads N, through gatepiers and down through a half-timbered link by a wide Bramantesque stair with the first half of the steps convex-semicircular and the second half concave-semicircular – so that the landing is a circle. This link connects with a c 17 house of half-H plan, with gables to the N, dormers to the forecourt, which Lutyens converted into servants' rooms and nurseries.

Instead of continuing here it is better to return to the Hall range and turn s round the range. The s view is specially fine. From l. to r. the gable end of the Hall range rises but does not descend again, because of an addition made in 1652. This projects, two-stepped in plan, and consists of a flat-topped balustraded part and a big shaped gable at the r. end. Below the gable a canted bay-window, in the gable a stepped three-light window.‡ The extension of 1652 turns the corner to the E and has a straight gable. The E front now exhibits a symmetrical Jacobean façade. This however is due to Lutyens,

* The necessary alterations to this text have been made from notes supplied by Sir Gyles Isham and Bruce Bailey.

‡ In the Hall end wall a doorway with shouldered surround and cherub keystone of c. 1700, acting as overture to the garden here, which has four stone figures, badly weathered, of the seasons and a central one of Atlas, also probably c. 1700 (BB).

who in 1909 designed – probably not with much pleasure – the central part and the N gable repeating the S gable of 1652. Lutyens made this range the axis for his fine GARDEN with a sunk canal, herbaceous borders, and, at r. angles to the N, an ingenious BRIDGE of three stone arches with a demonstratively heavy superstructure.* The N end of this Lutyens range is a little confusing. A bay-window cuts across a large window behind. The window belongs to the North or Stone Hall, a room of 1909–10 continuing the axis of the Dining Room to the E. What is more confusing still is that the E front then runs on, recessed as against the Lutyens façade but projecting a little as against the E window of the Stone Hall, and that it runs on by means of a timber-framed C17 house which was bought by the second Lord Wimborne at Ipswich and re-erected (not with Lutyens's approval, it is said). The IPSWICH HOUSE stood in Cow Street. It is of two storeys with an overhang, built of closely set uprights and occasional diagonal braces. Beyond this projected until 1968 *Lutyens*'s NORTH WING of 1923–4.‡ Now that this has been removed the Ipswich House acts as terminal to the E front. The N side is now a service approach. Turning S we are brought back by the Bramantesque stair into the forecourt and to the main entrance.

Of the INTERIORS the screen on the N side of the Entrance Hall introduces one to Lutyens's ingenuities. It leads down some steps to the newly created DINING ROOM and so to the STONE HALL of 1909. This was designed as a two-storey hall with open roof, but in 1969 was divided horizontally. (In the upper room Lutyens's splendid steep timber roof now springs effectively from floor level.) Originally the axis turned here, and one passed from the W end of the Stone Hall through an arch into the Dining Room of 1904,§ which had a tunnel-vault decorated by imitation-Jacobean plaster-work. This room has now been converted into a kitchen, with a false ceiling. Beyond this is the DINING ROOM of 1924, with a coved plain ceiling and classical unfluted Doric columns. Chimneypiece with pedimented overmantel and marble fire-

* Beyond the garden, by the lake, a marble statue of Apollo, apparently English, *c.* 1730, brought from the site of Ashby Lodge in 1972 (BB).

‡ This had kitchen and servants' hall below, twelve servants' bedrooms on a mezzanine floor, and guest rooms and the master's bedroom above. It had a good masculine front with canted oriel windows and block-shaped chimneystacks.

§ This was designed not by Lutyens but by *Thornton Smith* (N. Taylor).

place surround. Finally the E range. In the STUDY in the SE corner good panelling of the first half of the C17, with primitive Corinthian pilasters and flat carving. Next to the study a C17 staircase. N of this Lutyens's MUSIC ROOM, then another C17 staircase, rebuilt, and N again the CARD ROOM with late C17 panelling, not *in situ*, and a good chimneypiece.

(In the village THE COTTAGE, a small Jacobethan house by *Lutyens*, 1912, built for Lord Wimborne's agent. H-shaped plan, with central projecting porch. Also by *Lutyens* a picturesque row of COTTAGES, 1908–9, with sweeping thatched roofs, asymmetrically placed windows, and Lutyens's typical battered buttresses and bold chimneys.)

(1 m. NW on the A361 the former LODGES to the now demolished Ashby Lodge. The lodges are mid C18, with an early C20 portico in between. BB)

ASHLEY

7090

ST MARY. Ironstone and grey limestone. Ashlar the tower top and the S porch. Dec tower with spire on broaches. The exterior almost rebuilt; by *Sir G. G. Scott*, 1867.* The old material re-used by Scott indicates a date *c.* 1300. Quatrefoil piers, dog-tooth hood-mould over the S doorway. The chancel is entirely by Scott, and the most interesting part of the church. Very expensively done, for the Rev. Richard Pulteney, rector from 1853 till 1874 and squire as well. Polished pink granite shafts in the chancel arch, various colours in the triple arches between chancel and organ chamber. – REREDOS of alabaster. – PAVEMENT of marble and encaustic tiles. – Very richly detailed CHANCEL RAIL of brass. – Painted WALL DECORATION by *Clayton & Bell*, who also did the STAINED GLASS. – FONT a solid block of pink marble.‡ – The Gothic CHANDELIERS of iron are by *Bodley*. – PLATE. Silver-gilt Cup, 1570; silver-gilt Cover Paten, *c.* 1590; Breadholder, 1717; silver-gilt Paten, 1720; Cup, 1811; silver-gilt Almsdish, 1866; silver-gilt Flagon, 1869.

The Rev. Richard Pulteney did a good deal also to beautify the village. He was responsible for remodelling the MANOR HOUSE (by *E. F. Law*, dated 1865), got *Sir G. G. Scott* to design a handsome Gothic SCHOOL (of 1858) and master's house (date 1865), and built a number of substantial cottages, or

---

* Pre-restoration drawings by George Clark suggest that, apart from the chancel, Scott followed what was there (BB).

‡ According to the Rev. L. E. Brown it cost £2000 in 1865–8.

rather semi-detached houses. *Law* designed some of these (1865–6) and also made additions to the RECTORY in 1871 (BB).

(YEOMANS, Green Lane. Medieval and later. L-shaped, one wing cruck-framed, originally an open hall. Stone external walls. DOE)

ROMAN REMAINS were found in Alderstone Field during C19 railway construction. The site lay beside the Roman road from Ratae (Leicester). Excavations in 1969–71 have shown the existence of a villa and outbuildings of the C3–4 (J. M. Steane).

7040   ASHTON
                1¼ m. SE of Roade

ST MICHAEL. W tower of 1848 with saddleback roof (by *R. C. Hussey*). Restoration by *E. F. Law*, 1895, when much was rebuilt (BB). N arcade of two bays, with octagonal pier and double-chamfered arches, C13 or early C14. Dec chancel and N aisle windows, the latter worth a special glance for their lopsidedness. – PULPIT. Jacobean, with two tiers of the well-known blank arches. – PLATE. Flagon, 1672; Cup and Cover Paten, 1682; Breadholder, 1700. – MONUMENTS. Effigy of a cross-legged Knight. Of wood, early C14. Said to be Sir Philip de Lou. – Sir John de Herteshull, *c.* 1365. Alabaster effigy on a tomb-chest with panels and a ballflower frieze. The earliest alabaster effigy in the county. – Robert Marriott † 1584 and family. Tomb-chest with brasses, the figures 2 ft 6 in. long.

0080   ASHTON
                ¾ m. E of Oundle

CHAPEL AND SCHOOL. 1705. Oblong with four tall round-arched windows of two lights. The first three belong to the chapel, the fourth to the school room. W front with a round-arched doorway in a heavy oblong frame. Three-light window of stepped round-arched lights under one big round arch and framed by volutes. – REREDOS with fluted pilasters and pediment.

(MANOR HOUSE. Partly C15, partly C16 and later. L-shaped, with blocked two-light arched window in the NW gable-end. DOE)

ASHTON WOLD. The house was built and the village rebuilt in 1900 for the Hon. Charles Rothschild, second son of the first Lord Rothschild, to the design of an architect called

Hackvale. Two cottages were added to the village in 1945. The house is in the Tudor style with straight-sided gables and mullioned and transomed windows, large and essentially *See* p. 517 symmetrical. The village is emphatically a model village. The cottages are also in the Tudor style, rock-faced and thatched. They were built with local materials and local labour. Great care was taken over the gardens. Also, every cottage, already in 1900, had a bathroom. All wiring is underground, an all too rare luxury which has a considerable effect on the undisturbed unity of a street or a village.

ASTON-LE-WALLS
4050

St Leonard. The oldest features are the bottom parts of the w tower – its w doorway, now hidden behind the later w porch, and a s window are round-headed – and the N doorway with a single-stepped pointed arch but still a scalloped capital. The tower ends in c13 bell-openings, of two lights with a shaft between. c13 also the s doorway and the (somewhat later?) N and s windows (pairs of lancets, Y-tracery, Y-tracery with a trefoil in the spandrel). Of *c.* 1300 the SEDILIA and the very pretty DOUBLE PISCINA (with a cinquefoil in fine bar tracery) and the tomb recess opposite (with a cinquecusped arch). Arcades of three bays. On the N a circular and then an octagonal pier, on the s an octagonal and then a circular one. Double-chamfered arches. The church was restored in the 1870s and in 1881–2 by *J. M. Townsend* (BB). – FONT. Square, Norman, three sides carved. On one a knot pattern, on the next intersected arches, on the third a very asymmetrical Tree of Life. – BENCHES. Square-headed with tracery panels between buttresses. – PLATE. Cup, 1682; Paten, 1713. – MONUMENTS. Effigy of a Priest; early c14; stone (chancel N). – Elizabeth Orme † 1692. Small bust at the top. The inscription ought to be read.

(CHAPEL (R.C.), SE of the church. 1827, Gothic with thin details, altered since (BB).)

MANOR HOUSE. W front of *c.* 1700. Seven bays and two storeys with a hipped roof.

ASTROP PARK
5030

¾ m. NE of Kings Sutton

Built by Sir John Willes after 1735. His house was seven bays long, of two storeys. Quoins, and also quoins to the five-bay

centre, which has a pediment. All windows with alternatingly
triangular and segmental pediments. Doorway with Gibbs surround. To this house *Sir John Soane* added one-storeyed
wings, heightened in the C19, which were removed in 1961.
Soane is also responsible for the four pairs of columns in the

*See
p.
517*
Dining Room.* Internally much is still later. The staircase,
however, is possibly Georgian.

(Astrop was the site of a famous spa, whose waters were
discovered in the C17. By the early C19 it had declined, and
all that remains now is a small well, sometimes called ST
RUMBALD'S WELL. It lies to the S of the house in a valley.
Round-headed niche with large keystone and rusticated
quoins; probably mid-C18. A replica stands by the road S
staircase, of the park. BB)

6040

ASTWELL CASTLE

1½ m. SW of Wappenham

Really Astwell Manor House. The term Castle is recent. Thomas
Lovett in 1471 arranged to exchange Astwell for Rushton. Of
this time the tower with the lower attachment on its l. Both
parts are embattled. The tower has an archway with a four-
centred head, two-light cusped windows, and a higher stair-
turret on the N side. The lower building has a quatrefoil
window to the S and one to the W. To the W a house was added
by George Shirley about 1606. Yet it still has mullioned
windows with arched lights. Inside a fireplace with a broad
frieze of simple geometrical motifs above the four-centred
arch. George Shirley's house was a large courtyard house with
over forty rooms. What remains is only a fragment.

5030

AYNHO

20 ST MICHAEL. Rebuilt in 1723–5 by *Edward Wing,*‡ much in
the style of Hawksmoor and Archer (cf. below). Only the Dec
tower remained of the medieval building. This has diagonal
buttresses with a niche to the NW and one to the SW, a doorway with many fine continuous mouldings, a three-light
window, and two-light bell-openings under a straight hood-
mould (cf. Kings Sutton). Battlements, pinnacles. The body

---

* This piece of information comes from Miss Dorothy Stroud.

‡ And 'by the Pious care, Generous encouragement and prudent manage-
ment' of Mr Cartwright of Aynhoe Park, as the architect says on a drawing
of which the Rev. Vivian Banham kindly told me.

of the church is broad and somewhat squat. Seven bays treated as a symmetrical composition – not as a procession from W to E. Two storeys of windows, round-arched and segment-headed. Flat frames. Bays one and seven project a little and are emphasized by giant Doric pilasters. Bays three to five are again stressed by giant pilasters and have in addition a pediment. The centre of its footline is broken by an arch, a motif from Baalbek used for instance at St Alphege, Greenwich, but also already by Sir Christopher Wren e.g. in the transept front of St Paul's. E end with four giant pilasters, three big round-arched windows, and a middle pediment. The interior is disappointing.* It is just one large, uncomposed unit. – Fine, dignified WEST GALLERY on coupled Tuscan columns. – Also original PULPIT and BOX PEWS. – FONT. Ornate bowl on a baluster. The details of the bowl have a Gothic touch. – STAINED GLASS. E window initialled by *Thomas Willement* and dated 1857. With a very Victorian vine border and three religious roundels. – In the S wall two *Kempe* windows of 1898 and 1899. – PLATE. Cup, 1602; Paten, 1677; Flagon, *c.* 1729. – MONUMENTS. Many tablets. The best are the two identical ones to Mr and Mrs Chapman † 1686 and 1684 and to Matthew Hutton, 1711. The latter is by *Edward Stanton*. The former two are attributed by Bruce Bailey to *William Stanton*. – (In the S chapel a fine free-standing tomb to members of the Cartwright family, erected 1654.)

AYNHOE PARK. The house represents essentially four periods: Jacobean, Carolean, the early C18, and the early C19. Three names are connected with it: *Edward Marshall*, master mason to the king from 1660 to 1673 and sculptor of monuments, *Thomas Archer*, one of the triad of truly Baroque English architects, and *Sir John Soane*. Richard Cartwright, whose descendants owned the house until the 1950s, had bought the estate in 1615, and though the house was set on fire in 1645, a certain amount of it may have survived. The Jacobean house seems to have been of E-shape, facing S. *Marshall* filled in the space between the formerly projecting wings with their canted bay-windows in the end-walls. The wings were of three storeys, the infilling piece of two. It looked like a separate five-bay house. All this we know from a drawing of 1683. Much of Marshall's work can still be seen in the present S front. The

---

* No doubt due to the restoration of 1863. The grisaille glass dates from this time (BB).

windows were of the cross type and are now, it is true, sashed, but their pediments, triangular on the ground floor, segmental on the first floor, are Carolean, and so is the arched upper middle window with its characteristic surround of two Corinthian columns carrying pieces of jutting-forward entablature and decorated between these with garlands.

The quoins also date from the 1660s. The top storey on the other hand, which replaces Marshall's balustrade and is crowned by a big pediment across the whole width, belongs to the work attributed to *Archer*, as does the entrance below the central window and repeating its columned frame. The columns are Tuscan. Archer worked at Aynhoe from 1707 to 1714. He also refaced the fronts of the former wings, renewing e.g. their canted bay-windows. Moreover, Archer added seven-bay wings of one storey which continue the line of the s façade. The windows are arched, and the arches rest on pilasters. The inward-turning volutes of their capitals ought to be noted as an Archer mannerism copied by others of his generation (cf. the Bastards of Blandford). The two attachments were built for the Library and the Orangery.

The N front is much simpler. It consists of a raised three-storeyed five-bay centre with pediment, and three-bay, three-storeyed side pieces. There is no display of decoration. But Archer's principal contribution to Aynhoe is the detached Stables and Offices flanking the entrance courtyard and placed at r. angles to the N front. They are of eleven bays and two storeys, with a slightly higher pedimented five-bay centre. What is here unmistakably Archerish is the doorways. They are arched, and the arches stand on oddly moulded shafts. Their mouldings are continued in the arch, and the arch is separated from the shafts not by capitals but by a block with hardly any detail. Moreover, the whole of this is surrounded by a frame with diagonally placed, tapering pilasters without proper capitals carrying an entablature the centre of which curves back concavely.

The whole group is architecturally impressive, though visually somewhat forbidding, an impression due largely to the cementing of the brick structure.

The wings were joined to the centre by *Soane*. His work at Aynhoe dates from 1800–5. The motif he used is the triumphal arch, i.e. an open archway flanked by blank bays with niches. The bays have Tuscan columns with projecting fragments of entablature. The whole does not blend well with the rest and cannot be called one of Soane's successes. On the garden side Soane added the upper floor of the Orangery and Library and rebuilt the W end. His incised Grecian ornament is unmistakable. The two-bay pediment towards the W is a licence worth noting.

The INTERIOR also combines work by Archer and by Soane. In the Entrance Hall the screen of Roman Doric columns is by *Archer*, and so is the Staircase behind it, a very handsome piece, of wood, with three slim balusters for each tread: twisted – fluted – twisted. The tread-ends are carved. The newel-posts are fluted Corinthian columns. The treads have some inlay. The decoration of the walls with attached unfluted Ionic columns however is *Soane's*. Soane in 1801 had planned a much more thorough remodelling of the staircase with ashlar or imitation ashlar walls and a segmental tunnel-vault. Soane also remodelled the Garden Hall in the middle of the S front, an exceedingly delicate design with shallow apsed ends, very shallow wall arches, and a groin-vault the groins of which disappear towards the corners, the Dining Room, which has a serving alcove apsed at both ends and separated by unfluted Ionic columns from the dining room proper, the Library with a dainty Gothic cornice of tiny fans and a bay beyond a segmental arch, the White Staircase with a circular glazed opening, and the Vestibule to the staircase with typically Soanian recesses covered by segmental arches or short tunnel-vaults. One more Soane room must be mentioned: the Cold Bath, near the E end. But this was largely remodelled in 1952 and now has strangely swelling attenuated Tuscan columns carrying a groin-vault. The plan is, on a minute scale, the Byzantine plan of the inscribed cross.

The PARK was landscaped by *Capability Brown* in 1761–3 (D. Stroud).

THE VILLAGE of Aynho is neat and exemplarily kept. Of individual buildings the following deserve notice.

GRAMMAR SCHOOL. 1671. Five bays. Originally two doorways. These have four-centred arches. Tall two-light mullioned windows – an early case of this motif. The windows are partly altered.

ALMSHOUSES, N of the Grammar School. 1822. Grey and brown stone. Two-storeyed, with tripartite windows and pedimented doorways. The centre bay carries a rather starved pediment.

STOCKS. N of the E end of the road to Deddington.

BADBY

ST MARY. W tower of 1707 with arched windows and bell-openings. The latter have the flat bands of Y-tracery which are so characteristic of the C18. Lower down also a vertically placed oval and a circular window. As for the body of the church, much outside is due to the restoration by *E. F. Law*, 1880–1. The chancel windows seem of *c.* 1300, the N aisle windows certainly are, and the N arcade with its octagonal piers, responds with ballflower, and double-chamfered arches also fits the date. The S arcade, if anything, looks earlier. The clerestory with its extraordinarily closely set straight-headed two-light windows is Perp. – PULPIT. Simple, C17. – COMMUNION RAIL. C18. – STAINED GLASS. S aisle E by *Ward & Hughes*, 1881. – (Chancel S. Late C15 roundel. – Nave N clerestory. Inscription and arms, C15. RM) – PLATE. Cup, undated; Cover Paten dated 1662.

INSTITUTE, formerly School, facing the Green. By *James Wyatt* (Baker). Ironstone, symmetrical. Five bays, one-storeyed, the centre a two-storeyed porch-tower. Cross-windows, and in the tower a window with Y-tracery.

BADBY HOUSE, 1½ m. N. Early C19. S front of five bays and two storeys. On the E side entrance with unfluted Doric columns *in antis*.

LANTERN HOUSE (or Fawsley Lodge), on the Banbury–Daventry road. Two-storeyed, octagonal, early C19. Derelict (1972).

BARROW, ¾ m. N of the village on the Daventry road. Now much spread by ploughing. This is all that remains of a group which lay N of the village.

IRON AGE HILL FORT. On Arbury Hill, 1 m. W of the village, lies a single-rampart hilltop camp roughly square with sides 600 ft long. There is now practically no sign of a ditch and bank, and, apart from a slight feature in the NE corner, no evidence for an entrance; nevertheless the prehistoric date of the fort seems clear enough.

MEDIEVAL REMAINS. Remains of a moated grange of Evesham Abbey, to the E of the village, were excavated in 1965–8. There was evidence of work from the C13 to the C16.

BARBY

ST MARY. Mostly of pink sandstone. The windows are nearly entirely C19. Inside, W of the S doorway, a re-set small Anglo-

Saxon window. The chancel N windows belong to the late C13, the bell-openings and the top frieze of the W tower too. Inside the chancel, arcade of three bays to the S chapel. Low piers of quatrefoil section. Double-chamfered arches. Probably late C13 or early C14. The doorway and windows are all C19. The nave is flanked by two aisles. The N arcade has four bays with octagonal piers carrying capitals with big faces, shields, etc., and double-chamfered arches. The S arcade was pulled down and re-erected farther S. This gives the interior an uncomfortably lopsided appearance. Not that one comes to notice this easily; for the interior is perhaps the darkest in the county – due to a very complete set of STAINED GLASS by *Kempe & Tower*, starting from 1901. – (N aisle E. Nativity (restored), *c.* 1310. RM) – COMMUNION RAIL. C18.

RECTORY. 1869. Red brick with yellow diapering. Gabled, Tudor – like so many others in the neighbourhood.

MOTTE of a castle, N of the village. There does not appear to be any bailey.

BARNWELL

ST ANDREW. Externally mostly of the later C13. The priest's doorway looks early but is probably re-made out of bits from All Saints (*see* below). C13 W tower. Doorway with three orders of shafts and pretty fillets. W window of two lights with a quatrefoil over. A little higher up on the S side a circular window with dog-tooth. Bell-openings wildly decorated with dog-tooth and ballflower. Spire tall with small broaches. Three tiers of lucarnes. They show that by then the C14 was under way. C13 S doorway (shaft-rings, dog-tooth, hood-mould on flower stops) and S aisle (E lancet – inside accompanied by two fine big Perp niches). Late C13 clerestory with two-light windows with pointed quatrefoils over. Corbel-frieze with closely-set heads. Late C13 N aisle W window. The other N aisle windows after 1300, one with a big circle in the tracery filled by three spherical triangles, the other with reticulated tracery. Very good Dec N doorway. Two orders of shafts, but instead of capitals a frieze of nobbly leaves sprouting out of a face. Late C13 arcades inside, except for one raw earlier circular pier. The rest of quatrefoil section with fillets and double-chamfered arches. Tower arch triple-chamfered and dying against the imposts. Chancel arch with groups of three short detached shafts on corbels. Perp chancel windows. The chancel completely remodelled by *Sir G. G. Scott* in 1851. In the chancel poor Dec SEDILIA with little tipped-up vaults and flat ogee arches. At the E end of the N aisle a splendid Dec REREDOS, very unusual in composition. Tripartite with a wider centre. Extremely rich ogee arches with big cusps filled with big leaves. Finials and a frieze of fleurons and faces against the back wall. – FONT. Dec. Octagonal with eight flat crocketed gables and flowers at the foot. – PULPIT. Jacobean. – PLATE. Cup, 1570; Dish, 1636; Paten, c. 1694. – (STAINED GLASS. Chancel s. Canopies and Saints, c. 1400–25. RM) – MONUMENTS. Christopher Freeman † 1610. Brass plate with small kneeling figures. – The Rev. Nicholas Latham † 1620. Frontal demi-figure with a book on a desk representing the reading desk of a pulpit.

In the wall between the church and the RECTORY, several C13 fragments from All Saints (*see* below), including a window head with cusped intersected tracery and others of two lights with foiled circles.

To the SE of the church LATHAM'S ALMSHOUSES, founded in 1601 and rebuilt in the appropriate style in 1874.

ALL SAINTS. Only the chancel remains, with a C13 chancel arch and big Perp windows. It was left undisturbed because of the Montagu monuments, when the rest of the church was pulled down in 1825. – REREDOS. C18, with Corinthian pilasters. – MONUMENTS. Henry Montagu † 1625, a most unusual and attractive monument covered with pathetic and quaint inscriptions. The monument is a tall obelisk on a base. Its lowest part is opened as a niche or tabernacle and in it stands Henry, who died at the age of three, dressed as a little man. He holds a scroll which reads: Lord give me of ye water. But below we are told that he died 'immature per aquas'. The upper parts of the obelisk have five tiers of heraldic shields. Immediately below the niche two big feet. On one it says: 'Not my feete only', on the other 'but also my hands and head'. In the middle an opening as of a village pump with the inscription: 'Poure on me the ioyes of thy salvation'. At the very foot of the monument: 'Vita brevis, merces aeterna'. – Dame Letice Montagu † 1611. Severe tall oblong monument without figures. Framed inscription and framed shield above. At the top obelisk on a disk with a shell motif. – (Dorothy Creed † 1714, by her mother *Elizabeth Creed* (*see* also Titchmarsh). Oil on slate. An armorial lozenge and swags. E. Croft-Murray)

BARNWELL CASTLE.* The castle is of great architectural interest and far too little known. If it was really built in or about 1266 by Berengar Le Moyne, who ceded it to Peterborough Abbey in 1276 (although he went on living in it), then it represents the first example in Britain of the most monumental type of castle architecture, the type with a more or less square plan and round corner towers.‡ The type is more famously represented in Britain by Harlech of 1284 etc. and derives from France and Italy where, on Roman town-planning precedent, it had been used from about 1220 or 1230 onwards. Barnwell has four mighty round corner towers, the only irregularity being that the NE and NW towers are really trefoiled to the outside, because the two halves of the curved projection are separated by a smaller curved staircase projection. The other irregularity is that the gatehouse is not in the middle of its side, the E side, but immediately next to the SE tower. The gatehouse again has two round towers. The arches are double-chamfered, the gateway inside has a pointed tunnel-vault. Grooves for the portcullis. In the tower of the gatehouse ground-floor rooms with two bays of vaults with single-chamfered ribs. Curiously enough the doorways of these rooms and all others are round-headed and plainly single-chamfered – an anachronism in 1266. Above the gateway was a room with large windows. Otherwise the windows are small and there are many cross-slits, some with two horizontal slits. In the SE tower remains of a pointed rib-vault on the ground floor, in the NE tower a garderobe shoot.

At the Dissolution the castle was bought from Peterborough Abbey by Sir Edward Montagu. He built a new house in the outer courtyard. Camden in 1586 calls it 'of late repaired and beautified with new buildings'. It is gabled with mullioned and transomed windows and has been much added to c. 1890 and in 1913 (by *Gotch & Saunders*) and later.

RAILWAY STATION. In the Old-English style. By *Livock*, 1845. Now disused.

BARTON SEAGRAVE

ST BOTOLPH. An impressive Norman parish church. Nave, central tower, and chancel. Herringbone masonry. N doorway

* To the NW of the castle a strong motte marks the position of an earlier fortification.

‡ The date is based on the statement of a jury in 1276 that he had illegally built a castle ten years ago.

with one order of shafts and a tympanum which must be wrongly assembled. Two friezes. Below head (of Christ ?) between two beasts. Above a jumble of stones with saltire crosses, stars, etc. The hood-mould also is decorated. One blocked upper N window. With a big shaft, saltire crosses in the abaci, and a strong roll moulding in the arch. The rest here of *c.* 1300, i.e. cusped intersected tracery and a clerestory of spherical triangles. In the tower N side again a Norman window, much like the nave window. The tower top Perp. In the chancel N side a similar Norman window. The chancel otherwise has two widely separated lancets on the s side and a splendid, if vastly restored, display of blank arcading. This is of the late C13, as the naturalistic foliage of the few original capitals proves. The arcading covers the E, N, and s sides and even returns on the w side. It can do this because the chancel arch is Norman and narrow. With the Norman w arch of the tower it makes a good show. Tall shafts, primitive volute capitals, one also with primitive upright leaves, another with birds. Arches with roll mouldings and an outer billet frieze. All these Norman motifs together indicate a date *c.* 1120 or 30. s arcade C13. Two bays, octagonal pier, double-chamfered arches. The aisle itself dates from the restoration of 1878 by *Carpenter & Ingelow*. – READER'S DESK. With two good linenfold panels re-used. – STAINED GLASS. w window by *H. Hughes*; bad. – One N window by *Kempe*, 1890. – PLATE. Christening Bowl, 1763; Set, 1832. – MONUMENTS. Jane Floyde † 1616. Brass plate with kneeling figures. – John Bridges † 1712. Tablet with pilasters and open segmental pediment. – John Bridges, the county historian, † 1724. Tablet by *John Hunt*. – John Bridges † 1741. Tablet with side volutes and a pretty pediment with a top consisting of two ogee curves and a crowning segmental curve. – The Bridges family lived at the Hall.

RECTORY. Of *c.* 1700. Six bays, two storeys, hipped roof. The s side of 1806 (*Gentleman's Magazine*).

BARTON SEAGRAVE HALL, N of the church, on the A-road. Rain-water heads 1725, but clearly structurally older. E-plan with two gables. Only the porch has a pediment of 1725. Eleven-bay front of two storeys, all windows sashed and with flat frames. Porch doorway with segmental pediment on fluted Doric pilasters. Lower wing to the E. One-storeyed with pedimented dormers. w front entirely Georgian. Five bays, two storeys, doorway with pediment on corbels. – ORANGERY, to the w. An exquisitely beautiful little building of the late c18. Five bays, the middle three in a shallow canted projection. These have round arches, the outer bays segmental arches. The arches are separated by immensely elongated, almost Pompeiian, cast-iron columns. The glazing bars of the windows are also of iron and form charming classical or Adamish patterns. In the roof three glazed domes, two small, the middle one bigger.

w of the church and alongside the river are two MOATED AREAS of rectangular form, of which the more southerly appears to be the site of the castle.

(HOUSE. An attractive small house of c. 1600 opposite the church. L. M. Gotch)

BENEFIELD

9080

ST MARY. 1847 by *John Macduff Derick*, paid for by the Watts-Russell family of Biggin Hall. 'An important specimen of the sumptuous Tractarian church' (Goodhart-Rendel). w tower with broach spire, interior with much sculpture. Encaustic tiles on the floor throughout. – ROOD SCREEN with loft and rood by *Comper*, 1904, but the screen earlier. – NORTH SCREEN. Assembled in 1926, with a splendidly carved open-work centre of c. 1700 with the Russell coat of arms, from Biggin Hall. – REREDOS. 1897. Small, also by *Comper*. – STALLS by *Derick*, with MISERICORDS said to have come from Fotheringhay. These have a lion, a green man, and a foliage sprig. – STAINED GLASS. E window of c. 1847, in a pre-Pugin style, with painted panels of St John Baptist and the Evangelists. – PLATE. Cup and Cover Paten, 1570; Paten, 1637; Set, 1843.

RECTORY FARM. 1877–8. Tall and gabled.

CASTLE. Of the castle, licensed in 1208, only the moated platform is left, immediately w of the church. It has been derelict since 1315 or earlier.

BIGGIN HALL. *See* below.

FERMYN WOODS HALL. *See* p. 216.

BIGGIN HALL

0080

1½ m. E of Benefield

The core of the house is of c. 1700: five bays and two storeys. It shows in the middle of the w front and is partly hidden be-

hind the fine portico of *c.* 1750 on the E front.* This is the
show-side. Basement and two storeys. Portico reached by a
wide open staircase. Four giant columns and pediment slightly
in front of the rest of the façade. Behind each of the two outer
columns another column and, outside these, pilasters to make
up the width of the old house. Then three-bay one-storeyed
connecting links and three-storeyed end pavilions in the tradition of Houghton, Holkham, Hagley, etc. The end pavilions
have Venetian windows on the ground floor, tripartite windows
with pediment over the middle part on the first floor. The w
side has an entrance with a shell-hood typical of *c.* 1700 and a
three-bay pediment. The end pavilions also have pediments
to the w. The shell-hood and the central pediment are an
addition of 1911. To the same date belongs the raising of the
connecting links to two storeys. Much C20 work also in the
interior, all in the appropriate style; partly of *c.* 1911 and partly
of *c.* 1938. Original the SE room with a fine stucco ceiling and
a chimneypiece of the mid C18.

BLACKGROUNDS see CHIPPING WARDEN

BLACKLANDS see KINGS SUTTON

6050
BLAKESLEY

ST MARY. Chiefly of ironstone, but the w tower of rough grey
blocks. The tower is of *c.* 1300. Tower arch with triple
responds, the main one with a fillet. Bell-openings of two
pointed-trefoiled lights. Dec arcades of two continuous sunk
quadrant mouldings, an unusual sight. Dec also the chancel
arch. The chancel itself was rebuilt in 1897 by *Edmund Law.*
Perp clerestory and battlements. The roof is supported on
angels making music. Late Perp s chapel. Money for its
building was left in 1500. Continuous mouldings to the arches
to w and N. Straight-headed windows. – SCULPTURE.
Pelican, medieval, of wood (over the tower arch). – PLATE.
Set, 1793. – MONUMENTS. Brass to Matthew Swetenham,
Bowbearer to Henry IV, † 1416. The figure is 3 ft 2 in. long. –
William Wattes † 1614. Hanging monument with four kneel-
ing figures in two tiers. They are headless.

See BLAKESLEY HALL. Demolished in 1957-8.
p.
517

* The alterations of *c.* 1750 have been attributed to *Hiorne* of Warwick,
who designed similar but unexecuted alterations to Stanford Hall, Leicestershire.

HOUSE in the SE corner of the churchyard. Dated 1689. Upright two-light mullioned windows. Circular window in the gable.

GLEBE FARM, W of the church. Incorporating a Perp doorway and the upper part of a two-light Perp window.

THE SYCAMORES, a little S of the church. Dated 1670. Symmetrical front with four-light mullioned windows, those on the ground floor higher in proportion to width than they would have been earlier.

(KENDAL HOUSE. C18 and later. Formerly an inn. GI)

(SEAWELL FARM. One of the Grafton Estate farms of c. 1840, see Introduction, p. 67.)

BARROW. At Woodend, 250 yds E of Green's Park Farm.

BLATHERWYCKE

HOLY TRINITY. Norman W tower with unmoulded arch towards the nave and small W doorway. Norman S doorway with one order of shafts; simple. E.E. N arcade of two bays with minimum capitals and slightly chamfered round arches. The E respond has a stiff-leaf capital. Of c. 1300 the fine arcading towards the N chapel. Three bays. Quatrefoil piers, double-chamfered arches. Of about the same time the S side. The chancel follows. With its windows with reticulated tracery and the two niches l. and r. of the (new) E window, it is Dec. – STAINED GLASS. By *Clayton & Bell*, 1858. Quite good, with medallions in the C13 style and clear colours. * – PLATE. Cup and Paten, 1659; Almsdish, 1821. – MONUMENTS. Humphrey Stafford † 1548 and wife. Brasses set in a coarse architectural surround. – Probably Sir Humphrey Stafford † 1575, the builder of Kirby Hall. The C19 inscription is wrong. Two upright panels framed with egg-and-dart. In the panels in relief the kneeling figures of Sir Humphrey, if it is he, his wife and children. Surround with columns, top with strapwork and achievement. – Thomas Randolph, poet. By *Nicholas Stone*, 1640. A very simple, completely classical tablet with a frame with ears at top and bottom. Poem in an oval laurel wreath. The monument was commissioned by Sir Christopher Hatton, *musarum amator*. The poem reads as follows:

---

* The window with the Corporal Works of Mercy is from a cartoon by *J. R. Clayton* himself (R. Hubbuck).

Here sleepe thirteene together in one tombe
And all these greate, yet quarrell not for roome.
The Muses and ye Graces teares did meete.
And grav'd these letters on ye churlish sheete;
Who having wept, their fountaines drye,
Through the Conduit of the eye,
For their freind who here does lye,
Crept into his grave and dyed,
And soe the Riddle is untyed,
For which this Church, proud that the Fates bequeath
Unto her ever-honour'd trust,
Soe much and that soe precious dust,
Hath crown'd her Temples with an Ivye wreath;
Which should have Laurell been,
But y^t the greived Plant to se him dead
Tooke pet and withered.

BLATHERWYCKE HALL by *Thomas Ripley* was demolished in
1948. NE of the church a large stable building survives, with
the inscription D, OB 1770 (for Donatus O'Brien). Depressed
entrance arch.

7050

BLISWORTH

ST JOHN BAPTIST. Perp W tower. The chancel S windows are
late C13, the E window of a very strange Dec design (renewed,
but correctly), the N window Perp, the S aisle rebuilt 1926. The
arcades are both of the C13, the N one partly earlier. Five bays,
octagonal piers, double-chamfered arches. There is an evident
difference between the E and the W parts. The earlier work is
the E bays. The S arcade is shorter and also not of one build.
The E bays and the arch across the aisle are earlier, the W pier
with its rare quatrefoil and trefoil frieze looks C15. The
church was restored in 1856 by *E. F. Law*. – SCREEN. Tall, of
one-light divisions, Perp. – COMMUNION RAIL. Later C17;
dumb-bell balusters. – STAINED GLASS. In the tracery heads
of a chancel N window C15 figures. – (Chancel S: C14 and C15
fragments.) – MONUMENT. Tomb-chest with shields in
quatrefoils, linked by knob-patterns. On the lid brasses to
Roger Wake † 1504 and wife. The figures are 2 ft 4 in. long.
Close by is an ogee-headed recess.

BLISWORTH HOUSE, E of the church. Of c. 1700. Seven bays,
two and half storeys, the windows in flat frames.

RECTORY, W of the church. Symmetrical Tudor; 1841.

STONEACRES C17. Singled out by the DOE as the 'best
example in the district' of the enthusiastic use of local

materials. Bands of limestone and ironstone, dressings of a yellow freestone, thatched roof. There are other houses as well with the handsome bands of limestone and ironstone, e.g. one on the Stoke Road, where the gable end has on the ground floor and the first floor three-light stepped mullioned windows.

CANALS (*see also* Stoke Bruerne). The Grand Union Canal near Blisworth enters a tunnel to Stoke Bruerne (opened in 1805). The VENTS, circular, of vitrified bricks are beacons by the road. The Northampton Branch Canal has seventeen locks between Blisworth and Northampton.

(RAILWAY BRIDGE across the A43. 1837–8. An elegant stone arch. A viaduct was intended. BB)

BODDINGTON *see* UPPER BODDINGTON

BOROUGH CLOSE *see* IRCHESTER

BOROUGH HILL *see* DAVENTRY

BOUGHTON

7060

OLD CHURCH, 1 m. E. In ruins already in Bridges's time. It then had a spire, which collapsed in 1780. What remains is now smothered in ivy. No detail of special interest.

ST JOHN BAPTIST. In the village, along the road, without a new churchyard – i.e. an urban position. In existence by 1546, according to Baker. The church began as a chantry. The W tower is Late Perp. Repairs are recorded to it in 1599 and in 1653 (BB). The body of the church was re-done in 1806 and enlarged in 1846 (date on the E gable). Tall two-light windows (three lights at the E end) with arched lights and hood-moulds. No structural division between nave and chancel; no aisles. – STAINED GLASS. The W window by *Kempe*, 1897. – MONUMENT. Mary Tillemont † 1706. Tablet with curly open pediment. Two cherubs' heads at the foot.

SCHOOL to the N of the church tower. 1841. With tall pointed windows and doorway.

BOUGHTON PARK. The house of the Wentworths has gone. The present house was built in 1844 'in the domestic style of English architecture' (Wetton, 1849) – i.e. Tudor. The architect was *William Burn*.* The second Earl of Strafford (second

* Inside the porch splendid ROYAL ARMS, of stone, re-coloured. Perhaps brought from Holdenby House. E of the house, early C18 gatepiers with splendid lead heraldic supporters with the Wentworth arms. Returned to Boughton in 1972 (BB).

creation), a friend of Horace Walpole, had spent his time building medievalizing FOLLIES on his estate. A good many of them still exist. Main GATE LODGE on the Leicester Road, known also as the HAWKING TOWER, a castellated tower with ogee-headed windows and the familiar large quatrefoils. The wall rises to its s to support an outer staircase to the top floor. Former ARCHWAY from the village, plain and castellated. Similar ARCHWAY into the kitchen garden. The tower is mentioned in a letter of Walpole's of 1756.

The other buildings appear to date mostly from the 1770s. A Gothic Lodge of 1770 is mentioned in the Dryden MSS as being not far from Bunkers Hill Farm.* Further afield to the N is a barn dated 1770 (formerly castellated). To the E of this BUNKERS HILL FARM (taking its name from the battle of 1775). It has a plaque 'S.1776' and is castellated, with quatrefoil and circular openings in its s façade. On the E side of the park towards Moulton are THE SPECTACLES and HOLLY LODGE, quite close together, each with an archway with rounded turrets. Holly Lodge is the more substantial structure. Its road façade has two pretty stone panels carved with cherubs. Behind this rises a much taller, equally medieval house with a tall thin tower. This was built c. 1861. In addition there is a GROTTO to the N of the house in a spinney, and quite on its own, an OBELISK, ½ m. s. This was erected in 1764.

BARROWS. One lies just s of Bunkers Hill Farm, and a second in the angle of the lane to Boughton Grange.

8080

BOUGHTON HOUSE

Boughton may be chiefly remembered for its noble N façade and the other work done by the first Duke of Montagu, who inherited the estate in 1683 and died in 1709. But there are in fact behind that façade substantial remains of a house of c. 1500 and of the alterations made by the first Montagu owner, Sir Edward. The estate was purchased by him c. 1530. He became a leading lawyer and one of Henry VIII's executors. The house behind the deceptively simple N front has an oblong W court, called Fish Court,‡ with the principal ranges around, smaller, less regular E courts of which the one further

---

* The following account has been expanded from information provided by Bruce Bailey.

‡ Until c. 1900 there was a fish pond in this court.

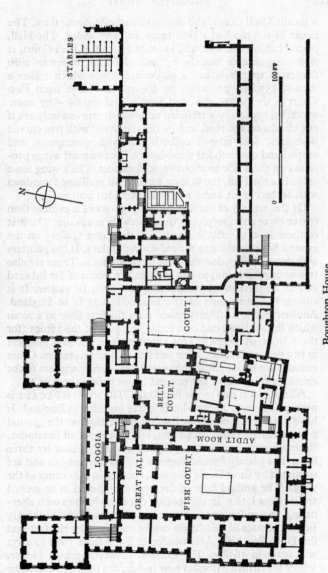

Boughton House

(Redrawn by courtesy of Messrs Batsford)

N is called Bell Court, and extensive outbuildings to the E. The house of c. 1500 had a Hall range and two wings. The Hall, placed behind the N façade, i.e. at the N end of Fish Court, is now recognizable mainly by one elaborate doorway with decorated spandrels and a gadrooned frieze which makes a date c. 1550–60 probable, by the gables visible from Fish Court – they have moulded shanks and finials – by some windows, especially a trefoiled one, which one can only see if one climbs on the roof, and by the roof itself with five curved tie-beams, four cusped collar-beams with queenposts, and cusped and quatrefoiled wind-braces. The original wings projected on the S side to about equal distances. The E wing has a gable like the Hall, the W wing some small mullioned windows with arched lights and a roof with moulded purlins.

Of the activity of the first Montagu no more is evident than two or three chimneypieces, quite possibly not *in situ*. The first of these is in the Audit Room, i.e. the Long Gallery on the ground floor continuing the old E wing to the S. It has pilasters with pretty foliage decoration in its sunk panels. There are also two inscriptions and, as one of them is a motto of Sir Edward and as he died in 1557, this fireplace must be earlier. It is among the *incunabula* of the Elizabethan style in England. Another mid-C16 chimneypiece is on the first floor in a room which lies at the SE end of a projecting part of the S front (for the S front *see* below). This chimneypiece also has pilasters in two tiers with sunk panels and fine foliage decoration. Other rooms have Elizabethan chimneypieces bearing witness to the existence of much of the present house before the C17.*

90   All the rest is due to the first Duke. The NORTH FAÇADE is perhaps the most French-looking C17 building in England. It has such French motifs as banded rustication on the ground floor, a mansard roof, and a complete absence of all ornament. Recessed nine-bay centre, projecting wings of four by three bays. The plainly framed upper windows have sashes and are separated by short Doric pilasters, coupled at the corner of the wings. The ground floor of the centre is opened in an arched arcade from l. to r. In the roof are dormer windows with alternating triangular and segmental pediments. The strikingly French climate of this façade can be explained by the fact that the Duke had been Ambassador in Paris from 1669 to 1672 and again in 1678–9. His London house, Montagu House, where the British Museum now stands, was built in 1674-80 by

* They are illustrated in *Country Life*, LXXII, 1932.

Robert Hooke and called by Evelyn 'after the French pavilion way'. It was burnt in 1686 and rebuilt, according to *Vitruvius Britannicus*, 'in the French manner' by the otherwise unknown French architect, *Pierre Pouget*.* Dr Whinney has also pointed to the similarity of the Boughton façade to a plate in the so-called *Petit Marot*.‡ Equally French was the layout of the estate, of which the avenues can still be recognized. (The formal gardens were laid out by the first Duke, who employed a Dutch gardener, *Van de Meulen*. They were modified and extended from *c.* 1720 by the addition of a court and a pond and by a network of avenues and rides.)

The rest of the work of the first Duke appears curiously bitty after this restrained grandeur. Behind the loggia on the ground floor runs the front line of the time before the N front was erected. It continues to the E and is there exposed. Its front is of ashlar, but its back is of exposed brick with rubbed brick dressings. To the front seven bays, two storeys, still with cross-windows. Pedimented dormers in the roof. Further E continuation somewhat set back: eleven bays, two storeys, and the same windows and dormers. No string-course. This branch merges into the outbuildings (*see* below).

The STABLES almost join up. They are a fine composition, stone to the W front, brick to the E back. The centre is a tunnel-vaulted archway. This has a pediment to the W with an attic over crowned by a very squat four-sided lead dome.§ The windows are of the cross-type, the quoins of even length, to go with the banded rustication round the archway and in the N façade. S of the stables are more OUTBUILDINGS including three different late C17 brick houses. The E side of the house proper needs no comment. It contains among other things the kitchens. One storey, hipped roof with dormer windows.

Nor does the irregular SOUTH SIDE call for study. The WEST FRONT also, though evidently taken more seriously, was not regularized. It starts from the N with the four bays of the wing of the N façade, recedes and continues with three bays, changes its direction slightly and runs on with five bays and a top balustrade instead of the mansard roof, and then settles

* John Cornforth suggests that Pouget may be the architect *Bouget* known from drawings in the Smithson Collection at the R.I.B.A. (*Country Life*, 3 September 1970).

‡ In front of the N façade run two tunnel-vaulted parallel tunnels. They are about 6 ft high and run from E to W. What was their purpose?

§ The pediment has carving by *Duchesne*, completed in 1704 (J. Cornforth).

down to an eight-bay front which is a little higher, also
finishes on top in a balustrade, and has on the ground floor in
the middle a four-bay loggia on arches. This is now glazed.
In the same years the Duke remodelled the s front of the
C16 Hall. He gave it five tall two-light windows with two
transoms.

The INTERIOR is almost entirely his. In the old Hall the
C16 roof was hidden by a vaulted ceiling on which *Chéron*
painted Aurora and an assembly of the gods.* To its E is the
Egyptian Hall, with a ceiling by *Chéron*, to the w of the Hall
the Little Hall with a chimneypiece the big overmantel of
which displays the family tree of the first Lord Montagu
(creation 1621), another *Chéron* ceiling, and a balcony on the
w side with thin twisted balusters to act as a connexion between the first-floor rooms of the new N front and of the older
w range. (In the Drawing Room a C16 stone fireplace with two
orders of columns possibly from Brigstock Manor.) N of
the Little Hall the spectacular Stone Staircase with wrought-
iron balustrade, wall-paintings in gilt paint, and another
Chéron ceiling. The State Rooms are on the first floor facing N.
In the NW wing are two plus two rooms; the corresponding
arrangement in the NE wing, however, was never carried out,
and the wing remains gutted to this day. Some painted
panels made for this wing survive. The State Rooms also
have painted ceilings. One has a small fireplace placed diagonally as they were provided at the same time also at
Hampton Court and at Drayton (*see* p. 57). Near the E end
of the State Suite is a subsidiary staircase with turned balusters
running through all floors. In a first-floor room in the w range
near the Stone Staircase is a specially pretty chimneypiece (not
in situ),‡ the overmantel of which displays the armorial bearings
of the first Lord Montagu connected by a graceful ivy trail.
The title was conferred in 1621, Lord Montagu died in 1644.
The architectural decoration is indeed of the transition between the Jacobean and the Jones-Webb style. (At the end of
the s range the Chinese Staircase with a shield with the family
coat of arms on each tread, probably of *c.* 1740. Another curious example of chinoiserie at Boughton should be mentioned:
the late C18 portable tent of oilskin, formerly in the garden of
Montagu House.)

* The panelling and fireplace were put in only after 1910.
‡ Possibly brought from Barnwell (J. Cornforth).

BOZEAT

ST MARY. Of grey stone. Late Norman W tower (rebuilt in
1880–3), see the arch towards the nave, round, single-stepped
on simple imposts, and also the plain windows to the nave and
the shafted S window. Twin bell-openings with a separating
polygonal shaft and a round hood-mould with nailhead decoration. W doorway and W window Perp. The spire has broaches
and two tiers of lucarnes, making an unhappy pimpled outline.
Late C13 doorway. Two orders of shafts, foliage capitals, deep
arch mouldings. Late C13 also the chancel 'low-side' lancet
and priest's doorway. Otherwise the chancel is Dec with reticulated tracery in the E window. Dec also the aisle windows,
straight-headed with ogee lights, the small quatrefoil S aisle W
window, and the pretty N aisle E window with the figure of a
four-petalled flower in the tracery head. Dec arcades of three
bays. Octagonal piers, double-chamfered arches, the N capitals
looking a little earlier. The arches die into the W and E imposts
(no responds). – SCREEN. Unusually ambitious, four-light
divisions, with the main mullion running into the apex of the
four-centred arch. Each two lights taken together under an
ogee arch. Busy minor tracery. On the dado panels PAINT-
INGS illustrating the Expulsion, the Annunciation, the Adoration of the Magi, and the Baptism. – BENCHES. Square-
topped with buttress shafts. – CHANDELIER. Brass, Georgian,
small (chancel). – STAINED GLASS. In the E window by W.
Holland, 1859. – PLATE. Cup and Paten, 1636.
ROMAN BUILDINGS. ¾ mile NW of Bozeat a circular Roman
building of the C2 was excavated in 1964–5. It was 48 ft in
diameter with four central posts and internal partitions. Building work on a housing estate at Bozeat led to the discovery
of two C1 kilns and a C3 settlement which consisted of five
stone buildings, three rectangular and two circular.

BRACKLEY

ST PETER, Old Town. The Norman church which once existed
here is now represented only by the S doorway, with one order
of shafts, decorated capitals, zigzag in the arch and hood-
mould of a motif like flattened dog-tooth, and in addition by
the impost of the NW arch of a transept which exists no longer.
To this Norman church a fine W tower was added in the C13.
It has a doorway with stiff-leaf capitals, a lancet W window
with cusped niches to the l. and r. in which are still original
C13 seated figures, bell-openings of two lights with a shaft

between and blank arches to their l. and r., a pointed-trefoiled top frieze, and later battlements. To the C13 also belongs the s arcade of four bays. This has w and e responds with stiff-leaf capitals and three piers, of which the first two have circular capitals of the style corresponding to the responds, but the third has an octagonal one which corresponds to the third pier and must be a later addition, dating from the time when the arches were renewed and the N arcade was built. That time was probably the early C14, to which the s and N aisle windows belong. The easternmost window of the aisle has a very unusual tracery pattern.* But before that time was reached the chancel had been rebuilt and connected with the nave and aisles by a short, low arch. The mouldings around here are late C13 and very good. The same moulding also characterizes a respond at the NE end of the s aisle, meant to carry an arch across the aisle and open into the former transept. When the N aisle was built such a respond was also provided in the corresponding N position. A Dec chapel was added to the chancel in the early C14. The tracery of part of the N aisle windows is identical with that of the s chapel. – FONT. Square, on a big base, with chamfered corners and filleted shafts in these corners. Below the top an oak frieze. Early C14. – STAINED GLASS. At the e end of the N wall two windows by *O'Connor*, 1868 and 1869. – In the s chapel one window by *Kempe*, 1901. – PLATE. Set, 1776. – MONUMENT. Defaced effigy of a priest; in the churchyard.‡

ST JAMES. Built as the chapel of the Hospital of St James and St John founded *c.* 1150 by the Earl of Leicester. It was originally for resident brothers, was refounded in 1423 for travellers, and was sold in 1484 to William of Waynflete, who handed it on to his Oxford foundation, Magdalen College. In 1869–70 it was restored by *Buckeridge* for the use of Magdalen College School (*see* Perambulation, below, p. 118). It is difficult to follow the evidence of the building in its present state. The w front has a Late Norman doorway with zigzag also at r. angles to the wall, with foliage in the resulting lozenges. Above it is a late C13 window of three stepped lancet lights with dog-tooth decoration. To its l. and r. are niches with C14 statues (cf. St Peter, above). Recessed on the N side is a short tower. The bell-openings are plain single lan-

* That to its w is Victorian.

‡ At the w door of the church turn l. and pass through a gap in the hedge. The effigy is then immediately to the r.

cets. Only on the w side there is a blank arch to the l. of the lancet. The s side of the chapel has much disturbed masonry, including doorways, leading presumably to the hospital localities. The windows are lancets, and in the chancel stepped three-light lancets. On the N side there was a short aisle and a long chapel, the former of one bay, w of the tower, the latter of four to its E. Of the aisle the tall quatrefoil pier still exists and the springing of the arch, of the latter the quatrefoil piers with fillets and in addition thin shafts in the diagonals. Some little nailhead decoration. In the s wall SEDILIA and DOUBLE PISCINA with pointed-trefoiled arches and dog-tooth decoration. To their w a big recess with many shafts and mouldings. There is in all this no evidence later than the early C14, though how much the C19 has done is not certain. – FONT. Circular, Norman, with intersected arches and below them a band of long barbaric trail. – PULPIT. By *E. P. Warren*, *c.* 1890. – PLATE. Cup, 1570; Cup, 1580; Paten, 1623.

METHODIST CHURCH, High Street. *See* Perambulation, p. 118.

TOWN HALL. Built by the first Duke of Bridgewater in 1706. Two bays to the s, five to the E and w. To the N blank except for a middle projection and a broken pediment. In the projection a Victorian doorway and a window over with a curly open pediment. Two storeys throughout, hipped roof and cupola. Arched ground-floor windows; originally an open ground floor.

PERAMBULATION. Coming from the church and the old town* *See* p. 517 one's first impression of the HIGH STREET is the ALMS-HOUSES facing St Peter's Street. They were founded by Sir Thomas Crewe (*see* Steane) in 1633. The six dwellings have ingeniously been turned into four flats.‡ The range has one storey and dormers, three pairs of two, above the windows not the doorways of the dwellings. The High Street has trees on both sides. On the same side as the Almshouses (w) follows WINCHESTER HOUSE SCHOOL, at one time a Woodard School. This is the manor house much enlarged. The manor house was a one-storeyed dormered C17 house of which only the doorway and the mullioned window to its l. survive (now chapel). The enlarging was done by Lord Ellesmere in 1875–8. It is also in the Jacobean style and has gables and mullioned and transomed windows. The upper quadrangle was originally

---

* The name old town was used for the area around the church already in the C13, presumably to distinguish it from the settlement which had grown up around the castle to the s. The castle itself was destroyed in 1173.

‡ The conversion was done by *Blackwell, Storry & Scott*, 1969–70.

stables. After Winchester House School, No. 20, the former
CONSERVATIVE CLUB, dated 1737, but with a Victorian
cast-iron trellis porch. Opposite, the thatched PLOUGH INN,
and also a tactful stone-faced POST OFFICE of 1964. The
trees continue, but there are now grass bands as well. The
Town Hall is in the middle of this N–S axis. The view has
recently been opened up by removing some houses. On the E
side now No. 7, early C18, with a good doorway with an open
scrolly pediment. The house belongs to MAGDALEN
COLLEGE SCHOOL, whose chapel is St James (see above)
and whose own buildings begin here. The school was founded
in 1548. The buildings are largely Victorian, but there is
evidence of the hospital premises in the house lying back
from the street to the S of St James and of the later C16 in the
chimneybreast, the masonry, and a two-light window of the
main building. Opposite the METHODIST CHURCH, typical
Nonconformist Gothic of c. 1900 with an asymmetrically
placed short tower with a cross. Then (No. 6) a fine early C18
house of five bays and two storeys, unfortunately heightened
later. Doorway with Gibbs surround. The trees and grass
end now, and the elongated MARKET PLACE is reached. Its
centre is the Town Hall. The houses are uneventful but pleasant, more of brick than of stone, and often of chequered red
and blue brick. On the W side the CROWN HOTEL with a
central carriageway (now filled in) and a Venetian window
above it. Finally on the E side No. 2 BRIDGE STREET, an
C18 house of three widely spaced bays with a middle projection in which a Venetian window, and a lunette above it
set in a pedimental gable. Its neighbour, No. 4, is of five bays
and two and a half storeys, Early Georgian. It is well to look
back from here to get the S view of the Town Hall. Opposite,
some nondescript new shops intrude on the scene. So far the
rest of the High Street is marred only by the traffic, but there
are some ominously empty buildings (1972).

BRADDEN

ST MICHAEL. Short, broad, unbuttressed C13 W tower – see the
bell-openings. N arcade, except for the Perp W bay and S
arcade, also C13. The N arcade was apparently built before the
W tower, the S arcade takes the tower into account. Octagonal
piers, double-chamfered arches. The rest of 1858 (by *William
White*). – PLATE Cup and Cover Paten, 1570; Set, 1827.

MANOR HOUSE. Rain-water heads 1819, but the building history is more complicated. There was a pre-Reformation house here, and it had the projecting wings which the present house has. The W front of this looks earlier Georgian than 1819. At present the two wings have pediments. The ground-floor windows were altered fairly recently.

BRAFIELD-ON-THE-GREEN

8050

ST LAWRENCE. Norman W tower. Small S doorway. One upper S window. Arch towards the nave C19. The bell-stage is Perp, and to build it three big, clumsy, but impressive buttresses were erected. Two-light transomed bell-openings, battlements, pinnacles. Chancel rebuilt 1848 by *J. M. Derick*, N aisle and arcade 1850, porch 1911. The S arcade is interesting. It must date partly from the late C12 and partly from the early C13. The first pier has a highly unusual section. Big keeled shafts in the diagonals, fine coupled shafts in the cardinal directions. The capital has stiff-leaf and faces at the corners. It is clearly much restored but seems basically original – of the early C13.* The second pier is earlier: circular with a square abacus whose angles are cut off. The capital has water-leaf but is less trustworthy. The E respond has, again much re-cut, upright leaves. – FONT. Big, Norman.
(HOUSE, on the Green. C15. Possibly a priest's house. Formerly with Tudor wall paintings, which could not be preserved when the house was restored. GI)

BRAGBOROUGH HALL *see* BRAUNSTON

BRAMPTON ASH

7080

ST MARY. Chancel of the late C13 with an interesting E window of four lights (two plus two lights, in the spandrels tiny encircled trefoils, in the main spandrel a bigger encircled trefoil), contemporary N windows, SEDILIA and PISCINA, and a chancel arch on triple shafts. The rest Perp, especially the W tower and the arcades inside. The former has clasping buttresses, a big top frieze of cusped lozenges, and a broach spire with two tiers of lucarnes.‡ The arcades have slender piers with a long hollow-chamfered projection to nave and

---

* Is the pier perhaps wrongly erected?
‡ The Rector kindly told me that the tower was originally vaulted inside.

aisles and shafts with capitals to the arch openings. Perp also the N porch with side windows and the two handsome niches to the l. and r. of the E window. It has been pointed out that the details of the nave are very similar to Islip, and that Simon Norwich inherited Brampton Ash and a manor at Islip in 1427. He is indeed buried in the church. – BRASSES to him († 1468) and his wife on the floor in front of the chancel. The figures are 2 ft 10 in. long. Next to them the fragmentary brasses to Sir John Holt and his wife (?). Under ogee-sided gables, the figures 3 ft 2 in. long. – COMMUNION RAIL. C18. – PLATE. Cup and Cover Paten, 1631; Breadholder, 1694; Almsdish, 1826. – MONUMENTS. For the brasses, *see* above. – Charles Norwich † 1605. Two kneeling figures under an arch. – George Bosworth † 1804. Tablet. Two weeping willows bending over an urn.

BRAUNSTON

ALL SAINTS. By *R. C. Hussey*, 1849 (GR). Restored by *Butterfield*, 1874 (P. Thompson). A big, prosperous-looking church in the Dec style with a heavily crocketed spire and plenty of pinnacles. Some original Perp work in the S chapel. – FONT. Circular, Norman, with an almost defaced rope-moulding at the top. – LECTERN with 'Celtic' figures. By *Trevor Cox*, 1956. – SCULPTURE. Cross-head of a churchyard cross with the Crucifixus and three other figures, badly defaced. – STAINED GLASS. S chapel by *Wailes*, 1849; chancel N by *Hughes*, 1863. – PLATE. Cup and Cover Paten, 1570; Cup and Paten, 1657; Cup, 1720. – MONUMENTS. Excessively cross-legged Knight, a gabled flatly trefoiled canopy above his head, a big shield by his side. Of *c.* 1300.

E of the church in the main street on the N a TOWER MILL of brick, sail-less but castellated. On the S a little further on a COTTAGE with heavy timber-framing and the head of a cusped two-light window, pre-Reformation, and perhaps C14.

RECTORY, S of the church. 1839, by *H. J. Underwood* of Oxford. Cement-rendered, with a colonnade of Tuscan columns and square piers.

BRAGBOROUGH HALL, 1½ m. E. Early C19, of three wide bays with tripartite windows.* Porch of two pillars and two unfluted

---

* Plans dated 1841 at the Northants Records Office. They are signed by the builder, *William Thomson*. The architect is unknown. Information kindly supplied by Mr King.

Greek Doric columns. Entrance hall with two Tuscan columns leading to an ante-room with an open circle in the centre and with access on the r. to the staircase, which ascends in one arm and returns in two. Very simple iron balustrade. Fine late C18 fireplace from a house at Twickenham.

(CANAL BRIDGE. Of the hump type, with fine sweeping approaches. Balustrade of cast iron, signed by the Horseley Iron Works. NMR)

BRAYBROOKE   7080

ALL SAINTS. Mostly of c. 1300 and Perp. Chancel E window with intersected tracery, arcades of three bays with octagonal piers and double-chamfered arches. The detail differs. It will be noted that the W responds of the fourth bay have rather strange foliage of an earlier date. They probably belong to the C13, and they must have opened into transepts. Of c. 1300 also the S doorway. Perp the ambitious S chapel of three bays with four-light and five-light windows.* Perp also the slender W tower. Top frieze of cusped lozenges, broach spire with two tiers of lucarnes. – FONT. Square, Norman, with rosettes, beaded intertwined monsters, and on one side the incongruous combination of a cross and by its side a figure holding two fishes and placed horizontally, not vertically. How can such a thing be explained? – SCREEN. To the S chapel, Perp, coarse, of one-light divisions.   PULPIT AND COMMUNION RAIL. C18. – SCULPTURE. Big, somewhat Rabelaisian medallion containing the head of a military man. More than life-size. He has a walrus moustache and a goatee and wears a wreath. Probably c. 1575, and perhaps from Braybrooke Castle, which belonged to the Griffins (cf. Dingley). – WALL PAINTINGS (S aisle). St Anthony with his pig (?). A Knight to the l. – (STAINED GLASS. Nave S: C14 Trinity shield. Griffin Chapel: fragments, late C15–early C16. RM) – PLATE. Cup and Cover Paten, 1570; Flagon, 1703; Cup, 1764; two Breadholders, 1829. – MONUMENTS.‡ Splendid Elizabethan monument to members of the Griffin family, c. 1565–70. Base 55

* Mr Bruce Bailey draws attention to similarities between the S chapel and work at Whiston church and suggests a date of c. 1520–30 or later.

‡ The cross-legged Knight thought to be Sir Thomas le Latymer † 1333, of oak, is now on loan to Northampton Museum, as are the VAMPING HORN, 5 ft 6 in. long, to rouse the village choir to more fervent singing (cf. Harrington), and the FUNERAL HELMET which hung near the Griffin monument.

with short pilasters with roundels and a cartouche with scrolls. Main tier with four bulgy Ionic balusters, the outer ones trebled and set out in front of the others. Their bases are shorter balusters, and they carry another set of short balusters. Centre panel with shield in a gadrooned frame. Top with urns and a semicircular centrepiece containing a shell and crowned by an urn. No figures at all. Sir John Summerson suggests that the *Thorpe* family of masons were responsible (cf. Dingley and Kirby).

BRIDGE, to the SE. Begun by Sir Thomas Latimer *c.* 1400, completed in 1402–3. Of brown stone. Three pointed chamfered arches. Two massive cutwaters on the E side. Low stone parapets (GI).

CASTLE. To the E of the village, on the N side of the Desborough road, extends the complex of moated and banked platforms of the castle. The ditches are dry almost everywhere, but were once supplied from a wide artificial pool covering the N of the position. The whole area is about ¼ m. long, and many of the enclosures are very weak; in fact it is unlikely that there was any intention of defending anything except the castle proper against a serious attack.* This part of the area is occupied by a farm, whose business has inevitably done a good deal of damage to the earthworks; but the central island appears to have been double-moated, with a strong bank between the moats. Its stone defences have vanished.

BRIGSTOCK

9080

4 ST ANDREW. The Saxon tower of course is the chief object of curiosity at Brigstock. Its more than semicircular W extension, almost like an East Anglian round tower, remains most puzzling. Why is it so big if it had not been intended to contain more than a staircase, and where would so prominent a staircase have led? The problem is the same as at Brixworth. The W tower itself has long-and-short quoins, and long-and-short quoins also indicate the width and height of the Saxon nave. They are visible outside at the NW and SW end and inside at the SE end. It was a Saxon church of substantial size. The tower top is Dec. So is the spire. Low broaches, three tiers of lucarnes. Mighty Saxon tower arch, remarkably tall, with the same cyclopic unmoulded blocks representing capital and abacus as at Wittering in the Soke of Peterborough and with

* Some of the earthworks may in fact be the remains of fishponds (J. M. Steane).

the familiar raised band running up parallel with the jambs and round the arch at a distance which excludes any thought of structural expression. The tower arch is clearly Late Saxon, late C10 or C11. But Dr H. M. and J. Taylor have suggested that the lower part of the tower and the body of the church are Early Saxon, the early work being characterized by the single-splayed windows with radial voussoirs (cf. Monkwearmouth) on the N and S sides of the tower (the S one behind the clock) and the head of a similar one above the N arcade. The upper windows of the tower are double-splayed and less carefully constructed, and the long and short quoining at this level is also slightly different. Inside the tower, the small triangular-headed entry to the staircase was perhaps a W door before the stair-turret and upper part of the tower were added. Inside, the turret holes in the wall suggest an original spiral stair of wood. The unmoulded N tower arch must be a Norman insertion. During the Late Norman decades a N aisle was added to the Saxon nave. The arcade consists of two bays. Circular pier, flat capital with broad flat crocketed leaves, square abacus, round, single-stepped arches. The details point to c. 1190. Somewhat later the S doorway with thin shafts, and a round finely moulded arch. C13 also the SEDILIA in the chancel with their mature stiff-leaf capitals and the N chapel with its slim quatrefoil pier and double-chamfered arches. Of c. 1300 the low tomb recess outside the S aisle. Dec the S arcade (octagonal piers, double-chamfered arches) and the E extension of the N arcade. This and the E arch of the S arcade seem to take into consideration a Norman transept of which there is no other evidence. Dec also the chancel E window (four lights, reticulated tracery). Perp in conclusion a number of features: the chancel arch (of the four-shafts-four-hollows type), the exterior of the N side with a turret halfway down the N chapel and a big, damaged niche inside the E window, the exterior of the S side with the two-storeyed porch, its entrance with pierced traceried spandrels, See p. 517 and the picturesque turret at the NW angle of the porch. – SCREEN to the N chapel, a fine Perp piece. Said to come from Pipewell Abbey. – PLATE. Cup, 1569; Cup, 1638. – MONUMENT. First Lord Lyveden. By *Matthew Noble*, 1876. Recumbent marble effigy on a sumptuous tomb-chest.

MANOR HOUSE, W of the church. The core is a hall range of before the Reformation. The hall itself has always been one-storeyed and there was a chamber over it. The windows have four-centred heads and are of two lights with a transom, the lights two-centred and cusped, also below the transom. On the garden side is the original buttressed porch. The porch on the opposite side is recent. Jacobean extensions to the N and S, and in addition a larger S extension by *Gotch & Saunders*, 1890. Inside a Jacobean staircase (vertically symmetrical balusters), a fireplace of *c.* 1750, and a room with Adamish decoration. The house was surrounded by a moat.

MARKET CROSS. Square, bevelled shaft, head with dates 1586, 1705, 1778, and 1887. The head looks as if the cross might be medieval and remodelled. Bridges says it dates from 1586.

In SCHOOL LANE the CONGREGATIONAL CHAPEL of 1798, simple with arched windows, but some C19 alteration, and LATHAM'S SCHOOL, rebuilt by *Blomfield* in 1873.

On the road to Corby FACTORY (now of Wallis & Linnell), built in 1873–4, but still in the early C19 tradition. Thirteen bays by only two, four storeys, all windows arched. In the middle a pedimental gable with a bell.

7070

BRIXWORTH

ALL SAINTS.* 'Perhaps the most imposing architectural memorial of the seventh century surviving north of the Alps' (Clapham). That the building belongs essentially to the C7 is convincing though not conclusively provable. All we know from the C12 chronicle of Hugh Candidus of Peterborough is that around the time when Saxulf was made Bishop of the Mercians – that is in 675 – from the abbey of Peterborough many monasteries were founded . . . as at Brixworth. The church is predominantly Anglo-Saxon to this day, but not predominantly of *c.* 675. At that time it consisted of a wide and tall nave with aisles (*see* below), a spacious presbytery, as wide as the nave, a polygonal apse, and at the W end a two-storeyed porch with *porticus*, i.e. chambers, l. and r. The church, with an external length of 140 ft and an internal width across the nave of 30 ft, surpasses all other Anglo-Saxon churches in England. What survives of this is as follows. First the nave with four tall arches to the aisles. The pillars are eight-foot wide chunks of solid wall. The arches are built up of two rings of Roman bricks not used strictly voussoir-wise, that is wedge-

21

---

* The re-use of Roman tiles in the arc.   of All Saints, and finds in the neighbourhood of the church of Roman pottery and coins, indicate a settlement as yet unidentified.

wise, but rather haphazardly. At what time the aisles were pulled down is unknown. It also seems that the aisles remained normal aisles only for a short time, and that at least part of them was then subdivided to form *porticus*, i.e. separate chambers (as they are familiar from St Augustine Canterbury, Deerhurst, etc.). This was however not done consistently, as excavations in 1958 by the late Mr Dudley Jackson and Sir Eric Fletcher have proved.* So we are entitled to think of the original C7 building as a basilica in the Early Christian sense, that is as a nave with aisles and a clerestory and an apse at the E end. The clerestory windows survive, also with Roman brick arches. They are placed above the spandrels and not the apexes of the arches. The presbytery was divided from the nave by a tall arcade of three arches – as at Bradwell-juxta-Mare of *c*. 655 and at Reculver of *c*. 670. The existence of this arcade has been proved by excavation, and the l. springer of the N arch is still visible. The present W tower with its stair-case tower to the W is later in its upper parts (probably C10). It was originally a two-storeyed porch. Its tall western entrance arch can be seen inside (towards the staircase tower). The original entrance was from here – as at Monkwearmouth in 675. The *porticus* to the l. and r. can be recognized from the bits of wall running N from the NW and S from the SW angle of the W tower. The doorways from the W tower into them are *See* p. 517 also still there, again with Roman brick arches. There is a door above the tower doorway which is now blank, but is supposed to have led to a wooden W gallery (cf. Wing, Buckinghamshire). The presbytery had a low N doorway to yet another *porticus*, again with Roman brick voussoirs. The apse is narrower, and shortly after its completion a half-sunk ambulatory or outer ring-crypt was added, of a type which has been much discussed by scholars recently. The ring – or semicircular – crypt inside and below an apse is first found at St Peter's in Rome *c*. 590; outer crypts or ambulatories outside the apse are characteristic of Carolingian and Ottonian architecture in France and especially Germany. They begin, according to the most recent German paper, about 820, and culminate in the C10 and C11. No outer crypt exists or is recorded on the Continent of as early a date as that of Brix-

* Evidence was found for dividing walls between the first two bays of the N aisle, but there was no division between the third and fourth bays from the E. A dividing wall at the E end of the S aisle was discovered in 1966. (See *Journal of the British Archaeological Association*, XXIV (1961) and XXX (1967).)

worth. The ambulatory was entered by oblique stairs l. and r. of the apse arch and had a tunnel-vault, of which traces can still be seen on the s side. Mr Ralegh Radford dates the ambulatory to the late c8 or the c9.* In the c10 or early c11 the apse was rebuilt of tufa. At the time, as Mr Radford could prove, the ambulatory was in ruins. Original the N lesenes or pilaster strips which, by coming so close to the E windows of the presbytery, show that the windows are of a later date. Original also part of the large N window. The chancel was rebuilt with a square E end in the c15, but restored to its apsidal form in 1865.

The tower was raised over the porch also in the later Saxon period and given the big w stair attachment (cf. Brigstock). The pretty triple opening from the tower into the nave was made too, with its turned baluster shafts. It cuts into the arch of the earlier doorway below it. The masonry of the tower and stair-tower includes herringbone courses.

Brixworth ceased to be a monastery after the Danish devastation of 870. As a parish church it was given its Norman s doorway (two orders of shafts, roll mouldings) and its handsome two-bay s chapel of c. 1300. One bay has semi-octagonal responds, the other keeled semicircular ones. There are two tomb recesses in the s wall. In the c14 the Saxon tower was heightened. Ashlar pinnacles, broaches, and a spire with two tiers of lucarnes.

FURNISHINGS. RELIQUARY. Small, of stone, with on each side a cusped arch under a crocketed gable. The date of the piece is probably c. 1300. It is now exhibited close to the pulpit, but was found in the s chapel, with a relic inside. – SCREEN. To the s chapel, but formerly rood screen. Much restored. With tall one-light divisions and panel tracery above. – SCULPTURE. Inside the w jamb of the s doorway the Eagle of St John in relief, Saxon and perhaps from the top of a cross. The suggested date is c. 800. – Also part of a Saxon cross-shaft with a combat, almost entirely defaced. – STAINED GLASS. On the s side, 1888. – PLATE. Cup and Cover Paten, 1700. – MONUMENT. Cross-legged Knight, c. 1300 (s chapel).

METHODIST CHAPEL. 1811, enlarged 1860. Still entirely of the Georgian type with pedimental gable and arched windows.

BRIXWORTH HALL, the house of the Saunders family, has been demolished. But the stables, now LAKE HOUSE, have sur-

* But Dr Taylor now considers that the crypt is of the same date as the original building.

vived, though adapted to domestic use. Nine bays with a three-bay projection, low, square windows and oval windows over, the centre raised and in the middle of this raised portion a vertically placed bigger oval window.* At the entrance to the estate from the E THE LODGE, a good small modern house (1957 by *J. C. C. Warren*).

(MANOR HOUSE. Early C17 and later. L-shaped, some mullioned windows. Inside a remarkable large wooden staircase ascending round a central newel post. G1)

(VILLAGE CROSS. Base and part of the shaft survive. Late C14.)

(RURAL DISTRICT OFFICES. Built as the WORKHOUSE in 1836.)

(PYTCHLEY HUNT KENNELS, 1 m. W. By the *Wyvern Design Group*, 1965–6.)

ROMAN VILLA, ½ m. N. C2, with a small bath suite.

BROCKHALL

6060

ST PETER AND ST PAUL. Small, close to the Hall, with the village houses the other side. Of *c.* 1200 the S doorway and the two bays of the S arcade with circular piers, simply moulded capitals, square abaci, and round arches with a slight chamfer. The W bay was added when the W tower was built, and a further bay to embrace the tower. The tower has a W lancet window, and in the S aisle is also a window with two lancets under one hood-mould. The chancel arch corresponds. The chancel was rebuilt in 1874 by *E. F. Law*. In the S aisle the big cusped arch of a tomb recess, decorated with much ballflower, i.e. early C14. – FONT. Plain, octagonal, Perp. On the underside of the bowl fleurons. – DOOR SURROUNDS of the N and S doorways inside. Gothic, probably *c.* 1830–40. – (STAINED GLASS. Nave N. Two late C14 roundels. RM) – PLATE. Cup, 1662. – MONUMENTS. Many tablets to Thorntons, e.g. Thomas † 1783 by *William Cox*.

BROCKHALL HALL. An impressive if somewhat forbidding Elizabethan S front. Originally it had two gables and three dormers instead of the straight top it has now. Three storeys, half-H shape, with short wings and bay-windows in the re-entrant angles. Three- and four-light windows, transomed on the ground floor. The windows all have arched lights. The principal doorway is not original. It leads into the middle of

* *William Smith II* refronted the house in 1743. Presumably he did the stables (G1).

the Hall. Originally it would have led into its end. The Hall bay-window survives, and its opposite number. In the Hall now a fine fireplace of c. 1740. Several original fireplaces remain, with four-centred openings, not all *in situ*. The E side continues the Elizabethan house. Part of it was a tower. The N front is late C18 Gothick with pointed windows, including pointed Venetian windows. The W front had the same character, but was adjusted about 1900 to fit the Elizabethan façades. Inside several fine late C18 interiors, especially the staircase with a very elegant and unusual iron balustrade of single unconnected fern-like stems. The Dining Room has a classical stucco ceiling, but a Gothick frieze below the ceiling. The staircase and the Gothick alterations were designed by the owner, *Thomas Reeve Thornton*. (The Drawing Room has a good ceiling in the Adam style, by *C. Wood*, 1889.)

STABLES to the E, C18, three sides of a courtyard, with cupola, 1799. The garden was replanned at the same time on picturesque principles.

MANOR HOUSE, E of the stables. A fine, regular house, dated 1617. Half-H shape, mullioned windows.

MUSCOTT. *See* p. 308.

8070

BROUGHTON

ST ANDREW. Informally placed. Of ironstone. Mostly early C14, except for the SW angle of a former Norman aisleless church and the S doorway, which is also Norman. One order of colonnettes with primitive scallop capitals. Arch with zigzags on, and at r. angles to, the wall surface, making lozenges. One moulding has beads in the lozenges. Norman also the SW buttress and the E quoins. The W tower has in the W window as well as the bell-openings forms of the late C13 but with ogee arches. Broach spire with two tiers of lucarnes. N aisle W window and doorway, blocked S aisle S lancet, and both arcades (octagonal piers, double-chamfered arches, differing details) are of the early C14. The chancel is earlier, but was rebuilt in 1828. E window of five lights with intersected tracery leaving the top out to fit a circle in. The chancel arch corresponds in date. – FONT. Octagonal, with panelled stem and nodding ogee arches against the bowl; C14? – STAINED GLASS. E window by *Powell's*, 1855; still in the tradition of the early C19. – (S aisle E. Coats of arms, c. 1500; heads, c. 1420–40. RM)* –

---

* Also in the S aisle a late *Morris & Co.* window of 1919 (BB).

PLATE. Paten, 1632; Cup, 1683; Paten, 1721; Flagon, 1770. – MONUMENTS. Two of 1631, one in a tradition of certain monuments of divines, the other in a more recent, more courtly fashion. Robert Bolton, rector. Frontal demi-figure, praying, his hands on the bible, the bible on a pillow. The figure is in a shallow arched niche. – Harold Kynnesman. Bust in an oval medallion surrounded by fleshy, curly ornament no longer indebted to the strapwork convention.

THE GABLES, SW of the church. 1685. Still in the Jacobean style, irregularly gabled.

YEOMAN'S HOUSE, W of the church, on the A-road. Jacobean. Tall, of ironstone. Steep gable to the street, smaller gable at r. angles to it, to the S. Barn S of the house.

(In CHURCH VIEW two quite distinguished neo-Queen Anne houses of 1903 by *J. Blackwell*. BB)

BUGBROOKE

6050

ST MICHAEL. Fine early C13 S arcade of four bays. Circular piers, capitals of which two have stiff-leaf foliage (one, it seems, only set out and not completed), pointed arches with one slight chamfer. The N arcade (octagonal piers and double-chamfered arches) is somewhat later, but still C13, the one-bay N chapel perhaps of the same date as the N arcade. The S chapel is of the late C19. Lancets at the W ends of both aisles, also a pair of lancets in the N wall of the N aisle. Perp three-light clerestory windows. Dec W tower with recessed spire (two tiers of lucarnes). – FONT. Octagonal, Perp. – SCREEN. Good, with two-light divisions, the mullions reaching up into the apex of the arches. Ribbed coving. – PLATE. Flagon, 1803; Paten, 1804; Breadholder, 1805; Cup, 1821. – (MONUMENTS. Two good tablets to the Whitfield family, 1704 and 1734. BB)

(RECTORY, W of the church. Early C19, yellow brick. Tuscan porch. BB)

A number of good houses at the SE end of the village, e.g. one of 1706 with sashed windows; one of the late C17 still with mullioned windows but symmetrically placed; and a Georgian ten-bay group canted twice round a corner. The BAPTIST CHURCH is of 1808. Front with two doorways and segment-headed windows. The yellow brick cottages E of the church beyond the brook were built in the Gothic style in 1844 by *E. F. Law*. They were the NATIONAL SCHOOL with dwellings for the master and, it is said, the policeman.

At the NE end of the village the MANOR HOUSE with a wide arched entrance to its yard. (A restoration in the Tudor manner in 1881 by *E. F. Law* makes the house look comparatively new. BB)

On the top of the hill on the road to Kislingbury, BUGBROOKE SECONDARY SCHOOL, by the County Architect's Department (*A. N. Harris*), 1966–8, extensions (by *John Goff*) 1971–2. The first purpose-built comprehensive school in the county. A large, powerful composition in brick and concrete, with effective black mullioned staircase windows.

(CLAPPER BRIDGE. C16. Damaged by river widening. GI)

₉₀₉₀   BULWICK

ST NICHOLAS. Tall Perp w tower with clasping buttresses. Two tall two-light bell-openings with transom. Quatrefoil frieze below the battlements. Recessed spire with roll mouldings up the edges and two tiers of lucarnes in alternating directions. Late C13 chancel. The E window of five lights is specially characteristic. Intersected tracery cusped, but with a circle at the top to break the regularity of the intersections. The window is shafted inside. Late C13 also the SEDILIA and PISCINA, and probably the doorway into the N aisle too. Two orders of stone shafts with shaft-rings; moulded arch. The principal aisle windows are Perp and remarkably big. On entering the church it is seen that it was originally provided with transepts (see the pieces of wall after the first two orders of the arcades). The N arcade is earlier than the rest, say of *c.* 1200. Two wide bays with a short octagonal pier. Capital with short upright stiffleaves. Pointed double-chamfered arch. The s arcade is Dec. Both arcades were lengthened by incorporating the former transept arches. The heights and details of these and the chancel arch differ. The church was restored by *Slater & Carpenter*, 1870 (N. Taylor). – BENCH ENDS. Carved by the Rector of 1862–92, the Rev. *J. H. Holdich.** – (STAINED GLASS, nave N. C14 and C15 canopies and grisaille work. RM) – PLATE. Paten, 1638; Cup and Cover Paten, two Flagons, Breadholder, all 1702. – MONUMENTS. Henry Fowkes † 1612 (date not filled in) and his wife who died in 1609. With kneeling figures facing one another across a prayer-desk. – (Admiral Lord Tryon † 1893. Bronze plaque with portrait medallion.)

BULWICK HALL. 1676, but remodelled in the mid C18 and

---

* Information from the Rev. C. J. Ough.

later.* The date 1676 is on the handsome arcade with a balus-traded balcony which runs to the s at the e end of the house. Rusticated segmental arches. The house itself has cross-windows to the e which go with its date. The s front however is sashed. Two storeys, twelve bays plus a bow-window attached on the l. Small doorway with Gibbs surround. No other enrichment. (In the Hall a fireplace which may be Early Elizabethan. Very tapering columns, the shafts decorated with the pattern of connected circles and squares familiar e.g. from the Tresham buildings and a gadrooned cornice (NMR); fine wrought-iron GATES into the park (L. M. Gotch).)

FINESHADE ABBEY. *See* p. 218.

BUNKERS HILL FARM *see* BOUGHTON

BURNT WALLS *see* DAVENTRY

BURTON LATIMER

8070

ST MARY. Externally the church is much too restored. The tower was rebuilt in 1866.‡ So we start inside, with the strange nook-shafted respond in the N arcade; for the shape of the pier to which it belongs is evidence of the transept of a cruciform Norman church. Only thus can it be explained that there are two nook-shafts (with stiff-leaf capitals, *see* below) to the N and a round arch to the E. To this cruciform Norman church of which no actual feature remains, a s arcade was added still in the C12, and of that we have two and a half arches from the w. Circular piers, square capitals with many scallops and one with upright leaves, the arches (from the w) unmoulded, then with a thin angle roll,§ then with zigzag. The N arcade, also with a half-arch, follows in the early C13. One pier is circular with a circular stiff-leaf capital, the next is square with four demi-shafts (cf. Rothwell) and stiff-leaf. The piece of wall indicates the junction between aisle and transept, the stiff-leaf respond to the N the arch into the transept. The C13 arches are pointed and single-stepped. The s doorway also is of the early C13. The arch is still round, but complexly moulded.

---

* There were alterations in 1805 by *W. D. Legg*, and in 1838 (P. I. King, H. M. Colvin).

‡ By *Slater*, who also restored the church (R. Hubbuck).

§ Similar to the N transept arch.

Next came the tower, cutting off half the first arcade arches. The tower has to the N and S and, at a lower level, to the W blank arcading of three large arches on each side. The tower arch towards the nave has clustered shafts as responds and is triple-chamfered. The bell-openings are of two lights and heavily shafted. They are of after 1310. Battlements, recessed spire with two tiers of lucarnes. About 1280 or 1290 the former chancel was taken into the nave, and the arcades were correspondingly lengthened. Three bays, quatrefoil piers, double-chamfered arches. At the same time a new chancel was built. The E window is of 1867, but the side windows are late C13. Y-tracery with foiled circles. Perp most of the other windows, and Perp the N porch with a niche over the entrance. – SCREEN. Perp, much restored. Of two-light divisions. Good, clear tracery. – NORTH DOOR. Studded, dated 1500. – (CHEST, dated 1629.) – WALL PAINTINGS. On the N aisle wall fragments of a cycle of St Catherine, C14. Near the W end Martyrdom of the Saint; further E St Catherine led away from the judge. – (In the spandrels of the nave arches, figures representing the tribes of Israel, in scrolled cartouches. Late C16. E. Croft Murray) – STAINED GLASS. (E window 1896.) – N aisle E by *Capronnier*, 1874. – PLATE. Cup and Cover Paten, 1569; Paten, *c.* 1682; Flagon and Almsdish, 1774. – MONUMENTS. Boyvill Brass (E end of nave). Only a group of children remains. The parents were in shrouds. Probably early C16. – (Edward Bacon † 1626. Only part of the brass survives.) – Margaret Bacon † 1626. Brass in a large, tall stone frame with fluted pilasters, a fluted frieze, and a top with three obelisks.

SCHOOL, W of the church. 1622. Oblong, one-storeyed, with two three-light mullioned windows on each side of a doorway which has a four-centred head and flanking pilasters. Above it a big ogee-sided gable with finials. Inscriptions over door and windows. (Fine oak roof. VCH) To be converted into a private house (1972).

BURTON LATIMER HALL. Jacobean. Originally of half-H shape. Cross-windows and mullioned and transomed windows; gables. The original staircase remains with balusters with Ionic heads. The doorways by the staircase with their carved frames look rather later C17. So does the large Hall fireplace. Also of the later C17 the two windows in the E wing opening S. The upper one has the typical arch inserted in the middle part of a tripartite window below the lintel. The W wing was lengthened in 1873. Behind it, the w front towards the road received a new face some time early in the c18. Five bays, two storeys, pedimented doorway.

BYFIELD

HOLY CROSS. Essentially Dec, and an ambitious building. Tall chancel with fine, slender two-light windows. The tracery is [12] of the intersected type, but the heads of the windows are segmental – quite a piquant effect.* The aisle windows and doorways are also Dec. The w tower has a sumptuous portal with ballflower in a continuous moulding, a crocketed ogee hoodmould and pinnacles, a two-light window above, and niches with nodding ogee arches to its l. and r. A third niche above it. The upper part of the tower is Perp. Two widely set, tall bell-openings linked by an arch of the basket or *anse de panier* type. Battlements and a recessed spire. The spire is not tall, but has two tiers of lucarnes in alternating directions. The big s porch entrance repeats the design of the w portal. The sides of the porch have small two-light windows. Dec again the arcades of four bays (octagonal piers, double-chamfered arches). – BENCHES. With tracery panels on fronts, backs, and ends. – STAINED GLASS. By *Kempe*, 1893 (w), 1897 (E), and 1902 (chancel s). – PLATE. Patens, 1696 and 1698; Cup, 1697; Flagon, 1763; Strainer Spoon, 1827.

MANOR HOUSE, ¼ m. NW, at the main crossing. Five bays, two storeys, quoins. Doorway with an open segmental pediment. A small cherub's head in the opening. Probably early c18.

CALDECOTT see CHELVESTON

CANONS ASHBY

ST MARY. A fragment of the church of an Augustinian priory founded *c.* 1150. What remains is two bays of the nave and N aisle and the big NW tower added to the N of the aisle in the mid c14. This has tall two-light bell-openings, still Dec, and battlements and pinnacles. The nave front is distinguished by a splendid portal, richly shafted and with a richly moulded arch. To its l. and its r. are two bays of blank arcading. Rounded quatrefoil heads under richly moulded arches. The shafts have stiff-leaf capitals. All this must be of *c.* 1230–40.

---

* The flowing tracery of the E window is Victorian.

The big window above is Perp, the s windows and the E
window are post-Reformation. The church never had a s aisle.
The cloister was attached immediately to the nave. It was surrounded by the usual buildings, including a long oblong
chapter house. On the N side however an aisle existed, erected
probably a little after the nave and its W end. The aisle front
at least has blank arcading typical of the late C13 (pointed-
trefoiled arches) and the shafts of the window above look *c.*
1310. The arcade inside certainly does not contradict this
dating. Very tall and substantial piers. The first is circular
with circular abacus, the second octagonal with octagonal
abacus. The arches have three hollow chamfers, and there are
conical foot-pieces. Doorway to the tower with the typical
Dec moulding of two sunk quadrants. The nave was originally
96 ft long and was followed by a long aisleless chancel. –
FONT. Octagonal, with patterns of window tracery as if from
a pattern book. They are both Dec and Perp. – READER'S
DESK. With Jacobean panels. – COMMUNION RAIL. Probably
late C17. – ARMOUR of Sir Robert Dryden † 1708, 'the most
elaborate funeral achievement in the county'. Large banner,
two pennons, helmet and crest, wreath and mantling, tabard,
shield, gauntlets, spurs, sword. – MONUMENTS. Brass to John
Dryden † 1584 (a 23 in. figure). – John Turner Dryden † 1797.
By *Rossi*. In the Bacon style, with a large female figure seated
at the base of an urn. – John Edward Turner Dryden, 1818 by
Rossi (Murray). Standing, mourning Grecian woman holding
a garland to lay on an altar.

WELL-HOUSE, NNE of the church and E of the house, in an
orchard. Small, with a pitched roof and an arched entrance.
Tunnel-vaulted inside.

CANONS ASHBY. After the Dissolution a house which has now
gone was made by Sir John Cope out of the buildings of the
priory. Another house was built in the mid C16, possibly
on the site of the guest house of the priory, by the Dryden
family, who married into the Cope family in 1551. This is the
house which survives in its essential and its most interesting
parts. It stands immediately by the road and is built round a
smallish courtyard. It is of ironstone but with much brick,
especially on the E side, which faces the road. Sir John Dryden,
who came into the property in 1632, seems to have done much
in a still unquestioned Jacobean style, and then came Edward
Dryden, who made important alterations in 1708–10. The
present approach is from the W, though it was originally prob-

ably from the s in the place where there is now only an elementary doorway. The w side is mostly of 1708-10, with sashed windows arranged as regularly as could be managed in the presence of a big tower of the c16 building.* This rises now in an unexpected way above the Queen Anne skyline. The tower has mullioned windows with arched lights, and so have all John Dryden's windows. In this and, it seems, all other important respects, the building begun in the 1550s was still entirely pre-Renaissance. At the foot of the tower is Edward Dryden's doorway with an open segmental pediment. At r. angles to this range, i.e. facing N, is the Hall range, and the Hall remains, though ceiled and no longer open to the roof. All that survives is the doorway to the N with a four-centred head and the two doorways inside which once led from the screens passage to the kitchen and buttery. The Hall windows are Jacobean to the courtyard as well as the N, and the N front is indeed essentially Jacobean, i.e. Sir John's, with the exception of the doorway in the middle, which, with its segmental pediment, is clearly of 1708-10. The front is symmetrical with projecting ends, that to the w with the c16 windows, that to the E with the square-topped mullioned and transomed windows of Sir John. One can assume that the w projection is the work of John Dryden and contained the Parlour and the Guest Chamber above it, but that the E projection was remodelled by Sir John. The E range is quite irregular. To the courtyard its N piece is of one build with the Hall and ends in a broad buttress. The joint here is very evident. The piece contains at the N end the Servants' Hall and then, down some steps, the Kitchen. The Bakehouse follows s of the joint. The back staircase N of the kitchen with flat, openwork, tapering balusters is again Jacobean. To the E the façade is given more dignity by canted bay-windows at the N and s ends. Nothing much need be said about the s side. This also is irregular. Its only ornament is an oriel window near the r. end under the gable. This was added by Sir Henry Dryden, the antiquary, in the c19. He rebuilt the E side of the s front to correspond with the c16 E front.‡

Of INTERIORS the only outstanding one is the Drawing Room in the w range on the first floor. It has a very grand fireplace with Ionic columns flanking the opening and three

* Mr L. M. Gotch informs me that J. A. Gotch considered the tower to be prior to 1551.
‡ Information from Sir Gyles Isham.

pairs of Corinthian columns in the overmantel. The decoration is chiefly foliage and arabesque. There is only very little strapwork. The style looks decidedly Elizabethan, in spite of the arms of Sir John. The first John died only in 1584 – could it still be his, and could it perhaps be re-set? What is certain is that the ceiling of the room is later and does not fit it. It is a gorgeous ceiling, highly coved, decorated with plasterwork with the patterns of broad bands usual in the early C17, and culminating in a big openwork pendant with four demi-figures of women like galleons' heads. This dates from the time of Sir John, who, as we have seen, succeeded in 1632 – an oddly late date. Of the time of the same Sir John is probably the main staircase in the tower, with remarkably fat vertically symmetrical balusters. To its N a room with Queen Anne panelling including a curious and amply curved mirror above the fireplace. At the S end of the W range is the Painted Parlour, with Corinthian pilasters feigned in paint.* The room above it has a Rococo ceiling.

There are to the N as well as the W several fine sets of GATEPIERS, both Jacobean and Queen Anne. (In the garden a fine lead figure of a shepherd boy, the only survivor of several lead figures made for Edward Dryden by *John Nost*, *c.* 1700. BB)

BARROW, ¼ m. due N of the church. A Late Bronze Age spearhead was found in it.

CASTLE ASHBY

ST MARY MAGDALENE. The church lies immediately next to the balustrade of the terrace of the E garden of the house and with its other side even nearer to the Orangery. Rarely is a church made so much part of the private garden furnishings of a mansion. The church is entered from the terrace by the N porch, which has a re-set Late Norman or earliest E.E. doorway, very sumptuous and very much restored. It has as the elements of the decoration of its arch zigzag and lozenges (i.e. two zigzags meeting) as well as fully developed dog-tooth, a rare (and historically instructive) combination. The zigzag and lozenges are set parallel to the wall surface as well as at r. angles to it. The church otherwise has a Dec N aisle with flowing tracery and a Perp W tower (doorway with traceried

---

* Mr Louis Osman suggests that the decoration may be by one of the *Creed* family (cf. Titchmarsh), who were related to the Drydens.

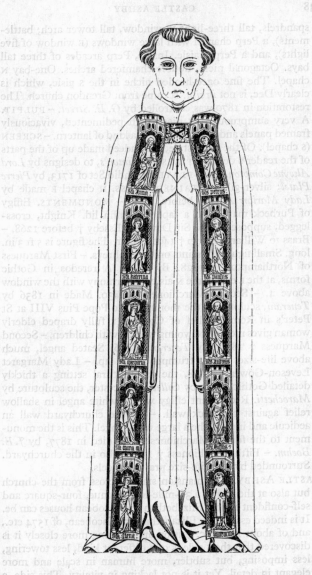

Castle Ashby church, brass to William Ermyn † 1401

spandrels, tall three-light w window, tall tower arch, battlements), a Perp chancel with large windows (E window of five lights), and a Perp s aisle. Inside, Perp arcades of three tall bays. Octagonal piers, double-chamfered arches. One-bay N chapel. The fine ogee-headed niche in the s aisle, which is clearly Dec, is not *in situ*. It came from Grendon church. The restoration in 1870 was controlled by *G. E. Street*. – PULPIT. A very sumptuous C17 piece with pedimented, vivaciously framed panels and a tall tester with a kind of lantern. – SCREEN (s chapel). Of the same style, and indeed made up of the parts of the reader's desk. – (TILES by *Minton's*, to designs by *Lord Alwyne Compton*. BB) – PLATE. Splendid Set of 1713, by *Pierre Platel*; silver-gilt. – STAINED GLASS. N chapel E made by *Lady Marian Alford*, before 1888. – MONUMENTS. Effigy of Purbeck marble on a tapering coffin lid. Knight, crosslegged, supposed to be Sir David de Esseby † before 1268. – Brass to William Ermyn † 1401, rector. The figure is 5 ft 3 in. long. Small figures of saints on the orphreys. – First Marquess of Northampton † 1828. By *Blore*. A reredos in Gothic forms, at the E end of the N aisle, in harmony with the window above it. – Second Marchioness † 1830. Made in 1836 by *Tenerani*, sculptor of the monument to Pope Pius VIII at St Peter's in Rome. Relief of Charity: a fully draped elderly woman gives money to a young woman with children. – Second Marquess † 1851. By *Tenerani*, 1866. Seated angel, much above life-size, with a trumpet in his lap. – Lady Margaret Leveson-Gower † 1858, the architectural setting a thickly detailed Gothic recess by *Gillet* of Leicester, the sculpture by *Marochetti*. Recumbent effigy with a white angel in shallow relief against the back wall. – In the churchyard wall an aedicule and in its niche a large white angel. This is the monument to the fourth Marchioness, who died in 1877, by *J. E. Boehm*. – Fifth Marchioness † 1902. Also in the churchyard. Surrounded by four life-size praying angels.

81 CASTLE ASHBY. The mansion stands across from the church but also at the end of a 3½-mile-long avenue, four-square and self-confident as only Elizabethan and Jacobean houses can be. It is indeed essentially Elizabethan and Jacobean, of 1574 etc., and of about 1600 etc. But on approaching more closely it is discovered that the s side is of a different kind, less towering, less imposing, but subtler, more human in scale and more elegant in detail. Yet it is not lacking in vitality. This side, a screen to close the Elizabethan courtyard, is work of 1625–35

and possibly by *Inigo Jones*.* The later contributions are important inside but not outside. The house is of Weldon stone.

Castle Ashby had been a castle from the C11, but when Leland saw the place in the 1530s he wrote that it was 'now clean down'. By then the estate had been bought by Sir William Compton, a personal friend of Henry VIII and hence a very rich man. But Sir William did not at once do anything to the building; for in a survey of 1565 it is still called an 'old ruined castle'. Work was started by the first Lord Compton in 1574 when a long-drawn-out litigation was settled, but no doubt before his wife, whom he had married only in 1572, had died in the same year 1574. Her and his arms still appear together on the spandrel of the doorway to the s w tower. Lord Compton's house occupied three sides of a long courtyard. Externally it is a little wider than it is deep, but the sides of the wings to the courtyard are longer than the recessed middle range, a type familiar from such mid-c16 houses in East Anglia as Long Melford and Rushbrooke. In common with them also is the placing of polygonal staircase turrets near the ends, but not quite at the ends, of the courtyard fronts of the wings. Of this Elizabethan work, the s ends of the wings meet one as one approaches the house. They were heightened later.

But the principal impression of the s side is the SCREEN. The attribution to *Inigo Jones* comes from Campbell's *Vitruvius Britannicus* vol. 3 (1725) and Bridges. Can it be accepted? Not by Sir John Summerson, and not by Oliver Hill and John Cornforth. Yet I am still tempted to defend the attribution. The s front is of two storeys, i.e. lower than the rest of the house, and ashlar-faced. It is nine bays wide with a wide tripartite and pedimented centre and the end bays a little projecting. All along the façade there is articulation by pilasters or attached columns, Tuscan with three bands of rocky rustication below, slender unfluted Ionic above. The centre has in addition an archway with segmental head and the same bands of rocky rustication, niches to its l. and r., and, on the first floor, a Venetian window also with niches l. and r. The Venetian window was an innovation in England at that time. Inigo Jones had used it for the first time in the Queen's Chapel in London in 1623. The foot-line of the top pediment recedes slightly above the Venetian window. To the l. and r. of the pediment balustrade with lettering. It reads Dominus

* The arms of the first Earl, who died in 1630, are above the entrance.

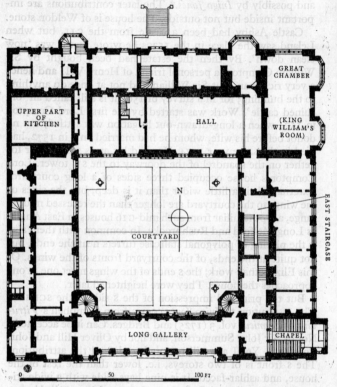

Castle Ashby
(Redrawn by courtesy of Messrs Batsford)

custodiat introitum tuum. On the inside of the screen building the text is Dominus custodiat exitum tuum. This balustrade lettering is a speciality of Castle Ashby, and more will be said of it later. The internal front of the building is identical with the external except that it is only seven bays wide, because the last bays disappear behind the stair-turrets of *c.* 1574, and that it has attached columns throughout, also where the s façade has pilasters. Campbell illustrates a scheme for the whole s front according to which Inigo Jones was to have extended his system of pilasters to the faces of the E and W wings and to have replaced the – still brand-new – balustrade with its quaint lettering by a plain balustrade and a plain parapet. Scholars have objected to the attribution, because of certain licences in the design. But we are getting used to the idea of a less pure Inigo than the Queen's House and the Banqueting House alone would make one expect. Incidentally, the second Earl of Northampton, who succeeded in 1630 and died in 1643, was closely attached to the court, having accompanied Charles on his adventurous trip to Spain in 1623. The ground floor of the screen range is filled by a loggia open to the courtyard. The s wall has niches with pediments on Tuscan pilasters.

The motif of a screen wall across the entrance side of a COURTYARD is French in origin (Bury), but had been adopted by the Elizabethans and Jacobeans and occurs in Northamptonshire also at Rushton and, long before Castle Ashby, at Kirby. Again in the usual way the Hall range of the Elizabethan Castle Ashby was the range facing the screen, i.e. the N range. The three ranges were originally two-storeyed, except for the Hall, which rises through both. The windows are mullioned and transomed. Those in the ground floor in the Hall range have two transoms, all others one.* There are six bays on the w, five on the E side. On the w side in the centre is a later C17 doorway with an oval opening above, placed vertically. Shortly before 1624 a third storey was added with windows of a different design and in a different rhythm and with a top balustrade on which one can read these lines from Psalm 127: Nisi dominus custos custodiverit domum frustra vigilat qui custodit eam. Nisi dominus aedificaverit domum in vanum laboraverunt qui aedificant eam. 1624. The idea of openwork inscriptions on parapets is probably French. It occurs in the apse of the church of La Ferté Bernard in 1535–44. In England other examples are Felbrigg Hall in Norfolk (c. 1600), and Temple Newsam (c. 1630) and, somewhat later, the gatehouse at Skipton Castle in Yorkshire (c. 1660). The SE and SW stair-turrets were also heightened, and one of them has at the top the date 1635, so that work must have gone on at the same time in the Jacobean and the Inigo Jones style. The heightening was begun by William Lord Compton, who entertained James I at Castle Ashby in 1605, 1612, and 1616 and became the first Earl of Northampton in 1618.

* The first window from the w is smaller, and there is a small doorway below it with a four-centred head.

Now for the external faces of the three wings. The EAST FAÇADE is a composite job. It is ashlar-faced, while the rest of the façades is of rubble. Starting with the Elizabethan work near the N end, the two big bay-windows here correspond in their two-transomed upper parts with the Elizabethan Great Chamber. There follows to the S a ten-bay part which had on the ground floor originally an open loggia like Burghley, Longford Castle, Cranborne, Audley End, and other Elizabethan and Jacobean houses. The loggia was of five wide bays, the arches separated by coupled diamond-banded pilasters with a niche between. The motif of the niches repeats on the upper floors, separating pairs of windows from each other. The whole of this part of the façade is stylistically a transition from the Jacobean to the Jonesian. Near the S end of the front is the big Venetian window of the Chapel. This was put in by the third Earl after the Restoration (*see* below). At the same time the loggia was converted into rooms. The NORTH FAÇADE, i.e. the N side of the Hall range, originally had a recessed centre corresponding to the N wall of the Hall and offices, and projecting wings. The centre was filled in in 1719–22. The former E wing remains, with a bay-window and the large, six-light, two-transomed N window of the Great Chamber. The corresponding W bay-window is an addition made for symmetry's sake in 1719–22. The new centre has five bays. Open stairs to the doorway. All windows segment-headed, but curiously enough still with mullion-and-transom crosses. Below the parapet horizontal oval openings, another conservative motif. The lettered parapets here and on the W range were added in 1827.

The Elizabethan WEST SIDE must have been quite informal. Only the N and S ends are part of it. The rest was recessed and filled in about 1630–5. The fenestration is conservative (and irregular because of the W staircase behind).

The INTERIOR must be described chronologically. All that remains of Elizabethan interiors is the rib-vaulted UNDERCROFT of the Hall and the Great Chamber (N range centre and NE corner). It looks decidedly older than 1574. Of *c.* 1625–30 is first of all the splendid plaster ceiling of the GREAT CHAMBER (first floor, NE corner, also known as KING WILLIAM'S ROOM). It is no longer strictly Jacobean; that is, the main division is panels with frames in strong relief, though the cartouches etc. in the panels still exhibit strapwork. Pretty coving with allegorical figures in cartouches. The tremendously elaborate chimneypiece is of about the same time but comes from Northampton House, Canonbury, London. There are six small allegorical figures in the overmantel and two larger caryatids l. and r. of the fireplace opening. Everything ornamental is overcrowded. Nothing here strikes one as post-Jacobean. The date of the chimneypiece is indeed 1601. The panelling and door-frames of the room are later C17. Of c. 1625–30 the OLD LIBRARY, in the SE corner on the second floor. This has a plaster ceiling in the same style as the Great Chamber, though, in accordance with the lower proportion of the room, the relief is less bold. But the combination of semi-classical framing with strapwork continues. Again of c. 1625–30 the WEST STAIRCASE. It runs through all storeys. Its style harmonizes with that of the other two rooms. It has open-work panels, a motif more characteristic of the second than the first half of the century, but they are not yet filled with acanthus foliage (see East Staircase, below), but with strap-work.* The posts are square and end in Jacobean pendants below but in plain balls above. On the ground floor in the w range at its s end is the BOWER, a charming cabinet with panelled walls and a plaster ceiling. The plasterwork here is of the usual broad-banded Jacobean type. The wall panelling is painted, with charming ribbonwork, little trophies, bunches of fruit, etc. Perhaps by *Matthew Gooderick* (E. Croft-Murray).

Much redecorating was done by the third Earl, who died in 1681. He made the three DRAWING ROOMS N of the chapel, in the E range on the ground floor, where he had closed the former Loggia, the splendid EAST STAIRCASE behind them, which is more spacious than the West Staircase and has open-work panels of luxuriant acanthus foliage with flowers, and the STATE ROOMS on the first floor above the Drawing Rooms. The lush wood carving here is in the style of Grinling Gibbons.

A certain amount of minor work dates from the late C18 (fireplace in the DINING ROOM, N end E wing, ground floor), but it was only about 1880 that major work was again undertaken. Now *Sir T. G. Jackson* redecorated the CHAPEL (SE corner) in a neo-Wren style‡ and the LONG GALLERY which

* This motif occurs at Radclive, Bucks in 1621, at Cromwell House, Highgate, London, in 1637–8.
‡ PLATE. Silver-gilt Breadholder of 1664 and Set of Cups, Cover Patens, and Flagons of 1677.

forms the upper floor of the Jones screen. This is tripartite and has a refined fireplace of 1771 which came from the Hall. Pairs of Ionic columns, the fluting replaced by green inlay in white. The HALL was redecorated in 1884. Original only the chimneypiece, dated 1599, which was brought from Canonbury (*see* above).

Much is to be seen in the gardens and outbuildings. STABLES; to the w. Jacobean, with mullioned and transomed windows and doorways with four-centred heads. Close by a peculiarly hideous Victorian WATER TOWER, built in 1865, probably by *Sir Matthew Digby Wyatt*. The great avenues in the grounds were laid out immediately after the visit of William III, which took place in 1695. Specially spectacular the wide and long SOUTH AVENUE, which ends towards the house with wide GATES. They were designed by *Sir Matthew Digby Wyatt* in 1868. The elaborate iron gates are said to have come from Italy. The piers are of *Blashfield's* terracotta, a material much favoured by Sir Matthew. The style is derived from the Certosa of Pavia or similar Lombard work. Also of terracotta the balustrading of the TERRACES to the E and N. This has inscriptions on the pattern of the Jacobean inscriptions of the house. One of them says 'The grass withereth and the flower fadeth but the word of God endureth for ever', the other 'Consider the lilies of the field how they grow they toil not neither do they spin and yet I say unto you that Solomon in all his glory was not arrayed like one of them'. This inscription ends with a reference to the death of the third Marchioness in 1865.

The E and N gardens are both in the Italian style. The gardener was a Mr *Thomas*. Long before Wyatt's time, in 1761–7, *Capability Brown* had landscaped the grounds of Castle Ashby. Of his time remain the pretty TEMPLE to the NE with a semicircular centre, four columns, and a semidome, the DAIRY, immediately NW of the house, with a wooden veranda and a horizontally placed oval in the parapet, the BRIDGE (with a balustrade of *c.* 1865), and the AVIARY behind the temple, now a private house. By *M. D. Wyatt*, of 1861–5, the large free-Italianate ORANGERY, S of the E terrace, facing E. It is thirteen bays long with raised and arched centre and end bays. Balustrading throughout. Above the three middle bays a terracotta frieze of figures. Aisled interior. Facing the Orangery to the S at some distance a SCREEN or Gloriette of nine arched bays with the centre arch raised.

Between this and the Orangery the ITALIAN GARDEN of c. 1860. The walls of the very large KITCHEN GARDEN to the s of the church are partly by *M. D. Wyatt* and partly by *Edward Godwin,* who worked on the garden in 1868–70. Also by him the French Renaissance ENTRANCE SCREEN (1868) across the South Avenue (on the A428) and the picturesque STATION LODGE (1869) facing the road to Earl's Barton, with a tall arched entrance and a small circular turret (BB).

SCHOOL in the village. By *G. E. Street.* The plans approved in 1856. Picturesque Tudor, banded and with steep roof and a big chimneybreast on the front.

CATESBY

5050

OLD CHURCH. In the churchyard obelisk MONUMENT to John Parkhurst, 1765. The ball on top was originally gilt.

ST MARY. 1861–2 by *Gillet* of Leicester. The SEDILIA and PISCINA with crocketed gables and pinnacles are original and of c. 1300. – C17 furnishings from the old church: big Jacobean PULPIT with tester. – Also Jacobean panels in the STALLS and the READER'S DESK. – COMMUNION RAIL. With strong twisted balusters; late C17. – STAINED GLASS. Mixed C14–15 fragments in the w window (the Virgin and Saints). – PLATE. Cup and Paten, 1632; Flagon, 1635; Breadholder, 1635.

COTTAGES, N of the church. A row of four which looks as if it had been built as almshouses. Mullioned windows with arched lights.

STABLES, SE of the church. Red brick, large, with a turret. They belonged to Catesby House.

HOUSE, E of the old church. Its doorway is a re-used C13 piece. Two orders of shafts and three roll mouldings.

CATESBY HOUSE. 1863 and 1894. With shaped gables. Inside fitments from the preceding house. This in its turn had been preceded by a Benedictine NUNNERY, founded c. 1175. Canons and lay-brothers were attached to it until after 1310. The house which followed the priory was built in the late C17. From it comes the fine staircase with strong twisted balusters and the panelling in one room. Linenfold panelling in the staircase hall may come from the priory itself, which was dissolved in 1536.

CHACOMBE

4040

ST PETER AND ST PAUL. Essentially a Dec church, over-restored. The arcades are original and interesting. They are low, of three bays, and although their piers are octagonal, the capitals are quatrefoil and typically Dec. Double-chamfered arches. Again, though the windows are all renewed outside, the continuous filleted moulding inside accredits them. Their forms are of *c.* 1300–30 (cusped lights and a cinquefoiled niche, reticulation, etc.). The w tower is not of special interest. The s porch, whose entrance arch is clearly Dec, has its stone roof supported on two big single-chamfered transverse arches. – FONT. Circular, Norman, with intersected arches. – SOUTH DOOR. Battened and with ironwork. – BOX PEWS. – PLATE. Cup and Paten, 1712. – BRASS. Michael Fox † 1569, but made *c.* 1545. Small, a quatrefoil with concave curves connecting the lobes (chancel, N side, in the floor, *c.* 8 in. in size).

There was a PRIORY of Augustinian Canons at Chacombe, founded in the mid C12. Nothing is known about its exact site, but the house called The Priory has to the N of its E end a short building known as the Chapel which is medieval. It has on its ground floor a plain doorway and a two-light window, both apparently late C13, and on its upper floor a two-light window with cusped ogee lights. The house otherwise has a big Elizabethan porch with a balustrade of vertically symmetrical balusters near the top, interrupted at the corners by spiral-fluted shafts, and a top cresting of a pair of S-curves. To the l. and r. four bays and an outer bay all apparently Georgian. The staircase is of the late C17. It is reached past two wooden Corinthian pilasters and has massive twisted balusters.

CHAPEL BRAMPTON

7060

An attractive ironstone village, with Althorp estate housing of 1848 (*see also* Church Brampton). E of the A50 CEDAR HYTHE, a better-than-average small housing estate, designed by *R. H. Stobbs*, 1967–71. Nicely grouped monopitch roofs.

CHARLTON

5030

INDEPENDENT CHAPEL. 1827. With arched windows and pedimental gable.

THE COTTAGE, opposite. 1912 by *Alan James*, for F. E. Smith, first Earl of Birkenhead. Three-bay centre with giant angle pilasters and a pedimented doorway. Lower symmetrical wings, the whole in a revived late C17 style. On the garden side three gables.

CHARLTON LODGE. Victorian Gothic; asymmetrical.

(CEMETERY. Altar tomb of F. E. Smith, Earl of Birkenhead, † 1930. Designed by *Lutyens*, carved by *Broadbent*. N. Taylor)

CHARWELTON

HOLY TRINITY. Far W of the village. Big Dec W tower. Chancel mostly of 1901–4. Good Dec N arcade of three bays with tall piers continued straight into the arches. Two piers have wave-chamfered projections to the four sides. Lower and rather coarse S arcade with octagonal piers and double-chamfered arches. Perp S porch, two-storeyed, the lower coarsely rib-vaulted. But the S aisle W window of three steeply stepped lancet lights seems to be of *c.* 1300. – FONT. Octagonal, with square stem. On bowl and stem closely scattered individual leaves and flowers. Is this C15 work? – PULPIT. With Jacobean parts. – COMMUNION RAIL. With slender dumb-bell balusters; late C17. – PLATE. Cup and two Patens, 1696. – MONUMENTS. Brasses to Thomas Andrewe † 1496 and wife, good 4 ft figures; to the wife of Thomas Andrewe † 1490 (he died *c.* 1530; 3 ft figure); and to Thomas Andrewes † 1541 and wife (2 ft 1 in.). – Sir Thomas Andrew † 1564 and two wives. Alabaster. Free-standing tomb-chest with shields, some in roundels, separated by pilasters with flat baluster decoration. At the foot end shield with kneeling children l. and r. Three good recumbent effigies. – Thomas Andrew and family. An outstanding relief of fine white stone. The centre is a relief with twelve figures, mostly kneeling. The attitudes are well rendered, especially sensitively in the standing smaller children on the l. side. Tapering caryatids l. and r. Inscription below and, to its l. and r., roundels with profiles. The whole monument looks rather 1570–80 than 1590, which is the date on it.★

PACKHORSE BRIDGE, W of the station. Only 3 ft wide. Two pointed arches; one cutwater.

★ Mr Bailey points out that this is one of a series of very similar mural monuments. Others are at Harrington, Nether Heyford, Welford, and Thorpe Mandeville.

MANOR HOUSE, W of the church. A fine house of five bays and two storeys; ironstone; hipped roof. The façade probably early C18. Two ranges of outbuildings in front at r. angles. (Inside much early C16 panelling (cf. Abington Manor House, Northampton), a fireplace of *c.* 1620, and a fine late C17 staircase.) Behind a stone SUMMER HOUSE with a pyramid roof.

9060

CHELVESTON

ST JOHN BAPTIST. Mostly C13. The tower stands on the N side. It has blank arcading at ground level to the N. The S arcade – the N arcade is of 1849–50 by *E. F. Law* – has four bays with octagonal piers and double-chamfered arches. The last bay of the aisle is singled out transept-wise. The same appears on the N side where it connects with the tower. The clerestory, though restored, is also C13. It consists of single small lancets.

4040

CHIPPING WARDEN

ST PETER AND ST PAUL. Mostly Dec and Perp. The chancel is early C14, with its three-light windows with richly detailed intersected tracery. The E window of four lights is Early Perp (two-centred arch, ogee details). 'Low-side' window of before 1300. It is of two lights separated by a shaft and has pointed-trefoiled lights and a quatrefoil pierced through the spandrel. In all probability it is re-set. Dec S aisle windows of strange varieties of tracery developed from reticulation. The N aisle windows are again different, but equally unusual. They culminate in a large circle with a wheel of four mouchettes. Perp W tower. The doorway has one order of fleurons and a crocketed ogee hood-mould. Battlements and pinnacles. The most interesting element however is the arcades inside. They are probably of the same date as the E window, i.e. Early Perp with still much of memories of the Dec. They are tall and wide, of four bays, separating a wide nave from wide aisles. The piers consist of four main shafts and four subsidiary shafts, all with such broad fillets that they are more than fillets. The arches are many-moulded, and the bases and capitals are overloaded with mouldings. The aisles embrace the tower. In the S aisle SEDILIA and PISCINA with shafts with fillets and a fragment of former dog-tooth. The chancel poses a further problem. On the N side are two tall blocked round arches, one of them cut into by the chancel arch. Do they represent a former chancel, of *c.* 1200, reaching further W? Behind this wall a vestry consisting of two rooms, one E of the other, but with W walls to both which may possibly not be medieval. In the W room is a Perp window (and in the S wall a PISCINA), in the E room a Dec E window. The division of the two rooms is not axial with the blank arches inside. On the S side, outside, the wall is very disturbed, and one can recognize traces of a small round-headed doorway. – FONT. Simple, probably of the 1660s. – The PULPIT with back panel and tester, open BENCHES, and BOX PEWS in raised tiers (at the W end facing E) are of the C18, but very early, it seems. – SHELF, of stone, N of the altar, embattled, on a good head corbel; C14. – (Some good Art Nouveau metalwork, e.g bronze eagle LECTERN of 1902, in the style of *Henry Wilson*, and Celtic ALTAR CROSS, brass, by *John Williams*, 1901. BB) – PL..E. Cup, 1570; Paten, 1742. – BRASS to William Smarte, Rector, † 1468 (chancel floor, a 13 in. figure).

MANOR HOUSE, E of the church. Apparently part of a C16 house including a tower. But the S side with a rain-water head dated 1668 no longer has mullioned windows but cross-windows. The house deserves study.

ROMAN VILLA at Blackgrounds, on the N bank of the Cherwell, ¼ m. E of Edgecote House. Investigations in 1849 revealed only a detached bath house measuring 36 by 18 ft. Four inhumation burials found here may also have been related to the settlement. The coin evidence gives a date in the C3–4 A.D.

ARBURY BANKS. Just S of the village, on the W side of the Wardington road, lie an extensive ditch and bank. The monument is roughly circular and measures *c.* 600 ft in diameter, with an entrance to the SE. Its date is doubtful, but it is presumably Iron Age.

CHURCH BRAMPTON

ST BOTOLPH. Not an important church. Mostly Dec, but the chancel rebuilt in 1860. Only the S porch entrance looks earlier than Dec. Four-bay arcades inside with octagonal piers and double-chamfered arches. The chancel arch has triple shafts and sunk quadrant mouldings. The W tower is Dec too. – (ROYAL ARMS. Of Edward III, carved, according to Sir Gyles Isham, indeed in the C14. – STAINED GLASS. Nave N. C14 grotesque. RM) – PLATE. Cup and Cover Paten, 1632; Breadholder, 1636; Flagon, 1760.

ALMSHOUSES. 1858 by *John Wykes*. Built by Earl Spencer. Neo-Tudor, gabled.

Much substantial gabled neo-Tudor estate housing of the Althorp estate. The houses are dated 1848. The same houses and date also at Chapel Brampton (*see also* p. 146). (They were designed by *Blore*. BB)

CLAPTON *see* CLOPTON

5070
CLAYCOTON

ST ANDREW. Disused, and threatened with demolition (1971). Dec w tower, unbuttressed; very short recessed spire with one tier of lucarnes. Fine tall Dec chancel window of two lights. The rest mostly of 1866 by *E. F. Law*. – BENCH ENDS. Broad, straight-topped. Tracery patterns and small panels below. One end has a Knight instead. – PLATE. Paten, 1656; Paten, 1682; Cup and Flagon, 1720.

MILESTONES *see* Stanford.

CLIFTONVILLE *see* NORTHAMPTON, p. 347

7080
CLIPSTON

ALL SAINTS. Except for the priest's doorway, which may be of *c.* 1200, there is nothing earlier here than the arcades. They belong to the early C13.* Three bays, circular piers, moulded capitals, circular abaci, keeled responds, double-chamfered pointed arches. The tomb recesses in the N and S walls are somewhat later. Dec the S aisle with its doorway and the (rebuilt) w tower. The w window is ogee-headed. Spire with low broaches and two tiers of lucarnes. Clerestory and roof are of 1470. The exterior of the church is heavily restored (1884–5). – SCREEN. To the S chapel from the w. A very good Elizabethan piece. Open low arches. – PLATE. Cup, *c.* 1562; Paten, 1632. – MONUMENTS. Many of the Buswell family, a family of London merchants. George † 1632. Frontal demi-figure, his hands on an upright book. Tapering pilasters l. and r. – Elizabeth † 1636. Tomb-chest (S aisle E) with a fine frieze of macabre symbols. Originally with a 'busto' above (Bridges).

---

* Mrs E. C. Fisher (*Clipston*, Kettering 1926) gives 1245 as the date but does not explain why.

– John † 1659. White marble bust, hand on heart, in an oval, wreathed niche. Open pediment. Long Latin inscription. – Sir George † 1668. Cherubs at the foot. Open segmental top, and a fine portrait bust in it. – Hester † 1706. Urn and two standing putti. Inscription with drapery and two putto heads at the top. – Eusebius † 1730. Purely architectural.

BAPTIST CHAPEL, Chapel Lane. 1803. The brick side with the three arched windows belongs to that date. The gross and townish front of 1864 is by *E. F. Law.*

SCHOOL AND HOSPITAL, W of the church. 1667–73. Designed and built by *Matthew Cole* of Clipston. The frontage is in its original state, the interior and back were completely altered in 1926. E front with short wings and a broad flat central projection. Three straight gables. Two storeys with a third in the gables. The three doorways have four-centred heads. The windows are of broad cross-type, except for the one above the central entrance, which is of four lights and has a transom. Originally the centre had the headmaster's lodging on the ground floor, the school-room on the first, and the hospital, which was for twelve men, occupied the two wings. The central staircase has fine strong balusters.

Opposite the School THE ACACIAS, Georgian, of five bays and two storeys. This is ironstone; THE CHESTNUTS in Chapel Lane is brick. It also has five bays and two storeys.

CLOPTON

ST PETER. 1863 by *Richard Armstrong.* In the late C13 style. W tower with saddleback roof. – PLATE. Silver-gilt Cup and Cover; Paten of 1548, a very early post-Reformation date; silver-gilt Paten, 1740. – (MONUMENT. Dame Judith and Mary Williams, *c.* 1750–60. Two fine portrait medallions, reminiscent of *Cheere* or *Taylor.* BB)

CLAPTON MANOR.* The present stone-built neo-Jacobean house dates from 1907. Some C18 panelling inside. In the grounds a roofless, five-bay wing of the manor house of the Dudleys, apparently of the late C17, and probably built by Sir Matthew Dudley, who succeeded in 1670 and died in 1721. There is also a rather earlier square, roofless GATE-HOUSE of two storeys, with coats of arms including that of the

* Details from Sir Gyles Isham.

Dudleys (who owned the property from the C14 until 1764).
C18 gatepiers.

8060

COGENHOE

ST PETER. The S and N doorways are a late C12 survival. The
N doorway is plain, the S doorway shafted. Scalloped capitals.
Round, slightly chamfered N arch, pointed, single-step S arch.
The chancel belongs to the early C13. Paired side lancets, and
at the E end three lancets, stepped and under one hood-mould.
Inside, the chancel has tall, deep blank arcading. The shafts
are triple, the middle one with a fillet. Simplest moulded
capitals. The arches have only a slight chamfer. The shafting
of the E window is interfered with. Two aumbries and a
pointed-trefoiled niche above them in the N wall. C13 also, but
a little later, the N chapel arch. One bay, cutting into the
arcading. Arch on moulded corbels. The chapel itself was replaced by a vestry in 1869, but its W arch with a filleted shaft
is also original. The next stage in the development of the
church remains a mystery. The arcades of three bays have
double-chamfered ironstone arches, but they stand on oölite
piers which are extremely curious. They belong to the four-
shaft-four-hollow type, with the early wide hollow (in the
Perp style all members are finer). But they are set diagonally,
with the main shafts in the diagonals and the hollows frontal.
They don't fit the arches at all. Were they perhaps set up
wrongly, when it was decided to re-use them? Hartshorne
dates them before 1281 on armorial evidence, and one ought
perhaps to remember that this Perp type of moulding occurs
in the mid C13 in the tower arch at Higham Ferrers. In any
case the responds go with them and are of ironstone. They go
with them especially in the charming motif common to them
all of heads and shields at capital level. Only the shafts have
moulded capitals proper, the hollows are terminated by the
heads and shields. Hartshorne's date is based on the heraldry
of the shields. In one S pier a half-broken-off bracket for an
image, carried on a small standing figure. The chancel arch
corresponds to the arcade. Dec a S aisle window and the S
porch. Tall Perp W tower with thin diagonal buttresses, W
doorway, tall tower arch, two-light bell-openings with transom. – PLATE. Cup and Paten, c. 1682; Flagon inscribed 1743.
– MONUMENT. Knight, cross-legged, late C13 (Sir Nicholas
de Cogenhoe † 1281 ? cf. arcade shields).
Several houses with dormers and mullioned windows.

See
p.
517

COLD ASHBY

St Denis. Simple, of w tower, nave, and chancel. No aisles, but a clerestory. Norman the inner arch of the N doorway. Perp the s doorway with traceried spandrels and the fine roof. The Dec E window is C19. – FONT. Octagonal, Perp. Panelled stem. Fleurons against the underside of the bowl. Top battlements. – PLATE. Paten, 1639; Cup, 1651. – The church has a High Victorian stone LYCHGATE, dated 1883, by *John A. Hanley* of Chester (GI).

COLD HIGHAM

St Luke. C13 W tower with a saddleback roof that could be original (cf. Maidford). The tower arch was originally narrower than it is now. The arch is too wide for the imposts. The chancel has a Dec tomb recess outside. The s chapel poses a problem. It has a very elementary 'low-side' window of lancet shape, framed as primitively as if it were Saxon, and it is blocked inside by the only important piece in the church, a Dec MONUMENT. Is this not *in situ*, or has the window been shifted? The monument consists of an oaken effigy of a slender cross-legged Knight, said to be Sir John de Pateshull † 1350. The effigy looks earlier, but the surround may well be so late. Tomb-chest with ten ogee-headed panels containing shields. Big ogee arch with ballflower decoration. – PLATE. Cup, 1570; Paten, *c.* 1682.

COLLINGTREE

St Columba. A C12 church, according to the evidence of the chancel s doorway, the low round-arched recess to its E with an arch, only slightly chamfered, and the E parts of the N and s arcades with a circular pier with square abacus and corresponding E responds. The arcades were then extended to the W in the C13 (circular piers, circular abaci) and then or yet later received their double-chamfered arches. The N aisle was pulled down in 1808. Dec chancel windows and SEDILIA with very thin shafting and ogee arches. Perp w tower and five-light E window. – FONT. Circular; against the underside of the bowl a king's head, a monster, a winged figure, and a quite unrecognizable motif. The suggested date is the C13. – STAINED GLASS. In a N lancet by *Powell*, 1871. – In the chancel N by *A. Stoddart* of Nottingham, 1916.

s of the church on the road to Milton a HOUSE with a date 1631 but largely a C20 rebuilding. Symmetrical three-bay composition of three-light mullioned windows and a central dormer. (Italian Renaissance wellhead. G1)

(COLLINGTREE GRANGE, 1875 by *E. F. Law* for Mr Pickering Phipps, the Northampton brewer, has been demolished. Its entrance lodges and gateway on the A508 survive.)

COLLYWESTON

9000

ST ANDREW. The s wall of the chancel seems to be Saxon; see the small window exposed inside. Dec chancel arch. Otherwise mostly Perp. Good w tower similar to Easton-on-the-Hill and Stamford: ashlar, clasping buttresses, big crocketed pinnacles, probably early C16. Perp N arcade of two bays. Perp also the most handsome feature of the church, the s doorway with an ogee-arched head, big fleurons in a broad moulding, and a crocketed top with finial and thin pinnacles. – PLATE. Cup, *c.* 1570; Flagon, 1671; Cover Paten, late C17; Breadholder, 1683. – MONUMENT. Elizabeth Follett † 1508. Brass, the figure 18 in. long.

W of the church lay the mansion. It belonged to Lord Cromwell, Henry VI's Treasurer (of South Wingfield and Tattershall), and then to the Lady Margaret Beaufort. All that survives is some terracing, a BARN with attached DOVECOTE dated 1578, and a very handsome C18 SUNDIAL in an alcove in a garden wall. Ashlar, with a segmental apsed top.

BRIDGE. Three pointed arches and three segmental arches of which one is dated 1620.

MANOR HOUSE, ¼ m. SW of the church, on the A43. Dated 1696. Simple, already classical. Five bays, two storeys.

In the main street a former INN, small, with two gables and two pretty canted bay-windows beneath; C17.

(ROMAN ?) SANCTUARY. In the s part of Collyweston Great Wood, 1¾ m. SE of the village, a group of buildings was excavated in 1954. Three of the buildings were circular in plan, one was octagonal, and one hexagonal. An isolated section of tessellated paving was also found. Occupation seems to have ranged from the C1 to the C4 A.D., with a peak in the C2.

Collyweston is known principally by the stone slates for roofing which are still quarried here.

Corby is a village and a New Town. It was designated a New Town in 1950. As in the cases of the other New Towns, it took a long time for anything like an urban character to develop anywhere on the site. Factories and housing came first, and at Corby in contrast to most of the other New Towns the principal factory, the Corby Steel Works, was there. The population of Corby was 15,000 in 1951. In 1960 it was *c.* 35,000. In 1963 the designated area was increased from 2696 to 4298 acres, and by 1970 the population had risen to *c.* 49,000.

St John Baptist, Old Town. s arcade of two bays built *c.* 1200. Octagonal pier, tall capitals with upright stiff-leaf. Pointed double-chamfered arches. About 1300 the w bay was added. Of *c.* 1300 the s aisle windows with cusped and uncusped intersected tracery, the s doorway, and the s porch. The porch is remarkable inside. It has later* chamfered transverse stone ribs rising right up to the roof and standing on chamfered stone posts along the w and e walls. In addition the ribs are connected, as if they were of timber, by a ridge rib and stone purlins. n arcade of *c.* 1900. Much in the church is Dec, namely the w tower (tower arch with continuous mouldings, quatrefoil frieze below the spire, spire with low broaches – the charming pairs of little heads ought to be noticed – and two tiers of lucarnes), and the chancel (bar tracery with a spherical triangle in the head, reticulated and flowing tracery, sedilia and piscina with ogee arches). In the chancel a large tomb recess without an arch, just with a big crocketed gable. – font. Circular, with six low dogtooth arches at the bottom of the bowl; c13. – stained glass. c14 fragments of canopies etc. in the chancel n and s windows and nave s aisle. – Several windows by *Morris & Co., c.* 1920, i.e. long after the deaths of Morris and Burne-Jones. – plate. Silver-gilt Cup and Cover, 1601; Flagon, 1662; Paten, 1718; c18 Chalice, presented in 1928. – monument. Perp tomb-chest with coped roof and quatrefoil and shield decoration. In the churchyard, s of the church.

The recent New Town churches partake of the current trend in avoiding traditional plans.

The Epiphany, Elizabeth Street. 1961–2 by *D. F. Martin-Smith*. Greek-cross plan. High gables over the arms, a folded

* See the former roof-line.

star roof with clerestory lighting over the centre, slender spirelet above.

ST PETER AND ST ANDREW, Beanfield Avenue. 1966–7 by *Dodson, Gillatt & Partners*. A Latin cross with pointed arms, the church hall occupying the 'nave'. Tall pitched roofs reaching nearly to the ground. Large triangular gables jazzily echoed by other triangular motifs; even the bell tower is a triangle. Was Rushton Lodge the inspiration?

ST NINIAN (Scottish Church), Beanfield Avenue. 1968 by *Gotch, Saunders & Surridge*. More restrained, and consequently more successful. Hexagonal church with split-pitched roof, linked by a vestry to a hall at 45 degrees to the church. In front a free-standing brick bell-tower.

CORBY NEW TOWN

The TOWN CENTRE is c. ½ m. W of the station. Its spine is CORPORATION STREET, running E–W. It is the shopping centre, but was not originally planned as a pedestrian reserve (a fault which is being remedied twenty years later; *see* below). In it CARDIGAN HOUSE, by the Corporation Architect, *H. Schofield*, of five storeys with the typical mid-C20 low-pitched roof and many Festival-of-Britain motifs. S of it is a small pedestrian shopping precinct. Corporation Street leads W to GEORGE STREET. On the N corner a six-storey complex of shops with maisonettes above, by *H. Schofield*, 1960. To the S a HOTEL, with a chunky tower above a podium. This faces the well grouped but disappointingly drab buildings of the CIVIC CENTRE. All are by *Enrico de Pierro*, 1960–5. The Civic Centre has a smooth curtain-walled range of offices along George Street. Behind, a taller monopitch-roofed range containing the Council Chamber projects on stilts into a large paved area. There is a fountain beneath. On the r. the CIVIC THEATRE, linked by a light bridge, and beyond the courtyard a SWIMMING POOL. W of this a park with a boating lake. E of the Civic Centre the TECHNICAL COLLEGE, 1955–8 by the County Architect's Department (*A. N. Harris*), still the best building of the town to date, especially the steel and glass block at its E end, four-storeyed and clearly of Miesian derivation.* Beyond this the LIBRARY, with a projecting windowless upper storey with zigzag relief pattern, 1959–60. At the E end of Corporation Street, branching off to the N, the

---

* The steel unfortunately no longer painted black throughout.

MARKET SQUARE, architecturally a nonentity. To the s major buildings by the Development Corporation (Consultant Architect *John Stedman*) are in progress (1972) which should transform the town centre when complete.* Around ELIZABETH STREET an unintegrated miscellany: CROWN HOUSE by the Department of the Environment (Architect: *I. J. Pennycook*), 1967–70, large. Opposite a small but elegant office block, red brick and black steel, by the Development Corporation's Architect's Department (*John Stedman* Chief Architect), 1965–6. Further N the indifferent POLICE STATION (1954–6) and COURTHOUSE (1957–8) by the County Architect's Department (*A. N. Harris*). Round the corner in STUART ROAD first the LUTHERAN CHURCH, uninspiring, then the CENTRAL HEALTH CLINIC, with a pierced screen in front of the entrance, again by the County Architect's Department (*A. N. Harris*), 1966. The screen is by *William Mitchell*.

Corby's industrial areas are to the N and E. In WELDON ROAD Stewart and Lloyd's offices (now BRITISH STEEL CORPORATION) by *J. Douglass Mathews & Partners*, 1960–2. Two powerful blocks, one of eight storeys, one of four. Heavy brutalist details; projecting floors, shuttered concrete bands on top. At EARLSTREES INDUSTRIAL ESTATE good, simple factories of the 1960s, designed by the Development Corporation's Architect's Department.

To the N the older housing, without architectural interest. In this area also:

R. C. SECONDARY SCHOOL, Occupation Road. By *Gotch, Saunders & Surridge*.

MATERNITY HOSPITAL, Cottingham Road. By *R. Llewelyn Davies & Weeks*, 1959–61. Small, of brick, adjoining the NUFFIELD DIAGNOSTIC CENTRE. The roofs are treated with unusual variety because one looks down on the hospital from the road.

S of the town centre around OAKLEY ROAD, which cuts through the area in an E–S W direction, chiefly flats of the 1950s. Some motifs are again on the playful side (cf. Corporation Street). The GRAMMAR SCHOOL, Oakley Road, is by the County Architect's Department (*A. N. Harris*), 1953–5.

Further on to the S W is the most recent part of the town, with some

* Corporation Street and Market Square will be closed to traffic. The new buildings will be arranged round a pedestrian precinct, with access for service vehicles beneath.

housing which is of interest on a national level, and is certainly some of the best recent work in the county. KINGSWOOD, by the Development Corporation (Chief Architect *John Stedman*), dates from 1965–72. Approaching from the N, along Gainsborough Road, the identity of the area is first declared by the 103 jagged roof-lines of the four-storey flats along LINCOLN WAY, which create a sense of momentum so often absent in low-rise suburban housing. Lincoln Way, entirely pedestrian, runs E–W through an intricate, densely knit complex of houses and flats. Along its route plenty of variety on a small scale: two squares, shops, community buildings, and a pub. Alleyways branch l. and r. to the lower houses on either side. The houses are of traditional construction, mostly yellow brick. Eighty per cent have gardens. The seemingly random grouping of windows is the result of a carefully worked out system to ensure maximum privacy. To the S a surprise, a generous open area with trees, and two SCHOOLS by the County Architect's Department. Further S is the later housing of Kingswood (SOWER LEYS), the units larger and less tightly packed, but the views along the pedestrian ways again full of originality. At COLYERS, W of Sower Leys, CANADA SQUARE, the main shopping centre for the area, under construction in 1971–2.

BEANFIELD LAWN, NW of Kingswood, is a small area within BEANFIELD (1957–63), planned on similar principles to Kingswood, but system-built. Flat roofs, walls partly weatherboarded. The rest of Beanfield is more traditional. S of Kingswood will be DANESHOLME (work starting 1971). Here there will be some private housing (by the *John Stedman Design Group*).

Many new schools in this area, e.g.:

KINGSWOOD GRAMMAR SCHOOL, Tower Hill Road. By the County Architect's Department (*A. N. Harris*), 1964–6. Red brick and glass. A well balanced group: two long two-storey ranges, one four-storey cube, lower buildings in front. The arrangement of the windows adds individuality. The technical block was added by *John Goff*, 1969–70.

BEANFIELD SCHOOLS, Farmstead Road. By *A. N. Harris*, 1960–2. A crisp series, nicely scaled. PRIMARY SCHOOL of one storey, brick; JUNIOR SCHOOL of two storeys, curtainwalled; SECONDARY SCHOOL, again of two storeys, much larger, with dark boarding and white fascia. This has extensions of 1969–70 by *John Goff*.

POPE JOHN XXIII R.C. SCHOOL, Tower Hill Road. A large group of buildings, mainly faced with pale green panels. The main block on slightly tapering piers. By *Reynolds E. Scott*, 1965–8.

COSGROVE

7040

ST PETER AND ST PAUL. Badly over-restored.* It seems however that the N doorway and the N aisle are original early C13 work. The arcade has five bays. The piers are quatrefoil. The arches are double-chamfered and have hood-moulds with small zigzag at r. angles to the wall surface. At first sight it appears to be nailhead. The same motif in the simple, blocked N doorway. The tower arch is even more tampered with. In its present form it looks as if it might have been C14 work. The tower itself is Perp. (Gilded copper WEATHERCOCK. It 'may well be medieval'. *North. P. & P.*, 1954) – COMMUNION RAIL. With twisted balusters; late C17. – (STAINED GLASS. Nave S. Three shields, C15–16. RM) – PLATE. Cup, 1569; Cover Paten, *c.* 1680; Almsdish, 1704. – MONUMENT. Pulter Forester † 1778. With an open book in front of the familiar obelisk. By *William Cox Sen.*

THE PRIORY. In the house a most sumptuous SCREEN of the 72 time of Henry VIII. It is supposed to have been bought in Devon. Two archways. In the spandrels leaves, also a man lying on his back. The panels to the one side normal linenfold, to the other a very uncommon variety with cusping and little grapes.

CANAL BRIDGE. In 1800 the two halves of the Grand Junction Canal met here. It had been started at Braunston and at Brentford in Middlesex. The bridge is in the Gothick taste and very charming. The arch has nice blank cusping. The cutwaters end in little half-cupolas. There are also ogee-headed niches and blank arches and quatrefoils. Reconstruction is in progress (1972).

COSGROVE HALL. Originally a half-H plan. Early C18.‡ Seven bays, two storeys. The garden side has Doric pilasters in two orders, the entrance side Corinthian ones. On this side the centre was later filled in. (The interior was much altered soon after 1800. One room has late C16 or early C17 panelling. GI)

* The result of *E. F. Law* in 1864 trying to regothicize what had been made plain Georgian in 1770–4 (BB).

‡ H. M. Colvin suggests that the house may be by *John Lumley* of Northampton (GI).

ROMAN BUILDING, in front of the Hall and 600 yds SE of the church, on the S bank of the Grand Union Canal and 1 m. NE of Watling Street. In 1958–9 a bath-house complex was discovered, including two hypocausts, one lined with box tiles, *calidarium*, *tepidarium* with window glass and painted wall-plaster fragments, and *frigidarium* with an apsidal end. One of the baths had originally been lined with lead.

6070

COTON

½ m. s of Guilsborough

COTON HALL. Dated 1662. With gables – one banded in ironstone and grey oölite – and mullioned windows. C20 addition. In a room on the first floor above a fireplace a fragment of a large metope frieze with, in the metope, a bucranium and a rosette. The frieze was no doubt originally outdoors. It is said to come from Holdenby House.

0090

COTTERSTOCK

ST ANDREW. The thrill of the church is its Dec chancel, tall, wide, airy, and with large windows with flowing tracery. That on the E, of five lights, is especially sensational. The side windows are of three lights and simpler. The chancel looks out towards the river Nene. It is higher than the rest of the church. SEDILIA and PISCINA inside with ogee arches and crocketed gables. This chancel was built in connexion with the foundation of a college at Cotterstock in 1338. The founder was John Giffard, Canon of York. Mr Dickinson thinks the foundation may have been the largest private one in England.* The next piece to be admired is the C15 S porch. Elaborate entrance, tierceron-vault with ridge ribs and fine bosses. The Dec S doorway is disappointing by contrast. After that one will pause by the W doorway, a Late Norman piece with one order of scalloped capitals and a round arch with much zigzag, also at r. angles to the wall surface. The bell-openings of the tower are C13 (two lights with a shaft), the parapet is Perp. Now for the interior. Tower arch a little later than the tower doorway. Nailhead decoration, double-chamfered pointed arch. Early C13 arcades of two bays with circular shafts,

---

* A provost and twelve chaplains.

octagonal capitals, and double-chamfered pointed arches. (The stripped stonework is the result of *G. E. Street*'s restoration of 1877. BB) The detail on the S side (angle spurs of the bases) is a little earlier. – FONT. Octagonal, Perp, with panelled stem and elaborately cusped quatrefoils etc. against the bowl. – (TILES in the chancel. C19. Perhaps by *Lord Alwyne Compton* ? BB) – (STAINED GLASS. Nave N. C14 canopies and coat of arms. RM) – MONUMENTS. Fine brass to Robert Wintringham, Canon of Lincoln, † 1420. The figure is 3 ft 1 in. long and stands in a fragile architectural frame with a concave-sided gable on thin shafts and tall pinnacles. The whole of this is balanced on a shaft as if it were a monstrance (chancel). – Defaced effigy of a Canon ?, C13 (under the tower). – John Simcoe † 1760. By *Edward Bingham* of Peterborough. Inscription between strongly tapered pilasters, almost as if they were Elizabethan. At the top obelisk with, at its foot, what Mr Gunnis calls a 'naval still-life'. – (S aisle. Lt. Kenneth Dundas † 1915. With scenic reliefs, angels, and foliage. Mr Barley suggests an attribution to *Mrs G. F. Watts* (cf. Courteenhall).)

RECTORY, W of the church. Dated 1720. Six bays, two storeys, classical, but completely unadorned.

Opposite a Regency house with pretty iron verandas, and a little to the E a MILL, badly damaged by fire recently but restored in 1972. Three- and four-storeyed, with the miller's house close at hand. Probably also early C19.

COTTERSTOCK HALL. Probably a Jacobean house, though it was altered in 1658 (date on the central gable) and later. E-shape. Straight gables l. and r., the gable behind the porch with ogee-volutes and flat strapwork. The porch has two floors and a balcony. Mullioned and transomed windows, except for four large Georgian windows on the W front. The work of 1658 must be the porch entrance. Semicircular pediment with thick foliage on the big volutes. Also of 1658 the fine stone fireplaces inside. One in particular with big volutes is much of the type of Thorpe Hall. Entrance hall with arcading l. and r. Three arches on Roman Doric columns of wood. They are presumed to have been open into the principal rooms originally. Big staircase projection at the back with windows with two transoms. The staircase itself is a C19 imitation. The subsidiary staircase is Jacobean. The alterations of 1658 were due to John Norton.

COTTESBROOKE

ALL SAINTS. A long, cruciform church – only the N transept
is pulled down – and all of c. 1300. Much restored, most
recently in 1959–60 by *Lord Mottistone* (of *Seely & Paget*). The
big windows with Geometrical tracery cannot be trusted with
certainty. They may have been foliated originally. In a trustworthy state the s doorway, the w tower with its beautiful
pairs of two–light bell-openings with Y-tracery (circular
mullions), the shafting of the windows inside, their capitals
(some left undetailed), and some of the small head-stops
outside. The two E windows must be Georgian (called 'recent'
in 1849). The nave roof is ceiled and has, in the coving, painted
imitation-plasterwork. This ceiling and painting was done in
the C18. During the recent restoration the plaster ceilings
were removed from the chancel and s transept, revealing the
C15 roof timbers. – REREDOS and COMMUNION TABLE by
Lord Mottistone, Wrenian, set half-way down the chancel (so
that a vestry is formed behind). – FONT and FONT COVER. Of
wood, C18.* – Fine three-decker PULPIT, BOX PEWS, and
STAIRCASE to the raised family pew in the s transept, all
Georgian. – PLATE. Cup and Paten, 1635; two Flagons and
Breadholder, 1665. – MONUMENTS. John Rede † 1604
(s chapel). Alabaster and marble recumbent effigy on a half-
rolled-up mat. Flat arch between two columns. Big cartouche
under the arch. On the ground ten kneeling children. – Sir
John Langham † 1671 and wife. The Langhams bought the
estate in 1637. It had previously belonged to the Saunders
family. Sir John Langham was a London Turkey merchant.
The monument is by *Thomas Cartwright Sen.* and he was paid
£290 for it in 1676 (Gunnis). Free-standing. Of white and
grey marble. Tomb-chest with good fleshy cartouches. Recumbent effigies, lively carving (s chapel). – Mrs Mary Langham † 1773 (chancel). With a classical urn. By *Moore*. – Sir
James † 1795. Long inscription; standing female figure by an
urn. – The following four by *Bacon Jun*. Lady Langham
† 1807. Standing figure of Faith. – Marianne † 1809 (made in
1810), simple, with a draped urn. – Lady Langham † 1810.
With columns and the rock of Golgotha. – Sir William † 1812
(made in 1815). Free-standing in the nave. *Coade* stone (BB).

---

* The new and unremarkable font designed by *Street* and made in 1853
is now in Uppingham parish church.

COTTESBROOKE HALL. Built for Sir John Langham in 1702–13. It has recently been convincingly suggested* that the architect was *Francis Smith* of Warwick. The house belongs to the type of the former Buckingham House, London, and Cound in Shropshire, both of almost exactly the same years as Cottesbrooke. The type is continued in the later houses designed by the Smiths of Warwick. It is characterized by the use of brick with stone dressings, articulation by giant pilasters, stressing the angles as well as the angles of the centre bays, and a top balustrade. At Cottesbrooke the width is seven bays, the height two storeys. The centre is three bays wide, the pilasters are Corinthian. The only other emphasis is on the doorways, to the garden with a plain pediment, to the entrance with an open curly pediment on Corinthian columns.‡ The detail is exquisitely carved. The entrance side is in addition given more prominence by blank quadrant walls leading to one-storeyed outbuildings with hipped roofs. They have segment-headed windows, large doorways to the forecourt (open segmental pediments on Doric pilasters), and central broken pediments reaching up into the roof on the sides facing the approach. About 1770–80 a bow-window was added on either of the short sides. This made the doubling of the giant pilasters on the garden front necessary. At the same time the one-storeyed square LODGES and SCREEN with decorative *Coade* details at the w entrance were put up,§ and the handsome BRIDGE was erected. The work of *c.* 1770–80 is by *Robert Mitchell.*

Beautiful INTERIOR, kept in perfect condition. Three-bay Entrance Hall with mid-C18 stucco work and a fireplace of *c.* 1770–80. To its l. and r. the Dining Room and Drawing Room, both redecorated when the bows were added. Charming corridor with little domes from the side entrance towards the staircase. Garden Hall redecorated by *Mitchell* and altered in the C20. Library with a good mid-C18 fireplace. Finally the Staircase, the most beautiful ensemble in the house. Rococo 97 papier-mâché decoration on walls and ceiling. Wrought-iron handrail with addossed S-curves. In one of the wings a Ball-

* By Sir Gyles Isham and Bruce Bailey in *Country Life,* 19 February 1970.

‡ The circular motif in the broken pediment can be compared to a similar feature at Chicheley Hall, Bucks, now known to be by Smith.

§ They were originally on the Leicester Road and were moved to their present place and enlarged between the two wars.

room was contrived between the wars (by *Gerald Wellesley*). Its fine fireplace of *c.* 1740 comes from Woburn Abbey.*

(In the Yew Walk s of the house four statues by *Scheemakers*, of Homer, Lycurgus, Epaminondas, and Socrates. They were formerly at Stowe, Buckinghamshire. BB)

Cottesbrooke Hall is one of the candidates for being the pattern of Jane Austen's *Mansfield Park*.

(OLD RECTORY. Built *c.* 1735–40, perhaps by *William Smith II*. Five bays, two storeys, with hipped roof. Stone, with a Gibbs doorcase. Good pine staircase with twisted balusters. Drawing room with Regency features (cf. Lamport Rectory) and marble chimneypiece, perhaps by *John Whiting*. Some C19 additions and modern C18-style windows. GI)

LANGHAM'S HOSPITAL AND SCHOOL. On the road to Brixworth. Built in 1651. One-storeyed. Three-light mullioned windows.

(CALLENDER FARM, 1 m. w. Earthworks remain from the Premonstratensian cell of Kayland founded *c.* 1155. J. Steane)

8090 COTTINGHAM

ST MARY MAGDALENE. Of ironstone. The story begins with the W wall inside. This has a Norman window and traces of a former roof-line. The two need not be contemporary. Then follows the N arcade, which will be remembered by any visitor to the county. It is of a mid-C13 date, and has the unique feature of capitals decorated by human figures placed without qualms horizontally: two ladies, in opposite directions, their wimples meeting, two knights with characteristic helmets, a bishop, etc. In addition the responds have stiff-leaf foliage, very damaged in the E respond. One respond has typically E.E. grotesques. But the existence of this respond poses a problem. The first arch is separated from the second by a piece of wall, always a sign of a former cross-wall. What can that wall have been, if the Norman W wall ran one bay further W? The only answer which suggests itself, and it is a doubtful answer, is that it was the E wall of a Norman tower. If so, the C13 aisle embraced the tower, until it was replaced by the present tower. This was begun in the late C13. It is a very fine piece indeed, with angle buttresses, tall, shafted two-light bell-openings with quatrefoiled circles, and a spire with low

* In the Oak Sitting Room Elizabethan panelling from Pytchley Hall. This had been moved to Sulby Hall when Pytchley was demolished.

broaches on which stand short pinnacles and two tiers of lucarnes in alternating directions. The s arcade is of *c.* 1300: three bays with quatrefoil piers and double-chamfered arches (but the E window has flowing tracery). The chancel, again of *c.* 1300, has a very interesting, if only copied,* E window of four cusped lights, consisting of two plus two with Y-tracery and a big quatrefoiled circle in the spandrel between the two super-arches. Big, low, shafted recess inside the N wall (keeled mouldings). – PLATE. Paten, 1626 (?); Flagon, 1770; Bread-holder, 1773.

(BURY HOUSE. C17 and later. The main front early C18, of seven bays, the two at each end slightly projecting. Three storeys (the top one blind). Simple mid-C17 staircase inside. DOE)

At MIDDLETON, w of Cottingham, in the main street a stately Georgian HOUSE of five bays and two and a half storeys with a graceful doorway; late C18.

COURTEENHALL 7050

ST PETER AND ST PAUL. The strange s doorway with a tre-foiled head under a blank round arch, though much restored, may be of before 1200. Contemporary the E pier of the three-bay N arcade (circular, with square abacus). Of the C13 the fine s arcade (single-chamfered arches, octagonal piers), then the w continuation of the N arcade (double-chamfered arches) to make it even with its opposite number. Also still C13 the arch from the chancel into the N chapel. The chancel windows early C14. SEDILIA and PISCINA have ogee heads, the piscina also a pretty piece of blank flowing tracery. The w tower is Dec with a Perp parapet. The N aisle windows late C17. – WALL PAINTING. Upper halves of female figures against the w side of the w pier of the s arcade. – PLATE. Cup and Cover Paten, 1603. – MONUMENTS. Tomb-chest with black marble lid. On it indents of brasses to Richard Ouseley † 1599 and family. Rhyming inscription. – Sir Samuel Jones † 1672 and wife. Black and white marble. Ionic columns with big open segmental pediment. Large kneeling figures nearly facing one another – that is the convention of Elizabethan and Jacobean monuments. But the figures are now much more at ease. Behind black panel with a putto head and garlands l. and

* By *Albert Hartshorne*, 1879–80 (BB).

r. The monument has been attributed to *William Stanton*. – Sir Charles Wake Jones, 1769. By *William Cox Sen*. A pretty architectural tablet. Above the inscription a skull surmounted by a baldacchino with draperies. – Iola Campbell † 1852. Porcelain baby, her mouth open, about 18 in. long, in a niche.

RECTORY. s of the church. Built *c.* 1805. Front with a canted bay-window and pointed windows.

FREE GRAMMAR SCHOOL (former), ¼ m. w. Built *c.* 1680 under the will of Sir Samuel Jones († 1672). Oblong, with a fine big eared doorway with open segmental pediment in the N wall. Hipped roof. The w side with three windows, tall, of the wooden cross type. On the E side at r. angles the school house adjoins. This is of three bays and two storeys. Inside the schoolroom forms and desks are preserved. They run along the walls, and at the foot of the desks run lower benches for smaller children. Raised seat with desk for the master.

COURTEENHALL HALL. Built in 1791–3 for Sir William Wake. The architect was *Samuel Saxon*, a pupil of Chambers. It is a house of moderate size and treated architecturally and internally with great restraint. The entrance side is almost forbidding. Seven bays, two and a half storeys. The ground-floor windows in blank segment-headed panels. The tripartite doorway (with Tuscan columns) is treated in the same way, so that it seems slightly recessed. The garden side has a three-bay pediment, and the principal windows below it on the ground floor are treated again slightly recessed with Ionic columns and segmental arches. In the Entrance Hall a screen of two tall Roman Doric columns at the back. Frieze with fine, slender garlands. The Dining Room has a frieze of vine garlands and at the back a screen of Corinthian columns. In the Library the end is a segmental apse with two curved niches set out with columns with palm-frond capitals. The ceiling is in the Adam fashion. Finally the Staircase with a very reticently designed cast-iron balustrade and a glazed oval dome. The marbled walls are part of the original decoration. On the first floor the centre of the house is a corridor reached by a door from the staircase and lit by another glazed oval dome.

STABLES. Palladian, *c.* 1750, with the characteristic raised angle bays with pyramid roofs. Arched lower windows. Three-bay pediment. The main range runs N–S. Behind it not a complete courtyard, but lower individual ranges.

The GROUNDS were laid out by *Repton* before 1794 (mentioned in his *Sketches* published in that year).

CRANFORD ST ANDREW

ST ANDREW. N arcade of *c.* 1200. Three bays. Very plain circular piers. Round single-stepped arches. Late C13 W tower. Shafted, finely moulded doorway. Two-light bell-openings with quatrefoiled circles. Lively tower arch. Battlements. The clerestory with pointed-trefoiled spherical triangles must be of *c.* 1300 or a little later. – PULPIT. With late C16 Flemish panels with biblical stories (cf. Cranford St John). – STAINED GLASS. An assortment of Netherlandish bits; also one kneeling English C15 figure (E window). – PLATE. Cup, *c.* 1570; Paten, 1813; Flagon, 1835. – MONUMENTS. Brass to John Fossebrok † 1418 and his wife, nurse to Henry VI; 20 in. figures. – Brass to John Fosbroke † 1602 and wife. – Sir William Robinson † 1679. Tablet with twisted columns. Bust at the top in an open segmental pediment. Attributed to *Hardy* by BB.

CRANFORD HALL. Early Georgian with later alterations. Of seven bays and two and a half storeys. Towards the entrance one-storeyed porch with two pairs of Tuscan columns. Towards the garden the same motif, but in attached columns. Pedimented central window. Terrace. (The interior much altered when converted into flats in 1950. Original Drawing Room. GI) STABLES to the E.

To the W a circular DOVECOTE, probably C15.

CRANFORD ST JOHN

ST JOHN. No solution has yet been offered for the earliest piece of architecture in the church, the Norman W arch of the N arcade, round with one step only, on the simplest imposts and made of ironstone. It is followed by a stretch of wall and then the late C12 arcade of two bigger arches with rich, rather wild stiff-leaf capitals and round arches with one step and one slight chamfer. A stretch of wall in an arcade usually means the position of a former cross-wall and thus a lengthening beyond this previous wall, and the VCH does indeed explain the arch as a lengthening of the existing arcade to the W. But it is in style emphatically earlier than the arcade. How can that be so? The only answer seems to be that the Early Norman arch is a re-used piece. A reason for this procedure can perhaps be given. The W tower of the church was begun in the C13 (see the ironstone lancets in the lower part), the chancel at the end

of the C13 (see the window of three lights with cusped intersected tracery and the two-bay arcade to the N chapel with its
octagonal pier). The Early Norman arch in question might
either have been the arch of a preceding Norman w tower
which fell and whose ironstone materials were re-used in the
new w tower in other places, or the chancel arch. It does in
fact not quite fit its present position. The s aisle is almost
entirely of 1842, especially the arcade capitals. The pier shapes,
the first a square with four demi-shafts, the second round, are
probably correct and of the same date as the N arcade, and the
arches may also be old. Dec the upper part of the w tower and
the triple-chamfered arch towards the nave. Two-light transomed bell-openings. Frieze of wheels of three mouchettes. –
PULPIT. With two Flemish C16 panels with religious stories
(cf. Cranford St Andrew). – SCREEN. Jacobean; base only. –
STAINED GLASS. Assembled Netherlandish bits; also three
early C19 figures. – PLATE. Cup and Paten, 1569; Paten, c.
1682.

MANOR HOUSE. C18 front of three bays, but inside fine
Jacobean staircase through two storeys. Flat openwork
balusters. Newel posts with, at the top, openwork arches.
String with carrot-like gadrooning.

HOUSE, w of the corner of the A-road and the street to Cranford
St Andrew. Inside a large pre-Reformation fireplace has
been discovered. Castellated beam, castellated side supports.

8070

CRANSLEY

ST ANDREW. Big Perp w tower, ashlar-faced. Clasping buttresses. Pairs of two-light bell-openings with transom. Quatrefoil frieze, battlements, pinnacles. Recessed spire with two
tiers of lucarnes. Most of the body of the church of c. 1300–30,
i.e. the s aisle, s doorway, windows l. and r. of it, E window of
three lights with a quatrefoiled circle, low tomb recess, the
chancel arch (triple shafts), the SEDILIA in the chancel, the
tomb recess opposite and the chancel doorway (the E window
tracery is C19*), and the arcades with their octagonal piers
carrying capitals which in the N arcade have ballflower en-
richments. Perp clerestory and roof (low pitch, tie-beams on
arched braces, wall-plate decorated with quatrefoils, and
longitudinal arched braces above the clerestory windows). –
FONT. Baluster type; C18. Spiral-strigillated stem, Corinthian

* 1870 by Slater & Carpenter (N. Taylor).

capital, the bowl marked no more than if it were the abacus. –
STAINED GLASS. C14–15 fragments (Cranes for Cransley),
S aisle W window. – E window by *Kempe*, 1900. – PLATE. Cup
and Cover Paten, 1618; Flagon (by *Fawdery*), 1707; Breadholder, 1723. – BRASS to Edward Dallyson † 1515 and wife
(S aisle E), 25 in. figures. – (Incised slab to Edward Barnewell
† 1557 (?) and wife; a skeleton.)

CRANSLEY HALL. Built in 1677,* the S and E fronts of 1708–9.
The house is five by five bays – except for the W front, where
there are four irregularly spaced bays, two-storeyed, with
quoins and a hipped roof with pedimented dormers. On the E
side quoins also to the middle bay. The doorway here has a
segmental pediment. On the S side there is a canted bay in the
middle, a Georgian addition. On the W side the segmental
pediment of the doorway rests on columns. (Dining Room
with excellent decoration of *c.* 1740–50. Overmantel with
openwork basket set in an open scrolly pediment. Thick
acanthus scrolls l. and r. of the mirror. NMR)

Small MOTTE, NW of the church.

CRICK

5070

ST MARGARET. A fine Dec church with little restoration and
little that is earlier or later.‡ Earlier the first two bays of the S
arcade and the re-used E respond. These are E.E. Circular
piers, stiff-leaf capitals, circular abaci. When the W tower was
built the S arcade was linked up with it and a N arcade built.
Octagonal piers, double-chamfered arches. The tower has
Y-tracery and a broach spire. Three tiers of lucarnes. The
lowest of the lucarnes have ballflower decoration. The lucarnes
are curiously arranged, the lowest in the cardinal directions,
the two upper in the diagonals. The tracery in the aisle and
chancel windows is interesting. It culminates in the five-light
E window and the crazy S aisle E window with very low lights
and an oversized circle at the top. The S aisle windows have
mostly a large five-petalled flower as their principal motif. Inside the chancel SEDILIA and PISCINA with ogee arches, the
N doorway with an ogee arch on two head corbels, large
beasts, monsters, and heads on corbels to the window arches.
The chancel arch also rests on head corbels. – FONT. Circular,
Norman. The foot is three kneeling figures, an Italian motif. 36

* Information kindly given by Sir Gyles Isham.
‡ The restoration was by *R. C. Hussey*, 1840.

On the bowl vertical chains of big beads, three or four in a chain, and top border of zigzag. – SCREEN. The two-light top parts are preserved above the chancel arch. – ORGAN. Of *c.* 1800. – STAINED GLASS. Flemish bits in a N window. – MONUMENT. Stone effigy of *c.* 1300, a slender lady. – (CURIOSUM. A sentrybox-like shelter for the priest at funerals. R. Hubbuck)

EX-SERVICE MEN'S CLUB, S of the churchyard. Victorian Gothic, of diapered brick, with a turret. Built in 1847 as the school.

(E of the church is a late C17 HOUSE, six bays, three storeys, with cross-windows. A. Gomme)

(VYNTNER'S MANOR. 1652, but much altered about 1925. Vaulted cellars said to be medieval. DOE)

RUGBY RADIO STATION, 2 m. N. Main building brick, by the *Ministry of Works,* 1955. In addition dozens of masts, mostly in Warwickshire.

5030   CROUGHTON

ALL SAINTS. Some minor Norman evidence in the chip-carved stones with saltire crosses etc. to the S of the tower arch inside. The N arcade is of three bays and must date from the later C12. It is continued to the E by one half of a round arch with a slight chamfer. This may represent the transept of the Norman church. The arcade itself has circular piers, flat capitals with trumpet scalloping and one with flat leaves, square abaci, and single-step arches which are pointed. The unbuttressed W tower seems to belong to the same time. Its E arch is un-moulded but pointed. The S arcade is E.E., with circular piers and circular abaci. The E respond has small, early, upright stiff-leaves. The windows are mostly renewed, but point to work of *c.* 1300 etc. This included the clerestory. Nave roof with tie-beams. Tracery above the arched braces. – FONT. Circular, C13, but re-carved in the C15 (and by a rector in the first half of the C19, BB). Friezes of dog-tooth, pointed arches, naturalistic leaves, and also tiny medallions with figures, symbols, and animals. – PULPIT. C17; simple. – SCREEN. Perp, of one-light divisions. – COMMUNION RAIL. C18. – BENCHES. Square-topped, with tracery panels, also the chalice and wafer. – PANELLING, N aisle. From a screen or bench fronts. – WALL PAINTINGS. Discovered *c.* 1921, and restored again *c.* 1960. A memorable series of the early C14 in the style more familiar from illuminated manuscripts. The pictures represent the following scenes. s wall from E, upper zone: the Rejection of Joachim's Offering, the Meeting at the Golden Gate, the Birth of the Virgin, the Presentation of the Virgin, the Virgin leaving her House, the Espousals of Mary and Joseph; then in the lower zone: the Visitation, the Nativity, the Angel and the Shepherds; then over the arch of the door: the Magi before Herod and the Adoration of the Magi; then the Massacre of the Innocents, the Flight into Egypt (two specially well preserved scenes), the Presentation of Christ; and after that the Angel giving the palm to the Virgin, the Virgin giving the palm to St John, the Arrival of the Apostles, the Death of the Virgin, the Funeral of the Virgin and the Miracle of the Jews, Christ and the Apostles at the Tomb of the Virgin, and the Assumption. On the N wall from the w, upper zone: Entry into Jerusalem, Last Supper (well preserved), Betrayal, Christ before the High Priest, the Mocking (not recognizable), the Scourging, Christ carrying the Cross, the Crucifixion; then in the lower zone: Deposition, Entombment, Harrowing of Hell, Resurrection, the Angel and the Virgin, Annunciation. Finally, of the C15, the Last Judgement above the chancel arch. – (STAINED GLASS. E window: arms of England, pre-1340; s aisle E: C14 fragments. RM) – PLATE. Cup and Cover Paten, 1570; two Patens, 1700. – MONUMENTS. John Clarke † 1603 with the inscription in a bold cartouche of three-dimensional strapwork. Steep pediment. – (Rev. William Freind † 1689. Good tablet, which must date from c. 1720. BB)

BARN, NW of the church. Good stone barn, 68 ft long, recently converted into a house.

CULWORTH

5040

ST MARY. Externally entirely new looking except for the unbuttressed w tower, in its lower parts probably late C13, in its upper Perp. What in the body of the church can be trusted points to c. 1300 or a little later. But inside, both arcades (of three bays) are of c. 1200, lengthened in the C13. The earlier part has on the N side an octagonal pier with a many-scalloped capital, on the s side with flat broad single leaves. The abaci are octagonal too. The continuation has round piers with round abaci and double-chamfered arches. In the s aisle a tomb recess with ballflower decoration. The shafts have nobbly or still naturalistic capitals, i.e. again c. 1300 or a little later.

Chancel rebuilt in 1840; other alterations and refitting c. 1880 by *E. F. Law* (BB). – FONT. Small, octagonal, dated 1662, mostly with simple fleur-de-lis panels. – PULPIT. Jacobean. – BENCHES. With tracery on ends, fronts, and backs. – PLATE. Cup, 1681. – MONUMENTS. To members of the D'Anvers family, erected 1790. By *Thomas Burnell & Sons* of London. White, brown, and grey marble. Short sarcophagus with an urn standing on it. Two standing cherubs. Big obelisk on top.

RECTORY. 1854, with additions and alterations of 1869 by *E. F. Law*. Very elaborately Gothic.

DANVERS FREE SCHOOL, N of the church. Built c. 1795. Five bays with four upper windows and a cupola.

DANVERS HOUSE, near the w end of the village. Said to have been built with materials from the large mansion of Sir John Danvers (succeeded 1673, died 1744). The window frames with the pendant pieces and the giant angle pilasters with un-moulded blocks instead of capitals might indeed be of c. 1700 or a little later.

MORAVIAN CHAPEL, E of Danvers House. 1810. Red brick, very simple three-bay front.

CASTLE. Close to the church is the ringwork of a small castle.

(The D O E lists mention some other good houses, especially THE OLD MANOR, a courtyard house, mostly C17, W front with wooden cross-windows; and WESTHILL HOUSE, C17 and C18. Inside good panelling, and a Jacobean overmantel with Doric columns. C17 BARN and GRANARY near by.)

DALLINGTON *see* NORTHAMPTON, p. 356

5060

DAVENTRY

19 HOLY CROSS. 1752–8 by *David Hiorne*. The only C18 town church in Northamptonshire, and a remarkably monumental building for a small town. Of ironstone. Broad W front with giant pilasters at the angles and the angles of the centre bay. The porch here was added in 1951. Tripartite lunette window over. The aisle fronts have doorways with Gibbs surrounds and arched windows over and end in a balustrade. The tower stands on the centre bay, four-square with its rusticated lower stage and its bell-stage articulated by widely spaced pairs of pilasters. Small octagonal clock-stage and obelisk spire. Along the s side all is giant pilasters, arched windows, and a top balustrade. On the N side no pilasters. The chancel projects and has a Venetian window. Inside Tuscan columns on high

bases and with far-projecting pieces of entablature. Round
arches and plaster groin-vaults. Only the chancel is tunnel-
vaulted. Three wooden galleries. Mr Whiffen has pointed out
that the arrangement in the nave combines those of Gibbs's
Derby Cathedral and of his St Martin-in-the-Fields. –
REREDOS. Tripartite, with coupled Roman Doric columns. –
PULPIT. With very fine marquetry and fretwork. Stairs with
twisted balusters. – READER'S DESKS. Also with fretwork. –
STAINED GLASS. E window by *Wailes* (TK), quite unsuited in
its style to its setting. – PLATE. Cup and Cover Paten, 1588;
Cup and Paten, early C17; Breadholder, 1709; two Flagons
and Dishes, 1742.

N of the W end of the predecessor of Holy Cross lay the Cluniac
PRIORY of Daventry, founded in 1090 at Preston Capes and
moved to Daventry in 1107–8. It depended on La Charité-sur-
Loire. Nothing of the buildings remains. The W range was
immediately attached to the church.

CONGREGATIONAL CHAPEL, Sheaf Street. Structurally of
1722, but certainly much altered – internally completely.

METHODIST CHURCH, New Street. 1824. Broad three-bay
front with arched upper windows and a pedimental gable.

MOOT HALL, Market Place. 1769. Ironstone, three bays, two
and a half storeys, the ground-floor windows arched. Pedimental gable right across; cupola. The adjoining house is of
1806 and contains the main entrance, with a porch. The
staircase of the Moot Hall is now at Welton Manor House.

Former GRAMMAR SCHOOL, New Street. Until recently an
R.C. church. Built in 1600. The front has been altered, but the
side with its two four-light windows in two storeys is original.
The windows still have arched lights. Attached on the l. is a
late C17 house.

NATIONAL SCHOOL (Abbey Buildings), of ironstone, immediately NW of the church and part of the market place. Gothic.
Built in 1826, with additions of 1870.

HOSPITAL, including the former WORKHOUSE. Red brick, of
c. 1838, still classical and with a central pediment. At the side
a simple brick Gothic CHAPEL, with a small apse. Interior
with an ornamental iron roof and decoration of 1956 by *Henry
Bird*.

HEALTH CENTRE. Well sited on the slope in front of the
hospital. Red brick, one storey, with projecting roof-lights
of various shapes. By the County Architect's Department
(*A. N. Harris*), 1969.

POLICE STATION AND COURTHOUSE, New Street. The former a nondescript brick block.* The latter with some late C17 allusions: an ironstone wall along the street, strongly projecting eaves, a hipped roof, and a cupola. By the County Architect's Department (*A. N. Harris*), 1958–9.

FIRE STATION AND WEIGHTS AND MEASURES OFFICE, Staverton Road. By the County Architect's Department (*A. N. Harris*), 1966.

The MARKET PLACE and the church are in a convincing and entirely urban relation to one another. In the Market Place the Gothic MEMORIAL CROSS of 1908. At the w end of the Market Place NEW STREET branches off to the l. Apart from the former Grammar School (for which *see* above) it has nice minor Georgian houses, the nicest No. 5, and No. 9 with a pretty Late Georgian doorway. The area between New Street and the High Street will constitute the first phase of the Daventry Town Development Scheme (by the *City of Birmingham Public Works Department*). Plans for the central area were approved in 1969 and work started in 1971. Although New Street is losing some of its houses, the HIGH STREET is to be preserved as a historic core in the redeveloped town centre. The High Street, the major street of Daventry, runs straight w. In it quite a number of worthwhile houses of ironstone, especially No. 17 with a Gibbs surround to its doorway; then No. 27, late C17, with a porch and low, broad windows on three storeys; No. 29, a three-storeyed higher and plainer house of seven bays, no doubt Georgian; No. 39, Early Victorian with Ionic columns framing its doorway. Opposite the INTERNATIONAL STORES, 1968 by *A. W. Walker & Partners* (which repeats the three canted bays and gables of its C17 predecessor). Again on the former side No. 59, statelier than the others. Seven bays, two storeys, with quoins and a three-bay pedimented centre with quoins. Doorway, not in the centre, with Gibbs surround. Facing the end of the High Street, i.e. at the corner of Tavern Lane and SHEAF STREET, No. 2, an early Victorian Tudor fantasy, castellated and extending in a rambling fashion along Tavern Lane. In Sheaf Street Nos 47–9, an eight-bay frontage of chequered brick with the archway which leads to the Congregational Chapel. The house was Doddridge's Academy, where

---

* It replaces the old Police Station of 1860, which was of brick with very gay dark blue diapering and an equally gay asymmetrical composition.

Priestley was a pupil. At the end of Sheaf Street, the WHEAT-SHEAF HOTEL, whitewashed, long, with irregular fenestration, but held together by the fine large Ionic lettering. Finally in BROOK STREET the SARACEN'S HEAD, dated 1769, with a good courtyard of that date, including Venetian windows and a Venetian doorway. Pretty staircase with three slender turned balusters to each tread and carved tread-ends. Sheaf Street, Tavern Lane, and Brook Street will all be affected by later stages of the redevelopment scheme, although the buildings mentioned above are to be preserved.

A word on the STREET LIGHTING remodelled in the late 1950s. It is done by standards with vertical lighting units or by brackets attached to houses, also with vertical lighting units – a most gratifying contrast to the usual disturbing or messy arrangements.

Daventry is expanding rapidly as an overspill area for Birmingham. The population, now c. 12,000 (1971), has doubled in six years, and is expected to increase to 36,000 by 1981.

The main industrial areas lie to the SE, and to the NW (e.g. Ingersoll factory by *H. Sheppard Fidler & Associates*, 1969; and the Ford Motor Company). In the northern suburbs FALCONERS HILL SCHOOLS (Primary and Junior, 1962–5), and further E in Greenhill Crescent, the Headlands, a nice group of OLD PEOPLE'S FLATLETS, 1970–1, tile-hung, with split-pitched roofs (cf. Desborough), all by the County Architect's Department (*A. N. Harris, John Goff*).

To the SE on the edge of Borough Hill is the pleasantly laid out SOUTHBROOK ESTATE, designed by *J. A. Maudsley* (City of Birmingham Architect's Department). This is the first comprehensive neighbourhood unit designed for the town expansion, and was begun in 1966. The houses are grouped in short terraces, mostly in cul-de-sacs. The focal point is SOUTHBROOK COMPREHENSIVE SCHOOL by the *Consortium of Private Architects*, of Northampton, 1969–72. The main blocks are faced with white plastic cladding panels with projecting windows. Hexagonal hall with conical roof. To the W the GRANGE ROAD ESTATE, also with cul-de-sacs, 1968–70.

BOROUGH HILL. Here lies an Iron Age hill fort of at least two periods. To begin with it was restricted to the N end of the hill, where an area of $4\frac{1}{2}$ acres is enclosed within an impressive bank and ditch with counterscarp bank. The S side is protected by a double bank and ditch. An entrance to the SE, guarded by an overlapping section of ditch and bank, may be original. Subsequently a slighter earth-bank has been added, extending along the 600 ft contour line and enclosing some 150 acres; this is best observed on the w, close to the golf course.

ROMAN VILLA. In 1823 and 1852 an extensive range of buildings, measuring 70 by 145 ft, was discovered at the N end of the hill fort. These apparently represented part of a large villa, including the *calidarium* of the baths, a hypocaust, two rooms with mosaic floors, much painted wall-plaster, and 'terra sigillata' and Castor ware, as well as a quantity of C4 A.D. coins. Excavations in 1972 revealed a number of farm buildings, and three native huts datable to the second half of the C1 A.D.

BURNT WALLS. s of Borough Hill, between the railway and the main road, is a ditch and banked enclosure. It is roughly triangular, measuring 600 ft on the long side and 300 ft at the w end, with a central entrance strengthened by a counterscarp bank. Its low-lying position and well preserved earthworks suggest a medieval date.

7030

DEANSHANGER

HOLY TRINITY. By *B. Ferrey*, 1853. Nave with bellcote, N aisle, chancel. Lancet windows and windows with plate tracery.

CARPENTER'S CHARITY HOMES, overlooking the Green. Built in 1823. Eight bays in a 2-4-2 rhythm. The ground-floor windows have hood-moulds, the upper windows are lunette-shaped.

ROMAN BUILDING, s of the village. Excavated in 1957. A tiled, timber-framed structure on stone foundations comprised an 150 by 50 ft corridor with a veranda, which, together with a group of outbuildings, lay within a walled courtyard measuring 250 by 200 ft. A C1 A.D. phase was followed by rebuilding in the C2. Occupation lasted until the C4.

9090

DEENE

ST PETER. Mostly the work of *Sir Matthew Digby Wyatt*, who in 1868–9 restored the church and rebuilt the chancel. The whole conception of a church of unified design placed entirely on its own like a model on a table is highly Victorian. Original work the w tower. It is of the C13. w doorway with stiff-leaf capitals and dog-tooth. Two-light bell-openings with shafts and quatrefoils over. Parapet. Recessed broach spire with ribbed edges, and one of the earliest recessed spires in the country. The lower lucarnes are very tall and have two tiers of windows, the lower trefoil-headed with cusps, the upper of two lights with a shaft and a trefoil over. Very small second lucarnes higher up in the diagonals. C13 arcades with tall circular piers, circular abaci, and double-chamfered arches. Dec aisle windows. M. D. Wyatt extended the nave to the E and added his extremely ornate E.E. chancel and chapels. *Maw*'s tiles on the chancel floor. The stencilling and other decoration of the chancel 1890 by *Bodley*. – REREDOS, Brudenell Chapel. 1635, i.e. of the time when the Brudenells were Catholic. Three oval medallions, corn-ears and paten, the Heart of Jesus, and vines and chalice. – STAINED GLASS. E window by *Lavers, Barraud & Westlake*, c. 1868. – S aisle window by *Anning Bell*, 1919. – PLATE. Cup, 1568; Set, 1716. – MONUMENTS. The monuments of the Brudenells fill the S chancel chapel. They are, in approximately chronological order: Sir Robert † 1531 and two wives, alabaster effigies of fine quality on a sarcophagus with coarse Renaissance balusters and still Gothic quatrefoil panels between. – Brasses of c. 1580 (Edmund † 1585), of 1586 (Sir Thomas † 1549), and of c. 1606 (John † 1606). – Plain blank arches without figures: Agnes Lady B. † 1585 with Ionic pilasters and a top with cartouches, arms in a wreath, and obelisks. On the base simple geometrical shapes connected by bands. – With Doric pilasters John † 1606 and Edmund † 1652. – Robert † 1599. Tomb-chest, used as an altar. With three shields connected by coarse arabesques. The inscription still in black letter. – Thomas † 1664. Odd, fragmentary-looking monument. Front one open arch with Ionic pilasters. Sides two half-arches. No figures.– Anne Duchess of Richmond † 1722. By *Guelfi*. Bust on an [61] inscribed base surrounded by an exquisitely designed and detailed frame with egg and dart and two young caryatids outside it in profile. Metope frieze and pediment. The frame is taken from the frontispiece of Kent's Palladio edition of 1730. (The frame was carved and signed by *John Bussom*. BB) – Countess of Cardigan † 1826. By *Sievier*. Tablet with lush, somewhat French, Grecian decoration. – Seventh Earl of Cardigan † 1868. By *Sir J. E. Boehm*. Recumbent effigies on a big sarcophagus. Bronze reliefs on this and bronze seahorses at the bottom corners.

DEENE PARK.* The Brudenells had lived for at least two
hundred and fifty years in Northamptonshire when in 1514
Sir Robert bought Deene Park. The house is still in the family.
Most of what we see now was done by the Brudenells and
first of all by the two owners after Sir Robert: Sir Thomas,
who married a Fitzwilliam of Milton, took over Deene Park
in 1520, and died in 1549, and Sir Edmund, who entertained
Queen Elizabeth I at Deene in 1566 and died in 1585. While
it is this C16 work which makes the house architecturally
important and enjoyable, it is the remains of the pre-Brudenell
house which make the layout so interesting. The house is,
however, not without problems.

It is large and built round a spacious courtyard. It is
approached from the N, and the N range is of the C17, with
cross-windows and castellated. The tall four-storeyed tower
at the NE angle belongs to the E rather than the N side. As one
passes through the archway and enters the courtyard, one
faces the Elizabethan Hall range. One should, however, look
at the E range first. Within the E wing, on the ground floor,
in what is now the Billiard Room, are the earliest visible
remains from pre-Brudenell days, the jamb of an archway of
C13 or C14 date. By the C15 a large Hall, open through two
floors to the roof, had been formed as the E side of a courtyard
house. A plan of c. 1745 in the house shows that the entrance
was from the W. It is this hall with its bay-window which we
see as the E courtyard range, remodelled probably by Sir
Thomas Brudenell in the C16. In the large canted bay-window
the top lights only have four-centred arches. There is also a
small doorway with four-centred head and hood-mould. The
gables are a C17 addition (see also the E front and the NE
tower).

The solar wing of this early Hall lay to the S. It too was
remodelled in the C16, and became a two-storey block above
a high cellar, extending to the SE. Of this the corner towers
and buttressed walls survive as part of the S front, and a number of doorways and fireplaces inside.

We can now return to the Elizabethan Hall on the S side
of the courtyard. This is the work of Sir Edmund and has on
the porch his arms and those of his first wife, who died in
1572.‡ The composition is still entirely asymmetrical, the
porch to the r. of the centre, the hall bay-window in the angle

* This entry has been revised and expanded by Bruce Bailey.
‡ A note by Sir Edmund states that he began the Hall in 1571.

between this side and the E side of the courtyard. Inside, this
links the new Hall with the older house. The bay-window has
two transoms, the other windows one. All have lights with
four-centred heads, also below the transoms. Parapet with
semicircular merlons instead of the normal battlements.*
This is so far the only faint sign of Italian influence. The porch 74
on the other hand is almost wholly Italian. The doorway has a
round arch and busy foliage in the spandrels. To the l. and r.
are pilasters with a decoration by vertically linked oblongs and
ovals which is specially characteristic of Northamptonshire at
this moment. Ionic capitals. Frieze with handsome foliage
scrolls and little naked figures holding the coat of arms. The
pilasters on the upper floor have guilloche decoration and
Corinthian capitals. The pilasters repeat singly on the sides of
the porch.

Before discussing the interior the other external fronts
should be noted. In the courtyard the W range is an Elizabethan refacing of the earlier entrance range, with some later
remodelling, including C17 gables. The S front, overlooking
the terrace and park, consists of three parts: the E third is
buttressed work of the C16, but with sash windows of c. 1725,
the centre third is of c. 1800–10 in a neo-Tudor style, a
slightly larger edition of its earlier neighbour; the remaining
third contains the Ballroom added in 1865, somewhat over-
poweringly treated with transomed windows and a large bay.
The W side of the house is totally irregular, and since the
demolition of the mid-C18 laundry block in 1968 has no
features of note.‡ The E front is the most interesting and the
most unexpected. It is also the most picturesque, as it appears
across the lake or foreshortened from the fine C18 bridge.
The front is completely asymmetrical, demonstrating almost
every period of the architectural history of the house. The
centre is the pre-Brudenell Hall. The dominating tower at the
NE corner was formed by reducing the length of the N wing
and heightening the walls, during the first half of the C17.
Of a similar date are the gables, and the curious little stair-
turret with its heraldic window piercings half-way along.§
The showpiece of the S front is in all probability not *in situ*.

* This motif had appeared at Dingley already in the 1550s.
‡ The laundry was a two-storeyed, seven-bay building with a one-bay
pediment.
§ The display of heraldry is reminiscent of Sir Thomas Tresham's work
at Rushton. In fact the Tresham arms appear here, as Thomas Brudenell,
first Earl of Cardigan, married Sir Thomas Tresham's daughter, Mary.

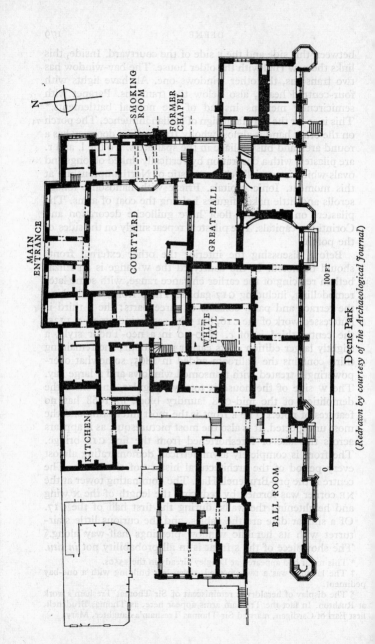

Deene Park

(Redrawn by courtesy of the Archaeological Journal)

It is a two-storeyed, eight-light-bay-window with a truncated 75 ogee-sided gable stuck against the E wall of the pre-Elizabethan house. All the lights of the bay are transomed and all are blocked (because the window stands against an internal chimney flue). The eight lights are arranged in pairs, each pair making a cross-window and being divided from the next by fat fluted Ionic columns. The mullions of the cross-windows are slenderer Ionic columns. The oddest thing is that the Ionic capitals do not carry the frieze but are part of it. Lively strapwork cartouches in all the sill panels. In the gable a three-light window and a rosette or wheel above it. All this supports an Early Elizabethan date, and there are indeed the initials of Sir Edmund and Agnes his wife, who died in 1572. Just S of this curious frontispiece, and partly overlapping the staircase turret, according to C18 illustrations, the Chapel projected. This also had a truncated ogee gable like the frontispiece, and there was a gap between the broad SE projection and the Chapel. The NE corner of the SE range was a large mid-C17 loggia, whose arcades were filled in early in the C18. A number of windows in this front were, probably in the early C19, converted back to mullion-and-transom from C18 sashes.

It now remains to consider the INTERIOR. The largest room inside is the Great Hall of the 1570s. It has a splendid roof with alternating single and double hammerbeams, pendants, and ogee wind-braces. Fine wall panelling of the dais wall, the lower tier with Doric pilasters, the upper with caryatids and volutes and small panels with inlay patterns. The fine chimneypiece with the date 1571 was moved in 1966 from the ground floor of the E wing. The fireplace frame is still in the Perp tradition of mouldings, but it is flanked by pilasters with sunk panels and roundels and lunettes in the Venetian fashion. These repeat in the overmantel. The centre here is a coat of arms within an elegantly detailed frame. The proportions and decoration of the fireplace, all totally appropriate to the Hall, make one wonder whether it is now back in its original position. The early house lay to the E and NE of this Hall. The present Billard Room takes up most of the ground-floor area of the first Hall. Within it is the C13 or C14 arch already mentioned, and also the sill and base of the bay-window. The curious internal arrangement behind the E front bay-window centrepiece was to some extent revealed when the fireplace was moved recently, and shows considerable signs of not being in its original form. Simple moulded beamed ceiling of the early C18. Above the Billiard Room the Tapestry Room, whose ceiling (for which *see* below) hides remains of an early C16 flat timber roof with heavily moulded beams. Above this is the original C15 open timber roof with collar-beams on arched braces. The division of this wing into two floors and attic probably dates from the early C17. The subdividing floor cut across the top of the 1571 chimneypiece.

The principal Staircase E of the Great Hall has a balustrade with simple, somewhat coarse geometrical openwork panels, probably *c.* 1625. The way it cuts across the planning of this part of the house suggests that it may not be *in situ*. Just beyond the staircase, in what was the loggia room of the C17, a Chapel was formed in 1971. At the top of the stairs above the first Hall the Tapestry and Tower Rooms, with splendid Jacobean plaster ceilings. They have short pendants. The pattern in the Tapestry Room is specially attractive. The pendants here are the hub of large circles divided into four quarters with framed strapwork cartouches.

The rooms in the SE wing are still basically early C16 in layout, and many have contemporary fireplaces with four-centred heads. The very thick spine wall running E–W through this wing may originally have been an outside wall. On the upper floor part of a timber-framed partition, cut into by the staircase, and King Henry's Room with fine but re-arranged early C16 panelling, including linenfold. Sir Thomas Brudenell, later Lord Brudenell and yet later the first Earl of Cardigan, who died in 1663, was so convinced that Henry VII slept here before the battle of Bosworth that he set up Henry's arms in the room.

Now from E to W along the S front. On the ground floor, a small room with a fine early C18 moulded plaster ceiling; then a suite of large rooms of *c.* 1800–10, with simple Regency decoration, including the White Hall with a fine open-well staircase with iron handrail and an octagonal glazed dome, and finally the Ballroom at the SW end with its monstrous alabaster fireplace by *Crace*. The last room that need be mentioned is the Long Gallery in the N range with a heavy fireplace of *c.* 1650–60.

(ENTRANCE LODGE on the A43. By *John Crake*, 1841 (Colvin). Tall archway with turrets and battlements.)

(SEAHORSE INN, NW of the house. Two three-bay wings on either side of a central projection. The W wing is C17 (mullioned windows), altered when the rest was built *c.* 1720. E

wing with mullion-and-transom-cross windows. In the centre
a Venetian window with pointed centre arch. Dormer
windows with alternating segment-headed and triangular
pediments. Interiors of unusually high quality. In the w wing
a panelled room with arched recess, in the E wing a room with
two arched recesses. Gotch suggested that the house was the
former dower house. BB)

DELAPRÉ ABBEY see NORTHAMPTON, p. 352

DENFORD

9070

HOLY TRINITY. Close to the river Nene. Fine C13 w tower
with lancets, tall two-light bell-openings with spherical triangles over, a blank arch l. and r. of them, and a tall spire with
two tiers of lucarnes. The spire is both broached and recessed
behind a parapet with pinnacles. C13 chancel of bands of ironstone and grey stone. The windows are renewed but represent
the late C13. Only the E window of four lights is Perp. Inside
the original SEDILIA and PISCINA, and, on the N side, blind
arcading of the same design. Above this a mysterious relieving
arch with small holes in the tympanum made for acoustic jars.
One of these survives. Late C13 also the N aisle NE and the S
aisle SE windows, equally typical in their tracery, the S porch
(entrance with nailhead decoration), the simple S and N doorways, and the arcades of four bays with quatrefoil piers and
double-chamfered arches. The details differ. Good Dec
window in the S aisle, straight-headed with reticulation units.
Perp N chapel. – (STAINED GLASS. S aisle E. C16 and C17
Flemish roundels. RM) – PLATE. Cup, c. 1570; Paten, inscribed
1682; Cover Paten, c. 1700.

DENTON

8050

ST MARGARET. Unbuttressed C13 w tower. The body of the
church rebuilt in 1827–8.* Aisleless with pointed windows.
However, the w responds of the former aisles have been
allowed to remain, and so have the C13 chancel and two C13
lancet windows, re-set in the vestry.‡ – FONT. Circular with
bold, coarse, large cross patterns. What is the date? – PLATE.
Cup, 1570; Cover, c. 1650; Paten, c. 1682.

* By *Charles Squirhill*; so Mr Hartley tells me.
‡ The present coal-store has a PISCINA and a blocked opening to the
church. It is supposed to have been an anchoress's cell. (Information kindly
given by the Rev. H. C. R. Eltoft.)

A house near the church has a Georgian Ionic porch but mullioned windows in three storeys. In a field a little more to the w a circular DOVECOTE with a C17 lantern.

(COMPTON HOUSE, Vicarage Lane. Built for the son of the fifth Marquess of Northampton by *Wade* in 1893, in elaborate brick and stone Jacobean. BB)

8080　　　　　　DESBOROUGH

ST GILES. One-bay nave and wide transept. Originally probably two bays and no transept. Of that date the C13 quatrefoil pier on the N side with a curious stiff-leaf capital, the leaves emanating from diagonally placed long, bare stalks. Then the transept was formed, the second N arch re-used over a wider distance, and the s bays were built (octagonal pier). The short, wide plan is due to the peculiar site of the church. The N doorway belongs to the quatrefoil pier or may be yet earlier. The date of the transepts can be read from the windows. They have Y-tracery cusped, three-light cusped intersected tracery, and also two lights and a trefoiled circle. The chancel SEDILIA and PISCINA again clearly late C13. Ashlar-faced Perp w tower. It looks C15, but a donation to its building is recorded for 1529. Clasping buttresses. Pairs of two-light transomed bell-openings under one big ogee arch (cf. Arthingworth). Frieze of cusped lozenges. The battlements fade into broaches, the pinnacles do the same. Spire with two tiers of lucarnes. Perp clerestory. Very pretty stone representation of a roof above the rood stair, probably Perp. – SCULPTURE. Part of a Saxon cross shaft with two addossed beasts and interlace. Also a second Saxon fragment. – PLATE. Cup, 1570; Paten, 1724. – MONUMENT. Mrs Pulton † 1779. By *Mrs Coade*, i.e. of Coade stone. With two putti on a sarcophagus.

CHURCH HOUSE, to the N of the church. Five bays, of *c.* 1700. The original wooden cross-windows have recently been replaced by sashes.

A little further NE, in Paddock Lane, a FACTORY, five storeys, ten windows wide, very shallow. The date is uncertain.

At the corner of the HIGH STREET, SERVICES CLUB, an elegant stuccoed C19 house. Porch with Doric columns in antis. Further N HAZELAND, old people's flatlets, by the County Architect, *John Goff*, 1970–1, in brown brick and wood, with split pitched roof, nicely in scale with what still remains of the town centre.

By the N end of the High Street the MARKET CROSS, a
rusticated C18 pillar with a ball finial.

DINGLEY

7080

ALL SAINTS. Close to Dingley Hall. Nicely overgrown with
creeper. The s arcade is C13 (octagonal piers, double-chamfered arches), the N Perp. The rest seems much remodelled in
the C17, though there is no published evidence. The windows
look of that date, and the arches of the N arcade and the s
chapel. – PLATE. Silver-gilt Cup and Paten, 1679; Flagon and
Almsdish, 1707; Glass Flagon, 1807; Glass Cruet, 1809. –
BRASS to Anne Boroeghe † 1577, a former nun who settled at
Dingley. Kneeling figures and interesting inscription.

DINGLEY HALL. The years between 1550 and 1560 are rare
years in English domestic architecture. The style is no longer
Henry VIII and not yet Elizabethan. What it is can be learned
in few places as interestingly as at Dingley.

There was a preceptory of the Knights Hospitallers of St
John here which was dissolved at the Reformation. It is possible that parts are incorporated or re-used. The house in the
form in which it survived up to 1961 is due to Edward Griffin
and Sir Edward Griffin, the one dating work in 1558 and 1560,
the other building in the 1680s and, according to Sir Gyles
Isham's convincing supposition, using as his architect *Hugh
May*, who was a relation of his wife. Edward Griffin was
Attorney General to Edward VI and Queen Mary and
according to the inscriptions on his building a fanatic Catholic
– a forerunner of Sir Thomas Tresham in the architectural
demonstration of his faith.

The house was a courtyard house. The w wing was pulled
down in 1780–2. The E wing was partly demolished in 1972.
It is approached from the s through a gateway still flanked
by polygonal towers, although these towers are not made into
a showpiece as was usual under Henry VII and VIII and
Queen Elizabeth. The archway has a four-centred head, the
spandrels a little foliage decoration. Round the arch run two
lines of writing. They read as follows: 'What thing so fair but
Time will pare. Anno 1560. Sorte tua contentus abi. Ne sutor
ultra crepidam. Emeri pro virtutem proesta quam per dedus
vivere. That that thou doest do it wisely and mark the end and
so forth. Invigilate viri, tacito nam tempora grassu / Diffu-
giunt, melloque sono convertitur annus / Si Deus nobiscum

quis contra nos. God save the King 1560' – that is King
Philip of Spain. So that could still be written in stone so
publicly two years after the accession of the Virgin Queen.
The window above the archway is of three lights, transomed,
and has no arched lights, although many windows in the rest
of the house have. Above the window a characteristically steep
pediment. To the l. and r. of the archway are pilasters, and
they carry corbels instead of capitals. On the corbels stand
strips, and pilasters which are set diagonally, as if they were
buttresses. All such details are eloquent of the fancifulness,
the lack of discipline, and the brimming-over inventiveness
which precede the Elizabethan Settlement. The gatehouse
and the wing to its l. which linked up with the w wing have
instead of battlements round, or rather more than semicircular
merlons.

After passing through the archway one is in the courtyard
and, turning round, sees that the archway went through the
73   last of four arches of a short arcade or cloister placed rather
inorganically. It occupies only the l. half of this façade; the r.
half is closed, and ends in a polygonal tower, again with the
rounded merlons. The arcade arches are four-centred, not
round. The windows here have mullions and arched lights,
and the cresting is not merlons but elongated half-decagons
with concave sides and shell or arms infillings. The arcade
arches are separated by elongated Ionic columns with an excessive entasis, clearly derived from the baluster and candelabra
shapes so popular in the 1530s and 1540s. On the upper floor
the columns are indeed balusters. Foliage grows up their
bulbous lowest parts.

What the E and W sides were like we cannot now say, and
the present appearance of the N side, which contains the Great
Hall, is also mute. However, the entrance to the Hall exists; it
has been re-set against the w end of the Hall and converted
into a porch.* It is a showpiece which one is not likely to forget.
The doorway has a four-centred head and scrolly carving in
the spandrels. To the l. and r. are coupled fluted Corinthian
columns. Turning round the corner single columns flank a
window (cf. Kirby Hall). On the capitals stand semicircular

* Mr Bailey points out that drawings by George Clark in Northampton
Public Library show that the porch originally was opposite the arcade. When
it was rebuilt many details were misplaced. He also suggests that the decoration is so close in style to work by the *Thorpe* family (cf. Kirby Hall) that it
seems probable that they were employed here.

projections, and they carry thin fluted shafts. The upper window is altered, but has its original steep pediment. At the foot of this a cornice runs to continue along front and side, projecting in a curve above the shafts. Above it the shafts continue. To the l. and r. of the window and the pediment heavily moulded small panels with rosettes etc. Top pinnacles of bulbous shape and a heavily moulded flourish above the entrance bay with volutes and a shell, all encrusted with decoration.

Of the C16 house in addition a tall, tower-like mass stands upright, slightly behind the N front, and more has become apparent with the partial demolition of the E range in 1972. It again has mullioned windows with arched lights, but is embattled. Sir Edward Griffin in 1685 rebuilt the E wing and much of the S wing. These parts were gutted in 1972. His (or May's) work is very simple, but dignified. Two storeys, quoins, tall windows with moulded frames (sashed, which must be a later alteration), hipped roofs. The S front has a pedimented three-bay centre and a doorway with a segmental pediment on corbels.

Nothing is now left of the original interiors, which had already been altered in the 1930s.*

The house became derelict after it was sold in 1961. The C16 parts are now being converted into two separate residences, leaving May's house as a shell.

(STABLES. By *Hakewill*. BB)

DITCHFORD
2½ m. E of Wellingborough

9060

BRIDGE. Probably C14. 14 ft wide. Massive cutwaters.

DODFORD

6060

ST MARY. The S wall is Norman. Two windows remain, one of them visible only inside, and some herringbone masonry. C13 W tower, see e.g. the bell-openings of two lancets under one arch, C13 N aisle with an arcade of four bays (octagonal piers,

---

* There was panelling of 1560 on the first floor of the S range, and a fine chimneypiece with monkeys and garlands, of c. 1730, was in a first-floor room projecting to the E of the S range. There was also a good late C17 staircase.

double-hollow-chamfered arches) and lancet windows (the one
in the w wall is unrestored). Dec s windows with transom.
Perp s porch, two-storeyed, the lower storey heavily rib-
vaulted. Chancel 1850 by *Philip Hardwick* (BB). The church
was restored by *Butterfield* in 1878–80 (P. Thompson). –
FONT. Circular, Norman, with lunettes upright and upside
down, their outlines beaded. They are linked up, and the
links are beaded too. Foliage in the lunettes. – SCREEN. Of
one-light divisions. Given in 1740 by Sir John Cressy. –
PULPIT. Jacobean. – STAINED GLASS. E window by *Clutter-
buck*, in the style of the German or Dutch C16. – PLATE. Cup
and Paten, 1570; Breadholder, 1658; Cup, 1750. – MONU-
MENTS. Brasses to John Cressy † 1414 and wife (19 in. figures);
William Wylde † 1422 and wife (18 in. figures); and Bridget
Wyrley † 1637 (19 in.). – Beautiful Purbeck-marble effigy of a
cross-legged Knight (Sir Robert de Keynes † 1305?), the
slab on which he lies still with tapering sides like a coffin lid. –
Early C14 tomb recess (N aisle) and in it oak effigy of a Lady.
Pushed in front of it stone tomb-chest with five small figures
of mourners against it. On the tomb-chest effigy of a Lady with
angels by her pillow, said to be Wentiliana de Keynes † 1376.
In the arch PAINTING of a soul taken to heaven by angels,
and the hand of God. – Sir John Cressy † 1444. Free-standing
alabaster monument with recumbent effigy. Against the tomb-
chest at the head-end two kneeling angels holding a shield,
against the sides stiffly frontal angels with shields and
between them smaller mourners in arched panels. – (Benson
family. Architectural monument erected after 1730. Probably
from the yard of the *Smiths* of Warwick. BB)

To the N at the foot of the hill VICARAGE, Georgian, five bays,
two storeys, with parapet. One-bay pediment. Below it a
Venetian window. Two-bay addition on the l. To the r.
PORCH HOUSE, with a two-storeyed Jacobean porch.

(GLOBE FARM. Plain late C17. Seven bays, two storeys, stone.
A. Gomme)

DRAUGHTON

ST CATHERINE. w tower late C12, still with a small round-
arched w window, but also with an arch towards the nave
which is pointed though unmoulded and stands on responds
with nailhead. The top looks C17. Early C13 arcades, both
with octagonal piers and double-chamfered arches, but other-

wise differing. The s side has a little nailhead enrichment. The simple s doorway and two windows of the s aisle in the same style. Chancel of *c.* 1885. – (The N transept window, formerly the E chancel window, is Georgian Gothick of *c.* 1770–80, perhaps by *Wing* of Leicester (cf. East Carlton). BB) – FONT. C18. Baluster with a serpent winding round the stem. – BENCHES. With uncommonly inventive tracery panels. (Some late C17 ones with carved arm rails.) – STAINED GLASS. (Chancel: by *C. E. Moore*, 1933. GI) s aisle E window by *Kempe*, 1895. – PLATE. Cup, 1570; Paten, *c.* 1682.

DRAYTON HOUSE   *9070*

At Drayton House one sees centuries through centuries until one *69* reaches right back to 1328, the year in which Simon de Drayton was granted licence to crenellate his house. It was a rectangle of considerable size, and the forbidding s wall at the end of the early C18 forecourt with its splendid iron GATES marks the s extent of his property. Only his gatehouse was made more inviting by a new arched portal dating from the late C17.* The wall can be seen to return on the E side, where it is continued by C15 walling with different buttresses. It can also be seen on the w side between irregular C18 projections of which one, with a pointed roof, holds the kitchen. This dates from the early C18.‡

As one entered the oblong courtyard of the house of Simon de Drayton one would have had the porch to the HALL opposite. But this Hall, of which the thick outer walls survive, although all the rest is of *c.* 1700, is not Simon's Hall. It is the Hall of the house existing on the site when he applied for his licence to crenellate. The walls of the Hall do not help in arriving at a date, but to the E of the Hall there is the so-called CRYPT, i.e. the undercroft of the original Solar, and this with its two naves separated by three short octagonal pillars, and its rib-vault with chamfered ribs, perhaps suggests the late C13 or early C14. (The two-light window at the s end is however C19. H. M. Colvin) In addition one can see in the s wall of a room on the upper floor of the N range a blocked

---

* The gateway has a surround of rustication in alternating sizes, niches l. and r., and a handsome domed interior. It displays the arms of the Earl of Peterborough.

‡ It forms part of the contract with *Talman: see* below.

upper window of the Hall. This is of one light with a cusped head and a hollow chamfer.

In 1361 Sir Simon's son conveyed Drayton to Sir Henry

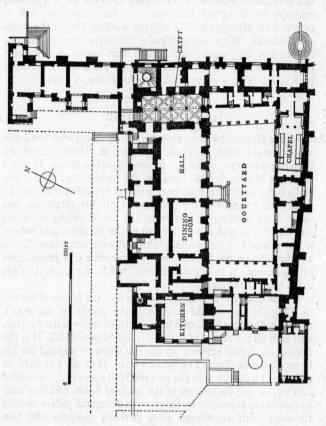

Drayton House
(Redrawn by courtesy of Messrs Batsford)

Greene (*see* Lowick, p. 297). The later Henry Greene who lived at Drayton in the mid and later C15 added much to its embattled pile. Due to him is much of the N view with crenellated turrets, especially the central one of a complicated stepped polygonal form. Below it is an early C18 doorway. To Henry Greene's extension also belong the polygonal turrets in line with the s front of the Hall range to its E and w. There are two on the E and two on the w side.

Next in order of time comes Lord Mordaunt of Turvey, who extended the E side of the house by a wing projecting to the N and by wings projecting along the w and E sides of the courtyard to the old s wall. The NE wing has a date 1584. The new work had mullioned and transomed windows of no great regularity. The chimneyshafts are very tall and pillar-shaped. Lord Mordaunt also marked the s end of his wing, i.e. the NE corner of the old house and its NW corner, by dominating towers. The western tower had to be partly rebuilt at the beginning of the C18, and both towers received their pretty cupolas then. In the Elizabethan E front is a doorway with a Gibbs surround, and along part of its side runs an outer staircase with iron railing. These are additions of c. 1705. In the Elizabethan wing the only room still in its original form is the CELLAR, curiously medieval-looking with its short octagonal piers and chamfered ribs. The LONG GALLERY on the second floor is structurally intact, but the Venetian N window is Early Georgian and altered in the early C20 (by *Gotch*), and the canted ceiling is C20 too.

The architectural history of the house continues now with some minor work. Jacobean mantelpiece in a room close to the Chapel Gallery and Jacobean staircase with vertically symmetrical balusters behind the N front to the w of the centre. Then, in 1653, *John Webb*, Inigo Jones's pupil, designed two fireplaces for Drayton. The drawings are preserved at the R.I.B.A., and one of them is in the STATE BEDROOM at the N end of the Elizabethan wing. It has characteristically heavy classical forms with an open scrolly pediment and thick garlands. Not much later than Webb is probably the POWDER CLOSET next to the Long Gallery on the second floor. The large, somewhat bald S-scrolls in the coving are particularly characteristic. Above the State Bedroom is a genuine PRIEST HOLE below a closet and accessible by lifting two loose floor boards (the fourth Lord Mordaunt was a Catholic and died in the Tower three years after having been arrested in connexion with the Gunpowder Plot).

The next phase was the last of major changes. It covers the last years of the C17 and the first of the C18. The ownership of the estate at that time went through strange vicissitudes.

The Earl of Peterborough, still of the Mordaunt family, died in 1697. His daughter, the Duchess of Norfolk, took over. She lived at Drayton with her lover Sir John Germaine, whom she married in 1701, after the Duke's death.* She herself died in 1705 and he married in 1706 Lady Betty, daughter of the second Earl of Berkeley. Lady Betty was born in 1680 and died in 1769. A contract with *William Talman* of 1702 exists according to which Talman was to build the kitchens (*see above*), and to build or remodel the W tower and the façade of the Hall towards the courtyard and also the Grand Staircase (*see* below). The Hall was internally modernized as well as re-faced. The façade is very lively and very characteristic of Talman.‡ It has broad fluted angle pilasters blocked at frequent intervals, six tall windows with alternating pediments, and a doorway with detached columns and a trophy over. Between the capitals and abaci of the doorway a figural keystone and some thin and playful swags. The windows immediately l. and r. of the doorway are also more playful than the others. Instead of pediments proper they have thin, shallow, scrolly, rather pert token pediments with foliage and small heads. Moreover, above all the windows, on the level of the trophy above the doorway, runs an attic divided by blank panels, in the same rhythm as the windows, and against each panel stands a little bust on a bracket. Finally there is a top balustrade, rising in the middle into a broken pediment carried by caryatid girls and housing a large coat of arms. The ultimate source of the forms is no doubt the Italy of Borromini, but the most similar forms are to be found in Bohemia about twenty years later. In England also the rare cases where such details have been preserved are that much later (Wentworth Wood-house, w front, Kettlethorpe Hall Wakefield).

The sides of the courtyard have colonnades of Roman Doric columns reminiscent of those by Wren at Hampton Court. At Drayton they can be dated by the Berkeley and Germaine arms as of between 1706 and the year of Sir John's death, 1719. The chapel in the s range, to the E of the archway, was completed in 1725.

The interior of the Hall is Sir John's, with its giant wooden Ionic pilasters and its coved ceiling, hiding the rafters of the preceding hall. The other principal interior of the same years

---

* Their monuments are at Lowick, *see* p. 298.

‡ Mr John Harris draws my attention to similar details in Talman's designs for a Trianon for William III – i.e. of before 1702 – and for Welbeck.

is the STONE STAIRCASE to the NE of the Hall. This has an iron balustrade and paintings by *Gerard Lanscroon* filling the walls and, without any caesura, the coving and the ceiling. People are agitating and tumbling over the whole space, a questionable scheme favoured in England at that moment – cf. Burghley House and Hampton Court. The paintings were done in 1712 and represent Heaven and Hell with only children eligible for Heaven, where Mercury, Minerva, etc., give them toys and lessons. In the scenes of Hell Hercules and Justice are recognizable. The allegory on the ceiling is un-identified. Much more satisfactory is the GEOMETRICAL STAIRCASE in the NE tower. It is of wood, but constructed on the principle of Inigo Jones's Tulip Staircase at Greenwich and Wren's Geometrical Staircase at St Paul's, that is as a flying staircase. Wren's staircase dates only from *c.* 1707, that at Drayton is of *c.* 1705.* Strong twisted balusters; the tread-ends exposed but not carved. The noblest room on the first floor is the KING'S DINING ROOM, above the C13 undercroft. This is also of the 1690s, i.e. the time of Lord Peterborough. It has big panelling and a ceiling with restrained plasterwork. The centre is a circular laurel wreath. Also of the time of Lord Peterborough the CHINESE CABINET next to the State Bedroom on the E. This has panels with garden scenes in lacquer.

No more need be added except the second Earl of Peter-borough's STABLES, flanking the S forecourt on the W, long and low and by no means large for such a house, the second Earl's two plain square SUMMER HOUSES at the far end of the formal E garden (whose remodelling by *Nesfield c.* 1850 has recently disappeared), a tiny room on the second floor off the Gallery which has the cipher of the Duchess of Norfolk, the interior of Lady Betty's CHAPEL with a reredos flanked by Corinthian columns, big stucco scrolls and garlands on the walls and a fine COMMUNION RAIL,‡ and the rooms re-decorated in 1771–4 by *William Rhodes*. These are the DINING ROOM next to the Hall in the place where the medieval buttery and pantry must have been, and the DRAWING ROOM, wh ch is the principal room of the Elizabethan N wing. The Dining Room has a fine plaster ceiling with pretty but conventional Adamish motifs, and a chimneypiece by *Edward Foxhall*. The Drawing Room

---

* Information from S. Blutman.
‡ The chapel is not in use and has been dismantled (1971).

ceiling has an unusual scheme of octagonal coffering with a circular centrepiece set in a square. The design is derived from a plate in Robert Wood's *Ruins of Palmyra*.*

Finally a last word on the IRONWORK at Drayton. It is of superb quality, dates from *c*. 1700, and may well be by *Tijou*. It begins out to the S, along the great avenue, with a series of gates and gatepiers with urns. The S boundary of the fore-court has magnificent gatepiers with garlands and eagle termin-als, and gates and rails with acanthus cresting and coronets. These are dated 1701. (They have been attributed to *William Winde*. BB) On the E side of the forecourt a large rusticated arch with another gate, and more out in the garden to the E. A gate from the garden to one of the eastward avenues is dated 1699. (In the garden LEAD URNS and statuary, possibly from the yard of *John Nost* or *John Cheere*. BB)

9000

DUDDINGTON

ST MARY. The appearance of the church has been quite spoiled by the ugly Victorian chancel. This is an over-restora-tion of 1844. In addition the tower stands in a baffling position: at the E end of the S arcade. This arcade was built at the same time that the tower was begun. Two bays, circular piers, water-leaf capitals, circular abaci, double-chamfered round arches: i.e. late C12. The ground floor of the tower has round-headed slit-windows and a simple N doorway. The arch to the aisle has a little nailhead decoration and is double-chamfered and pointed; that to the nave is similar. Higher up the tower is clearly C13. Two-light bell-openings with a shaft between the lights. Spire not high, with very low broaches and two tiers of C13 lucarnes. The S doorway into the church must again be of *c*. 1190–1200. The capitals still have waterleaf, but the finely moulded arch is pointed. But the oldest piece in the church is 22 the N arcade. It must date from *c*. 1150–75. Two bays, circular pier, scalloped capitals, big square abaci, big round arches with roll and zigzag mouldings, the zigzag being placed on the wall surface as well as at r. angles to it. The third bay on the N and S were added as a later enlargement, *c*. 1225. The arches are still round. C14 S porch and clerestory. – DOOR. The S door could well be of the time of the S arcade. – COMMUNION RAIL. Mid-C17, with vertically symmetrical balusters. –

---

* J. M. Robinson pointed this out.

STAINED GLASS. E window by *Baillie* (TK), 1852. – PLATE. Cup and Cover Paten, 1605.

BRIDGE. Probably C14, but much altered. By the bridge picturesque WATERMILL of 1664, restored, and now used as offices.

An attractive village (a by-pass is under construction in 1972). (Several noteworthy houses, e.g. the MANOR HOUSE, with a date 1633 in one gable, but mostly gothicized in the C19, and with a relief of St Hubert above a fireplace. DOVECOTE and BARN late C16. STOCKS HILL FARM has mullioned windows, some with arched heads, and a date 1601. NMR)

DUSTON *see* NORTHAMPTON, p. 358

EARLS BARTON

ALL SAINTS. The prime interest is of course Saxon, the secondary is Norman. The Late Saxon w tower is a mighty 3 piece, unbuttressed, but with three setbacks. The angles have long-and-short work and, as this appears at all four angles, it seems that the tower was originally not followed by a nave, i.e. a wider vessel, but by a chancel, i.e. a narrower vessel. The tower has its main entrance on the w. As usual the capitals and abaci of the responds are one block, entirely unmoulded. However, at Earls Barton they are decorated with blank arcading. Also the arch of the doorway is moulded, competently enough to be Norman. The jambs and arch are, however, accompanied in the accepted Saxon way by a raised flat band. The same raised flat bands become lesenes up the walls of the tower. The walls are very thoroughly decorated in that manner, and the same bands run diagonally and form triangles and even combine to form X-patterns. The whole taste may well be derived from timber customs. There are three external doorways, and there are windows in many irregular positions. The most interesting ones are on the first floor, complete to the s, incomplete to the w. They have very short turned balusters and shallow arches decorated with a cross. On the s side these windows are filled by mid-wall slabs, each pierced by a cross-shaped opening. The bell-openings, a most unusual enrichment, have five narrow arches, each again on turned balusters. There is no indication of any w attachment. The plan can therefore not have been like Barton-on-Humber with the tower in the middle of a tripartite plan. There is no known parallel to a tower nave with narrower chancel.

The Normans enlarged the church in two campaigns, in the early and the late C12. Of the former time the W quoins of the nave and responds of the chancel arch with shafts carrying one-scallop capitals; of the latter the remodelling of the tower arch with responds with many-scalloped capitals and a curious arch displaying a surfeit of billet-work. This arch was re-used and made pointed later. Of the later C12 also the S doorway. Two orders of shafts with horizontal zigzags and spiral decoration. The inner moulding is continuous zigzag. One arch moulding has beakhead, the other zigzag. In addition the chancel received some very ornate blank arcading with rich zigzag. It includes the stepped SEDILIA.

Later work matters little at Earls Barton. The arcades of three bays are of the late C13 (S, octagonal piers, double-chamfered arches) and the early C14 (N, piers with four shafts and four thinner shafts in the diagonals, arches with two sunk quadrants). The chancel E end is C13. Three stepped inSee
p.
517dividual lancets, shafted. There were originally three 'low-side' lancets. The aisles have Dec windows with reticulation. – PULPIT. C17, heavily moulded panels. – SCREEN. Tall, of two-light divisions, much restored in 1892. The painted panels are by *Henry Bird*, 1935. – PLATE. Set, 1814. – BRASS. John Muscote † 1512 and wife. The figures are 2 ft long.

The churchyard forms the point of a fairly well-marked ridge. To the N, towards the higher ground, stands a conspicuous and quite unmistakable Norman CASTLE-MOTTE. It is so close to the church that it stands partly in the churchyard; on this side it appears to have been cut back to make more room. To the N it is protected by an unusually fine ditch. As a result of its position, the motte is completely overlooked by the Saxon church-tower. From this it has been argued that the motte itself (contrary to the received opinion on these earth-works) must be older than the church; in all probability, however, the castle was founded at the Conquest or soon after, and its builder ignored the existing church – which from its position must have been in his bailey – intending to take it down at his leisure, an operation which he never carried out. The rounded shape of the motte suggests that it was disused at an early date.

EAST CARLTON

ST PETER. 1788 by the younger *Wing* (cf. King's Norton, Leics.). In the Decorated Gothic style, handled remarkably

seriously, with a real attempt to reproduce medieval tracery
patterns. W tower and E end ashlar. The tower with the
quatrefoils so beloved of the C18 gothicists. Quatrefoil frieze
below the battlements, and frieze of cusped lozenges below
the top of the other parts of the church. Flat ceiling on tie-
beams with quatrefoil tracery. Pointed arches inside with the
fluted capitals typical of the late C18. – (FONT. 1860 by *Kirk*
of Sleaford. BB) – Two-decker PULPIT, BOX PEWS, COM-
MUNION RAIL with attenuated balusters. – (Sanctuary
DADO with typical late C18 frieze. – STAINED GLASS.
In the S chapel heraldic panels, one dated 1659. – S window of 1892. BB) – PLATE. Paten, 1638; Almsdish, 1683;
Cup and Cover Paten, 1721; Flagon and glass Cruet,
1724. – MONUMENTS. Sir Geoffrey Palmer † 1673 and Lady 59
Palmer. Two upright figures of alabaster in their shrouds in
a black shrine with open arched doors. Segmental pediment.
Attributed to *Joshua Marshall* by Mr Gunnis on the strength
of the close similarity to the Noel monument of 1664 at
Chipping Campden. – Many minor tablets.

EAST CARLTON HALL. 1870 by *E. F. Law* (replacing a Late
Palladian house by *John Johnson* of Leicester, 1778). Red
brick and ironstone. Symmetrical façades. Italian detail but
French pavilion roofs. Well handled.

(ALMSHOUSES, near the church. Rebuilt in the Tudor style in
1866 by *E. F. Law*. The RECTORY of 1873 is also by *Law*.
BB)

EASTCOTE

BARTON HEAD. C17, though one window in the gable end has
arched lights and may be older. In the same wall an inscription referring to Richard Barton, son of John Barton. A date
1674 on the house, a date 1640 in the former dairy. The bays
towards the E were added in 1922.

EAST FARNDON

ST JOHN BAPTIST. Dec and Perp. Perp chiefly the upper part
of the W tower, slender, with battlements and pinnacles and
with an arch towards the nave which has capitals decorated
with fleurons. The same motif in the capitals of the two-bay S
chapel. Dec the chancel arch, the S doorway, and the S arcade
with piers of the type of Stanford and Leicestershire, i.e. a

slender chamfered projection to nave and aisle, a broader one
to each arch opening, and continuous mouldings throughout. –
PLATE. Cup, 1633; Paten, c. 1700. – MONUMENTS. Brass to
Daniel Halford, rector, † 1622. Brass plate with standing
figure in gown. – Slate slab to commemorate a whole family
tree of the Lee family, from one who died in 1693 to one who
died in 1804.

The EARTHWORK near the Hall is probably not prehistoric but
dates from the Civil War.

EASTFIELD see NORTHAMPTON, p. 341

6060

EAST HADDON

ST MARY. Of the Norman church the responds of the chancel
remain, double-nook-shafted, with little leaves and waterleaf
in the capitals. The chancel arch and the rest of the chancel
probably remodelled in the C14. But the windows are over-
restored.* PISCINA with ogee arch. The basin stands on a
half-projecting pillar. Perp W tower with a top of 1673,
and possibly all rebuilt at this time. The bell-openings have
arched lights still. Battlements and pinnacles. Perp the big N
windows and the later S aisle windows. The S arcade has octagonal piers and double-chamfered arches. – FONT. Circular,
C13. With a frieze of intersected arches and one of foliage trails
with a man holding two affronted dragons (cf. Brackley). –
STAINED GLASS. Chancel N and S by O'Connor, 1861. –
Chancel S by Kempe, 1883. – PLATE. Cup, 1570; Paten,
c. 1700; Paten, 1714. – MONUMENTS. Several nice tablets,
e.g. Clarke Adams † 1776, by William Cox.

EAST HADDON HALL, N of the church. Built in 1780–1 for
the Sawbridge family. The contract signed by the builder,
John Wagstaff Jun. of Daventry, survives. The design has
been attributed to John Johnson of Leicester. Of five bays and
two and a half storeys with a rusticated ground floor, a centre
pediment, and, beneath it, a tripartite window with a blank
segmental lunette decorated with thin garlands. The original
doorway, which survives inside the porch added c. 1910, is
similar to one that existed at Johnson's Kingsthorpe Hall.
Inside, a fine staircase with wrought-iron balusters, top-lit;
good fireplaces and plasterwork. The C19 servants' wing has

* The restorations were by Mackesey, 1872–4, and E. F. Law, 1877 (BB).

recently been removed, and the vaulted cellars ingeniously converted into a garage.* Fine C18 ENTRANCE GATES from Stoke Doyle Manor, later at The Berrystead, Oundle. At the entrance STABLES of 1663, on an E-plan, with three gables. The porch entrance has a round arch, and there is a big, vertically placed oval window above it. The GARDENS were laid out by *Gertrude Jekyll* and *Lutyens* in 1897, but only a fragment of the formal rose garden survives (with metal reliefs on the sundial of 1905) (NT).

(VILLAGE PUMP. Under a thatched roof.)

EASTON MAUDIT

8050

ST PETER AND ST PAUL. Of grey stone, not big, mainly Dec. Fine tower with graceful spire. In the tower a small quatrefoil and a small pointed trefoil opening. Perp bell-openings. The spire is connected with the tower pinnacles by flying buttresses of openwork quatrefoils. Also parapet with openwork quatrefoils in lozenges. Three tiers of lucarnes. The body of the church has all its windows renewed, but they represent the Dec style too (some straight-headed with ogee lights). The restoration was by *W. Slater*, 1859–61. Dec N doorway and doorway into the N chapel. Arcades of four bays, quatrefoil piers, arches with sunk quadrant mouldings. The chancel arch has the same mouldings. Tower arch with Dec capitals and a triple-chamfered arch. N chapel of one bay. The arch to the chancel dies into the imposts. To the N aisle instead a strainer arch of openwork quatrefoils etc. of exactly the same type as at Rushden and Finedon, i.e. with up-curved top and down-curved bottom. – FONT. Beautiful gadrooned bowl of stone on a square base; C18. – PULPIT. 1860. With panels carved with elaborate naturalistic foliage. – (COMMUNION TABLE, S aisle. Jacobean.) – DOOR. With ironwork, probably also early C14. – TILES. 1859–60, made by *Minton's* and designed by *Lord Alwyne Compton*. – (STAINED GLASS. E window by *Clayton & Bell*, 1906.) – PLATE. Silver-gilt Cup and Paten, 1630; silver-gilt Almsdish, 1661; silver-gilt Flagon, 1672; silver-gilt Almsdish, 1676. – MONUMENTS. Two big, self-confident Yelverton monuments. The mansion of the Yelvertons was demolished early in the C19. It stood

* Information for the revised entry for East Haddon Hall was kindly provided by Sir Gyles Isham.

to the N of the church. Sir Christopher † 1612 and wife. Six-poster, very plain, uncouth pillars (altered*) carrying a pair of coffered cross-arches. Strapwork and vases at the top. Recumbent effigies, the children in relief, kneeling along the base. – Sir Henry Yelverton † 1631 and wife. The effigies semi-reclining on their elbows, he above and behind her. The back wall behind him a pattern of books standing upright with their edges, not their backs, showing (cf. Dr Bodley's Monument at Merton College, Oxford, 1615, and the Catesby Monument of 1636 at Hardmead, Buckinghamshire). Above this, ribbonwork round the inscription with a skull, a shield, and other emblems. To the l. and r. the surprising motif of two nearly life-size standing statues of hooded and bearded bedesmen carrying cushions, and on these the superstructure – a mixture of a Sluter and a Floris motif. Arch and five small allegorical figures at the top. The children again kneel against the base. – (Thomas, Bishop Morton, † 1659. Shields surviving from this destroyed monument are on the N side of the chancel.)

In the former VICARAGE Thomas Percy lived as vicar at Easton Maudit from 1753 to 1782. He published the *Reliques* in 1765. The house was much altered in the C19. The s wing dates from 1852. (Good C18 staircase.)

EASTON NESTON

ST MARY. Perp w tower, Perp s side, except for the fine s aisle w window, which is of the late C13 and has bar tracery of three stepped lights and three foiled circles over, all daintily detailed with bars, circular in section. The chancel has a blocked priest's doorway in the middle of a broad, buttress-like projection. Arcades of three bays. Octagonal piers, double-chamfered arches. – FONT. Octagonal, with a band of fleurs-de-lis leaning forward and treated in a stiff-leaf manner. Is it C13? – COMMUNION RAIL. Of *c.* 1700, with twisted balusters. – PULPIT, a two-decker, with a little marquetry, BOX PEWS, and ORGAN PROSPECT, all C18. – STAINED GLASS. The E window, it is said, designed by *Sir F. Shuckburgh* and made by *F. & C. Crace.* The other windows are clearly by the same. – PLATE. Breadholder, 1671; silver-gilt Cup and Paten, 1712;

---

* Sir Christopher Yelverton († 1654) directed that his grandfather's tomb was 'to be hansomely repaired and set up' (GI).

silver-gilt Flagon, 1735. – MONUMENTS. Richard Fermor
† 1552 (chancel s). He bought the manor early in the C16.
Tomb-chest with brasses, the figures 2 ft 3 in. long. The
brasses are palimpsest of brasses of c. 1480–1525. – Sir John
Fermor † 1571 (chancel s). Small with two kneeling figures,
facing one another. – Sir George Fermor † 1628 (chancel N).
Alabaster. Two recumbent effigies. Children kneeling in relief
against the front of the tomb-chest (some renewed). Arch
behind and a splendid peacock's tail of ornamental panels
separated by sixteen pennons. Columns, obelisks, achievements. Attributed to *Jasper Hollemans* (M. Whinney). – Sir
Hatton Fermor, erected in 1662 (chancel s). A hanging
monument, but very large. Two standing figures, he in a very
mannered attitude, and a bust between them. Columns and
cornice. On it three frontally praying demi-figures. Obelisks l.
and r. The monument has been attributed to *Pierre Besnier* on
the strength of a comparison with his monument of 1656 at
Shuckburgh in Warwickshire. – Second Earl Pomfret, erected 66
in 1819 (s aisle). Grecian relief, a scene of bidding farewell.
By *Chantrey*. – Third Earl Pomfret † 1830. By *E. H. Baily*
(chancel N). Life-size seated relief figure of a man by an urn. –
Peter Denys † 1816 and Lady Denys † 1835. Also by *Baily*.
Relief with urn and two sarcophagi. Three female genii above.
At the top acroteria and an urn. – First Lord Hesketh † 1944.
Large neo-Georgian aedicule. – Second Lord Hesketh
† 1956 (N aisle). Of alabaster. No figures.

EASTON NESTON. Built for Sir William Fermor (later Lord
Lempster) c. 1685–95, and remodelled c. 1700–2 by *Nicholas
Hawksmoor*. Mr Colvin has recently shown that the original
design and the interior may owe as much to *Wren* as to
Hawksmoor.* Wren was consulted on the house in 1682. His
letter of that year may refer to the wings, of which one survives,
according to the letter by no means necessarily designed by
Wren. The wing is of nine bays, built of brick with stone
dressings, and has a hipped roof. The middle bay is ashlar-
faced and pedimented. Doorway with segmental pediment
on brackets. Tall windows in stone frames and with two
transoms. More building of the same type behind towards
the stables. But Hawksmoor was also involved already in the
1680s, as a memorandum of his survives dated 1686. Hawksmoor was born in 1661 and from the early 1680s was an office

* H. M. Colvin, 'Easton Neston Reconsidered', *Country Life*, 15 October
1970.

boy, an assistant, and then a close collaborator of Wren for about twenty years. He was Clerk of the Works at Kensington Palace and Greenwich Hospital.

The final form of the exterior appears to be Hawksmoor's own independent work. The house is entirely faced with ashlar from the Helmdon quarries. It was formerly of brick, and the design of the house as first built was probably similar to the splendid model of wood at the R.I.B.A. It differs from the present building in that it has two superimposed orders instead of the consistent giant order which endows the house with its unparalleled nobility. Morton in 1712 calls the stone 'the finest building stone I have seen in England'. One is tempted to agree. Hawksmoor's design combines grandeur with urbanity to a degree rare in England and perhaps only matched at Chatsworth. Yet Hawksmoor's is very different from Talman's style. The source of Hawksmoor's is no doubt Wren's office about 1700. But there is no executed work of Wren's that could be compared with Easton Neston. Hawksmoor's own style in addition changed towards a more Baroque ideal immediately after Easton Neston, and indeed inside Easton Neston. This change is often attributed to the influence of Vanbrugh, under whom he worked and with whom he collaborated at Castle Howard from 1699 onwards. But the particularly Vanbrughian conceits inside Easton Neston are earlier than any comparable ones in Vanbrugh's œuvre. So the credit for them must go entirely to Hawksmoor and to Wren. Bridges calls Hawksmoor the architect of Easton Neston, and Hawksmoor left 95 drawings for the house when he died. However Mr Colvin refers to a letter of 1708 which mentions that the staircase was designed by Wren and Hawksmoor, and Sir Gyles Isham has discovered a document of c. 1766 in the Duke of Northumberland's collection which states that Wren built the Hall. So the interior may have been worked out jointly by Wren and Hawksmoor.

91　　The house is nine bays wide and two storeys high above a basement. A balustrade finishes the composition at the top. The middle bay projects a little as against the rest and the third and fourth and sixth and seventh bays project again a little as against the outer pairs of bays. The windows are simply framed and have slightly projecting hoods on the ground floor. The basement has banded rustication and the windows are segment-headed. Above the basement on both fronts, w and e, rises the giant order, of Corinthian pilasters all along, except that on the entrance side (w) the middle bay projects slightly and has attached columns instead of pilasters – the only Baroque motif of the exterior. Here the balustrade is replaced by a segment-headed piece of attic too, with a coat of arms – a Late-Wren motif. In the frieze the Italian motto of the Fermors, Hora e sempre. A curved two-arm staircase with a fine iron railing rises to the arched entrance, and there is an arched window of the same size above it. The garden side (E) is identical, but has pilasters flanking the central bay as well. In the frieze is the date 1702, and there is no attic achievement. The s side is of five, the N side of seven bays. The s side is regular and has giant pilasters only to flank the whole side and the middle bay. Also there is an extra storey tucked in between the first floor and the balustrade. The N side is not meant to be seen. Here the composition is curiously restless, of two storeys in bays one, four, and seven, of one and a half plus one and a half, i.e. with two mezzanines or one mezzanine and an attic, in the other bays. Broken pediment over the middle bay, in which the large, tall arched staircase window.

The INTERIOR has been much altered, especially the Hall, which was originally tripartite with screens of columns to separate the parts. The centre went up through two storeys, an excessive height in comparison with width and breadth, and one that must have had an almost menacing character with its tall, stone-faced walls.* The hall is now horizontally sub-divided and an Entrance Hall has been created out of an adjoining room and the N quarter of the Hall. Only the s screen and s quarter of the original hall remain. Beautifully carved Corinthian columns. In the centre part large grey marble and stone chimneypiece with alternating blocking of the flanking pilasters in their lower halves. The N screen originally created a proper screens passage – that is a survival in Hawksmoor's design of the English medieval hall plan. The Staircase is a splendid, spacious composition rising with an intermediate landing straight on from the centre of the house to the centre of the N side and there reaching the main landing, from which it returns and, again with an intermediate landing, arrives at the first floor. 'Flying' steps. Noble wrought-iron balustrade, chiefly with lyre-shaped patterns. At the top landing however a cypher and leaves instead. Tunnel-vault with

* Old photographs, taken before the ceiling was inserted, show that the central part of the hall had a series of large niches, with statuary, divided by Corinthian pilasters (BB).

rich plasterwork. Monochrome wall paintings from the life of Cyrus; by *Thornhill*, between 1709 and 1711.* This is an arrangement infinitely more satisfactory than the coloured wall and ceiling paintings of Hampton Court, Burghley, Boughton, and Drayton. The other most ornate room is the former Dining Room in the SE corner. The decoration here must date from *c.* 1730–40. The house is indeed called 'not quite finished' in 1731. Baker mentions *Kent* for certain work done for the then owner, the first Earl of Pomfret, and this may well refer to the Dining Room. Ceiling with lively stucco work. The centre is a large oval panel with Venus and Adonis. On the walls stucco panels with freely double-curved frames, though strictly symmetrical. But while they are in themselves symmetrical, they differ in size according to the size of the hunting pictures framed by them, and with size position also was made to differ. One for instance is an overdoor panel, another partly over a door, but carried to the l. of the door so that a hunting-trophy had to be fitted below this overhanging l. part of the frame to restore balance. The total effect is gay but curiously restless. Noble, very classical chimneypiece of black and white marble with slender volutes up the sides of the opening and a pulvinated frieze. The corridor or gallery on the first floor is again tunnel-vaulted, and the small room between the staircase and the garden exit has a groin-vault. The delight in vaulting inside private houses is also something one connects primarily with Vanbrugh, although its appearance at Easton Neston antedates that in any of Vanbrugh's buildings. One of the smaller Drawing Rooms on the E side was redesigned as a Library in 1967 by *David Hicks*. It has heavy projecting piers, and a dark green colour scheme (based on Hawksmoor's Codrington Library at All Souls, Oxford). In the room is a late C18 chimneypiece with, above, a fine marble plaque of *c.* 1730, formerly in the Hall, showing putti playing with a donkey.

Plain C18 STABLES. To the NE of the house a TEMPLE with rain-water heads dated 1641. Three bays with two broad windows and a broad doorway with segmental pediment. Between the windows Tuscan capitals, but no pilasters. Pronounced quoins. Tall one-bay attic with pediment on wildly Jacobean, rather Dietterlin-like pilasters. The side bays have quarter-circle curves leading up to the attic. Behind this façade a room two windows deep. Except for the fanciful

* Sir Justinian Isham says in his diary in 1708 that the staircase wall 'is to be painted'.

upper pilasters, the façade is in the Inigo Jones style, and ought to be compared with the summer house at Ecton, and also with Lamport.* Probably of the same time the GATE-PIERS w of the w façade. They are of a strange Baroque composition. Alternating bands of rocky rustication. Niches towards the house. Fragments of segmental pediments at the top. In the gardens much statuary from Stowe. The canal, pool, and avenue E of the house belong to the original layout, but the formal gardens were made in the early C20.

The NW and SW LODGES on the road to Towcester are by *John Raffield, c.* 1822. Also of about the same date the more extensive GATE SCREEN which is now the entrance to the Towcester Racecourse. This is signed by *William Croggan,* 1822, and made of *Coade* stone (BB). Archway with Corinthian columns. Lower screen of five bays. Urns on it. One-storeyed, one-bay lodges.

EASTON-ON-THE-HILL

A perfect hill village of the oölite band (many houses restored recently). The church lies at the N end in trees.

ALL SAINTS. Norman one nave window on the s side, exposed inside. In the late C12 a s aisle was built. The arcade is of three bays. Circular piers, octagonal abaci, double-chamfered round arches. The s doorway is also round-arched, but has many deep mouldings. In the early C13 a vestry was added on the s side of the chancel. It had a tall shafted E window and an arch to the s which is less easily explained. The trefoiled PISCINA is probably not *in situ*. The s chapel is also early C13, see e.g. the nailhead decoration of the arch. Below the s window is a slab with an inscription in French commemorating Richard de Lindon, who died *c.* 1255, and his wife. Good straight-headed Dec window in the chancel N wall. It has reticulated tracery. In the same wall an inscription recording Henry Sampson and his wife as founders of a chantry, and Robert Senkel, rector, who in 1411 registers this foundation. Dec N chapel. Fine Perp w tower, ashlar-faced, with clasping buttresses, a quatrefoil frieze below the battlements, and tall crocketed pinnacles. It is modelled on St John Stamford. The N aisle dates from 1856. – FONT. Octagonal, Perp, with shields and tracery. – SCREENS. Two stone screens, different in design, to the N and s chapels. – BENCH ENDS. Simple, straight-headed. One is

* But could it be a later pastiche made up of pieces from the old house?

dated 1631. Many BOX PEWS. The two-decker PULPIT goes with these. – SCULPTURE. A finely detailed piece of a Perp stone frieze, perhaps from a reredos or a monument (s aisle). – (STAINED GLASS. Chancel N. Head of Christ and foliage fragments; C14. RM) – PLATE. Cup, 1662; Almsdish, 1772; Cover Paten, 1776; Cup, 1777. – (MONUMENT. Incised slab to a Lady, upper part lost; c. 1340.)

PRIEST'S HOUSE, W of the church, some distance away. Until recently used as a stable, but now converted for a meeting room and museum. Probably late C15. Two storeys, windows with arched lights. A projection contains a newel stair which leads to the upper room. This has a fireplace and an open timber roof (restored). The ceiling of the ground-floor room has moulded beams.

OLD RECTORY, N of the Priest's House. Georgian (five bays, two storeys), but the basement still with mullioned windows. Many good houses in the village. (At the corner of Church Street an elegant house of c. 1820–30. Five bays, three storeys. In the centre bay a pretty Gothic window below a curved gable. Gothic pinnacles and frieze. Nearer the main road, SCHOOL and SCHOOLHOUSE, 1867 with Gothic turret. BB)

8060

ECTON

ST MARY MAGDALENE. Of ironstone, large, and away from the street. Built in the C13 to early C14. The W tower is prominent and out of the ordinary. Cusped almond-shaped window above the W doorway. Dec bell-openings, then a truncated pyramid roof and on it, ashlar-faced, another storey with bell-openings. They are Perp, pairs of two lights each, with a transom. Quatrefoil frieze, battlements, pinnacles. The low arcades of the aisles are C13, of four bays, i.e. three plus a fourth different one. The first three bays on the N change from octagonal to round piers; on the S they are octagonal, and very rough. The fourth bay represents the former transepts and has continuous chamfers. Late C13 jambs of the chancel E window and N recess in the chancel. Late C13 to early C14 the S porch and the doorway. – FONT. Circular, defaced; the raw tracery may indicate the C14. – PULPIT and BOX PEWS. Shortly before 1825 (Cole). – COMMUNION RAIL. Later C17. – STAINED GLASS. Chancel N by *Morris & Co.*, but as late as 1924. – FAMILY TREES of the Palmer and Whalley families, built up of slabs of marble and fitted into the spaces of pointed arches. – PLATE. Cover Paten, 1569; Cup, 1591; Almsdish, 1673; Flagon, two Cups, and Paten, 1728. – MONUMENTS. Samuel Freeman † 1707, Dean of Peterborough (chancel w wall). Elaborate cartouche, urn at the top, two cherubs' heads above, two below. – John Palmer. Erected in 1732. By *Rysbrack*. With an excellent terracotta bust at the top and very fine architectural detail. – John Palmer † 1761, with another terracotta bust by *Rysbrack*. Signed also by *H. Cox*, who probably carved the surround. The same general scheme, but with a Rococo cartouche below. Books l. and r. of the bust. It stands against a banded obelisk. – Catherine Whalley † 1817. By *Rossi*. Oddly Victorian in its Quattrocento inspiration. Two kneeling angels holding a circular medallion. – In the s chapel: Ann Isted † 1763. Coloured marble. An urn above a tablet flanked by two standing putti.

ECTON HALL. The foremost example of the Early Gothic Revival in the county.* The front is dated 1756. The scheme with the canted bays in the gabled wings and a porch in the middle is traditional Tudor and not specially Gothic. The gables in fact are self-consciously in what Horace Walpole once called 'King James' Gothic'. The porch on the other hand is pure Gothick, small, with an ogee head and with prettily shafted niches inside with little rib-vaults. The front also displays the large blank quatrefoils which were so popular at the beginning of the Gothic Revival. It is, needless to say, castellated. The windows on the other hand are sashed and simply Georgian. Inside fine Entrance Hall with restrained plaster decoration including overdoors with the medallions of Homer, Julius Caesar, and Cicero. Ambrose Isted, who built the house, was a poet and translator. The fireplace has diagonally placed volutes and big eagles on the pediment. In another room a good mid C18 fireplace. Most of the additions made in the Tudor style in the 1880s and 1890s were removed *c.* 1966. The house is uninhabited and becoming derelict.

In the grounds to the NE a SUMMER HOUSE worth a careful look. It has recently been well restored. Its style places it in the second third of the C17, and quite probably the 1630s. It is purely classical and built on an oval plan, which is remarkable for its date. Tuscan pilasters and Ionic pilasters over. On the ground floor opened in three bays by means of Tuscan columns. The third bays have upright oval windows.

* The front is very much in the style of, and very likely by, *Sanderson Miller* (H. M. Colvin).

Access to the room on the upper floor by an outer staircase. The upper windows have ears. They are partly framed by close laurel garlands, partly given some oak foliage above the lintel.

RECTORY (ECTON HOUSE), N of the church, now a retreat and conference centre. 1693. Built by Thomas Palmer. Seven bays, two storeys, hipped roof. Lower two-bay attachments. Along the front a trellis veranda. Additions by *Talbot Brown, Panter & Partners*, 1966–8. (In the entrance hall *Rysbrack*'s terracotta study for the bust for the monument to John Palmer of 1732.)

Many good ironstone houses in the HIGH STREET. On the E side, set back, the former SCHOOL, built by John Palmer. The inscription has the foundation date 1752 in black letter. Further S on the W side the MANOR HOUSE. 1694. Still with mullioned and transomed windows, but they are now completely symmetrically arranged. Three-bay front, two storeys. Steep pediment above the doorway.

EDGCOTE

ST JAMES. The church, surrounded uncommonly closely by trees, and the house form one picture. The oldest features are the simple S doorway and the S arcade of three bays. They are early C13. The arcade has circular piers with circular abaci and pointed double-chamfered arches. One capital is decorated by rather timid crockets and small heads. Dec the N side, Perp the W tower, though its W doorway with crocketed ogee hoodmould and pinnacled buttresses is a Dec design. Perp W window, transomed bell-openings, and battlements. Perp also the big S windows of the chancel and the NE vestry, originally two-storeyed. – PULPIT and BOX PEWS, C18. – (FAMILY PEW on the N side of the chancel, a separate room.) – PLATE. Set, 1768. – MONUMENTS. A remarkable series of monuments to the Chauncey family, including four by *Rysbrack*, though three of them are architectural tablets for which the family might just as well have gone to a less distinguished man. The series of the Chauncey monuments starts with Toby † 1579 and two wives and William † 1585 and wife. Both are free-standing, of alabaster, with effigies on tombchests. The decoration of the chest fronts with flat balusters and especially a species of spiral-gadrooned balusters shows that they are by the same hand. The N side of Toby's has nine children in relief. – The architectural tablets begin with another Toby, † 1662. Those by *Rysbrack* are William † 1644 (E end S wall), the children of yet another Toby (W end S wall), and Richard † 1734 (W of the S door). In 1760 Rysbrack made the much more ambitious monument to another Richard. This has an excellent bust, though it is perhaps not perfectly connected with the architectural background. – (Toby Chauncey † 1724. Architectural tablet in variegated marbles attributable to the *Smiths* of Warwick (cf. Lamport, Fawsley). BB) – Julia Cartwright † 1856. Gothic triptych with two allegorical figures. Unsigned.

EDGCOTE HOUSE. Built in 1747–52 for Richard Chauncey by *William Jones*. The stables however, which lie to the l. of the entrance side and are, in a very Age-of-Reason manner, balanced by the church, were built in 1747 and designed by *William Smith* of Warwick, who died in that year. It is likely that he designed the house as well. Jones received £250 as a fee and the house cost just over £20,000. The names of the craftsmen are all known: *Abraham Swan* for the woodwork, *Richard Newman* and others for the stone fireplaces, *J. Whitehead* for the plasterwork, and *Cobb* for furniture. The house is nine bays in width and two storeys plus a basement in height, of ironstone, with the dressings in a very fine-grained grey stone. Hipped roof. Three-bay pediment with a shield in a cartouche. Open staircase in two flights. On the principal floor the three-bay side parts have a pediment over the middle window. The doorway pediment is stressed by corbels. The arrangement on the garden side, which overlooks a lake, is essentially the same. The main rooms inside are the Entrance Hall, the Saloon in axis with it, and the Staircase. The staircase has a wooden balustrade of turned balusters bulbous at the foot, and a carved string instead of carved tread-ends – a conservative feature. Very tall lantern high up with a ceiling divided by frames into panels. The Saloon has the most sumptuous ceiling, in Rococo forms. The fireplaces, whether of wood or stone, are throughout of very high quality.

VICARAGE, S of the church. Simple Georgian, of five bays and two storeys.

EVENLEY 5030

ST GEORGE. 1864–5 by *H. Woodyer* and of some merit, not so much because of the rich decorative carving inside as because of some original architectural motifs, such as the detached

inner arcading in front of the low aisle windows. W tower with
shingled broach spire. – STAINED GLASS. E window by *Hardman*, probably of *c.* 1865. – PLATE. Cup, 1578; Paten, 1724. –
MONUMENTS. The statue of Sir Creswell Levinz † 1700,
attributed by Mr Gunnis to *Nost*, is not in its original setting.
There was an arched architectural background, and to the l.
and r. of his feet cherubs on the arms of an open scrolly pediment. – Pearne Family, big sarcophagus with very large urn,
in the churchyard. Erected before 1757. – H. Gwynne Browne
† 1803. By *R. Blore Jun.* Mourning woman by an urn.

EVENLEY HALL. Though much altered after a fire in 1897, the
house is still recognizable as a Georgian building of five bays
with a three-bay pediment and quoins. On the upper storey
four attached unfluted Ionic columns. The windows on the
main floor alternatingly with triangular and segmental pediments. Back with two bow-windows and a bare Venetian
window, somewhat Vanbrughian. Stable of half-H plan with
a cupola.

OLD MANOR HOUSE. C17. Symmetrical, of three bays with
four-light mullioned windows. Central porch with gable.
The GREEN has nice rows of two-storeyed cottages.

EVERDON

ST MARY. Mostly early C14, namely the W tower, the N doorway, the N aisle E window, the S aisle windows, of which that
at the E end has unusual tracery, and the sumptuous S doorway.
Three orders of shafts with nobbly leaf capitals, three orders
of voussoirs with foliage trail, ballflower, and fleurons,
crocketed ogee hood-mould with finial. The arcade probably
also Dec. The arches have one sunk quadrant moulding, and
that moulding is reproduced on the moulding of the piers.
They are thus circular with very wide fillets. The nave is wide,
and the arcade is tall. The chancel arch is the same, only with
a wave rather than a quadrant moulding, again taken up by the
responds. In the chancel simple SEDILIA with ogee arches and
crocketed gables, and opposite a low tomb recess also ogee-
headed. The chancel windows date from *c.* 1860. – FONT.
Octagonal, C13, of Purbeck marble, of a familiar, often supplied
type with two flat blank pointed arches to each side. –
SCREEN. Wide one-light divisions corresponding to two
panels of the base. Ogee arches and fine tracery above them.
A good piece, as Northamptonshire screens go. – (CHOIR

STALLS by *Bodley & Garner*, 1891–2. BB) – (STAINED GLASS. Fragments in several windows, including a Pelican in her Piety (nave N). RM) – PLATE. Cup and Paten, 1691. – MONUMENT. Thomas Spencer, 1606. Tablet with columns and without figures.

OLD HOUSE, Little Everdon. 1690. Mullioned windows and one blocked vertical oval window by the doorway. Inside, staircase with a balustrade of twisted balusters reproduced flat, that is by boards with undulating outlines.

EYDON

5050

ST NICHOLAS. Much of the church is the work of the restorer, *R. C. Hussey*, 1864–5. The S aisle and S porch were added at this time. The history starts with the N arcade. Its first two bays are original work of the early C13. Circular pier, square abacus, double-chamfered arches. The rest of the N arcade is C19. The W tower is early C14, see the doorway with two continuous sunk-quadrant mouldings and the arch towards the nave with three chamfers. Details of the chancel and the N aisle are also Dec. – FONT. Norman. The base is like an octagonal scalloped capital reversed (cf. Buckinghamshire fonts). Big leaf in the scallops. The bowl is circular and fluted with a band of foliage at the top. Foot and bowl are joined by a rope-moulding. – MONUMENTS. (Effigy of a Lady, *c.* 1340; in the vestry.) – Rev. Francis Annesley † 1811, by *Bacon Jun.* Very simple tablet above the S door.

EYDON HALL. Built for the Rev. Francis Annesley, 1789–91. Designed by *James Lewis* and illustrated in his 'Original Designs', published in 1797. A house of moderate size and great, if reticent, elegance. Only five bays, and only a basement and two storeys, but refined in proportions and details. Ironstone ashlar. The garden side has a four-column portico of attenuated Ionic columns and a pediment. The entrance side has no portico, but also a three-bay pediment. Above the doorway a frieze of thin garlands. The first and fifth ground-floor windows are set in blank arches. Parapet partly balustraded. The interiors are again delicately decorated. No display is made anywhere, not even in the ample staircase hall with its simple cast-iron stair balustrade and its oval glazed dome. ORANGERY of four bays, the upper parts by *Sir Herbert Baker*. STABLES. A successful design of *c.* 1925.

Outside the gates the STOCKS, well-preserved, and a C17 HOUSE with a two-storeyed, gabled porch.

FAR COTTON see NORTHAMPTON, p. 351

5030

FARTHINGHOE

ST MICHAEL. Norman the lower part of the tower, see the W doorway and the arch towards the nave, which is round, unmoulded, quite wide, and stands on the simplest imposts. Of the early C13 the S doorway and the fine S arcade. This is three bays long and has circular piers and circular abaci. One capital and the bits of decoration by the E respond are stiff-leaf. Double-chamfered pointed arches. The N arcade is different but roughly contemporary. One capital has stiff-leaf too, but the capital is flatter. Dec the N aisle, the S porch with its pretty pairs of small two-light windows, and the chancel (E window with reticulated tracery). The S aisle is Perp including a tomb recess. The higher S chapel is Late Perp. Perp also the head-corbels in the clerestory. The top part of the tower has an inscription referring to 1654 and a coat of arms framed by columns. – PLATE. Cup and Paten, 1570. – MONUMENTS. Tablets of 1684, 1694, and others. – A pretty tablet, now dissembled, to the Misses Henrietta and Catherine Rush † 1801. With a young woman by an urn. – George Rush † 1806. By *Charles Regnart* of Cleveland Street, Fitzroy Square, and according to Mr Gunnis his masterpiece. The conception is still one of the C18. Comfortably reclining figure on a sarcophagus, completely free-standing. The old gentleman wears night-cap and slippers and an ample kind of toga. He has been reading and is now looking up.

ABBEY LODGE, W of the church. Though the date-stone 1581 is Victorian, the house may well be of that date. What survives is the archway formerly leading into the front garden, the doorway and the back doorway and a doorway to the r. into the Hall, all three with four-centred heads, and the fireplace in the Hall, placed, against all local custom, against the screens passage. The surround has lozenge-shaped medallions.

(FARTHINGHOE LODGE, 1 m. SW. With Gothick windows. Two bows to the E. The middle windows to the E may have the only original Gothick detail. NMR)

FARTHINGSTONE

S T MARY. Simple N doorway of *c.* 1200. Late C13 chancel, see
the s windows and the doorway; also the SEDILIA. To their
w – an unusual position – a tomb recess with ogee arch. Dec
(but altered) the arch to the N transept. Its w respond is an
octagonal pier, i.e. the arch did not lead to a transept proper
but to a bay of a N aisle. C13 w tower. Unbuttressed. Narrow
triple-chamfered arch towards the nave. – PLATE. Cup and
Paten, 1570; Breadholder, 1728.

KING'S ARMS, opposite the church. Picturesque neo-Tudor.
Built before 1845. Reconstructed after a fire *c.* 1870.

PENSION ROW, s of the church. Two odd cottages with brick
door-frames and wider frames and giant arches round them.
The walling otherwise is faced with old crocks and plaster.

CASTLE DYKES, 1 m. N of the church. This large earthwork
represents a medieval castle of a comparatively unusual type.
The narrow main bailey is cut virtually in two by the ringwork which forms the inner stronghold. Large outer bailey.

ENCLOSURE. There is a double ditch and banked enclosure
beside the Stowe road, *c.* 1 m. N of the village. In poor condition, only readily visible from the N and w. It is probably
connected with the Castle Dykes motte-and-bailey (*see* above).

FAWSLEY

S T MARY. The church lies in the middle of the spacious ornamental grounds of the Hall,* facing it at a distance and overlooking the beautifully curving double lake. The earliest item
is the two C13 bays of the arcades, with octagonal piers and
double-chamfered arches. They may be contemporary with
the intersected tracery of the chancel E and s aisle E windows,
but are earlier than the Dec w tower, with which they were
linked by a new bay. The tower has an ogee-hooded niche and
cusped Y-tracery in the bell-openings. Dec also the re-used
arch of the N doorway. The clerestory could be C16 or C17.
(Mr Bailey compares the C17 Hall brewhouse windows; Mr
Marks the C16 clerestory at Great Brington.) The chancel was
rebuilt in 1690 (H. M. Colvin). – FONT. Originally probably
C13, but the big heads certainly re-worked. – WOODWORK.
Late Perp and Early Renaissance panels, some ornamented,
some with heads in medallions or with grotesques; re-used
in the pews. – STAINED GLASS. Many imported Flemish

* But the village was formerly close to it.

roundels; also heraldic glass in the s aisle w window. –
PLATE. Cup and Paten, 1582; Breadholder, 1688; Flagon,
1713. – MONUMENTS. Thirteen are worth attention, all to
members of the Knightley family. They follow each other
roughly chronologically like this: Brass of Thomas † 1516
(nave; 18 in. figure). – Sir Richard † 1534 and wife. Alabaster;
free-standing. An outstandingly fine monument, especially in
the small figures of the mourners standing against the tomb-
chest under broad, flat ogee arches, four daughters to the N,
eight sons arranged in pairs to the s. They are delicately
characterized and move with ease. At the head end two praying angels and a shield. – Brasses to Sir Edmund † 1542 and
wife, the builder of the Hall. The figures are 3 ft long. His
head lies on a helmet, hers on a pillow. – Sir Valentine † 1566,
Sir Richard † 1615, and Sir Valentine † 1619. Standing
monument, broad, with a big sarcophagus high up, supported
by two praying caryatids. Between them, lower down, small
recumbent effigy on a slab supported by tall brackets. Two
putti in the sarcophagus. Top with metope frieze and pediment. – Five large architectural tablets, all in the chancel,
recording deaths of Knightleys in 1661, 1670, 1728 and 1738
(nearly identical), and 1731.* They make interesting stylistic
comparisons. Only the one of 1731 (Jane Grey Knightley) has
a figural element: a small bust on top. – Devereux † 1681 and
Elizabeth † 1715 (N aisle). Two very similar standing monuments on a tall pedestal. Again a comparison is enlightening.
The later monument is richer, and the skill in the carving of
the four garlands deserves notice. – Lucy † 1805, by *Richard
Westmacott Sen.* Architectural, without any figures. Very
finely detailed and still entirely pre-Grecian. – Selina † 1856.
By *John Gibson* of Rome. She is being received by an angel.
(Both the latter in the s aisle.)

FAWSLEY HALL. A Hall and various other ranges remain of
the building of Sir Edmund Knightley. The buildings were
taken over by a factory in the 1960s, and have suffered sadly.
The house is now derelict (1972). The whole group remained
more or less in the state in which Knightley left it until
Anthony Salvin for another Knightley added in 1867–8 more
commodious reception rooms and a whole three-storeyed
block as well. They face E, and the front of the Hall appears

71

---

* The monuments of 1728, 1738, and 1731 have been attributed to
Francis Smith.

between them. This has a width of five bays separated by buttresses. The first three and the fifth have a three-light window with arched lights high up, the fourth is the bay-window. Its base is decorated by shields in lozenges or quatre-foils. The window itself has two embattled transoms, and there is an embattled upper storey above it reaching above the eaves of the roof. What can it have contained, and how can it have been entered? Finials on the end gables. Access to the Hall was in the first bay. The exit into the courtyard behind still exists. The screen has gone, but the roof survived until 1966, when it was scandalously destroyed on the occasion of the re-roofing of the house.* Huge stone fireplace, about 12 ft wide, with a big quatrefoil frieze over, then a foliage frieze as fine as in any wooden rood screen, and finally a cresting. There are windows high up to the courtyard as well as the outer world, and one of them, originally open, stands right above the fireplace. The flues were conducted to its l. and r. (*see* Morton, 1712). The bay-window has panelled jambs and a fan-vault. The spandrels of the panelling and of all window lights are prettily decorated. To the C16 building also belong the Parlour, facing s with a buttressed front and a two-storeyed oriel window, the Kitchen and Bakehouse, w of the parlour, i.e. at an angle to the Hall, with their big fireplaces, and the long range known as the Brewhouse, which runs parallel with the Hall range, from the Bakehouse to the N.‡ At its N end is a large transomed oriel window on a big corbel. This and the other windows of this range also have arched lights. The three ranges so far mentioned enclose an inner court. Its fourth (N) range has a date 1732, but was altered by *Cundy* in 1815, and then extended by Salvin into a three-storey range.

To the N STABLES, C18, of red brick, three sides of a court, with a cupola. This and the 1732 block have been attributed to *Francis Smith*.

DOWER HOUSE, ¾ m. NE. A small house, already in ruins *c.* 1710, in the middle of the estate. Brick and ironstone. Brick the tower (with dark blue diapering) and what remains of the moulded and ornamented chimneyshafts. The windows again with arched lights. Also later straightforward mullioned windows. The house seems to belong to the same time as the

* It had elegant arched braces supporting a collar-beam, and wind-braces.
‡ The interior of the Parlour, with its coved ceiling, and the kitchen arrangements with the Cook's Loft, still survive (BB).

Hall, and may even be a little earlier, that is, it is the earliest example of brick in the county.

FAXTON

7070

Now deserted. The village had declined after c18 enclosures. Excavations have produced evidence of settlement from the late c12 onwards. The church of ST DENIS was demolished in 1958.*

SHORTWOOD LODGE. *See* p. 402.

FERMYN WOODS HALL

9080

2 m. SW of Benefield

An Elizabethan centre of E-plan, successfully disguised by extensive neo-Elizabethan extensions of *c.* 1850. The c19 w wing has now been demolished. It was in fact a remodelling of a wing of 1788. The s side of the stables has as its centrepiece the GATEWAY from Lyveden Old Bield (*see* p. 299). Archway with paired niches l. and r. Three shields above each pair. Crowning with openwork geometrical motifs, volutes, and arms.

FINEDON

9070

ST MARY. An exceptionally beautiful, large church. Ironstone with ample grey stone dressings with battlements. All Dec, and built quickly. The joint between tower and nave shows that a start was made from the E as well as the tower and that the latter work met the former when the tower was already standing to a certain height. The w tower has a doorway with an ogee surround flanked by pinnacles, pairs of tall bell-openings, a quatrefoil and an ogee frieze, battlements, and a very fine recessed spire with two tiers of lucarnes. The body of the church is embattled, the windows are mostly Dec, and mostly with tracery of a tall, elongated, uncusped variety of reticulation. Others have three steeply-stepped lancet lights under one arch. Many are shafted inside. The chancel E window has five instead of three of the stepped lancet lights. The chancel, incidentally, was first intended to have a different

* The FONT is at All Saints Kettering. The PLATE, and a mural tablet to Mrs Raynsford † 1763 by *William Cox*, are at Lamport. The MONUMENT of Judge Nichols († 1616), a tablet by *John Hunt*, and another by *John Bacon Jun.* are in the Victoria and Albert Museum.

fenestration, see the priest's doorway and the shafted 'low-side' window, cut into by the present windows, yet not much earlier. Also, the chancel was intended to be vaulted, as the interior proves – a great rarity in English C14 parish churches. The two W springers stand on head corbels. The S porch is two-storeyed, with big gargoyles (as they also pop out from other parts of the building). Its lower floor is vaulted (a quadripartite vault) and leads to an unusually tall doorway. The arcades are of three wide bays, the N side with quatrefoil piers and arches with two sunk mouldings, the S side mostly new (square piers with four demi-shafts). There is an irregularity at the transept, where the N pier has six shafts and six hollows, the S pier a cluster of six shafts which gives them an odd oblong shape. The S pier and the triple-shafted responds of the chancel arch have big leaves in the capitals. The clerestory is also Dec. Across the nave runs a strainer arch very similar to that at Rushden, curved top and bottom, and with the sinking top curve incongruously embattled. In the spandrels circles with the motif of the four-petalled flower inscribed. At the foot of the arch l. and r. angel busts facing W as well as E. This may well be as late as *c.* 1400.* In the chancel a handsome though badly mutilated SEDILIA arrangement. They have little tipped-up vaults on shafts with leaf capitals, but in front of them the shafts of the blocked S window are carried down as clustered shafts with leaf capitals. – FONT. C12, reworked in the C15 (?), octagonal. On one side of the bowl a group of the Annunciation. – BENCH ENDS. Simple, straight-topped, panelled. – ORGAN CASE. Of 1717, a very fine, sumptuous, famous piece, with both leaf carving and open segmental pediments. By *Shrider*. – IRON GATE, C18, in the S porch entrance. – STAINED GLASS. Chancel S, 1847; probably the window by *Wailes*, mentioned in *R & P.* 1853. – (N transept. By *Kempe & Tower*, 1919.) – PLATE. Silver-gilt set, 1683; mother-of-pearl Christening Bowl and Almsdish, foreign, presented in the C18. – MONUMENTS. (N transept. Rev. James Affleck † 1784 by *J. F. Moore.* – N aisle. Lt. William Roberts † 1747 by *John Hunt.* BB) – In the vault at the E end of the church, visible from the E outside, with many others: Mary Dolben † 1710, Elizabeth Dolben † 1736, with busts by *John Hunt.*

(FINEDON HALL. Something of the Elizabethan house is said

---

* The church was restored by *Slater c.* 1858 (R. Hubbuck).

to remain on the NW side, but mostly the house is a Gothic-cum-Tudor fantasy of William Mackworth-Dolben.* Dates 1835, 1851, 1856, 1859, and 1872. Also big Gothic inscription. Many gables, straight and otherwise. Stables with a tower sporting shaped gables and a pyramid roof. The grounds were landscaped by *Repton* and are mentioned in his 'Sketches' published in 1794.)

Several notable buildings close to the church. They are the VICARAGE, dated 1688, of ironstone, three plus one plus three bays, with wooden cross-windows; the former BOYS' SCHOOL (now disused), endowed in 1595, with gable and mullioned windows; the small oblong house to the E of the church with a C14 window; the handsome group at the beginning of CHURCH STREET, including the GIRLS' SCHOOL of 1712, with its seven bays and its doorway with a big segmental pediment, and THINGDON COTTAGE, very Gothic, of 1862. Mr Mackworth-Dolben built more houses in the village, indulging his peculiar Gothic taste, especially the BELL INN of 1872, to the S of Thingdon Cottage. In CHURCH STREET a little further on the ALMSHOUSES with their dormers and the row of gabled cottages of 1847, Nos 5–19.

TOWN HALL, Berry Green. 1868. Two storeys, Gothic, with trefoil-headed first-floor windows.

(MACKWORTH GREEN. A little square of ironstone houses dated 1840. DOE)

WELLINGTON TOWER, on the Thrapston Road, c. 1 m. from the church. Built to commemorate the Battle of Waterloo.

(WATER TOWER, E of the A6 road to the S. Octagonal, of polychrome brick, in a freely adapted Norman style. Probably late C19. A. Cox)

9090

FINESHADE ABBEY
2¼ m. NNE of Bulwick

The remains of the Augustinian priory were destroyed in 1749. Only a fragment survives of the Georgian mansion, mostly demolished in 1956. The late C18 STABLES remain, with a cupola above the entrance.

At various points around the site of the house, and particularly on the SW, are visible the remains of the earthworks of the

* The pre-Mackworth-Dolben house is shown as a plain half-H-shaped house in a George Clarke drawing (GI).

CASTLE of Hely or Hymel, deserted before the foundation of the monastery in the early C13.

FLORE

6060

ALL SAINTS. Mainly of the C13, i.e. the exquisite arcades of three wide bays, with triple shafts to the four sides, twelve in all. One pier and one respond have stiff-leaf capitals. Of the C13 also the S doorway with two orders of shafts with stiff-leaf capitals. About 1300 may be the date when the W tower was begun and the aisles continued to embrace it. Of the same date the N aisle windows and doorway. Dec the continuation of the W tower, the S aisle windows, and also the N aisle E window. The chancel has a late C13 W part with a heavily dog-tooth-decorated doorway and windows with intersected tracery, and a Perp E end. – SCREEN. Of three-light divisions, that is one unit l., one r. of the entrance.* – PLATE. Cup and Paten, 1570; Dish, 1669. – BRASSES. Thomas Knaresburghe † 1450 and wife † 1498 (23 in. figures); Henry Michell † 1510 and wife (26 in. figures); Alyce Wyrley † 1537 (of the cross which was the centre of the composition only the foot remains).

FLORE HOUSE. Partly Jacobean, but much altered and added to. The oldest windows are mullioned with arched lights.

OLD MANOR, NE of the churchyard. Late C17. Ironstone. Five bays, two storeys, hipped roof, cross-windows of stone.

FOTHERINGHAY

0090

FOTHERINGHAY CASTLE was built probably by Simon de St Liz, first Earl of Huntingdon and Northampton, c. 1100. It was largely rebuilt by Edmund Langley, Earl of Cambridge and son of Edward III. It is remembered chiefly as the place where Mary Queen of Scots was held prisoner from 1586 to her execution on 8 February 1587. Little remains but the powerful motte and bailey on which it was rebuilt in the late C14; the earthworks themselves are almost certainly of the C12. There is an outer bailey which was probably never walled. Leland still called it 'fair and meately strong with double ditches and a kepe very anncient and strong'. He also mentions 'fair lodgyns'. But Stukeley, writing in the early C18, says that the castle is 'mostly demolished'. It is not known when the decay set in and the destructions took place. We cannot now easily visualize Fotheringhay as it must have

* Formerly part of an organ case built by *Holdich* (BB).

looked in the C15, when not only the castle towered over the village, but when also the college buildings stretched to the s of the church.

ST MARY AND ALL SAINTS. Edmund Langley conceived the idea of a college attached to Fotheringhay Castle about 1370, but he died in 1402 and his son Edward of York decided to establish the college in the church. The college was founded finally in 1411, but Edward fell at Agincourt in 1415. The college consisted of a master, twelve fellows, eight clerks, and thirteen choristers. A grand and ambitious chancel was built. The nave was rebuilt according to a contract between Richard Duke of York and the freemason *William Horwood*, a contract dated 1434. The nave was to be of the same height and width as the chancel. The same was stipulated for the aisles. The chancel was pulled down in 1573 by Dudley, Duke of Northumberland, to whom Edward VI had granted the college.*

What remains now is this: w tower with broad w doorway. Eight-light w window with ample Perp tracery. Four-light bell-openings. Polygonal turret-pinnacles. The tower here turns octagonal. Another set of eight tall three-light bell-openings with transom. Battlements, pinnacles, no spire. The arch towards the nave is exceptionally tall. Behind it appears a beautiful fan-vault, dated 1529. The aisles embrace the tower. On the N side in addition a two-storeyed porch at the w end. Four-light aisle windows, four-light clerestory windows. Bold slender flying buttresses curved not only below but also above. The last N bay has a three-light window, the last s bay is disturbed. The passage to the cloister went off from here. Heavily buttressed E wall where the chancel started. The interior is wide and airy, decidedly East Anglian in character. The chancel must have been lower than the nave, as there is a nave E window. Piers of a complicated Perp section. The shafts towards the arch openings are the only ones which have capitals. The shafts towards the nave run right up to the roof. The roof has curved braces and curved collars continuing the same curve, a noble conception. – FONT. Octagonal, Perp. Panelled stem, bowl with quatrefoils and big leaf motifs alternating with animal faces on the underside. – REREDOS. Gothic, probably early C19. – PULPIT. A very good Perp piece, recently repainted, with a Perp rib-vaulted

* Information from Malcolm Airs.

tester slightly tipped and a larger Jacobean tester. – BOX 39
PEWS. – PLATE. Paten, 1640; Set, 1827. – MONUMENTS.
Two identical, grand and restrained Elizabethan memorials to
Edward, second Duke of York, and Richard, third Duke of
York, erected in 1573 by Queen Elizabeth. Big base, coupled
attached Corinthian columns, big attic. In the centre arms in
a strapwork cartouche. No figures at all.

OLD INN, E end of the main street, on the S side. Transformed
into cottages. In the middle, passageway with original four-
centred doorway, flanked by a large room on either side.
On the w side a large fireplace and a blocked doorway.
(Originally ranges extended back on either side of a courtyard. On the upper floor of the front range on the l., large
room with arch-braced roof of two bays. A coat of arms
recorded in 1821 may date the building to the reign of
Edward IV. W. A. Pantin)

NEW INN, opposite the Old Inn. Good C15 gateway with a four-
centred arch and traceried spandrels. Quatrefoil frieze. Two-
light window above. Two buttresses. On the l. projecting wing
with blocked windows and doorway. The New Inn had two
courtyards behind.

ESTATE COTTAGES. Early C19. Plain.

FURTHO 7040

ST BARTHOLOMEW. Disused and derelict (last used as a parish
church in 1921). Mostly of 1620. To this belong the straight-
headed windows and the round tower arch and chancel arch.
– PLATE. Now at Potterspury.

DOVECOTE. Probably C15 (cf. Harlestone). Circular, with a
bold string-course at the top of the bottom stage. The upper
stage is only partly preserved. Conical roof later.

GAYTON 7050

ST MARY. Norman the w tower below the bell-openings. One
round-headed arch and one pointed window. The arch towards
the nave is pointed too and has one step and one slight chamfer. The upper part of the tower is C19. The rest of the church
is Dec externally. The windows are much renewed. Sumptuous
E window with flowing tracery. N chapel with a curious w
entrance squeezed into the wall behind a broad buttress. C13
arcades inside. Three bays, octagonal piers, arches of one
chamfer and one hollow chamfer. The details differ between
N and S. The S arcade is probably earlier. The N arcade was

built more closely to the tower and out of symmetry with the
w wall. Dec chancel chapels. The s chapel of two bays has a
quatrefoil pier with fillets on the projections and an arch with
one chamfer and one wave, the N chapel of one bay has
responds with fillets and an arch like the other. In the N chapel
an ogee-headed recess. – FONT. Circular with intersected
arches – that is seemingly Norman. But the resulting pointed
arches are cusped. Is it a remodelling of a Norman font, or an
example of archaism? – REREDOS. Linenfold panels, early
C16, probably not *in situ*. – ROOD SCREEN. Only a stone base
survives. – STALLS. Perp, with six MISERICORDS. They
represent the Virgin of the Misericord, a lion and a dragon, a
seraph astride two figures, three seated female figures, Christ
in Majesty, Christ's Entry into Jerusalem, and a small praying
figure. – PULPIT. Jacobean, with two tiers of the familiar
short, broad blank arches. – STAINED GLASS. In the N chapel
assembled glass, including some that is heraldic and a number
of Netherlandish roundels. – PLATE. Cup and Paten, 1570;
Breadholder, 1707; Flagon, *c.* 1757. – MONUMENTS. In the
N chapel a C13 coffin lid with an uncommonly lushly foliated
cross. – Between the chancel and the N chapel an ogee arch
with buttresses and finial and beneath it a tomb-chest with six
ogee-headed crocketed panels. On the tomb-chest effigy of
oak, a cross-legged Knight, supposed to be Sir Philip de
Gayton † 1316. – N chapel, N recess. Effigy of a Lady on a
plain tomb-chest. Above her on corbels a tiny effigy with an
inscription beneath. The large effigy is supposed to be
Scholastica de Gayton † 1354, the small effigy is Mabila de
Murdak, early C14. – In the chancel s wall Perp tomb recess
with an almost flat arch and battlements. Purbeck marble.
Probably *c.* 1500. – Francis Tanfield † 1558 and wife (N
chapel). Tomb-chest with shields in lozenges. Incised alabaster
slab, attributed to the *Roileys* of Burton-on-Trent. – Lock-
wood family by *Robert Blore*, the latest date 1759. Architectural
frame, long inscription.

MANOR HOUSE. Built by the Tanfield family. A very interesting
house, probably of the third quarter of the C16. The shape is
roughly that of a Greek cross and the building is three-
storeyed, including the gables. All windows with arched lights.
To the S, E, and W there are canted bay-windows in the middle
of the ends of the cross. To the N a flat staircase projection.
The E and W bays are of four lights plus the one-light canting,
but they taper at the gable level to three lights only. The bay-

window gable is placed in front of the gable of the cross-arm, slightly lower and narrower. On the s side the bay-window has three lights and tapers to two. Compact interior, well preserved. Staircase with busily detailed vertically symmetrical balusters.

GAYTON HOUSE was demolished in 1972. It was probably early C18, but with a SE front with two-storey porch and bay-windows added by Roger Eykyn, who acquired the property in 1874. The windows had the Eykyn arms (G1).

(THE WEIR, at the SW end of the village. C17. Of two storeys. In the s front four-light mullioned window and a massive double buttress disguised as a porch, complete with fine doorway. DOE)

ROMAN BUILDING. The site lies in the Warren, by the crossroads c. ½ m. SE of the village. Partial excavation in 1840 revealed a portico with four column-bases in a front 66 ft long, with evidence for subsidiary wings. Amongst the finds was a bronze Cupid, and coins mostly of the C4 A.D. The building seems most probably to have been a temple.

GEDDINGTON

ST MARY MAGDALENE. Interesting evidence of a Saxon nave. A frieze of triangle-headed arcading ran along the outer walls and is now visible from the aisles. Also a window and long-and-short quoins at the E end of the nave.* This nave was enlarged by a N aisle in the late C12. The arcade consists oddly enough of two and a half bays, and it must be assumed that the intention was to pull down the Saxon E wall and to continue the arch, but that this was given up. Circular piers, volute and waterleaf capitals. Square abaci. Single-stepped round arches. The next part of the church is the C13 S aisle. It has three full bays, which shows that by then the position of the Saxon chancel arch was accepted. The arcade has quatrefoil piers and double-chamfered arches. To this aisle belong the s doorway (two orders of shafts with renewed rings). After the s arcade the chancel. N window with two lights and a spherical triangle which looks late C13, but s window with ogee-headed lights in spite of intersected cusped tracery. The splendid five-light E window also has ogee-headed lights. It culminates in a big circle filled with three pointed trefoils without ogee arches.

---

* The window on the N side cuts into the arcading, and therefore appears to be a Late Saxon insertion.

Good head stops. L. and r. of the E window head corbels. Clerestory windows, below the main Perp ones, in the form of alternating quatrefoils and spherical triangles. All this might well be called *c.* 1300, but the ogees in the lights make it necessary to add another ten or twenty years. One would not be tempted to add more. Yet in an inscription in Lombardic lettering along the foot of the chancel walls the date 1369 is explicitly quoted. It refers to the death of 'Wilhelmus Glovere de Geytyngton Capellanus', who 'fecit scabella eius are et pavimentare istum cancellum' and who 'obiit in festo Corpus Christi anno domini MCCCLXIX'. The inscription continues without a break into the s chapel, and there records 'Robertus Launcelyn de Geytingtoune', who 'fecit istum cancellum'. The s chapel to which the second inscription refers looks, just like the chancel, *c.* 1300, and certainly not later than *c.* 1320. Two bays, quatrefoil piers, double-chamfered arches, one big s lancet window. The E window is Perp, but its internal shafting looks *c.* 1300 too. How is one to explain this? Did the two men do their good deeds fifty years before the death of one of them? That seems unlikely. If they left the money, one would have to assume that forms which for the whole of England one has every reason to call *c.* 1310–20 were used in Northamptonshire fifty years later, which is just as unlikely. Does the truth lie in the middle? There is evidence in other places of conservatism in tracery. The chancel arch with its thin responds belongs in any case to the rest of the chancel.

The w tower is Perp and has clasping buttresses, two pairs of two-light bell-openings with transom, a quatrefoil frieze, and a recessed spire with three tiers of lucarnes in alternating directions. – REREDOS. In the chancel, stone, Perp, with a quatrefoil frieze, thirteen blank arches, the middle one much wider, and crenellation. – SCREENS between chancel and s chapel, of the early C14 (or *c.* 1370?), cusped pointed arches and shafts with a ring. – Screen between s aisle and s chapel, formerly the rood screen. Dated 1618. A most interesting piece of early Gothic Revival. The carver has faithfully repeated the tracery of the chancel E window, only filling all the spaces with small scroll-work of his own. – (WARDROBE, in the vestry. Made of BENCH ENDS, one dated 1602.) – STAINED GLASS. Chancel N and s by *Clayton & Bell*, 1860; chancel E by *Comper*, 1903, still entirely in the Victorian tradition; s aisle by the *Rev. J. S. H. Horner* of Mells in Somerset. – PLATE. Paten and Cup, *c.* 1570. – MONUMENTS. Effigy of a

Priest, C13, the lower part of his body covered by a shield. – Brass of Henry Jarmon and wife, c. 1480, 18 in. figures.

ELEANOR CROSS (cf. Hardingstone, p. 353). Erected shortly [67] after 1294. Of the three surviving Eleanor Crosses, this is the most modest and the best preserved. Its shape heralds the end of the classic Gothic moment and the coming of Dec capriciousness. Triangular and carrying on at the top, by means of six pinnacles, to a recessed hexagonal star with more pinnacles. Close diapering in the lower parts. The three figures in the three niches characteristic also of the end of the crisp and sharp carving of up to 1275–80 and the heavier flow and broader masses of 1290 etc.

There was a royal hunting lodge at Geddington. It lay NE of the church.

PRIORY, SE of the church. L-shaped, with the projecting part dated 1588 (mullioned windows), the recessed part late C17 with early sash-windows.

BRIDGE. C13, with large cutwaters on one side. Two pointed arches, the round one of 1784. Much repaired.

GLAPTHORN

0090

ST LEONARD. Mostly a C13 church. Early C13 S aisle of two bays. Low circular pier, octagonal capitals, round, double-chamfered arches. Late C13 the replacement of a pre-existing N aisle by one with round pier and round abacus and pointed double-chamfered arches. The base of the pier includes two reversed scalloped Norman responds of the preceding aisle. Before the present N arcade the E extension of the aisles, also still C13. The place where the original E wall was is marked between the W and the E parts of the arcades. Late C13 chancel with bar tracery, Y-tracery, and cusped intersected tracery. Also a PISCINA with dog-tooth. Bar tracery also in the N chapel E window. This corresponds to the chapel arch towards the chancel. One demi-shaft and one continuous chamfer. Finally, late C13 the masonry of the lower parts of the unbuttressed W tower (Y-tracery in the W window). The top is Perp. The windows at the E end of the S aisle are Dec. – FONT. Octagonal, Perp, with panelled stem and quatrefoiled bowl. – FONT COVER with a re-used Perp finial. – PULPIT. With Jacobean panels. – READING DESKS. With some re-used linenfold panels and a Perp band. – COMMUNION RAIL. Jacobean or a little later. – WALL PAINTINGS. Many traces, most clearly discernible the large St Christopher on the N wall of the N aisle. – PLATE. Cup, Paten, and Almsdish, 1813.

GLENDON HALL

The house consists of two parts, with a third not originally belonging to it. This third component is chronologically the first. It is the porch from Pytchley Hall, which was pulled down in 1824. It is a very noble piece of Elizabethan design, probably begun c. 1578 (see also Pytchley, p. 380). Arched doorway. Roman Doric columns to the l. and r., frieze of very wide metopes, fluted Ionic columns on the upper floor with two small beaded bands across. Cross-windows, also one on each of the sides of the porch. Balustrade of vertically symmetrical balusters. The porch is set in front of the later part of the house. Its earlier part looks Jacobean. Doorway with four-centred head. Cross-windows on the ground floor, large mullioned and transomed windows on the first floor. One wide canted bay-window. The later part of the house was probably built after 1758. Red brick, two and a half storeys, three-bay pediment now partly hidden by the Pytchley porch. Side with a canted bay-window. Towards the S also a canted bay-window, mediating between the new and old parts.* In the garden by the pond two STATUES from Boughton (Aeneas and Anchises, Hercules and Cacus), attributed by Gunnis to *Andreas Kearne* (BB).

STABLES. Late C17. Gabled sides, pedimented centre with cupola.

GRAFTON REGIS

ST MARY. Mostly Dec. The N arcade however is early C13 work. Four bays, low, with circular piers and circular abaci. Hood-moulds with small zigzag at r. angles to the wall surface. In the chancel SEDILIA and PISCINA are Dec – an interesting composition, with the priest's doorway between and all three ogee-arched. The chancel windows are Perp. Dec tomb recess in the S wall. W tower completed, according to the inscription on his monument (*see* below), by Sir John Woodville ('campanile peregit'). – (SCREEN. A panel of the former rood screen now above the vestry door.) – FONT. Of tub shape, Norman. With intersected arches. – PAINTING. Betrayal of

* Some Flemish STAINED GLASS in an upper room may come from the demolished church at Glendon (GI).

Christ. Probably part of the former rood screen (above chancel s doorway). – PLATE. Silver-gilt Cup and Cover Paten, 1683. – MONUMENTS. Tomb-chest with panels and three semi-octagonal piers. – Tomb-chest with seven ogee-headed panels and on it the incised slab to Sir John Wydevyl, c. 1415 (both N aisle, W end). – Charlotte, Countess of Euston, † 1808. By *Flaxman*. Grecian tablet with Faith and Hope at the corners, placed diagonally – which a pure Grecian would not have done. – Lord James Henry Fitzroy † 1834. By *William Behnes*. Tablet with a draped urn.

(MANOR HOUSE, near the church. An oblong outbuilding has a buttress to the street and some mullioned windows with arched lights, i.e. is of pre-Reformation date. It is a relic of a large royal house built by Henry VIII. H. M. Colvin)

WOODVILLE MANOR HOUSE. Excavations on a site W of the A508 in 1964–5 revealed medieval buildings, apparently monastic in origin, arranged round a cloister, with a small church on the S side. They were converted to secular use in the C15. In the E end of the church were tiles with the Woodville arms.

The Grafton Estate in the early C19 built a number of model farms, all characterized by formality of layout and by low-pitched slated roofs. The houses are of three bays and have lower wings continuing in line with the house or recessed or at r. angles, and the farm buildings are grouped in a rational relation to them. Cf. Abthorpe, Green's Norton, Paulerspury, Stoke Bruerne.

GRAFTON UNDERWOOD

9080

ST JAMES. Late C12 N arcade of three bays with circular piers carrying square capitals with leaf volutes and crockets, square abaci, and single-stepped round arches. Still later C12 S arcade with circular elementary stiff-leaf capitals, circular abaci, and round arches of one step and one chamfer. C13 chancel arch (pointed, double-chamfered, some nailhead) and C13 W tower (arch towards the nave single-stepped but pointed, lancet windows, twin bell-openings under a round arch). Recessed Perp spire with two tiers of lucarnes. Chancel higher than the nave, in its E part Dec. The four-light E window is odd but possible, though the mullions are a little suspicious. Flowing tracery. At the top the motif of the four-petalled flower, each petal quatrefoiled and the whole in a depressed circle. On the s side one Dec window with flowing tracery and one later C13 one with normal bar tracery. Big niche inside to the N of the E window with ogee arch, thick finials, heads, and ballflower. Smaller, similar niche to the S. Ogee-arched SEDILIA and PISCINA. – PULPIT. Simple and nice, dated 1728. – SCREEN. Perp, base only. – STAINED GLASS. E window, 1884, signed by *E. R. Suffling* of London. – PLATE. Cup and Paten, 1664; Almsdish, 1690; Breadholder, 1704; Flagon, 1836. – MONUMENTS. Family of Lord Gowran to the second Earl of Upper Ossory † 1818. By *Westmacott*. Two kneeling women bending over and holding a medallion with a portrait of the Earl. – Lady Anne Fitzpatrick † 1841. By *Westmacott Jun*. Large relief with a charitable lady offering bread to a child, a kneeling mother, and a *vieillard*. Gothic arch, but the relief in a sentimental classical style.

(Former RECTORY, W of the church. 1869. A large stone house in Renaissance style. BB)

HOUSE in the main street, dated 1653. Stepped three-light mullioned windows in the gables.

GREAT ADDINGTON

9070

ALL SAINTS. Mostly late C13 to early C14. Arcades with octagonal piers, except for the E pier on the N side, which is quatrefoil. The arches, with ironstone and grey stone voussoirs, are double-chamfered. Contemporary chancel arch and one-bay N chapel. In the S wall a tall tomb recess with Dec mouldings. The chancel is Dec too, in spite of its Perp windows – see the ANGLE PISCINA and the N doorway. The tower is Dec. Above the doorway a niche with a nodding ogee arch. Strange lozenge-shaped windows to W and S, with mouchette tracery and cusping respectively. Bell-openings of two lights. Pretty frieze of little ogee arches with quatrefoils in the spandrels. Battlements with cross-slits (why?). Arch towards the nave with three continuous chamfers. The entrance to the S porch has not yet been mentioned. This must be re-set and belong to the predecessor of the present building. Round arch with zigzag, former shafts whose leaf-crocket capitals survive: i.e. *c.* 1190–1200. – FONT. Of tub shape, on five supports. At the corners projecting heads. C13. – PULPIT. Late C17; simple. – SCREEN to the N chapel; one-light divisions. Unusual tracery, based on two crossed diagonals. – (STAINED GLASS. N chapel: Virgin and Vere arms, *c.* 1490; nave: C13 grisaille

fragments. RM) – PLATE. Almsdish, 1832; Cup, 1835. –
MONUMENTS. John Bloxham, c. 1519. A 2 ft brass figure
with a scroll emanating from his head. On a plain tomb-chest.
– Sir Henry Vere † 1493. Alabaster effigy. He had founded a
chantry in the church, the chaplain of which was Bloxham,
and he willed that his 'towmbe be made in oure lady chapell
. . . of alabaster'.

ADDINGTON MANOR. A gabled Jacobean house with extensive
neo-Jacobean additions. The old centre has an E-shaped front
with very little space between porch and wings. At the back a
straight wall with three gables in line.

GREAT BILLING see NORTHAMPTON, p. 349

GREAT BRINGTON

6o6o

ST MARY. What endows the church with a far higher than
regional importance is the Spencer Chapel, one of the great
storehouses of costly and self-confident monuments of the
C16, C17, and C18. The rest can be treated briefly. The church
is approached by GATEPIERS of 1840 from the W as well as the
E. The W gatepiers have handsome cast-iron GATES. The
church is large, of ironstone, and has a C13 W tower. The bell-
openings are two lancets under one arch. Perp doorway and
large W window. The S doorway is of c. 1300, and not far
from it in the S wall is a gabled outer tomb recess with dog-
tooth decoration which must be of about the same time.
Dec N windows, Perp S chapel, chancel, and N chapel. The
chancel is known to have been rebuilt at Sir John Spencer's
expense, the N chapel was to be the family chapel (see below).
See p. 517
Fine Dec six-bay arcades with octagonal piers. The N arcade
has octagonal piers and double-chamfered arches, the S arcade
taller piers with concave sides and double-hollow-chamfered
arches. S porch of 1832 by *Blore*. – FONT. Circular, of Purbeck
marble, with flat, blank pointed arches and in the spandrels
crosses and flowers. Stone base with dog-tooth. C13. –
BENCHES. Made up in 1846, but incorporating earlier ones
including a large number of the C15 and of 1606. All with
poppy-heads. – POOR BOX on raw column; C17. – COM-
MUNION RAIL. C17. – SOUTH DOOR. Studded, probably
the original door. – STAINED GLASS. St John Baptist and
the other remains in a chancel S window are the original work
done under the will of Sir William Spencer (1532). – E

window by *Morris & Co.*, 1912. – PLATE. Flagon, 1605; Cup and Cover Paten, 1715; Almsdish, 1775. – MONUMENTS in the chancel. John de Clipston † 1344. Brass with demifigure of priest. – Laurence Washington † 1616. Tombstone with shield in relief.

SPENCER CHAPEL. Sir John Spencer, who died in 1522, added the N chapel. The design has been attributed to *Thomas Heritage*, who was rector of Great Brington and later Surveyor of the King's Works. He had been given the living by Sir John in 1513.* The chapel is three bays long. The exterior was rebuilt in 1846 by *Blore*. There is a pretty polygonal bay-window to the N. This has a fan-vault in imitation of those of Henry VII's Chapel at Westminster. The chapel has its original STAINED GLASS by *Ward*, who was advised by *Winston*. One window apparently by *Morris & Co.*, but late – cf. the E window of the church. In the chapel the SPENCER MONUMENTS, re-arranged, except for those between chancel and chapel. The iron RAILINGS are original. The monuments are described here in chronological order.

See p. 517

52   Sir John Spencer † 1522 and wife (SE of chapel). Two effigies, at the feet of the lady two tiny puppies. The effigies lie on a tall tomb-chest with three quatrefoils with shields. The monument is placed under a canopy with a broad fourcentred arch panelled inside. Against its apex, almost detached,

53   the beautiful figure of an angel in the Doric peplos worn by the angels on Torrigiano's tomb of Henry VII – the only indication of the Renaissance here. Big attic with quatrefoil etc. friezes.

Sir William Spencer † 1532. Below the E window. Low, long tomb-chest with quatrefoils. No effigies left. The inscription tablet is Elizabethan or Jacobean and belongs to a general labelling which must then have taken place.

Sir John Spencer † 1586 and wife (w of Sir John). By *Jasper Hollemans* of Burton-on-Trent, but judging by his name clearly from the Netherlands. Tall tomb-chest with shields separated by very curious, coarsely ornamented strips. Effigies recumbent, she with an excessively heavy hood. To the l. and r. big obelisks covered with strapwork. Round arch and pediment over.

Robert, first Baron Spencer, and wife (w of the above).

* But as he only became involved in the King's Works *c.* 1530 the attribution cannot be certain (H. M. Colvin).

Erected in 1599 and also made by *Hollemans*. He is in armour, she wears an even bigger and heavier hood. The lower half of her body is covered by a heraldic coverlet, trefoiled in section, and making her look as if she were in a pulpit or a chariot. It is a most uncommon, if not a unique, feature. They lie on a sarcophagus painted with strapwork. To the l. and r. fluted Corinthian columns. Depressed round arch. At the top three obelisks continued downwards as pendants hanging into the arch.

Sir John Spencer † 1599 and wife (NE corner). Also by *Hollemans*. Although now standing against the wall, before 1846 this was a detached monument. It is the tallest in the chapel. Four-poster on thin square pillars covered with close and dainty arabesques. Diagonally outside the pillars four tall detached black columns with Corinthian capitals carrying supporters. The centre of the monument carries openwork strapwork and small obelisks. The lady wears the same curious hood as the others. Inscription plate against the E wall of the chapel.

William Lord Spencer † 1636 (NW part of the chapel). By *Nicholas Stone*. Completed in 1638. He received £600 for it (including apparently the materials) and paid £14 of this to *John Hargrave* for carving the effigy of the lord, £15 to *Richard White* for the effigy of the lady – not a very generous apportioning (but possibly these were only extra gratuities). Noble detached eight-poster. Black marble columns with white marble capitals, connected along the long sides by small arches. Tomb-chest of black and white marble. White effigies on a black moulded lid.

Sir Edward Spencer † 1655 (in the SE corner). 1656 by *John Stone*. Very curious indeed. Demi-figure rising out of the Urn of the Resurrection. To his r. the square pillar of the Word of God, to his l. the column of Truth. On it lies the Bible.

John Earl Spencer † 1783. By *Nollekens* (w of the bay-window).* A large hanging monument. Female figure standing on clouds and holding a medallion with the profile of the Earl, also on clouds. Big cornucopia at her feet. The poem ought to be read.

Georgiana Countess Spencer † 1814. By *Flaxman* (w wall), originally designed as a base to the Nollekens monument.

---

* The design is by *Cipriani*. The drawing is at Althorp; so Earl Spencer told Mr Bruce Bailey.

Big oblong tablet. Architecturally extremely simple. The inscription in the middle. To the l. Faith, to the r. a noble and lovable figure of Charity.

Capt. Sir Robert Cavendish Spencer (E of the bay-window). 1833 by *Chantrey*. White marble bust on plinth.

In addition numerous small brass coffin plates let into the floor of the bay-window, and many HELMS, CORONETS, SWORDS, GAUNTLETS, and HATCHMENTS.

CHURCHYARD CROSS in the churchyard, with concave-sided shaft.

OLD RECTORY. By *Blore*, c. 1822 (Murray), picturesque Tudor with a polygonal tower and spire at the back.

GREAT CRANSLEY see CRANSLEY

7070

GREAT CREATON

ST MICHAEL. Short Dec w tower. Re-set in the N vestry a transomed C13 'low-side' lancet window. The surround of another in the chancel s wall. Windows lancet, Dec, and Perp, mostly renewed. Late C12 N doorway. One order of shafts, one waterleaf capital, the arch steeply pointed. The s aisle added in 1857.

(ALMSHOUSES. Founded 1825, rebuilt 1897. BB)

Pleasant village green.

(HIGHGATE HOUSE, ¾ m. s at Little Creaton. An C18 inn turned into quite an impressive late C19 Tudor residence. Now a conference centre. Good Italian wrought-iron gates. GI)

8060

GREAT DODDINGTON

ST NICHOLAS. The lower part of the tower is of the C12, with a round-headed window to the W as well as into the nave. The fine double-shafted w doorway was inserted about 1200, at the same time perhaps that the thin E buttresses were provided which are now cut into by the nave arcades. The tower top has a date 1737.* The rest of the church mostly early C14, except for a Norman scallop capital just inside the s doorway (not *in situ*). Windows with cusped intersected and with reticulated tracery. The chancel SEDILIA of c. 1300. There are three 'low-side' lancets and a priest's doorway.‡ The upper windows are

---

* But may only have been re-worked then.

‡ Mr Cromwell considers the priest's doorway and the adjoining 'low-side' window as of the late C12, one N lancet as E.E.

straight-headed and Dec. The E window is C19, but a correct restoration: four lights, with a top circle with three spherical triangles in it. Shafted inside. Tall s doorway with many fine continuous mouldings. Arcades of four bays dating from c. 1300. Octagonal piers, double-chamfered arches. On the s side one pier is earlier and probably re-used. It has a little nailhead. On the N side the Norman transept angle is recognizable. Triple-chamfered tower arch of c. 1300. – FONT COVER. C15, but much re-done. – SCREEN. Minor parts, re-used in various ways. – PULPIT. Jacobean, with two tiers of the usual short, broad, flat arches. – HOUR GLASS STAND. Also Jacobean. – STALLS. Four with poppy-heads and MISERICORDS with leaves etc. and a carver at work. – COMMUNION RAIL. With twisted balusters; late C17. – DOOR. The s door is of the C15; traceried and with original ironwork. – WALL PAINTING. Good Crucifixus with the Virgin and St John, a large head of Christ above (s of the chancel arch). – STAINED GLASS. Nave N: C14 coat of arms; nave S: C15 roundel. RM) – (SCULPTURE. Satan and the apple of Eden. Supposed to be late C12. In the vestry.) – PLATE. Cup and Cover Paten, 1569; Almsdish, 1683; Flagon, 1721.

VICARAGE (former Manor House). C17, small, of half-H shape and well preserved. In the recessed part the doorway with a four-centred head and the Hall window to its l. The projecting wings are gabled. No transomed windows. The staircase (with vertically symmetrical balusters) is original but not *in situ*.*

(TOP FARM. The main range possibly of 1588, with a re-used C14 window. In a wing with the date 1661 is an upper room with C17 panelling. J. T. Smith)

GREAT EVERDON see EVERDON

GREAT HARROWDEN

8070

ALL SAINTS. Of ironstone, except for the tower of grey ashlar. In the w wall of the nave the remains of a Norman window and the responds of the Norman tower arch. The tower was rebuilt in 1822. It had had a spire which, however, had collapsed in the C18. The rest is of the C14. The arcades are specially interesting, that on the s side having been blocked when the s aisle was demolished. Both arcades have the four-

* On the house a date stone 1510. I am grateful to the Rev. R. H. Cromwell for much information on Great Doddington.

shafts-and-four-hollows section which is so familiar from the Perp style, but both are clearly pre-Perp. The s arcade is earlier. The shafts are very fine, the hollows wide, and the capitals round. In the N arcade the shafts are stronger and the capitals polygonal. That may mean *c.* 1300 *v.* the mid C14. The intersected tracery of the s windows, which were re-set when the aisles were pulled down, bears out a date of about 1300. Dec chancel with beautifully slender two-light windows and a grand five-light E window. The tracery in both cases is reticulated. The NE vestry is also Dec. – SCREEN. Perp, of two-light divisions, the mullions reaching up into the apexes of the arches. Fine, crocketed ogee gables. – WALL PAINTING. Above the chancel arch. Doom, only partially recognizable. – (STAINED GLASS. Chancel s. Early C14 grisaille glass. RM) – PLATE. Cup, 1635; Paten, 1675. – BRASSES to William Harrowden † 1423 and wife. Fine large figures, 3 ft 7 in. long. The architectural surround has not survived.

HARROWDEN HALL. The dating is well documented. The house is not mentioned by Morton in 1712. Bridges about 1720 calls it 'new built', and rain-water heads proclaim 1719. But the panelling inside and two very boldly and largely detailed fireplaces look like 1690 at the latest. There is also a fireplace with the date 1667, and the wall paintings on the upper parts of the staircase in the *Verrio* style certainly look more at home about 1690 than about 1720.* The exterior on the other hand is clearly of *c.* 1720. Completely plain five-bay centre of two and a half storeys with three-bay two-storey attachments l. and r., equally plain. Fine staircase of *c.* 1719 with three stone balusters to the treads and carved tread-ends.‡

Very beautiful gardens. On the gatepiers and the fine iron GATES the Watson arms. Thomas Watson Wentworth, later first Marquess of Rockingham, bought the house in 1694. He died in 1723. In the gardens a CHAPEL built by the then Lord Vaux in 1905, a copy of the school at Higham Ferrers. Also

* E. Croft-Murray attributes the paintings to *Lanscroon*.

‡ Sir Gyles Isham points out that there is evidence to suggest that the present house was built on earlier foundations. (This might explain the off-centre entrance doorway.) J. A. Gotch noted that there were remnants of stone arches and vaulting in the cellars. It is possible that the late C17 interior features date from the time of Charles Knollys, Earl of Banbury, who inherited Harrowden in 1674 and sold it in 1694, and that they were re-used in the house of 1719. Sir Gyles suggests an attribution to *Francis Smith* for the latter work.

in the gardens three groups of LEAD STATUARY probably contemporary with the house, one of them a copy of *Giovanni da Bologna*'s Samson and the Philistine, now in the Victoria and Albert Museum, but formerly at Hovingham Hall, Yorkshire, and originally in Florence.

BARROW. W of a moated enclosure.

GREAT HOUGHTON

7050

ST MARY. Built in 1754 by *David Hiorne*, and alas restored by the younger *Hakewill* in 1878, when the Georgian windows received their painful Norman two-light subdivision. Fine W tower, strong and square, with an octagonal peripteral order of Tuscan columns at the top, each carrying a volute and a strange projecting piece of entablature which originally each carried an urn. The volutes lead up to a spire. Aisleless body of three bays, the middle bays stressed by pediments. Projecting chancel with an undetailed Venetian E window. Flat ceiling. – PLATE. Silver-gilt Cup, 1553, a rare date; Cover Paten, 1606; Paten, 1740. – MONUMENTS. Two tablets † 1778 and 1782 by *William Cox Sen.*; and two identical tablets, † 1825 and 1833, with inscriptions on flat urns.

GREAT OAKLEY

8080

ST MICHAEL. The church lies to the S of the house, in its grounds. Small C17 W tower with arched lights and battlements. Big nave roof of Collyweston stone slates, reaching on the S side right down to the eaves of the aisle. E wall also late C16 or C17 with four decorated battlements.* S arcade originally of three bays, then – soon after – lengthened to the W by another three, an odd enterprise. Both parts have octagonal piers and double-chamfered arches with foot-pieces. The earlier part has one capital with a little nailhead, i.e. is C13, the later may be of the C14. The only original early window is in the N wall of the nave. Two lights and a lozenge over, i.e. late C13. In the same wall a low tomb recess.‡ – SCREEN. Perp, and remains of another re-used in the S pew and the stall fronts. – STALLS. From Pipewell Abbey. Four with little heads on the arm ends and MISERICORDS of Father Time with the Scythe and Hour Glass, a head, an angel, and a pelican. – COMMUNION RAIL. Jacobean, with vertically symmetrical

---

* On the porch roof medieval ridge tiles (J. Steane).

‡ The church was restored by *Slater* (N. Taylor).

balusters. – (STAINED GLASS. Chancel N. Two angels' heads, early C16. Flemish or German? RM) – MONUMENT. Sir Richard Brooke de Capell Brooke † 1829. With a draped cross. By *Francis* of London.

GREAT OAKLEY HALL. Bridges gives the date as 1555, a credible date. The original house was L-shaped, with the Hall in the recessed wing. The S wing was added in 1893. The original work has all mullioned windows with arched lights and hood-moulds. The recessed centre has five bays in three storeys, all windows on the ground floor and the first floor of four lights. The centre is divided by a slight step back. To the l. of it ashlar, to the r. rendered. To the l. the top storey has three-light, to the r. four-light windows. The Hall was evidently single-storeyed from the beginning. Four gables connected each time by one semicircular merlon (cf. Dingley). Finial on each gable. Elaborate porch with coupled, bulgy, fluted Doric pilasters, a round-headed entrance, shields to its l. and r., and a heavy balcony. Can all that be of 1555 too? It is more than unlikely. The interior nowhere in its original state. Jacobean parts of overmantels. Some pretty C18 plasterwork (*c.* 1750) and fireplaces. C18 staircase with twisted balusters. Much Victorian alteration by Bishop Trollope, who placed verses from the Bible wherever he could find places for them and added much highly Elizabethan detail.

(Victorian FOUNTAIN from Market Harborough, re-erected in 1962. GI)

ROMAN BUILDING. The stone foundations of an aisled building have been excavated 1¼ m. NE of Great Oakley. The building was 112 ft long by 41 ft wide and dated to the first half of the C2 A.D. In the second half of the century a roughly circular hut was erected over one corner of the building.

7080   GREAT OXENDON

ST HELEN. Oddly proportioned W tower. Buttresses only below, upper parts receding in steps. Battlements; pinnacles. The tower arch has capitals with flowers. Exterior of the rest of the church varied, but no feature of individual interest. Inside, C13 S arcade, early C14 N arcade, the former with circular piers, circular capitals and abaci, and double-chamfered arches, the latter with quatrefoil piers with ballflower enrichment. Half-arches are thrown across the N aisle. Early C14 chancel arch, renewed. – FONT. Of tub shape; Norman, with

raw vertical zigzag. – STAINED GLASS. E window 1870 by
Powell. The single figures in the tracery lights deserve notice. –
PLATE. Paten, *c.* 1682; Cup, 1696.

MILL MOUND. N of the village.

GREAT WELDON

9080

ST MARY. Internally older than externally. Later C13 S arcade
of three bays with quatrefoil piers, stiff-leaf capitals, and an
arch with one chamfer and two fine rolls, one with a fillet. In
the same style the S chapel. In it SEDILIA with shafts and
filleted arches. The chancel SEDILIA are similar. Triple shafts.
At the E end of the S chapel a tall early C14 squint with
crocketed gable and finial. The N arcade is Perp. Piers with a
hollow chamfer towards nave and aisle and shafts towards the
arch openings. Only the latter have capitals (cf. Lowick). The
N chapel was added in 1862.* Externally to the same period as
the S arcade etc. belongs the sumptuous S porch. Entrance
arch with filleted rolls. Wall arcading with triple shafts. The S
aisle windows point to *c.* 1300–20, i.e. have cusped intersected
as well as reticulated tracery. Reticulated also the tracery of
the chancel S window. Flowing tracery in the N aisle W and E
windows. The N windows are straight-headed, but also Dec.
Pretty frieze of tiny heads at the top of the wall. Battlements,
also on the S aisle, S porch, and clerestory. Dec also was the W
tower, see the doorway, but it was rebuilt at an unknown date
in the C18. Unbuttressed. Bell-openings round-arched with
round-arched lights and a circle over. Obelisk pinnacles.
Handsome glazed, wooden cupola with a scrolly iron weathercock. – REREDOS. S aisle. Perp. A horizontal band of blank
tracery. – BRACKET. Fine Perp bracket against the N side of
the chancel arch. – STAINED GLASS. In the W window a complete Flemish early C16 representation of the Adoration of the
Magi. According to Murray, once a gift from Sir William
Hamilton to Nelson. It was installed here in 1897. – (In the
vestry, heads of *c.* 1350 and an early C16 figure. RM)

LOCKUP. On the green, circular, with a conical roof. Probably
C18.

MANOR HOUSE, E of the church. Late C17. Symmetrical range
of three bays with gabled porch. Mullioned windows. Projecting wing on the r., also with mullioned windows.

* Restoration designs were published by *Preedy* in *The Ecclesiologist* in
1861 (R. Hubbuck).

HAUNT HILL HOUSE, W of the church, on the A43. Date-stones 1636 and 1643. It was built by *Humphrey Frisbey*, one of a local family of masons. The house might well be called a folly, if one sees it only from the s. The front is symmetrical, of three bays, with low mullioned and transomed windows and a porch with an ogee-headed doorway. But the s, i.e. the gable, side has fat volutes l. and r. of the ground-floor as well as the first-floor windows, and in the gable a stepped three-light window. The whole would not surprise somewhere near Halifax or Huddersfield.

The Weldon limestone quarries were reopened recently. Weldon stone was widely used in the Middle Ages and later. The workings are to be seen on either side of the A43, w of the village.

(Many good stone HOUSES* and two INNS, one late C16 or early C17, the other with attractive bay-windows of *c.* 1740. L. M. Gotch)

ROMAN VILLA. Chapel Field, on the N side of the A 42, 150 yds N of Ise Brook, marks a site first discovered in 1738 and re-examined in 1955–6. Within an area 380 by 240 ft was a N-facing main block with attendant buildings, enclosed by a courtyard wall with an arched entrance. This was preceded by two earlier structures: a wooden building of the C1–2 A.D., and a half-timbered block built *c.* 200 A.D. The third and main building phase was in the C4 A.D. The frontage of the N–S corridor block, which contained two mosaic-decorated rooms, measured *c.* 100 ft.‡ Behind it was a separate circular workshop, 27 ft in diameter, containing a furnace perhaps for ironsmith-ing. To the s was a separate bath suite, 46 ft long, which underwent several alterations during the course of the settle-ment's occupation. In the SE corner of the yard was a 120-ft-long stable, to the w of which was a section of paving perhaps related to the second building period. To the NE was a barn measuring 64 by 28 ft. This was twice burnt. In a w enlarge-ment constructed between the fires, a coin of A.D. 388 was found; this and a scattered hoard of coins belonging to the mid C4 mark the end of the settlement. 25 yds N of the main block were found two inhumation burials, one with C4 Castor ware.

* Many of these now derelict (1972). The King's Arms has been de-molished.

‡ One of the pavements is now on a wall of the administrative block of the British Steel Corporation, Corby (J. Steane).

GREATWORTH

St Peter. Externally of no architectural interest. W tower, nave, and chancel. The lower part of the W tower is of *c.* 1300 (see the arch towards the nave). The chancel is of the C13 (see the pointed window). The chancel arch by *H. R. Gough*, 1882. – plate. Cup, 1570; Paten, 1633; two Cups, 1688.* – monument. Charles Howe † 1741. A most Rococo conceit. Asymmetrical cartouche and asymmetrical surround, as if to fit into the spandrel between an arch and a straight wall. The carver must have enjoyed this restriction.‡

Gatepiers. The Manor House at Greatworth was destroyed by fire in 1793. The gatepiers remain, and especially the inner ones, with their wondrously large pineapple finials, are splendid things.

GREEN'S NORTON

St Bartholomew. Interesting Saxon remains, namely the long-and-short work of the NW and SW quoins of a tall and wide nave and the jambs of a window now high up in the E wall of the nave above the chancel arch. This has a triangular head (not visible from the nave). There are also traces of blocked windows above the N arcade (H. M. and J. Taylor). Next to this in interest is the W tower, whose upper parts (pointed bell-openings with Gibbs surrounds) were repaired probably after 1718, when the tower and spire were described as cracked and dangerous. The spire was rebuilt in 1807 and again in 1957. Chancel rebuilt in 1890–1, when the church was restored by *Edmund Law*. Flowing tracery in the N and S windows. Arcades inside which prove that the church at some stage was cruciform. The first two bays are separated from the third by pieces of wall where the W arch of the crossing (i.e. the Saxon wall) ran. The third bays opened into transepts. The arcades have octagonal piers and double-chamfered arches. – font. Circular, Norman, decorated with beaded lozenges filled with flowers. – pulpit. With Jacobean panels. – stained glass. E window by *Kempe*, 1896. Two more, later Kempe windows. – plate. Cup, 1570; Paten, *c.* 1636; Breadholder, 1723. – monuments. Brass to Lady Greene (Sir Thomas † 1417). The figure is 20 in. long (S aisle E). –

---

* A Flagon of 1688 was sold in 1960.

‡ The composition is not unique, cf. e.g. Norwich, St Giles and Melton Constable, Norfolk.

Sir Thomas Greene † 1457 and wife. Alabaster effigies. – Sir Thomas Greene † 1462. Brasses of good quality, 3 ft 6 in. long. The monument is inside a big recess with a four-centred arch. The tomb-chest has shields in pointed quatrefoils. – William Hicklinge † 1606, but the monument must be of c. 1620–30. It is good enough for *Nicholas Stone*.* Small kneeling figures below a baldacchino which curves forward. The draperies are lifted up by two fine large standing angels, in the best Netherlandish Mannerist tradition. At the foot two corbels in the shape of caryatid heads with Ionic capitals.

BENGAL MANOR. 1698. The elegant doorway is of 1934, but the windows and the four oval windows in the W gable are original. Is the spiked frieze of brick original too? Good gate-piers.

Near Green's Norton are two of the farms built by the Grafton estate about 1840 (*see* Introduction, p. 67). They are CAS-WELL and FIELD BURCOTE, and they are characterized by a house of three widely spaced bays with a low-pitched, hipped slate roof and lower wings, the whole very formally arranged. In addition Grafton farms may have a pedimental gable or a doorway with columns, a metope frieze, and a pediment.

8060.

GRENDON

ST MARY. The story of the church begins inside. The first three bays on both sides are Late Norman. W imposts with many scallops, circular piers with many slightly enriched scallops, circular abaci – an early case (but cf. Holy Sepulchre, North-ampton) – and unmoulded round arches. Next in order of time the late C12 S doorway with one order of shafts carrying simple moulded capitals and an arch with a thick roll moulding and a flat face decorated with saltire crosses and palmette leaf. Early C13 the simple N doorway close to a pair of lancets. The E bays of the arcade come after that, Dec presumably. Much taller with octagonal piers and double-chamfered arches. The pointed trefoil-headed PISCINA in the S aisle wall must be earlier, but the chancel may well be contemporary – see the chancel arch, the crocketed SEDILIA, the simple EASTER SEPULCHRE, and the tall (much renewed) straight-headed

* Mr John Goff has kindly drawn my attention to a family connexion that provides some circumstantial evidence in support of an attribution to Nicholas Stone: William Hicklinge's wife's brother married into the Spencer family, and Stone was employed on the tomb of William Lord Spencer (*see* Great Brington, p. 231).

two-light windows. Two of them are of the 'low-side' type. C14 S porch. Perp W tower, of banded brown and grey stone. Money was left to the fabric of the *campanile* in 1453. Tall arch towards the nave. Slim diagonal buttresses. Big doorway and W window. Battlements, pinnacles. – PLATE. Cup and Cover Paten, 1655. – BRASS. Lady and two Knights, late C15.

GRENDON HALL (County Youth Centre). Fine E front, early C18. Three-bay centre and two-bay projections, restrained detail, doorway with segmental arch, quoins, hipped roof. The S side of four bays corresponds. The N side is older, probably later C17. Mullioned windows with straight architraves (no longer hood-moulds). The transomed staircase windows create a break in their pattern. Pedimented dormers. Inside some rooms with early C18 panelling. Staircase with twisted balusters, rather late C17 than early C18. Stables to the N of the house, and oblong dovecote to their N, both C18. The stables were converted into a residential block by the County Architect's Department (*A. N. Harris*), 1964.

Off MANOR ROAD, to the SW of the church, the PARSONAGE, 1850 by *S. S. Teulon*, picturesque Tudor with an odd lantern with cupola, then MANOR FARM HOUSE, C17, handsome, gabled, with mullioned windows. (A house NW of the church has a garden porch created from an archway from Holdenby. Archway flanked by Corinthian pilasters. Previously in St Giles Street Northampton. BB)

GRETTON

9090

ST JAMES. The story starts with an aisleless Early Norman church of which two blocked windows remain in a fragmentary state. There follows soon, about 1130, the W part of the N arcade, with a circular pier, capitals with three and four scallops, a square abacus, and arches with fat rolls. The W part of the S arcade follows after that, a little later, but still Norman. The difference in time can be measured by the development at Peterborough Cathedral. The difference in form is that the scallops are livelier. In the C13 both aisles were extended to the E and a new chancel and new transepts built. Evidence of the C13 chancel is the blocked lancet windows on the S side.* The puzzling thing about the transepts is that they are not in line with the E bay of the arcades. Does that indicate that they

---

* The chancel was raised by four steps in the C18, when the Hatton family vault was established.

were a rebuilding of Norman transepts? But they can hardly
have been in line with the Norman nave to which the W bays
of the arcade were added. In detail the new E bay has on the N
side a round pier and round abacus, on the S an octagonal pier.
The E respond has nailhead decoration here. Both arcade extensions have pointed double-chamfered arches. In the N
transept there are one E lancet window and three stepped
(renewed) single N lancets. In the S transept are an E lancet,
remains of a W lancet visible from inside, and, inside also, some
sumptuous and baffling arcading. One arch, trefoiled with a
pointed moulding to the N. Stiff-leaf capitals and dog-tooth.
A second at r. angles to it, to the E, was probably a squint.
It has dog-tooth decoration too, but the arch-head is simply a
curved line rising to the l. to join up with the arch round the
corner. Next in order of time the chancel E window of four
lights with reticulated tracery, i.e. of a Dec date, and the
equally Dec clerestory. The clerestory windows are foiled
circles and cusped spherical triangles. Finally the W tower,
which is of ironstone and Perp, and the short ironstone arches
which connect the arcades with it. The tower is tall and has
slender clasping buttresses. Two-light bell-openings with
transom. Ashlar battlements and pinnacles. – FONT. Octagonal, Perp, with shields and panelling. – SCREEN. Jacobean,
with vertically symmetrical balusters. Now in the tower arch. –
COMMUNION RAIL. Of c. 1700, with strong balusters. – Some
Jacobean PANELLING in the N transept. – C18 chancel
PANELLING, PULPIT, and BOX PEWS, handsomely receding
in a curve to the l. and r. to leave more space in front of the
chancel. – PLATE. Silver-gilt set, 1638. – MONUMENTS. The
Ladies Hatton, 1684 by *William Stanton*. Two identical tablets with draperies and a cherub's head at the foot. – Viscount
Hatton † 1706. Grey sarcophagus. Two cherubs on white
volutes. White obelisk and inscription.

STOCKS AND WHIPPING POST, on the Green S of the
church.

NATIONAL SCHOOL, SE of the church. 1853. Five bays, one
storey; classical.

HOUSES. A house W of the church has mullioned windows and
one horizontal oval window, i.e. must be late C17. Another on
the way to Great Weldon is dated 1699, and also has such an
oval window.

GRETTON HOUSE in the High Street is Georgian (five bays,
two storeys) but has a large neo-Jacobean addition. Opposite

is MANOR FARM, with mullioned windows and bands of iron-stone, dated 1675.

HARBOROUGH HILL HOUSE, ¼ m. N. An arch from Kirby Hall is built into the w side. Rusticated pilasters and spandrels. Archway with ears and volutes. Shield in cartouche with swags – i.e. the 1640 phase of Kirby.

GUILSBOROUGH

6070

ST ETHELREDA. w tower and spire E.E. in style, but the spire dated 1618, and the complete structure probably all of this date. The bell-openings are two lancets.* Low broaches, spire with two tiers of lucarnes. Arcades of four bays with octagonal piers and double-chamfered arches with cone-shaped foot-pieces. Chancel arch with fleurons in the capitals and double-hollow-chamfered arches. The nave roof has the low pitch usual in the county, tie-beams, and carved corbels and bosses, mainly with big heads. – (FONT of terracotta, Perp. Dated 1823. According to Wetton's *Guide*, by *Grimes*, 'an amateur'. BB) – REREDOS and ALTAR SURROUND. These are Gothic of 1846. The PEWS of 1815 include some in rising tiers at the w end of the aisles. – (TILES of 1868.) – STAINED GLASS. The chancel windows are by *Morris* and *Burne-Jones*. They commemorate Adelaide Countess Spencer † 1877. Much transparent glass with dainty Gothic patterns. In the E and N windows the figures stand isolated against these patterned quarries, in the s window they have a pale brown background panel. The subject of the E window is Christ crucified, with the Virgin and St John. – s aisle SE and s by *Morris & Co.* after Morris and Burne-Jones were dead and the original inspiration had left the firm. – N aisle E by *Burlison & Grylls*, 1894. – PLATE. Two silver-gilt Cups, *c.* 1650; two silver-gilt Patens, *c.* 1700; silver-gilt Flagon, *c.* 1750. – MONUMENTS. Thomas Lucas † 1756. Obelisk with inscription in a medallion on it. Signed by *Henry Cox* of Northampton. – Also several other tablets, with and without obelisks, by *Samuel Cox Sen.* († 1741), *Wiliam Cox Sen.*, and *Henry Cox.*

GUILSBOROUGH HALL. Demolished in 1959.

GUILSBOROUGH HOUSE, E of the church, on the main road. An C18 part of two storeys and five bays with a later E addition.

GRAMMAR SCHOOL. Converted into flats (1972). Founded by Sir John Langham of Cottesbrooke in 1668. It was a most

* Double-lancet bell-openings appear also at St Giles Northampton, 1619, and Wicken, 1617 (BB).

generous foundation as C17 schools went – for fifty boys, a master, and an usher – and the building is correspondingly large. It is of ironstone, seven bays wide, with a middle porch of four storeys and to the l. of it one storey, plus another behind the dormers, and on the r. two plus one. The part to the l. of the porch was the Master's House, that to the r. was the Schoolroom, with bedrooms above.* The windows are mullioned in the dormers, mullioned and transomed otherwise. The porch doorway is round-headed. The sides of the porch on the ground floor have vertically placed oval openings. It leads to a passage at whose end was the projecting staircase, going up square in a narrow well through all floors. Square, tapering balusters.‡ The style of the building is decidedly conservative. No echo can yet be heard from Lamport Hall, or even semi-classical mid-century endeavours.

ROSE MANOR, at the NE end of the village. 1686. Of ironstone. A very handsome five-bay front of two storeys. Two-light, upright, mullioned wooden windows. Doorway broad, with a pediment. In the frieze below it the date and horizontal laurel leaves l. and r.

In the village several Late Georgian brick houses which deserve a glance, e.g. the SUN INN and a house facing the GREEN, both of which have the Midland motif of the middle bay being stressed by a blank giant arch.

COMPREHENSIVE SCHOOL, at the NW entry. 1955–9 by the County Architect's Department (County Architect *A. N. Harris*). Very different from the normal architectural character of mid-C20 schools in England. An oblong two-storeyed block, faced in its upper storey with stone from the demolished Guilsborough Hall, with a tower in a notched-out corner crowned by an odd top, with one-storeyed attachments for laboratories, for kitchens etc., and for library etc., and with formal fenestration in pairs of upright windows. (Large extension by *John Goff*, 1967–8. Three storeys, curtain walling and brown concrete panels.)

7070   HANGING HOUGHTON
                        ½ m. sw of Lamport

SCHOOL HOUSE. Built in 1775 according to the will of Sir Edmund Isham. Seven bays, two storeys.
(THE LODGE. By *J. Milne*, 1837. GI)

---

* See M. Seaborne: *The English School*, 1971, p. 67.
‡ The staircase is to be re-erected elsewhere.

HANNINGTON

8070

ST PETER AND ST PAUL. A two-naved late C13 church, and as 28
such a great rarity in England.* On the Continent occasional
examples can be found in Germany (St Nicholas Soest, St
Eucharius Nuremberg), and the Blackfriars had not infre-
quently adopted the two-naved plan (e.g. Paris, Toulouse,
Frankfurt, Pirna) which may derive from monastic rather than
church buildings. At Hannington, which at the time was in the
gift of Sempringham, the Gilbertine mother house, the two-
naved plan is specially interestingly handled. There are two
tall circular piers with circular abaci and double-chamfered
arches. The E arch runs against the wall above the chancel
arch, the W arch against the projection in the W wall which
corresponds to the slender W tower. When this received its
bell-openings the Dec style had arrived. The windows of the
rest of the church have consistently intersected tracery, i.e. on
the N and S sides and in the chancel. The SEDILIA in the chancel
have dog-tooth decoration. Only the S doorway with its round
arch with two slight chamfers and its simple capitals is
evidence of a predecessor of the present church. It must be of
c. 1180–90. – PULPIT and SCREEN. Perp, with the same
dainty tracery. Probably by the same carver. – PLATE. Cup
and Cover Paten, c. 1570.

(HANNINGTON HOUSE, the former Rectory. Stone; 1861. BB)

HARDINGSTONE see NORTHAMPTON, p. 353

HARDWICK

8060

ST LEONARD. Unbuttressed C13 W tower. Lancet in the W wall.
Two-light bell-openings. Battlements. C13 also the S arcade of
four bays. Circular piers, circular abaci, double-chamfered
arches. C13 the original chancel too, see the 'low-side' lancet,
the priest's doorway, and the chancel arch. Dec windows
(mostly renewed), also in the clerestory.‡ – PULPIT. 1860, with
a display of mosaic. – STAINED GLASS. In the W window
damaged figure of a saint; C14? – PLATE. Cup and Cover
Paten, 1570. – MONUMENT. Sir Francis Nicolls † 1642. Brass
panel with kneeling figures in an alabaster surround.

---

* But cf. Stretford in Herefordshire of the early or mid C13, Wootton
Bassett, Wiltshire, also C13, and Caythorpe, Lincolnshire, early C14.

‡ Restoration designs by *Slater* were published in *The Ecclesiologist* in
1867 (R. Hubbuck).

MANOR HOUSE. In the NE gable a two-light C14 window. In the SE gable a Jacobean bow-window, shallow and heavily detailed. Its top floor recedes slightly. (Inside a wooden overmantel with Ionic pilasters. VCH)

HARGRAVE

0070

ALL SAINTS. Mostly C13. The earliest piece is the s doorway, shafted prettily with one order in front of two others, and with half-dog-tooth, dog-tooth, and horizontal chevrons in two orders in the arch. The hood-mould rests on twisted corbels. Then the arcades, of four bays, of which the fourth represents former transepts. Circular and octagonal piers. Double-chamfered arches. The E responds run together with the chancel arch. The W tower* has an excessively tall lancet window, two-light shafted bell-openings, and a broach spire with two tiers of lucarnes in the cardinal directions and the third in the diagonals. Some of the windows are also of the C13, e.g. N aisle w, s aisle E, and one s. Cf. also the N doorway and the chancel s doorway. – FONT. Octagonal, C13, with small faces on two sides. – SCREEN. Perp, one-light divisions. – BENCHES with tracery on the ends and the fronts and backs of whole blocks. Also linenfold panelling on some ends. – WALL PAINTINGS. Traces of a St Christopher on the N wall of the nave. – (STAINED GLASS. Nave. C14 and C15 fragments. RM) – PLATE. Cup and Cover Paten, 1618.

7060

HARLESTONE

ST ANDREW. The church is all Dec – with the exception of the Late Perp clerestory and the E window, which is in the style of 1275 and was designed by *Sir G. G. Scott*, who restored the church in 1853. The Dec work, has the privilege, rare in parish churches, of being datable. In his estate-book, Henry de Bray, who owned the manor in the early C14, writes: 'Magister Ricardus de Het [the rector] ipse de novo fecit cancellam A.D. 1320.' He adds that 'tota ecclesia facta fuit', A.D. 1325, he himself providing the stone and timber and Johannes Dyve the carpenter's work. Dec the unbuttressed w tower, though evidently earlier than the rest. The tower arch is quadruple-chamfered. The bell-openings are two pointed-trefoiled arches under one arch. Henry de Bray records in fact

---

* Rebuilt in 1868–70.

the purchase of the bell-rope in 1294. Dec the tall s doorway with its continuous mouldings and the reticulated tracery of the s windows, Dec the more restored N windows, and also the N doorway. The chancel has two transomed 'low-side' lancets, that on the N better preserved. SEDILIA with cusped arches and crocketed gables. The PISCINA is in the SE angle and rests on a big head corbel. Arcades of two bays with octagonal piers and double-hollow-chamfered arches. The responds are concave-sided (cf. Great Brington). Below the chancel a CRYPT of two bays with chamfered ribs in the vault. – FONT. Circular, plain, but from the foot project four heads. Early C13? – PULPIT. This incorporates fine Flemish panels of c. 1500. – COMMUNION RAIL. Jacobean, with vertically symmetrical balusters. – WEST GALLERY. Above the tower arch. Later C17, with fat vertically symmetrical balusters. – STAINED GLASS. E window by *Burlison & Grylls*, 1897. – PLATE. Cup and Paten, 1824. – MONUMENTS. (Portrait bust of a man with flowing hair, part of a lost memorial to Robert Andrew † 1667, recorded by Baker.) – Many tablets, including Sir Salathiel Lovell † 1713 by *Edward Stanton*, with Ionic columns and an urn; Robert Andrew † 1739, coloured marble; probably by *Smith* of Warwick (*see* Lamport). – Lady Lovell † 1718 with Corinthian pilasters and baldacchino, probably also by *Stanton*, and Maria Townsend † 1743, a copy of the former monument.

RECTORY. Of c. 1700. Two gabled parts and a slightly recessed centre. Quoins. Finely framed doorway. The window above it connected with it and distinguished by leaf volutes.

HARLESTONE HOUSE was demolished in 1940, but the big Palladian STABLES remain, just above the church. There is a ground plan of house, offices, stables, gardens, etc., at Althorp, signed by *Humphry and John Adey Repton*, 1808–11. The grounds are indeed referred to in Humphry Repton's 'Fragments' of 1816. The stables have the familiar quadrangle with corner pavilions with pyramid roofs (cf. e.g. Courteenhall). Harlestone House is one candidate for Jane Austen's Mansfield Park.

Also near the church the SCHOOL by *Devey*,* and the RECTORY, a substantial early C18 house, H-shaped. Central doorway with eared surround linked to an upper window with volutes and pediment. On the A28 Althorp ESTATE HOUSING of

* Information from Earl Spencer.

c. 1850, and the FOX AND HOUNDS, Late Georgian, five bays. The OLD MALTING HOUSE opposite is a conversion from outbuildings (1972).

At UPPER HARLESTONE, 1¼ m. SW of the church, weather-boarded VILLAGE HALL of 1924, GRAFTON HOUSE, L-shaped with mullioned windows, and PARK FARM HOUSE, after 1834, of five bays and two storeys, ironstone with quoins. At the W end, a DOVECOTE, probably of the C15. Circular, of two stages separated by a bold string-course. Conical roof.

SHARAOH. On the N side of the stream to the E of Nobottle Wood, beside the road from Bannaventa (*see* Whilton) to Duston, which runs through Nobottle Belt, lies a ROMAN BUILDING which was partially excavated in 1927–9. It consisted of a rectangular block on heavy foundations. In the building was found a large hoard of 814 coins, ranging in date from the reign of Hadrian to Honorius. The majority lay within the late C4 A.D. The pottery, on the other hand, was mostly of the C2 A.D., with a little 'terra sigillata'.

6060   HARPOLE

ALL SAINTS. Norman the S doorway (decorated capitals, single-step arch), the S chancel doorway (waterleaf capitals, single-step arch), and the chancel arch (scalloped capitals). Of *c.* 1200 the N doorway (moulded capitals, pointed arch with one step and one slight chamfer) and the N aisle W lancet. Of the C13 the W tower (quadruple-chamfered arch, on the W front above the doorway three blank arches, bell-openings of two lancets, corbel table, later battlements and pinnacles), the chancel arch, and the N chapel. In this twin tomb recesses with pretty leaf capitals of *c.* 1300. Dec arcades of three wide bays, short octagonal piers, double-chamfered arches. The detail of the N arcade is more primitive. Perp chancel windows. – FONT. Norman, circular, very closely entwined leaf trails and dragons; a remarkable tangle. – PLATE. Cup and Paten, 1737; Breadholders, 1779 and 1786.

(HARPOLE HALL. Early C19 with massive Doric porch. GI)

HOUSES. At the SE end of the village a sequence of good houses. One (No. 35) has a porch on primitive pillars. Mullioned windows are continued into the C18; but a house of 1731 has them no longer.

ROMAN REMAINS. (1) ¾ m. N of the village and the same

distance SE of the Harlestone villa, on the S side of the Duston branch road, is the site of an extensive building with tessellated flooring. Excavations in 1966 revealed the SE corner of the villa where a C4 structure overlay C2 robbed walls. 40 ft to the E a Roman stone cistern was discovered during road widening. (2) SE of the village and W of Halfway House is a villa site examined in 1846–9. It contained a fine polychrome square mosaic with central Greek cross. Considerable tesserae and other building materials, together with potsherds, can still be picked up in the area.

HARRINGTON   7070

ST PETER AND ST PAUL. S tower of 1809 with round-arched bell-openings, attached to the S transept. The rest externally almost entirely Perp. Ironstone, but the tower grey ashlar, with ironstone buttresses, a curious idea. The interior shows that the church was originally aisleless and had transepts. The W walls of the transepts were partly caught on corbels when the aisles were built. The N corbel is of simple but playful shape. The narrow aisles are of the early to mid C14. Arcades of four bays. Quatrefoil piers, the foils connected in a single curve by a deep hollow. At the W corner of the transept sexfoil piers instead. The quatrefoil piers have fine capitals with big leaves, standing or lying. The sexfoiled piers have moulded capitals instead. The arcade arches with two hollow chamfers, and the chancel and transept arches the same. All this fits a date c. 1300–50. – SCREEN. Tall, of two-light divisions, each with a middle mullion reaching up into the apex of the arch. Much fine tracery and crocketing. – TILES. In the chancel, called Norman, but of the C14 to C16.* – VAMPING HORN (cf. Braybrooke). 5 ft long. – PLATE. Paten, 1696; Cup, 1834. – MONUMENTS. Laurence Saunders † 1545. Grey marble. Tomb-chest with three shields in lozenges. The arch of the recess almost a lintel. Jambs and soffit panelled. Back wall with kneeling brass figures (15 in. tall). – Saunders Monument, dated 1588. Not in its original state. Of very fine quality. The 54 family in relief is represented kneeling on two panels facing each other. Two allegorical figures called Spes and Fides in shallow niches to the l. and r. Fine foliage at the top. Very little strapwork is used.

* Letter from Miss Nora Whitcomb.

(EARTHWORKS. Extensive remains of terraces and fishponds.
There was a preceptory of the Hospitallers of St John on the
site, and later a large house erected by Lord Stanhope. The
latter was demolished in 1740. GI)

₉₀₉₀   # HARRINGWORTH

ST JOHN BAPTIST. The W tower must have been begun before
1200, see the waterleaf capitals and the pointed arch with two
steps and one chamfer towards the nave. Clasping buttresses,
lancets below, twin bell-openings of two lights separated by a
shaft. Spire with low broaches. Big heads above the broaches.
Three tiers of lucarnes. They look early C14. Wide nave and
chancel. The chancel arch and doorway are of c. 1300, but the
rest of the chancel is Perp. Big five-light E window and big
gargoyles. Early C14 S aisle, S porch, and N aisle and arcades.
The windows range from two lights with a circle or a spherical
triangle or a pointed quatrefoil to reticulated tracery. Dog-
tooth on the S porch entrance. Handsome early C14 N doorway with shafting inside as well as outside. The S doorway
also early C14, but partly blocked when a smaller C15 doorway
was set in, with big leaves in the spandrels. The nave is wide,
and the arcades have low octagonal piers and double-chamfered arches. Dec SEDILIA and PISCINA in the S aisle below a
straight-headed Dec window. – FONT. Square, with two
shallow ogee arches on each side, c. 1300. – PULPIT. Dated
1605, of the usual type with broad blank arches in the panels.
Brought from Barrowden, Rutland. – SCREEN. Perp, tall, with
one-light divisions and ribbed coving. – PANELLING. Some
of Jacobean date. – BENCH ENDS. Some square-headed Perp
bench ends with tracery, loose at the W end of the S aisle. –
HELMET. In the N aisle. From the monument to Lord George
Zouche † 1569 in the former family chapel between church
and manor house. – (STAINED GLASS. Chancel. C14 fragments and C15 angel's head. RM) – PLATE. Cup and Cover
Paten, 1570; Cup and Paten, two Flagons, and Breadholder,
1705. – MONUMENTS. In the N aisle, sunk by some steps, the
family vault of the Tryons, the platform on top raised by four
steps. The vault was built c. 1650. Excellent wrought-iron
RAILINGS. Only one monument need be mentioned: to four
generations of Tryons, probably c. 1710. Hanging monument
with two standing cherubs, two cherubs' heads at the foot.
Garlands and a shield at the top.*

* Mr Bailey suggests an attribution to the *Stanton* yard.

VILLAGE CROSS. Possibly erected in 1387. Shaft of eight clustered shafts of alternating girth. Capital and square abacus. The top of 1837.

SWAN INN. With a blocked two-centred archway and windows with arched lights; early C16.

OLD MANOR HOUSE, NE of the church. Of the medieval manor house of the Zouches, originally much larger than the present building, there survives on the first floor of the S range one two-light window with cusped ogee heads. Behind is a shorter parallel range with mullioned windows. (C17 staircase inside. DOE)

MANOR HOUSE, N of the Swan Inn and S of the church. Late C17, five bays, two storeys, cross-windows, hipped roof, flat quoins, rusticated door surround.

COTTAGE, at the corner of the Laxton and Uppingham roads. With a C14 or C15 chimney.

WELLAND VIADUCT. Brick, of eighty-two arches, about ¾ m. long; 1874–9. The viaduct dominates the whole W aspect of the village.

HARTWELL   7050

ST JOHN BAPTIST. 1851, by *C. Vickers & Hugall* (GR). Neo-Norman with a lower neo-E.E. chancel. Ornately carved S doorway. The arcade inside is original work of the latest C12. Four bays. Circular piers, square abaci. Capitals with leaves and dragons, stiff-leaf crockets, and less foliate crockets. Unmoulded round arches.

HASELBECH   7070

ST MICHAEL. The W tower is Perp.* It has pairs of two-light bell-openings with an ogee super-arch. Quatrefoil frieze, battlements, of the pinnacles only the stumps. Most windows are new, but the W windows of the aisles seem original C13 work. The arcades inside are low, of three bays. They both have quatrefoil piers, but the N arcade, where the four foils are more like independent shafts, is C13, the S arcade C14. The capitals are not consistent. Both arcades have double-chamfered arches. The eastern parts are all C19. N chapel 1872 (by *Salvin*, built for Viscountess Milton, who painted the windows herself. They are not good. BB). Chancel restored by *W. Slater*, 1859–60, and elaborated by *Butler*, 1881. Very ornate

* Mr Bailey suggests a date of *c.* 1500 (cf. Arthingworth and Desborough).

French Gothic decoration. The carving of all the details, with stiff-leaf, animals, birds, and portrait heads, was done by *J. Forsyth*, at the expense of Elizabeth Pym. Equally ornate s chapel. With arms surrounded by Gothic ornament in the gable outside and a SE entrance. – PULPIT. Jacobean, complete with back panel and tester. – BENCH ENDS. Perp. With two tracery panels to each end and framing buttresses. – (TOWER SCREEN. Elaborate; continental Gothic in style, one panel dated 1842. BB) – CHANCEL GATE. Tall. Of wrought iron, C18, of domestic origin. – (STAINED GLASS. E window by *Alan Younger*, 1966. R. Hubbuck) – PLATE. Paten, 1683; Cup, 1706; Flagon, 1727. – MONUMENTS. George Ashby † 1802. By *Benjamin Button*. Pretty. – (Albert Pell † 1907. Delightful iron work at the base. BB) – Charles Bower Ismay † 1924. In the churchyard, N of the tower. Block-like sarcophagus with an incised frieze of animals, rather Egyptian in inspiration. By *A. H. Gerrard*.

HASELBECH HALL.* N front of three bays and three storeys, with Jacobean gables and a projecting two-storey central porch. The E side was pulled down in the 1960s. The original house is known to have been built just before 1678 by *Henry Jones* for Randolph Wikes, but the present Jacobean building is the result of alterations made in the mid C19 and in the early C20. The house was gutted by fire in 1917, and rebuilt for Captain Bower Ismay by *Crawley*, who added the Jacobean gables. STABLES, E of the house. Brown stone with brick facings (converted into a house in 1971). In the same style as the SCHOOL in the village, which was built by Viscountess Milton in 1872.

HELLIDON

ST JOHN BAPTIST. Dec, but much redone by *Butterfield* in 1845–7. Also a N aisle added in 1867. The piers are square with a slight chamfer, and the chamfered arches die into them. It looks more like late than like mid C19. – PLATE. Cup, 1599.
(THE GRANGE (former parsonage) by *Butterfield*, 1852. SCHOOL also by *Butterfield*, 1867. P. Thompson)
LATCHETTS (HELLIDON HOUSE). Late C18 front of five bays. Porch of pairs of unfluted Doric columns. In the s gable a mullioned window.
WINDMILL. Tower mill, ½ m. SE. Derelict.

* Information from Sir Gyles Isham.

HELMDON

5040

ST MARY MAGDALENE. W tower rebuilt in 1823. Dec chancel, long and tall. 'Low-side' windows to the S and N. SEDILIA and PISCINA with leaf capitals and crocketed ogee arches. N doorway with ogee top, aumbry with ogee top. Nave arcades of standard elements. Three bays, octagonal piers, double-chamfered arches. The details vary. The N arcade is taller. In the S wall a tomb recess. – STAINED GLASS. Original fragments in the heads of the Y-tracery including an early C14 stonemason donor figure in the nave. – PLATE. Cup and Paten, 1570; Flagon, 1771.

RECTORY. In the porch the lintel of a wooden fireplace with a carved dragon, a date 1533 (or 35), and initials.

HEMINGTON

0080

ST PETER AND ST PAUL. Perp W tower. The rest 1660, but gothicized in 1873 by *Carpenter & Ingelow* (BB). – FONT. Square, with chamfered corners. On the chamfers four faces. Short circular foot with nailhead, like a section from a pier; C13. – STALLS. From Fotheringhay College. With splendid ends, their tops forming a swan's-neck curve. Tracery and leaves below on the ends. Misericords including the hawk in fetterlock (the device of Edward IV), a publican with a jug, a mermaid, an owl, a tumbler. – PULPIT. Incorporating fragments from a screen. – PLATE. Cup and Cover Paten, c. 1683; Paten and Flagon, 1699. – BRASS to Thomas Montagu † 1517 and wife. The figures 18 in. long (in front of the pulpit).

MANOR HOUSE. Jacobean. Probably only one wing of a larger mansion. Gable, mullioned and transomed windows.

HIGHAM FERRERS

9060

Higham Ferrers Castle stood N of the church. It was built in the late C11 by a Peverel, then came into the hands of the Ferrers, and in 1266 was granted by Henry III to his son Edmund Crouchback, Earl of Lancaster. The castle, town, and manor remained with the Lancasters and shared their vicissitudes, until under Henry IV, son of John of Gaunt, Duke of Lancaster, they went to the Crown. Higham Ferrers is still part of the Duchy of Lancaster. While this connexion with the house of Lancaster accounts for the early greatness of Higham Ferrers, its later architectural achievements are connected with Archbishop Chichele, who was born at Higham Ferrers about 1362. He founded a college in 1422, and built a new bede house and a new school in connexion with this. Both bede house and school had however been in existence before Chichele's time. The college was for a master, seven chaplains, four clerks, and six choristers. Two of the chaplains or clerks were to teach grammar and singing.

ST MARY. A very grand church, spacious with its two naves and dominant with its superb spire. Two periods chiefly contributed, the C13 – c. 1220–80 – and the second quarter of the C14. Rebuilding apparently began at the E end, but of the C13 chancel there is no more evidence than the nook-shafts of the E window and the priest's doorway. The S arcade is mid-C13, of four bays, with ironstone detail, quatrefoil piers, and double-chamfered arches. The S doorway has four orders of colonnettes, the capitals with upright leaves, the arch containing two hollow chamfers. The W tower follows. Professor Bony has shown that its building followed that of the nave immediately, and that a change of plan occurred after the NE stair-turret and the middle buttresses outside the S wall had been begun. There is also a change of masonry and of capitals (foliated instead of moulded) between the lower stages of the tower on the N side, indicative of a further change of plan.* However, the whole is the work of one generation: c. 1250–80. The style is closely connected with Westminster Abbey, especially in the sculpture. The tower has recessed buttresses. The W portal is recessed too. The recess has two bays of cusped blank arcading with leaf capitals (corresponding to the upper parts of the tower) and a pointed tunnel-vault with a chamfered arch across and floral diapering. There are two W doorways with a *trumeau* between. The doorways have segmental arches (cf. Sainte Chapelle Paris and the early work at Westminster Abbey), and jambs and arches are decorated with small figures in the way of the French cathedral voussoirs. In the middle of the tympanum is a modern image of the Virgin on a leaf corbel. The rest of the tympanum has roundels with sacred stories, including some of an inorganically fragmentary shape (N: the Meeting at the Golden Gate, the Annunciation, the Three

* The Rev. C. S. Ford points to considerable C17 rebuilding of the steeple and asks for this to be taken into consideration. (The spire and part of the tower collapsed in 1631, and were rebuilt by 1632 by *Richard Atkins*. BB)

Magi, Christ among the Doctors, the Baptism of Christ; s: Joachim and his flock, the Crucifixion, the Annunciation to Joachim, the three Maries at the Sepulchre, the Harrowing of Hell). The motif of such roundels derives no doubt from illuminated manuscripts and stained glass. High up, on the bell-stage, is more sculpture, e.g. a Christ in an almond-shaped glory, and this may come from a former porch gable. Below the bell-stage a two-light w window. On the N side at ground level blank arcading with a two-light window with, in the spandrel, a charming little figure of a man making music. The bell-openings are of two lights, transomed (which is rare in the C13) and richly shafted.* The top parts are of the Dec building period: an openwork frieze, pinnacles, and the beautifully slender, recessed, crocketed spire with three tiers of lucarnes. The pinnacles are connected with the spire by flying buttresses with openwork quatrefoils. Towards the nave, inside the church, the arch has to w and E seven shafts in the responds. The moulding with a hollow between the shafts heralds that which became popular in the Perp style.

The church was spacious in this form, and its tower ambitious, but the volume of enlargements which was em-barked upon some time after 1327 was much more so. This may be due to the second Earl of Lancaster († 1345) or to Laurence St Maur, rector of Higham Ferrers († 1337; see below). What was done was that the chancel was remodelled with large Dec windows, and a N aisle was added (four bays, octagonal piers, double-chamfered arches), made as wide as the nave, endowed with its own (outer) N aisle, and continued in a Lady Chapel as spacious as the chancel, projecting as far as the chancel, and ending like the chancel in a five-light window with reticulated tracery. The altar stands some 8 ft w of the E wall and E window, and behind it space was left for a sacristy. Against the E wall of the tower, to cover the wall left bare when the N arcade was pushed further N than it had been in the C13, a blank arch was placed, with some nailhead en-richment. The outer N arcade is similar to the inner, but the piers are taller. They also have some nailhead enrichment. Between the chancel and the Lady Chapel a wide opening was made to contain no doubt the tomb of the man responsible for all this (see below). The arch has filleted mouldings, and inside at the apex a (recent) boss. Shafts l. and r. ending in brackets with dainty little heads – coarser heads, really demi-caryatids,

* These transoms may however date from the C17 rebuilding.

against the tomb-chest.* As for window tracery, it ought to be remembered that, in spite of their date, the N aisle to the W and the Lady Chapel to the N still have windows with cusped intersected tracery. Straight-headed N aisle windows with ogee lights. s aisle windows with reticulated tracery. Flowing tracery in the E window of the outer N aisle. Perp clerestory and tie-beam roof with kingpost and two queenposts. The church was restored by *Slater, c.* 1857 (R. Hubbuck).

FURNISHINGS. FONT. Octagonal, C13. On one side a cross with stiff-leaf, on three others short gables with fleurs-de-lis etc., also nailhead. – SCREENS. A large number, though none of prime interest. The rood screen is much restored (the original entrance arch now under the tower). It is tall and has two-light divisions with pendant arches. The loft and rood by *Comper.* – Other screens, all of one-light divisions, to the s aisle E bay, to the Lady Chapel (big, the entrance with embattled capitals), and to the outer N aisle E bay. – STALLS. Twenty of the collegiate stalls survive, with MISERICORDS (Archbishop Chichele's portrait accompanied by two clerks on the Master's and Vicar's stall, the Chichele arms on the Sub-Warden's stall, the Vernicle, a pelican, a lion, an angel with a shield, etc.). – (AUMBRY with tracery grille, by *Comper.* R. Hubbuck) – TILES. In the chancel; of the mid C14. – STAINED GLASS. Several windows by *Kempe & Tower,* see their signet, the wheatsheaf and tower. – ARMOUR, outer N aisle wall. Several pieces of *c.* 1600. – PLATE. Two Cups and Patens, 1653. – MONUMENTS. Tomb-chest between chancel and Lady Chapel. Four panels with shields; buttresses with small heads at the top. No doubt the most important monument in the church. But whose was it? The brass now on it does not belong to it. It is of Laurence St Maur, † 1337, a priest. It is one of the finest English brasses. The side shafts have saints, and of the canopy there remains a strip of five arches; the middle one with the deceased's soul held in a napkin by angels. The figure is 5 ft 4 in. long and lies under an ogee arch. – In the Lady Chapel many more brasses, the best that of Archbishop Chichele's brother † 1425 and his wife, under ogee gables, 4 ft 3 in. figures. – Also Archbishop Chichele's father † 1400 and mother, a foliated cross with Christ in the centre and the Symbols of the Evangelists in the ends. – William Thorpe † 1504, wife, and children (near the Chicheles), 2 ft 1 in. figures. – Also three brasses without any

* These are re-used corbels or C17 imitation.

1. *Village:* Polebrook
2. *Town:* Northampton, Market Square

3. *Church Exteriors, Saxon :* Earls Barton, tower

4. *Church Exteriors, Saxon :* Brigstock, tower

5. *Church Exteriors, Norman*: Pitsford, south doorway

6. (below) *Church Exteriors, Norman and Transitional*: Spratton, tower

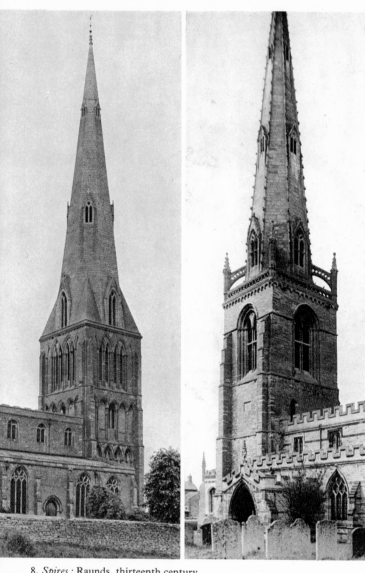

8. *Spires*: Raunds, thirteenth century
9. *Spires*: Higham Ferrers, *c.* 1250–80

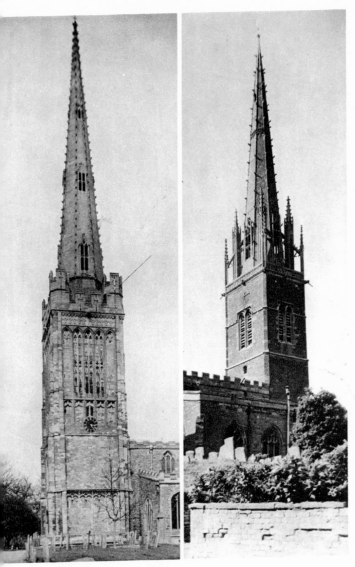

10. *Spires*: Oundle, fourteenth century
11. *Spires*: Kings Sutton, fourteenth century

12. *Church Exteriors, Decorated :* Byfield, chancel
13. *Church Exteriors, Decorated :* Milton Malsor

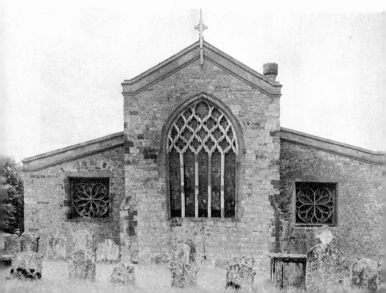

14. *Church Exteriors, Perpendicular:* Titchmarsh

15. (below) *Church Exteriors, Perpendicular:* Lowick, late fourteenth to late fifteenth century

16. *Church Exteriors, Carolean*: Kelmarsh, east window of the north chapel

17. (below) *Church Exteriors, Seventeenth Century*: Lamport, north chapel, by Henry Jones(?), 1672

18. *Church Exteriors, Seventeenth Century :* Northampton, All Saints, by Henry Bell(?), mainly of 1676–80

19. *Church Exteriors, Eighteenth Century :* Daventry, by David Hiorne,
1752–8
20. *Church Exteriors, Eighteenth Century :* Aynho, by Edward Wing,
1723–5

21. *Church Interiors, Saxon :* Brixworth, late seventh century and later
22. *Church Interiors, Norman :* Duddington

23. (top) *Church Interiors, Norman :* Northampton, St Peter
24. *Church Interiors, Norman :* Wakerley, capital
25. (right) *Church Interiors, Norman :* Northampton, Holy Sepulchre
26. (below right) *Church Interiors, Transitional and Early English :*
Rothwell

27. (left) *Church Interiors, Early English :* Warmington

28. (right) *Church Interiors, Early English :* Hannington, late thirteenth century

29. (below) *Church Interiors, Early English :* Cottingham, capital, mid thirteenth century

30. *Church Interiors, Perpendicular :* Kettering

31. (below) *Church Interiors, Perpendicular :* Whiston

32. *Church Interiors, Seventeenth Century*: Northampton, All Saints, by Henry Bell(?), 1676–80

33. (below) *Church Interiors, Twentieth Century*: Wellingborough, St Mary, by Sir Ninian Comper, begun 1908

34. (left) *Church Furnishings* : Little Billing (Outer Northampton), font, Saxon
35. (below left) *Church Furnishings* : West Haddon, font, Norman
36. (below) *Church Furnishings* : Crick, font, Norman
37. (below right) *Church Furnishings* : Clopton, cup and cover paten, 1548

38. *Church Furnishings*: Stanford, stained glass, *c.* 1330–40

39. (below) *Church Furnishings*: Fotheringhay, tester of pulpit, Perpendicular

43. *Church Furnishings*: Stanford, organ, sixteenth or early seventeenth century(?)

44. (below) *Church Furnishings*: Towcester, organ, French or Belgian, eighteenth century

45. *Church Furnishings:* Middleton Cheney, stained glass in the east window, by William Morris and his firm, 1864–5

46. (below) *Church Furnishings:* Oundle School Chapel, stained glass by John Piper and Patrick Reyntiens, 1955–6

47. (opposite) *Church Furnishings:* Northampton (East), St Matthew, Kettering Road, Madonna and Child, by Henry Moore, 1944

48. (left) *Church Monuments :* Stowe-Nine-Churches, Sir Gerard de l'Isle(?) †*c.* 1287
49. (below left) *Church Monuments :* Paulerspury, oaken effigies, mid fourteenth century
50. *Church Monuments :* Warkworth, a knight (Sir John de Lyons?), *c.* 1350

51. *Church Monuments*: Lowick, Lady Greene, from the monument to
Sir Ralph Greene, by Thomas Prentys and Robert Sutton, 1415–20
52. (above right) *Church Monuments*: Great Brington, Sir John
Spencer †1522 and wife
53. (below right) *Church Monuments*: Great Brington, Sir John
Spencer †1522 and wife, detail

54. (above left) *Church Monuments*: Harrington, members of the Saunders family, 1588

55. (left) *Church Monuments*: Braybrooke, members of the Griffin family, *c.* 1565–70

56. (above) *Church Monuments*: Apethorpe, Sir Anthony Mildmay †1617

57. (right) *Church Monuments*: Easton Maudit, Sir Henry Yelverton †1631 and wife

58. *Church Monuments:* Great Brington, Sir Edward Spencer, by
John Stone, 1656
59. (above right) *Church Monuments:* East Carlton, Sir Geoffrey
Palmer †1673 and wife, by Joshua Marshall(?)
60. (right) *Church Monuments:* Stowe-Nine-Churches, Dr Thomas
Turner †1714, by Thomas Stayner

61. (above left) *Church Monuments*: Deene, the Duchess of Richmond
†1722, by G. B. Guelfi
62. (left) *Church Monuments*: Stoke Doyle, Sir Edward Ward, by
J. M. Rysbrack, *c.* 1720–5
63. *Church Monuments*: Warkton, Mary, Duchess of Montagu, by
L. F. Roubiliac, 1753

64. (left) *Church Monuments:* Warkton, Mary, Duchess of Montagu, designed by Robert Adam, sculpture by P. M. van Gelder, 1775

65. (right) *Church Monuments:* Kings Sutton, Thomas Langton Freke †1769, by John Bacon Sen.(?)

66. (below) *Church Monuments:* Easton Neston, the second Earl Pomfret, by Sir Francis Chantrey, 1819

67. (left) *Secular Monuments:* Geddington, Eleanor Cross, shortly after 1294
68. (below left) *Secular Monuments:* Hardingstone (Outer Northampton), Eleanor Cross, by John of Battle, statues by William of Ireland, begun 1291, detail
69. *Secular Architecture:* Drayton House, 1328 and later

70. (left)
Higham Ferrers,
Bede House, 1428

71. (below left)
Fawsley Hall, hall,
early sixteenth
century

72. (right) Cosgrove,
The Priory, detail
of the screen, *temp.*
Henry VIII

73. (below right)
Dingley Hall,
cloister, *c.* 1550–60

74. Deene Park, porch, *c.* 1570
75. Deene Park, east front, bay-window, *c.* 1570

76. Kirby Hall, porch, 1572, 1575, and 1638
77. Kirby Hall, pilaster from the north range, c. 1570 etc.

78. (above left) Rothwell, Market House, by William Grumbold, given by Sir Thomas Tresham, 1578
79. (below left) Rushton, Sir Thomas Tresham's Triangular Lodge, 1594–7
80. (above) Rushton Hall, east front, Elizabethan and Jacobean
81. Castle Ashby, south front, 1574 etc., *c.* 1600–20, and the lower connecting wing possibly by Inigo Jones, *c.* 1625–35

86. (top) Lamport Hall, by John Webb, *c.* 1655
87. Dingley Hall, south wing, probably by Hugh May, *c.* 1680
(before gutting in 1972)

88. (below) Northampton, Sessions House, by Henry Bell(?), 1676–8
89. (right) Northampton, Sessions House, plasterwork by Edward Goudge, 1684–8
90. (below right) Boughton House, north front, *c.* 1690–1700 (*Copyright Country Life*)

91. Easton Neston, west front, by Nicholas Hawksmoor, *c.* 1700–2
92. (right) Drayton House, hall entrance, by William Talman, *c.* 1702

93. (left) Aynhoe Park, window in one of the service wings, by
Thomas Archer, *c.* 1710 (*Copyright Country Life*)
94. (above) Potterspury, Wakefield Lodge, by William Kent, *c.* 1745

95. Upton Hall,
hall, stucco work by
Giuseppe Artari,
1737

96. Althorp, entrance hall, probably by Roger Morris, 1733 (*Copyright Country Life*)

97. Cottesbrooke Hall, staircase, mid eighteenth century

98. (above left) Laxton Hall, by George Dance, completed by about
1811, hall
99. (left) Weedon, barracks, begun 1803
100. (above) Northampton Town Hall, by Edward Godwin, 1861–4

101. Northampton, New Ways, by Peter Behrens, 1925
102. (right) London-Birmingham Motorway near Kislingbury, 1959

103. Corby, Kingswood estate, Lincoln sector, by John Stedman, 1965–72

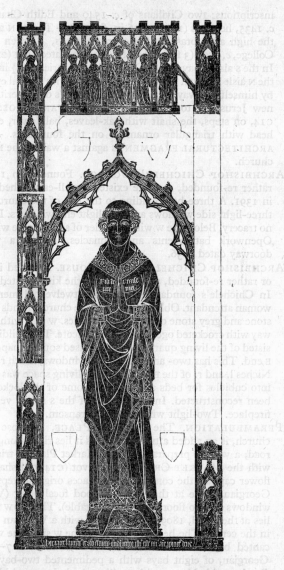

Higham Ferrers church, brass to Laurence St Maur † 1337

inscriptions: two Civilians of *c.* 1540 and Edith Chancellor, *c.* 1435, headless (12½, 17, 26 in. figures). – To the N and S of the high altar brasses of Richard Walleys, Warden of the College, *c.* 1500 (3 ft 6 in.) and a Civilian, dated 1501 (22 in.). – In the S aisle E bay Henry Denton † 1498, priest (19½ in.). – In the N aisle E chapel Thomas Rudd † 1656 with several epitaphs by himself ('Always looking up to Christ's only merit/Hopes new Jerusalem to inherit'). – CHURCHYARD CROSS, early C14, on steps, the shaft with oak-leaves, ballflower, etc., the head with triangular ornament on the four faces. – Some ARCHITECTURAL FRAGMENTS against a wall to the N of the church.

ARCHBISHOP CHICHELE'S SCHOOL. Founded in 1422, or rather re-founded, as there existed a well-established school in 1391. A three-bay building to the NW of the church, with three-light side windows and five-light end windows. Little or no tracery. Below the W window a tier of small single windows. Openwork battlements and pinnacles. Inside, a wooden doorway dated 1636.

70 ARCHBISHOP CHICHELE'S BEDE HOUSE. Founded in 1428, or rather re-founded, as a hospital of the kind existed before. In Chichele's foundation it was for twelve old men and a woman attendant. Oblong block S of the church, bands of ironstone and grey stone on the N and W sides. W side with a doorway with crocketed ogee arch and a bellcote. The building consisted of the living quarters and the raised square chapel at the E end. This has two- and three-light windows, much restored. Niches l. and r. of the E window. The living space was divided into cubicles for beds and lockers. Some of the lockers have been reconstructed. In the middle of the S side a very large fireplace. Two-light windows with transom.

PERAMBULATION. The MARKET PLACE, so close to the church, is an added attraction, or, as it lies right along the A6 road, a worthy preparation. The Market Place is triangular, with the MARKET CROSS as its pivot (C14, tall shaft, ballflower capital; the conical base replaces original steps) and a Georgian house at the N end, a good focal point (Venetian windows on two floors, pedimental gable). The TOWN HALL lies at the S end, 1809, of three bays, with a Venetian window in the centre. The best houses are on the W side, one with two canted bays and mullioned windows, and Nos 7–8, mid-Georgian, of eight bays with a pedimented two-bay centre. On the E side No. 11 with mullioned windows and No. 12 of seven bays, C18, altered later. From the S end of the Market Place to the E WOOD STREET, with at the end the MANOR HOUSE, L-shaped with a three-storeyed, gabled, mullioned bay-window. From the N end of the Market Place to the N COLLEGE STREET, so called after Archbishop Chichele's COLLEGE, founded in 1431. What remains of this is as follows. First the S range. The E part of this is called the chapel and is single-storeyed; the E window is apparently reduced in size. The W part is horizontally subdivided into two storeys, of which the upper oversails into the chapel – if it was a chapel.* Second the gatehouse and a lodging to its S. The gateway has a four-centred arch and three niches over. Thirdly part of the W range, which seems to have contained the hall.‡

Opposite COLLEGE HOUSE, consisting of one part, dated 1633, with a gabled porch and a canted, dormered bay-window, and another of the late C17, with wooden cross-windows in four bays and two storeys.

Massive ditches, the remains of its moat, mark the site of the CASTLE that once stood near the church. Stone from the castle was taken to Kimbolton House in 1523.

ROMAN BUILDING, Vine Hill Drive, on the W side of Higham Ferrers. A small C4 stone building, 36 by 26 ft, with rounded corners, on the site of a C2–3 stone building, probably aisled. There have been several other Roman finds in the vicinity.

HIGHAM PARK

9060

2 m. SE of Rushden

HIGHAM OLD HALL has one four-light mullioned window with arched lights; probably early C16.

HIGHGATE HOUSE see GREAT CREATON

HINTON see WOODFORD HALSE

HINTON-IN-THE-HEDGES

5030

HOLY TRINITY. Norman W tower, the arch towards the nave unmoulded. Early C13 upper parts. Two-light bell-openings with a shaft under a round arch. Corbel table. Late C12 or early C13 N aisle. The arcade of two bays has a circular pier with a multi-scalloped capital and a pointed double-cham-

* Excavations in 1966 indicated that as first planned, the N range was to have been much larger. When the plans were reduced in scale, it is possible that part of the domestic S range was converted into the chapel.

‡ Information kindly given by Mr S. E. Rigold.

fered arch. The external evidence of the church is disturbed by restoration. Early C14 N doorway. In the jambs of the S doorway nice, dainty, very small pieces of C16 (?) carving. – FONT. Tub-shaped, C13. With friezes of stiff-leaf, intersected arches, and dog-tooth. – SCREEN. Perp, with one-light divisions. – PULPIT. Jacobean, an unusual arrangement of usual motifs. – (STAINED GLASS. Chancel S. Coronation of the Virgin (reversed), c. 1400–30. RM) – PLATE. Cup, 1570; Paten, 1658. – MONUMENTS. Sir William Hinton (?) and wife. Later C14. Tomb-chest with quatrefoil frieze. His head still on the pillows usual in the C13. By her pillow two angels. The effigies are now separated. – Reynold Braye † 1582. Brass inscription plate. Good architectural surround with Corinthian demi-columns and entablature. Top achievement. – Salathiell Crewe † 1686. Tablet with open scrolly pediment. Attributed to *William Stanton* (see Mrs Esdaile; but not in Gunnis).

OLD RECTORY. 1678, gabled and symmetrical. The windows are altered.

HOLCOT

3 m. SE of Brixworth

ST MARY AND ALL SAINTS. Dec windows (Y-tracery cusped, also reticulated – see the well preserved window at the end of the N aisle now inside the church). Dec arcades of three bays. Very short piers with four shafts and four subsidiary shafts in the diagonals. The capitals on the N side look earlier than those on the S side. The chancel arch is of the same period and again a little different. Two-light bell-openings with transom. Battlements. – WALL PAINTINGS. At the W end of the S aisle Ascension, Pentecost, Coronation of the Virgin (?), and adjoining these Incredulity of St Thomas (?). Near the S door Resurrection. In the N aisle Martyrdom of St Thomas Becket, St Catherine before the Emperor, etc. In window splays single Saints, in the window arches scrolls. A representation of the Descent of the Holy Ghost, unique in English wall painting, has faded away. All C14. – PLATE. Cup and Paten, 1834.

HOLDENBY

ALL SAINTS. The church, now disused (1972),* belongs to the house more than to the village, i.e. the village was removed

* It is likely that the church will be declared redundant, but will be preserved.

when the house was built. From both it can be reached only by footpaths. All is green around it. Chancel rebuilt in 1843 to the design of *Sir Henry Dryden* of Canons Ashby. Restoration by *Sir G. G. Scott*, 1868. So the church now appears mostly C19. Dec however the arcades of three bays, the S side with octagonal piers and double-hollow-chamfered arches, the N side with taller piers and normal double-chamfered arches. The S aisle is remarkably wide. – FONT. Perp, octagonal, much recut. – STALLS with simple MISERICORDS. (One stall is apparently French of *c.* 1720, with dainty ribbonwork.) – SCREEN. The rood screen, the tower screen, and the REREDOS are said to have formed part of the former hall screen of Holdenby House. It must have dated from the late C17. Roman Doric columns, metope frieze, slender columns to fill the sections above the dados. The top with a middle arch with tapering pilasters flanked by two splendid foliage volutes with openwork. They especially make an earlier date impossible. – WALL PAINTINGS. Handsome long inscription panels with strapwork surrounds. Most probably Jacobean. – STAINED GLASS. W window by *Powell*, 1871. – (Chancel S, Coronation of the Virgin, *c.* 1290–1300. RM) – PLATE. Plate, C16; Cup and Paten, 1570; Breadholder, 1718; Flagon, 1720. – MONUMENT. Incised alabaster slab to William Holdenby † 1490 and wife (S aisle E).

HOLDENBY HOUSE. The house was built by Sir Christopher Hatton, who became Lord Chancellor at the age of forty-seven in 1587. The work was begun after 1570, and in 1583 he seems to have completed his great house; for this is the date on the two surviving archways. They led into the Green or Base Court. The mansion had two principal courts in addition and was 350 by 225 ft in size. This compares with the *c.* 475 (or *c.* 320) by *c.* 165 of Theobalds and the *c.* 475 by *c.* 300 of Audley End. The fronts were symmetrical, the windows mullioned. There was two-storeyed open arcading with coupled Roman Doric columns (Buck), and there also were large bay-windows. James I bought Holdenby in 1607, as he had bought, or rather exchanged, Theobalds in the same year. In 1651 it was bought by Capt. Adam Baynes and demolished except for part of the offices. In 1873–5 a new house about one-eighth the size of the Elizabethan house was built on the site in a style reminiscent of the old. Into this house the remains of the part left standing by Baynes were incorporated. The architects were *R. H. Carpenter* and *W. Slater*. The house

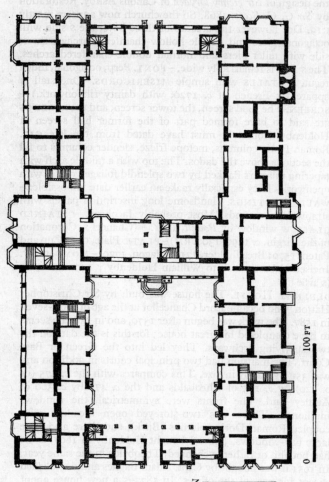

Holdenby House
(By courtesy of Mrs Ian Hodgson)

was enlarged in 1887–8 by *W. E. Mills*. The only important architectural remains of Hatton's palace, however, are the two archways already mentioned. There is a third archway, almost identical, to the N of the house. This has the date 1659, and a defaced coat of arms. It must have been erected by Baynes, when he had completed his destruction to give access to the small house he had made in place of the palace. The original arches now stand on an ornamental lawn. They are tripartite, with two orders of lesenes dividing the tall main arch from the blank outer bays with arched niches. Top achievement of clumsy outline.*

HOLLOWELL

6070

ST JAMES. 1840 by *Kempthorne*. Lancet style with a polygonal apse and a bellcote. The apse arch is shafted and has nailhead decoration. Quite ambitious triple-shafted W portal. Wheel window over (with STAINED GLASS designed by *Moberley* for *Powell*'s. G. Hamilton). – MONUMENT. R. M. Dukes, some time curate of Hollowell, † 1843. Brass on the floor, a cross surrounded by an inscription border.

VICARAGE. 1698. Of ironstone. Two storeys, seven bays, those l. and r. of the centre being very narrow (cf. Lilbourne). Quoins. Broad, rather low windows in flat frames. (Staircase with strong turned balusters. NMR)

THE LAURELS (formerly Manor House), at the W end of the village. Dated 1665. Mullioned windows. Georgian doorway, pilasters and pediment. (A circular DOVECOTE in the stable yard.)

(MANOR HOUSE. Late C17, five bays, stone. GI)

HOLLY LODGE *see* BOUGHTON

HORTON

8050

ST MARY. C13 W tower – see the pointed, very slightly chamfered arch towards the nave. The upper parts of the early C18 (pre-1720). Splendid tall curly weathervane. The rest of the church almost rebuilt in 1862–3 by *E. F. Law*. S arcade of three bays, probably of *c.* 1300. Octagonal piers, double-chamfered arches. – MONUMENTS. Brass to Roger Salisbury † 1491 and two wives; 2 ft figures. – Lord Parr † 1546, Catherine Parr's

---

* Part of an external frieze is at Coton Hall, *see* p. 160. Other fragments at Grendon (p. 241) and (?) Boughton (p. 109n).

uncle, and wife. Free-standing tomb-chest. At the foot a foliage frieze with hunting dogs. Five flat niches with balusters between them. Mourners in the niches, including bedesmen. Shields at the short ends. Two recumbent effigies. – Sir William Lane and family, c. 1580. Tablet with small kneeling figures. – Edward and Henrietta Montagu, 1756. By *James Lovell*. Architectural tablet, with two chaste urns in arched niches.

HORTON HALL was pulled down in 1936. What remains is the two LODGES, two-storeyed with giant pilasters and no doubt Victorian, and the STABLES, red brick, C18, of two storeys with a raised centre of three bays and an archway in the middle, which, like the six doorways in the lower wings, has rustication of alternating sizes.

The grounds between the lodges and the stables were built upon in the 1960s. At the end of the drive, near the site of the hall, and next to a splendid cedar, a striking house by *A. A. J. Marshman*, built for himself from 1966. The dominating features are the broad curving eaves of the shingled roofs, and the taller circular service cores and chimney of local yellow stone. In plan the house is a comma, with a full stop linked by a bridge. The tail of the comma, open on the ground floor, with bedrooms above, shelters a paved garden. The broad end has service rooms and entrances below, and a circular living area above, which has views in all directions.

Further afield are some of the garden furnishings of the old house. The MENAGERIE lies to the SE, a one-storey building with corner pavilions and a raised centre which has a semi-domed canted bay containing the entrance and a broken top pediment. The windows to the l. and r. of the bay have Gibbs surrounds and pediments. Above them lean-to roofs in the manner of Palladio's church façades. The whole is quite a dynamic composition, reminiscent of Kent. It has been attributed to *Daniel Garret*, who worked at Horton for Lord Halifax in the 1730s, but more recently to *Thomas Wright* working after 1739.* Inside, fine plaster ceiling, with Father Time, the four winds, and signs of the Zodiac. The building is in need of repair. Proposals to convert it into a private house are under consideration (1972). To the E THE ARCHES, a tripartite triumphal arch with Ionic pilasters. The arches and the frames of the medallions above the side arches are rustica-

* See J. Cornforth, 'Horton House', in *The Country Seat*, ed. J. Harris, 1967. (Garret was, however, still at Horton in 1750. H. M. Colvin)

ted. Also to the E THE TEMPLE, with a fine Ionic portico carrying a pulvinated frieze and a pediment. Probably Early Georgian. A farmhouse to its l.

HOTHORPE HALL
6080

Built in 1801. Six-bay front with two-bay pediment. Round the corner five bays with a one-bay pediment and a porch of coupled columns. The apsed CHAPEL (Lutheran Council of Great Britain) was added in 1894. Coffered tunnel-vault and coffering in the apse.

HULCOTE
7040

The estate village to Easton Neston. A group of eight very lovable and a little funny houses along two sides of a green. They are largish, two storeys with a third in the gable, of chequered brick and with pointed Gothick windows. Four of the houses are simply gabled, four have lower one-bay wings with half-pediments reaching up to the main block. (They were built by the third Earl of Pomfret, *c.* 1800–20. BB)

HUNSBURY CAMP *see* HARDINGSTONE,
NORTHAMPTON, p. 355

IRCHESTER
9060

ST KATHARINE. Mainly C13 to early C14. The only older pieces are the W responds of the nave arcade, both late C12 with leaf crockets in the capitals, a nook-shaft in the W wall of the N aisle, probably of a former doorway, and the bases of the first two N piers. So there were clearly aisles at that time. The S aisle W wall has an early C13 pair of lancets. The arcades are also C13. The piers are octagonal and have double-hollow-chamfered arches. C13 also the chancel, see the very low SEDILIA with leaf capitals, the trefoiled N doorway, the surprising niche to its r.,* and the chancel arch. A little later the N chapel with odd, very complex responds to the chancel and a low tomb recess in the N wall, and the shafted S and N aisle doorways. Fully Dec the W tower. Bands of ironstone and grey oölite. Pairs of two-light bell-openings. Spire with low broaches and three tiers of lucarnes. Perp chancel windows and S porch with entrance framed by buttress shafts and side

* It has a chimneyshaft.

windows. – FONT. Octagonal, with flat trefoiled arches. In
them barbaric demi-figures, faces, and stiff-leaf; C13. –
SCREEN. Rood screen, much restored. Wide one-light divisions with ogee arches. – Parclose screen to the s chapel. With
tall linenfold panels. – PULPIT. C17, with coupled little
balusters at the angles. – BENCH ENDS. Straight-topped, each
with two traceried panels and angle buttresses. – BREAD
SHELF. Very pretty. Jacobean or a little later. With small,
vertically symmetrical balusters (s aisle w). – WALL PAINT-
ING. Traces of a C15 Doom above the chancel arch. –
(STAINED GLASS. Several windows with fragments of c. 1340
and of the C15. RM) – MONUMENTS. Brasses to John Glynton
† 1510 and wife, 19 in. figures (N aisle, s wall). – Thomas
Jenison † 1681. Double inscription tablet flanked by Corinthian columns. The pediment is consequently wide. At the
foot shield and branches.

HOUSE, s of the church. Towards the church a gable wall with
a large ogee-headed window.

CHESTER HOUSE, ½ m. N. On an L-plan. Mullioned and sashed
windows.

KNUSTON HALL, 1 m. NE. The history of the house is not clear.
There is a Jacobean piece to the s and a projecting block to its
w which would correspond to a plan made by *J. B. Papworth*
in 1817 (R.I.B.A.). Although this range was built, it has since
been remodelled in a heavy Early Victorian way.* In addition
a tall gabled w block, added in 1865. To the N of this Georgian
offices.

ARKWRIGHT SCHOOL. NE of Knuston Hall, pleasantly sited
on a slope, among trees. A residential school for girls by the
County Architect, *John Goff* (Architect in Charge *J. R. Wool-
mer*), 1968–70. A series of self-contained three-storey units,
linked in an informal range, with lower buildings at r. angles.
Tile-clad slightly projecting upper walls and monopitch
roofs. The total impression not at all institutional.

ROMAN TOWNSHIP. Borough Close, the site of this unidentified settlement, lies N of the village, between the main road
and the town. The rectangular ditch and bank cover an area
of c. 720 by 900 ft and enclose c. 20 acres. Only parts of the
N side are still visible at all on the ground. Camden mentions
the site, and C18 accounts refer to walls still standing, while
excavations in 1878–9 uncovered foundations of central gates
to the s and w with roads leading to s and E entrances. A

* A drawing by George Clarke shows a tall Georgian house (BB).

number of buildings were also located in the centre of the settlement, while circular foundations in the s w corner may have supported a bastion. Amongst the finds was a tombstone, painted wall plaster, much 'terra sigillata' and Castor ware, slate from the Collyweston quarries, and coins ranging in date from Claudius to Constantine. Excavations in 1962 indicated that the settlement spread outside the walls, and that occupation began in the Early Iron Age. E of Chester House were the remains of further buildings with, to the NE (now under the railway line), a cemetery of at least 300 graves, discovered in 1873.

IRTHLINGBOROUGH

9070

St Peter. A quite remarkable sight, lying as it does between the village, centre of a now industrial town, and the river. The church is large and at first seems quite incongruous. What appears to be incongruous is however the survival of not only the church, but also the very tall and dominant tower to the w of the church which belonged to the college founded by the widow of John Pyel, a mercer of London, in 1388. The manor had been conveyed to John Pyel in 1354 and he had obtained licence in 1375 to make the church collegiate. The tower, which was rebuilt correctly in 1887–93, was probably begun shortly after 1354. It is of ironstone and grey stone. Recessed buttresses, turning clasping higher up. Lancet openings, one a doorway to college buildings to the N. Two Dec bell-openings with tracery on each side, a niche between them. Polygonal turret pinnacles (not according to the original) and battlements. Then two octagonal storeys, the upper one with straight-headed three-light windows with reticulation motifs, and battlements again. Of the buildings of the college to the N there only remain two undercrofts, with rib-vaults, one of two quadripartite bays, the other with ridge ribs as well. The former are in line with a room to the E of the tower which has two storeys and connects directly with the church porch, that is a room with entrances from the N, the S, the W, and of course also the church to the E. The openings are again lancets, looking decidedly earlier than 1300, but the doorway to the E has sunk rounded mouldings and a sunk chamfer, the same details exactly as in the N, S, and W doorways. The church is of two phases in the C13 and of c. 1300–50. The arcades come first, mid C13, with quatrefoil piers and double-chamfered arches in voussoirs of ironstone and grey stone. The N piers are stronger, the S piers slenderer. Transepts independent of the arcades. In the S aisle and the W wall of the S transept contemporary lancets. Two-bay chancel chapels, again quatrefoil piers and again different details. Late C13 the E end of the chancel, with a low cusped recess on the N side (naturalistic leaves in the capitals) and remains of the SEDILIA opposite. Typical late C13 chancel E window (five steeply stepped lancet lights under one arch), N transept N window, S aisle W, and others. Of *c*. 1300 the strange large, triple-shafted recess filling the E wall of the N transept. What was its purpose? It is surely too big for a reredos. Dec windows with reticulated tracery in the S transept on the S side and a straight-headed one in the S aisle; Dec window with flowing tracery at the W end of the nave. The W doorway under the porch is flanked by two niches. Dec also an elaborate aumbry in the N chapel.* The exterior of the N chapel is Perp and has a parapet decorated with shields. – FONT. Perp, octagonal, with traceried panels, embattled. – STALLS. Eight survive, the fronts with poppy-heads. One MISERICORD only, with a shield held by an angel. – STAINED GLASS. E window by *Kempe*. – PLATE. Set, 1832. – MONUMENTS. Alabaster effigies of a Civilian and a Lady, *c*. 1490. Tomb-chest with quatrefoils containing shields. At the head end angels holding a shield. – Alabaster effigy of a Lady, *c*. 1490. – Re-set monument of grey marble. Tomb-chest and recess with pendant arches (the colonnettes are C19 replacements). Panelling and remains of pendants inside. Indents of brasses on the back wall.

ALL SAINTS. In ruins already in the C16. Excavations in 1965 revealed that the earliest building, possibly mid-C12, had a nave, chancel, and apse. In the C14 the chancel was lengthened and aisles and a W tower were added. Nothing now remains.

LIBRARY AND HEALTH CENTRE. By the County Architect, *John Goff*. Under construction in 1971–2.

CROSS SHAFT in the square. On steps, with crockets.

BRIDGE across the river Nene. Of ten arches, mostly pointed; C14. Several arches with chamfered ribs. Cut-waters. Widened in 1922.

BARROWS. Two, on the E side of the Nene, N of the weir.

---

* The VCH calls all this Dec work in church and tower *c*. 1385. Stylistically such a date must appear too late. Shortly after 1354 would be more convincing. But do the documents allow this?

ISHAM

ST PETER. The first two bays of the arcades are Late Norman. Circular piers, N with many scallops, S with horizontal leaves and heads at the corners. Square abaci. Unmoulded N, single-stepped S arches. The third bays belong to the same period as the chancel and the openings into the chapels, i.e. the C13. Dec a number of windows and the ambitious recess in the N aisle. Ogee arch and pinnacles, a quatrefoil frieze at the back. Finally the W tower, Dec to Perp, with a top frieze of cusped lozenges and battlements. – SCREEN. Perp; only the base remains. – PULPIT. Jacobean, with its back wall and a small ogee tester. Very primitive figure carving. – COMMUNION RAIL. Jacobean, with vertically symmetrical balusters. – PLATE. Cup and Cover Paten, c. 1680; Breadholder, 1683.

Remains of Pytchley Hall, demolished in 1824, are worked into a façade of a three-bay house N of the church and a cottage next to it. Doorway with three vases. The door surround also looks as if it does not belong. Also in a cottage to the SE of the churchyard a fireplace with a four-centred head.

ISLIP

ST NICHOLAS. A Perp church. Simple windows. The W tower is the only ornate piece. It is similar to Lowick next door, but has a spire instead of the octagon. W doorway with traceried spandrels. Clasping buttresses. Top frieze of cusped lozenges. Tall, square, panelled pinnacles. The spire is recessed and crocketed. Two tiers of lucarnes in alternate directions. Interior with arcades of four tall arches. Piers with a deeply hollow-chamfered projection without capital to nave and aisles and slim shafts with capitals to the openings. Ogee hood-moulds. Angel corbels for the roof, also in the chancel. – STAINED GLASS. E window by *Kempe*, 1886 (with C15 Pelican in her Piety). – N aisle E by *Clayton & Bell*, c. 1878. – PLATE. Cup, 1570; Paten, c. 1682. – MONUMENTS. The big and fine-looking brasses on the chancel floor are a re-creation by the *Rev. H. Macklin*, author of one of the standard books on brasses. – Dame Mary Washington † 1624 and Catherine Curtis † 1626. Tablets with brief inscription between two coarse columns (cf. Lowick, † 1625).

ISLIP HOUSE, by Thrapston Bridge. Georgian, of seven bays and two and a half storeys.

KELMARSH

St Dionysius. Perp w tower with clasping buttresses, pairs of bell-openings with a transom, and broach spire with two tiers of lucarnes in the cardinal directions. Otherwise the only item of interest externally is the N chapel with the most extraordinary Carolean tracery in the E window, consisting of lozenges and circles. The N window is perfectly normal Perp (transomed). Top frieze and pinnacles, at once recognizable as Jacobean. The interior is all rich High Victorian, owing to Mrs Naylor of the Hall. The date is 1874, the architect *J. K. Colling*. Aisle arcade with circular piers of pink granite. Foliage capitals, foliage corbels, foliage on the PULPIT and the BENCHES. The chancel is particularly rich. Blind arcading all round with panels of marble allegedly taken from ancient buildings of Rome. Marble flooring. – WALL DECORATION by *Powell's*, designed by *Wooldridge*. – STAINED GLASS by *Lavers, Barraud & Westlake* (E) and *William Pepper* (N and S). – FRONTAL and ALTAR RUG by *Morris & Co.* – SCREEN in the tower arch. With late C16 or early C17 panels of Netherlandish (story of Esther) and German origin. – PLATE. Cup and Paten, 1696; Flagon, 1698; Paten and Cover, 1736. – MONUMENTS. Brasses to Morrys Osberne † 1534, the figure in its headless state 23 in. long. – Sir John Hanbury † 1639. In the N chapel no doubt built for it. Big standing monument with two figures kneeling and facing one another across a prayer desk. Big drapery opened above them, baldacchino-like. Open pediment. – William Hanbury † 1768. Very tall inscription base, *c.* 9 ft high. Strigillated sarcophagus above; no figures. – William Hanbury † 1807, by *Chantrey*. No figures. Grecian altar with drapery and two interlocked wreaths. – First Lord Bateman † 1845. By *Samuel Cundy*. Outside the church, E of the chancel. Coped tomb-chest with low 'basket' arches of the shape the French call *anse de panier*.

Kelmarsh Hall. By *James Gibbs*, *c.* 1727–32. In 1956 *Sir Albert Richardson* removed all C19 additions and restored the house to the appearance it has in Gibbs's original drawings at the Royal Institute of British Architects. Of red brick, and more Home Counties than Northamptonshire in looks. A perfect, extremely reticent design. Seven-bay centre of two storeys connected by one-storeyed quadrant wings with two-storeyed pavilions of five by four bays. The centre has a three-bay pediment, ground-floor windows with triangular and segmental pediments, a doorway with a segmental pediment on fluted Corinthian columns, and a parapet at stretches replaced by balustrading. The garden side (w) is more or less like the front, except that the three-bay centre projects and the doorway receives less stress. The quadrant arches have Ionic pilasters and a pedimented doorway. The pavilions also have pedimented doorways. Their roofs are visible and hipped. The whole is done in an impeccable taste which also applies to the original interiors, i.e. the staircase, and especially the Entrance Hall. This is one and a half storeys high. The back wall here is an arcade of three arches, and above it there are corridor windows as if they were in an outside wall. Very restrained stucco work. The stucco work is somewhat richer in the staircase. The handrail is of wrought iron, with lyre-shaped units. In the s w room a fine Kentian chimneypiece. Gibbs's designs for the other rooms are recorded, but most of them appear to have been decorated some forty years later. The Drawing Room is probably the work of *James Wyatt*, c. 1778. The Dining Room was redecorated by *Saxon Snell*, and the library by *W. Delano* in 1928. The Ballroom at the N W end was added in the C19 and redecorated in 1928–9.

ORANGERY, s of the house. Of stone. Late C18. Five arched openings. The building used to stand at Brixworth Hall and was re-erected at Kelmarsh not many years ago.

LODGES and GATES. Built to *Wyatt*'s design in 1965–6.* Each lodge has a pedimental gable, and a window framed by an arch. Rusticated gatepiers with urns.

KETTERING

CHURCHES

ST PETER AND ST PAUL. The siting at a distance from the main modern street of the town and along an avenue of trees gives the church a curiously ungenuine look, as if it were an imitation or re-erected. Yet the tower is indeed seen in this way to its best advantage and certainly deserves it. Very tall (179 ft), Perp, with a spire not too short and not too long. Set-back buttresses. Four stages with altogether five friezes of quatrefoils or cusped lozenges. w doorway with tracery in the spandrels, a crocketed gable, and pinnacles, framed by a quatrefoil frieze. Five-light window with transom. Then a tall

* Wyatt's original drawing of 1778 was discovered in Northampton Public Library.

all-panelled stage. Bell-stage with three fine, slender bell-openings with transom. Battlements, polygonal turret pinnacles. Recessed spire with crockets and three tiers of lucarnes. The rest of the church is Perp too, with the exception of the early C14 N doorway and the Dec E parts of the chancel with the odd E window. Its basic forms are Geometrical (unfoiled circles), but the lights have ogee arches. That may seem the fault of the drastic restoration,* but Billings in 1843 shows it such. Perp aisle windows of three lights with transom (embattled in the N aisle), doorways in the first bay, and on the N side in addition a two-storeyed porch. Entrance with traceried spandrels. Three niches above it. The aisle E of the doorways has five windows, i.e. the arcades inside are of six bays. Piers with the usual four-shafts-and-four hollows section. Arches with two sunk quadrant mouldings. The same details in the chancel chapels. They have five-light E windows. The S chapel is ashlar-faced. Perp clerestory. The tower must have been built before the nave, as its buttresses, fully decorated, appear inside. – SCREEN, N chapel. Classical, not Gothic. 1926 by *Martin Travers*. – (Wrought-iron GATES of the 1960s by *W. F. Knight*. GI) – WALL PAINTING, N aisle. St Roch, now unrecognizable. – STAINED GLASS. In the S chapel assembled original bits. – W window by *Kempe*, 1893. – PLATE. Cup, *c*. 1663; Plate, 1716; Flagon, 1756.

ALL SAINTS, William Street. Built in 1928. – FONT. From Faxton (*see* p. 216). Plain, Norman.

ST ANDREW, Rockingham Road. 1869 by *G. E. Street*. Ironstone, in the Late Geometrical style. A polygonal bell-turret over the nave. Wide nave. Arcades with octagonal piers carrying arches which die into them. Roof with arched braces and collar-beams. – STAINED GLASS. E (1893) and S (1906) by *Kempe*.

ST EDWARD (R.C.), London Road. Brick, with broad W tower and round arches. By *E. B. Norris* of Stafford. Opened in 1940.

ST MARY, Fuller Street. 1893–5 by *Gotch & Saunders*. Ironstone, Gothic, with a bell-turret on the nave.

FULLER BAPTIST CHURCH, Gold Street. 1861–2 by *Sharman* of Wellingborough for Sir Morton Peto. Late Classical façade of ashlar with a big pediment, but the details such as the round-arched one-storeyed portico and the small round-arched windows above it, and especially the bits of mosaic friezes, are Victorian all right.

TOLLER CONGREGATIONAL CHURCH, Gold Street. 1723, but

* By *Slater* (N. Taylor).

little recognizable of that date. The side with the ironstone facing and the arched windows on two floors looks Late Georgian; the terrible red-brick façade with two short towers is of 1875. Up Meeting Lane TOLLER CHAPEL SUNDAY SCHOOLS, 1883. Also of red brick with two towers.

CONGREGATIONAL CHURCH, London Road. 1898. Red brick with two short polygonal turrets and details typical of a neo-Gothic Nonconformist chapel of c. 1900. By *Cooper & Williams*.

CEMETERY, London Road. The chapels are of 1861. They are separated by a thin spire.

PUBLIC BUILDINGS

CORN EXCHANGE (former), Market Place. 1853 by *E. F. Law*. Red brick, two storeys, three bays with giant blank arches. The upper floor was designed as the Town Hall (JS).*

MANOR HOUSE (now part of the Public Library), s of the church. Georgian façade, of four bays and two storeys, concealing C17 parts.

PUBLIC LIBRARY and ALFRED EAST ART GALLERY. The two buildings in Sheep Street, with the church with its formal appearance near by, form a beginning of an effort towards a Civic Centre. The library is by *Goddard, Paget & Catlow*, 1904, the gallery by *J. A. Gotch*, 1913. The former is a half-H in plan, red brick, gabled, with mullioned windows and a pretty little cupola on top. The latter has grouped Tuscan columns and stone walls without any windows.

MUNICIPAL OFFICES, Bowling Green Road. Built as the Grammar School by *Gotch & Saunders*. Opened in 1913. Large, of red brick, neo-Georgian. The porch was added when it was converted to offices.

TECHNICAL COLLEGE, St Mary's Road. An instructive contrast between the 1950s and 1970. The older building (by the former County Architect, *A. N. Harris*, 1955) has a façade facing the road, with curtain-walling between symmetrical brick towers and, to add interest, a selfconsciously off-centre curved ironstone wall to the l. of the porch. The new block (by the County Architect, *John Goff*, 1968–70), of concrete, largely on stilts, is ruthlessly functional. It faces inwards around a grassed courtyard.

GRAMMAR SCHOOL, Windmill Road. 1960–2. Four-storey

* This and other details marked JS we owe to Mr J. M. Steane.

main block with cream spandrel panels; various lower ranges. Ceramic MURAL by *William Mitchell*.

HIGH SCHOOL, Lewis Road. 1964. This and the Grammar School are by the County Architect's Department (*A. N. Harris*). On a slope, so the four-storey main building is reached at first-floor level by a bridge, and is linked by another two-storey bridge to a lower range on the l.

SECONDARY SCHOOL, Montagu Street. Opened in 1892. By *Gotch & Saunders*. Red brick, Tudor, with gables. Tall, asymmetrically placed tower with odd, original tracery details and a top with four gables. New additions behind.

(BISHOP STOPFORD SECONDARY SCHOOL, The Headlands. By *J. M. I. Scott*, 1965. Red brick.)

(HENRY GOTCH SECONDARY SCHOOL, Deeble Road. Extensions by the County Architect's Department (*John Goff*), 1970–2.)

(POST OFFICE BUILDINGS, Gold Street. 1887 by *Gotch & Saunders*, large, red terracotta. Next door the former VICTORIA HALL, 1888 by the same firm. JS)

POLICE STATION AND MAGISTRATES' COURT, London Road. By the County Architect's Department (*A. N. Harris* and *John Goff*), 1968–71. A large, quite formal composition. Low central block with steps in front, with one-storey links to the two-storey Magistrates' Court on the r., and to the more elaborately detailed three-storey Police Station on the l. This has a porch, and the motif of beam ends slightly projecting beyond the brick walls.

ST MARY'S HOSPITAL, London Road. The old part was the former WORKHOUSE, 1837, Latest Classical. The characteristic raised octagon in the centre was taken down in 1971, when the building was altered by *Gotch, Saunders & Surridge*. The front has been reduced to one storey throughout, and the three-bay central pediment lowered.

GENERAL HOSPITAL, Rothwell Road. Redevelopment to the w of the railway was begun in 1958 by *Gollins, Melvin, Ward & Partners*, with a nurses' training school, nine-storey residential tower, and recreation hall in the w corner of the site. Phase 2, completed in 1965, to the s of the original hospital, consists of a one-storey outpatient department and a three-storey wing. Phase 3 was begun in 1971. Two- and three-storey wings for operating theatres, administration, etc., will link Phase 2 with a five-storey rectangular ward block.*

* For the Roman remains which lie E of the hospital, *see* below.

STATION. 1857. Small, red brick and light brown terracotta. Shaped gables.

THE TOWN

There is remarkably little of architectural note at Kettering, and no perambulation can be made of it. What can be mentioned is as follows.

In SHEEP STREET, SAWYERS ALMSHOUSES, of 1688, very humble opposite the budding Civic Centre. Then the MARKET PLACE. Here SILVERS, the chemists, early C19. In the HIGH STREET the GRANADA CINEMA, good 1930s style brick, with circular turret. On the other side a Victorian façade (now FOSTERS) with upper floor with continuous arcading. The date is 1880 (JS). Further N at the corner of Lower Street and Gold Street, a block of shops, with roof-lines stepped up the slope of Gold Street. This is by *Shingler Risdon Associates*, 1967–71, and is the first phase of a redevelopment plan which will drastically affect this part of the town. Further on in Lower Street first the BAPTIST MISSION HOUSE, a stately early C18 house of seven bays and two storeys, then the former CHESHAM HOTEL, of *c.* 1762, with a charming doorcase.* (Off to the l. in TANNER'S LANE, BEECH HOUSE. Five bays, early C18, brick, with a stone wing of *c.* 1790.) E of Gold Street is MONTAGUE STREET with the CONSERVATIVE CLUB, and s of this in DALKEITH PLACE the former LIBERAL CLUB (now Trustee Savings Bank), both of 1888, the former by *S. Perkins-Pick*, a very good example of its date, the latter by *Gotch & Saunders*, in a free Tudor with certain motifs not authorized by tradition, but without real originality. This is what the Conservative Club undoubtedly possesses. Tall l. part with a big gable ending in a half-timbered top triangle, lower r. part with the doorway crowned by a nice feathery foliage cartouche. (Further w in GREEN LANE, STAPLES FACTORY, built as a shoe warehouse in 1873, extended in 1885 and 1891. Round arches, slightly Italian-Venetian. JS)

In SILVER STREET the pretty RISING SUN, 1892, with Jacobean gables, and MARTINS BANK, a good small infill job by *A. W. Walker & Partners*, 1960s.

Finally two houses by *J. A. Gotch*, the Kettering architect who, until recently, has remained the leading English authority on houses from Henry VIII to Charles I. SUNNYLANDS, The

* This and the Chesham Hotel are threatened with demolition.

Headlands (St Peter's School), is red brick, Tudor, and really of no interest. THE CONVENT OF OUR LADY, Hall Lane, of *c.* 1900, is more successful. Red brick and pebbledash. L-shaped, mullioned and transomed windows. Hipped roof with dormers.

The main concentration of the ROMAN INDUSTRIAL CENTRE lies E of the hospital (*see* Introduction, p. 26). Considerable foundations, tesserae, coins, etc., have been recorded on the N side of the town on the track between Weekley Hall Wood and Boughton Park.

5070

KILSBY

ST FAITH. Unbuttressed C13 W tower with later small recessed spire. One tier of lucarnes. The body of the church is over-restored (in 1868–9 by *E. Christian*, and again in 1895) and of no architectural interest. Inside tall arcades of four bays with octagonal piers and double-chamfered arches. – BOX PEWS. – (STAINED GLASS. E window by *Powell & Sons*, 1869, with Crucifixion by *Doyle*.) – PLATE. Cup and Paten, 1731.

CONGREGATIONAL CHAPEL. Said to be of 1764. The façade of the stone building with the pedimental gable and the tripartite lunette window in it could be of that date.

RAILWAY TUNNEL. 2400 yards long. By *Robert Stephenson*. Part of the work of the London–Birmingham Railway, opened in 1838.

0090

KING'S CLIFFE

ALL SAINTS. Norman crossing tower, see the twin windows with dividing shaft and round arch. The upper parts, including the broach spire, are of the late C13. Two tiers of lucarnes, the lower starting below the broaches. Two lights, Y-tracery, dog-tooth. The nave W window is Dec and has flowing tracery. Above it appears the roof-line of before the addition of the Perp clerestory. Mostly Perp also the rest of the exterior. Inside, the W and E crossing arches are a C13 remodelling, the N and S arches are Perp. At the W end of the chancel on the N side about 1300 a N chapel was started. Triple responds with fillet. C14 aisle arcades with octagonal piers and moulded arches. Embattled abaci. Perp roof on good corbels. – FONT. C14. Rounded with four plain raised medallions and four with quatrefoils. – BENCH ENDS. From Fotheringhay; C15. –

STAINED GLASS. Some fragments from Fotheringhay, including angels with musical instruments. – (Nave N windows with early C16 fragments possibly from Barnack Manor House. RM) – S aisle, window by *Kempe*, 1904. – PLATE. Two Breadholders, 1691–2; Set, 1751. – MONUMENT. Thorpe family, 1623. This is the family of masons whose only famous member is John Thorpe, born *c.* 1566 and living till 1655, whose sketchbook is at Sir John Soane's Museum and has led to the erroneous attribution of many Elizabethan houses to him. Very simple architectural frame with Doric pilasters and an open pediment and obelisk at the top. At the foot 'Thomas, Thomas, Thomas', recording three generations, proavus, avus, pater. Of the proavus nothing is known, the avus died in 1558, the pater in 1596, the famous John being one of his sons. – W. Pyemont † 1759. Floor stone, recording him tellingly as a 'Faithfull Diligent and Allways Resident Rector'. – In the churchyard William Law † 1761, in the form of a writing-desk.

Around BRIDGE STREET several charitable and educational buildings established by the Rev. William Law and his disciple Mrs Elizabeth Hutcheson. To the N in SCHOOL HILL, LAW'S LIBRARY. This is a house of *c.* 1700, converted into a Master's house in 1745. Law's books were kept here from 1752. Over the door the inscription: Books of piety are here lent to any persons of this or ye neighbouring towns. Symmetrical three-bay front. Upright mullioned windows. Adjoining the house the BOYS' SCHOOL, 1748, and to the E WIDOWS' ALMSHOUSES, dated 1749. Later almshouses to the W. S of Bridge Street the former GIRLS' SCHOOL, a building of 1752, with rooms for the mistress on the ground floor and a schoolroom above. The original staircase, and panelling in the schoolroom (now divided), survive. To the W SPINSTERS' ALMSHOUSES, 1754.*

JOHN THORPE ALMSHOUSES. 1668. One-storeyed. Mullioned windows with straight hoods.

RECTORY (formerly OLD MILL HOUSE), SE of the church. Georgian, of three bays, simple. DOVECOTE to the SW.

(MANOR HOUSE. Unpretentious front to the main street with two early C17 projecting mullioned bays (possibly originally taller). An older part to the E. Early C19 garden front. Inside, a graceful early C19 staircase.

* This paragraph has been expanded from information in M. Seaborne: *The English School*, 1971.

In the garden a stone screen and a good circular DOVECOTE.
GI)

(HALL YARD FARMHOUSE, E of the church. Dated 1603,
altered later. Inside, on the r. of the W door, Dr Law's
MUSIC ROOM, with a high coved ceiling with Adamish
decoration. Near by is LAW'S CHAPEL, C18 altered,
originally with three open arches on the ground floor.
Pediment on the S side. Hall Yard is the site of a medieval
royal manor. Traces of fishponds remain in the adjoining
fields. DOE, H. M. Colvin)

(In gardens opposite the cemetery two doorways from Fotheringhay, one with a two-centred head and blank quatrefoil
tracery above it, the other with a four-centred head. NMR)

KING'S HEATH see NORTHAMPTON, p. 357

4030

KINGS SUTTON

11 ST PETER AND ST PAUL. Kings Sutton has one of the finest,
if not the finest, spire in this county of spires. The W tower is
tall. To its W is a porch with its own pinnacles and three
niches above the entrance. The inner W doorway has tracery
panels, and the porch a tierceron-vault with the tracery pattern of the four-petalled flower as its central motif. The bell-
openings are of two lights with a straight hood-mould and
Dec tracery. So while the porch is Perp, the tower is Dec.
Below the battlements runs a frieze of cusped lozenges. At the
top corners thin, tall pinnacles connected by thin, short flying
buttresses with more substantial and taller pinnacles which
keep close to the spire. This is crocketed, and the tall, sturdier
lower lucarnes are transomed. High up a tracery band and yet
higher another set of tiny lucarnes. The spire is probably of
the late C14. It had to be partly rebuilt in 1898, in 1968 was
repaired again, but is now in good order. Beasley in 1848 says
that the greatest thickness of its walls is 9½ in. The total height
of the steeple is 198 ft. As for the body of the church
it is mostly Dec. Only the chancel E window, the N aisle W
window, and the S porch entrance are Perp. Dec are the
chancel side windows, Dec the S aisle windows culminating
in the fantastic tracery of the E window, which has at the top a
circle with a trefoil of three segments, Dec the N aisle.
Internally the picture is different. The greater part of the
chancel turns out to be Norman, and this is borne out by

the corbel table outside. Inside there is blank arcading along both walls. The shafts are original, the arches with their zigzag Victorian. As for the nave and aisles, their grandeur and airiness, it is true, are due to the early C14, but the S arcade is considerably earlier. It makes a strange impression. Its piers and arches are earlier than is its general character. This can only be explained by the re-use of the piers and arches, and indeed the outer hood-mould of nailhead. The piers are circular, the abaci square. One capital has many scallops, the E respond waterleaf. The arches are unmoulded. This points to the late C12. But the proportions are the same as those of the N arcade, with quatrefoil piers and arches with a moulding of two slight chamfers – which is C13 work. Actually the moment when the S arcade was readjusted can be determined by the fact that the one capital which is not late C12 in style has some ballflower decoration, an unmistakable sign of the early C14. – FONT. Rough, plain, Norman. The lead-lined bowl measures 2 ft 8 in. internally. – SCREEN. By *Sir G. G. Scott*, who restored the church in 1866. – PLATE. Cup and Cover Paten, 1569. – MONUMENT. Thomas Langton Freke 65 † 1769. Of plaster. Attributed to *Bacon*, but much in the Roubiliac tradition. Not *in situ*. At the bottom rocks, on them Christ triumphing over a recumbent skeleton, the hollow chest with the ribs hideously exposed. To the r. a kneeling angel.

MANOR HOUSE, on the S side of the Green. With gables and mullioned windows. Mid C17.

The STOCKS are between the Manor House and the Bell Inn.

A little further E COURT HOUSE, half stone and half timber-framed with an oversailing upper floor of *c.* 1500, altered in the C16 and C18. Great Chamber on the first floor, probably used as the Court Room, with heavily moulded tie-beams and large fireplace. C16 wooden window surrounds and staircase.

BLACKLANDS, ½ m. N of the village, on rising ground, is the site of a large Roman settlement. Though never excavated, the site has produced considerable small finds, the commonest coins being of C4 A.D. date.

KINGSTHORPE *see* NORTHAMPTON, p. 339

KIRBY HALL

Kirby Hall was begun in 1570 for Sir Humphrey Stafford.* The mason was in all probability *Thomas Thorpe* ('pater' – *see*

* It is of Weldon stone.

Thorpe Monument at King's Cliffe). The better-known *John Thorpe*, a future surveyor and author of a book on the 'plus fameux bâtiments' of England which was never completed and never went into print, laid the foundation stone at the age of about five. But the designer of the house is unknown. Sir Humphrey died in 1575. Dates 1572 and 1575 occur on the principal porch. The estate was bought by Sir Christopher Hatton, one of the Queen's handsome young men, and he must have continued work side by side with that on his principal house at Holdenby (*see* p. 261), which seems to have been completed in 1583. Kirby is in several ways one of the most important and interesting houses of its date in England. It is also a visually rewarding house, in its rather bleak situation with ironstone mining close by and no village or church to relieve its loneliness.*

The architectural significance of Kirby lies in the fact that it represents a style different from that which established itself at Longleat and Burghley House in the 1570s and became the accepted style of the Elizabethan Settlement. The source of this Elizabethan style *par excellence* was the Lord Protector Somerset's London mansion of *c.* 1548–52, and Kirby also owes a debt to this. But the masons of Longleat and Burghley made something different of the Somerset House innovations. At Kirby they are enriched by much that seems to be local in style and derives from such work as that at Dingley about 1558–60, and in addition by certain motifs as up-to-date in the Continental sense as those of Somerset House but not made use of there. The principal of these motifs is the giant order of pilasters, a motif derived from Delorme's St Maur of 1541–4 and illustrated in his *Architecture* in 1567. There is also a drawing of the relevant façade by Ducerceau. The giant pilaster never became popular in Elizabethan England (whereas it became popular in France), but gives Kirby its distinguishing character.

The principal range of Kirby Hall, with porch, hall, kitchen, etc. on one side, parlour, etc. on the other, is the s range. It is one-storeyed. To its N is a courtyard with E and W ranges of two storeys containing sets of lodgings. The N range is occupied by a loggia with a gallery over and the main gateway from the N. This range was altered in 1638–40, and the combination and confusing interaction of the 1570s with the 1630s is what faces the visitor.

* The former church lay to the sw of the house.

He approaches Kirby Hall by a forecourt entered through one of two identical arched GATEWAYS. The arches are framed by niches in two tiers; the tops are damaged. They are reminiscent of the gateways of 1583 at Holdenby. In the N wall of the forecourt is a smaller archway, no doubt of 1638–40. This has sides with alternating blocks of stalactitic rustication and an open pediment with a shield. The N front of the N range of the house appears mostly of 1638–40. It is thirteen bays wide and two storeys high. The lower windows are segment-headed with eared frames. The top balustrade rises in alternating pediments carried on volutes. There are horizontally placed ovals below the pediments. The three centre bays are higher by one storey, and the middle bay has a high attic in addition. Archway with rusticated surround. Niches l. and r. This work of 1638–40 is attributed traditionally to *Inigo Jones*; but there is no evidence to confirm the attribution. On the other hand it is known that *Nicholas Stone*, the sculptor, did stone-work at Kirby in 1638–9, and this ought to be remembered, as one watches for further alterations made in these years.

It is only when one enters the courtyard that one recognizes the N range to be structurally part of the main building scheme of the 1570s. The upper windows have, it is true, the alternating pediments of the 1630s, but the giant pilasters and the arcading of the ground-floor loggia are clearly of a piece with the principal s range. The N front of this, as the centre of the whole composition, must now first be described. The façade here is of nine bays, of which the middle one contains the two-storeyed porch with its tall blank attic and gable, whereas the angle bays are distinguished from the others by being narrower and projecting as if they were bay-windows. They start right above the base courses and have four transoms. So have the adjoining windows of bays two and eight, but the windows of bays three, four, six, and seven start somewhat higher up, so that they have only three transoms. The justification for the enlarged window in bay eight is that it represents the dais end of the Great Hall. But there is no justification for the same height in bay two, let alone the projecting bays. In all these the guiding idea was symmetry, and indeed visual impressiveness altogether; for the projecting bay nine marks no more than a passage from the Hall to the W range, and in bays one and two neither the enlarged window nor the projection has any functional meaning. The large windows with their grid of

verticals and horizontals belong to the Elizabethan style of
Longleat and Burghley, but the giant pilasters, already mentioned, do not, and the porch does not either. The giant
pilasters are fluted and have fanciful Ionic capitals. A thin
frieze of foliage and a solid parapet are carried by them. The
76   porch is much gayer, and if the giant order comes from such
French châteaux as St Maur, the porch is indigenous English
work at its most unacademic. It carries a date 1572, and in the
pediment of the clearly altered upper window a date 1638. The
porch has a round-arched entrance framed by coupled Ionic
pilasters. A third pilaster is set round the corner to the E and
W, but has – rather painfully – no counterpart close to the wall
of the range, as one would expect. A foliage frieze follows, and
then, on the upper floor, instead of the Corinthian pilasters
which ought to be there, fluted Corinthian columns on
brackets. They cause a projecting and receding of the frieze
above which prepares for the fun and games of the attic and
gable. The whole of their surface is decorated with foliage,
strapwork cartouches, and geometrical motifs. In addition, set
against the attic, are seven Corinthian colonnettes (and again
one to the W and one to the E round the corner). Above each
of them the frieze again juts forward. The gable consists of
two concave curves and a semicircular top with a shell-motif.

The E and W ranges are two-storeyed, with four-light
windows (two plus two lights) and one transom, and low
broad doorways flanked by Ionic pilasters. The friezes, as on
the porch and above the giant pilasters, are continued above
the ground floor and the first floor. Tall chimney with coupled
polygonal shafts. The S side of the N range takes up again the
motif of the giant pilaster. The two flanking the entrance from
the N are singled out by bold broad candelabra decoration. Sir
John Summerson has demonstrated that such decorative
motifs at Kirby Hall were taken from recent books, especially
Serlio, John Shute (1563), and Hans Blum. The interior of
the loggia was remodelled later with niches. Mr Chettle
attributes the alteration to the late C16.

At that time – i.e. the time of Sir Christopher Hatton –
important alterations were also made to the outside façades of
Kirby Hall. The most important of these are the Great Staircase projecting from the W side and the two twin semicircular
bay-windows on the S side. These are a strange addition,
breaking the logic of the courtyard house of the 1570s and not
part of a logical composition of their own date either. Semi-

circular bays are more usual about 1620 than before 1600.
They are here fully glazed, of ten lights (in groups of two),
with two transoms to the ground floor, one to the upper floor.*
In the roof dormers, also bent semicircularly. The windows
here are of six lights, stepped so that the centre has a transom.
Curly volutes on the sides and at the top. These are taken up
in the other contemporary parts of the w side. The s side continues to the r. (E) with the back doorway of *c.* 1640 to the Hall
and then another staircase block, added in brick in the C17.
The chimney wall of the kitchen lies just E of this.

As for the INTERIOR, the position of the kitchen shows that
at Kirby in the accepted English medieval and Tudor way the
porch led into a screens passage with the Kitchen, Buttery,
Pantry etc. on one side, the Hall and living quarters on the
other.‡ The Hall has a beautiful canted ceiling with double-
curved wind-braces, all the timbers carved with foliage. This
must be of *c.* 1575. C17 E gallery on big corbels, E doorway
of *c.* 1640 with pediment. w doorway with segment-headed
pediment. Through this door to the Great Staircase with a solid
newel rounded at the angles. Moulded stone handrail partly
recessed in the wall. The staircase led to the Long Gallery,
which ran all along the w range above the ground-floor
lodgings. A fragment of its plastered tunnel-vault remains at
the s end. Very broad ribs with large circles. The date probably Jacobean.

Gardens on the w side laid out *c.* 1685 on a formal plan;
recently reconstructed.

KISLINGBURY

7050

ST PETER AND ST PAUL. Mostly Dec and very fine, especially
the chancel. This has a splendid five-light E window with
interesting tracery based on intersected ogee arches. The same
principle is used for three-light windows on the N and s sides
of the chancel. A fleuron frieze runs all along the s side below
the eaves. Inside the chancel the N doorway is a piece of
unusual and very attractive design. A continuous order of
leaves with knotty branches and a continuous order of flowers

---

* Mr Bailey points out that the ground-floor windows have been lowered.
They originally had one transom, like the upper windows. It has been suggested that these bays are part of the alterations and additions of *c.* 1610–20.

‡ There is some evidence both in the building and in documents for a house
at Kirby prior to Stafford's work of the 1570s. This may explain the siting,
and possibly part of the structure of the kitchen wing (BB).

with the same kind of branches (cf. the capitals at Radstone). Hood-mould on head-stops. SEDILIA and PISCINA are ogee-cusped and have crocketed gables. The finials reach above the window sill. Canopies of former statues l. and r. of the E window. Dec also the W tower with a recessed spire (two tiers of lucarnes). The tower restored in 1717. Dec the aisle W windows, the N doorway and the S porch with its side windows, and the pretty S doorway with one continuous order of fleurons and ballflower and a hood-mould on head-stops. The straight-headed aisle windows might well be as late as c. 1717. Dec finally also the arcades of four bays. Octagonal piers, double-chamfered arches. Responds with head-corbels. – FONT. Octagonal, Perp, with shields in quatrefoils. Panelled stem. – CHEST. Of c. 1500, with blind arcading and many big rosettes. – CHANDELIER. Of brass, two tiers; C18. – PLATE. Cup and Cover Paten, 1562. – (CURIOSA. Leather Fire Buckets of 1743. L. M. Gotch)

RECTORY. One of the finest in the county. Attributed to *Francis Smith* (cf. Cottesbrooke Hall, Lamport rectory); built probably c. 1710–20. Ironstone. Five by three bays, two storeys, quoins, hipped roof. The windows in finely moulded frames, the doorway with an open curly pediment. Staircase with twisted balusters and carved tread-ends. A fireplace of c. 1740 with a sun-face. Good wrought-iron garden gate. The rectory BARN has a cupola, and in it are over 1,300 nesting-places for pigeons.

KNUSTON HALL *see* IRCHESTER

LAMPORT

7070

ALL SAINTS. Close to the Hall, but now across the road. Externally a medieval tower and a C17 and C18 church (with, alas, a S vestry of 1879 – alas, even though it is by *Bodley*), internally a medieval nave and aisles under an C18 ceiling and leading to an C18 chancel. The low W tower is Late Norman and was buttressed later. The arch towards the nave has keeled responds. The bell-openings of two lights are C13. Of the C13 also the three-bay arcades. Octagonal piers, double-chamfered arches. To this church Sir Justinian Isham added a N chapel in 1672. The chapel, which was built probably by *Henry Jones* of Walgrave, who later lived at Lamport, opens towards the chancel in three arches. The E window is still in its original state. It is of cross-type, with the transom remarkably high up. Segmental pediment on corbels. This is clearly influenced by Webb's work at the Hall. It is even possible that *Webb*, who died only in 1672, designed the chapel. He had designed a circular, domed family mausoleum in 1654, but this was not carried out. Then, after 1737 (completion 1743), *William Smith* of Warwick rebuilt the outer walls of the aisles and nave and most of the chancel, placing at the E end a fine Venetian window with Doric pilasters. His other windows are round-headed, heavily and bluntly framed, and have that Y-tracery which was the C18 favourite of all Gothic tracery. By Smith also the S porch, rusticated and pedimented. The plasterwork inside is by *John Woolston*, alderman of Northampton. It is simple in the nave – three circles with emblems, that in the middle circle being the eye of God surrounded by cherubs – and richly Rococo in the chancel. Especially happy the cartouches above the spandrels of the arches to the chapel and the ROYAL ARMS of George II over the chancel arch. – FONT and FONT COVER, tall, designed by *Bodley*, 1869. – COMMUNION RAIL. Of wood, no doubt of c. 1745. – IRON SCREEN, between chapel and chancel. 1965 by *W. F. Knight*. – PROCESSIONAL CROSS. Found at Lamport Hall in the late C17. It is of bronze, gilt, with champlevé enamel medallions. Charles Oman dates it c. 1475, although the drapery of the Virgin and the figure of the angel of St Matthew look earlier. The cross is made so that it can stand on the altar or be fixed to a staff. – STAINED GLASS. E window, Resurrection, by *Warrington*, 1847, very strong, in dark colours and with heavy figures. – Other glass c. 1865, designed probably by *Sir Charles Isham*, who was certainly capable of this, as he also illustrated books. – PLATE. Cup and Cover Paten, 1653; Paten, 1720; Flagon, 1717. Also a Cup and Paten of 1670 from Faxton. – MONUMENTS. Now that the organ has been removed, those in the chapel can be appreciated. All of Ishams. Mrs Jane † 1638. Slab with, at the top, three putti with three wreaths. By *Thomas Stanton*, according to a drawing at Lamport Hall. – Sir Justinian by *William Stanton*, paid for in 1699–1700. Tablet with twisted columns. The price was £64. – Elizabeth † 1713. By *Edward Stanton*. Big tablet with fluted pilasters and at the top two putti l. and r. of a coat of arms in a scrolly surround. The price was £55. – Sir Justinian † 1730. A fine architectural tablet, making use of variegated marbles, known from documentary sources to be by *Francis Smith*.* – Sir Justinian † 1737. The powerful bust by *Scheemakers*. Volutes to the l. and r. of the bust. Corinthian columns and open pediment. – John † 1811 by *Henry Westmacott*.– Mrs Raynsford † 1763. By *W. Cox* (from Faxton church).

RECTORY, E of the church. Built in 1727–30 for the then rector, Dr Euseby Isham, by *Francis Smith*. Handsome five-bay front of two storeys. Doorway pedimented. Good staircase inside with three slender turned balusters to the tread and carved tread-ends. Ground- and first-floor rooms panelled. The library (formerly the drawing room) was altered in 1819, when the panelling was covered up and a coved ceiling and new fireplace (by *John Whiting*) were added. The original fireplaces are of red Derbyshire marble.

LAMPORT HALL. The Ishams have lived at Lamport ever since 1560. Their Elizabethan house had its front E of the present large porch and facing NW towards the church. Lamport was only one of the Isham houses; Pytchley was the other. The core of the present building was built for Sir Justinian, who succeeded his father in 1651 and got married in 1653. He was the great-grandson of the Elizabethan Isham who had died in 1595 and had been three times warden of the Mercers in London. The designer of the house was *John Webb*. Enough correspondence is preserved to be sure of many details for which one is in the dark in the case of most Stuart houses. The letters start in 1654 and end in 1657. Webb signs himself 'your assured ffreind', which shows that he and his client considered one another as of equal social status. Webb's house is only five bays wide and two storeys high, that is a *villa* in the sense in which the Queen's House at Greenwich by Inigo Jones, Webb's master and his relative by marriage, is a villa. Webb wanted first to give it a portico, a feature he liked, but that suggestion was not accepted. He then suggested a porch, but that also was not built. Webb's front was ashlar-rusticated throughout, with raised quoins and a top balustrade, that is it was infinitely purer in its Italism than e.g. the exactly contemporary Thorpe Hall. Actually a small dormer-like pediment was added as early as 1657. This was hidden by another bigger pediment about 1730–40. The present pediment is of 1829 and stands rather awkwardly behind the balustrade. Webb's doorway has an open segmental pediment, and the

---

* Similar monuments e.g. at Harlestone, Fawsley, Edgcote, Dodford, consequently may be attributed to the Smiths (BB).

windows to the l. and r. are given pediments of alternatingly
segmental and triangular shape. The windows themselves are
now sashed but originally in all probability had mullion-and-
transom crosses similar to those of the N chapel in the church.
On the top frieze below the balustrade the (later) inscription:
In things transitory resteth no glory. The Entrance Hall, now
called Music Hall, is structurally Webb's work, though almost
entirely re-decorated. It is noteworthy that with all his Italism
Webb still allowed this hall to be entered not in the middle
but close to one end, that is in the medieval and Elizabethan
way. The chimneypiece was designed by Webb and made by 84
'Mr Keyes'.* Webb's drawing for it exists. He would, he
writes, have preferred 'to employ our own countrimen'. It is
a splendid piece, with big, powerful forms, grand though
somewhat restless in the same way in which the details at
Thorpe Hall are so much more restless, that is e.g. an open
segmental pediment and in it a smaller triangular one, or the
mantelshelf projecting in three places and fruit panels squeezed
into the parts of the frieze of the shelf where it does not project. The decoration has thick, compact fruit and leaf garlands
and also two swans, the sign of the Ishams. Only the lower
part incidentally is of stone; the overmantel is of wood. The
simple door frames are also designed by Webb. The panelling
of the walls was re-done in 1686. Originally the walls had
straight-headed niches with wax figures by one *Andrew
Kearne*, Nicholas Stone's brother-in-law. He was a German,
and therefore probably Kern. He may well be a member of
the Kern family of Würzburg and Württemberg. Of Webb's
time also the handrail of the former Staircase. The panels are
now kept at the level of the upper landing of the present staircase. More are stored away. They have, like those of Thorpe
Hall and others of about 1660 and after, openwork foliage
scrolls. At Lamport these scrolls are a little flatter and more
formalized than at Thorpe.

The Elizabethan house remained independent of the new
one, which faced s w and was screened from the old building
by hedges. The first addition was the Stables. They date from
1680. There were originally two ranges forming a generous
forecourt to the NW. The w range, which had a small cupola,
was pulled down in 1829. The E range consists of two parts,
that nearer the house structurally Elizabethan – see the

* Probably *Caius G. Cibber*, who is known to have designed for Lamport
in 1670.

windows at the back – the other of 1680. Seven bays, two storeys, cross-windows, large round-headed archway. The archway in the Elizabethan part is re-set and comes in all probability from the w range. The stable quadrangle behind was built in 1907.

The next addition was more momentous. In 1732 a N wing, in 1741 a S wing was begun to widen Webb's w façade from its original five bays to thirteen and thereby totally altering its character. Yet the *Smiths* of Warwick, *Francis* on the N, *William* on the S wing, kept very tactfully to the style of their Palladian, Jonesian predecessor. Only the window details and the balustrade details differ. At the back of the surprisingly shallow S wing William Smith made an open arched garden hall. The work of the Smiths inside is more spectacular. It culminates in the splendid redecoration of the Music Hall, i.e. the former Entrance Hall. This dates from 1738. The stucco work was done by *John Woolston*. Attic with beautiful lettering and above it panels containing 'trophies' of musical instruments alternating with profile busts in roundels.* Big coving and flat ceiling with three large plaster panels. The middle one is circular, and has a bold wreath of foliage and fruit and three frolicking cherubs in the centre. On the l. and r. panels mermaids. The style of the wreath is only superficially similar to Webb's. The foliage is in fact much looser and more deeply undercut.

Of the time of the Smiths also the Staircase. Slim turned balusters, two to the tread, and carved tread-ends. Elegant plaster ceiling.‡ Similar ceilings in the adjoining corridors. On the upper landing the situation is complicated not only by Webb's stair panels (*see* above) being displayed here, but also by neo-Jacobean work of 1907. The Oak Room is also neo-Jacobean, though it has an original Jacobean fireplace with overmantel, the origin of which is not known. Again part of the Smith work is the Library in the N wing. The fireplace and the flanking giant pilasters are of 1732, the rest is a remodelling of 1819, i.e. it is by *Henry Hakewill*. At the same time Hakewill built a new neo-Tudor N front which was replaced later, the quadrant porch at the back of William Smith's S wing (Tuscan columns), and the pediment above Webb's façade. He was followed by *Goddard* of Leicester, who in 1842

* The lettering is Victorian. It is by *Sir Charles Isham*, the tenth baronet.
‡ Stained glass from Pytchley Hall, dated 1596. The staircase was moved to its present position in 1825.

added the mildly Jacobean lower part of the s front, and Goddard was followed by *Burn*. Burn's is the N front. He wanted to go Jacobean, but was prevented by the then owner, who thus succeeded in keeping the original character of Lamport safe through the dangerous Victorian decades. Burn in 1861–2 added the massive Tuscan porch, the low, rather weak square tower, and the lower range beyond. Extensive restoration work on the house is now in progress (1972).

GATES on the Northampton road by *Hakewill*, 1824. ROCKERY, SE of the house, by *Sir Charles Is   m*, 1847.

LODGES 1849–50, probably by *J. G. Blan* who designed LAMPORT MANOR (Home Farm) in a similar Tudor style. In the village a number of polychrome brick ESTATE COTTAGES, dated 1854, and a DOVECOTE of 1735, later converted to a bakehouse (hence its inscription), and now a cottage.

SHORTWOOD LODGE. *See* p. 402.

LAXTON

ALL SAINTS. Exterior much restored, partly by *Lord Carbery* († 1894), who was a talented amateur carver. Is the E window design e.g. due to him, with its archaeologically inaccurate combination of Dec and Perp motifs? He certainly designed the cast-iron GARGOYLES in the shape of dragons. Norman parts of the s doorway, i.e. the two orders of strong shafts with weird volute capitals. Late C13 the w tower with bell-openings of two lights separated by a shaft and with a blank cinquefoil over. Short spire with low broaches and two tiers of lucarnes. Double-chamfered arch on head corbels to the nave. Late C13 also the three-bay s arcade with quatrefoil piers and double-chamfered arches. The N arcade is C19. – PULPIT. Carved by *Lord Carbery* in the style of 1700. – PLATE. Cup, 1694; Paten, 1724.

LAXTON HALL. Built by about 1811 (rain-water head) by *J. A. Repton* and altered in 1867–8 after the seventh Lord Carbery had succeeded in 1845. The garden side has a central bow-window, the entrance side had a portico or porte-cochère. The columns of this were removed after 1845, and the front now looks very bleak, with its excessively broad Doric pilasters and the weird detail round the doorway. Inside a beautiful Hall by *George Dance Jun.* of *c*. 1812. Square, with four Ionic columns in a row on the upper floor, facing one as one enters. Segmental arches, pendentives, and a circular dome on a glazed lantern. Very restrained plaster work. To the l. ample Staircase Hall. Oblong staircase with open well. Cast-iron handrail with honeysuckle motif. Oblong glazed lantern. – CHAPEL (formerly Orangery). Built *c.* 1845. Portico with four columns. – STABLES with cupola, the bell dated 1805. – GATES on the E side of the estate, on the A-road. Two pedimented lodges and a tripartite archway with attic.

LAXTON PARK HOUSE, in the grounds, near the entrance from the village. Gothic. With a façade like that of a church. Stepped gable with finials.

The VILLAGE was rebuilt by the Evans family, Lords Carbery, beginning before 1800 (*Beauties of England and Wales*). Gabled stone cottages, mostly in pairs. Bargeboarded gables.

LICHBOROUGH *see* LITCHBOROUGH

5070
LILBOURNE

ALL SAINTS. Unbuttressed W tower with Perp arch towards the nave. Dec chancel. The windows have ogee-headed lights under a fine segmental arch. Hood-moulds on small heads outside as well as inside. The arcades are interesting. The first one and a half bays on the S side come first. They have a circular pier with circular abacus and double-chamfered arches. They date from the C13, and the first arch was cut into when the tower was built. The rest of the S arcade comes next, with the piers and arches in a continuous moulding of the Stanford and Leicestershire type (North Kibworth, Misterton), i.e. with piers with slender chamfered projections to nave and aisle and broader ones to the arch openings. That is Dec. C14 also the N arcade, all of a piece – with octagonal piers and double-chamfered arches. Nave roof of low pitch with tie-beams and carved bosses. – PULPIT. C18, with its tester. – SCREEN. Perp; only the base survives. – COMMUNION RAIL. C18. – PLATE. Cup, 1734.

STONE HOUSE FARMHOUSE. Of the late C17 (cf. Hollowell Vicarage of 1698). Five bays, two storeys, hipped roof. Three bays are widely spaced, but the middle one has flanking, much narrower windows. Doorway with heavy pulvinated frieze. Staircase with dumb-bell balusters.

CASTLE. Site of a motte-and-bailey castle, N of the village and E of the church, close to the river. A second smaller bailey was to the NE of the motte. It was a small but well protected castle. To the E is a ditch, measuring 84 ft across. Another small motte with a single, rather feeble bailey lies ½ m. W.

LILFORD

St Peter. *See* Thorpe Achurch, p. 427.

Lilford Hall. Fine s front of *c.* 1635, with a wing carrying
that date at the back on the w side. The wing was supple-
mented by an identical one on the n side in 1656. Much was
done to the interior by Sir Thomas Powys, who bought the
house in 1711. Finally, the wing of 1656 was enlarged in 1858.
The front is nine bays wide, of which the first and the last are
generous bow-windows, and the middle one is a one-storeyed
porch with Roman Doric columns and a balcony. The bow-
windows are of two storeys and also end in balconies. The railing is of an unusual design with arches from which stalactites
hang down. The windows between are tall and slender and of
cross-type. Three big gables with convex and concave parts
and an open ring as a finial. The two w windows of four lights,
but a tripartite form, with the centre two lights in their lower
part made into one wide arch, is so typical a motif of *c.* 1660
that it must belong to the work of 1658. So also does of course
the oval window on the e front. Of the external changes of
1711 etc. the most prominent on the front is the spectacular
row of thirteen chimneys connected by arches. At the back
the even fenestration with smaller cross-windows belongs to
1711 etc. Seven bays, two storeys. In addition two identical
stable and office blocks were built on this n side, both with
projecting wings and a cupola – a very handsome composition,
surprisingly formal. Inside fine Entrance Hall of *c.* 1730 by
Flitcroft.* Even finer contemporary staircase with stucco
panels, garlands, etc. Two Ionic columns on the ground
floor, two Corinthian ones on the first. Of the same time the
centre s room on the first floor. Victorian Ballroom. (Over the
chimney in the s wing of the courtyard a fine mid-c17
achievement with crest and mantling and the Elmes arms,
re-erected in 1909. GI)

LITCHBOROUGH

6050

St Martin. Dec almost throughout: w tower, chancel with
reticulated tracery in the n and s windows (the e window is
Perp), clerestory with quatrefoil windows, n doorway and s
doorway, and s arcade of four bays with octagonal piers and
double-chamfered arches. – RECTOR'S PEW. – STAINED

* The designs are in the County Record Office (H. M. Colvin).

GLASS. S aisle E, *c.* 1850. – (Nave windows with early C14 Annunciation and Trinity Shield. Chancel N: C14 foliage work. RM) – PLATE. Cup, *c.* 1570; Almsdish, 1637; Paten, 1695; Breadholder, 1706; Cup, 1809. – MONUMENTS. Sir John Needham. Erected in 1633. Noble alabaster effigy on a very large tomb-chest. The VCH says this has the latest 'military pillow' in the county. Behind the monument, on the wall, inscription tablet with two columns and some foliage decoration. – Frances Simpson Grant † 1907. White marble angel with raised arm – like a monument in a churchyard.

LITCHBOROUGH HOUSE, by the church. C17 house embedded in neo-Tudor work of 1838 (by *George Moore*).

LITTLE ADDINGTON

9070

ST MARY. Of the late C13 to mid C14. Of the latter date the W tower, embraced by the aisles. Sumptuous doorway with figures up the jambs and a crocketed ogee gable with flanking pinnacles. The bell-stage is treated as a recessed panel. Quatrefoil frieze, battlements, recessed spire, not high, with two tiers of lucarnes. Of the windows the chancel E window has a reticulation motif, and the 'low-side' window has tracery below the transom. To the earlier date belong the arcades, similar but not identical. Four shafts (or quatrefoil) with thin keeled shafts in the diagonals. The proportions differ, and the slenderer N arcade has fillets on the main shafts, while the S arcade has not. Fine S doorway with two orders of shafts and a many-moulded arch. Heavily vaulted N porch. Late C13 tracery in the windows of the W parts of the aisles.* – PULPIT. Perp, with traceried panels. – SCREEN. Of two-light divisions, based on the Y-type of arrangement. – (STAINED GLASS. Nave N. C14 fragments.)

LITTLE BILLING *see* NORTHAMPTON, p. 351

LITTLE BRINGTON

6060

ST JOHN. By *P. C. Hardwick*, 1856 (GR). Built by the Spencers of Althorp. Only the W tower stands now, E.E. in style with a proud broach spire.

BAPTIST CHAPEL. Built after 1837. Brick chequer, red and yellow. Arched windows.

SCHOOL. 1850 by *Hardwick*. A proud building with its two large,

* The church was restored by *E. F. Law*, 1857 (R. Hubbuck).

very Perp four-light windows in the facing gable-ends. Red brick.

Some of the substantial Althorp ESTATE HOUSES of 1848. Semi-detached, with gables, patterned chimneys, and leaded lights (cf. Church Brampton). Also an ALMSHOUSE, 1851, and a LODGE, both by *John Wykes*.* See p. 517

LITTLE CREATON *see* GREAT CREATON

LITTLE EVERDON *see* EVERDON

LITTLE HARROWDEN

8070

ST MARY. Late Norman s doorway with three orders of shafts carrying volute capitals. Three roll mouldings and an outer zigzag moulding. Chronologically there follows the third bay of the s arcade. This is of ironstone and must have been a transept arch. Then, late C13 to early C14, the other s bays and the three N bays, the s aisle windows, the grand chancel E window of four lights consisting of pairs with cusped Y-tracery and a sexfoiled circle in the head. The Dec w tower was demolished recently (the spire had fallen in 1703). A small vestry is on its site. Carved fragments from the top of the tower are in the churchyard.‡ The tower had two-light bell-openings and a quatrefoil frieze below the battlements. – SCREEN. Perp, of one-light divisions. – COMMUNION RAIL. Jacobean. – PLATE. Cup and Cover Paten, 1569. By *Thomas Buttell*.

LITTLE HOUGHTON

8050

ST MARY. s doorway of *c.* 1200. One order of shafts with leaf-crocket capitals, round arch with two flat steps. C13 w tower. What was the bell-stage then has five blank arches with two lancet windows. The Perp top stage has two-light bell-openings, a quatrefoil frieze, and battlements. The rest of the church was almost rebuilt in 1873 by *Buckeridge*. The windows were all renewed, the N aisle was built, and the s arcade restored at that date. Three-bay arcade with octagonal piers and double-chamfered arches. One-bay chancel chapels to the N and s. – FONT. Circular, with flat shafts carrying rough single-scallop capitals. Is it Norman or an imitation ? – STAINED GLASS. E window by *Clayton & Bell*, *c.* 1873. –

* Information from Earl Spencer.
‡ Information from A. S. Ireson.

PLATE. Breadholder, C17; Cup, 1685; Paten and Flagon 1721. – MONUMENT. Pretty tablet to William Ward and family, erected in 1775. By *William Cox Sen.*

STOCKS, SE of the church on the S side of the road to Bedford.

LITTLE HOUGHTON HOUSE, on the Bedford Road, at the E end of the village. Mainly of after 1825, added by the Smyth family to an earlier house, which survives as a five-bay, two-storey wing. The newer part is of three storeys, with five bays on the E front, four on the S front. S porch of 1848, with a pediment added in the 1950s, made up of stone from the demolished Horton Hall. Good staircase. To the W of the house SUMMER HOUSE dated 1685, with Latin verses commemorating the Ward family's support of James II.

THE MERE, at the W end of the village. Built as the dower house for Little Houghton House *c.* 1838. Five bays, two storeys, with parapet.

Nice HOUSES S of the church along the main road, e.g. an L-shaped one whose one arm is C17, the other of *c.* 1700. There is a date 1702 and also a vertically placed oval window. Moreover, the windows of 1702 are no longer mullioned. At the E exit is a house of 1691 with a flat front and mullioned windows, those on the ground floor under relieving arches.

CLIFFORD HILL, *c.* ½ m. N of the village, on the banks of the Nene. This is a large MOTTE, which is remarkable in several ways: first for its size, as it is one of the largest mottes in the country; secondly because it appears that there is no historical record of the castle which stood upon it; and finally because with any considerable motte it is reasonable to expect a bailey. Clifford Hill has nothing but a counterscarp bank, well-marked to N and S, destroyed or vague on the other two sides. A disturbed area on the W may mark the position of some sort of dependency, but certainly not that of a bailey worthy of so splendid a mount. Part of the S side of the motte appears to have collapsed at some date (not recent), and it is possible that this may have led to the early abandonment of the castle.

8080

LITTLE OAKLEY

ST PETER. Fine early C13 chancel. Lancet windows, the group of three stepped ones at the E end shafted inside, the shafts with stiff-leaf capitals. C13 S arcade of quatrefoil piers, broadly detailed, and double-chamfered arches. Early C14 N arcade of the same elements, but with more mouldings in the capitals. Perp W tower with clasping buttresses, tall bell-openings, and battlements. The church was restored by *Slater & Carpenter*, 1867 (N. Taylor). – SCULPTURE. Figure of an archer with arrow, inside the N wall of the church. It is very weather-worn.*) – PLATE. Cup and Paten, 1569; Paten, 1618. – MONU-MENTS. A member of the Montagu family, *c.* 1575. An uncommonly fine and noble design without any figures or inscriptions. Three pairs of coupled Roman Doric columns on high bases with garlands and grotesques. Between the columns strapwork cartouches and shields. Simple roof-like top storey with a shield between pilasters. Two supporter dragons l. and r. – William Montagu, 1620. With a big kneeler between columns. In the foot-piece lies a putto. Inscription: Hodie mihi cras tibi.

MANOR HOUSE, W of the church. Similar in its windows to Great Oakley Hall and so also probably of *c.* 1550–60. Gabled, with mullioned windows with arched lights.

LODDINGTON

ST LEONARD. Of ironstone. C13 W tower. Bold W doorway with a tall gable, representing in relief the end of a stone-tiled roof. The portal beneath has three orders of shafts, two of them with shaft-rings. Later (grey stone) frieze of cusped lozenges, big gargoyles, and broach spire with two tiers of lucarnes. C13 also the S aisle, see the SW lancet and the arcade of three bays with one octagonal and one quatrefoil pier. C13 again the S chapel of two bays and its elegant little doorway. The chapel arcade has a circular pier with four attached shafts (cf. Roth-well). The arches have two hollow chamfers and an inner roll with a fillet. The chancel is of *c.* 1300, see the intersected tracery in the E window, the S window of two lights with a circle, and perhaps the SEDILIA. The latter are either severely restored or C19 work. (There was a restoration in 1859 by *E. Christian*.) Tomb recesses in the S chapel and S aisle. Niches l. and r. of the S aisle E window. Perp clerestory. – SCREENS. Perp. Of the rood screen only the base remains, but the parclose screens to the S chapel are complete. They differ in design. – STAINED GLASS. In the chancel in a S window glass by *Morris & Co.*, *c.* 1891. – PLATE. Cup or Porringer, Cup or Mazer, and Paten, all of 1671.

LODDINGTON HALL. Jacobean, on an E-plan, with a large N extension of 1893. The original work has mullioned and mul-

* The Rev. A. M. Somes kindly drew my attention to this.

lioned and transomed windows and many gables. The doorway into the Hall is original, the porch may be a later addition.
In the Hall fireplace with strapwork. The fireplace in the
Kitchen (to the W of the hall) has the date 1615. Big C18
GATES. The Hall is now a school. To the N is an attractive
new building for the school by the County Architect *John
Goff*, 1970–1. It is faced with simulated ironstone with
vertical channelling. Thick mullions on the ground floor, and
some boxed-out windows. Irregular roof, because of the top
lighting. Inside, this makes the gymnasium, workshop, and
central corridor agreeably light and airy.

LONG BUCKBY

6060

ST LAWRENCE. Of ironstone. The W tower is of the C13. Very
flat, thin, set-back buttresses with a shaft at the exposed angle.
W lancet in a projection. Two-light bell-openings separated by
a shaft. Pointed-arched top frieze. Battlements. Dec arcade of
four bays. Octagonal piers, double-chamfered arches. Dec
probably also the aisle walls and the chancel. But the windows
are too renewed to be of use. The aisles had in fact been made
Georgian in 1774 (restoration by *G. G. Scott*, 1862–3, and by
W. Bassett-Smith, 1883–7). Dec cinquefoiled clerestory
windows. On the N side an arch resting on corbels with
fleurons. There was no doubt originally a monument here.
In the chancel SEDILIA, the backs of the seats deepened into
little niches. – STAINED GLASS. E window († 1858) by the
Evans Brothers of Shrewsbury. The window commemorates
the daughter of a Shropshire vicar. – MONUMENT. Cilena
I'Anson Bradley † 1726. By *John Hunt*. With a small but
charming marble bust.

(At BUCKBY WHARF a small MISSION CHURCH of 1875.
BB)

CONGREGATIONAL CHAPEL, SW of the Market Place. Dated
1771. Three-bay front with arched windows and doorways,
segment-headed below, round-headed above. Two-storeyed
fenestration also along the sides. Three galleries internally and
a blank arch behind the pulpit. The MANSE to the l. is of three
bays and two and a half storeys.

BAPTIST CHAPEL. Dated 1846, but still in the same classical
tradition.

In KING STREET, on the way from the Market Place to the
church, a handsome L-shaped group of two houses, dated
1734.

CASTLE. In the middle of the village, a little distance to the sw of the church, is a rather curious earthwork consisting of an oval ringwork in the middle of a triangular bailey. Excavations have indicated that the ringwork is of mid-C12 date, partly overlying an earlier enclosure. A stone wall around the bailey was added later.

LOWICK

9080

ST PETER. A very good Perp church, built chiefly at the expense of members of the Greene family of Drayton, namely Sir Henry who succeeded at Drayton in 1369 and died in 1399, Ralph who died in 1415, and Henry who died in 1467–8. The nave and aisles probably came first. The chancel has the arms of the Greenes and of John Heton, rector from 1406 to 1415. Ralph is buried between the chancel and the N chapel, Henry in the southern transeptal chapel. The tower was probably completed only after 1470. Earlier than the Greene period only the early C14 S doorway (hood-mould on angels with shields) and probably the SEDILIA in the chancel as well as the blank arch at the E end of the N aisle. They have the ogee arches and crocketed gables with elongated pointed trefoils characteristic of c. 1330–40. The nave is divided from the aisles by four bays of tall octagonal piers with double-chamfered arches (tall vertical pieces at the springing of the arches). The chancel arch is of the same design. The aisles have tall transomed windows of three and four lights with embattled transom and four-centred arches to the individual lights. In the N aisle a cusped segment-headed tomb recess. The same windows in the S transept, except that the two-light S window has two transoms. The E window however is quite different and much prettier. It has nice cusping below the transom, and in the top the motif of the four-petalled flower. The chancel even has panel tracery below the transoms of the windows, and the same motif is used in the N chapel. And so to the W tower, a beautifully erect and vigorous piece, not too much opened up. Clasping buttresses. Big W doorway with tracery in the spandrels. Three tiers of quatrefoil or cusped-lozenge friezes. Big two-light upper windows, perhaps once intended for bell-openings. Battlements with tall square panelled pinnacles. Then an added top storey between the pinnacles, octagonal and with its own eight pinnacles. This and the new wide, three-light, transomed bell-openings provide a splendid finale to the church.

FURNISHINGS. BENCH ENDS. With fleur-de-lis poppy-heads. Some poppy-heads have heads instead of the two side pieces. One has in addition two mitred heads as the top piece. – STAINED GLASS. Sixteen beautiful figures in the N aisle windows. They come from a Jesse window and seem to be of c. 1310–30. There is also a donor knight. – PLATE. Set, 1723–4. – MONUMENTS. Sir Ralph Greene † 1417. The contract of 1415 for the monument exists. It pledges 'Thomas Prentys and Robert Sutton, kervers of Chellaston' (the village in Derbyshire with the famous alabaster quarries) to make two images, a counterfeit of an esquire and a lady in her open surcoat with two dogs at her feet and two angels by her pillow. Husband and wife were to hold hands, and there were to be angels along the sides and an alabaster arch above, the whole to be gilded and painted. The delivery date was Easter 1420, and the price £40, to be paid in five equal instalments. The arch has gone, but the tomb-chest has indeed six by three angels. They stand stiffly frontal in an identical attitude, each holding a shield. Excellent effigies. Over their heads canopies with lierne-vaults. At their feet a mastiff and a puppy. – Henry Greene † 1467. Tomb-chest with shields in quatrefoils. On the lid good brasses, 3 ft long. – Edward Stafford, second Earl of Wiltshire, † 1499. Alabaster effigy on a tall tomb-chest with lozenge panels inside cusped square panels. – William, son of the first Earl of Peterborough, † 1625, 82 days old. Two columns with very unorthodox capitals. Short inscription. No figures. – Lady Mary Mordaunt, Duchess of Norfolk, † 1705. Semi-reclining white figure in contemporary dress. No background. – Sir John Germaine † 1718. Young-looking, semi-reclining, in armour. Three semi-reclining figures oddly and perhaps wrongly arranged. No background. – Fifth Duke of Dorset † 1843. By R. Westmacott Jun. White tomb-chest. The Duke's mantle lies and hangs over it, his shield leans against it, his coronet stands on the ground. At the foot of the tomb-chest a big, white, life-size but lifeless seated angel.

(SCHOOL (former), Drayton Road. Of one and two storeys, with a coat of arms over the door. Founded in 1717–25 by Sir John and Lady Germaine for twenty poor children. M. Seaborne, DOE)

LUDDINGTON-IN-THE-BROOK

ST MARGARET. C13 W tower with clasping buttresses, bell-openings with Y-tracery, and a short broach spire with one tier of lucarnes. Perp s aisle with piers of a characteristic section. Long chamfered projections to nave and aisle without capitals, attached shafts with capitals to the aisle openings. Perp s porch, two big Perp N windows. Chancel in the C13 style; 1875 by *Carpenter*. – BENCHES. C16; straight-headed, with linenfold panels. – SCULPTURE. In the chancel N wall some C13 diapering. – STAINED GLASS. Remains of C15 canopy work. – PLATE. Silver-gilt Cup and Cover Paten, 1640.

LUDDINGTON-IN-THE-WOLD *see* LUTTON

LUTTON

1080

ST PETER. Perp w tower with clasping buttresses, four-light bell-openings with transom, and battlements. Late C13 chancel with an interesting four-light window with one trefoiled and one quatrefoiled circle and a spherical triangle above them. The s arcade of about the same time, the N arcade fifty years earlier. N arcade of three low bays. Circular piers with octagonal abaci, nailhead enrichment, double-chamfered pointed arches. In the aisle w wall one lancet. s arcade with piers of quatrefoil section. Responds on head corbels. Hood-moulds with small head-stops. – EASTER SEPULCHRE. Four-centred arch above six blank panels. The two middle ones stop halfway down to allow for a blank tablet to be set in them. – SCULPTURE. In the tower N wall some Anglo-Saxon interlace. – PLATE. Cup and Cover Paten, 1570; Paten, 1637; Paten, 1706. – MONUMENTS. Robert, William, and Robert Apreece, 1633. Three frontally kneeling figures, their hindparts left out. – Adlard Apreece † 1608. Small figure kneeling in profile, as usual.

(MANOR HOUSE. C17, altered later. Two storeys, with mullioned windows. DOE)

LYVEDEN

9080

OLD BIELD. Lyveden belonged to the Treshams (*see* Rushton) as early as the mid C15. Sir Thomas Tresham, the fervent Catholic who built the Triangular Lodge (*see* Rushton), also owned Lyveden, and, late in his life, created a new building at some distance from the old house. The old house (or Old Build or Bield) was remodelled by Sir Thomas. Preparations for work on the house are recorded in 1604, and probably continued under Sir Thomas's son, Sir Lewis, but the house now contains little that can be connected with that period. One wing with mullioned and transomed windows survives. The windows in the upper storey had two transoms, one window in a lower annexe is older and still has arched lights. After the confiscation of Rushton following the Gunpowder Plot, the Old Bield was the main Tresham house. Much of the work, including the gateway, which has been removed to Fermyn Woods Hall (see p. 216), and the early C17 staircase now in America, dates from the time of Sir Lewis Tresham, i.e. is Jacobean or Early Carolean (GI).

NEW BIELD. A large summer house rather than a house proper. It is situated some distance to the s of the Old Bield and can be reached only by a rough lane. Remains of terracing and a regular arrangement of ponds and mounts between the two. Work was being done on the building already in 1594, but it was unfinished at Sir Thomas's death in 1605. Sir John Summerson has shown that the house was probably designed by *Robert Stickells*. The building is drawn in John Thorpe's famous book of plans and elevations of houses and has therefore wrongly been assigned to him. The rigid symmetry of the plan and the symbolism of the details are equally characteristic both of the date when it was built and the man for whom it was built. Greek cross with, at each end, a canted bay-window rising to full height. Two storeys above a basement. Mullioned and transomed windows. The entrance with a round arch was by an open staircase into the s bay. The plan consists of three rooms on each floor and the staircase in the s arm. The two rooms in the w–e axis are larger than the others. They are the Hall and Parlour on the raised ground floor, and the Great Chamber and a bedroom on the upper floor. The Kitchen and Buttery were in the basement below Hall and Parlour. On the ground floor three arches on piers connect the staircase with the Hall and the Parlour. The cross-shape of the building is an allusion to Christ's Passion. Stickells's surviving design shows that this remarkable conceit was intended to be crowned by an elaborate two-storey lantern surmounted by a domed roof with a large ball.* The metope frieze above the ground floor and the frieze above the upper floor are Catholic

---

* The ball was never erected, but some kind of roof may have been completed as timbers in the house survived until the Civil War. In the mid C18 there was a scheme to Palladianize the unfinished building by completing the walls and adding a large dome and cupola. The designs, signed by *Dougal Campbell*, are in Northampton Public Library (BB ,GI).

demonstrations, referring in particular to the Passion and to the Mater Dolorosa.* In the metopes the ⚒ sign, the IHS sign, the Instruments of the Passion, and Judas's money-bag, in the upper frieze the following inscription partly remains:

Iesus mundi Salus – Gaude Mater Virgo Maria – Verbum autem Crucis pereuntibus quidem Stultitia est. – Iesus, Beatus Venter qui te portavit. – Maria Virgo Sponsa innupta. – T. eam. alt. – Benedixit te Deus in aeternum Maria. – Mihi autem absit gloriari nisi in Cruce Domini XP.

MAIDFORD
6050

St Peter and St Paul. A c13 w tower with its original saddleback roof. c13 also the s aisle, see the w lancet. Three-bay arcade. Octagonal piers, double-chamfered arches. – screen. The tops of two lights attached to the responds of the chancel arch. – stalls. They are plain Perp benches from Eydon church. – communion rail. c18. – plate. Cup and Paten, 1712.

Manor Farm. In the gable towards the street a large, blocked medieval window with a two-centred arch.

MAIDWELL
7070

St Mary. The first items chronologically are the s and n doorways, with plain single-stepped round arches and no responds: that is c12. Then follows the w tower, which must be of the c13. It is unbuttressed, but has the unusual feature of nook-shafts at the angles. One upper lancet window. The bell-openings of 1705. c13 single lancets and two-light windows with a quatrefoiled circle also in the n and s walls, shafted inside. The chancel was rebuilt in 1891 by St Aubyn. The clerestory was removed at this time. – font. c18, of baluster type. – stained glass. Several windows by Kempe, 1892 (E) to 1906. – plate. Paten, 1658; Cup, c. 1680; two Flagons, 1709. – monuments. Catherine Lady Gorges, erected in 1634 by her husband, Edward Gorges, Lord Dundalk. Standing monument. Two recumbent effigies, she a little higher than him and behind him. Two kneeling figures not in situ. Shallow coffered arch. Cartouche with strapwork. Open broken pediment above, framed by halves of an open broken pediment. –

* For further details of the symbolism see Sir Gyles Isham: 'Sir Thomas Tresham and his Buildings', Northants. Ant. Soc. Reports and Papers, LXV (1966).

(Haslewood family. Cartouche. Erected in 1695 by Elizabeth Viscountess Hatton.*)

MAIDWELL HALL. The porch is of 1637. Two storeys, with a balcony on top whose balustrade is vertically symmetrical. Shaped gable behind. The rest is mostly by *Gotch*, 1885, was gutted by fire, and rebuilt in 1902.

MALLOWS COTTON *see* RAUNDS

5040

MARSTON ST LAWRENCE

ST LAWRENCE. Spacious interior. The S arcade is of the C13. Four bays, circular piers, circular abaci, double-hollow-chamfered arches. Much else is Dec: the N arcade of two continuous chamfers, i.e. no break between piers and arches, the N aisle and doorway, the chancel arch (two continuous sunk chamfers), the SEDILIA, EASTER SEPULCHRE, and niches l. and r. of the E window, all with pretty little vaults behind the arches, and also the chancel windows, although the E window is clearly of the later C14, i.e. has passed the frontier to the Perp. The N and S windows are tall, of two lights, with cusped Y-tracery, and transoms. Perp W tower and Late Perp aisle. – FONT. Octagonal, with crocketed blank arches – Dec or Perp ? – SCREENS. Those to the N chapel are Perp and simple, but the tower screen, dated 1610, made up from a reredos, is an uncommonly good example of Jacobean carving. Four columns with ornament and diamond studding. Four figures and cartouches at the top. – PLATE. Cup and Cover Paten, 1621; Breadholder, 1739. – MONUMENTS. Sir John Blencowe † 1726. Signed by *Edward Stanton* and *Horsnaile*. Architectural tablet. Sir John was a Baron of the Exchequer and 'as a just reward had his salary continued to him during his life'. – John Botry † 1728 (N chapel). Yet still with the cartouche form, the drapery, and the putto head at the foot, as had been customary thirty years before. – (John Blencowe † 1777, by *Thomas Burnell & Sons* of London. BB) – William Walmesley † 1809. Signed by *R. Westmacott* (later Sir Richard), but still in the style of his father. – (John Jackson Blencowe † 1852. Signed by *M. W. Johnson*. A scroll with books and a branch of willow. BB) – Many other lesser tablets of the C18 and C19.

MARSTON HOUSE. A large house on a strangely irregular plan.

* Perhaps by *William Stanton*, who made monuments for Viscount Hatton's family at Gretton (BB).

The plan is specially puzzling because the principal features on the entrance and the garden sides are of about the same date – some time between 1700 and 1730 – but do not connect in plan. One is the doorway on the entrance side, with a characteristic open curly pediment, the other the doorway on the garden side, which has a Gibbs surround. The garden side is on a half-H plan, and this is certainly of Elizabethan or Jacobean origin; for in one of the wings is a panelled room apparently *in situ*, with one very rich overmantel which carries the date 1611. Georgian staircase with slim turned balusters, three to the tread, and carved tread-ends.

(VICARAGE, Georgian, the N side earlier than the S side. The latter is of three bays and two storeys, with the outer windows tripartite. Handsome oval dining room.)

MARSTON TRUSSELL   6080

ST NICHOLAS. Tall Perp w tower with clasping buttresses, ironstone and ashlar. Pairs of two-light bell-openings with transom. Battlements and pinnacles. Tall arch towards the nave. The nave arcades differ. The S arcade is of 1300 at the latest. Quatrefoil piers, double-chamfered arches. The N arcade (octagonal piers) is later. The chancel encroaches on the S arcade, see the last pier, now half embedded in the chancel wall. Windows and doorways are mainly of the late C13 to early C14. The N porch is timber-framed. Its entrance is of extremely heavy timbers. – FONT. Octagonal, Perp, with quatrefoils. – (STAINED GLASS. S clerestory. St Peter, C14; Trussell arms, C14–15. RM) – PLATE. Cup, 1570; Dish, 1661; Paten, 1719. – CHEST. Of the dug-out type; C14. – MONUMENT. Mark Brewster † 1612, a London merchant who died 'in the city of Mosco in Russia'. Big kneeling figure.

HALL. The building seems externally all Victorian. At the back some late C17 windows. The staircase with twisted balusters goes with them. Exceedingly fine late C17 gatepiers and large wrought-iron gates from Brampton Ash Hall (demolished in the C18).

MEARS ASHBY   8060

ALL SAINTS. S doorway (round single-stepped arch) and chancel S doorway of c. 1200, the rest mostly C13 to early C14. Low w tower. The two bell-openings on each side are placed in three blank arches. Of c. 1300 the S aisle windows (Y-tracery), the blocked outer recess, and the low arcades of four bays. Octagonal piers, double-chamfered arches. The details differ. – FONT. Norman, octagonal. With rosettes, interlace, etc. The carving is detailed and so sharp that it appears to be re-tooled. – SCULPTURE. Saxon wheel cross-head. – WALL PAINTING. Doom, above the chancel arch, unrecognizable. – STAINED GLASS. Chancel E by *Clayton & Bell*, s by *A. Lusson* (1859). – (w window by *Clayton & Bell*, 1860 (R. Hubbuck). – (Four windows by *Lawrence Lee*, 1959–60. GI) – PLATE. Set, 1685; Flagon, 1702.

Immediately s of the church, facing the churchyard, with a doorway with four-centred head, is an oblong HOUSE with mullioned windows.

VICARAGE. Steeply gabled. This is of 1860, by *Buckeridge*, who had restored the church the previous year (information from A. J. Saint).

MEARS ASHBY HALL. Fine front of 1637. E-shaped, but with very little space between the wings and the porch. The wings have big straight gables, the recessed pieces little ones, the porch an ogee-sided gable into which an ogee-sided three-light window is squeezed. The other windows are of three and four lights. No transoms. The doorway has coupled Roman Doric columns. Large added Tudor wing of 1859–60, by *Salvin*. Adjoining to the w STABLES dated 1647, a square SUMMER HOUSE with a pyramid roof, and a DOVECOTE.

MANOR HOUSE, w of the church. Early C18. Three widely spaces bays, two storeys, hipped roof.

MIDDLETON *see* COTTINGHAM

4040

MIDDLETON CHENEY

ALL SAINTS. Much restoration work by *Sir G. G. Scott* in 1865. Tall Perp w tower with a doorway with the two figures of the Annunciation and tracery in the spandrels, a moulding enriched with fleurons, and a top frieze of angel-busts. Three-light w window. Tall panelled battlements, pinnacles, recessed spire with a band of pointed quatrefoils and two tiers of lucarnes. The total height is *c.* 150 ft, and the proportions are exceptionally good. Most of the windows in the body of the church are Geometrical or in the style of *c.* 1300, but they are renewed. Original s doorway of *c.* 1300. The steep stone roof of the s porch is supported by a transverse arch with a sunk quadrant moulding and big bold tracery motifs above it. Four-bay Dec arcades with piers of quatrefoil section, but with separate narrow hollows in the diagonals. The arches have one chamfer and one hollow chamfer. Above the chancel arch a blocked window and a circular trefoiled window above that. The Dec contributions have been assigned to the years when the future Bishop Edington was rector (1322–35). Prettily painted roof on Perp head corbels.

All this is interesting enough, but what makes Middleton Cheney a place of unforgettable enjoyment is the STAINED GLASS by the *William Morris* firm. It is so beautiful and so important that it deserves a detailed record.* It was put in during the incumbency of W. C. Buckley, a personal friend of Burne-Jones. The E window was designed in 1864 and fitted in in 1865 as a memorial to William Croome, who died in that year. In it, below the small figures in the tracery lights, a frieze of the white-robed twelve Tribes of the Apocalypse and then, again below, Adam, Noah, David, Isaiah, St Peter, St Paul, St Augustine, and St Catherine, and, below once more, Abraham, Moses, Eve, the Virgin, the Magdalene, St John, St Alban, and St Agnes. The Censing Angels, the Seraph, St Peter, St Augustine, St Catherine, Eve, the Virgin, the Magdalene, and St Agnes are by *Morris*, the four beasts and the twelve banners by *Philip Webb*, the Adoration of the Lamb and St Alban by *Burne-Jones*, St Paul and St John by *Ford Madox Brown*, the twelve Tribes, David, Isaiah, Abraham, and Moses by *Simeon Solomon*.‡ In a chancel S window, apparently of 1866–70, panels from the Old Testament (*F. M. Brown*, tracery glass by *Webb*). In two chancel N windows scenes from the Gospels. These are a memorial to Buckley († 1892) and designed by *Burne-Jones* in consultation with Buckley himself. In the N aisle E window (1880) St Mary by *Burne-Jones*, St Anne by *F. M. Brown*, St Elizabeth by the same, the Annunciation by *Morris*, and shields etc. probably by *Webb*. In the N aisle NE window (1880) Samuel by *Burne-Jones* and Elijah by *Morris*,§ and in the W window (1870) the three young men in the fiery furnace by *Burne-Jones*. They

45

* The following is based on long letters from the rector, the Rev. C. E. Glynne Jones, and from Mr A. C. Sewter, the leading authority on Morris glass.

‡ Mr Sewter is less positive on these attributions than Mr Glynne Jones. He has documentation for the Eve and the Virgins as by Morris, the Elders as by Burne-Jones, the banners and some angels as by Webb. For Solomon's contribution there is, according to Mr Sewter, a great probability.

§ Mr Glynne Jones suggests *Rossetti*.

are the most striking of the series. The Dove in the gable window is by *Webb*. – MOSAICS by *Powell & Son*, the longer one (N aisle) designed by *Holiday*. – FONT. Plain, Perp, octagonal. – PULPIT. Perp, with simple panels. – SCREEN. Perp; but the canopy by *Sir G. G. Scott*. – BENCHES. Perp, plain, with buttresses. – DOOR. The S door is medieval and has its original wicket. – PLATE. Cup and Paten, 1752; Flagon, Almsdish, Breadholder, 1764. – MONUMENT. Gothic shrine in the churchyard to the Horton family, designed by *William Wilkinson* of Oxford, made by *Earp*, 1866–7 (A. J. Saint). (VICARAGE. C17 stone, altered by *Scott*, whose Dec N wing is to be demolished. N. Taylor)

THE HOLT, a large stone manor house by *Wilkinson*, 1864 (A. J. Saint), was demolished in 1973.

BAPTIST CHAPEL. 1806. Quite large, of stone, with pedimental gable and arched windows.

7050

MILTON MALSOR

HOLY CROSS. Of the C12 the bases of the N arcade piers, and the lower courses (limestone) of two of them. The rest seems to be of the late C13 to mid C14. Late C13 are the aisle W walls with their windows and the lower parts of the unbuttressed W tower with a doorway with three continuous chamfers. Later battlements and pinnacles. Then a short recessed octagonal stage and a short crocketed spire with two tiers of small lucarnes. The principal windows in the aisles and the chancel are all Dec, specially noteworthy the square one at the E end of the S aisle with an inscribed wheel of radially set two-light arches. The N chapel has a good N window. The E window in the chancel is of five lights with reticulated tracery. The arcades are of the late C13. Four bays with tall slender circular piers carrying octagonal abaci and double-chamfered arches. The same details in the tall chancel arch and the lower N and S chapel arches. – PLATE. Cup, 1570; Paten, 1700; Flagon, 1722; Cup, 1810. – MONUMENTS. Mrs Sapcoates Harington † 1619. Tablet with some strapwork. – Richard Dodwell † 1726. With garlands down the volutes l. and r. of the inscription and two cherubs' heads at the foot.

BAPTIST CHAPEL, W of the church. 1827.

MILTON HOUSE, SW of the church. Built in 1777. Five bays, two storeys, doorway with Tuscan columns and a broken pediment.

Opposite Milton House to the E a similar but earlier seven-bay
HOUSE. The windows are in flat frames.

Opposite this house and to the E of Milton House a gabled C17
HOUSE with a later E front. This is of chequer brick and incomplete. It has three giant pilasters with brick bands.

MANOR HOUSE, W of the church, in a lane off the A-road to the E.
Five-bay, two-storeyed painted front of the early C18. The
windows are in flat frames. Inside an uncommonly fine mid or
later C17 staircase with openwork acanthus scrolls, comparable
with the C17 work at Lamport Hall and Castle Ashby. It
runs through two storeys.

CREMATORIUM, N of the village. A large domed Renaissance
building of the early C20.

MORETON PINKNEY

ST MARY. Of c. 1200 the simple N doorway and the N arcade.
This is of three bays and has circular piers with square abaci.
The arches are pointed but unchamfered. C13 the S arcade
(rebuilt correctly). Circular piers with octagonal abaci, single-
chamfered arches. The PISCINA inside cannot be much before
1300. Also C13 the W tower. Lancet windows and bell-openings. To the N two blank arches l. and r., both trefoiled, but
one rounded, the other pointed. The chancel was rebuilt in
1846, but probably also correctly. Its style is again that of the
C13, as is proved by the single lancets to the N and S, the three
stepped lancets to the E, shafted inside, and the DOUBLE
PISCINA inside. Late C13 foliage capitals and foliage hood-
mould stops. – SCULPTURE. Fragment of an Anglo-Saxon
cross shaft with some simple decoration, now in the SE corner
of the churchyard. – PLATE. Almsdish, 1787; Cup, 1814;
Paten, 1815.

MORETON PINKNEY MANOR. Mainly of 1859 and 1870. At
the turning to Weston, turreted LODGE and impressive
entrance arch, 1859 by E. F. Law. The archway has a rope-
work surround and heraldry of the Barons Sempill.

An attractive village, the cottages a mixture of brown and grey
stone. Wide verges and two greens. (Facing the N one,
chequered brick BAPTIST CHAPEL, by the southern one,
near the church, SCHOOL dated 1822 (enlarged 1876). BB)

MOULTON

ST PETER AND ST PAUL. Of ironstone. There was an aisleless
Norman nave, of which the arch of one window has been ex-

posed inside. To this about the end of the C12 was added a N
aisle. This has low square piers with four demi-shafts and one-
step round arches. About 1300 much was done to alter and
enlarge the church. Witness of this is the S arcade, with
octagonal piers and double-chamfered arches. Witness also is
the start made in the N aisle to encase the old piers, no doubt
with a view to reconstructing the whole arcade. There cannot
be many examples in existence where medieval building procedure can be seen so interestingly. Of *c.* 1300 also a number
of windows (intersected tracery, Y-tracery) and the arches to
the N and S chapels. Dec W tower with Perp, ashlar-faced top
storey. Pairs of two-light bell-openings with transom. Quatrefoil frieze. Battlements. The spire was taken down in the C17.
– FONT. C18. Plain baluster, small gadrooned bowl. – COM-
MUNION RAIL. C18. – SCULPTURE. Fragment of a Saxon
cross shaft. A beast biting its tail. Interlace below. – PLATE.
Cup, 1607; Paten, *c.* 1685; Breadholder, 1735.

METHODIST CHAPEL. 1835. With steeply pointed windows and
doorway and a steep gable. Very pretty glazing bars.

SECONDARY MODERN SCHOOL. 1952–4 by *A. N. Harris*
(County Architect) and *John Goff*. Three-storeyed classroom
with curtain walling all round. The horizontal bands between
the window bands faced with vertical wood slatting. To the W
and E assembly hall and gymnasium, the former connected
with the classroom block by a concourse, the latter by a one-
storey service and workshop range.

(MOULTON COLLEGE OF AGRICULTURE. The main building
is of the 1930s by the then County Architect, *G. H. Lewin*.
Administrative and teaching block 1964, hostels 1967–8, conference hall and library 1968, and other buildings, by the
County Architect's Department (*A. N. Harris* and *John Goff*).)

(ROMAN BUILDING. In 1970 remains of a C3–4 circular building, 18 ft in diameter, were found E of the Northampton-
Kettering road. J. Steane)

MOULTON GRANGE *see* PITSFORD

6060

MUSCOTT

½ m. NW of Brockhall

Of a pre-Reformation house the GATEWAY remains with a stone
ground floor and an upper floor originally probably timber-
framed (suggestion of the D O E). Inside a doorway with two-
centred head. In the present farmhouse one cross-slit. It is

said that it and the core of the farmhouse were part of a barn.

NASEBY

6070

ALL SAINTS. The finest part of the church is the S arcade, as far as it is early C13. It is of three bays and has quatrefoil piers and stiff-leaf capitals and double-chamfered arches. The N arcade is of the C14. Four bays, also quatrefoil piers and double-chamfered arches. The lower parts were encased in the C17 or C18. The fact that the W bay on the S side is later, but on the N side is not, dates the beginning of the W tower, with which the S arcade was to be connected. Its ground floor is indeed Dec. The upper parts are Perp. Pairs of tall two-light bell-openings with transom. Battlements, and a recessed spire (added by *W. Slater* in 1859–60, when the church was restored) with crockets and three tiers of lucarnes. The chancel arch is of the same date as the N arcade, the chancel E window has intersected tracery. – FONT. Circular, Late Norman, with blank arcading and, below the arches, individual flowers. – TABLE. Called Cromwell's Table. Perhaps from Shukbrugh House, the manor house which was partly pulled down in 1773. What remains of it is now Shukbrugh Farm (completely altered). The story of the table is that the King's Life Guards supped at it the evening before the battle. – STAINED GLASS. W window by *Clayton & Bell*; chancel S, *c.* 1872, by *Lavers, Barraud & Westlake*. – PLATE. Cup and Paten, 1683. – BRASS. To John Olyver † 1446 and wife, the figures 2 ft 2 in. long.

In the churchyard a big copper BALL. This came from the stump which was added to the tower about 1780. It is said that it was originally brought from Boulogne in 1544 (Kelly) and that it holds 60 gallons of ale.

(NASEBY HALL (The Wooleys). The house altered by *E. F. Law* in 1859 was damaged by fire in 1948. It has been reconstructed on a smaller scale, re-using some of the old materials. GI)

(MANOR FARM, formerly New Hall. Georgian. The spring which is the source of the river Avon is in the garden of Manor Farm.)

OBELISK. Put up in 1823 to commemorate the Battle of Naseby, but not on the site of the battlefield.

See p. 518

NASSINGTON

0090

ALL SAINTS. Saxon nave, see the SW angle (inside the S aisle) and the W wall with a round-headed and a triangle-headed

opening. Then followed the W tower; for the tower arch is
Late Norman with a demi-shaft, capitals with some leaf
details, and a double-chamfered round arch, and there are
straight joints outside between the tower and the aisles. The
(re-set) N doorway is late C12 too, see the waterleaf capitals
and the hood-mould with small flowers. The W doorway into
the tower would be a little later, say early C13. It has dog-
tooth mouldings and is pointed. Later quatrefoil window
above it. The upper parts of the tower are Perp. The top storey
turns octagonal half-way up the bell-openings. These are of
two lights with an embattled transom. The octagonal part has
big pinnacles in the diagonals and battlements. Behind these
rises a recessed spire with big leaf crockets up the edges. Two
tiers of lucarnes.* Aisles were started in the C13, at about the
time when the W doorway was made. The tower is embraced
by slightly narrower chambers W of the aisles – see the dog-
tooth moulding in the W part of the S aisle, the W lancets, and
the fine E arch of the first S bay (nailhead), and the S porch,
also with much dog-tooth. The rest of the aisles is later C13.
Octagonal piers, triple-chamfered arches. The N windows
with Y-tracery, intersected tracery, and three stepped lancets
under one arch. The S windows are Dec (reticulated tracery).
Perp chancel (with later C13 chancel arch). – FONT. Octagonal,
early C14, with two tiers of small, flat arch-heads. – CROSS
SHAFT. Anglo-Saxon fragment. Crucifixion with sun, moon,
and soldiers. Also a demi-figure, and much interlace. –
WALL PAINTINGS. Last Judgement above the chancel arch. –
N arcade and N aisle figures and scenes, e.g. Wheel of the
Works of Mercy, all c. 1350.

PREBENDAL HOUSE, SW of the church. Early C13 Hall with
original doorways at the N end. The W doorway has a round
head with a single chamfer, the E doorway a pointed chamfer.
The porch here is probably later. The heads by the entrance
are not *in situ*. To the l. of the W doorway two partly blocked
C13 windows under round hood-moulds. The hood-moulds
have square stops. More windows are visible inside. They
have segmental pointed rere-arches.‡ The S range, projecting
to the W to form an L with the Hall, probably contained the

---

* The spire is dated 1640 (BB).

‡ According to Margaret Wood: *The English Mediaeval House*, the window
on the E side of the Hall with a squint commanding the entrance is the earliest
known precursor of the well known later medieval arrangement of a bay-
window at the dais end of the Hall.

offices below, the Solar above. Just s of the w doorway are two internal C13 doorways, one with a round, the other with a segmental head.

MANOR HOUSE, N of the former. Of c. 1500. Pretty oriel to the N. To the E arched entrance and windows with four-centred arched lights.

NETHER HEYFORD

6050

ST PETER AND ST PAUL. C13 the N aisle and the s doorway. The doorway has one order of shafts, a single-step arch, and some dog-tooth decoration. The aisle arcade of five bays has single-chamfered arches on octagonal piers. In the N wall a low tomb recess. The windows are lancets, one of two lights with a circle over. The s arcade is Dec (four wider bays, octagonal piers, arches with two sunk quadrant mouldings). Dec also the chancel windows and probably the clerestory windows in the shape of a pointed quatrefoil placed diagonally. Dec the w tower too. – PLATE. Set, 1698. – MONUMENTS. Sir Walter Mauntell † 1467 and wife. Good figures, 4 ft long, holding hands. – Sir Richard Morgan † 1556. Hanging monument. Kneeling figures facing each other. To the l. and r. allegorical figures in niches on elaborate brackets. Only the r. one, Spes, survives. Sumptuous foliage frieze beneath the relief.*

(Former RECTORY. Yellow and grey stone, Gothic, c. 1870. GI)

MANOR HOUSE. Early C18. Five-bay front of two storeys, with quoins. Doorway on Doric pilasters set against rustication; metope frieze. Lower three-bay wings with, above the ground-floor windows, horizontally placed ovals. (Staircase with turned balusters and carved tread-ends. NMR)

ROMAN BUILDING. In Horestone Meadow, E of the village, is a site first discovered in 1699. It yielded part of a fine floor mosaic, wall-plaster fragments, and 'terra sigillata' and other pottery. In 1821 the building was estimated at 100 ft maximum length.

NEWBOTTLE

5030

The manor house and the church in the trees and a few houses – that is all that remains at Newbottle. The village has disappeared.

ST JAMES. C13 chancel with E window of 1865, Dec tower, and Late Perp s aisle. Internally it becomes clear that the tower is

* Other memorials of this form are at Welford, Harrington, Thorpe Mandeville, and Charwelton (BB).

basically of *c*. 1190–1210. The arch towards the nave has many-scalloped imposts and a pointed arch with two slight chamfers. Dec four-bay N arcade. Octagonal piers, arches with two sunk quadrants. The S arcade has double-chamfered arches. – PULPIT. Simple, with little lozenges in inlay. Dated 1584. – SCREEN. With heavily detailed Perp tracery, probably still C14. – STAINED GLASS. E window by *Kempe*, 1893. – PLATE. Cup and Paten, 1591; Cup and Breadholder, 1627. – MONUMENTS. Peter Dormer † 1555. Brasses. He is 12 in. long; to his l. and r. his two wives kneeling. – John and Elizabeth Cresswell. By *John Stone*, 1655. Sarcophagus with a very Roman foliage scroll. On it the inscription base and on this two free-standing busts. The architectural surround with a big arch and looped-up draperies has disappeared.

MANOR HOUSE. Centre and W wing only; the E wing no longer exists. The centre has mullioned windows with arched lights and probably dates from the time of Henry VIII. Doorway with four-centred head near the l. end and symmetrically grouped upper windows. The Hall fireplace also survives. The W wing is a C17 addition. Library panelling of *c*. 1730. DOVECOTE to the W. Stone, lined internally with brick. Octagonal. (With an open lantern on eight oak posts.)

RAINSBOROUGH CAMP. This is an oval Iron Age hill fort on the S edge of the parish, W of Camp Farm. Excavations in 1961–5 revealed that the Early Iron Age fort had a three-tiered rampart construction faced with drystone or turf walls, a V-shaped ditch, and a counterscarp. The W entrance was inturned and had guardrooms set into the passage walls behind the gates. In the early C4 B.C. the fort was deliberately burnt, and in the late C2 B.C. it was re-fortified with a double bank of dump construction, U-shaped ditches, and simple entrances. In the C4 A.D. a 10 ft square building was built over the deliberately filled-in ditch, and the entrance passage was remodelled. In the C18 the inner bank was heightened, the ditch deepened, and beech trees planted.

5050 NEWNHAM

ST MICHAEL. The W tower is opened as a porch to N, S, and W. Tall, wide, double-chamfered arches. Pink and brown stone. Rib-vault inside with ridge ribs and a large bell-hole. To the E an arch into the church and in addition a smaller doorway to the tower stairs. It looks almost like the arrangement usual for medieval domestic archways into courtyards. A niche with a nodding ogee arch to the w. Set-back buttresses. Recessed spire with two tiers of lucarnes in alternating directions. Perp s doorway with two orders of fleurons. Fine chancel of *c*. 1300 with a large five-light E window. Cusped intersected tracery interrupted to allow for a trefoiled circle at the top. Chancel arch of two continuous sunk quadrant mouldings. Perp aisle E windows. But the arcades differ in date, though both are slim. On the N side two quatrefoil piers of *c*. 1300. The third bay and the whole s arcade Perp. The NE respond is a bust of an angel. – BOX PEWS in the aisles. – PLATE. Cup and Paten, 1638. – MONUMENT. Brass to Letitia Catesby. Her husband died in 1467. Also a shield in a scroll surround. The figure is 2 ft long. – To the l. of the altar an inscription, now illegible, with two putti standing on skulls l. and r. and two praying angels above. This was in the churchyard.

MANOR HOUSE, s of the church. Gabled, with mullioned windows.

NEWNHAM HALL, ¼ m. NE. Whitewashed Regency house with a bow-window to the s. On the opposite side a Greek Doric porch. (To the N an EYECATCHER of *c*. 1850. DOE)

NEWTON BROMSWOLD

9060

St PETER. Small. Dec and Perp. Dec or a little earlier the w tower, Dec the chancel (five-light E window with reticulated tracery) and the N doorway. Internally Dec or a little earlier the SEDILIA and PISCINA in the chancel, part of a simple scheme of blank arcading, and the recess opposite. The N arcade however is Perp, of the four-shafts-four-hollows type. One capital with upright leaves. – BENCH ENDS. Plain, straight-topped, with little buttresses. – FONT COVER. Simple, Jacobean. – STAINED GLASS. Head of a Bishop, nave N. Heads of Apostles, chancel N. All *c*. 1430. – PLATE. Cup and Paten, 1570; Almsplate, 1656. – BRASSES. William Hewet † 1426, rector, 14 in. figure, and Roger Hewet † 1487, chaplain, 2 ft figure.

NEWTON-IN-THE-WILLOWS

8080

St FAITH. All alone in the meadows.* Dec to the N and s, short Perp w tower (two-light transomed bell-openings, deeply recessed broach spire), chancel of 1858 (by *Slater*). The arch on

* Now disused and derelict (1972).

corbels with naturalistic vine and oak. – STAINED GLASS. In the chancel by *Clayton & Bell*, 1858. – PLATE. Cup, 1672. – MONUMENTS. Brass to John Mulsho † 1400 and wife. A very attractive type of composition with small kneeling figures looking up to a large cross and throwing up, as it were, inscribed scrolls which issue from their mouths. In the cross St Faith. The kneeling figures are only 13 in. long. – Richard Tresham † 1433 and wife. Large incised alabaster slab of the mid C16.*

DOVECOTE. The only relic of a mansion of a cadet line of the Treshams (*see* Rushton). The Tresham trefoil is on it. A large oblong building nearly 60 ft long. With two compartments each with its own lantern. There are nests inside for 2,000 pairs of pigeons. The date must be Late Elizabethan (as it has the initials of Maurice Tresham; GI). Below the dovecote was the house. Traces of the terraced gardens survive.

* Mr Greenhill suggests that 1433 should read 1533.

INTRODUCTION

Northampton was an important town in the Middle Ages. Traces of pre-Conquest settlements have been found on the site of the castle. In the castle, of which hardly anything remains (*see* p. 328), the trial of Thomas Becket took place, and many councils and parliaments were held at Northampton. The town had a large Cluniac priory colonized from La Charité-sur-Loire at the end of the CII, near the present Priory Street, the Augustinian abbey of St James established *c.* 1105, and houses of the Greyfriars (N of Greyfriars Street, founded in 1225), Blackfriars (NE of the Castle, before 1233), Whitefriars (between Abington Street and Princes Street, 1271), and Austin Friars (NW of St John's Hospital, before 1275), and short-lived houses of the Friars of the Sack and the Poor Clares. The first extant charter dates from 1189. The medieval town was largely destroyed in the fire of September 1675. Rebuilding began immediately, and an Act of Parliament of December 1675

established a body of Commissioners to draw up regulations
and carry out planning improvements. It seems that *Henry
Bell* of King's Lynn was involved in this work.* Defoe calls
post-fire Northampton the 'handsomest and best town in all this
part of England'. All Saints and the Sessions House are the
finest buildings of those years.‡ Already in 1712 Morton says
that 'the Principal Manufacturie is that of shoes whereof
mighty Numbers are, and have been, sent to Foreign Planta-
tions, and to the Army in Flanders'. But the trade remained
small until the Grand Junction Canal reached Northampton in
1815. In 1801 the town had only 7,000 inhabitants, in 1821
10,000, in 1831 15,000. Even that is only a moderate size. The
London–Birmingham railway touched a point 5 m. s of Northampton (Blisworth) in 1838, and the town received its own
railway station at last in 1845. The line went to Peterborough.
Law's very informative map of Northampton was issued in
1847. Growth speeded up so that in 1861 the figure of 33,000
inhabitants was reached. The shoe trade differs from most others
in that for a long time it did not encourage either the introduction of machinery or the creation of large units of production.
Machinery, according to Mr Hatley, began to appear only in the
1860s and 1870s, and large units are a yet younger phenomenon.
In 1960 Northampton was still characterized by the many small
factory buildings of brick scattered over most parts of the town.
Now, in 1972, these are beginning to be swept away for large-
scale shopping and office areas and for an inner northern ring
road. This transformation of the centre of Northampton is only
one aspect of the changes which are just becoming noticeable.
In 1969 a plan for the expansion of the town was published
by *Hugh Wilson & Lewis Womersley*. The population is to
increase from 130,000 (1969) to 230,000 (1981). 30,000 new
dwellings are to be built. The new areas of housing will be mostly

* An anonymous biographical essay published in 1728, referring to his
interest in architecture states that 'the town of Northampton, which was
Re-built agreeable to his Plan, and pursuant to his own Direction, is a
Testimony sufficient to evince his Masterly Hand in that Noble Science to
succeeding Ages'. See H. M. Colvin and L. M. Wodehouse, *Architectural
History*, 4–5 (1961–2).

‡ The medieval town plan survived the rebuilding, but is now disappear-
ing beneath recent developments. The curving line of Bath Street–Silver
Street–College Street and Kingswell Street probably indicates the site of pre-
Conquest defences. The town expanded w, and the line of the medieval
walls can be traced along St George's Street, Campbell Street, Upper and
Lower Mounts, Cheyne Walk, and Victoria Promenade.

See
p.
518

to the E and S of the present town (see Outer Northampton, pp. 349 and 355).

INNER NORTHAMPTON

The area circumscribed by, and including, the main-line S–N railway, Grafton Street, Campbell Street, Upper and Lower Mounts, York Road, Cheyne Walk, Victoria Promenade, and St Peter's Way. This corresponds roughly with the walled medieval town.

CHURCHES

ALL SAINTS. The medieval church was burnt in the fire of 1675, except for the W tower and the crypt below the chancel. The lower parts of the masonry of the tower may go back to the C12, the crypt could be of the C13. In 1232 an indulgence was granted to contributors to the building of the church. The crypt lies below the W part of the present chancel and has a central octagonal pier and four compartments with simply chamfered rib-vaults. The tower is mostly of the C14 including the triple-chamfered arches to the N and S, dying into the imposts.* The upper part was repaired in 1617 and received its balustrade probably in the late C17. The pretty cupola is of 1704, the details of the bell-openings of the C19. The rest of the church was rebuilt in 1676–80. The architect was per- 18 haps *Henry Bell* of King's Lynn.‡ The portico was added in 1701. This lies in front of the tower and the rooms to its l. and r. It is of eight unfluted Ionic columns carrying an entablature with inscription along the frieze. In the middle a rather under-sized STATUE of Charles II by *John Hunt*. The motif of the portico comes from Inigo Jones's former W portico of St Paul's, but the scale at Northampton is modest as compared with that of St Paul's. The portico at Northampton is two bays deep. The church is entered by three arched doorways with two small niches between. The W tower rises behind the portico in the somewhat awkward way later made the rule by Gibbs (St Martin-in-the-Fields etc.).

* The tower was originally a central tower.
‡ *Henry Bell* was certainly associated with the rebuilding work, as a document of 1676 now in the Northamptonshire Record Office records the appointment of Mr Henry Bell and Mr Edward Edwards, 'two experienced Surveyors now residing in . . . Northampton', as 'managers' of the work on the church, to which was allocated one-tenth of the money collected for the rebuilding of the town after the fire.

32   The church itself is in the form of a square, about 70 ft across, composed on the pattern of Wren's St Mary-at Hill (1670–6), i.e. with a domed central space, four arms of equal length and height, and four-flat-ceilinged lower corner pieces. The centre rests on four monumental unfluted Ionic columns and opens into a dome with a lantern. The four arms have segmental tunnel-vaults. All this is stuccoed. The vaults are not of stone. The chancel was redecorated in 1888 by *E. F. Law* in imitation of the original style but a little grander and richer.* The N and S sides of the church are externally symmetrical, of five bays with an oval window under a segmental pediment above the centre. The same motif repeats above the E end of the nave. The windows have curious tracery throughout, with pointed lights and circles in a kind of plate tracery. The War Memorial Chapel is an addition by *Sir A. Blomfield & Sons* and *A. J. Driver*. The late C17 church was highly admired at the time, and is indeed one of the stateliest of its date outside London. Morton in 1712 called the most eminent 'Public Structures' in the county Peterborough Minster for the 'Greatness and Beauty of Gothic Architecture' and All Saints for 'the Conveniences and Ornaments of the modern Improvement of that Art with relation to Buildings of this kind'.

The wooden GALLERIES spoil the interior, partly because they introduce a longitudinal motif in a central plan and partly because they were cut back in 1865. Originally they came forward to the four giant columns. – The REREDOS is of 1888 (PAINTING of the Crucifixion by *P. H. Newman*). The original reredos with the PAINTINGS of Moses and Aaron is now above the W gallery. – FONT. Of marble, given in 1680, the base altered in 1888. – PULPIT. Wood, of *c*. 1680. Originally in front of the altar. The stand is not original. – The former SCREEN was removed a long time ago. – MAYOR'S CHAIR. A splendid piece, dated 1680. – COMMUNION RAIL. Of *c*. 1680. Turned balusters. Half-way up each baluster an openwork bulbous motif. – DOORCASES of the three W doorways into the body of the church. Of *c*. 1680 and very fine, especially the middle one with open segmental pediment. – THRONE with coat of arms above (E end of N aisle). Formerly in the Consistory Court in the W vestibule of the church. – PLATE. Two Cups, Cover Paten, Flagons, Almsdishes, and Breadholder, all of 1677; Cup and Strainer Spoon, 1718; Cup, 1740. –

* The moulded arch on Ionic columns in the chancel, and the giant pilasters at the E end of the nave are his additions.

MONUMENTS. Many, all minor, e.g. Mrs Beckett and Mrs Sargeant † 1747 and 1738 by *S. Cox* (with a charity child standing against an obelisk), and Richard Backwell, 1771 by *William Cox* (with some rocaille ornament). – In the church-yard to the E WAR MEMORIAL by *Lutyens*, 1926. Two widely spaced obelisks and an altar between them.

ST ANDREW, St Andrew's Street.* 1841–2 by *E. F. Law*. Iron-stone. Big. In the lancet style. Pairs of tall lancets along the sides. W tower with pairs of lancet bell-openings. Wooden galleries inside. Small rectangular apsidal chancel.

ST GILES, St Giles' Street. The dominant element is the tall crossing tower. This is Norman, but its upper parts fell in 1613 and were rebuilt in 1616. The top was again renewed in 1914. The church is long, with a nave of five bays, of which the two W bays are an addition of 1853–5. It has aisles, a clerestory of the C17, and an outer aisle rebuilt also in the 1850s. The aisles extend to where the Norman transepts were. The chancel has N and S chapels. The earliest remaining parts are the Norman arches of the crossing. The tall W and E arches were unblocked in 1853–5 and reconstructed on the basis of re-mains of the original E arch. They have two orders of shafts and capitals with leaf volutes. Traces of the Norman N arch survive. The W doorway is of the same time, but even more restored. It was re-set when the church was lengthened. It has a continuous inner order of zigzag and two outer orders with shafts and more zigzag. To the N of the tower is a stair-turret. The simple late C12 doorway of this survives inside the N aisle. The staircase itself has a rotating tunnel-vault. With the turret doorway goes another doorway, on the S side of the chancel, close to its E end. That proves the chancel to be to its full length of a date earlier than the present early C13 lancet windows. The difference in masonry is indeed clearly visible outside. The two flat buttresses on the E wall should also be noted. They break off where the masonry changes. The big E window has C19 tracery. Of the chancel lancets one remains to the S, close to the C14 S chapel, and one and part of a second on the N side can be seen inside. It will be noticed that the N wall of the C13 chancel was slightly pushed N as against the Norman one, whose position can be guessed from the relation to the chancel arch. The N crossing arch was reduced in size about 1300. (The other crossing arches were blocked in the C17.) The present arch to the N is triple-chamfered and

* Now demolished.

dies into the imposts, while the inner order of the double-chamfered s arch rests on two head-corbels. Of about the same time is the s arcade, as far as it is medieval, i.e. in its three E bays. Octagonal piers, double-chamfered arches. The old parts of the N arcade were damaged when the tower fell, and coarsely renewed in 1616. Of the C14 the arches to the N and s chapels, that of the N chapel triple-chamfered and dying against the imposts, that to the s chapel very tall and of three hollow chamfers. The N chapel windows were re-done in 1512. They have four-centred arches and simple panel tracery. The C19 work is by *E. F. Law*. It was based on a report made in the 1840s by *G. G. Scott*, whose brother was curate of the church. – FONT. C15 with blank Perp windows as motifs of the panels. Much re-cut. – REREDOS. Stone, alabaster, and mosaic. By *Law*, 1883. – PULPIT. Jacobean. – CHANDELIER (N chapel). Brass, 1745. – STAINED GLASS. W window by *Powell's*, c. 1858. – E window *Clayton & Bell*, 1876. – N aisle *Hardman*, 1869 and 1884. – N aisle w window *Heaton, Butler & Bayne*, c. 1883. – MONUMENT. Alabaster tomb-chest of the C15 with figures under shallow tripartite cusping and separated by thin buttresses. They are alternatingly angels and bedesmen (N aisle E end). – Several tablets by *Hunt* and the *Coxes*.

St JOHN BAPTIST (R.C.), Bridge Street. Part of the medieval Hospital of St John, founded c. 1137. The hospital had prob-ably at first an infirmary hall and aisles for the beds and an aisleless chapel to the E. The chapel was allowed to remain but, when the infirmary became an almshouse, the domestic quarters were built on the site of the former s aisle. It is for this reason that the NE angle of the former almshouse just touches the sw angle of the chapel. The almshouse building was in 1955 converted into an R.C. church, with a new chancel. The old chapel, which had been restored in 1881 by *S. J. Nicholl*, thus became a side chapel. The master's house lay further to the N and was destroyed when the (now de-molished) railway station was built. The chapel has a Perp five-light w window and doorway (traceried spandrels) and an early C14 E window (three lights, intersected, cusped). The s wall was rebuilt in 1853. In it a simple original early C14 doorway, now connecting the chapel with the former alms-house. Good traceried W DOOR. The almshouse (now church) has an early C14 front to the street, with a tall blank arch on shafts with moulded capitals and a smaller doorway set into it.

This has a re-set arch with deep mouldings. Above the blank arch a handsome rose window filled by a saltire cross of pairs of pointed arches. The building before conversion consisted of a two-storeyed W part, a two-storeyed E part, and a one-storeyed centre. The latter must have been the Hall. It has Late Perp windows. The other windows are Elizabethan or later. Roof with tie-beams and queen-posts. The W gallery incorporates the balusters from the former staircase. – STAINED GLASS. Upper part of a C15 figure. – St John (nave S window). It comes from the chapel of Ashby St Ledgers. – Three complete figures of c. 1845; good. From *Pugin*'s original church of St Felix, now R.C. Cathedral; see p. 338. – (In the chapel Munich glass by *Mayer*, of the Crucifixion. G1)

ST PETER, Marefair. The most interesting Norman church in Northamptonshire, large, and with a number of unusual features. The exterior appears long in relation to the relatively stumpy W tower. This was rebuilt in the early C17, but contains much that is Norman work. In the W wall an original flatly carved arch containing saltire crosses, knots, etc. Above, blank arcading to the N and S in two tiers. Scalloped capitals. The curious thing about the tower is the angle buttresses. They are semicircular in plan and have on either side a semicircular companion. Along the N and the S of the church the most remarkable fact is the absence of any structural division between nave and chancel and the emphasis on this fact by an uninterrupted row of blank arcading all along the clerestory. Every so often a Norman window under one of these blank arches. N and S doorways Norman and simple. The E end was rebuilt by *Scott* in 1850, but it is affirmed that he had sufficient evidence for the semicircular buttress in the middle of the E wall. Most of the windows are probably of the C17. One Perp window in the S chancel aisle.

The interior is outstandingly ornate and distinguished by 23 the use of alternating supports, a motif familiar in cathedrals and abbeys (Jumièges, Durham, Peterborough transept, etc.) but highly unusual in parish churches. Is the ambitious conception of St Peter connected with its situation close to the castle ? The alternation is between quatrefoil and round piers. The round piers have broad waistbands or shaft-rings. The quatrefoils consist of a shaft towards the nave which rises without any break to the roof and no doubt supported the main Norman beams. This also is a motif often used in major and rarely in minor churches. The shaft towards the aisle seems to have supported a transverse arch. There is no evidence for vaulting in the aisles. The nave consisted originally of three such double bays, but half of one was cut off when the tower was rebuilt in the C17. Extremely elaborate tower arch, obviously reconstructed. Three orders of shafts, decorated with lozenges, zigzag, and fluting. Decorated abaci, arches with much zigzag. One would like to think that this was the original chancel arch. But there would not have been space for one. The continuity of the arcades, only changing from double to single bays, is again most unusual. Chancel aisles of three bays. Circular piers, the second ones with shaftrings – a hint at the alternation of supports in the nave. All arches with zigzags. The capitals are of many types, with thin curly trails, with broader bands, with volutes, with palmette leaves. The clerestory windows are not in line with the arcade arches. The date suggested by all these particulars is *c.* 1150 or a little later. In the S aisle an early C14 tomb recess.

FURNISHINGS. FONT. Octagonal, Perp. Stem and bowl in one. Blank windows with tracery as decoration. – REREDOS. By *J. Oldrid Scott*, 1875–9. – SCULPTURE. In the S aisle recess two Anglo-Saxon fragments with interlace decoration (the cross shaft is of the C9 according to Sir Thomas Kendrick), re-used as Norman bases. – Norman sepulchral slab, mid-C12 with big trails, partly emanating from the mouth of a bearded man. Also 'inhabited' scrolls, i.e. with beasts in them (S aisle E end). – STAINED GLASS. In two S windows by *Sanders*, 1891, nothing special. – PLATE. Paten, 1709; Cup and Paten, 1711; Breadholder, 1713; Flagon, 1715. – Processional Cross and Almsdish, 1917 and 1919, by *Omar Ramsden*. – MONUMENTS. William Smith, the creator of modern geology, † 1839. Bust of marble by *M. Noble*. – (John Smith, the mezzotint artist, † 1742, by *John Hunt*. BB) – Many other minor tablets by *Hunt* and the *Coxes*.

HOLY SEPULCHRE, Sheep Street. A Norman round church with a C14 W tower and a long C13 chancel. Round churches are a rarity in any country. They were favoured by the Knights Templars and Knights Hospitallers in memory of the rotunda which formed part of the church of the Holy Sepulchre in Jerusalem. In Britain a round Templars' church survives in London, and remains or records tell us of more: in London on the first site of the Templars, in Holborn; in Bristol; at Dover; at Asleckby and Temple Bruerne in Lincolnshire; and at Garway in Herefordshire. There are also remains of St John at Clerkenwell, London, belonging to the Hospitallers, and of St Giles Hereford, a hospital dependent on the Hospitallers, and also the C14 church of the same order at Little Maplestead in Essex. But the round church at Northampton, just like that at Cambridge, though called Holy Sepulchre, is a parish church and always has been one.* Holy Sepulchre at Northampton was founded about 1110 by Simon de Senlis, Earl of Northampton, who had taken part in the First Crusade. The church then consisted of an oblong chancel in addition to the round nave. Of this chancel windows can still be traced inside the present chancel aisles, and long stretches of the corbel table, partly re-set, also remain. The nave has a circular central space and a circular ambulatory. [25] They are separated by eight strong round piers with circular, many-scalloped capitals. The two to the E have square abaci, the next two square ones with the corners notched back, the four to the W circular abaci, perhaps the earliest ones in England. The arches and the octagonal upper storey were remodelled in the C14. The arches are tall and single-chamfered. The elaborate ROOF of the rotunda dates from 1868, that of the ambulatory from 1879. The ambulatory is said to have been originally two-storeyed with a vaulted lower floor. The springing of the vault is still in places visible against the outer wall, but it is difficult to visualize how the vault would have met the circular piers. There are, however, remains of Norman ambulatory windows on a lower and an upper level. There is also a mysterious built-in Norman shaft, just N of the W entrance into the ambulatory. It is taller than the springing-points of the surmised vaults. Externally the only Norman feature apart from the windows is some remaining flat buttresses.

The chancel was gradually rebuilt and enlarged by aisles and an outer N aisle from c. 1180 to c. 1330. The N arcade comes first. Two bays are original. The responds have three shafts separated by r. angles and leaf capitals. The pier is circular with four thin tripartite groups of shafts in the cardinal directions and moulded capitals. The difference in style has made Professor Bony suggest that the pier was replaced about the middle of the C13. The arches are pointed and have two slight chamfers. Two splendid image brackets from the E wall

* A circular nave also exists at the chapel of Ludlow Castle and another has been excavated beneath the parish church of West Thurrock in Essex.

are set in the present E wall. They are big leaf capitals on the heads of a King and a Bishop. An outer aisle was added in the late C13 (rebuilt by *Scott*). It consists of three instead of two bays, and has quatrefoil piers with slenderer subsidiary shafts in the diagonals, moulded capitals, and double-chamfered arches. A PILLAR PISCINA in the E respond. Renewed Purbeck shaft and a little nailhead decoration. The S aisle is assigned to the C14, but cannot be in its original state. The arches are earlier than the clumsy square piers, and their mouldings do not go with the shapes of the piers. The ambulatory is connected with the chancel aisles by triple-chamfered arches. Of the C15 roof of the chancel 'nave' the CORBELS remain, carved with figures playing musical instruments (bagpipes, portative organ, hurdy-gurdy, kettle-drum, etc.). The whole E end of the church, including the semicircular apse, is by *Scott* and dates from 1860–4. It is a typically High Victorian attempt at improving on the Middle Ages. Scott introduced polished shafts and a greater variety of flora in the capitals. Finally the W tower, a very impressive piece of the early C14. Very big diagonal buttresses with five set-offs. Recessed spire with three tiers of lucarnes. Deeply moulded doorway with continuous mouldings. Also moulded frames of the W window and the bell-openings.

FURNISHINGS. BANNER-STAFF LOCKER. C14? In the ambulatory S of the chancel arch. Such lockers were usual in East Anglia, but are rare otherwise. They are simply very tall recesses. The one at Holy Sepulchre is 11 ft high. – SCULPTURE. Norman trefoiled tympanum with the bust of a man between a small human figure and a dragon. Early C12 (ambulatory, W wall). – In the S wall of the churchyard, near the SW corner, head of a churchyard cross, C15, with Crucifixus on either side. – (CHANCEL SCREENS. By *J. Oldrid Scott*, 1880. – Victorian TILES in the rotunda by *Lord Alwyne Compton*, 1861.) – STAINED GLASS. (Tower W window by *Hardman*, 1878.) – In the outer N aisle, W window Battle of Richard Coeur-de-Lion by *Mayer* of Munich, 1883. – S aisle, another by *Mayer*, 1899, and one by *A. J. Dix*, 1903. – N chapel E window by *Kempe*, 1887. – (S chapel E window by *Burlison & Grylls*, 1887.) – BRASS to George Coles † 1640 and two wives, all modishly dressed. Still cut-out figures, as in the Middle Ages.

NONCONFORMIST CHAPELS. Brief remarks on some in inner Northampton, in chronological rather than topographical order. The sequence starts with the DODDRIDGE STREET CONGREGATIONAL CHURCH, where Doddridge preached for twenty-two years. Square, secular-looking stone building of 1695, enlarged in 1862. Pyramid roof. Two-storeyed. Three by six bays. (Interior with galleries and box pews. – MONUMENT. Philip Doddridge † 1751. An asymmetrical pyramid of the *Cox* type, although signed by *John Hunt*. BB) Then the COMMERCIAL STREET CONGREGATIONAL CHURCH of 1829 (by *John Davies*) (now disused), stuccoed, three bays with a three-bay pediment and arched windows. Later porch. The same scheme still in the GRAFTON STREET BAPTIST CHURCH of 1868. Brick, five bays, two storeys, the upper windows arched. Three-bay pediment. Also the same scheme, but now gone grand, in the COLLEGE STREET BAPTIST CHURCH, 1863 (by *William Hull*), where the pediment rests on detached giant columns.* Compare also Outer Northampton.

PUBLIC BUILDINGS

TOWN HALL, St Giles's Square. The present assertively 100 Gothic façade consists of two parts, the seven E bays with the symmetrically placed tower by *Edward Godwin*, 1861–4, begun when he was only twenty-eight, and the additional w bays with the big gable by *Matthew Holding*, with assistance on the interior from *A. W. Jeffery*, 1889–92. The style is Gothic of the late C12, and in general Franco-English, but with allusions to Italian Gothic as well. (The *Illustrated London News* called it 'Continental Gothic'.) Godwin himself stated afterwards that he was strongly influenced by Ruskin's *Stones of Venice*, which he read just before the competition.‡ Rich texture, with plenty of reliefs and statues (the reliefs in the porch by *Nicholls*, the statues by *R. L. Boulton* of Cheltenham). Inside, a corridor leads through the building from the main entrance. The impressive GREAT HALL is on the r. Walls with arcading below, large circular windows above. The panels under arches decorated in 1925 by *Colin Gill* with paintings of famous men connected with Northampton. The columns of the blind arcading are of cast iron and have elaborate capitals of iron foliage. They carry cast-iron brackets also with foliage, and on these rest the wooden arches for the roof. Arched recesses

* The one Gothic building, the PRINCESS STREET BAPTIST CHURCH of 1890 (by *Dyer*), brick, with asymmetrical turret, was demolished in 1970.

‡ See *The British Architect*, 1878, Vol. 2, p. 210. Mr Gordon Hamilton kindly gave us this information.

at both ends of the hall. On the l. of the corridor a small winding staircase (stained glass on the landing by *Heaton, Butler & Bayne*) leads up to the former Council Chamber (now COMMITTEE ROOM A) in the centre of Godwin's building. This has its original table and chairs and two fireplaces, all by *Godwin*, in a heavy style reminiscent of Burges. A corridor leads E to the present COUNCIL CHAMBER in Holding's extension, a fine room richly decorated on all four sides with Gothic arcading in white and brown stone, sculptured frieze, and naturalistic capitals. STATUE of Spencer Perceval, M.P. for Northampton, 1817 by *Chantrey*. From All Saints. At this end of the building a strange, cramped Gothic staircase (which divides in two despite its size) leads to the ground floor. Here also much carving, the capitals illustrating trades and industries, etc. Godwin's building has a rear façade to Dychurch Lane which originally housed a Fire Station, Reading Room and Museum.

88 SESSIONS HOUSE, George Row. 1676–8. The architect is a problem. The building has been attributed to *Henry Bell* (*see* Introduction to Northampton). There is a contemporary account that it was 'contrived and layd out' by *Sir Roger Norwich*, head of the Committee of Justices of the Peace, but that may only mean that he was responsible for the plan. The accounts also mention a payment of £100 to *Mr Edward Edwards*, surveyor. Five-bay N front, the l. and r. bays stressed by attached unfluted Corinthian columns and segmental pediments. The three bays between have large windows with carved surrounds and flat wooden mullion-and-two-transom crosses. Hipped roof, originally with a cupola and pedimented dormers with oval windows. To the w one bay treated like the first and last bays to the N, but with coupled pilasters. This forms an excellent picture with All Saints as one approaches from the w. Inside, splendid plaster ceilings by *Edward Goudge*; 1684–8. First the w ANTEROOM with a wreath of flowers and fruit. Partitioned off to the E is the NISI PRIUS COURT, to the s is the CROWN COURT.* These both have ceilings with central wreaths with deeply undercut leaves, and even more daringly undercut flowers etc. in the spandrels. At the end of each ceiling a fat boy Justice between cornucopia, and also an angel's head and a devil's head. Goudge did equally prodigious work at Cambridge. Behind the Sessions House was the GAOL, built in 1791–4 by *Brettingham*.

* The partitions between the courts are later additions.

Enlarged in 1846 by *James Milne*. Largely pulled down in 1930. What remains is a big range, almost entirely rewindowed, which stretches s to Angel Street and ends in a broken pediment with a lunette. To the w of the Sessions House the COUNTY HALL, an extension in a remarkably ornate Palladian style. Of five big bays. Rusticated ground floor with short pilasters. Upper floor with attached unfluted Ionic columns and heavily pedimented windows The building was originally a private house. It was entirely rebuilt in 1845 by *James Milne*, remodelled in 1890 by *Edmund Law*, who designed the half-oval Council Chamber, and altered again c. 1900 by *Aston Webb*, who redesigned the entrance, vestibule, octagonal ante-chamber, and staircase.*

COUNCIL OFFICES, Guildhall Road. Designed in 1934 by *G. H. Lewin*, then County Architect, and *J. A. Gotch*; plain neo-1700.

POLICE, FIRE STATION, PUBLIC BATH, Upper Mounts. A group of 1938–41. By *J. C. Prestwich & Sons*. Ashlar stone, not in any period style, severely block-shaped, especially the l. and r. buildings, i.e. the Police and Bath. The Fire Station is desperately uninspired. The swimming bath has big round concrete arches and side windows in three diminishing tiers.

MUSEUM AND ART GALLERY, Guildhall Road. 1883, 1889 (remodelling), and 1934. It occupies part of the former gaol (*see* above).

PUBLIC LIBRARY, Abington Street. 1910 by *Herbert Norman*. Palladian. Statues of Northamptonshire worthies. The interior remodelled in 1969–70 by the Borough Architect, *Leonard Howarth*.‡

TELEPHONE EXCHANGE, Spring Gardens. The large extensions under construction are by *F. L. Mason* of the Department of the Environment, consultant architects *Leonard J. Multon & Partners*. Plans were accepted in 1971.

CASTLE STATION. Rebuilt in 1963–4 by *R. L. Moorcroft* of the London Midland Region's Architect's Department. An attractive glass-walled gabled range with booking office etc. at r. angles to the track. A small courtyard behind. The other stations have been demolished.§

* Information from Bruce Bailey.

‡ Exhibited in the Library is a large series of Northamptonshire drawings by *F. L. Griggs*.

§ ST JOHN'S STATION was of 1872 by *Alexander Milne* of Northampton. Porte cochère with excessively fat pillars and columns. BRIDGE STREET STATION was of 1845 by *W. Livock*; brick, Jacobean, symmetrical.

CASTLE. Of the great castle, obliterated by the railway, virtually nothing remains. It appears to have been a motte and bailey, walled in stone, and with a great semicircular earthwork covering its gate. It was founded in the late C11 or early C12. Leland mentions its 'large kepe'. Excavations in 1961 revealed that the C12 defences included a ditch 90 ft wide and 30 ft deep, and a bank 80 ft wide and 20 ft high. Remains of stone buildings within the bailey were also found. All that remains is a minor archway with continuous chamfers, re-erected in the wall towards Marefair. The castle was one of the most famous Norman castles in England.

PERAMBULATION

The centre of Northampton is All Saints church, and fortunately
2 not the Market Square. The MARKET SQUARE is just sufficiently linked with it not to be a backwater, and yet sufficiently isolated to retain an unmistakable identity, something of the character of market places in Holland or Belgium. Another reason for giving that impression is that only three streets (and three passages) enter it, and that the streets enter it at the corners. Also no building is too dominant – if the Town Hall had been placed here, the square would have become its forecourt – nor any too awful. That was the impression in 1960. But since then several good buildings have been demolished. The replacements have so far been mediocre. The fountain in the centre has disappeared, and so, alas, has the most distinguished and conspicuous building, the PEACOCK HOTEL on the E side.* It has been replaced by a sadly nondescript block with shops, depressing evidence of this century's aesthetic standards compared with the efforts made in the town after the 1675 fire. A passage through leads via a shopping precinct to Abington Street. By *Leslie Cook*, 1960–1. N of this on the E side No. 32, ironstone, Georgian, of four windows and two

---

* The FOUNTAIN was of cast iron, erected in 1863 and somewhat like a green candelabrum. It was designed by Mr *Atkinson* (G. Hamilton). The commemorative panels have been preserved, and are at Abington Museum. The PEACOCK HOTEL was of 1676 and later. It was eleven bays wide with a top cornice of upright acanthus leaves proving that all eleven already formed part of a whole by 1700 at the latest. Most of the fenestration however was Georgian. The carriageway was not in the middle. Above it a wide sumptuously framed window with open segmental pediment and the complicated details of Thorpe Hall in the Soke of Peterborough. Another window of the same date above it. The windows to the l. appeared in their proportions to be the earliest.

and a half storeys. In the middle a pretty Gothick oriel. Adjoining, the WELSH HOUSE, one of the few that escaped the fire. It is dated 1595 and has above a spoiled ground floor some gay Elizabethan overdoor decoration and an inscription in Welsh. (Good staircase inside.) After much discussion, permission to demolish Welsh House was refused in 1972, and there are now plans to restore it to its original appearance.* The building stands just to the N of the Market Square proper, in what was a street called Newland. The rest of this street has now vanished beneath the enormous GROSVENOR CENTRE (architects: *Stone, Toms & Partners*; consultants: *Percy Thomas Partnership*), on which work started in 1972. The centre will extend N to Lady's Lane and E to Wood Street, with pedestrian shopping malls on two levels, and a car park and ten-storey office block behind.‡ The entrance will be just beyond Welsh House, and the redevelopment also includes the rebuilding of most of the N side of the Market Square (stone-faced façades, ground floors with segmental arches) and the destruction of its centrepiece, the EMPORIUM ARCADE.§ W of this, in PARADE, the ROYAL INSURANCE COMPANY, 1850 by *E. F. Law*, has been replaced by a new building by *Sir John Brown, Henson & Partners*, 1960–1.|| Next to this is the former CORN EXCHANGE (now Gaumont Cinema), by *Alexander* and *Hull*, also 1850, classical, but stuccoed and with a giant Ionian order *in antis* above a rusticated ground floor.¶ On the W side, at the N corner, VICTORIA HOUSE, probably of *c.* 1840, stuccoed too, and with a giant

* The neighbouring house (now demolished) had a broad doorcase with fluted Doric pilasters, and a pediment, probably from Welsh House. (Information from Mr Hatley.)

‡ Excavations in 1972 around the former Greyfriars Street (i.e. S of Lady's Lane) revealed remains of medieval buildings which must have been part of Greyfriars. They included a double-vaulted structure, *c.* 30 by 120 ft, which was probably a N–S claustral range, and floor areas with glazed tiles, no doubt part of the church. (Information from Mr John Williams.)

§ This was of 1901 by *Mosley & Scrivener*. A grand archway decorated with *Doulton*'s tiles (preserved, and now stored) led to an engagingly off-centre octagonal space with a glass dome. The whole could have been re-habilitated as a shopping precinct leading to the bus station planned in Lady's Lane. Instead this will be reached by a dull new passage from the Market Square.

|| *Law*'s building was only three bays wide but remarkably monumental, by means of an unusual restraint. The style was Italian Cinquecento. Tall rusticated ground floor (the vermiculated panels were a Victorian favourite), first floor with windows in pedimented aedicules.

¶ The iron gates from the Corn Exchange are at the Museum at Abington.

order too, but here pilasters, very elongated, through two and a half storeys. Nice C18 and early C19 houses follow.* The s side starts on the r. with DRURY CHAMBERS, stately, Early Georgian, but probably re-faced. Five bays, three storeys, giant upper pilasters. Two windows on the first floor with curly open pediments. Its neighbour No. 18 is much humbler, but much more genuine. Later C17, with pilasters through the upper storeys. The Ionic capitals have garlands connecting the volutes. Thick garlands also below the upper windows. Broad proportions of the windows. No. 19 is early C19, stuccoed, with a pleasant C19 ground-floor window (formerly a Savings Bank, DOE). The SE corner is now occupied by NORWICH UNION HOUSE, 1962–5 by *A. W. Walker & Partners*. Five storeys, much too large and clumsy for its site.‡ This faces into the narrower s continuation of the Market Square which links it to the traffic milling round All Saints. To the E of the church, and more aware of its surroundings, is the MIDLAND BANK, 1963–7 by *Whinney, Son & Austen Hall*. A slightly concave front faced with yellow Casterton stone. Ground floor with arched windows, top floor set back. For the other buildings around the church see pp. 326 and 334.

The Perambulation now turns NE along ABINGTON STREET, where there is much variety but little quality. No. 1 at the corner of Market Square is dated 1677. Altered ground floor, but first floor with eared window surrounds (the plaster swags are C20).§ The street is now the town's main shopping area. On the N side, Nos 15–29, up to the corner of Wood Street, are being redeveloped (1972) by the Prudential Assurance (architect: *K. C. Wintle*). N of this, in Wood Street, the Grosvenor Centre reappears (*see* Market Square).‖ Opposite, between Wood Street and Wellington Street, the depressingly massive NORTHAMPTON HOUSE, a mediocre office block of ten storeys now visible from all over the town. By *Stone, Toms & Partners*, 1971–2. Back in Abington Street the most dominant recent buildings are BRITISH HOME STORES, extended by *Beecroft, Bidmead & Partners*, 1967–70, and

* The building housing the Northampton Development Corporation is a tactful rebuilding of 1968–9.

‡ It replaced WATERLOO HOUSE, stuccoed, with giant pilasters, probably of *c.* 1830.

§ The best small building, No. 23, one bay with bow windows on two floors, has been demolished.

‖ In Princes Street, off Wood Street, was the MASONIC HALL, 1889 by *Ingman & Shaw*, Jacobean, symmetrical, stone.

MARKS AND SPENCER by *Monro & Partners*, 1968–9. Tucked away to the N of Marks and Spencer, in WELLINGTON STREET, is the QUAKER MEETING HOUSE, early C19, altered, red brick, hipped roof, with a single-storey porch on the N side. Back in Abington Street the most conspicuous older building, with neither variety nor quality, is the long barrack-like brick front of the CONVENT OF NOTRE DAME, built in 1871 by *William Hull*. Then ANGLIA BUILDING SOCIETY by *Rolf Hellberg & Maurice Harris*, 1962–5. Standing forward from the main block is a tall glass-walled lobby. Inside, a double-height hall with gallery. More visible round the corner in LOWER MOUNTS. Here the building is of five storeys with marble-faced spandrel panels and a brick staircase tower. Between the two parts the original building by *Mosley & Anderson*, 1891 (extended 1930). Abington Street continues with Abington Square (*see* Outer Northampton, p. 343). Turn NW along Lower and Upper Mounts. Between the two EARL STREET runs NE. Here the former church of ST CRISPIN, now a warehouse. In the C13 style, with plate tracery and a flèche. 1883 by *Holding*. In Upper Mount all that matters is public buildings, but on the l. in CAMPBELL SQUARE are the earliest surviving major industrial premises of Northampton. The one with the tall recessed Italianate tower was built for Manfield's, the shoe manufacturers. As Mr Hatley has found out, it was erected in 1857, when during a strike it was referred to as the rising 'monster warehouse' and Mr Manfield assured strikers that it would not be used for operating machinery. The architect is unknown, but the adjoining brick building on the l., with the rounded corner, was illustrated in *The Illustrated London News* in 1859 and the architect is mentioned there, *William Hull*. Mr Hatley in addition discovered an advertisement of the architect in the *Mercury* in February 1857. The strike meeting was in November 1857. So both buildings went up at the same moment. The former Manfield building is stuccoed. It has three storeys. Symmetrical façade of nine bays, turning in a typically Victorian way to double the number on the top floor. Extension on the r. Then REGENT SQUARE, the junction of Campbell Street and Sheep Street. (Near Grafton Street, the former CHINESE LAUNDRY, early modern of the 1930s, by the local architect *Lawson Carter*.*) Back to the centre by SHEEP STREET (for Royal Terrace, Barrack Road,

* Information from Mr John Goff.

see p. 339). Good, even flow of Georgian houses, with quite a
number of nice doorcases. Behind No. 47, the Ex-Servicemen's
Club, a new CONCERT HALL is being built, by *Rex Bryan &
Pennock*, 1972. No. 57 of five bays and three storeys has a pair
of doorcases with Roman Doric pilasters. Above, a Venetian
oriel and above this a Venetian window. Nos 18–24 looks late
C17. It has heavily tapered pilasters on the first floor. The main
motif, l. of the centre, is the niches flanking a window
(altered). This was once an inn, then the town house of the
Earls of Halifax, and, after 1740, the seat of Dr Doddridge's
Academy for Dissenting Ministers. Opposite, much devastation (1972).* The s continuation of Sheep Street is DRAPERY.
On the W side the NATIONAL WESTMINSTER BANK, 1841
by *E. F. Law*, a remarkable building, restrained, grand, and
pure. Palladian, with upper giant columns and a pediment.
Next door ADNITT'S, 1958–62 by *Deacon & Laing*, Northampton's first large store in the modern idiom. Turquoise
spandrel panels. On the E side of Drapery several commendably
discreet recent buildings (e.g. No. 50, SKIPTON BUILDING
SOCIETY, 1968–9 by *Sir John Brown, Henson & Partners*,
brown brick with hipped roof, and No. 48, GLYN MILLS
BANK, 1965–6 by *John & Michael Chaplin*). Towards
the s end No. 12 (W. & R. SHIPMAN) is early C18 and
later. Only one bay wide. Good C19 shop-front with
square bay-window above.

So back to All Saints and now off in an easterly direction. In
ST GILES'S SQUARE immediately to the l. of the Town
Hall a gabled four-bay office building in the so-called Queen
Anne style as made fashionable by Sir Ernest George. Brick
and rubbed brick. Superimposed pilasters. By *Matthew
Holding*, 1886. Opposite, BARCLAYS BANK, 1888 by *Charles
Dorman*, extensions by *Rex Bryan & Pennock*, 1971. Off St
Giles's Street to the s in CASTILIAN STREET, MEMORIAL
HALL, by *A. E. Anderson*, 1919. Scottish Baronial in minia-
ture. Doorway with curly pediment between two turrets; on
the l. a corbelled-out, stepped gable. Further E along ST
GILES'S STREET No. 74, ST THOMAS'S HOSPITAL,
castellated and stuccoed. Built in 1834. Opposite a terrace of
houses again in the Ernest George style (Nos 81–7, also 73).
This is also by *Holding*. Round the corner to the N ST GILES'S
SCHOOL, very Gothic, stone with brick dressings, by *Law*,

* In BEARWARD STREET were Nos 10–14, a pleasant early C19 stuccoed
group, and some humbler C18 houses on the other side.

1858–61. In SPENCER PARADE, s of the churchyard, first a castellated (Nos 1–3) then a gabled (Nos 4–5) Tudor house, both stuccoed, and then a neo-Jacobean house (Nos 6–7). We are clearly here in the Early Victorian developments of a still suburban, i.e. leafy, kind. In fact, according to Mr Hatley, the houses are on a map of 1841 but not on one of 1836. E of the churchyard a terrace first mentioned in 1838, the angle bays with giant pilasters, the centre house with a Greek Doric porch *in antis*, the end houses with thickly ornamented cast-iron porches.

Turn s down CHEYNE WALK (including Melbourne Crescent on the w). Here the houses are detached. The northernmost is High Victorian Gothic (of 1868, by *Law*). Then the Y.M.C.A., a nice design, 1957–8 by *Nicholls & Moodie*. The villas further s probably of *c.* 1845. A little to the E along the BEDFORD ROAD is ST THOMAS'S WELL, a gabled Gothic recess in the c13 style; 1843.

Back to the centre along DERNGATE. At the corner is EAST-GATE HOUSE, facing SE. Stuccoed, a grand composition but trailing off in the l. third. Opposite, i.e. at the SE corner of Derngate, BECKET HOUSE and No. 82, with a prettily ornamented cast-iron porch. No. 78 is a c19 terrace house remodelled in 1916 by *C. R. Mackintosh* for Bassett Lowke (cf. New Ways, p. 346). Mackintosh added bay-windows at front and back and moved the staircase so that it rises between front and back rooms. The partly openwork screen decorated with glass geometric panels, between the stairs and front room, survives; also a little of the wall decoration. Originally the front room had a frieze of rather jazzy triangular leaf motifs and a black ceiling. In the back room a Mackintosh fireplace. Many nice houses in Derngate, Nos 54–64 with identical doorcases.* No. 44 (part of the GIRLS' HIGH SCHOOL) has a tall (altered) doorcase with fanlight. The school buildings next door are by *W. Cecil Young*, the range behind facing Victoria Promenade by *A. W. Walker*. More recent additions of the 1960s facing Albion Place by *F. H. Allen* (top storey by *Stimpson & Walton*). Also in ALBION PLACE a brick terrace of *c.* 1830. Then followed the VICTORIA

---

* Nos 54–64 date from *c.* 1815–20, as Mr Hatley could prove from rent-books and newspapers.

Opposite, Nos 59–69 are being redeveloped for Sun Alliance. Architects: *Leach, Rhodes & Walker*, 1972. The plans look sympathetic to the character of the street.

DISPENSARY.* Another brick terrace of *c.* 1835 leads down to Victoria Promenade. Cast-iron porches and an unusually beautiful cast-iron first-floor veranda with big honeysuckle motifs (Nos 17–18). Beyond this, an acceptable new office building, ALBION HOUSE, by *A. W. Walker & Partners*, 1964–6. Four storeys, with a projecting wing neatly containing the porch. White mosaic panels, black mullions. So back to Derngate. On the N side NEWILTON HOUSE by *R. A. Barker* of Wilson Properties, 1961–3. Then just to the s in GUILD-HALL ROAD, No. 9, Gothic, brick, of 1872–3,‡ and the REPERTORY THEATRE, formerly the Opera, by *C. J. Phipps*, 1884. The original auditorium survives, small but lavish. Finally GEORGE ROW. E of the Sessions House the JUDGE'S LODGING, a dignified flat-fronted Georgian house of five bays. Then w of the Council offices the COUNTY CLUB. Five bays, porch with rusticated pillars, tiny central pediment. It dates from after the 1675 fire and so is associated with *Henry Bell*'s activities. Inside a fine late C17 staircase survives, with a stair-well ceiling of *c.* 1740. Below, late medieval vaulted cellars; octagonal piers, quadripartite rib-vaults.

To the s only BRIDGE STREET. At the E corner LLOYDS BANK, classical, 1924 by *F. W. Dorman*. Further s No. 7, a one-bay C18 house with two storeys of bow-windows. On the w side the former BLUE COAT SCHOOL and ORANGE SCHOOL. Two houses, of brick, both dated 1811 on prettily lettered name-plates over the doors. The s part higher, three bays, three storeys, stucco quoins and lintels. The N part lower, with big windows on the upper floor separated by niches. The two Charity Children at present in Northampton Museum probably lived in these niches. For ST JOHN'S HOSPITAL, a little further s, *see* p. 320.

Finally to the w. In GOLD STREET at once on the N side the former offices of Phipps's Brewery, three bays, brick and stone, tall, three tall upper bay-windows with round corners. The style is a mixed Dutch and French C17. Built in 1881 by *S. J. Newman*. Off to the s in KINGSWELL STREET the BECKET AND SARGEANT CHARITY SCHOOL, 1862 by *Law*, brick and stone, five bays, symmetrical Gothic. In Gold

---

* This was built as a public bath. 1844–5 by *George H. Willcox*. A lively façade. From l. and r. first one bay, then a two-bay projection, then in the middle a bow. The bow had Doric pilasters in two tiers, the two-bay part a colonnade of elongated Roman Doric columns. White and arcadian-looking.

‡ By *Law*, as Mr D. H. Holliday kindly tells me.

Street soon the GRAND HOTEL, by *Charles Dorman*, 1889–92, of no architectural interest. Off to the N up COLLEGE STREET and W along St Katherine's Street to the MEMORIAL SQUARE, really a public garden, made in 1951.* To the S ST KATHERINE'S HOUSE, by *Newman, Levinson & Partners*, and next to it and along HORSEMARKET, SCOTTISH LIFE HOUSE, by the *Philip Goodhew Partnership*, both under construction in 1972.‡ Horsemarket has been widened. Further N is the SAXON INN HOTEL, 1971–2 by *Ivan Nellist & Ian Blundell*. It has a distinctive roof line formed by a series of canopy-like arches. The same motif is repeated on the single-storey part to the E. N again a multi-storey CAR PARK, by the Borough Architect's Department (Borough Architect *Leonard Howarth*), under construction 1972. To the NW is an area of council housing. ST MARY'S COURT, the point-block of ten storeys (the first in the town), is by the then Borough Architect, *J. L. Womersley*, 1952. More blocks since. Back to the junction of Horsemarket and MAREFAIR. The W side of Horsemarket and the N side of Marefair are now dominated by BARCLAYCARD HOUSE, the first really large development in the town to date, but one that heralds the scale of the transformation that is beginning to overtake much of the town centre. Significantly, it is by the London firm of *R. Seifert & Partners*, 1969–72. A very long low range to the street, contrasting painfully with the small varied frontages opposite that still survive at the time of revision and broken only by a passage through to a central courtyard. A recessed taller part at the end, and more taller parts at the back, which is more satisfactory. Here the upper storeys step out over the lower ones. On the S side of Marefair, No. 33, HAZELRIGG HOUSE, dates from the C17. Altered later, and reduced in size. Coursed rubble, three big dormers with the semicircular gables typical of the mid C17. Tall mullioned windows. Irregular fenestration. Doorway with flat classical surround. Staircase with twisted balusters, probably later. There are plans for the development of the area round Hazelrigg House, between Marefair and St Peter's Way, as a series of linked courts, by *Marshman, Warren & Taylor*. The perambulation ends at the Castle Station, on the site of the CASTLE (p. 328).

* The STATUE by *Frank Dobson* (Seated Nude with a Fish) has been damaged and is now stored.

‡ The one Georgian building in Horsemarket, the SPENCER HOTEL, of five bays, has been demolished.

OUTER NORTHAMPTON

The strata of Outer Northampton consist of firstly, the old villages and mansions now within the town boundaries (Abington, Great and Little Billing, Dallington, Delapré Abbey, Duston, Hardingstone, Kingsthorpe, Weston Favell); secondly, the suburban development of the C19 and early C20 (the earliest to the N, the most interesting and affluent to the E); thirdly, the mid-C20 housing estates (Eastfield, E, and King's Heath, W); and fourthly and most recent the development just beginning for the expanded town (E and S). It is simpler, however, to describe Outer Northampton topographically rather than chronologically, and the area has been divided up as follows. Churches and Public Buildings will be found in their appropriate sector.

NORTH

(a) THE AREA S OF KINGSTHORPE GROVE

ST LAWRENCE, Duke Street. By *Burder & Baker*, 1877–8, in the Pearson style and notably good and progressive. Tall, of red brick, with nave and chancel under one roof. No tower. Lancet windows. The brick is exposed inside. Wide nave with low aisle passages and very tall clerestory. Tall s chancel chapel of two double bays, the subsidiary piers octagonal and as slender as in Pearson's St Augustine, Kilburn. The arcade repeats on the N side for the organ chamber. Straight E end with lancets in groups.

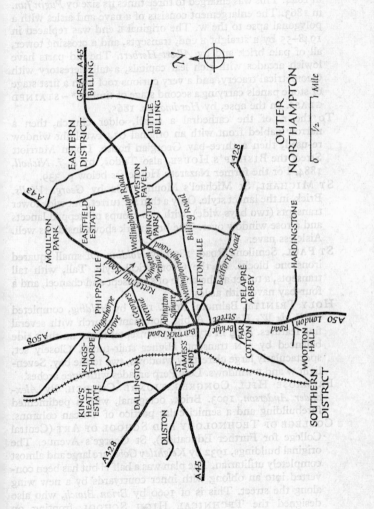

OUTER NORTHAMPTON

1 Mile

0   ½

St Mary and St Thomas, R.C. Cathedral, Kingsthorpe Road. A small church of St Felix was built by *A. W. N. Pugin* in 1844. This was enlarged to three times its size by *Pugin Jun.* in 1863. The enlargement consists of a nave and aisles with a polygonal apse to the w. The original E end was replaced in 1948–55 by a straight E end, transepts, and a crossing tower, all of pale brick and by *Albert Herbert*. The old parts have lowish arcades with rich leaf capitals, a tall clerestory with Geometrical tracery, and a very curious roof with a first stage of stone panels carrying a second stage of timber.* – STAINED GLASS. In the apse, by *Hardman*, c. 1865.

To the r. of the cathedral a small, older church, then a narrow gabled front with an original C14 two-light window re-used, then a three-bay Georgian house. Down Marriott Street the BISHOP'S HOUSE, also Tudor, by *S. J. Nicholl*, 1884. For the former Nazareth House *see* below p. 339.

St Michael, St Michael's Mount. 1882 by *George Vialls*. Brick, in the lancet style. Only a thin sw turret, but wide lower transepts (two bays wide), with two groups of stepped lancets and a rose window over. The brickwork shows inside as well. Aisleless nave.

St Paul, Semilong Road. 1890 by *Holding*. Of small squared ironstone blocks. In the Geometrical style. Tall, with tall transepts, a turret at the angle of s transept and chancel, and a four-bay nave with aisles.

Holy Trinity, Balmoral Road. 1909 by *Holding*, completed by *E. de W. Holding*. A big, dominant church with several fine features. Perp in style. Big transeptal tower on the s side balanced by a N transept. Higher stair-turret. Closely set, spectacularly large clerestory windows, two to the bay. Seven-light w and E windows. Low Perp arcades with ogee arches.

Primrose Hill Congregational Church. By *Alexander Anderson*, 1903. Brick, octagonal, with a pedimented forebuilding and a semicircular portico of Tuscan columns.

College of Technology and School of Art (Central College for Further Education), St George's Avenue. The original buildings, 1932 by *Keightley Cobb*, are large and almost completely utilitarian. The plan was a half H but has been converted into an oblong with inner courtyards by a new wing along the street. This is of 1960 by *Brian Bunch*, who also designed the TECHNICAL HIGH SCHOOL fronting on

* PAINTINGS. Resurrection and Assumption by *Heinrich Hess*, large, now stored.

Trinity Avenue. Tall block and lower ranges, one of them containing the Hall. Brick which much glass, a lively group.

NORTHAMPTON SCHOOL FOR GIRLS, St George's Avenue. 1915 by *Sharman & Archer*. Part of the group of Technical College and Technical School. Symmetrical, neo-Georgian, with a turret. Brick, but the centre, including a segmental pediment, stone-faced. Nice ranges of the 1950s behind.

LEICESTER UNIVERSITY CENTRE, Kingsthorpe Road. Formerly Nazareth House, and part of the R.C. Cathedral complex (*see* above). 1876–7 by *F. W. Tasker*. Elizabethan with some Gothic details. Attached to it in Marriott Street the former chapel with lancet windows and a flèche.

MILITARY ROAD PRIMARY SCHOOL. 1885 by *C. Dorman* and *W. Talbot Brown*. Pretty, low, symmetrical, of brick, with gables and a middle lantern. Decayed plaster decoration on the principal gables.

BARRACKS, Barrack Road. The oldest part of 1796, ashlar-built. The rest 1877–8, brick. Threatened with redevelopment (1972).

DRILL HALL, Clare Street. 1859. Brick with round towers and lancet windows, entirely like an American armoury.

The early C19 development of the town can be followed N along BARRACK ROAD. First ROYAL TERRACE, three storeys, stuccoed, of *c.* 1830.* REGENT HOUSE follows, three storeys, three bays, with central two-storey porch. Then LEICESTER TERRACE and, a little grander, ADELAIDE TERRACE. Nos 1–3 Adelaide Terrace are treated as one composition with a recessed centre with balcony. Opposite on the E side THE POPLARS with a porch with Ionic columns and a pretty veranda at the side; LANGHAM PLACE, beginning in the 1840s, three-bay houses with projecting porches; and then a succession of terraces with progressively fussier details, ending with the BARRATT SHOE FACTORY. This is of 1913, by *Anderson*. It has crude Baroque motifs in terracotta.

(b) KINGSTHORPE

ST JOHN BAPTIST. An aisleless Early Norman church is recognizable by its windows above the arcades in the nave as well as the chancel. About 1170–80 aisles were added, first, it seems, to the chancel on the N side, then to the nave on both sides. The chancel aisle has two bays, circular pier with

* The earliest newspaper advertisement is, according to Mr Hatley, of September 1827.

square abacus, many-scalloped capitals, and unmoulded round arches with a hood-mould decorated by nailhead. The same arches continue in the three-bay nave arcades. The piers are circular too and the abaci square, but the capitals are very shallow and have leaf motifs. The chancel was lengthened after 1300 – see the one ogee-headed lancet in the N chapel. A rib-vaulted CRYPT with a central octagonal pier lies below the E end (cf. All Saints Northampton). The ribs are chamfered. The wide one-bay chancel chapels are of the early C14. Externally the most noteworthy feature is the two square-headed S windows of the S chapel. They are Dec. The lights have ogee heads, and the windows are framed on three sides by fleuron friezes. Dec but simpler the aisle windows and the N doorway. Fine W tower of the C14, refaced in its upper parts. Doorway with continuous mouldings, tall tower arch. Tall two-light bell-openings. Recessed spire with lucarnes in three tiers.* – PULPIT. Jacobean. – STALLS. Some in the chancel, with poppy-heads, are original. – (STAINED GLASS. Nave N. Early C14 grisaille. RM) – PLATE. Set, 1678. – MONUMENT. Edward Reynolds † 1698. Oval cartouche surrounded by excellently carved flowers etc. Two putti.

ST AIDAN (R. C.), Manor Road. 1963 by *J. S. Comper*. The exterior red brick, the interior whitewashed, aisleless, in a minimal Gothic. Spatially quite effective. Domed Lady Chapel in the SE corner.

BAPTIST CHAPEL, High Street. 1835. Still classical.

KINGSTHORPE GROVE SCHOOL. A large single-storey building decorated with bright red terracotta. Art Nouveau drain-pipes and glass. By *Law & Harris*, 1905.

(CHURCH OF ENGLAND PRIMARY SCHOOL, Knights Lane. By *A. W. Walker & Partners*, 1962.)

KINGSTHORPE HALL. By *John Johnson* of Leicester, late C18.‡ White stone, five by five bays, two and a half storeys. In the main façade the ground-floor windows in blank arcading. Vaulted entrance passage. Very handsome spiral stair behind going all the way up. Wrought-iron balustrade. Pedimented STABLES behind the house.

N of the church No. 39 VICARAGE LANE, with a gable to the road, is of two storeys with mullioned windows. Derelict at the time of writing. More nice stone cottages behind, and further on (e.g. No. 47), but others have been demolished.

---

* The church was restored by *Slater* in 1863 (R. Hubbuck).

‡ Sir Gyles Isham suggests that *c.* 1775–80 is the most likely date.

Some of the survivors will be incorporated in a redevelopment scheme (1972). s of the church a pleasant group around the green. At the sw end in KINGSWELL ROAD, close to the entrance to Kingsthorpe Hall, the HOME FARM, old buildings including an oblong DOVECOTE.

From here MILL LANE leads to another centre on the main road, with THE COCK, careful gabled Tudor of 1893, and opposite, ST DAVID'S HOSPITAL. This is on the site of the Hospital of Holy Trinity, of which the last minor remains were demolished in 1928. The present house dates from 1882 and has since been added to.*

EAST

(a) ABINGTON SQUARE – KETTERING ROAD – EASTFIELD ESTATE

ST ALBAN, Broadmead Avenue, Eastfield. By *William Randoll Blacking*, one of his last buildings, consecrated in 1938. Brick, mildly Tudor, with a s tower close to the w end. Whitewashed inside. Square piers and unmoulded arches, no capitals or other moulding between pier and arch. – SCREEN. With classical columns, wide open.

ST EDMUND, Wellingborough Road. 1850 by *J. W. Hugal* of Cheltenham. The N aisle and clerestory by *Matthew Holding*. Of ironstone with a crossing tower and lancet windows. The finest motif is Holding's cross-gabled clerestory, each bay with a group of three stepped lancets. The interior is less rewarding. Lavish circular piers, stencilled walls. Steep roof on steep arched braces. – STAINED GLASS. Chancel E, with big figures, by *Hardman*, 1850–2.

ST MATTHEW, Kettering Road. 1891–4 by *Matthew Holding*. Big and prosperous, brown stone, cut into small regular blocks. Asymmetrically placed NW tower with a stone spire 170 ft high. Transepts, flèche, polygonal apse. Tall proportions, lancet windows and windows with plate tracery. The s porch continues the w front. Interior faced with white stone. Stone-vaulted chancel and apse (on Holding's dependence on Pearson, *see* Far Cotton, p. 351). The nave not vaulted but with a timber roof on big diaphragm arches. (Many contemporary furnishings: PULPIT, FONT, and REREDOS all of alabaster, by *W. Aumonier*. – TRIPTYCH by *C. E. Buckeridge*.

* To the N of this, No. 12a Harborough Road North is a decent flat-roofed brick bungalow by *Alan J. Ede*, 1966, for himself (N. Taylor).

– FONT RAIL and CHANCEL SCREEN by *G. R. de Wild*. – Also much STAINED GLASS: apse windows by *Clayton & Bell*; N chapel, and N and S aisle windows (1899) by *Alexander Hymers*; baptistery windows by *Pownall*; w window by *Burlison & Grylls*; later N transept window by *Kempe*.) But much more important the contributions of the C20. – SCULPTURE. *Henry Moore*'s famous Northampton Madonna. Made of Hornton stone in 1944 for Dean Hussey, then vicar of St Matthew. Dean Hussey shortly after commissioned a PAINTING as well: *Graham Sutherland*'s Crucifixion. This was unveiled in 1946. The Moore is in the N transept, the large Sutherland in the S transept. The Moore is as peaceful as the Sutherland is violent. Graham Sutherland must have been deeply impressed by Grünewald's Isenheim Altar. Background mauve, squarish shapes, to the l. and r. of the feet of Christ brick-colour. As for Moore's Madonna, the subtle way should be observed in which the colour variations and the veining of the stone have been used.

NONCONFORMIST CHAPELS. Quite a variety, as in Inner Northampton, though nothing noteworthy before 1875. The KETTERING ROAD METHODIST CHURCH of 1879 is reactionary. Red and yellow brick. Arched, i.e. Italian or Romanesque, windows. Sides with two tiers. Front with two starved towers. The KETTERING ROAD UNITARIAN CHAPEL, 1896 by *Charles Dorman*, is Gothic with an asymmetrically placed turret. Brick with stone dressings. Hall attached on the r. A typical Nonconformist design of *c.* 1900.

(COLLEGE OF EDUCATION, Moulton Park. By the *Consortium of Private Architects of Northampton*, under construction 1972.)

MANFIELD ORTHOPAEDIC HOSPITAL, Kettering Road. A substantial mansion begun for the shoe manufacturer Sir Philip Manfield by *Charles Dorman*, 1899–1902. Jacobean, with a large r. gable. Porch with heavy strapwork above. Inside, a staircase with lavish screen and large stained glass window.

ST EDMUND'S HOSPITAL (former WORKHOUSE), Wellingborough Road. 1837 by *G. G. Scott*. Brick, classical, starshaped, with pedimented façade.

CONSERVATIVE CLUB, Adnitt Road. 1892–4 by *Charles Dorman*. One of the best examples of the early Norman Shaw style in Northampton. Of three storeys, with projecting gables, towering over the surrounding terraces.

WAR MEMORIAL, Abington Square. 1937–8 by *Sir John Brown & Henson*. Memorial loggia. Light brick, the slim circular piers faced with gold mosaic. Long seat against the back wall, and above this inscriptions.

To the ENE the start is ABINGTON SQUARE with the War Memorial (*see* above) and the terracotta STATUE of Charles Bradlaugh, M.P., by *Tinworth*, 1894. Kettering Road runs NE. Off it, in ABINGTON AVENUE No. 19 by *Mosley & Anderson*, c. 1890, on a corner site with a rounded front and a pyramid roof. In HOLLY ROAD to the N a curiosity, HOLLY COTTAGE, 1892. A humble terrace house lavishly ornamented with sculpture by its builder and owner, *John Brown*, who worked on the Guildhall. The Prodigal Son over the doorway.

To the E of Kettering Road, PHIPPSVILLE, a spacious well-to-do suburb built up slowly from the 1880s in a variety of styles. Good examples in COLLINGWOOD ROAD, and in THE DRIVE, e.g. WESTBROOK, formal neo-Georgian, 1905, and Nos 1–3, probably by *Holding*.

1 m. N of Phippsville the EASTFIELD ESTATE. This was designed by *J. L. Womersley*, then borough architect, in 1953. In the New-Town style, with low-pitched roofs, terraces of cottages, and occasional three-storeyed flats. Pleasant if uneventful architecture. To see it at its best one ought perhaps to see the King's Heath rather than the Eastfield Estate (*see* p. 357).

(B) ABINGTON

ST PETER AND ST PAUL. Of c. 1200 the lower parts of the W tower, the S doorway, and the chancel. The tower is stone and unbuttressed. Some blocked original windows. Plain one-step tower arch. The bell-stage is Perp (two-light bell-openings with transom). Simple S doorway, the arch with two flat steps. In the chancel N wall small lancet. The nave had aisles, but these were ripped out in 1821 after a storm had damaged the church, and a wide nave was created. Large windows with pointed arches. The aisles were continued into transeptal chapels. They survive, with their W arches in line with the W arch of a former crossing. Perp SEDILIA (damaged). – FONT. Octagonal, Perp, the stem with blank tracery panelling, the bowl with quatrefoils, a rosette, a large leaf, etc. – FONT COVER. Octagonal, spire-shaped, with crockets up the angles. – PULPIT. A splendid piece of c. 1700, as richly carved in the Gibbons style and with as large a tester as that of any Wren church in the City of London. – COMMUNION RAIL. Of c.

1700, with dumb-bell balusters. – WEST GALLERY. Of *c.* 1938. – (ROYAL ARMS above, of *c.* 1660.) – PLATE. Cup, 1805. – MONUMENTS. Brass to William Mayle † 1536. Only the piece with the daughters survives (chancel floor). – Two tomb-chests with black marble tops, to Sir Edmund Hampden † 1627 and Dame Elinor Hampden † 1634 (N chapel). – William Thursby, 1730 by *Samuel Cox* (S chapel). Stiffly standing in barrister's robes below a baldacchino; Ionic pilasters l. and r. – Downhall Thursby, 1733, also by *Samuel Cox*. Tablet with bust at the top in an open pediment. – Several other tablets to the Bernards and Thursbys, including some by the *Coxes*.

CHRIST CHURCH, Wellingborough Road. Begun in 1904 by *Matthew Holding*, enlarged by *E. de W. Holding*. Of small, regularly cut ironstone blocks. The style is of *c.* 1300. To the W still incomplete. One more bay and a big W tower to follow. E end with transepts two bays wide. Chancel with S chapel.

ST GREGORY (R.C.), Park Avenue North. Incomplete. 1952–4 by *J. S. Comper*. Brick, neo-Byzantine. The interior unsuccessfully eclectic.

ABINGTON AVENUE CONGREGATIONAL CHURCH. 1910 by *Sutton & Gregory*. Entirely C. of E. in style. Ironstone, the same small regular blocks which Holding used. SW tower. The STAINED GLASS in the E window is by *Sir Frank Brangwyn*, 1921.

PARK AVENUE METHODIST CHURCH. 1924 by *George Baines & Son*, brick, in a free fancy Gothic, typical of Baines. Asymmetrically placed tower, flèche, lively skyline.

ABINGTON MUSEUM (former MANOR HOUSE). The S range is of before the Reformation. Hall with thin hammerbeam roof (the timbers renewed in 1951). To the courtyard tall four-light mullioned windows, one in the hall proper, one in the big square bay. They are probably a C17 alteration. (In the windows fragments of early C16 stained glass relating to the Bernard family, which therefore dates from the building of the Hall. In the spandrels of the entrance two roundels with Labours of the Months, of *c.* 1500. RM) The blocked doorway with its four-centred head may be original. Good stone fireplace of *c.* 1740. At the same time a new façade was set somewhat in front of the old, and a new E façade was built. (These are dated 1738 and 1743.) The architect was probably *Francis Smith* of Warwick. The S front has square projections in the middle and at the ends. Broad arched doorway with rusticated surround and rusticated pilasters. The Lobby between the façade and the Hall Gothic with a plaster vault. Another vault in the bay-window. These date from *c.* 1760–70. The E front of eleven bays with three-bay pediment. As for the other rooms, the Staircase with turned balusters must be mid-C17, although not in its original position, and the Oak Room has plenty of panelling, of *c.* 1500, from the house, but also not *in situ.** Mostly linenfold panels with figures of many kinds. In Abington Park, NW of the house, a TOWER dated 1678. Above, it is a dovecote, below, it has a well served by a water-wheel. (GATEPIERS towards Weston Favell, *c.* 1820. KEEPER'S COTTAGE (formerly the Rectory), C17, altered later.)

The PERAMBULATION proceeds anticlockwise around the Park.

At the NW corner of the Park ARCHWAY COTTAGES, two symmetrical sets of late C17 cottages with dormers and mullioned windows connected by an arch which now leads down to a courtyard with other cottages. Did the road once go through the arch? W of the cottages, just to the S of Abington Avenue, LOYD ALMSHOUSES, 1846 by *E. F. Law*, Tudor style, symmetrical, yellow and grey stone, with gables and dormers. Then a short detour down the WELLINGBOROUGH ROAD. At the corner of Roseholm Road THE ABINGTON (formerly Abington Park Hotel), 1898 by *Holding*, with lavish French Renaissance detail. Then opposite Christ Church (*see* p 344) the MANFIELD FACTORY, 1890–2 by *Charles Dorman*, long, low and symmetrical, one to two storeys, brick, Tudor style, with mullioned and transomed windows and gables with Dutch C17 decoration.‡ Back to Abington Park along CHRISTCHURCH ROAD, where THE NOOK and HILLCREST are oddities worth a look. THE COTTAGE and THE BUNGALOW round the corner in Sandringham Road are of the same vintage.§ Then along PARK AVENUE SOUTH, and E round ABINGTON PARK CRESCENT. ST CHRISTOPHER, the former Rectory is by *Law*, 1846, yellow and white stone, Italianate, with low-pitched roofs. Abington Park Crescent received its houses mostly in the first quarter of the C20. A number of them are pleasant to look at, notably TREETOPS (No. 23) by *Barry Parker*, 1923.

* Possibly from the Hall screens.
‡ The works were all on one floor, an advanced system of production for its date.
§ By *Anderson*, *c.* 1906 and later. Hillcrest was built for himself (BB).

There is an instructive variety of styles in this area. Back in WELLINGBOROUGH ROAD, ADELAIDE HOUSE, careful neo-Georgian by *Brown & Henson*, *c.* 1910. But by far the most important house is NEW WAYS, No. 508 Wellingborough Road, designed by *Peter Behrens* in 1925 for W. J. Bassett-Lowke. One room inside was re-installed from his preceding house, 78 Derngate (*see* p. 333), which had been altered and decorated by *Charles Rennie Mackintosh*. One does not know what to admire more, Mr Bassett-Lowke's discrimination in engaging Mackintosh at a time when his genius was no longer given adequate opportunities to express itself, or his courage in engaging Behrens, one of the earliest leaders of a completely new style of architecture then entirely untried in Britain and only just beginning to be publicized by one journal, *The Architectural Review*, which duly illustrated New Ways in 1926. How revolutionary this style must have appeared at the time is obvious, whether one looks at the house from the entrance or garden side; how prophetic it was of the future, i.e. the accepted style of the mid C20, can only be seen on the garden side. Here the two-storeyed white façade is divided into three parts, with the centre recessed. The side parts have on each floor just one large horizontal window without any surround or mouldings. There is in fact no more than an odd little hood-mould above the upper loggia to remind one of the early date of the house. It is different on the entrance side. Here the house is decidedly dated. That façade belongs to the passing phase of Expressionism in German architecture which comes between the earliest pioneer work of Behrens himself, Gropius, and others, and the mature, settled modern style which began in the mid twenties. Behrens himself sacrificed to the idol of Expressionism in his headquarters for the German Dye Trust at Hanau, built in 1920–4. The Expressionist (or as some would say jazzy) motif at New Ways is the triangularly projecting staircase window which cuts the front in half. This was topped by pylons with illuminated tops, and the white front has a curious top cresting 'redolent of Paris in 1925' (i.e. the Paris Exhibition of 1925), as the *Architectural Review* put it. Inside the house the floor of the Entrance Hall has an irregular geometrical pattern, designed by Behrens, and this is also very typical of the mid twenties, say of carpets and such-like work which came out of the Bauhaus. The Mackintosh room blended well with these Expressionist features owing to the historically remarkable fact that Mackintosh quite independently, and indeed prophetically, turned from his exquisite Art Nouveau of about 1900 to a private Expressionism, with cubistic and sometimes a little jazzy shapes, as early as 1907. The colour-scheme of the rooms was black furniture and walls with orange, grey, blue, and yellow stencilling.

(c) BILLING ROAD

GRAMMAR SCHOOL, Billing Road. 1911 by *H. Norman* and *A. McKewan*. Two-storeyed, of brick, symmetrical. Good additions of *c.* 1960 and later.

GENERAL HOSPITAL, Billing Road. The main building is of 1793. The architect was *Samuel Saxon*. Nineteen bays and three storeys, ashlar-faced. The rhythm is 3-5-3-5-3, with a three-bay pediment over the centre. Below this on the first and second floor are arched windows on short columns. Wing to the r. 1887–9, to the l. 1891–2. More later additions: Barratt Maternity Home 1936, Nurses' Home 1939, Outpatients Department 1959, all by *Sir John Brown & Henson*. The Pathology Laboratory by the Oxford Regional Hospital Board's Architect's Department, 1968, the Cripps Medical Centre by *Cartwright, Woollatt & Partners*, 1969. Nurses' Home, Cliftonville, by the Oxford Regional Hospital Board, 1971. – PLATE. In the Chapel: Cup and Paten of 1746.

ST ANDREW'S MENTAL HOSPITAL, Billing Road. John Clare lived and died here. The original building, by *J. Milne*, 1837, is of Bath stone, nearly a quadrangle and utilitarian in its details. Corridor 14 ft wide and 60 ft long (Wetton 1846). On the lawn in front two C18 lead statues. Separate CHAPEL to the r., Gothic, by *Sir Gilbert Scott*, completed in 1863. PLATE: Paten, 1721; Cup, 1759; Flagon, 1765. Beyond the chapel first ISHAM HOUSE by *Gotch, Saunders & Surridge*, 1971–2, an attractive long range, of two storeys, broken up by projecting windows, stairs, and a lift tower. Broad horizontal stone bands. Aluminium-covered roof, slightly sloping, with excrescences of various shapes. Then CHAPLAIN'S HOUSE (behind Isham House), a thatched Regency *cottage orné*; WANTAGE HOUSE, 1924–7 by *Law, Harris & Croft*; and GLOUCESTER HOUSE (Recreational Centre), 1962 by *Saxon Snell & Phillips*. To this is being added, approached by a covered way, a social centre, TOMPKINS HOUSE, by *Gotch, Saunders & Surridge*, under construction 1972.

Past the General Hospital (*see* above) BILLING ROAD and CLIFTONVILLE to the s were an expensive suburb built up from *c.* 1845. At the corner of Cliftonville BEAUMONT, a large Italianate mansion with a tower. Further s a house dated 1865 (now a Nurses' Home), Gothic, with elaborate conservatory at the side.* No. 43 Cliftonville Road is by *Holding*. Some good houses in the tile-hung Norman Shaw manner E of this in THE AVENUE (laid out by *Holding*, 1880–2). Back to Billing Road. On the N side No. 30 is elaborate Gothic of *c.* 1870, with a tower over the porch. Gothic details inside as well. Built for Shoosmith, the Town Clerk. Nos 36–9 are by *Holding*, 1880. Projecting bays and balconies. Then comes ST MARTIN'S VILLAS, brick with stone dressings, Gothic, of 1865, by *Godwin*. Opposite was *Godwin's* RHEINFELDEN, now replaced by flats.‡

(D) WESTON FAVELL

ST PETER. Of the C12 the lower part of the originally unbuttressed w tower with a rough blocked w doorway, the N doorway (shafts with scalloped capitals, segmental arch), and the s priest's doorway (one slight step in the arch) – i.e. the bones of the church. Of the C13 the chancel (good stepped lancets under one arch in the s wall) and most of the w tower (double-stepped tower arch, pair of lancets in the w wall, lancets in twos as bell-openings). The s and N windows are mostly C19. So is the N arcade. – FONT. Octagonal, Perp, with motifs such as rosette, shield, large leaves. – PULPIT. Jacobean. – BELFRY SCREEN by *A. A. J. Marshman*, 1971. – EMBROIDERY. A delightfully naïve Last Supper, dated 1698. It was in all probability a dorsal. – PLATE. Cup and Paten, given in 1674; Almsdish, 1724.

Excellent new VESTRY on the N side of the chancel. By *A. A. J. Marshman* (of *Marshman, Taylor & Warren*), 1969–71. In the style of the sixties, but in a yellow stone which tones well with the church. Low hipped roof with a prominent projecting drainpipe.

Some nice houses s of the church. First PRIORY HOUSE, with an early C19 Gothic front to the garden. In the garden an octagonal GAZEBO. Tucked away behind, No. 111, by *Stimpson & Walton*, 1967–9. One-storeyed. Brick facing panels projecting above the roof-line. To the w, across the road, the RECTORY, stone, partly faced with red brick, built

* To be demolished.

‡ This was a formidable Gothic red-brick villa of 1876–7. It had a towering centre with a circular turret covered by a conical roof.

shortly before 1758. Additions of 1777. More stone houses further s.

To the N of Wellingborough Road, between Weston Favell and the new Eastern District, the beginnings of an educational complex, e.g. WESTON FAVELL HIGH SCHOOL, with extensions in progress (1972) to turn it into a comprehensive school, and the COLLEGE OF FURTHER EDUCATION (stage one 1971–2), both by the Borough Architect's Department *See* (Borough Architect *Leonard Howarth*).   *See* p. 518

(E) THE EASTERN DISTRICT AND THE BILLINGS

The new Eastern District of Northampton (*see* also p. 316) lies to the E of Booth Lane, and, when complete, will cover 3034 acres, embracing Great and Little Billing. It is to be built up from 1971 to 1977 to house an estimated population of 44,400. The houses (both private and local-authority) will be grouped in twelve residential communities, each with its own shopping centre, lower school, and play park. There will also be larger parks, lakes, and woodland, connected by pedestrian routes. The first area to be built (1971–2), LUMBERTUBS, designed by *Wilson & Womersley*, consists of a series of rather dull rows of terrace houses with slightly broken frontages, running at r. angles to the slope of the hill. The LOWER SCHOOL, opened in 1972, and the LOCAL CENTRE with shops, community buildings, etc. (under construction) are by the Borough Architect *Leonard Howarth*. E of Lumbertubs, in the valley, will be LINGS. A little further N is THORPLANDS, designed by the Northampton Development Corporation (architect: *Gordon Redfern*), under construction 1972. This looks very promising. The varied heights, angles, and textures of the houses already begin to create the atmosphere of a village centre with an identity of its own. The LOCAL CENTRE, again in red brick, and by the Borough Architect, will include facilities used by the local SCHOOL. In the valley to the N a tree nursery and THORPLANDS FARM, with three octagonal brick buildings and a tall chimney.

GREAT BILLING

ST ANDREW. The church is attractively sited, away from the old centre.* The story starts with a Norman nave to which a

---

* It was near Billing Hall (now demolished), a house of *c.* 1776 by *John Carr*. The church parapets include C16 balustrading from the pre-1776 mansion. This and other information in this entry is from Bruce Bailey.

two-bay N aisle was added in the late C12. Circular pier, capital with flat, elementary leaves, square abacus. This aisle was extended to the W to meet a tower and to the E to meet a new chancel. The extensions have circular piers with circular abaci and double-chamfered arches. At the same time or a little later a S aisle was built with piers of an unusual and handsome type: triple shafts to each of the four sides. One arch has a nailhead hood-mould. All this is of the late C13 to early C14. The tower is also of this date, but the upper part was rebuilt after the spire fell in 1759. Much of the body of the church had to be renewed after this disaster (see the Georgian quoining at the ends of the N aisle). Perp S doorway with heavy hood-mould and a bust of an angel at the apex. Porch of after 1759. In the S aisle a very fine Dec tripartite REREDOS with wider and higher centre and ogee heads. The N chapel is dated 1687. In the E wall a tall blocked opening with an open segmental pediment. The chancel is largely a rebuilding of 1867 by *E. F. Law*. – FONT. Octagonal, Perp. Tall panelled stem, moulded top; no separate bowl. – STAINED GLASS. W window by *Powell*, 1870. – PLATE. Cup and Paten, *c.* 1682; Flagon by *John Bodington*, 1697; Breadholder, 1703. – MONUMENTS. Henry Earl of Thomond † 1691. By *John Bushnell*, according to Vertue. It was erected in 1700 and is shockingly inept.* The Earl and the Countess kneel behind a balustrade or a tomb-chest on which lies a baby. They have not enough room to kneel, and the foreshortening which would have been necessary to make the full-round heads and shoulders and the absence of the legs credible was not at Bushnell's command. Two kneeling children and more children kneeling in relief on the base. At the top draperies and what Mrs Esdaile calls 'two exquisite flying cherubs'. The whole group supported on an enormous Baroque tomb-chest. – Caroline Elwes † 1812 by *Flaxman* and Robert Elwes † 1852 by *Weekes*, both with women by urns, and neither specially memorable.

RECTORY. Partly 1678 (mullioned windows) and partly just before 1800.

The village centre has a number of good stone houses, notably the POST OFFICE, a building of 1703. Interesting for its date. Five bays, two storeys, quoins, doorway with straight entablature, but the windows still two-light mullioned. In a wall near by, bronze MEMORIAL to Gervase Elwes by *Arthur E. Vokes*.

* It was probably Bushnell's last work. He died, insane, in 1701.

(PEARCE'S TANNERY. 1939 by *Lawson Carter*. Early modern, the details quite functional, but with a formal entrance in the angle of the L-shaped office block.*)

LITTLE BILLING

ALL SAINTS. The church had a N aisle, but the arcade has been removed. According to Wetton's *Guide* it consisted of wooden posts on stone bases. Lewis Loyd of Overstone rebuilt the N chapel in 1849, and *E. F. Law* restored the church in 1852–4. The N tower owes its somewhat starved appearance to Law. The N chapel and the chancel both open now into the nave. – FONT. Plain, Norman, of tub shape, but of great interest 34 because of its inscription: '*Wigberthus* artifex atq. cementarius hunc fabricavit / Quisquis suum venit mergere corpus procul dubio cepit.'‡

MANOR HOUSE, N of the church. The fragment of a larger mansion of the Longuevilles. One circular quatrefoil window in the E wall, one four-light window with arched lights in the S wall.

OLD RECTORY. Mainly an enlargement of *c.* 1820 of an older building. Handsome panelled entrance hall and a pretty staircase.

SOUTH

(A) BRIDGE STREET AND FAR COTTON

ST MARY, Towcester Road, Far Cotton. 1885 by *Holding*. Prominent E view with tall NE tower crowned by a spire and tall semicircular apse with lancet windows only high up. The other windows also lancets or with plate tracery. Indifferent interior, but stone-vaulted throughout, as will be expected by anyone who knows that Holding was a follower of Pearson. No structural division between nave and chancel.

In BRIDGE STREET the extensive premises of the former PHIPPS'S BREWERY, redeveloped from 1971 for CARLS-BERG. The architect is *Knud Munk* of Copenhagen.§ The

* Information from Mr John Goff.
‡ Professor Talbot Rice drew attention to fonts with comparable Latin inscriptions at Potterne, Wiltshire, and Patrishaw, Brecon.
§ The oldest building of Phipps's was of 1866–7, by *Davison & Scamell* of London. To it was added the one facing the canal. This is of 1877. Tall, symmetrical brick front with a ludicrous, thin central turret covered by a concave-sided pyramid roof. At the N end of the Bridge Street front a building with an inset of curtain walling. 1956–7 by *F. C. J. Smith*.

brewhouse itself is a massive pile with a jagged roof line. Long low storage buildings running N–S.

(B) DELAPRÉ ABBEY

The house is now occupied by the County Record Office and the County Record Society. It stands in large grounds on the site of one of the only two Cluniac nunneries in England (the other was Arthington in the West Riding). Delapré Abbey was founded c. 1145 by Simon, the son of Simon of St Liz (or Senlis) who had founded the Cluniac priory of St Andrew about fifty years before. The present house is of four ranges round a nearly square courtyard. This in all probability represents the cloister, and the passage around the N, W, and E sides the cloister walks. The thick walls of the N range in that case represent the wall of the aisleless nunnery church. But no medieval feature survives, except perhaps two rectangular recesses in the cloister walk which may have served to keep lights in at night. The house came to the Tates of London after the Dissolution. Of the mid C16 three doorways, one from the courtyard to the E corridor, the other two in the N corridor. One of them leads to a spiral stair. They have four-centred arches or heads. Near in time comes the remodelling of the W wing, due to Zouch Tate, who was in possession from 1617 to 1651. His is the most conspicuous contribution to the house, the W front. This is of ironstone, E-shaped. The wings had big shaped gables of which only the l. one survives. The r. one was awkwardly replaced by a Library added about 1820, higher than the rest, stuccoed, and with medievalizing detail. Porch with arched entrance between Roman Doric columns. In the side walls blank, horizontally placed ovals in oblong frames. Embattled top. The rest of the roof is also embattled. Mullioned and transomed windows of two, three, and four lights. The E side of the house is irregular but was also remodelled by Zouch Tate. The N side is even more irregular. The jamb of one blocked window has been explained by Mr Pantin as belonging to the nunnery church. The s façade was made either c. 1750 or c. 1765. The s front was of twelve bays and two storeys. The two l. hand bays were replaced by the library addition already referred to. The two r. hand bays project, and the angles of this projection have quoining of even length. No specially interesting interiors. In one of the s rooms two columns separate the back part of the room. Most of the rooms were redecorated in a Raphaelesque mood, probably *c.* 1860–70. In the W range a minor staircase with vertically symmetrical balusters. The STABLES to the N with cupola are also of *c.* 1750 or *c.* 1765. They were renovated by *John Goff*, the County Architect, in 1971.

(C) HARDINGSTONE AND LONDON ROAD

ST EDMUND. Unbuttressed C13 tower. Broad, squat, double-stepped arch towards the nave. Bell-openings with cusped Y-tracery. Battlements. The body of the church over-restored. The windows mostly Late Perp. C14 five-bay arcades with octagonal piers and double-chamfered arches. The SEDILIA are very unusual – an Elizabethan segmental arch with some foliage decoration on the supporting pilasters.* At the apex of the arch an angel on clouds. – PLATE. Cup, 1810. – MONU-MENTS. Stephen Harvey † 1606. Alabaster. Kneeling figures in two tiers, two facing one another at the top, three more below, the central and r. figures placed frontally. – Sir Stephen Harvey † 1630. Recumbent effigy. Simple back architecture. – Bartholomew Clarke † 1746. By *Rysbrack*. With two oval medallions with busts in profile in front of an obelisk. Fine architectural detail below. At the foot a third medallion was added by Rysbrack to commemorate Mrs Clarke's brother Hitch Younge † 1759. – Also a large number of identical oval commemorative plaques to members of the Bouverie family of Delapré Abbey, eleven on the l., four on the r. of the altar. They go down to the 1870s.

CORFE HOUSE. Regency. Four bays wide, two storeys high, white. In the first and last bays doorways with Greek Doric columns *in antis*. On the first floor lesenes with Soanian incised ornament.

ELEANOR CROSS, London Road. Queen Eleanor had died at Harby in Nottinghamshire in November 1290. The king decided to set up crosses on lavishly decorated substructures at the places where the funeral cortège had halted overnight. The same had been done in France for the body of King Louis IX in 1271. The stopping places were Lincoln, Gran-tham, Stamford, Geddington, Hardingstone, Stony Stratford, Dunstable, St Albans, Waltham, Cheapside, and finally Charing Cross. Most of the places chosen had royal castles or monastic houses of distinction. Hardingstone really meant

* The Rev. W. L. Freeman tells me that the sedilia are a tomb rebuilt in the C19 with the front upside down.

Delapré Abbey (*see* p. 352). Of all these crosses only the three of Hardingstone, Geddington (*see* p. 225), and Waltham in **68** Hertfordshire survive. The Hardingstone Cross was begun in 1291 by *John of Battle*, *caementarius*, and, as far as the statues of the queen were concerned, *William of Ireland*, *imaginator* and *caementarius*, both artists in the employ of the king. William received £3/6/8 a figure. The Hardingstone (or Northampton) cross is octagonal. It stands high on (renewed) steps. It is in three tiers with a crowning terminal which does not exist any longer and whose original form is not known. It may have been a Crucifixus. The lowest tier has panelled buttresses at the angles and two-light panels with blank cusped Y-tracery between. Each light has a small flat ogee arch – a complete innovation in the 1290s – and below this a suspended shield with a coat of arms. On every second side there is an open book on a lectern against the two-light panel. Originally there was no doubt a painted text in the book, as the whole monument was painted. Above each panel is a crocketed gable, fantastically and quite illogically cusped. Above the gable is a frieze of big flowers, and then a piece of cresting again quite fantastic. It consists of concave curves. The second stage has four canopies containing four images of the queen. They differ in composition of the draperies but are all less crisp, with less sharpness of folds and clarity of distinction between body and mantle than statuary had possessed at Westminster Abbey some forty years before and at Lincoln some twenty or thirty. The canopies have thin buttresses instead of shafts, and crocketed gables with decoration by means of naturalistic foliage. Several kinds of leaf can easily be recognized. The arches below the gables have ogee heads and are ogee-cusped. Behind the gables appears the crocketed pyramid roof of the canopy. The third stage is square and retracted behind the canopies. It has a blank four-light panel on each side, made up of the units of Y-tracery. There are again buttresses, gables, and finial to link up with the missing terminal. The present broken column was placed on top by *Blore*, who removed various C18 accretions in 1840 (BB). The whole structure is memorable as the beginning of that development which was to lead to such superb excesses as the canopy of the monument to Edward II at Gloucester.

DIVISIONAL POLICE HEADQUARTERS, London Road. By the County Architect's Department (*A. N. Harris*), 1963.

WOOTTON HALL, W of the London Road. The county police

headquarters, red brick, neo-Georgian, built soon after 1911 on the site of an earlier house. Extensions are planned by the County Architect, *John Goff*. In the grounds extensive temporary single-storey offices of the 1960s for the County Council. These are to be replaced by a new building for the County Council.

The area w of the London Road will form part of the SOUTHERN DISTRICT of the expanded town.

HUNSBURY CAMP, 2 m. SW of Northampton. This is an Iron Age hill fort consisting of a bank, ditch, and counterscarp bank running round the 300 ft contour line and enclosing an area of *c.* 4 acres. Of three breaks in the fortifications on the NNE, NW, and SE, the first and last seem to be original. The ironstone workings of 1882–4 revealed some 300 storage pits, a few carefully lined with stone, as well as much additional material, the earliest consisting of a few flint arrows of Neolithic date. The general sequence of Iron Age settlement and construction, suggested by trial excavations in 1952, seems to be as follows. (1) An undefended Early Iron Age settlement possibly established by a group working the local ironstone. (2) C4 B.C. building consisting of a timber revetted wall of rubble covered with a vertical face in front (and presumably at the rear also) and incorporating roasted ironstone from the phase 1 settlement, with a berm and V-cut ditch; to this period belongs the earliest pottery with Fengate relationships (*see* Introduction, p. 22). (3) Rebuilding of the defences on the SE side near the entrance, the previous wall being converted into a glacis rampart; the now silted ditch contained some of the *c.* 150 Derby grit rotary querns. This period saw the manufacture of fine curvilinear pottery, and possibly the burial of a chariot-using chieftain. An outer ring work, traces of which were found 80 yds N in the original C19 investigations, is of uncertain date. (4) Following the abandonment of the fort in the early C1 A.D., a number of extended inhumations, possibly as late as Saxon in date, were deposited on top of the glacis rampart.

WEST

(A) ST JAMES'S END

ST JAMES, St James's Road. 1868–71 by *R. Wheeler* of Tonbridge. N aisle etc. by *Holding*, 1900. Tower 1920 by *G. H. Stevenson*. Red brick, in the lancet style. Big with a big and

heavy s w tower. From the w front projects a small baptistery.
The brick is exposed inside. Enrichment by black bricks.
Arcades with low circular piers of polished pink granite.
Foliage capitals, square abaci. Low aisles.

DODDRIDGE MEMORIAL CHAPEL. 1895 by *Mosley &
Anderson*. Brick and stone. Large gable with inscription.

(B) DALLINGTON

ST MARY. Late C12 doorway with one order of shafts carrying
early leaf capitals and a round, only slightly stepped arch.
C13 w tower with pairs of lancets as bell-openings. The
ground-floor lancet dates from the restoration of 1863. C13
also the N aisle, see the pair of lancets and the simple doorway.
The N or Raynsford Chapel was built in 1679 in a posthumous
Gothic style. The s aisle was rebuilt in 1877, the chancel in
1883. N arcade with simple octagonal piers and double-
chamfered arches, s arcade similar, though differing in details.
– FONT. Octagonal, Perp, with quatrefoil panels. – BENCHES.
Some, with poppy-heads, at the w end of the nave. – REREDOS.
1883, with statues by *Harry Hems* and mosaic. – PULPIT.
Jacobean. – SCULPTURE. A curious small Saxon fragment in
the inner N wall. Small human figure like an embryo, small
quadruped below. The stone has a triangular head. – STAINED
GLASS. E window by *Kempe*, 1892. – One s window by *Morris
& Co.*, but 1906, i.e. after the death of both Morris and
Burne-Jones. – PLATE. Strainer Spoon, 1597; Breadholder,
1658; Salver, 1660; Flagon, 1698; Paris-made silver-gilt
Paten with Crucifixus in relief, c. 1703; Cup and Cover
Paten, 1757. – Also four silver Badges for the inhabitants of
the Raynsford Almshouses, 1673. – MONUMENTS. Richard
Raynsford † 1678. Big base with, in the middle, inscription
surrounded by flowers. Big urn on top, with garlands. There
were putti at the top, but they have been removed (now N
aisle w end). – Three Raynsford daughters † 1657, 1662, 1664.
Inscription framed by black columns. Open segmental pediment. Both tombs may be by *William Stanton*, who made the
ledger stone to Dame Catherine Raynsford † 1698. – Two
large tablets with urns before obelisks, the earlier Rococo, the
later just a little chaster: Joseph Jekyll † 1752, Lady Anne
Jekyll † 1766.

DALLINGTON HALL (Margaret Spencer Hospital). Built by
Sir Joseph Jekyll, Master of the Rolls, who bought the estate

from the Raynsfords in 1720 and died in 1738. An attribution to *Francis Smith* has been suggested. The entrance side five bays and two storeys with basement. Giant angle pilasters, parapet, hipped roof, doorway with pediment on brackets. The garden side seven bays, with giant pilasters at the angles as well as the angles of the three middle bays. Similar doorway. The three windows above have pilasters and arches. Fine staircase behind the middle of the garden side. Three balusters to the tread, two twisted, one columned; carved tread-ends. To the N of the house the STABLES, their s end concealed by a pedimented front with a doorway flanked by two niches. The stables incorporate masonry from the C17 house of the Raynsfords. (In the gardens DOVECOTE, octagonal with ogee cupola, probably *c.* 1720.)

(DALLINGTON PARK SCHOOL. By the County Architect's Department (*A. N. Harris*), 1964.)

DALLINGTON GREEN. A pretty group with a stream across, the RAYNSFORD ALMSHOUSES to the N, a row of cottages to the s. The Almshouses date from 1673. Four dwellings, middle gable. The SCHOOL (now Village Hall) of *c.* 1840 to their r. continues the same motifs. To the r. of the school drive to the VICARAGE. This is dated 1741. Three bays wide, on the ground floor two minimum Venetian windows.

A few pleasant ironstone houses in RAYNSFORD ROAD, both w and E of the Green, e.g. THE BARTONS and DALLINGTON WEIR. Along the main Harlestone Road many prosperous Victorian and Edwardian houses, e.g. GREENWOOD SHIPMAN HOME at the corner of Bants Lane, Tudor and Renaissance, by *Charles Dorman*, and further W ELMLEIGH, by *Godwin*, 1885, but nothing special.

(c) KING'S HEATH ESTATE

Designed by *J. L. Womersley*, then borough architect, in 1950. Planned for 5,000 inhabitants. The plan is completely symmetrical, a kidney-shape being the basic motif. The centre is a green. In the curved ends two nursery schools (still to come). To its N two SCHOOLS of which so far only one has been built. Yet further N on the r. a HOME FOR OLD PEOPLE, and at the N end the CHURCH HALL of St Augustine. At the other end ST MARGARET'S CHURCH (R.C.) of 1960. The very successful pedestrian SHOPPING CENTRE is in the middle axis to the s of the Green. It is flanked along the green by flats, and these carry on along the curved ends of the green as well as s of the shopping centre to form the main approach from the s. These nicely-designed three-storeyed terraces of pale and dark red brick with balconies and moderately pitched roofs give the estate its character.

To the s an industrial area. In Gladstone Road the first tall office block of the town, for BARCLAYS, by *Green, Lloyd & Adams*, 1970–1. Ten storeys high.

(D) DUSTON

ST LUKE. Evidence of a late C12 building is the s doorway and the w respond of the s arcade. The latter is semicircular with a many-scalloped capital, the former has two orders of shafts with leaf capitals and a deeply moulded round arch, including keeling. Of the early C13 the fenestration of the C12 w wall. Three big lancets and a small one above. The aisles were added in the late C13, see the change of masonry in the w wall from mixed brown and grey rubble to bands of brown and grey; see also the aisle windows: three lancet lights under one arch, three intersected lights, Y-tracery, i.e. all late C13 motifs. The arcades of three bays probably of the same date: octagonal piers and double-chamfered arches. Clerestory with small windows of three different shapes, including quatrefoils. The E end of the arcades has no responds. Corbels on pairs of heads instead. The crossing tower is probably basically Norman, but the arches are again late C13. The E arch has the same corbels on pairs of heads. The narrow N and s arches are double-chamfered and die against their imposts. There is no trace of transepts. One-bay N and s chapels. Dec chancel and tower top. Of the former chancel roof the supporting C14 figures of musicians remain. – FONT. Norman. The lower half of the bowl fluted. – PLATE. Cup, 1570; Paten, 1682.

There is a Neolithic to Roman SETTLEMENT in the vicinity of Weedon Road, s of the church (*see* Introduction, pp. 21ff).

DUSTON SECONDARY SCHOOL, Berrywood Road. The main building neo-Georgian. Extensions in progress (1971).

ST CRISPIN'S HOSPITAL. Built as Berrywood Asylum in 1876 by *Griffiths* of Stafford. A large red-brick building with a prominent tower, vaguely Rhineland Romanesque in inspiration (GI). Many later additions. Separate CHAPEL, Early Gothic, four bays with aisles, redecorated in 1954 by *Henry Bird* and *G. H. B. Holland* with large panels depicting the Arthurian legend. The whole complex should be con-

trasted with the PRINCESS MARINA HOSPITAL, further W,
by *Stillman & Eastwick-Field*, 1964–72. This is the first
hospital in the country to be designed specially for severely
subnormal psychiatric patients. The buildings are arranged in
clusters, each group catering for patients with different needs.
There is also a community centre with a shop, and staff housing (the buildings with pitched roofs).

Several nice houses in DUSTON MAIN ROAD. At the corner of
Saxon Rise DUSTON HOUSE, large, early C19, stuccoed.
Porch with paired Corinthian columns. Further S the
NATIONAL WESTMINSTER BANK, a thatched one-storey
cottage. Near by the UNITED REFORMED CHURCH (formerly Congregational), with an attractive Church Hall with
three gables to the street, by *A. W. Walker*, 1967–8.

NORTON

ALL SAINTS. C13 W tower with Perp top. Otherwise mostly
Dec. The S doorway has small capitals to its shafts decorated
with faces. S arcade of six bays, an impressive sight. Quatrefoil
piers, arches of one chamfer and one sunk quadrant. The N
arcade with octagonal piers is also Dec, but a little later. –
FONTS. One C18, of baluster type. – The other circular, with
four faces sticking out. Probably a C13 piece, completely re-
cut. – WEST SCREEN. Three-storeyed. As high as the nave;
with pilasters and arches. The lower part is of 1810, the upper is
of the C18 and was formerly the reredos. Now much hidden by
the W gallery and organ. – PULPIT. C17. – STAINED GLASS. E
window signed by *Willement* and dated 1847. With three large
figures in somewhat gaudy colours. – What is the date of the
single figures and shields in the other windows? – PLATE. Cup,
1729; Paten, 1744; Flagon, 1745; Almsdish, 1835. – MONU-
MENTS. An uncommonly large number. Brass to William
Knyght † 1501 and wife, 23 in. figures. – Lady Elizabeth
Knightley † 1602. Large standing monument of alabaster.
Recumbent effigy. Arch with rows of coffering. Black columns,
outer obelisks. Not of specially high quality. – Nicholas
Breton † 1624. Tablet with two cherubs; very quiet, not really
Jacobean in style. – Ann Breton † 1635. Tablet. Banded
obelisks l. and r. A skull in the open segmental pediment. –
Elizabeth Verney † 1633. Large kneeling figure. On the broad
piers l. and r. two allegorical figures. Rustic quality. –
Nicholas Breton † 1658 and wife. Large standing monument,

progressive for its date. The centre has two busts. Big surround of pink and white marble. Open segmental pediment with shield and garlands. – Mrs Botfield † 1825. By *William Behnes*. A strange conceit. The only figure is her son, life-size, mourning her. Does this show filial piety, or also a wish to appear himself, close to the altar? Grecian style.

NORTON HALL was blown up in 1945.

BANNAVENTA. At Whilton Lodge on Watling Street is the site of a Roman settlement, extending on both sides of the main road and into Whilton parish, and covering at least 30 acres. Finds which have been made since reports of buildings in the C18 include much 'terra sigillata' and many coins, including several of Constantine found with a burial. Aerial photography and excavation indicate that this was a walled town. Excavations in 1970–1 showed that the defences consisted at first of a ditch with earth rampart. In the early C4 the ditch was filled, and a stone wall and further ditches beyond were constructed (J. Steane).

7070

OLD

ST ANDREW. Perp w tower with pairs of two-light transomed bell-openings, a quatrefoil frieze, and battlements. Very ornate Perp doorway with leaf spandrels, flanking buttresses with pinnacles, and ten fleuron motifs all along the hoodmould. Responds and windows of the S aisle late C13, arcade Perp. Four bays, wide arches, piers with four shafts and four hollows. Nave roof with good angel corbels of stone, single and in pairs, holding shields with the Instruments of the Passion. – STAINED GLASS. In a S aisle window medieval fragments (including a man with the devil on his back, *c.* 1520). – PLATE. Paten, inscribed 1683; Cup and Cover Paten, 1758.

RECTORY. Early C18, altered.* The street front seems to have had five bays and two storeys. The present doorway on the garden side may come from it. Now there is a late C18 canted bay-window in the middle. Hipped roof.

Opposite is a HOUSE dated 1731 which still has wooden crosswindows.

(Another largish FARMHOUSE has a date 1768 on a gable, but looks earlier. GI)

---

* But Sir Gyles Isham tells me of a beam in the kitchen dated 1616. He also has reason to believe that the later alterations date from *c.* 1835–50.

ORLINGBURY

ST MARY. 1843 by *Richard Charles Hussey* of Birmingham, partner of Rickman (GR). A remarkably serious, substantial job. Tall crossing tower with filigree battlements and very tall pinnacles (in 1970–1 lowered by 10 ft). At the E end a large rose window. The style is Dec throughout. The church was paid for partly by the rector and partly by A. A. Young of the Hall, and wall inscriptions of commemoration in Gothic framing are to the l. and r. of the S transept E window. – FONT. Also sumptuous, and also ogee. – (BENCHES with poppy-heads.) – PLATE. Cup and Cover Paten, 1637; Breadholder, 1673; Flagon, 1776. – MONUMENTS. Alabaster effigy of a Knight, *c.* 1375 (chancel N). – Brasses to William Lane † 1502 and wife (S transept), 18 in. figures. – Sophia Bridges † 1853. By *R. C. Hussey* (BB).

ORLINGBURY HALL. Bought by Richard Young in 1706 and rebuilt apparently immediately after.* The entrance side is original. Nine bays divided into three threes by giant Doric pilasters. Each pilaster carries one metope. Tall windows in flat frames. Pedimented dormers. The other sides and the interior are altered. C19 service wing. DOVECOTE.

RECTORY. On the Green, the entry close to that of the Hall. Dated 1703. Five bays, two storeys.

In the village a number of ESTATE HOUSES built by Mr Young 'after his own plans'. His architect was *R. C. Hussey*.

ORTON

ALL SAINTS. The church was closed in 1964. It is now used by the Orton Trust, formed in 1968, as a stonemasons' training centre. Short, unbuttressed Norman W tower. Later medieval top with battlements and pinnacles. Norman arch towards the nave, pointed. Norman also the chancel arch. The rest all over-restored. The original work points to the late C13, see the S arcade, the S aisle E lancet, and the S doorway. – FONT. Circular, with four faces – human and animal – like knobs. Is it C13? – COMMUNION RAIL. C18.

OUNDLE

CHURCHES

ST PETER. Scanty evidence of a Norman church. One chancel window with roll moulding visible from the N chapel, and the

* Justinian Isham mentions the house in 1709 (GI).

plinths of the crossing piers.* Nearly the whole church except
for its climax, the tower, is of the C13. Early the s arcade with
circular piers and circular capitals and abaci and pointed
double-chamfered arches. A little nailhead decoration. Both
chancel chapels of about the same time, see their arches. The
arch from the N chapel to the chancel is segmental. The N
arcade is of the later C13. Responds with fillets. Nailhead in
the arch to the N transept. Much of the outside is late C13, and
first the chancel N and s windows (two lights and a quatrefoiled circle). The E window is Perp, and so is the attached
two-storeyed vestry. Late C13 also the fine three-light window
with three foiled circles in the s chapel. The other windows of
the chapel are Dec. In the N chapel the large E window is Early
Dec with busy small tracery. The s transept E and W windows
are again late C13 (two cusped lights and a pointed quatrefoil
over). In the N transept the N window is typical of *c.* 1300:
five lights, intersected tracery, but at the top the tracery bars
simply left out. Of *c.* 1300 probably also the N doorway. The
N aisle windows are Perp, the s aisle has a splendid Early Dec
five-light window. Dec also the tower arch, and the identical
chancel arch and transept N and s arches – i.e. the C13 crossing
tower was removed at that time and arches were built while
the W tower was begun. The mouldings are the same as those
in the chancel of Cotterstock begun *c.* 1330. Ornate Dec
SEDILIA with crocketed ogee arches.‡ The s porch finally is a
dramatic Perp piece, paid for by Robert Wyatt and his wife
and built *c.* 1485. Two storeys with battlements and pinnacles.
Tierceron-vault with ridge ribs and a pendant. s doorway with
slanting reveals decorated with panelling.

10   So to the steeple, which dominates Oundle. It belongs to the
specially happy variety with a really tall slender tower and a
not too excessively tall recessed needle spire. The style is Dec.
W doorway with cusped ogee arch and gable. Niches l. and r.
Small panelled tunnel-vault inside the entrance (cf. Higham
Ferrers). Two-light window above this with identical blank
windows l. and r. The s and N sides have tall blank arcading
with ogee forms instead and a blank storey over this. Then a
shorter blank arcading. Beautifully tall and elegant bell-
openings. Three very slim two-light openings with transom
and identical blank windows l. and r. Quatrefoil frieze,

* In a room over the s porch two pieces of zigzag from an arch and a small
capital with similar moulding.

‡ A similar but more highly ornate PISCINA in the s transept.

fleuron frieze, battlements, and short, polygonal embattled turret pinnacles. Battlements and pinnacles have decorative cross-shaped arrow-slits. The spire is crocketed up the angles and has three tiers of lucarnes all in the cardinal directions. – FONTS. One oblong, early C18, like the plinth of a monument. No separate bowl. – The octagonal Perp font dates from 1909. – PULPIT. Perp, repainted in original colours in 1965. – SCREENS. Two Perp parclose screens and remains of a higher Perp screen now under the tower. – S DOOR. Perp, with tracery panels. – LECTERN. Fine C15 brass eagle, the same as at Urbino Cathedral, Southwell Minster, Newcastle Cathedral, Long Sutton Lincolnshire, Oxburgh Norfolk, etc. – AUMBRY (s chapel) with gilt canopy. By *L. H. Bond*, 1971. – SCULPTURE. In the room above the s porch two Anglo-Saxon fragments with interlace, probably from a coffin lid. – CHANDELIER. Of brass, two tiers. Dated 1685. – PLATE. Set, 1697; two Basins, 1729; two Plates, 1731. – MONUMENTS. Martha Kirkham † 1616. Back arch with cartouche no longer with strapwork. Achievement with two putti. On the l. and r. detached columns carrying obelisks. – William Loringe † 1628. Small, of alabaster, with black marble columns and a broken pediment with arms. Ten children praying beneath. – Sophia Whitwell † 1707 (E wall, exterior). Brass plate on a fully moulded sarcophagus base. – Mary Kirkham † 1754. Standing monument with obelisk and pretty carved decoration. – Rev. John Shillibeer † 1841. By *John Thompson* of Peterborough (BB). Elaborately Gothic.

JESUS CHURCH, West Street. 1878–9 by *Arthur Blomfield*. Now R.C. Byzantine 'quincunx' or inscribed cross plan. Square centre with octagonal tower on squinches. The piers carrying the tower are clustered and of red stone. The four low corner spaces have pointed arches. C13-style fenestration. Matching vestry added in the sw corner, 1971.

CONGREGATIONAL CHURCH, West Street. 1852. Still with a classical front with arched doorway and windows and pediment.

THE TOWN

The problem of the public school in the small town can be solved in several ways. At Harrow or Uppingham the school is the *Stadtkrone*, at Eton it is the great surprise at the far end of an undisturbed little town. At Oundle it is nowhere in prominence except in one place outside the main circulation; and the small, beautiful, stone-built town with its dominating church in the centre has it all its own way.

OUNDLE SCHOOL

The Free Grammar School of Oundle was founded by the will of Sir William Laxton, grocer of London, in 1556. It took the place of, or continued, a modest grammar school which dated back to the later C15 and was still extant in the mid C16. The school rose to having about 60–70 boys in the mid C17, but was hit hard by the Fire of London and the misfortunes which befell the Grocers' Company. It remained a small school in the C18 going through many vicissitudes and occasionally being almost in abeyance, until the mid C19, when, as in so many public schools, conditions and reputation changed rapidly. There were 26 boys in 1848, 132 fifteen years later, 217 in 1882. Then they went down again (1891: 104), but by 1909 there were 323. In 1971 there were 720 and about 100 day boys in Laxton School (the original foundation).

The centre of Oundle School is New Street with THE CLOISTERS on one side and School House on the other. The Cloisters is by *John Sebastian Gwilt* and dates from 1880. Gwilt and his father, the better-known Joseph Gwilt, were architects to the Grocers' Company, who are the governors of Oundle School. It is Tudor with a big gatehouse, asymmetrical, and with turrets at the s end. Through the gatehouse one enters a courtyard with a cloister. Above this a LIBRARY and classrooms have been added. These and the ART SCHOOL in the SE corner of the courtyard are by *Green, Lloyd & Son*, 1960. The N extension is by *A. C. Blomfield*, 1934–5. Opposite the gatehouse, on the E side, is the oldest surviving part of the school buildings. This is a house built in 1799. Its façade turns towards the churchyard and there, to its l., is an earlier Georgian house, a little more formal and of five bays. This was built in 1763. To the l. of the house of 1799 a Victorian Tudor addition, built in 1899. SCHOOL HOUSE on the opposite side of New Street is also Tudor and also asymmetrical. It is by *H. C. Boyes**; of 1887. The addition to the s with the two timber-framed gables is of 1909, by *A. C. Blomfield*. Opposite a three-bay Regency house and, to the N of School House, the GREAT HALL and Library, Perp, with an open roof and a Wrenish s gallery on columns. By *A. C. Blomfield*, 1907–8.

---

* Information from N. Taylor. Boyes was Gwilt's successor.

Then the pattern gets looser. In GLAPTHORN ROAD on the
r. a very dull CHEMISTRY BLOCK (Palmer), brick, by
L. R. Foreman of *Forsyth & Partners*, opened in 1958; duller
and older blocks behind it. But at the N end of the playing
field DRYDEN and SANDERSON, two well designed identical
big houses of 1932–8 with tall hipped roofs of dark tiles above
the light brick walls. They are by *W. A. Forsyth*. Opposite,
with plenty of space between, the SCIENCE BLOCK, 1914 by
A. C. Blomfield. Tudor, with mullioned and transomed
windows, and straight gables and a curved middle gable. To
its N, much smaller, the YARROW MEMORIAL, also Tudor
but simpler, 1918 by *Blomfield*. Much further back the
CHAPEL, 1922–3 by *A. C. Blomfield*, large, Perp, with low
aisles, an apse, and an ambulatory. The outstanding feature is
the STAINED GLASS in the apse, designed by *John Piper* and   46
made by *Patrick Reyntiens*, 1955–6. Nine large single figures,
not realistic, but recognizable, and in their entangled forms
and deep colours emotionally potent without being too exact-
ing. The nearest parallel is the German and Dutch Expressionism of the 1920s, but the style is undoubtedly quite
independent. The HANGING behind the altar was also
designed by *Piper*. The CROSS and CANDLESTICKS, good
simple designs by *Paul Morris*, 1966, are of bronze, finished
to look like steel. A FLOWER PEDESTAL, by *B. R. Williams*,
is to be added. Further N, beyond the former Workhouse (*see*
below), the Cricket Fields with a PAVILION by *Peter Bicknell*,
1957, two-storeyed with a lantern and cupola and a one-
storeyed curved attachment. Changing-rooms etc. below, a
large room for lunch and tea above. Across to the S from the
chapel in MILTON ROAD lies ST ANTHONY'S, 1925–8 by
Blomfield. Nine bays with a centre tower with four-sided
copper dome. The window with segmental head and foot is a
motif familiar e.g. from Herbert Baker. To the W of the chapel
SIDNEY and GRAFTON, 1907 and 1905 by *Blomfield*,
symmetrical, with a steep gable and a semicircular porch
hood, and LAXTON and CROSBY, also by *Blomfield*, Tudor,
with five gables and mullioned and transomed windows. W of
these, SWIMMING POOL and games complex by *Cartwright,
Woollatt & Partners*, 1969–71.

   Further N in Glapthorn Road a new JUNIOR SCHOOL is to
be built, by *Oliver Carey*. Plans are also being made (1972)
for an important new ART AND DESIGN CENTRE by
Powell & Moya. This is to be near the Great Hall.

For BRAMSTON HOUSE, BERRYSTEAD, COBTHORNE, LAUNDIMER HOUSE, NEW HOUSE, and other houses in the town belonging to the school, *see* the Perambulation.

PUBLIC BUILDINGS

TOWN HALL. 1826 in the Tudor style. Cruciform. Handsomely placed in the Market Place.

LAXTON GRAMMAR SCHOOL. Originally this and Oundle School were one foundation. They were finally separated only in 1876. The buildings of the Grammar School lie along the s side of the churchyard and then into North Street. They date mostly from 1881–5 and are by *John Sebastian Gwilt*. In North Street first a big Tudor block and then a Gothic one with a tower. This returns along the churchyard with a nice open ground-floor arcading. Further w neo-Tudor part of 1933.

(SENIOR COMPREHENSIVE SCHOOL, Herne Road. By the County Architect, *John Goff*, 1970–2.)

HOSPITAL, Glapthorn Road. Built as the WORKHOUSE in 1837 by the young *G. G. Scott*. Late Classical, with the usual raised octagonal centre. Red brick addition with pedimental gables, *c.* 1902. Separate chapel with lancet windows, by *Comper*, 1896, said to be his first work.

RAILWAY STATION, NE of the town. Now disused. In the Old English style. By *Livock*, 1845.

PERAMBULATION

It will be best to start in the MARKET PLACE. On the N side Nos 7–9, Late Georgian, ashlar-faced. On part of the ground floor a High Victorian Gothic bank. No. 13, opposite the Town Hall, is late C17. It has a colonnade on the ground floor with heavy Roman Doric columns. Broadly framed windows. Under the colonnade pretty Georgian shopfront. On the s side Nos 4–6, an ambitious double house of ten bays with, in the middle, an arched doorway with rusticated surround. The dormers with alternating pediments, however, look as though the houses might be of before 1700. Nice Georgian shopfront. Opposite the Town Hall No. 26, early C18, four bays, with aprons to the first-floor windows; No. 28, late C17, with broad, eared doorway and an oval plaque; BRAMSTON HOUSE, early C18, stately, of five bays and three storeys with giant Doric end pilasters and a balustrade.

From here NORTH STREET winds N. On the r. first the WHITE
LION, recently well restored by Oundle School, dated 1641,
with three canted bay-windows, the r. one one-storeyed, the
other two of two storeys. They end in gables, above the r. bay
a dormer in the roof. Bulgy finials. Opposite, the WELLAND
AND NENE RIVER AUTHORITY, formerly Rectory,
probably of 1845 and by *Donthorne*. Again opposite, i.e. on
the E side, BERRYSTEAD, early C18, set back from the road,
seven bays and two storeys, quoins, all to stress the three-bay
centre. Tall, slender windows in broad frames. No. 22,
LAUNDIMER HOUSE, early C19, ashlar-faced, of five bays.
Both belong to Oundle School. Behind, a REFECTORY by
Pick, Everard, Keay & Gimson, 1961. Then LATHAM'S
HOSPITAL. This was founded in 1611. The N court is original,
the S court a continuation of 1837 (by *J. W. Smith* of Oundle,
BB) in the same Jacobean style with mullioned windows and
gables. Wall to the street and in each court an archway in
Early Victorian medievalizing forms. Main doorway in the
old court with strapwork volutes. No. 34 has a curious doorway with an open pediment on tapering half-fluted pilasters.
Is that a mixture of C17 and C18 parts? On the W side No. 47
is again of the early C18. Windows with lintels curved on their
underside. At the N end of North Street, C18 MALTINGS
(now Oundle School Clerk of the Works Department).

Back to the Market Place and now to the W. First we must look
at the funnel-shaped opening of NEW STREET; for here
stands the TALBOT INN, the finest building in Oundle. It is
dated 1626. Two canted bay-windows of two storeys, mullioned and, on the first floor, mullioned and transomed
windows. Three dormers irregularly placed. Ball finials.
Central archway. Inside a fine big staircase. Its window to the
back is of six lights with the sill running down diagonally to
follow the staircase. So it has partly one, partly two transoms.
Then into WEST STREET. No. 2 is Georgian, of five bays, facing
up New Street. No. 14 has a pretty Georgian shopfront.
No. 3, on the other side, is of 1626. It has mullioned windows
and an C18 doorway with Gibbs surround. Again on the S side
No. 16, COBTHORNE, detached and recessed, built before
1660.* Big volutes carrying the pediment of the doorway, and
ears and volutes to the window above it. Five bays, two storeys.
No. 24 is of 1715. It is three-storeyed and very plain. Broad,
flat window frames. PAINE'S ALMSHOUSES are on the N side.

* According to Bridges (BB).

They were founded in 1801 by John Paine, who gave four tenements to house families of Protestant dissenters. Two ranges at r. angles to the street, connected by a wall with archway. Four-centred door-heads, mullioned windows, canted bay-windows to the street. At the far end of the gardens overlooking Milton Road, a GAZEBO, C18, with arched windows and pyramid roof. No. 58 seems to be Early Victorian. It surrounds the entrance to Danford's Yard with giant pilasters and a balustrade. No. 62 is small and has two two-storeyed canted bay-windows; No. 72 has another.

At the end of West Street MILL ROAD turns down to the s. Nos. 1–14 are a terrace of identical one-storeyed cottages, probably of the C18. To the sw in STOKE HILL, NEW HOUSE, another house with two two-storeyed bay-windows. It is dated 1640.

OVERSTONE

8060

ST NICHOLAS. Built in 1807 and remodelled in 1903. Ashlar-faced with a w tower. – STAINED GLASS. E window, French C16 glass; good, arranged by *Egington*. – PLATE. Bread-holder, 1689; Cup, Paten, and Flagon, 1735. – MONUMENTS. Frances Stretford † 1717 and Edward Stretford † 1720, both by *John Hunt*. On the later monument curly open pediment with two putti blowing trumpets.

OVERSTONE PARK. Of the Stretford house of the C18 no more than parts of outbuildings remain. The building which replaced them and was designed for S. Jones Loyd, first Lord Overstone, about 1860, defeats description and appreciative analysis.* The *Builder* guardedly writes (1862) that 'the style adopted is claimed to be that, in a simple form, of the age of Francis I'. It can safely be said, however, that it is neither simple nor Francis I. The architect was *William Milford Teulon* (1823–1900), brother of the more famous and more notorious S. S. Teulon. The front is done *asymmetricalissime*, with bays, gables, a tall tower, motifs from the Italian Trecento, motifs from the Italian Cinquecento, motifs from the French C16, Jacobean strapwork. The architect was careful to avoid the re-appearance of any major motif. The big s tower has an open top storey with coupled columns. A second

* Lord Overstone, the son of the Manchester banker Lewis Loyd, was described in 1865 as 'one of the wealthiest subjects in the world'. His fortune was estimated at five million.

tower on the E side further back was reduced in height some time ago. The house has double outer walls throughout, tied together by iron clamps. Inside, the principal rooms are the Staircase Hall and the Library with a sumptuous Jacobean ceiling. The large Stables are no less ornate. The girls' school which is at Overstone Park has had a dining hall added, simple with arched windows. This was done by *Sir Guy Dawber* in 1935.

GATEWAY, at the NW corner of the grounds. From Pytchley *See* Hall when this was pulled down in 1824, and therefore of $^{p.}_{518}$ *c.* 1590. Three arches, the middle one for carriages. This is flanked by attenuated Roman Doric columns. Frieze with wide metopes. Gable of two S-curves. A total of five obelisks at the top.

The village was moved in 1821 from near the house (earthworks survive) to the road outside the park. Estate cottages of 1821 and later (BB, J. Steane).

PASSENHAM

ST GUTHLAC. Late C13 W tower, the upper part rebuilt *c.* 1626. Doorway with fine continuous mouldings. The three niches above it have later ogee heads. Pairs of lancets as bell-openings. Parapet and pinnacles later. C13 nave, see the lancets on the N side. The fabric is perhaps earlier, as a string course on the N wall is interrupted by the windows. In the E wall of the nave, S of the chancel arch, an odd lancet-headed window has been revealed by the recent restoration. The S windows are C19. The chancel was rebuilt in 1626 by Sir Robert Banastre. The priest's doorway has a depressed arch of the type which the French call *anse de panier* and an inscription above. The Perp windows are of Sir Robert's time too, and so is the wagon roof visible in its tunnel-form also outside. – Very remarkable furnishings of *c.* 1626, especially the STALLS with MISERICORDS of 1628★ – no doubt a self-conscious archaism – and the WEST GALLERY, which has fluted Ionic columns and a frieze with affronted sirens, if that description be permitted. It was once part of the rood screen, or what Morton in 1712 calls 'the Wainscoted Partition betwixt the Chancel and Body of the Church'. Also part of the original scheme of decoration is the WALL PAINTINGS, large single figures in shell-arched niches divided by pilasters.

★ A lion, a unicorn, a monster, heads, etc.

They are in the style of the Venetian Late Cinquecento. Restored in 1962–6 by *E. Clive Rouse*; the backgrounds repainted by *Ann Ballantyne*. On the N wall Isaiah, Jeremiah, Ezekiel, Daniel, on the S wall the Evangelists (St Mark obscured by the monument to Sir Robert), on the E wall Nicodemus and Joseph of Arimathaea. – PULPIT with back panel and tester. Probably made up from Jacobean pieces *c.* 1800. – BOX PEWS. – STAINED GLASS. Three large single figures reminiscent of the work of Evans of Shrewsbury. – (In the nave N and chancel S, canopies of *c.* 1350. RM) – MONUMENT. Sir Robert Banastre † 1649. Demi-figure in an oval niche surrounded by a wreath. Volutes with compact garlands to the l. and r. Steep open pediment.

MANOR HOUSE. The manor house is likely to contain evidence of the time of Sir Robert. The front with gables l. and r. and a slightly recessed centre looks C17. The SE side of five bays is Georgian. Much C19 remodelling; attic nursery and re-roofing by *Lutyens*, 1935 (N. Taylor). By the manor house two BARNS at r. angles. The larger one is of pre-Reformation date. It is 110 ft long and has three collar-beams one on top of the other. The smaller is dated 1626.

(RECTORY. Late C17 and later. Five-bay front. Central window with moulded architrave. Central shallow gable. DOE)

6050

PATTISHALL

HOLY CROSS. The Anglo-Saxon nave can still be recognized in its NW angle (outside) and its NE angle (inside). Both are quoined in the unmistakable long-and-short work. The Saxon chancel was replaced by a Norman chancel whose arch remains. The church was then cruciform: for the N chancel chapel has respond mouldings which repeat in a respond in the N aisle. It must mark the arch from the aisle into the transept, which became useless when the present arcades were built without regard to a transept. The blocked N doorway, which is Norman, must be re-set. The arcades differ, but are both of the C13. The S arcade is of ironstone, the N arcade of grey oölite. Three bays, octagonal piers, double-chamfered arches. S windows and W tower of *c.* 1300 with the usual tracery forms based on the Y-motif. The tower was rebuilt in 1663. – PLATE. Silver-gilt Set of 1663 given by Duchess Dudley. The bowl of the chalice is richly embossed with flowers.

GEORGE INN, Fosters Booth. Dated 1637. The remains of pargetting, a rarity in the county, have now disappeared

(J. M. Swann). It had numerous arches, a huntsman, and dogs.

PAULERSPURY

7040

St James. Perp w tower.* The body of the church rebuilt with old materials in 1843–4 and further restored since. In the chancel the splendid SEDILIA and DOUBLE PISCINA are original early C14 work. Little vaults inside. Much crocketing. The top is a foliage frieze, then an ogee-arch frieze, and then battlements. The piscina has a six-pointed star in the spandrel (cf. the chancel stalls at Winchester Cathedral). The chancel must however be older than the sedilia; for the N chapel is of before 1300. Pairs of lancet windows provided with beautiful detached shafts inside. A little dog-tooth and nailhead decoration. The arcade to the chancel has an octagonal pier and double-chamfered arches. The nave arcades are of five bays, with the same elements, except that in the N arcade circular alternate with octagonal piers. – FONT. Circular, Norman, with lunettes upside down, their outlines beaded. Leaf capitals inside the lunettes and in the spandrels below (cf. Tiffield). – STAINED GLASS. The E window is by *Clayton & Bell*. – The chancel s window is also by *Clayton & Bell*, c. 1878. – PLATE. Brass Candlesticks, given in 1670; two Breadholders, 1671; Flagon, 1674; two Cups and Cover Patens, 1765; Pocket Communion Set, c. 1820–40 (inside the container, cruet fits into cup and cup into paten). – MONUMENTS. Oaken effigies, Knight and Lady, mid-C14. He is no longer cross-legged. Her pillow is supported by angels. Supposed to be Sir Laurence de Pavely, alive in 1329. – Sir Arthur Throckmorton † 1603 and wife. A most unusual and slightly ludicrous monument. Large, long base, and on it the two effigies *accubantes*, i.e. comfortably reclining on their elbows and so placed that their faces face each other and their elbows touch. His is a decidedly humorous face. Some funeral ARMOUR belongs to this monument. – (Benjamin Bathurst † 1704 and his wife † 1727, tablet of good workmanship, hidden behind the organ. – Joseph Spinnall † 1726 by *Hunt*. – Robert Sheddon † 1826 by *Theakston*. Information on these from Mr Bailey.)

School. 1860–1. Wildly Gothic, with a little spirelet standing on a highly unconventional flying buttress.

Stable House (Grafton Hunt Kennels), one of the Grafton

* Stair to the tower in the form of a very large buttress; unusual and effective (L. M. Gotch).

farms (see Introduction p. 67). Three bays, two and a half storeys. Grey stone with ironstone dressings. Doorway with Ionic pilasters.

PEEL'S QUARRY see YARWELL

PHIPPSVILLE see NORTHAMPTON, p. 343

8050

PIDDINGTON

ST JOHN BAPTIST. Strange and unsatisfactory w tower of the C13 to the C14. The strangeness is the spire, which starts with tall broaches and one tier of tall lucarnes (with Y-tracery) and then carries on with a big collar like a parapet. The second tier of lucarnes is small and set in the diagonals. The outlines of the collar look from a distance as if repairs were carried on with a suspended scaffolding. The body of the church is much rebuilt (mainly in 1877–8 by *E. F. Law* and in 1900–2 by *Edmund Law*, BB). All windows, except those of the Perp clerestory, are renewed. The probability is that the church was of *c.* 1300. Arcades of four bays with octagonal piers and double-chamfered arches. – PLATE. Cup and Cover Paten, 1570; Breadholder, 1789. – MONUMENTS. Many tablets of the C18, by such local carvers as the *Coxes* of Northampton and *Andrews* of Olney, mostly hung in the spandrels of the arcades – not a commendable arrangement. To mention one: Joseph Swayn † 1720, apothecary, pretty, with three heads at the top (chancel).

0080

PILTON

ST MARY AND ALL SAINTS. The church forms a fine group with the old manor house. The exterior mostly late C13. But the S doorway is of the late C12. Waterleaf capitals, arch with zigzags meeting at r. angles. Hood-mould with early dog-tooth. Late C13 first of all the W tower. Doorway with filleted shafts and arch mouldings, shafted bell-openings with Y-tracery, corbel frieze of small heads, spire with low broaches, two tiers of lucarnes. The lower has two lights with continuous roll mouldings and a quatrefoiled circle. Late C13 the S aisle, see the E window with three quatrefoiled circles in the tracery, and the corresponding two-light S window. The S porch entrance is also late C13. The N aisle has a three-light window with intersected tracery and a W lancet, i.e. is late C13 too. Dec clerestory. Inside, C13 arcades of three bays with octagonal piers and double-chamfered arches. At their springing little corner motifs like halved dog-tooth. Nailhead on one s pier. C13 chancel arch with stiff-leaf. The chancel is of 1862–4. – FONT. Octagonal, with leaf decoration on the foot. Not good. – STAINED GLASS. E window of *c.* 1864. Whom is it by? – TILES. With birds and animals. Late Victorian, perhaps by *Lord Alwyne Compton*? Sir Gyles Isham has pointed out that Lord Lilford, patron of the living, was a famous ornithologist.

MANOR HOUSE.* Built by the Treshams. After 1715 and until recently it was the Rectory. The external appearance Jacobean and picturesque. The SE part is the earliest, probably dating from the 1560s (cf. the dovecote at Newton). The SW part contains a good Jacobean staircase with vertically symmetrical balusters, and on the first floor a panelled room with an overmantel over the fireplace. This has handsome groups of three detached little columns, one standing in front of the other two. This part of the house was added *c.* 1620, when it became occupied by the Treshams of Newton. The mullioned windows were added in the 1840s.

OLD WATCH HOUSE (also known as the Bede House). With medieval fragments around the upper windows, such as a ballflower frieze and two shafts on head-stops, and a curious lookout, like a large chimney with a pyramid roof, at one end.

PIPEWELL

8080

1½ m. N of Rushton

Of the Cistercian abbey nothing is preserved. It was founded in 1143 from Newminster in Northumberland, which was founded in 1137 from Fountains Abbey, which was founded in 1133 from Clairvaux – so rapid was the spread of the Cistercian order in these early years. (Earthworks survive, possibly of a dam or fishponds; some may be remains of the village destroyed in 1143 (the earliest deserted medieval village in the county). The plan of the abbey was recovered in 1909. J. Steane)

(CHURCH. Erected in 1881–2 in what was then called the 'Norman' style, but in fact more rustic than Romanesque. BB)

(PIPEWELL HALL. Early C19. L. M. Gotch)

* This account was contributed by Sir Gyles Isham.

7060

PITSFORD

5 ALL SAINTS. Norman s doorway. Shafts with zigzag and two kinds of trellis, one of them beaded. Perhaps re-assembled wrongly. Outer arch moulding with beakhead, inner with zigzag. The tympanum represents St George and the Dragon, or perhaps Faith fighting Evil. The carver is always ready to lose himself in interlace. Thus e.g. there is a cock in the bottom l. corner, and his tail is interlace. Dec w tower. The ample buttresses have a nook-shaft all up the re-entrant angle, an unusual and successful motif. The bell-openings are of two lights, but to the N and s there is an extra cusped lancet asymmetrically at its side. N aisle E window with reticulated tracery. The arcades with their foliage capitals are of 1867, when the chancel was rebuilt too, and much else renewed. The architects were *Slater & Carpenter*, the carver *Gillet* of Leicester (BB). – FONT. Octagonal, C14. With flat gables. – PLATE. Cup and Paten of 1560, an early date; Paten, 1635.

VILLAGE HALL. Tudor. By *Morley Horder*, early C20.

PITSFORD HALL. By *John Johnson* of Leicester, before 1785. Originally a centre and two wings, but much altered since the Second World War. An additional storey was added and the garden side was changed sweepingly. Good staircase with wrought-iron balustrade. The building is now a school. A dormitory block was added by *Walker & Sturgess*, 1966.

SEDGEBROOK HALL, 1 m. SW. By a London architect (GI). Dated 1861. Façade with central pediment, and a grand porch with Ionic columns on the l.

(MOULTON GRANGE, ¾ m. E. Built just before 1830. Bald Regency classical, the s front Italianized *c.* 1850, the E parts extended in 1911–12. BB)

Possible NEOLITHIC LONG BARROW on Lymans Hill, *c.* 100 yds up the lane to the village, off the main Northampton road.

5040

PLUMPTON

ST JOHN BAPTIST. Small. Mostly a rebuilding of 1822, except that the tower arch and chancel arch seem to be re-used. – FONT. Could be of the 1660s. – (The original fittings of 1822 survive: BOX PEWS, BENCHES, and COMMANDMENT BOARDS. – REREDOS incorporating Jacobean carving. BB) – PLATE. Cup, 1684; Breadholder, *c.* 1693; exceptionally shallow Cup, 1694. – MONUMENT. Anna Moore † 1683. Tablet with drapery and a cherub at the foot.

MANOR HOUSE. C17. Two-storeyed, with a gabled porch and
fine rusticated gatepiers.*

POLEBROOK   0080

ALL SAINTS. An interesting rather than a beautiful church,
dating mostly from *c.* 1175–*c.* 1250, odd in shape, short, with
far-projecting transept and a tower at the SW end. The earliest
evidence is Early Norman. The church had a nave, a central
tower with or without a transept (see the piece of wall inter-
rupting the N arcade), and a chancel. To this was added *c.* 1175
a N transept and a N aisle. The chancel, or only the chancel
arch, was also rebuilt. The chancel arch, the transept arch, and
the aisle arcade exhibit circular, or in the responds semicircular, shafts, waterleaf capitals, square abaci notched at the
corners, and round, double-chamfered arches. In the arcade
there are also crocket capitals. Next followed the tower. It has
round-headed W and S windows decorated with dog-tooth.
The arches to nave and S aisle are triple-chamfered, round,
and have simple moulded capitals. So a S aisle was by then
also planned. In its execution it is a little later. The circular
pier and responds are much taller and slimmer, and the setting
out takes no account of transepts. Stiff-leaf capitals. Double-
chamfered round arches. Simple round-headed S doorway,
placed in the first bay E of the tower. The chancel and the
transepts in their present form must date from about the
same time. The priest's doorway still has a round, only slightly
chamfered arch. The chancel windows are lancets, including
two 'low-side' lancets and a fine group of three stepped
separate lancets at the E end. They are splendidly double-
shafted inside with shaft-rings. The chancel PISCINA is even
more splendid, if a little barbarically so. Two very odd decorative sub-arches rise above the pointed lights from the middle
in a single curve outward to meet the super-arch. Much dog-
tooth enrichment. Lancets are also in the S transept E wall and
the N transept W wall. Inside the N transept a startlingly
sumptuous display of blank arcading, covering the W wall and
part of the N wall. Detached shafts, plain capitals with dog-
tooth behind, deeply moulded arches, and leaf and rosette
stops. The same rosette or patera as here occurs also in the
hood-mould of the vestry doorway in the chancel and the

* Mr L. M. Gotch suggests that the house is of the late C16 but that the
front and the gatepiers date from *c.* 1650.

chancel piscina. Eaves courses with small heads in chancel and
N transept. The work in chancel and transepts takes us no
doubt into the second quarter of the C13, and so it is likely
that there is a connexion between this activity and the granting
of the church to Peterborough Abbey in 1232. The N porch
is a spectacular mid-C13 piece. Entrance with two orders of
colonnettes with lively late stiff-leaf capitals and three vertical
bands of dog-tooth. The arch must have been intended still
to be round. It has many fine mouldings. Eaves course of
dog-tooth. The tower now reached the stage of its bell-
openings. They are twins with a separating shaft and still
under a round arch. Spire with medium-high broaches and
three tiers of lucarnes. The S porch entrance is also shafted,
but has a pointed arch.

Of later contributions no more needs mention than the two
C14 E windows of the N transept with flowing tracery, the
Perp clerestory, and the nave roof (dated 1626) with tie-beams
and collar-beams on queenposts. – FONT. Octagonal, with
flat pointed-trefoiled arches; c. 1300. – SCREEN. Perp, minor,
with one-light divisions. – PULPIT. Plain, C17, the top panels
gadrooned. – BENCHES (S transept). Simple and raw, probably
Jacobean.

POLEBROOK HALL. Jacobean (1626 in the panelling of a room
on the upper floor) but much restored and remodelled. The N
front has two slightly projecting gabled wings. Inside was an
oblong courtyard, now glazed. The S front looks all Victorian,
except for the two-bay piece dated 1719, which is under a
Jacobean gable. Mullioned windows. Much panelling, the
finest in the ground-floor room behind the front of 1719. This
has strongly moulded panels and a coved ceiling with stucco
patterns of thin ribs. Many wooden chimneypieces, all with
flat carving. C18 staircase. C18 iron gates to the N and the E.
The garden was re-cast by *Sir Reginald Blomfield* 'early in his
career'.

OLD POST OFFICE, W of the church. Inside, one big fireplace
with a four-centred head. In the front garden two fragments,
probably from the church.

THE GABLES, N of the Hall. Dated 1698, but with a C16 doorway. The work of 1698 is purely classical.

POTTERSPURY

ST NICHOLAS. Perp W tower with a very elaborately moulded
doorway. The rest of the exterior is all Victorian. (There were

two restorations, firstly in 1848, and secondly in 1860–1 by *E. F. Law.* BB) The arcades are interesting. They are of three bays. That on the N side has its E pier clearly of the C12. It is circular and has a square abacus. The capital is flat and decorated with many scallops. The abacus has some dog-tooth. The W pier is octagonal and belongs to the C13. The arches date from the time of this. The S arcade is slenderer and has octagonal piers and arch mouldings indicating a Perp date. C13 N chapel of two bays. The chancel arch is striking. It is tripartite with two tall octagonal piers and a wide middle arch. The side arches die into the imposts. The arch cuts into the first bay of the N chapel. – FONT. Octagonal, Perp. Panelled stem, bowl with shields and pointed quatrefoils. – BOX PEWS. – PLATE. Cup, *c.* 1570; silver-gilt Paten, 1683; Set, 1728. – Also the Chalice and Cover, 1601, from Furtho church. – MONUMENTS. Gabriel Clarke † 1624, Cuthbert Ogle † 1633. Both with black inscription plates and both without figures.

CONGREGATIONAL CHAPEL. 1780. A very pretty two-storeyed brick range with dark chequer pattern. The first three bays are the manse and have a middle doorway, the next three were the chapel and have segment-headed windows. The school and manse were added in 1846.

GRAFTON TERRACE or Duchess Row, or also Factory Row, because it was at one time a lace factory. Terrace of eight houses. Another group of four houses is no doubt a little later. This is rock-faced, gabled, and bargeboarded and has leaded lights.

POTTERSPURY LODGE, I m. NW. 1664 with additions of 1899. The centre probably had seven bays with a three-bay projection, quoins, and a cupola. One room on the upper floor has Jacobean panelling. The staircase runs up in an open well. Twisted balusters with bulbous feet.

WAKEFIELD LODGE, 1½ m. WSW. Built by *Kent* for the second 94 Duke of Grafton, for whom he also built at Euston in Suffolk. Wakefield Lodge is a late work of his (*c.* 1745). It is a lodge indeed, a hunting lodge in Whittlewood Forest of which the Duke was ranger, but a cyclopean lodge. It is not actually large, only five bays wide, but the motifs used are all somehow oversized. They are not beautiful in themselves, nor is the whole beautiful, but the effect has power and a strange primeval attraction. Kent, Lord Burlington's protégé, is customarily regarded as the apostle of strict Palladianism. In fact he was nearer in spirit to Vanbrugh than to Palladio. The front has a recessed centre, which was two-storeyed originally, and the end bays are raised by a half-storey and covered with flat pyramid roofs. On the ground floor a three-bay portico of Tuscan columns with exaggerated entasis and a flat top. The windows are of the Venetian type, but they have depressed, actually three-centred, arches, and the same arches above all three parts. The upper floor has tripartite lunette windows, but they also have this squashed, three-centred shape. Big and unmoulded dentil frieze between ground floor and first floor. Inside there is one all-dominant room, the Saloon, filling the centre on both floors and surrounded by a balcony on brackets like the entrance hall in Inigo Jones's Queen's House at Greenwich. Kent was the editor of Inigo's works, and he has obviously taken his inspiration here from the Queen's House. That is equally clear in the very restrained panels of the stucco ceiling and in the circular, flying or geometrical, staircase with an iron railing – an echo of Inigo's tulip staircase at Greenwich.

STABLES of pale purple brick, fifteen bays wide, with a three-bay pediment.

The AVENUES to the W and the S can still be traced.

5050 ## PRESTON CAPES

ST PETER. Perp W tower with two-light transomed bell-openings and battlements. Several aisle windows of c. 1300–50. Inside, the S arcade is of the early C13, two and a half bays, circular piers and octagonal abaci, pointed arches and one slight chamfer. The N arcade is later (octagonal piers, double-chamfered arches) but also has a half-arch at the W end, i.e. was built before the tower. – FONT. With panels illustrating window tracery as if taken from a pattern book. – BENCHES. Some are original. They have traceried panels. – PLATE. Cup, Paten, and Breadholder, 1699.

GROUP OF COTTAGES built as an eye-catcher for Fawsley Hall. Red brick, two rows of two facing each other. Between the rows to the N a castellated archway. The battlements are then taken along the N side and along the E as well. The cottage roofs rise towards these E and W battlements in what is nowadays called monopitches.

CASTLE. A short distance to the E of the church is the ringwork of an C11 castle. Its only outwork is a bank on the side protected by nature; originally it seems to have had a bailey.

(MANOR FARM, on the SE side of the castle. The side facing

the road has a C17 façade, but at the back are mullioned windows and a late medieval corbelled-out bay-window.)

The Cluniac PRIORY founded at Preston Capes in 1090 was transferred to Daventry in 1107–8.

PRESTON DEANERY

St Peter and St Paul. Threatened with redundancy (1971), but preservation is likely. Norman w tower. Buttresses up the middle of the sides. To the l. and r. of the buttress a ground-floor window on the W, bell-openings on the E. Narrow round tower arch. The chancel arch is Norman too, round-headed and unmoulded. The chancel has a round-headed doorway of c. 1200 and a blocked 'low-side' window of c. 1300. – MONUMENT. Mrs Langham, 1773. By *Henry Cox*. Architectural tablet.

Preston Hall. Partly built after a fire of 1872, but mostly of 1933.

PURSTON

1¼ m. W of Farthinghoe

The E wing, the fireplace in the Hall in the middle of the S range, and the staircase (with vertically symmetrical balusters) are Jacobean, but the beautiful S façade is of the late C17. Three-bay centre with two-bay projections to the l. and r. Two storeys, hipped roof. Stone cross-windows. Doorway with a frame with ears and a steep open segmental pediment.

PYTCHLEY

All Saints. To record the history of the building one must start inside. Nave and aisles are comfortably wide. The arcades are not high. The first two bays of the N arcade are Late Norman (circular pier, capitals with horizontal scrolls and heads at the corners, square abacus, single-stepped arch with painted decoration). Then follows the S aisle. Its arcade has three bays. Quatrefoil piers with stiff-leaf capitals and double-chamfered pointed arches. That is C13. So is the S doorway and the strange recess in the N aisle with keeled mouldings. The chancel followed at the end of the C13, but was over-restored in 1861. The windows still have Geometrical tracery, but sedilia and piscina are Dec (ogee arches).* A

---

* Drawings by George Clark show that before 1861 most of the windows were of C17 mullioned form (BB).

little earlier the E continuation of the N arcade to link up with
the chancel. Quatrefoil piers, one with a moulded capital, the
other with big upright oak-leaves. Dec again the handsome S
windows E of the porch: three steeply stepped lancet lights
under an ogee arch. And essentially Dec the tall, unbuttressed
W tower. Transomed two-light bell-openings, battlements,
pinnacles. – WOODWORK. Much of various dates. The earliest
pieces are C15 SCREEN PANELS incorporated in the chancel
stalls. Jacobean the SCREEN in the N recess, PEWS in the nave,
COMMUNION RAIL with vertically symmetrical balusters, and
the PULPIT. The SEAT in the chancel is made up from C16 or
C17 pieces. – COMMUNION TABLE. Probably the one recorded
as made in 1704. – BOX PEWS. C18, cut down in 1844–5, when
the curious internal PORCHES were introduced.* – ROYAL
ARMS. Part of a painted 'tympanum', originally between nave
and chancel, dated 1661. – BOX PEWS. C18. – PLATE. Chalice,
Cup, and Cover Paten, 1570.

PYTCHLEY HALL. Built by Sir Euseby Isham about 1580–90.
Some stained glass preserved at Lamport Hall has the date
1596. The house was demolished in 1824. A gateway went to
Overstone (p. 369), the porch is at Glendon (p. 226), minor
fragments at Isham (p. 269), panelling from a room at Cottesbrooke (p. 164n), and a Vanbrughian fireplace at Shortwood
Lodge (p. 403). A small square GATEHOUSE with pyramid roof
survives E of the church. It existed already in 1820 (BB).

PYTCHLEY MANOR HOUSE. Dates 1633 and 1665, with good
chimneys, gables, and mullioned windows (L. M. Gotch).

(SCHOOL HOUSE. Mid C18. Red brick with stone dressings. Five
bays, two storeys. On the garden side a central doorcase with
pulvinated frieze, and a Gibbsian window above. BB)

7050

QUINTON

ST JOHN BAPTIST. Before the church received its W tower in
the C13, the nave ended to the W without a tower, as is testified
by the Late Norman pointed lancet in the W wall and the SW
quoin. The tower has two-light C13 bell-openings and above
them Perp bell-openings and battlements. Most of the rest of
the church was remodelled in 1801. The rounded corners of
the chancel and the porch and the similarly rounded chancel
windows are unusual. Early C13 S arcade of three bays with
circular piers and circular abaci. Keeled responds. Double-

* These details were supplied by Mr Bailey.

chamfered arches. The blank N arch indicates a former N transept. The chancel arch seems C13. – FONT. Disused. C18; of baluster type. – (MONUMENT (in the churchyard). Eleanor Maccallum † 1909. Of terracotta, with angels at head and foot. By her sister, *Mrs G. F. Watts*. BB)

RADSTONE

5040

ST LAWRENCE. Norman W tower, see the unmoulded round arch towards the nave, the blocked W window, and the blocked former bell-openings, which must be early C13. The later bell-openings are Dec. Early C13 also the chancel, see the S door-way with the small zigzag at r. angles to the wall surface and the two-lancet window. Early C14 S aisle and N aisle. Arcades of three bays, tall, with octagonal piers and double-chamfered arches. The SE respond and one S pier have very fine capitals decorated not only with oak leaves and acorns but also with knotty branches (cf. the doorway at Kislingbury). – FONT. Norman? Circular, with two tiers of flat round arches, the upper standing on the apexes of the lower. – PLATE. Cup and Paten, 1587.

RAUNDS

9070

ST MARY. The description must start from the ornate E.E. W 8 tower. Its proportions are exceptionally satisfying. Set-back buttresses. Shafted W portal set back behind an outer entrance, also shafted, a little higher than the portal proper and flush with the W wall of the tower. L. and r. small blank trefoil-headed arches. On the next stage two lancets in blank, nicely shafted arches and blank arches l. and r. Set out with a blank quatrefoil – one would like to know why. The question becomes more pressing on the stage above, where to the W there is a two-light trefoil-headed window placed under a gable filling nearly the whole height. To the l. and r. of it corresponding rising diagonals or half-gables towards the angles so that the whole stage has a letter W inscribed, as it were. More-over, blank quatrefoils are set in the surfaces, one in each of the four side triangles. The N and S sides are simpler. They have no quatrefoils, just noble blank arcading, on the N sub-divided Y-fashion by pendant arches on heads. The bell-stage has two pairs of shafted lancets and blank lancet arches l. and r., again subdivided Y-fashion. Broach spire with broaches reaching up about as high as the very tall tier of lucarnes.

There there are two more, and they are placed in alternate directions. The spire was rebuilt in 1826 by *Charles Squirhill* after being struck by lightning. The tower has a C15 CLOCK DIAL, stone-faced with twenty-four discs of the hours. The dial is held by two angels, and behind them kneel the donors, John Elen and his wife.

The interior is extremely puzzling. It clearly represents a development in various stages, but the differences in detail are such that re-use of older parts is also likely. The story certainly starts with the remains of a window above the S arcade, evidence of a Norman nave, and the shape of the last S pier but one, evidence of walls at that place which probably was the angle of the Norman S transept. There followed, begun *c.* 1225, the tower and the two semicircular W responds of the nave, evidence of the intention of E.E. aisling. But the Norman W wall must have been further E, and the fact that the first bay of the S arcade (*see* below) is wider than the others means probably that that arch, when it was built, bridged the distance between new tower and old nave. At the same time a new chancel was begun. A blank arch in the S wall shows that its wall had gone up to a certain height before a S chapel was added. This is of two bays with a circular pier with circular abacus and double-chamfered arches. The plan must have been to continue the arcading to the W beyond the then chancel arch, i.e. a chancel arch preceding the present one, but when a half-arch had been built, operations stopped for the time being. Of the C13 also the S doorway into the S chapel, with stiff-leaf capitals, and the N and S aisle doorways with the S porch. The N doorway has a slight chamfer, the S doorway is normally double-chamfered. Its details otherwise, especially the capitals, and the details of the S porch including its shafted entrance and the corner shafts for a rib-vault, correspond closely to those of the W doorway into the tower. The last glory of the C13 at Raunds is the splendid six-light E window, hardly possible before *c.* 1275, with cusped lights, six quatre-foiled circles, and a big octofoiled circle in the head. The S arcade was begun probably *c.* 1300. It has octagonal piers and double-chamfered arches. The irregularity of its wider W arch has already been mentioned. There are other irregularities too, due to the former W corner of the S transept. When the aisle reached the chancel arch, the idea of joining up with the half-arch of the chancel chapel had been given up, a new chancel arch, with finely moulded responds and ballflower in the arch, was built (and specially buttressed on the s side), and an awkward second half-arch was provided to finish the s arcade. The N arcade was probably only started when all these problems had been settled for better or worse. Its details are full C14, and it has no irregularities worth speaking of. The N windows have flowing tracery. The s windows, the chancel N windows, and the s chapel E window are Perp. Medieval ROOFS, the one over the nave with tracery in the spandrels.

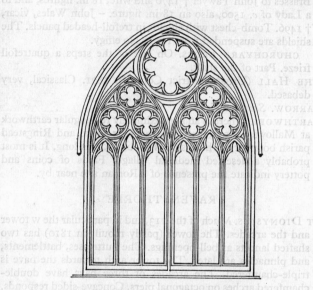

Raunds church, east window, *c.* 1275

– FONT. Circular, with one very realistic ram's head sticking out. Can this be C13? – SCREENS. Base of the rood screen; screens to the s chapel, one of them being C14 and having shafts with shaft-rings instead of mullions and ogee arches. – REREDOS (N aisle). Wooden panels with Flamboyant tracery. – BENCHES. Parts of late medieval benches are incorporated in the choir stalls of 1894. – PULPIT. The polygonal C18 TABLE was originally the tester of the pulpit. – COMMUNION RAIL. Jacobean, with vertically symmetrical balusters. – WALL PAINTINGS. Nave N wall Pride and her Six Children,

St Christopher, the Three Quick and the Three Dead. Over the N doorway St George, on the N aisle wall fragments of a Legend of St Catherine. Over the chancel arch angels with the instruments of the Passion. All C15. – STAINED GLASS. E window by *Kempe*, 1907. – (Chancel N St Elizabeth, C15. – Late C14 fragments in a window in the S aisle. RM) – CHANDELIER. Brass, given in 1762. – ARMOUR. Parts of two sets of the time of Charles I. – PLATE. Cup, 1687. – MONUMENTS. Brasses to John Tawyer † 1470 and wife, 18 in. figures, and to a Lady of *c.* 1500, also an 18 in. figure. – John Wales, vicar, † 1496. Tomb-chest with shields in trefoil-headed panels. The shields are suspended from roses. No effigy.

CHURCHYARD CROSS. On one of the steps a quatrefoil frieze. Part of the shaft.

THE HALL (Urban District Council). 1871. Classical, very debased.

BARROW. *See* Stanwick.

EARTHWORK. There is an approximately rectangular earthwork at Mallows Cotton, between the Hog Dyke and Ringstead parish boundary. The N side is about 200 yds long. It is most probably a deserted medieval village. Finds of coins and pottery indicate the presence of a Roman site near by.

RAVENSTHORPE
6070

ST DIONYSIUS. Much of the C13, and in particular the W tower and the arcades. The tower (partly rebuilt in 1810) has two shafted lancets as bell-openings. The buttresses, battlements, and pinnacles are later. The tower arch towards the nave is triple-chamfered. The arcades of three bays have double-chamfered arches on octagonal piers. Concave-sided responds. In the S aisle Dec doorway and W window. Also a low tomb recess inside. The chancel dates from 1866. – PULPIT. Jacobean. – SCREEN. Parts of the screen are Perp. – CHEST. Nearly 8 ft long, iron-bound. – ARMOUR. Said to have been found at Naseby. – PLATE. Cup, 1661; Paten, *c.* 1682.

(In the village several COTTAGES built of cob. M. Seaborne)

RINGSTEAD
9070

ST MARY. Good C13 W tower; not high. Unbuttressed with tall W lancet with stiff-leaf cusps. Shortish broach spire with high broaches and three tiers of lucarnes, the lowest very tall and with Y-tracery. Otherwise the exterior mostly Dec, i.e. the N porch entrance with ballflower decoration and an ogee gable, the simple doorways, the fine tall chancel windows (E five lights) with flowing tracery, the SEDILIA with ogee arches, also the s windows as tall as those of the chancel and with flowing tracery too, and the s porch with a quadripartite vault with ridge ribs. The ribs are round, not pointed. The N arcade

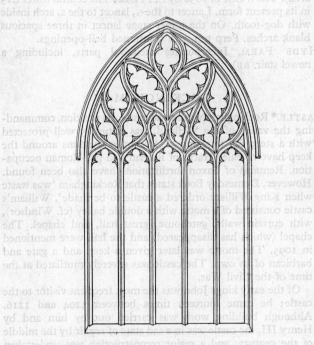

Ringstead church, east window, Decorated

inside is earlier. It belongs to the time of the tower. Five bays, quatrefoil piers, double-chamfered arches. The N chapel is of the same time again (circular piers and circular abaci, double-chamfered arches). – FONT. Octagonal, plain, with a stem with attached keeled shafts; c. 1300 perhaps. – SCREEN. Plain low stone base, also to the N chapel. – PLATE. Cup and Paten, c. 1682.

7050

ROADE

St Mary. Structurally Norman with a central tower. Norman two chancel windows and Norman the s doorway. Two orders of shafts, scalloped capitals. One arch moulding with a motif of two horns, the other with the beakhead motif. In the w wall a window of *c.* 1300 (three stepped lancet lights under one arch). The n aisle of 1850 by *E. F. Law*. The central tower c 13 in its present form. Lancet to the n, lancet to the s, arch inside with dog-tooth. On the upper stage lancet in three spacious blank arches. Perp top with transomed bell-openings.

(Hyde Farm. Incorporates medieval parts, including a newel stair. BB)

8090

ROCKINGHAM

Castle.* Rockingham was a royal castle. Its position, commanding the valley of the Welland, was naturally well protected with a steep fall to n and w. Recent excavations around the keep have revealed traces of Roman and pre-Roman occupation. Remains of Saxon fortifications have also been found. However, Domesday Book states that Rockingham 'was waste when King William ordered a castle to be made'. William's castle consisted of a motte with a double bailey (cf. Windsor), with curtain walls, gatehouse, great hall, and chapel. The chapel (which has disappeared) and the hall were mentioned in 1095. The motte was later given a keep and a gate and barbican of its own. The castle was severely mutilated at the time of the Civil War.

Of the early kings John was the most frequent visitor to the castle; he came fourteen times between 1204 and 1216. Although building work was carried out by him and by Henry III, the castle was in a sad state of repair by the middle of the century, and a major reconstruction was undertaken by Edward I in 1276–91. Of this time there survive the additions to the gatehouse, some of the e wall to its s, and remains of the reconstructed hall, which lies at r. angles to them, with its main entrance on the n. The Gatehouse is of Weldon stone. It has two strong semicircular towers with cross slits. These semicircular parts were almost certainly added by Edward I to earlier towers, although the building accounts

---

* This revised entry is based on a detailed study by Sir Gyles Isham which was specially prepared in connexion with the new edition of this book.

do not survive to prove this.* The arches of the gateway are two-centred and have fine mouldings. The portcullis groove ought to be noted. Doorways to the l. and r. Another window of Edward I's time survives on the w side of the adjoining E wall, towards the s end. Of the HALL there are preserved the N and S doorways, that on the N being more elaborately moulded. Rolls with keels and fillets. Stiff-leaf capitals (very worn).‡ Big chimneybreast.§ In the adjoining PANEL ROOM to the w (formerly part of the hall) are fragments of two tall shafted windows, and of a C14 window which perhaps lit a gallery. Edward I also reconstructed the other domestic buildings and added a NW tower to the outer bailey. Of this work only the base of the latter is visible.

During the C15 and early C16 the castle was neglected, and Leland reported that 'Rockingham Castle faullith to ruine'. Apart from the medieval parts described, the existing buildings are conversions and additions chiefly of three periods, the later C16 and the mid C17, all unassuming work, and the C19. The castle now has buildings on three sides of its entrance courtyard. On the N it is open and the views from here and the w gardens are extensive. S of the hall range is a smaller courtyard, and between this and the medieval outer wall a narrow court still called the 'street' which used to lead to the keep.

In 1553 Edward Watson obtained a lease of the castle from the Crown and began to convert it into a private residence. He divided the Great Hall into two and inserted a ceiling (dated 1579), and added a w range at r. angles to the hall, with a long gallery in the N half. The gallery was rebuilt in the earlier C17 (fireplace dated 1634) and shortened and re-paired after Civil War damage. His son added the buildings E of the hall (1585). This work is gabled and has mullioned windows, and appears Late Tudor, although most of the stonework is earlier. WALKER'S HOUSE, to the N of the gatehouse, was also built at this time (it was used as a resi-dence by Edward Watson when the castle was being recon-

* The history of the gatehouse appears to have been as follows: first, two square towers flanking a gateway (see the round-headed arches at the back); secondly a square centre projection; thirdly the rounded fronts added to the two towers.

‡ Stylistically the doorways look later than 1216 but earlier than 1276. But that does not fit with the documented major building periods.

§ This was added when the ceiling was inserted (information from Mr K. J. Allsop).

structed), but was rebuilt as a steward's house in 1655 after being damaged in the Civil War. The house is of three bays with a hipped roof. Several of the C16 mullioned windows survive. Good staircase of 1655. Also of the C17 the LAUNDRY at the S end of the 'street'. The date is 1669, and it has cross-windows and small two-light windows, placed irregularly. The alterations to the S part of the W front must also date from this time. The dormers here have tall mullioned openings and pediments. On the ground floor the LIBRARY with Adamish decoration of c. 1900. Of the C17 internal alterations the PANEL ROOM W of the hall can be dated to between 1679 and 1689. It has pine panelling decorated with coats of arms. These were renovated by *Willement* in the early C19.

Further internal changes were made in the C18, but no major work was undertaken until *Salvin's* alterations of 1839 and 1851-2. His are the square S tower adjoining the W range and the large bay-window of the long gallery which forms the lower part of the Flag Tower towards the N end of the W range. On the N front of the hall he added a one-storey staircase projection, and was also responsible for placing heraldic shields from elsewhere in the building above the main entrance, where there had once been a window and balcony. Inside, his main STAIRCASE is disappointing. Salvin also added battlements to the gatehouse and removed its pitched roof and the Georgian excrescences against the curtain wall. In the 1960s extensive reconstruction work was undertaken, including an overhaul of the whole roof structure. At the same time various internal alterations for C20 domestic convenience were made by *K. J. Allsop* of *Gotch, Saunders & Surridge*.

ST LEONARD. Immediately below the N courtyard of the castle and in no connexion with the village. Small and irregular. Exterior all C19. Small NE tower with octagonal pyramid roof. Internally also nothing of architectural interest. – FONT. Dated 1669. Of the oddly bleak kind of so many of the fonts of the 1660s. Big volutes, a heart, etc. – PULPIT. Jacobean, of the usual type. – COMMUNION RAIL. Of wrought iron; C18. – STAINED GLASS. In the S chapel by *Hedgeland*, 1853; in the N aisle by *Kempe*, c. 1904 – PLATE. Cup and Paten, 1570. – MONUMENTS. Many, and some of outstanding quality. The Montagus of Boughton were more discriminating in their choice of sculptors. Sir Edward Watson † 1584 and † 1616.

See p. 518

Fragments of two monuments, re-assembled and jumbled up no doubt after the Civil War. Two recumbent effigies, the children kneeling against the tomb-chest. The effigies are of *c.* 1616, though the woman, Sir Edward's mother, wears the dress that belongs to her time (s chapel). – Anne Lady Rockingham † 1695 (chancel N). By *John Nost* (BB). Heavy standing figure. Roman Doric columns l. and r. Big Baroque pedimented top. Black draperies behind the whole monument. – Hon. Margaret Watson † 1713, by *William Palmer* (s chapel). Also with a standing figure, but this one slender, in a serpentine posture. Big drapery canopy or baldacchino. Fluted Corinthian pilasters l. and r. – First Earl of Rockingham † 1724 (chancel s). By *Delvaux*. Figures by *Scheemakers*. Big sarcophagus and standing figures to the l. and r., he in Roman dress, she wearing an ermine mantle. Dancing putto on the sarcophagus carrying a wreath and a toy trumpet. Broad architectural background. – Lady Arabella Oxenden † 1734. Free-standing figure on a pedestal, like a piece of Roman statuary in a museum. No architectural background.* – Lady Sondes † 1777 (s chapel s wall). Signed by *William Paine*. No figures, only a base and a sarcophagus with domed top, all in flat relief and with very restrained decoration. – Various members of the Sondes family, the last † 1795 (s chapel s wall). Inscription plate with draped urn on top. – Lady Sondes † 1806 (*ibidem*). Same composition. – Lady Sondes † 1818 (*ibidem*). Hanging monument, woman by an urn.

The VILLAGE of Rockingham lies to the N, at the foot of the hill along a main road. C17–18 houses and cottages, the earliest date 1663 on the SONDES ARMS, the latest 1795 on a farmhouse. The best house is CASTLE FARMHOUSE, at the NW end. Half-H plan. Two-light upright mullioned windows. Doorway broad, classical, with ears. The date is 1674.

ROTHERSTHORPE

ST PETER AND ST PAUL. Of the C13 the W tower and the arcades. The tower has bell-openings with Y-tracery, a saddleback roof, and an arch towards the nave with semicircular responds and a hood-mould with head-stops. The arcades have piers with the rare form of a circular core with four triple shafts, i.e. altogether twelve shafts (cf. Flore). Arches with two slight chamfers. The arches into the chancel N and s

---

* Of good quality, and in the manner of *Rysbrack*, Mr Bailey suggests.

chapels are probably Dec. The windows partly of *c*. 1300 (s aisle), partly Dec (N chapel N), partly Perp (chancel E). s doorway of *c*. 1300; good. – PULPIT. With tall, plain, unadorned panels. One panel is inscribed 1579 – an important date, as one would not expect such simplicity in the mid-Elizabethan decades. Small tester. – COMMUNION RAIL. To the side chapel. C17. – SCULPTURE. Cross head with a crude figure of the Crucifixus and stiff-leaf decoration. An E.E. cross head is a great rarity. – PLATE. Cup, 1570; Paten, 1591.

MANOR HOUSE. C17. With gables and mullioned windows.

DOVECOTE, at the crossing of the Kislingbury and Northampton roads. Circular, 20 ft diameter, with over 900 nesting places.

8080

ROTHWELL

Rothwell is one of the most attractive towns in Northamptonshire, a small town but decidedly a town. It has a splendid church, and few houses of special note. The *ensemble* is however what matters most.

HOLY TRINITY. A large church of ironstone, remarkably long in particular (with its 173 ft the longest parish church in the county), and with unmistakable marks of yet larger size originally. The blocked arches along the fronts of the transepts and the chancel chapels indicate a wholesale cutting-down. In the case of the transepts it took place in 1673; for the chapels no date is known. The Norman church which preceded the present one must already have been unusually long; for there remain on the S side of the chancel the corbel table and five windows high up, three visible outside, the other two only inside. This cruciform Norman church* also had a crossing tower. Evidence of this in the bulk and the irregular shape of the E piers of the aisle arcades, which were built about 1200. Both aisles were in fact added at the same time and to the same design. The interior resulting from this and a later alteration, to be described presently, is singularly beautiful in its tawny colour. The arcades look very imposing in their erectness, more so in fact than they did when they were first built; for the suggestion is convincing that they were heightened

26

* It ought to be noted however that the outer string course round the Norman windows is continued above the transept N arch, evidence, it seems, of no transept when the Norman windows were put in.

when the aisles were widened. What height they originally had is not at all certain. Possible evidence is (a) the fillets on the piers which (with the exception of the E imposts) end halfway down, (b) a respond with a stiff-leaf capital of slightly later date between the N aisle and the N transept, (c) a shaft with a damaged circular capital in the S crossing pier.* The arcade piers alternate in shape between a circular and a square core with four demi-shafts attached. The shafts are divided by rings. The capitals are of a very early stiff-leaf variety with small leaves, the arches are pointed and double-stepped. The aisles were originally narrower than they are now, although the original width cannot be taken from that of the CRYPT or charnel house below part of the S aisle, an early C13 room. The room is 30 ft long and only 15 ft wide, but it is its S wall that corresponds to the S wall above, whereas its N wall lies to the S of the S arcade. The crypt has two bays and is rib-vaulted. Single-chamfered ribs and transverse arch. When the arcades of the church were heightened we do not know. The only *terminus ante quem* is the splendid tower arch with the naturalistic foliage of its ample filleted shafts. This cannot be later than *c.* 1280–90. But that arch itself is a surprise, for the tower was started a good deal earlier. This is shown by the W doorway, although it should be said at once that the arch of this doorway is a re-set piece. It is Late Norman, say of *c.* 1170, and was no doubt originally round. It has rich zigzag and crenellation motifs. The doorway itself has five orders of shafts with shaft-rings and fully developed stiff-leaf capitals, say of *c.* 1225. The tower is sturdy and rather short, though it would look less so if its spire, which was struck by lightning in 1660, still crowned it. The tower has to the N on the first upper stage a blank pointed arch and a second with trefoiling inside the arch. A lancet window sits inorganically under one of them, and another, now blocked, was opposite on the S side.‡ The tower stair is approached through a contemporary door-way in the N aisle. The upper parts of the tower are later, see the pairs of transomed two-light bell-openings with tracery below the transoms.

After this digression the building history must be resumed. The Norman chancel, at the time when the aisles were built,

* Dr A. Gomme adds that on the third pier from the W in the S arcade, the masonry changes colour two-thirds of the way up.

‡ So the strange relieving arches on the S and W sides must be compara-tively recent.

received a s and shortly afterwards a n chapel. They had four bays. The first pier on either side is quatrefoil, the second bay has two demi-shafts instead of one towards the central vessel, the third, only partly surviving on the s side, had the same. The chapels themselves are altered now and partly demolished on the s side. The arches of the arcade are pointed and have one step and another with a thin roll moulding.

To the chapels and the nave arcade, or to a slightly later date, the s porch entrance seems to belong. It has shafts with rings, a round arch, and dog-tooth decoration. Later C13 the SEDILIA and PISCINA in the chancel with their handsome little quadripartite vaults inside the canopies.

The next problem is the widening of the aisles decided upon probably at the same time as the heightening. There is in fact one detail which would tell a date if it could be dated precisely: the n respond of the n aisle e arch. The s respond was (see above) early C13, this n respond looks later in the same century. In addition we have the windows. The s aisle windows have three steeply stepped lancet lights under an arch, again a sign of the late C13. The s transept and s chapel correspond in date too. But they pose their own problem. They originally extended further s than they do now. In the present s wall is a formerly free-standing pier. Its section is four major and four minor shafts. The s arches are now blocked, but the windows must have been moved back when the demolition took place for they are genuine late C13 work, two lights with a spherical triangle over, one uncusped, the other cusped. The n aisle windows may originally have been like the s aisle windows – see the shafts – but were made Perp later. The simple s doorway is in agreement. So are details higher up in the crossing, and that spectacular piece, the e window of the n chapel. This has three lights with intersection and much cusping, including a diagonally set cusped quatrefoil. Of the fully grown Dec style there is no example at Rothwell. Perp and quite grand the chancel e end with a five-light e window, the excellent n windows of the n chapel with embattled transoms,* the clerestory, the clumsy square pinnacles on the two shallow porches, and the tierceron-vault with a large bell-hole under the tower.

FURNISHINGS. FONT. Hexagonal, C13, probably not in its original shape. A larger, higher and a recessed lower piece. Angle shafts with rings. Dog-tooth decoration. – (SCREEN, N

* But the shafts inside the e window are C13, and probably mid-C13.

aisle. Made up from inlaid panels from C18 pulpits. BB) –
STALLS. With poppy-heads in the shape of figures and heads.
Traceried fronts. MISERICORDS with angels, heads, and a
winged lion. – COMMUNION RAIL. C18. – CANDELABRUM.
1733; of brass; two tiers. – PLATE. Silver-gilt Cup, Paten, and
Breadholder, 1707; Cup, 1709. – MONUMENTS. William de
Williamstorp † 1309, vicar. In the s porch. Incised slab, the
lower part not preserved. – William de Rothwell † 1361,
archdeacon, brass, a 3 ft 5 in. figure, angels by his pillow
(chancel floor). – Edward Saunders † 1514 and wife, also
brasses, the figures 1 ft 10 in. long (s transept floor). – Owen
Ragsdale, 1591. Plain big tomb-chest with a shield in a strapwork surround. Small brass plate with kneeling figure above.
– (Andrew Lant † 1694. Architectural. Ionic columns,
cherubs and garlands. – Magdalene Lant † 1694. Elaborate
hanging cartouche. Panel below with symbols of the Resurrection. BB)

MARKET HOUSE. Built by Sir Thomas Tresham (*see* Rushton). 78
The agreement of 1578 exists with *William Grumbold*
(Grumball) 'for certain buildings at Rothwell Cross' to be
executed to the 'plot' drawn by Grumbold. Oblong with
four oblong projections, i.e. a cruciform shape with extruded
angles. The symmetry disturbed only by the big spiral staircase in one angle. Two storeys with pilasters in two orders.
They are decorated with the trefoils of the Treshams or with
bands of oblongs and ovals linked together (cf. Rushton).
Inscription frieze above the ground floor, frieze of heraldic
shields above the first. The ninety coats of arms are those of
landowners of Rothwell Hundred, and of some other Northamptonshire families. The ground floor was open. Mullioned
and transomed windows above. The building remained incomplete for more than three hundred years. It was finally
roofed in 1895 by *J. A. Gotch*.

JESUS HOSPITAL, SE of the church. Founded by Owen Ragsdale
in 1591. He was a schoolmaster and fellow of Magdalen
College. The two two-storeyed buildings at the entrance date
from the C18 (r.) and 1840 (l.). Between them the original
archway, four-centred, and with three finials at the top. The
main buildings are a long s range and two L-shaped wings
coming forward to the N, but not from the ends of the s range.
The shorter (N) wings of the L rebuilt in 1833. The rest
original. To the s three gables, one above the archway (with
the date 1593), the others oddly at the head of the chimney-

breasts. Even the two-light windows under the gable are repeated. In the two halves l. and r. on each floor are a common-room and four sleeping cubicles. In the parts of 1833 a common-room and two cubicles. In the connecting bars of the L the staircase. The whole foundation was originally for twenty-six old men.

URBAN DISTRICT COUNCIL (Manor House). W of the church, along the prettily laid out street which leads to the tower. An uncommonly fine mid-C18 house. Five bays, two storeys, a pitched, not a hipped roof. The ground-floor windows have Gibbs surrounds. The doorway has Roman Doric pilasters, and the window above is of the Venetian type, with Ionic pilasters.

ROTHWELL HOUSE HOTEL (formerly the Vicarage), Bridge Street. Quite a grand late C18 house. Red brick, three bays, three storeys. The centre windows (one round-headed, one circular) framed by a giant arch.

In addition one more house, a cottage in DESBOROUGH ROAD, dated 1660. It has a narrow gabled porch with a four-centred doorhead and an upper window of three stepped lights.

RUGBY RADIO STATION see CRICK

RUSHDEN

9060

ST MARY. Some minor evidence of c. 1300, but essentially Perp, and a very grand Perp parish church. The early evidence is one chancel S window, the SEDILIA and PISCINA beneath it, the N transept E and W windows, oddly not all on the same level, the N transept N window with intersected, but not quite consistently intersected tracery, the S transept window, the delightful little top frieze of the S transept with tendrils, flowers, and heads (or is this a little later?), and the S porch entrance and S doorway. The N doorway with a trefoiled head looks earlier than anything else. Now the Perp contributions. The superb W tower will be described a little later. The S chapel is also a very fine piece. It was given by Hugh Bocher and Julian his wife, as can be read inside the W arch. This arch is very handsome. It has capitals with small heads and, as supporters of the hood-mould, two standing angels. The chapel has windows with crocketed ogee gables (as the chancel E window also has). The N chapel is Perp too with its polygonal stair-turret. So are the two-bay arcades of both chapels with four shafts and four hollows as the pier section, the much simpler nave arcades (two bays, octagonal piers), the narrow vestry behind the former altar of the N chapel, the clerestory and the panelled nave roof on angel corbels and with bosses, several windows, and the N porch, which has one open side with a three-light window, ogee gable, a niche over it, and a vault with ridge ribs and tiercerons. The porch is two-storeyed. On the upper floor a fireplace. Perp moreover the most memorable item at Rushden, the strainer arch across the nave. This has a curved top as well as bottom, which has curious results. The bottom is of course an arch. At its springing there are demi-figures of angels to the W and E. The spandrels are made into complicated tracery with, as its principal motif, circles enclosing wheel-wise six mouchettes. Along the upper curve run a quatrefoil frieze and battlements. The details are all Dec rather than Perp – an alarming fact for the historian eager to date.* Finally the W tower. Set-back buttresses. Doorway with gabled porch, playfully connected with the buttresses by tiny flying buttresses. Small quadripartite rib-vault with ridge ribs inside. Pairs of two-light bell-openings, quatrefoil frieze, frieze of little ogee arches over, battlements, and shafted pinnacles. Recessed tall, crocketed spire connected by small openwork flying buttresses with the pinnacles. The crockets are uncommonly big. Three tiers of lucarnes. Total height 164 ft.

FURNISHINGS. FONT. Octagonal. The bowl C13 (big stiff-leaf groups), the stem C14 (various tracery motifs). – REREDOS in the N chapel. Stone with a row of embattled ogee arches. – PULPIT. Perp, small. – SCREENS. Of different details, but all with single-light divisions: rood screen, parclose screens to the S chapel from the W, to the N and S chapels from the chancel, to N transept and S transept. – STAINED GLASS. All C15. Good tree of Jesse figures in the tracery lights of the E window, blue backgrounds. – Figures of apostles in the tracery lights of the N chapel E window, white and yellow. – Figures of apostles with creed scrolls in one N aisle window. – (DOORS. With medieval iron work.) – MONUMENTS. Perp tomb-chest with quatrefoiled circles. In the churchyard E of the chancel. To the Pecke family. – Robert Pemberton † 1608 and wife. Standing monument. Two large kneeling figures facing one another across a prayer-desk. The children kneel below in the base. – Sir Goddard Pemberton † 1616. Standing monument. Effigy semi-reclining under a flat coffered arch.

* The strainer arch under the tower arch is of the 1870s.

To the NE of the church is a building which is also medieval and has a Perp window.

NONCONFORMIST CHAPELS. Three ought to be mentioned as typically Victorian varieties: SUCCOTH CHURCH, High Street, 1864, the details 1893. With arched windows and a broad pediment. Then of 1900 the INDEPENDENT WESLEYAN CHURCH, High Street, by *Preston & Wilson*, still Italianate, with a broad pediment, though this is now broken; the windows have gone mullioned and transomed. Finally of 1900 the METHODIST CHURCH in Park Road. This is free Gothic with an asymmetrically placed tower. Brick with stone dressings. The minister's house is attached. It is of 1904–5 and by *Thomas Watson*.

RUSHDEN HALL. The oldest part is to the S, although the two-storeyed embattled porch and the square bay-windows are C19 alterations. The porch leads into the PANELLED ROOM. The arches from the screens passage into the original office quarters survive. The woodwork, much restored and altered, is not *in situ*. The E front is Jacobean or slightly post-Jacobean, and very handsome in a variation on the theme of the E plan. The wings have semicircular, two-storeyed embattled bays attached, and shaped gables, their tops open semicircles. An identical semicircular bay was added in the centre in the C19. Doorway to the r. of the middle bay; with a four-centred head. The building was restored and converted by *Talbot Brown, Panter & Partners*, 1970. It has been divided into flats, a refreshment room, and a public hall.

(GIRLS' SECONDARY SCHOOL, to the N, E of Higham Road. By the *Consortium of Private Architects* of Northampton, 1969–71.)

(BOYS' SECONDARY SCHOOL, Purvis Road, W of the town centre. By the County Architect, *John Goff*, 1971–2.)

No private houses need reference; but perhaps the QUEEN VICTORIA HOTEL, High Street, surprisingly urban, of red brick, with French pavilion roofs ought to be looked at for a moment, and the CARNEGIE LIBRARY, SE of the church, 1905 by *W. B. Machin*.

HIGHAM PARK. *See* p. 259.

ROMAN REMAINS. Excavations at Boundary Avenue have revealed remains of a major Iron Age and Roman pottery industry, which for a short time after the Roman invasions produced exotic slip decorated ware. The industry died out during the C3.

RUSHTON

ALL SAINTS. Of ironstone. A Norman survival the w wall of the nave with the deeply splayed window (now behind the organ). The rest of c. 1300–50 and of the restorations of 1853 and 1869 by *E. F. Law*. Of c. 1300 the w tower with the triple-chamfered arch towards the nave. Tall twin bell-openings with continuous mouldings. Perp battlements. Also of c. 1300 the N arcade and, a little later, the N chapel arcade, the former with circular, the latter with quatrefoil piers, and both with double-chamfered arches. The chapel is higher than the aisle and has Dec windows. Dec s side and s porch, all minor. But major indeed the SEDILIA with nodding ogee canopies, beasts, heads, nobbly leaves, and very rich crocketing. To the s of the chancel a vestry with pitched roof and, under it, a pointed tunnel-vault with a single-chamfered transverse rib. – (ORGAN CASE. By *Gotch, Saunders & Surridge*, 1966.) – STAINED GLASS. Remarkably good and restful glass in the s windows, by *Powell & Sons*, 1872–3. – PLATE. Set, 1663. – MONUMENT. Fine late C13 effigy of a Knight, cross-legged, of Purbeck marble. Naturalistic foliage at his head. – Sir Thomas Tresham † 1559. Alabaster effigy on a tomb-chest with shields in circular bands separated by twisted shafts. Bearded effigy in the dress of a Lord Prior of the Knights Hospitallers of St John of Jerusalem. He was given this honour by Queen Mary when she revived the Order. (The monument was probably erected in 1562, and may be by the Derbyshire sculptors *Gabriel* and *Thomas Roiley*. It was formerly in St Peter's Church (demolished 1799). GI)

MANOR HOUSE, E of the church. L-shaped, mullioned windows. Doorway with four-centred arch.

MANOR FARM HOUSE, ¼ m. SE of the church. Half-H plan, mullioned windows. Late C17, altered in the C19.

OLD RECTORY, N of the church. Georgian, of four bays and three storeys.

RUSHTON HALL. The Treshams were a distinguished family in Northamptonshire more than a century before the time of Sir Thomas, who must principally engage our attention. William Tresham was Attorney General to Henry V and Speaker in the House of Commons. He bought the Rushton estate in 1438. His son, Sir Thomas, lived at Rushton and was also Speaker. His younger son lived at Newton-in-the-Willows (*see* above, p. 314). Sir Thomas was beheaded after the Battle of Tewkesbury. His grandson, another Sir Thomas, is the one whose monument is mentioned above. He was succeeded by his grandson, the Thomas who interests us. This Thomas was born in 1534 and knighted in 1575. He was brought up a Protestant but turned Catholic in 1580. His Catholic zeal was exceptional. He was learned in divinity and a great believer in symbols and other conceits to demonstrate his faith. Among his books and papers there was, according to the calendar of the Rushton papers, 'A Roll . . . containing figures and signs apparently working out a religious anagram upon his name and that of his Patron Saint' and also 'Some mystical notes . . . on the Trinity with a ridiculous account of a miracle which happened to him'. He was imprisoned as a Catholic in 1580 and remained confined to the Fleet and other less rigorous places till 1593. He was again in prison in 1596–7 and in 1599–1603 (or a little earlier). He died in 1605, in the same year in which Francis, his son, died in the Tower after having been involved in the Gunpowder Plot.

Rushton Hall was sold in 1619 to Sir William Cokayne, skinner and Lord Mayor of London. In 1612 he had been the first Governor of Ulster. He also founded Londonderry.

Rushton Hall – now a school – is essentially a building of before and after our Sir Thomas. It consists of three ranges round an oblong courtyard and a screen closing the courtyard to the E. The wings are longer than the end (W) range. The screen and about one third of the wings date from the Cokayne years, the rest mostly from the time of Henry VIII. Sir Thomas Tresham only made some alterations. It is built of Weldon stone.

80   Rushton Hall is approached from the E through the SCREEN, which has a corridor behind. Broad middle entrance with round arch and slender niches l. and r. containing figures of rather picaresque-looking soldiers. Tapering fluted pilasters. To the l. and r. of the entrance four bays with unfluted pilasters and three-light windows. Top balustrade, over the centre with the Gothic-Revival motif of quatrefoils. On the centre of the balustrade statue of a reclining youth with a cornucopia. The N and S ranges of the house project, framing the screen. Broad, two-storeyed, arched bay-windows with a strapwork cresting. Large shaped gables with thin obelisks. In each gable a double-stepped six-light window, i.e. a window with two transoms, and two lights above the top transom, four between the two transoms, and six below the lower one.

On entering the spacious COURTYARD one is faced with a rich, stately picture, at first unified-looking but highly confusing in its details. What pulls the composition together is the attic storey and the gables. The attic has short pilaster strips with simple geometrical ornament, lozenges or vertical zigzags, and a balustrade. The gables are straight-sided except for the centre of the W range, where the gable and the window in it correspond to the E ends of the W and S ranges. There is a date 1595, i.e. a date of Sir Thomas Tresham's time, on one of the gables of the W range (and another on the outer, i.e. W side, of the same W range).* So the system just described is of the Tresham time and was continued by the Cokaynes. They dated the central gable of the W range 1627 and the gable above the Hall bay-window (*see* below) in the S range 1626.‡ The decorated pilasters are in fact similar to those of Tresham's Rothwell Market House.

However, Sir Thomas Tresham only heightened and modernized an older house. Its date is not certain. Gotch calls it on his plan late C15, in his text late C15 or early C16. The latter date seems more likely, and perhaps one should not go too early in the C16. The motif of the four-centred arches to the lights of the windows was established at that time. It remained in use with the Treshams but was discontinued by the Cokaynes. Its chief example is the bow-window of the GREAT HALL in the S wing, overlooking the courtyard. This has a total of eight lights, little buttresses, two transoms, and battlements. The interior of the Hall is somewhat confused by the fact that its S side received two more bow-windows in the C19 (*see* S front below). The bow-window which corresponds to the original one on the courtyard side is also C19 work. To have even one bow-window of so early a date is surprising enough. The semicircular plan for bay-windows as against the oblong or canted plan came into use only at the end of the C16 (cf. e.g. Kirby Hall). The Hall rises to the roof. It has hammerbeams with some tracery in the spandrels (restored) and fourlight windows to the l. of the bow. There is only one tier of them, whereas the living quarters the other side of the bow must from the beginning have been two-storeyed. The original entrance into the Hall must have been in line with the SE bow,

* From the Rushton papers it appears that Sir Thomas made a new gallery here, and added a bay-window with a great chimney. The masons were the *Tyrell* family.

‡ Sir Thomas's date 1595 is in the gable between these two.

and that makes it likely that the Kitchen and Offices of the C16 house extended further E in place of the Cokayne extension of the S wing.

The SOUTH FRONT of the S range dates from 1848. The Cokaynes (Viscount Cullen) had sold the house to W. W. Hope (the family of Thomas Hope of Amsterdam, London, and Deepdene) in 1828, and Hope remodelled the front.

Tresham seems to have been specially busy to the W of the Hall. Here there are doorcases with the same geometrically decorated pilasters as on the Rothwell Market House. There is also a room with a barbarically lavish fireplace surround and on the first floor an ORATORY with a plaster relief of the Crucifixion and many figures, a curious, somewhat naive piece with a long inscription and a date 1577. The STAIRCASE is Cokayne rather than Tresham, and probably of c. 1625–30 (see the dates in the gables). It has balustrading with square tapering balusters and a fine plaster ceiling with broad strapwork bands and a pendant with mermaids. Much else here and in other rooms is period work of the late C19 and early C20.

The WEST RANGE towards the courtyard has an asymmetrically placed canted bay-window, original but face-lifted in the C19, and towards the garden gables of which the southernmost is of 1595, the next of 1626 (see above). The Cokayne gables again have stepped windows. The most interesting detail is the work in ironstone which indicates the end of the earliest S range. The NORTH RANGE has two canted bay-windows to the courtyard. The range contained the Long Gallery, an apartment 125 ft long.

EAST LODGES. Gothic, early C19.

GROOM'S HOUSE. Early C18, of five bays and two storeys with some original wooden cross-windows and some segment-headed windows.

STABLES. Three sides of a quadrangle. Late Georgian.

DOVECOTE. Rectangular and gabled.

79 TRIANGULAR LODGE. At the NW corner of the estate. Built by Sir Thomas Tresham. It was begun in 1594 and completed in 1597, although the dates on the building are 1593 (date on the iron anchors of the ground floor) and 1595 (date on the chimneyshaft). The most perfect example in architectural terms of the Elizabethan love of the conceit. Everything about the little building is directed by the number three, i.e. allegorizes the Trinity. It was also a pun on Tresham's own name. The Treshams' emblem was the trefoil, and so there are

plenty of trefoils on the building. But the plan and most of the details are based on the equilateral triangle. The building is of alternating bands of light and darker limestone. Its sides are 33 ft 4 in. long, i.e. one third of a hundred. There are three storeys, each with three windows in each of the three sides. The principal room on each floor is a hexagon. The corner spaces are triangular. One contains the newel staircase, the others small rooms. The basement windows are small trefoils on all sides with a smaller triangle in the centre of each. On the raised ground floor the SE side has a very narrow entrance which has the figures 5555 written on the lintel and a very odd steep gable consisting of short straight sides and two-thirds of a circle standing on them. The windows on this floor are on all three sides roughly lozenge-shaped and consist of a cross with, at the end of the arms, four groups of three circles arranged as a trefoil. Coats of arms to make the lozenge into a square. On the upper floor the windows are trefoils, each with triangles set in them, but each with a different pattern. Only one window has a circle instead with groups of three elongated leaf-like almond shapes branching off it on all three sides. Above the upper windows an inscription broken up into single letters and reading MENTES TUORUM VISITA. On the frieze above the upper storey the continuous inscription (of 33 letters!) reads on the SE: Aperiatur terra et germinet salvatorem; on the N: Quis separabit nos a charitate Christi; and on the SW: Consideravi opera tua domine et expavi. On each side there are three gables with crockets, triangular top obelisks, emblems, and inscriptions. Among the emblems are the seven-branched candelabra, the seven eyes of God, and the Pelican. There are also the dates 1580 (the year of Tresham's conversion), 1626, and 1641, and the unexplained figures 3509 and 3898. The inscriptions add up to: Respicite non mihi soli laboravi. Sir Gyles Isham has pointed out that the building symbolizes the Mass as well as the Trinity. The triangular chimneyshaft has symbols of the Mass, e.g. IHS, the Lamb and Cross, and the Chalice. The initial letters near the gargoyles below the gables read: Sanctus Sanctus Sanctus Dominus Deus Sabaoth qui erat et qui est qui venturus est – i.e. quoting from the Preface to the Canon of the Mass. In addition, the chimney itself, mysteriously resting on no visible interior support, may represent the mystery of the Mass. Even the smoke holes are arranged in threes.

What does all this amount to? A folly? A bauble? A pretty

conceit? It cannot be treated so lightly. It is no more nor less
than a profession of faith in stone – of a faith for which
Tresham spent more than fifteen years in prison and confine-
ment. So one should look at the Triangular Lodge with
respect, unless one suffers from Mr Rowse's blinkers.

For Tresham's other principal buildings cf. Lyveden, p. 299,
and Rothwell, p. 393.

(MOTTE, Gaultney Wood. Possibly the castle mentioned in
1140 by Simeon of Durham, and the Galclint castle referred
to in 1148–53. D. Renn)

THE MOUNT. Excavation of this flat-topped conical mound
established that a stone circle, perhaps of ritual use and
constructed no earlier than the C2 B.C., lay beneath the barrow.
The barrow's primary burial had been robbed, but a secondary burial immediately outside its perimeter contained
twenty-four decapitated skeletons.

ST JAMES'S END see NORTHAMPTON, p. 355

8050   SALCEY LAWN
                   2 m. SW of Horton

The centre must date from the late C17. It is of five bays and two
storeys, with quoins and a hipped roof.

7070   SCALDWELL

ST PETER AND ST PAUL. Unbuttressed Norman W tower. C13
N aisle windows. S arcade of the later C13. Two bays, very
primitive octagonal piers, double-chamfered arches. The S
doorway, if correctly rebuilt, could be contemporary in spite
of its round arch, and the W lancet window certainly is. The
N arcade is taller and later. The N chapel was built at the same
time. Divers Perp windows. Extensive restoration in 1863 by
William Slater and *Gillet*.

Former RECTORY. 1716. The porch is an addition. The doorway with its pretty cartouche was originally flush with the
windows, that is, it was a normal five-bay front. Flat window
frames, pedimented dormers.

SEDGEBROOK HALL see PITSFORD

7070   SHORTWOOD LODGE
                   1 m. NE of Lamport

HAWKING TOWER. A three-storeyed tower of *c.* 1720 with
two-storeyed wings, their two storeys being as high as the

ground storey of the tower. The top storey is canted. The windows have flat frames, and there is a top balustrade. The front window on the third floor is surrounded by a strange piece said to be a chimneypiece from Pytchley Hall. If that is true, it was a chimneypiece of Vanbrughian dimensions. The piers l. and r. must be at least 6 ft high. Unmoulded blocks instead of bases and instead of capitals. Depressed arch, big keystone. At the back of the tower exceedingly heavy rustication.

SHUTLANGER   7040

CHAPEL OF ST ANNE, attached to the former School Room. 1884 by *Matthew Holding*. The chancel was added in 1886. – STAINED GLASS. The E window is by *Kempe*, 1887.

THE MONASTERY, opposite the chapel to the SE. Bridges, writing early in the C18, mentions a chapel converted into a farmhouse. What exists now is a house with a big porch vaulted with quadripartite single-chamfered ribs and a transverse ridge rib. Foliage boss apparently C14. In the side one low two-light window. To the r. of the porch two more, different two-light windows. The doorway seems to be of *c.* 1300. There is another doorway inside the house at r. angles immediately to the l., and this leads to a spiral stone staircase. This part then is apparently *in situ*. (In the roof are smoke-grimed late medieval timbers. The evidence suggests a domestic use of several centuries. BB)

(GROVE FARMHOUSE. One of the Grafton farms, *see* Introduction, p. 67.)

SHUTTLEHANGER *see* SHUTLANGER

SIBBERTOFT   6080

ST HELEN. Mostly of 1862–3, especially the S aisle with its terrible plate tracery outside and its piers etc. inside with much foliage. Architect: *Browning*. The chancel was originally of *c.* 1300 (see e.g. the E window). The N chapel is Perp, see the two separate arches leading into it, and the doorway with traceried spandrels. – SCREEN. In the chancel the top of the entrance part of the former rood screen, exceptionally richly decorated with twisted branches and top crocketing. – PLATE. Cup, 1702.   *See*
          p.
          518

CASTLE YARD, in a wood *c.* ½ m. NE of the village. A motte and bailey with the motte on the uphill side.

6040

SILVERSTONE

ST MICHAEL. 1884 by *St Aubyn*. Nave and aisles under one
tiled roof. On the roof a little E of the W front a shingled
wooden turret.

(Remains of FISHPONDS N of the churchyard may indicate the
site of a royal hunting lodge. It was ruinous by 1313. H. M.
Colvin)

(LODGES on the A43. Two small stone buildings with doorways
with hoods on carved consoles. Originally giving access to
Stowe. BB)

6040

SLAPTON

ST BOTOLPH. A memorably intimate, unspoiled church. Early
to mid C13 W tower, see the unmoulded pointed arch towards
the nave and the blank arcading of the bell-stage to the S.
Early C13 S arcade of two bays. Circular pier, square abacus.
Unmoulded pointed arches. Later third bay. Interesting tripartite chancel arch, the side parts now blocked except for two
small straight-headed two-light windows. Dec chancel E
window, and Dec N and S windows. In the chancel two
recesses, one with its arch on shafts, the other with an ogee
arch from the floor. – SCREEN to the S chapel; Jacobean. –
WALL PAINTINGS. Many have been uncovered. Restored
1971. They date from the later C14 and C15. They are:
Nave N side a large St Christopher, with delightful mermaid
and fishes, a Pietà to the l., another scene to the r. – Nave S
side a St Francis receiving the stigmata, a St Michael weighing
souls. Below and partly painted on top of this, a St George. –
In the arcade W arch two figures, in the middle arch the Mass
of St Gregory. – In the S aisle: to the E the Annunciation, to
the W a Martyrdom and St Anne teaching the Virgin. On the
S wall of the S aisle: to the E the rare subject of St Eloi, with a
horse being shod, the figures incised with firm lines before
being coloured. To the W, traces of the Three Living and the
Three Dead. – (STAINED GLASS, E window. Lucy arms and
grisaille; early C14. RM) – PLATE. Cup and Paten, 1570.

METHODIST CHAPEL. Brick Gothic, plain. 1844.

(On the road from Bradden but in the village three HOUSES.
One is of *c.* 1600 with mullioned windows, one of 1650 with
quoins and architrave, and one of 1775, three-storeyed and
cement-rendered, but bold and dignified.)

SLIPTON

9070

ST JOHN BAPTIST. Small, on its own, nave, chancel, and bell-cote. One Norman N window. Chancel arch probably C13.

SOUTHWICK

0090

ST MARY. C14 W tower with provision for a vault. Two-light bell-openings with reticulation motifs and a transom. Recessed spire with crockets up the edges. Two tiers of lucarnes. The nave and chancel were rebuilt in 1760, but unfortunately later received Victorian Gothic fenestration. The chancel arch remains of the C14. – PLATE. Cup, c. 1570; Cover Paten, C17; Flagon, 1667 (?). – MONUMENT. George Lynn † 1758. By *Roubiliac*. In a niche in the chancel of 1760. Grey and white marble. Big base and on it an obelisk in relief with the oval medallion of the deceased, bust with lively drapery, and ample drapery hanging down from the medallion. To the r. in front seated female figure in contemporary dress, her arm resting on a remarkably restrained, classical urn. Her slippers ought to be noted.

SOUTHWICK HALL. The house consists of a square tower-like part at the SW corner of the C14, with a smaller annexe with staircase on one side, and an Elizabethan house recessed on its other side. A NE addition was made in the C18. This has a Gothic wooden bay-window. The tower has on the lower floor single-chamfered ribs, both diagonal and along the ridges, two two-light transomed windows with a reticulation motif, and an original entrance towards what is now the Elizabethan part. On the upper floor a square-headed E window with Dec tracery, and a piscina, suggesting the room was used as a chapel. In the W wall is a fireplace with two big re-tooled heads. The annexe also has single-chamfered ribs. The windows here date from c. 1850 but there is an original chimneystack over the W gable. The Tudor doorway into the tower dates from 1909, when the tower was made into an entrance hall. It seems that originally it was an addition probably made by Sir John Knyvett, Lord Chancellor († 1381), to a house built by his father, for on the N side of the Hall is more C14 work, including a doorway to the former screens passage, and further W a spiral staircase which must have led to an upper solar. The anteroom to it again has single-chamfered ribs. Boss with a rose and corbels with roses. Two doorways with shouldered lintels. The Elizabethan rebuilding

See p. 518

carries the dates 1571 and 1580. The Hall range is of two storeys, with two straight gables, the upper floor having two large bedrooms with barrel ceilings. The w wing is of three storeys.

7070

SPRATTON

St Andrew. Of an Early Norman church the w wall remains with one (lengthened) window in the present tower. The ornate tower is Late Norman. Doorway with one order of shafts and zigzag in the arch. Hood-mould with Saxon-looking interlace.* Instead of a tower arch the former w doorway was allowed to stay. The arch is unmoulded, but the many-scalloped imposts were re-worked when the tower was built. On the next stage in the middle of the w side three blank arches, on the stage after that blank arcading all the way. When the bell-stage was reached, the E.E. style had arrived. The bell-openings are of two lights and still have a round super-arch, but they are pointed, and there is a blank pointed arch l. and r. The corbel table is followed by later battlements and a recessed spire. Two tiers of lucarnes in alternating directions. Norman also the s doorway, but over-restored. Of the ending C12 the N aisle with its doorway (round, single-stepped arch, capitals similar to waterleaf) and its arcade. Four bays, circular piers, capitals with upright leaves, square abaci, round arches with one step and one slight chamfer. The s arcade is C13, with circular piers and abaci and pointed double-chamfered arches. Most of the windows of the church are renewed, but those of the N chapel, which was built by John Chambre between 1495 and 1505, stand out, coarse but virile, as are also the details of the two-bay arcade to the chancel. Of Dec details the SEDILIA in the chancel, the three tomb recesses (the two in the s aisle have ballflower decoration), and the handsome ogee-headed REREDOS niche at the E end of the s side. Its pretty buttresses are diapered in its lower parts. Large corbels on heads to the l. and r. An interesting detail, also of the C14, is the large blocked E window of the nave above the chancel arch. – FONT. Octagonal, C13. Plain, with three blank trefoiled arches. – BENCHES. The ends have traceried panels and buttresses. Also prettily traceried fronts and backs. –

---

* Mr John Goff has drawn my attention to the interesting use of poly-chrome masonry (three different types of stone) which occurs in the C12 work, and suggests that the irregularity of the patterns produced by this is deliberate.

STAINED GLASS. E window 1899 by *Powell*. – PLATE. Two Cups, 1790. – MONUMENTS. Brass to Robert Parnell † 1464 and family (under the organ; the figures are *c.* 2 ft 3 in. long). – Tomb-chest with quatrefoils in panels. (On it formerly a wooden effigy. VCH) – Sir John Swinford † 1371. Alabaster, well preserved and of good quality. The jupon is laced at the side. The SS collar is said to be the earliest on any monument. The iron GRILLE is original. – Many tablets, the best among them the two identical ones to Francis and Elizabeth Beynon † 1778 and † 1770 by *William Cox*. They both have a cherub's head set against an obelisk.

SPRATTON HALL. Built before 1778 (information received from Sir Gyles Isham). The house is of ashlar, five bays, two and a half storeys. Between entrance hall and staircase a wide segmental arch with a pretty Adamish fanlight. The staircase has three slender turned balusters to the tread and carved tread-ends. Later additions to the house.

SPRATTON GRANGE. Of brick, 1848; gabled and bargeboarded.

STAMFORD ST MARTIN (STAMFORD BARON)

see The Buildings of England: Lincolnshire

STANFORD

5070

ST NICHOLAS. An imposing church, mostly of *c.* 1300–50 and hence unified in its external and internal appearance. In addition a veritable gallery of statuary. The exterior is determined by the very tall chancel window of three and, at the E end, five lights, all with intersected tracery. The same motif recurs in the S aisle and in the simpler Y-form in the bell-openings of the tower. Reticulation instead in the N aisle windows and the S aisle E and two S windows. The S and N aisle E windows are of four lights. Inside, the arcades are of five bays, with tall, very white piers and arches – an attractive contrast to the pale rose and grey of the chancel exterior. The piers have a slender chamfered projection to the nave and aisles and a broader one to each arch opening. There are no capitals at all; all mouldings are continuous. The type is not uncommon in Leicestershire (cf. North Kibworth, Misterton; also Lilbourne, Northants.). In the S aisle PISCINA with crocketed gable, and next to it a low stone bench below the window with a quatrefoiled front. Good roofs in nave and aisles with carved bosses. The nave roof has tie-beams with tracery over, and the tie-beams are supported on thin wall shafts which rest on carved brackets. Externally there is one more motif which deserves mention: the little square pinnacles at the corners of the E wall. The pinnacles on the W tower in contrast are coarse and may be C16 or C17.

An account of the FURNISHINGS must be divided into three parts: general, stained glass, and monuments.

FONT. C14 with simple tracery patterns. – PULPIT. Incorporating part of the rood screen. – SCREENS. The base of the rood screen is original, the upper parts come from Lutterworth in Leicestershire. – Under the tower arch a smaller Perp screen, with one-light divisions. – STALLS. With panelled fronts and simple poppy-heads. One MISERICORD with a flower. – CHOIR PANELLING. C16, with linenfold. – COMMUNION RAIL. Of wrought iron; C18. – WEST GALLERY. On Tuscan columns. On it the rightly famous ORGAN CASE. Tradition has it that it comes from the Royal Chapel at Whitehall. Excellent, very dainty scrollwork. It seems to be C16 or early C17, and the upper part different in date from the lower. – FRONTAL. Embroidered by Lady Eleanor Rowe, née Cave; it is said in 1613. – PLATE. Undated Cup and Cover; Paten, 1637; Almsdish, 1674; Flagon and Plate, 1712.

STAINED GLASS.* The glass at Stanford goes from the original early C14 glass to the C16. The first group can be dated heraldically to either 1306–7 or c. 1312–27. It includes the following: In the E window small Virgin and donors, Saint under canopies above, the Crucifixion in the centre lancet, the two Abbots in the tracery heads, and a seated Christ. In the chancel side windows ten beautiful Apostles under identical canopies and two Saints under different canopies. In the heads of the chancel N window a small seated Virgin and a small seated Christ from a Coronation of the Virgin. The next group is of c. 1330–40. This includes the Resurrection and Angels and the Crucifixion with the Virgin and St John in the N aisle E window and the canopies in the same window. Also St Anne and the Virgin Child and a Bishop again in the same. In the S aisle E window the figures in the tracery heads belong to the same group, and so do canopies and the two female Saints in the same window. Again to the same group belong the figures in the tracery heads of the SE window, a kneeling figure in the NW window, the Agnus Dei

_____

* I am indebted to Mr P. A. Newton's unpublished catalogues of the Stanford glass for the arrangement in which it is here presented.

in the N window E of this, and the two large Spires in a chancel N window. The next group is of c. 1500. Its hallmark is the yellow and brown medallions. To it belong the Virgin, the Assumption, and St John Evangelist in the SE window, the St Margaret, St George, and Visitation in the window W of this, and the seated Saint in the window following this. Yet another group is the donors in the S aisle windows. They are probably early C16. Then there are the members of the Cave family in the E window, datable by heraldry to c. 1558, and the Henry VII and Elizabeth of York from Stanford Hall, probably C19.

MONUMENTS. There are fifteen in the church worth discussing. They are in chronological order as follows. In the S aisle, under an arch which belongs in date to the time when the church was building, a Priest, defaced. The effigy lies on a low tomb-chest with quatrefoils on its front. To the l. and r. buttresses and finials. The top is Perp. Upper quatrefoil friezes. – Sir Thomas Cave † 1558. Alabaster, free-standing between N aisle and nave. Recumbent effigies on a tomb-chest with shields in roundels. Twisted shafts separate them. At the head-end two putti hold the roundel, at the foot-end small kneeling figures in relief in two rows. – Sir Ambrose Cave † 1568 (N aisle). Fine and quiet, of moderate size and without any figures. Broad panel with shield, flanked by two Corinthian columns which carry a wide pediment. Three roundels on the tomb-chest. No strapwork or any other ornamental display. – Henry Knollys and his wife Margaret Cave, c. 1600 (N aisle). She lies stiffly on her side, he lies behind and above her on a half-rolled-up mat. Two young daughters kneel to the l. and r. Simple, but big background with a flat arch. – Sir Thomas Cave † 1613 (chancel N). Alabaster. Two recumbent effigies on a mat. Kneeling children in profile against the tomb-chest. Two columns of touch support a coffered lintel. Coffered arch between and big strapwork cartouche against the back wall. – Richard Cave † 1606 at Padua. Like another kneeling child's, his monument is placed next to his parents'. He kneels frontally inside an arched canopy placed on a tall pedestal. Obelisk on top. – Dorothy St John † 1630 (N aisle). Small tomb-chest. Against it three shields in lozenge panels. Garlands between them. Black top. No effigy. Decidedly post-Jacobean. – Sir Thomas Cave † 1733 (chancel S). Attributed to *Smith* of Warwick (cf. Lamport) (BB). Purely architectural. – Sir Verney Cave † 1734 (chancel S). Good bust in front of an obelisk. – James Callen † 1751 (s aisle). Standing monument. Small grey sarcophagus, white Rococo volutes l. and r. Obelisk above. – Sir Thomas Cave † 1778 (chancel s), but the monument must be early C19. Profile in oval medallion. Otherwise inscription only. – Thomas Otway Cave † 1830 (chancel N). Said to be by *Kessells*, a Dutch pupil of Thorwaldsen. With a fine relief of the dying man, an amply cloaked woman seated at his couch, and a genius with an extinguished torch standing by his head. – Robert Otway Cave † 1844, by *Westmacott Jun.* (N aisle W). Large monument. Background a Gothic arch. The deceased lies asleep on a couch. An afflicted young woman kneels on the l. Books lean on the r. On one it says Scriptores Graec et Rom. Also some leaves by the books. – Third Lady Braye † 1862, daughter of Sir Thomas Cave, by *Thornycroft* (s aisle W). According to Mr Gunnis probably by *Mary Thornycroft*. As large as the previous monument. Gothic background with a steeper arch. She lies asleep on a half-rolled-up mattress. Behind, a kneeling young woman with a cross and book. Three angels in relief above. These are by *Gibson*. These two C19 monuments take up much more space than any other; they occupy positions not customary for such ambitious monuments, and go to the expense of white marble. – Edmund Verney. By *Felix Joubert*, 1896. It is surprising to find a Baroque scheme carried on or revived at that date. Obelisk with portrait in an oval medallion. In front to the l. an all-round figure of a hussar. To the r. military still-life.

STANFORD HALL (actually in Leicestershire). Built by Sir Roger Cave between 1697 and 1700. Nine by seven bays with big quoins and hipped roof. Brick; only the s front is ashlarfaced. Tall sash-windows in two storeys. Doorway with lower segmental pediment on corbels. The window above it with ears and garlands hanging over them. The other fronts show their brickwork. Two of them originally had cross-windows. They were later sashed. The N front has projecting wings; that to the E was remodelled at the time when the stables were built, i.e. c. 1735 (see below). The E front has a doorway with Doric pilasters reached by a (remodelled) double-flight twoarm staircase. The basement has a doorway in a Gibbs surround and below a curious wide blank arch also with Gibbs detail. The stables were built in 1737. They are of brick and consist of two quadrangles. The date 1769 on rain-water heads can have no relevance. The house is by *William Smith the Elder* of Warwick. His younger brother *Francis* worked in the house in 1730 (*see* below) and is in all probability responsible for the stables and E front. *William the Younger* in 1745 remodelled the saloon. This has a deep cove below the ceiling. Big shell-shapes in the corners of the coving, fine chimneypiece. The stucco-work is by *John Wright* of Worcester. Most of the decoration of the room – remarkably sympathetically done – is of 1880. Painting on cove and ceiling by *Felix Joubert*. The main staircase was inserted by Francis Smith in 1730. It is of the 'flying' type and has three slim balusters to each tread. Of *c.* 1745 the Dining Room (NW corner) and the Three-Children Room (W front centre). In the former an elaborate chimneypiece with ornate stucco decoration on the overmantel, in the latter stucco roundel with three putti.

IRON GATES. Three good C18 gates of wrought iron.

In the grounds P. S. Pilcher did his flying experiments in the 1890s and was killed in 1899.

(PARISH BOUNDARY MARKERS. On each road into the parish. Fine piers with finials. Especially fine the ones on the Yelvertoft Road, erected after 1839. BB)

DOWER HOUSE, E of the church. Georgian. Four-bay centre and two canted bay-windows. Two storeys. Doorcase with Ionic pilasters and pediment.

STANION

9080

ST PETER. Commanding Perp W tower. Set-back buttresses. Doorway with traceried spandrels. Two two-light bell-openings with transom. Slender broach spire with two tiers of lucarnes. Perp also the arcades of four bays. The piers have a long chamfer towards nave and aisles with a hollow in its centre and shafts towards the arch openings which alone carry capitals. Apart from these, admittedly important, contributions, the dominant style of the church is the late C13 – see the S aisle windows, cusped intersected or with a big circle surrounding three small spherical triangles. Along the top of the S wall a pretty frieze of heads. Late C13 also the S porch and S doorway and the N chapel. The E window of this has three quatrefoiled circles. A little earlier perhaps the chancel, which has on the S side two pairs of lancets and on the E side simple bar tracery. The chancel arch, the SEDILIA, the N chapel arcade (two bays, quatrefoil pier, double-chamfered arches), and the N chapel SEDILIA bear out this dating. Dec the simple straight-headed N aisle windows. – FONT. Perp, octagonal, very generously decorated. The most interesting thing is that the stem is switched by 22½ degrees against the bowl so that all the quatrefoiling, lozenging, etc., appears broken at the corners, and the little buttresses support the sides and not the angles of the bowl. – COMMUNION RAIL. Jacobean, with vertically symmetrical balusters. – Very complete C18 WOODWORK in the nave, i.e. a three-decker PULPIT and two-decker READER'S DESK, and BOX PEWS in the aisles set longitudinally and rising in tiers as in an auditorium. – WALL PAINTING. A delightful and iconographically mysterious piece of the late C15, with a kneeling stag and a kneeling unicorn worshipping the place where originally a sculptured image must have stood. – (STAINED GLASS. Nave N. Zouche arms and grisaille fragments, early C14. RM) – PLATE. Cup and Paten, 1569.

9070   STANWICK

ST LAWRENCE. The essential parts are C13, i.e. the W tower, the chancel (see the chancel arch; the windows are Perp) and the arcades. The latter are of three bays with quatrefoil piers and double-chamfered arches. The hood-mould to the E has nailhead, to the W zigzag at r. angles to the wall surface. To the N of the arch facing into the chancel a beautiful trefoiled niche with a seat (whom for?). The outer moulding is continuous, the inner has stiff-leaf capitals. The tower is the most interesting piece. It is octagonal from the ground, has a triple-chamfered W lancet with a pretty, heavily framed pointed octofoil above it, a triple-chamfered arch towards the nave, shafted twin bell-openings under a round arch in the cardinal directions and tall blank arcading of the same type in the diagonals, a pointed trefoiled top frieze, and battlements dying into the spire. This of course has no broaches. Three tiers of lucarnes, again in the cardinal directions. C13 also the S doorway and the (later) S porch. The doorway has a stiff-leaf capital.* – FONT. Perp, octagonal, richly panelled. The stem is missing. On the foot a real foot. – MONUMENT. John Atkins † 1669 with his wife and her 'isheu'. Inscription tablet and arms over.

RECTORY, W of the church. By *Sir James Burrough* of Cambridge (H. M. Colvin). Dated 1717 over the porch. Five bays, two storeys. Remnants of a good staircase. The house was allowed

---

* The church was restored by *Slater* in 1856 (R. Hubbuck).

to become derelict when the road was widened and is now in a sad state (1971).

STANWICK HALL, ¼ m. SW. Also early C18, five bays, two storeys.

STAVERTON
5060

ST MARY. Mostly early C14 and Perp. Earlier only the round-arched simple N doorway. Perp the W tower, quite big, with pairs of two-light transomed bell-openings and battlements. Also a S aisle window with panel tracery filling the whole upper half, and the chancel E window. Of c. 1300 the N arcade of seven low and narrow bays with octagonal piers and arches with one hollow chamfer and one sunk quadrant. Of c. 1300 also the N aisle E window and a S window. The N chapel is Dec. Three bays with octagonal piers and double-hollow-chamfered arches. Conical foot-pieces. Big ogee-arched SEDILIA and PISCINA. Reticulated tracery in the E window. – MONUMENT. Thomas Wylmer † 1580. Standing monument. Two short Ionic columns. Metope frieze with wide metopes. Brass plate with kneeling figures.

(VICARAGE. C18. S front of five bays and two storeys. Veranda across the ground floor. DOE)

(THE CROFT. Dated 1700. W front three bays, two storeys, with later three-light mullioned windows and central door. DOE)

STEANE
5030

STEANE PARK. The house is partly the Crewe mansion of the C17, partly Victorian. The original mansion was much larger and incorporated medieval parts.* It was mostly demolished after 1730, and the offices made into a farmhouse, which was embellished as a hunting lodge in the mid C19 and later (GI). The present house is gabled and has mullioned and tran-somed windows.

ST PETER. The chapel of Sir Thomas Crewe, built in 1620, is puzzling. Some parts, such as the W window, seem genuine medieval material re-used. The S doorway on the other hand, with unfluted Ionic columns and a big, open segmental pediment, must be later.‡ The chapel is only two bays

* There is a drawing in the Bishop's Palace, Durham, and one in the Eayre-Tillemas Collection (1719), showing an arcade with the house above it, flanked by two towers (GI).

‡ Sir Gyles Isham and Bruce Bailey suggest the mid C17. It may have been added by Nathaniel Lord Crewe when he was Bishop of Oxford.

long and has a S aisle, nearly as wide as the nave, and a N chapel for the Crewe monuments. The pier and responds have a strange section with four wave-chamfered projections. E respond on a corbel with grapes. Straight-headed windows, some with close panel tracery, others without any, simply with arched lights. Obelisks on the corners and the nave front and back. A small W doorway of 1620 in addition to the large later one. – COMMUNION TABLE. Of marble, given by Bishop Crewe in 1720. – ARMOUR. Banners, helmets, crests, spurs, swords. – PLATE. Cup, 1697; Paten, c. 1700; Almsdish, 1707; Flagon, 1720. – MONUMENTS. Sir Thomas Crewe, Speaker of the House of Commons, † 1633 and wife. Alabaster and grey marble. She is recumbent, he behind her rests on his elbow. Two columns, arch, obelisks, and achievement. – Temperance Browne † 1634. Signed by *John and Matthias Christmas* and dated 1635. Hanging monument. She is sitting up in her coffin, still in her shroud. Two columns, two pendant arches. Under them two small arched niches with allegorical figures. In the spandrel the angel blowing the last trumpet. Top square with arms of an open segmental pediment. On them cherubs. In the 'predella' 'Disce mori' and 'Mors mihi corona'. – John, first Lord Crewe, † 1679. Simple tablet. – Thomas, second Lord Crewe, † 1697. Attributed to *Catterns* by Mrs Esdaile.* Very pretty tablet, with cherubs' heads, cypher, two standing putti, garlands, etc. – Nathaniel Lord Crewe, Bishop of Durham, † 1721. Architectural tablet. At the head two coronets and a mitre, at the foot a grape. This was originally a skull, but as the monument was put up before the bishop's death, and as he disliked the skull, the change was made (*Gentleman's Magazine*, 1786).

8080   ## STOKE ALBANY

ST BOTOLPH. Mostly of c. 1300, i.e. the W tower with a window of three steeply stepped lights under a steep arch, a window in the form of a spherical triangle higher up and pairs of transomed two-light bell-openings, chancel with an E window with intersected tracery, and quite a variety of two-light windows with quatrefoils, quatrefoiled circles, round and pointed trefoils, and also two 'low-side' lancets, S aisle with similar windows (a little later, see the one window with reticulated tracery), a shafted doorway, and an interesting W window

* Bruce Bailey however suggests the workshop of *Edward Stanton*.

with a five-cornered star in a spherical quadrangle, N aisle with an E window with Y-tracery. Inside a wide nave and a wide S aisle. Both arcades are of *c.* 1300 (octagonal piers, double-chamfered pointed arches, but differing details). In the chancel a low tomb recess with a trefoil-cusped arch and SEDILIA and PISCINA. All this also of *c.* 1300. Perp especially the S aisle E window of five lights with much panel tracery.* – FONT. A raw baluster, dated 1681. – (STAINED GLASS. Chancel. Roos arms and grisaille, *c.* 1295. RM) – PLATE. Cup and Paten, 1570.

OLD HOUSE. Mostly C17 but with a window with Y-tracery in the N wing and a big buttress on the S side. Gotch thought the house may go back to the C14.

MANOR HOUSE, on the way to the A-road. Oblong, the l. half of before the Reformation, the r. of 1682. The l. half has buttresses, a doorway with two-centred head and two shields over. Window of two plus two lights, two-centred cusped heads.

STOKE BRUERNE

7050

ST MARY. Norman W tower, see the two windows and the pointed but single-stepped arch towards the nave. The upper parts are Perp. Perp also the chancel E window. The side windows of the chancel do not seem in their original state. What is trustworthy of the aisle windows is Dec. Arcades of five bays. The double-chamfered arches are continued down the piers on continuous mouldings. In the N aisle a cusped tomb recess. – SCREEN. Tall, Perp, one-light divisions, ogee arches, and panel tracery over. – COMMUNION RAIL. With dumb-bell balusters, C17, now used as stall fronts. – PLATE. Cup, 1661; Paten, *c.* 1666; large Set, 1776.

STOKE PARK. The house was built by Sir Francis Crane, head of the Mortlake Tapestry Works, in 1629–35. He died in 1636 after having entertained the King at his new house in 1635. Bridges says that Crane had 'brought the design from Italy and in the execution of it received the assistance of *Inigo Jones*'. Both statements are credible. Stoke Park is the earliest house in England on the plan of Palladio's villas with a central *corps-de-logis* connected by quadrant colonnades to end pavilions. Crane could just as well have brought this idea from an Italian journey as Inigo Jones might have brought it

* Restoration by *Slater* (N. Taylor).

after he had been in 1613–14 and studied Palladio with un-precedented intensity and zest. The elevations on the other hand pose some problems. The main building was of I-shape with the front serif larger than that at the back. It is possible that the house was an older building which was altered when the pavilions were added. Old photographs show that the back parts had very plain mullion and cross windows. The end walls of the front serif had curved Jacobean gables. This building was burnt down in 1886 and what we know of it – it is e.g. illustrated in Campbell's *Vitruvius Britannicus*, vol. III, 1725 – does not tally with Jones's style. Campbell says indeed that it was designed by 'another architect'. Yet it had the motif which is also the hallmark of the end pavilions and which was going to be a favourite motif in the Jones connexion and the circle of architects of 1700 and after: the giant pilaster. This was a motif used in the Cinquecento by Michelangelo (Capitol) and Palladio (Palazzo Valmarana) but with more enthusiasm in France (St Maur, then Long Gallery between Louvre and Tuileries, etc.), from where it migrated to Holland. In Dutch classicism it became popular at nearly the same moment as it appears at Stoke Park. The s front of Stoke Park was of five bays, grouped by giant Ionic pilasters in three parts with one, three, one windows. There was an attic storey above the giant pilasters and a cupola or belvedere on the roof. The windows had frames of rustication in alternating sizes and were vertically laced together. Campbell only says that the Civil War interrupted work on the house.

After the fire of 1886 a new house in an ornate Jacobean style was built, attached in a most unfortunate way to the r. end pavilion. This house has now been removed and the c17 pavilions have been restored They are faced with cream oölite and dark brown ironstone. The columns of the colon-nade are also of ironstone. The combination adds greatly to the beauty of the pavilions. They are of one and a half storeys, oblong, with a slightly narrower projection to the forecourt. The oblong part is of three bays with a one-bay pediment to the s. The Venetian window of the l. pavilion is a late c18 alteration. The corresponding window of the r. pavilion has been restored according to the illustration in *Vitruvius Britannicus*. (This pavilion has now been converted into a private house.) The giant pilasters carry an entablature with a pulvinated frieze. To the forecourt, i.e. the side where the two pavilions face one another, the middle projection has a loggia on the ground floor with Ionic columns carrying a straight lintel and set fairly close to the framing giant pilasters, a motif familiar from Michelangelo's Capitoline palaces, not a likely source for Inigo Jones. Above this, on the upper floor a large arched window. The roof above is now hipped, but it formerly had a small pediment on this side, and another on the s side of the projecting part of the pavilion. To the l. and r. of the projection a one-bay, one-storey loggia. Those facing N mark the start of the quadrant colonnades. In the w pavilion, according to Campbell, was the Library, in the E pavilion the Chapel. – In the gardens STATUE of Sir George Cooke of Harefield, Middlesex, † 1740. Probably by *Henry Cheere*.* The pose of Sir George is derived from that of James Cragg by Guelfi at Westminster Abbey. On the base two good reliefs with putti.

STOKE PLAIN. One of the Grafton farms of *c.* 1840 (*see* Introduction, p. 67). Of stone, three bays, with lower wings in line but recessed.

(STOKE GAP LODGE. Another Grafton farm. DOE)

CANALSCAPE. Close to Stoke Bruerne, the Grand Junction Canal, with LOCKS and TUNNEL (cf. Blisworth, p. 109), cottages, inn, and CANAL MUSEUM, converted in 1963 from a C19 grain warehouse. The exceptionally attractive CANAL BRIDGE, with two arches and robust curving brick and stone walls, was strengthened with commendable care in 1972 by British Waterways, in collaboration with the County Surveyor, by the insertion of a reinforced concrete structure invisible from the outside. The bridge probably dates from *c.* 1835–40, when the canal was widened and a double set of locks constructed.‡

STOKE DOYLE

ST RUMBALD. St Rumbald is a rare dedication (but cf. Astrop). The date of the church is 1722–5, and that is a rare date in Northamptonshire.§ Tower with angle pilasters at the top, a balustrade, and obelisk pinnacles. Arched w doorway with pilasters, arched bell-openings with pilasters. On the s side a doorway close to the w end with a rusticated surround and an

---

* Attribution by Dr Margaret Whinney.
‡ Information from Mr P. I. King and Mr G. Freeston.
§ Designs exist for the body of the building by *Thomas Eayre* of Kettering, but the tower is by another hand (H. M. Colvin).

open segmental pediment on Doric pilasters. Then four round-arched windows and a Venetian E window. Plain coved ceiling inside. – FONT. On baluster stem. – REREDOS and COMMUNION RAIL original. – PULPIT and BENCHES original. – ORGAN. Early C19, Gothic. – SCULPTURE. Two large, beautifully carved angels above the sides of the E window, bought about 1835–40. – CROSS BASE outside the S door. Square with corner spurs of a bulbous indeterminate form to carry over into an octagon. The date can hardly be guessed. – PLATE. Set, 1734. – MONUMENTS. Outside the church, to the E. Priest, C13, the head under a trefoiled canopy. – Mrs Frances Palmer † 1628. Hanging monument with columns, obelisks, and an achievement. She lies stiffly on her side, head on hand and elbow propping up the arm. Her husband kneels in front of her in profile – an unusual com-
62   position. – Sir Edward Ward † 1714, made soon after his arrival in England by that young and brilliant sculptor *J. M. Rysbrack*. He had arrived in 1720. Not signed. White and grey marble. Elegantly semi-reclining figure with wig. Reredos with Ionic columns and a pediment. – Mrs Roberts † 1819. By *Chantrey*. An instructive comparison with the monument to Mrs Palmer. The subject is almost the same, but taste and sensibility have changed. She lies on a Grecian couch. He bends mournfully over her hand. – More early C19 tablets.

STOKE DOYLE MANOR. The C18 gates are at East Haddon Hall.

(OLD RECTORY, E of the church. L-shaped. The entrance front with two canted bays, the N bay of two storeys, the S one with the date 1633. The S wing perhaps built as a Hall range. Alterations in 1731 and 1790. BB)

STONEACRES *see* BLISWORTH

6050   # STOWE-NINE-CHURCHES

ST MICHAEL. Tall Saxon W tower. The early date is recognizable externally by the lesenes on the bell-stage to the W and E and one W window, inside by the arch towards the nave with its unmistakable blocks standing for both capitals and abaci of the responds and the remains of the equally unmistakable band along the arch and the jambs running at a distance from the opening. (Above is a blocked round-headed Saxon opening, visible from inside the tower. In the W wall a blocked square-headed doorway. H. M. Taylor) The piece of Saxon interlace at the NW corner externally is not *in situ*. Small Norman N doorway. E.E. S doorway with dog-tooth in the hood-mould. The rest is externally mostly very Late Perp (1639) and internally so renewed as to be valueless. The E end was rebuilt in 1860. – SCREEN. Jacobean, to the S chapel. With arches on balusters. – REREDOS. Made up in 1971 of Early Renaissance(?) domestic panelling. – PLATE. Cover Paten, 1681; Paten, 1775. – MONUMENTS. Effigy of a cross-legged Knight on a slab tapering like a coffin lid. Purbeck 48 marble; extremely fine quality. Said to represent Sir Gerard de l'Isle † *c.* 1287. – Elizabeth Lady Carey, by *Nicholas Stone*, 1617–20. An extremely early case of the post-Jacobean style, and carved as beautifully as the best Dutch monuments of the time. Free-standing tomb-chest. Black and white marble. The white effigy is very realistic, yet not lacking in dignity. The monument was put up in the lifetime of the lady. – Dr Thomas Turner, President of Corpus Christi College, Oxford, 60 † 1714. Signed by *Thomas Stayner*. Large standing monument. Inscription, long, Latin, and laudatory, in the middle, below a baldacchino with opened draperies. Big segmental pediment on fluted pilasters. To the l. and r. two life-size figures, the President and Fides. He stands on a terrestrial globe, she on a celestial. – John Daye † 1757. By *John Middleton* of Towcester. Architectural tablet with curly open pediment.

(MANOR FARMHOUSE (formerly Manor House). C16, altered later. A long irregular S front with central projection with arched windows. C18 N front. DOVECOTE, C17 or C18. DOE)

(DOWER HOUSE (formerly Rectory). C16, altered in the C19. With two two-storey bay-windows. DOE)

ST JAMES, Upper Stowe. 1855 by *P. C. Hardwick*. Nave and chancel with extremely steeply pitched roofs. Bellcote at the W end. Lancet windows, those in the chancel E wall of five steeply stepped lancets. Timber porch.

EARTHWORK. An undated linear earthwork extends 300 yds up Church Stowe lane from the intersection with Upper Stowe road.

STRIXTON
9060

ST JOHN BAPTIST. A C13 church rebuilt in 1873 except for the *See* w wall, but with old materials and, it is said, correctly. The w p. 518 wall has a triple-chamfered doorway on two orders of shafts and a sexfoil window over with a wavy frame. Tiny cusped lancet to the r. The windows of the church are mostly pairs of lancets. At the E end three stepped separate lancets with a quatrefoiled circle in the gable, and, also in the gable, three blank quatrefoils placed diagonally. S doorway with a double-hollow-chamfered arch. Inside, PISCINA with some dog-tooth. – SCREEN. Perp. Simple, with one-light divisions. – COMMUNION RAIL. With heavy twisted balusters; c. 1700. – PLATE. Cup and Paten, 1628.

SUDBOROUGH

9080

ALL SAINTS. Mostly of the C13, and first the three-bay arcades with circular piers and circular capitals and abaci. The first piers N and S are sturdier and probably older than the others. Pointed arches of one chamfer and one hollow chamfer. Cross arches in the aisles on responds against the outer walls. Arches into the transepts too. Late C13 W tower, chancel, and transepts. The tower has a blocked circular window on the W, lancets on the N and S, bell-openings of two lights with, above them, a spherical triangle or a circle with four inscribed circles or cusped Y-tracery, a corbel table with dog-tooth and heads, and four thin (later) pinnacles. Tower arch with semi-octagonal responds with concave sides and abaci and hollow-chamfered arches – i.e. Dec and not late C13. The chancel has decorated buttresses. SEDILIA with triple shafts, fillets and head-stops, and a tomb recess opposite it with a nearly segmental arch. The windows are tall with cusped lights and straight-headed. One is a 'low-side' window. The S transept S window is specially fine and typical of its date. Four lights arranged as two-plus-two with cusped Y-tracery, and above a large spherical triangle with three small ones inscribed. Steeply pointed arch. The N doorway is also of c. 1300. – STAINED GLASS. E window by *Kempe*, 1892. – (S transept. Late C15 roundels and crown. RM) – PLATE. Cup, 1820. – MONUMENTS. In the recess in the chancel effigy of a cross-legged Knight, slender, late C13. – Brass to William West † 1390 and wife, 18 in. figures.

TOLL HOUSE, at the E corner of the village street and the A-road. Circular with conical roof. With a date-stone of 1660.

SULBY HALL

6080

The house of 1792–5 built by *Sir John Soane* was demolished c. 1948. There was a Premonstratensian abbey at Sulby.

SULGRAVE

ST JAMES. In the W tower a triangle-headed doorway, i.e. a Saxon relic, not *in situ*. The upper parts of the tower are E.E. Two-light bell-openings. Otherwise mostly C19. The S doorway is original Dec work, the S porch entrance (quatrefoils, initials, and the date 1564 in the spandrels) original Perp. S arcade of four bays with octagonal piers and double-chamfered arches. The N aisle was built in 1885. – FONT. Octagonal, with leaf ornament, probably of the 1660s. – PEW. The Washington Pew is an open bench with front and back, of the C17. – STAINED GLASS. In the S aisle E window, heraldic, brought in. – PLATE. Cup, 1734; Paten, 1810. – MONUMENTS. Brass to Lawrence Washington † 1584 and wife; 21 in. figures. – John and Moses Hodges † 1724; architectural tablet.

STOCKS. On the village green.

SULGRAVE MANOR. The manor house was bought by Lawrence Washington, wool-stapler and Mayor of Northampton, in 1540 and sold out of the Washington family in 1659. It consists of a centre with porch and a N wing added at the time of Queen Anne. Of the centre only the r. half with the porch is original; the l. half was built by *Sir Reginald Blomfield* in 1921 after it had been pulled down about 1780. The date of the original work is later than 1558 (arms of Elizabeth I on the porch), but need not be much later. The whole front consists of no more than three very widely spaced bays. The porch doorway has a four-centred head. Inside the hall, the fireplace is original, the screen C20. Behind the hall pretty, late C17 staircase with twisted balusters.

CASTLE, W of the church. Excavations in 1967–72 have revealed a remarkable timber hall of the early C11 beneath the Norman ringwork. The building was 80 ft long, with a service room, screen, and opposed entrances at the screen end – a very early example of the standard later medieval arrangement. At the opposite end to the screen a cross-wing which was on stone footings and therefore possibly of two storeys. A detached timber kitchen lay beyond the service room. On one side of the hall stood a stone building, whose walls survive to a height of 7 ft. After the Conquest the timber hall was replaced by a timber first-floor hall on a stone undercroft; the Saxon cross-wing was retained as a chamber block, and the free-standing stone building was used as a gatehouse in conjunction with the new earthwork defences. The site was abandoned *c.* 1125.

(WINDMILL, ¾ m. NW. A derelict tower-mill.)

BARROW. Below Barrow Hill, 1 m. N of the village, on the S side
of Banbury Lane.

7090 SUTTON BASSETT

ST MARY. Nave and chancel and bellcote. In the N wall of the
chancel a Norman window. The responds of the chancel arch
are also Norman. Curiously primitive abaci. Norman the S
doorway to the nave too. One order of columns with scallop
capitals. Tympanum with relief diapering (cf. Peterborough
Cathedral). On the S side two later C13 windows. The double
bellcote also could be C13, but there is no detail to go by.
Several houses with mullioned windows, e.g. one dated 1642.

6040 SYRESHAM

ST JAMES. The chancel arch is of c. 1200. The corbels still have
the Late Norman trumpet capitals. The arch has one hollow
chamfer. Hood-mould with nutmeg decoration. C13 W tower.
Two-light bell-openings with separating shaft. Short recessed
shingled spire. N windows Late Perp, S windows all renewed.
Arcades of four bays with octagonal piers and double-chamfered arches. – FONT. Circular, Norman, with a rope moulding
at the top. – PLATE. Cup, 1701; Breadholder, 1773; Flagon,
1788. – MONUMENT 'Petri Andrewe generosi' † 1612.
Tablet in an architectural frame.

GATE HOUSE, to the SW. The house is partly of stone, partly
of timber from old barns, with brick infilling; by C. H.
Biddulph-Pinchard, c. 1930 (BB).

(Two good Georgian houses, the RECTORY and a house on the
A43, both of brick. BB)

8060 SYWELL

ST PETER AND ST PAUL. Short late C13 W tower. Bell-openings
of two lights with a shaft between. The same motif repeated
in the windows on the S side below. The picturesque stair
projection in the middle of the W side is not medieval. The
interior is odd indeed. When the S arcade was rebuilt in 1870,
the E wall of the tower must also have been interfered with.
The tower arch now has a triple-shafted N respond, but
instead of a S respond a whole quatrefoil pier with thin diagonal
shafts which cannot have been there originally. No medieval
architect would have placed the corner of his tower on a pier.

Nor did *J. Manden*, the architect of 1870. He enforced the corner by setting close to the quatrefoil pier two round ones with square abaci, one of original late C 12 work (waterleaf and leaf crockets in the capital) and one imitated. The arcade then goes on with such imitated piers. Could the original late C 12 arcade have been of two bays with one more added in the late C 13 ? Original the s doorway, late C 12, pointed, with one slight step. Original also the C 14 tomb recess in the N transept. Chancel rebuilt in 1862. – STAINED GLASS. E window by *Willement*, 1839, a very handsome and civilized composition made up of heraldic glass dated 1580. – PLATE. Cup and Paten, 1816.

SYWELL HALL. Quite a long front, straight, with two small and one central larger gable, irregular mullioned windows. To the l., at the end of the front, three-storeyed porch. The doorhead is four-centred. Above the first-floor window a frieze of linked squares and circles (cf. Rushton Hall). The front must have gone on to the l. of the porch. The house seems to be Elizabethan.

HOUSES. Many houses in the village were rebuilt by Lady Overstone in the 1860s. The former SCHOOL was rebuilt in 1861, in 1862 the RECTORY enlarged. The latter is all gabled and very substantial. (The new SCHOOL, on the road to Overstone, is by *J. M. I. Scott*, 1964.)

TANSOR

ST MARY. The history of this building is one of the most intricate in the county. The existing literature, including the late Hamilton Thompson's account, has not fully explained it, nor can a full explanation be offered here. The history starts with the blocked window in the w wall of the church. This may be C 11. It is continued with the former tower arch and the w parts of the arcades. The date here may be *c.* 1125–50. After that came the E extension of the aisles. But here the problem begins. The Norman piers are of two kinds, one sturdier than the other and with heavier capitals (four instead of six scallops and less bits of decoration between them). Now these earlier-looking capitals belong to the second pier from the w on the N side, the third on the s, and the two E responds. The rounded arches with one step and one chamfer indicate aisles of three bays. If this is true, the E responds have been shifted to their present position further E. But why the third pier on the s side? The capital is not, as has been suggested, made up of two responds. What that looks like can be seen at Glapthorn. Were the aisles meant to be of four bays? Or was one of the old piers left unused when the slightly later slender six-scallop piers were decided on instead? The former tower arch, and with it the w tower, belongs to the aisles. Of the original chancel, before the aisles were lengthened, fragments of a scallop and a billet frieze are witness (s side, inside the s aisle) and a fragment of a N window with a roll moulding. Late C12 the N doorway. Two orders, one with shaft-rings and stiff-leaf capitals. Round arch, with rich zigzag decoration, also at r. angles to the wall surface. That looks like late C12.

Now the C13. Much happened and the order cannot be established, except that the N lengthening of the arcades must have preceded the s lengthening. Both sides have circular piers and circular capitals and abaci and pointed arches. On the N side the arcade ran to a pre-existing vestry; hence the odd rhythm of the double-chamfered pointed arches. The vestry arch was partly filled in by a wall, and in this is a pretty doorway with much dog-tooth. Dog-tooth is also the hallmark of the s doorway. In addition however it has a dog-tooth-like zigzag and so may be a little earlier. The s arcade has wider arches to reach the E line of the vestry, i.e. the link for a new chancel (which is however later, *see* below). The capitals have a little nailhead enrichment. Of the same time the pairs of lancets in the w part of the s aisle and the lancets in the N aisle. Later C13 the NW window of the N aisle with bar tracery (renewed). At the same time the w tower was continued – see the bell-openings with a shaft between the two lights. Also, as there are no buttresses (though recessions from stage to stage), the Norman tower was considered unsafe and the arch towards the nave was reduced in size by a new narrow arch. The new chancel dates from the later C13. The E window is Perp, but remains of the C13 window can be seen inside. The side windows are typical of their date. DOUBLE PISCINA. The aisle walls also have C13 elements. Inside the s aisle a tomb recess. Of the early C14 finally the E half of the s aisle. Windows of three stepped lights under one arch, the outer ones with rounded trefoil cusping.

FURNISHINGS. FONT. Plain octagonal bowl with, in the diagonals, four monstrously big ballflowers. Early C14. – SCREEN. Against the E wall of the s aisle part of the upper parts of the Perp rood screen. – STALLS. From Fotheringhay.

With good MISERICORDS. – PULPIT. Jacobean. – BRASS.
John Colt, Rector, † 1440. The figure is 19 in. long.
(WINDMILL, c. 500 ft NE. Shell of a tower-mill.)

TEETON
6070

1½ m. w of Spratton

TEETON HALL. In the disguise of a gabled Victorian house (by
W. Smith, according to Sir Gyles Isham) the remains of a fine
if small Georgian mansion with a quoined ironstone façade of
five bays to the garden and a brick entrance side. Red and
dark blue brick chequered. Inside fine staircase with slender
turned balusters, two to the tread. The plaster decoration of
the stair-well indicates a date in the second third of the C18.
The builder was *John Wagstaff* of Daventry. There is a quadrant wall to connect the house to a range of STABLES, also of
chequer brick. The bell in the stables is dated 1702.

TEETON HALL FARMHOUSE. A C17 house with mullioned
windows with a new front-block added late in the C17. Ironstone, three bays, two storeys. Stone cross-windows. Former
doorway with pediment. Fine mid-C17 gatepiers.

THENFORD
5040

ST MARY. Perp w tower with tall transomed bell-openings and
battlements. The rest externally mostly of c. 1300. The s
doorway however and the s aisle w and e windows point to a
date c. 1200, and this is borne out by the impressive s arcade.
Octagonal piers, a stiff-leaf capital, and a stiff-leaf respond,
both with early upright leaves, double-chamfered, pointed
arches. The s doorway has a round arch instead and, according
to the blank arch visible inside to its w, has been re-set. The
N arcade is of c. 1300. Octagonal piers and double-chamfered
arches, but triple-shafted responds, the middle one with a
fillet. The w and NW windows of the aisle have internally
corbels with naturalistic foliage. – SCREEN. Perp; simple. –
POOR BOX. On a foot; iron-bound; of rough workmanship. –
STAINED GLASS. In the N aisle e window some very good
early C15 glass (St Christopher and St Anne with the Virgin). –
PLATE. Cup and Paten, 1570. – MONUMENT. Fulk Woodhul †
1613. Recumbent effigy in a recess with a depressed arch.
Flanking coupled fluted columns of the Composite order.

THENFORD HOUSE. Begun 1761, according to a handwritten
inscription on an engraving of Michael Woodhull, who built

the house and was twenty-one when he started. Completed probably in 1765, the date on a lead rain-water tank. The house is of fine quality, but decidedly conservative for its date, not only because its decoration is still Rococo without a touch of the new Adam style, but even more because of its strange twin hipped roofs with a cupola or belvedere in between, of the kind fashionable in 1650–80 or 90. The house is two storeys high on a semi-sunk basement, with a quoined centre of seven bays, then one-storey three-bay linking walls, and then lower three-bay pavilions. Outside these another three bays of the same walls. The walls have blank arches and the pavilions a centre pediment and half-pediments leaning against the centre. The principal block has an open stair up to a doorway with Tuscan columns, a metope frieze, and a pediment, alternating pediments and balcony-like balustrades to the three middle windows on the first floor, and a three-bay pediment. The two hipped roofs look odd enough to the l. and r. of this. The garden side is simpler, with two canted bay-windows. Entrance Hall and Saloon in the middle axis. In the Entrance Hall a beautiful fireplace with long slender brackets set frontally as well as in profile. In the Saloon the windows are accompanied inside by volutes. Good Rococo plaster ceiling and fireplace. Several other good fireplaces. The Staircase has two slender turned balusters to the tread, starting in bulbous shapes at the bottom. The tread-ends are carved, and a running Greek frieze accompanies them diagonally. On the first floor a central corridor and another fine plaster ceiling in the room above the Saloon. Evidence of an earlier building is the re-used mullioned windows at the back of the wings. Their mouldings are apparently late C17.

ROMAN SITE, in the NE corner of the village, ¼ m. w of the cross-roads, beside the garden wall of Thenford House. Early reports of finds of foundations, a hypocaust, and parts of a tessellated pavement are borne out by a still recoverable surface scatter of pottery and other small finds. Coins give a date between the C1 and the C4 A.D.

THORNBY

ST HELEN. Of little architectural interest. W tower, nave, and chancel. The tower is unbuttressed, probably C14, with C15 battlements. The N aisle was added and the chancel rebuilt by E. F. Law in 1870. Some Perp windows remain. –

FONT. Circular, Norman, with saltire crosses, interlace, and (re-cut) leaves. – PLATE. Cup and Paten, 1682.

THORNBY HALL. Stone, Tudor style, gabled. Original C17 core. Additions of *c.* 1873 by *George Hart* (GS). More added in the C20.

STONE HOUSE. Of *c.* 1700, with additions. The front is of five bays and two storeys. Wooden cross-windows. Eared door surround with pediment.

THORNBY GRANGE, ¾ m. SW. By *Gotch*, 1911. Large, neo-Stuart, of ashlar.

THORPE ACHURCH

oo8o

ST JOHN BAPTIST. Interior mostly C19 (1861–3 by *William Slater*) and exterior mostly yet newer-looking. Late C13 W steeple. Spire with broaches and two tiers of lucarnes. W doorway with finely moulded segmental arch. Lancet windows and quatrefoiled circular windows. Bell-openings with Y-tracery and a circle in the spandrel fitted with three cusped spherical triangles. Similar the S transept S window. Here the lights have in their heads pointed trefoils, but the circle is normally quatrefoiled – i.e. *c.* 1300. The chancel buttresses also seem to be of *c.* 1300. They have at their top tiny blank arches with the Y-motif. Inside, the tower arch is triple-chamfered with the inner chamfer on head-stops. The N transept arch is also on head-corbels. The E respond has good upright early stiff-leaf of *c.* 1200. The S transept arch also looks original. – PLATE. Cup, Paten, and Flagon, 1669; Almsdish, 1713. – MONUMENTS. Arthur Elmes † 1663. Tablet under the tower. Inscription in big oval wreath. Skull and bones below, cherub's head above. – Sir Thomas Powys † 1719 (*see* Lilford Hall). By *Robert Hartshorne*. Big standing monument with detached Corinthian columns and an open segmental pediment. Putti and big asymmetrical drapery falling over it. The deceased semi-reclining and wearing a wig. Truth and Justice standing outside the columns. Both from Lilford church. – Charles and Henry Powys † 1804 and 1812. With a military still-life below the inscription. – Henrietta Maria Powys † 1820. With a still-life of bowls, chalice, and dish below the inscription.

Below the churchyard to the SW the re-erected remains of LILFORD CHURCH, which was demolished in 1778. They have been assembled picturesquely but hardly correctly, and show early C14 semi-quatrefoiled responds.

(RECTORY. The SE part is of 1633. In the centre a two-storeyed porch, at the ends two-storeyed bay-windows. Mullioned windows. The NW part is C18. DOE)

(Along the main road a row of identical estate cottages of *c.* 1830–40. DOE)

7080

THORPE LUBENHAM HALL

Basically Georgian but externally altered and added to. Brick with several bow-windows. More alterations in the 1960s.

8070

THORPE MALSOR

ST LEONARD. Of ironstone. Chiefly late C13 and early C14. Restored in 1877 by *Clapton Rolfe*; carving by *Harry Hems*. The N chapel was formed at this time, out of an older vault. Late C13 in style, but externally a later trefoil frieze at the top.* Late C13 W tower (clasping buttresses, pairs of lancets as bell-openings; later quatrefoil frieze and broach spire with two tiers of lucarnes). Dec chancel E window (of four lights consisting of two two-light parts with cusped Y-tracery and a big quatrefoiled top circle – all lights being ogee-arched; cf. Geddington) and N aisle windows. They are somewhat unusual: of two lights, straight-headed, with reticulation at the top. One has ballflower all along its frame – also internally – the other a hood-mould with dog-tooth. Much of this is renewed, but it seems correct. The S side much altered and made more 'interesting' in 1877. Attached to the S porch on the W a vestry and a picturesque turret, all in the E.E. style. Inside, the S arcade is of three bays and has quatrefoil piers and double-chamfered arches. That goes with the ball-flower windows. The N arcade, also of three bays, has the usual octagonal piers and double-chamfered arches. The N chapel has two arches separated by a piece of wall and a W arch on head corbels. The windows, though much renewed, indicate again a date about 1300. – FONT. Octagonal, C14. With crocketed ogee arches. – PLATE. Chalice, C16; Paten, 1764.

THORPE MALSOR HALL. Jacobean, on the E-plan, but with all windows sashed in the C18. The garden (S) side of 1817, ashlar-faced, with two storeys, a bow-window, and three bays to its l. and r.

* The SEDILIA and PISCINA in the chancel are also late C13 in style, but the Rev. J. Gordon Cox suggests that they are also C19 work.

WELL, in the middle of the main street. Placed in 1589. The inscription is in Greek.

THORPE MANDEVILLE

ST JOHN BAPTIST. Mostly early C14. Short W tower with pretty recessed saddleback roof. A small figure high up on the E side. S doorway with an ogee hood-mould on head stops. In the chancel windows of c. 1300 and a 'low-side' lancet with a transom. Dec N aisle windows, shafted inside. Three-bay N arcade with octagonal piers and double-chamfered arches. The chancel restored by A. Hartshorne, 1872. Of this date and by Powell & Sons the REREDOS and the STAINED GLASS in the chancel E and two-light S windows. – MONUMENT. Thomas Kirton, Common Serjeant to the City of London, † 1601, and wife † 1597 (his date of death is added later). Long relief with kneeling figures against a background of six dainty arches. Frieze of light foliage-scrolls below. Tapering caryatids l. and r. Achievement in an open scrolly pediment. On the pediment two reclining figures. (Cf. Heyford and Harrington.)

MANOR HOUSE. A very fine early C18 front of five bays and two storeys with quoins, also to the three-bay centre. Over this an excessively large open segmental pediment – an Archer motif. Doorway with open scrolly pediment. Good panelling inside and a staircase with twisted balusters two to the tread and carved tread-ends.

THE HILL, 1 m. W. By C. F. A. Voysey, 1897–8. Built for Mr Hope Brooke of the family of the Rajahs of Sarawak. Very typical of Voysey with its pebbledash, its happily informal composition, its battered buttresses at the corners, its wooden veranda on one side, and the way in which the screen wall on the r., with its brick coping rising above arched entrances, cuts off one bay of the house. The porch leads direct into the dining hall, which goes across the house. Adjoining to the S was the ladies' drawing room, to the N on the E side the study and then kitchen and offices.

THORPE WATERVILLE

CASTLE. Licence to crenellate was given to the Bishop of Lichfield in 1301. The castle was, it seems, no more than a fortified manor house. The farmhouse has one small lancet window re-used. Otherwise what survives is now a big barn

with two chamfered circular windows in one end-gable. In
between them a chimneyshaft with octagonal top. Single-
framed roof with tie-beams and kingposts with four-way
struts.

BRIDGE. Also early C14. With ribs under the arches, three
straight across and two oblique. Widened on both sides.

THRAPSTON

9070

ST JAMES. Dec W tower with doorway of continuous mouldings,
frieze of cusped lozenges, battlements, and a recessed spire
with three tiers of lucarnes. Dec chancel with tall transomed
two-light side windows and a five-light E window with reticulated tracery. The round-headed priest's doorway and the
string course which runs round it must belong to the early
C13 predecessor of the present chancel. Below the SE window
SEDILIA with ogee arches, their top cutting into the window.
DOUBLE PISCINA with blank quatrefoil in a circle. Nave and
aisles were rebuilt in 1841. They are of nearly the same height.
Tall quatrefoil piers with shaft-rings. Three wooden galleries.
– STAINED GLASS. E window by *Wailes* (TK), 1863. – PLATE.
Cup and Paten, 1570. – MONUMENT. Elizabeth Darnell
† 1831. By *Physick*. Woman seated on the ground and holding
a medallion.

BAPTIST CHAPEL, Huntingdon Road. The old front of 1787
still survives, in spite of additions. Red brick. Four bays, two
storeys, arched openings. Doorways in bays one and four.

FIRE STATION AND LIBRARY. By the County Architect,
John Goff. Under construction 1971–2. Yellow brick, split-
pitched roofs.

STATION. Demolished.*

BRIDGE. Of nine arches, largely medieval, widened later. The
arches rebuilt in brick. Some stone cutwaters remain. The
bridge is threatened with demolition.

There are no houses of major interest at Thrapston, although
quite a number of C18 cottages. Apart from these the following: At the beginning of the HUNTINGDON ROAD the
VICARAGE faces up the Oundle Road. It is big and Elizabethan and was designed in 1836 by *W. J. Donthorne*. In the
Huntingdon Road THRAPSTON HOUSE, built apparently
c. 1805 but looks Early Victorian. Of three tripartite bays with

---

* It was by *Livock*, 1845, and one of the most picturesque of his neo-Tudor
stations, with bargeboarded gables (*see* p. 69 n).

a porch with fluted Ionic columns. On the N side of the
HIGH STREET the entrance to the former CORN EXCHANGE,
a heavy doorway with Tuscan columns inscribed 'erected in
1850 by F. Roe'. Above it a wooden wheatsheaf and plough.
Further on, on the s side of the Market Place, OAKLEIGH
HOUSE, C18, two storeys and dormers, red brick front, five
bays. Windows with keystones, doorcase with fluted pilasters.

THURNING

0080

ST JAMES. Norman chancel arch, narrow, with short semicircular responds with four-scallop capitals. The arch has only
one slight step. N arcade of two bays, c. 1200. Circular pier,
circular capital and abacus. Double-chamfered round arch,
the outer chamfer with an applied roll. A w bay was added a
little later, beyond the line of the Norman w wall, but this w
part of the church was demolished at the time of the drastic
restoration by *Carpenter & Ingelow* in 1880, when the church
received its unattractive w face with a small spired bell-turret.
The E respond of this added bay has nailhead. The s aisle is of
c. 1300, see the E window (two pointed-trefoiled lights and
two pointed trefoils over) and the arcade with a quatrefoil
pier with fillets and double-hollow-chamfered arches. The w
arch here was added after the Norman wall had come down.
Of the C14 the chancel s windows with flowing tracery and the
odd N chapel openings towards the chancel. They are a
composition of two doorways of different size and an arch. All
have continuous mouldings with one wide chamfer with a
hollow set in it. The SEDILIA are only two seats with a stone
arm between, placed below the three-light s window. –
PULPIT. Plain; Jacobean. – PLATE. Early C15 Florentine
Chalice, silver-gilt and enamelled, given in 1924; Cup and
Cover Paten, 1569; jewelled, silver-gilt Ciborium, 1900.

TIFFIELD

6050

ST JOHN. Small. Unbuttressed Dec w tower. The body of the
church all renewed, the s aisle and porch in 1859 by *E. F.
Law*, the rest in 1873 by *H. C. Vernon*. The original gable
cross from the E end re-set in the s wall. The N arcade is early
C13. Three bays. Circular piers with octagonal abaci and single-
chamfered arches. – FONT. Circular, Norman, with upside-
down lunettes beaded along the rim and filled with leaves.

Leaves also in the spandrels below. The same design as at Paulerspury. – PLATE. Cup and Paten, 1689.

ST JOHN'S SCHOOL. Founded as a reformatory in 1856. The excellent recent buildings by *James Crabtree*, 1960–3, consist of a series of two-storey brick pavilions with shallow hipped roofs, pleasantly grouped down a gentle slope. Those at the top near the road are entered at first-floor level.

TITCHMARSH

0070

ST MARY. There cannot be many churches in England whose churchyards have as their boundary a ha-ha. There certainly

14 are not many churches either which can boast of a tower like the tower of Titchmarsh. F. J. Allen calls it 'the finest parish church tower in England outside Somerset'. It is unfortunate that we do not know who gave the money for it or when it was built. It is later than the aisles, as the relation of the buttresses to the aisle W wall proves – that is all we can say. It has setback buttresses. The base is decorated with three friezes of quatrefoils one on top of the other, and there are two more higher up and two friezes of cusped lozenges. On the W side the porch has quatrefoils in the spandrels. Niches flank it, and there are two more pairs of niches higher up. The arch towards the nave has responds with castellated capitals. The bellopenings are pairs of two-light windows with transom, and on the stage below, on each side, is one more such window. The crown is sixteen pinnacles of which three on the middles of the sides are set diagonally and the smaller intermediate ones have fanciful outlines. Most of the remaining exterior is Perp too, with windows of three, four, and even five lights, but certain details show that the structure is largely earlier. They are the chancel S doorway, a chancel N window, the N doorway, the N aisle NW window, and also the entrance to the S porch. Earlier still is the evidence of the interior. There is a Norman zigzag arch re-set in the chancel. The N arcade and N chapel arcade are C13 (circular piers and abaci, nailhead enrichment), the S arcade belongs to the early to mid C14 (circular piers, two with capitals with big individual upright leaves). In the S aisle a low tomb recess. – FONT. Octagonal, Perp, panelled. – STAINED GLASS. Two small panels by *Kempe* in the S aisle E window. – PLATE. Cup and Cover Paten and Flagon, 1670; Cup and Cover Paten, 1674; Almsdish, 1836. – MONUMENTS. In the N chapel two painted monuments by *Mrs Elizabeth*

Creed. The Rev. Theophilus Pickering † 1710 (her brother). Painted bust on tall pedestal between pilasters and under an arch. – John Dryden, the poet (her cousin), and his parents. Here the bust of the poet at the top is real. – Members of the Pickering family down to one who † 1749. White, grey, and pink marble. Column and a broken pediment. Pretty Rococo decoration, including two cherubs' heads. – Major and Mrs Creed † 1704 and † 1705. Two very tall inscription tablets, l. and r. of the S aisle E window. They are the shape of Dec or Perp niches. Above an urn, below on his side a military trophy, on hers a flower basket. – Col. John Creed † 1751. By *Edward Bingham.* – Mrs Creed, c. 1800. By *J. & J. Coles* of Thrapston and Huntingdon (Gunnis). A very plain urn on a black base, set against the window.

PICKERING ALMSHOUSES. 1756. On the S side of the church and the Green. Of one storey with dormers, thatched. Extensions l. and r.

CASTLE. On the SW of the village is the rectangular moat of a fortified manor house, licensed in 1304 but ruinous by 1363. It may not have been the first fortification on the site. (The excavations were published in the *Reports & Papers read at the Meetings of the Archit. Societies*, XXI, 1891–2.)

(BROOK HILL FARM. Dated 1628, enlarged in the later C18. GI)

TOWCESTER

6040

ST LAWRENCE. Up Church Lane, looking into fields. Ironstone. Perp W tower with a doorway decorated with fleurons up a moulding of jambs and arch and a frieze of panelling above. Tall arch into the nave. The body of the church externally over-restored. The windows are Dec in the chancel, Perp in the S aisle. The S doorway has many fine continuous mouldings, i.e. belongs to the early C14. Internally the evidence is, as so often, earlier. The chancel arch re-uses Norman shafts with zigzag and lozenge decoration. The arcades (of four bays) re-use three late C12 capitals, of which one has the unmistakable waterleaf motif. The chancel chapels are both of two bays and both C13, that on the S with a circular pier with four circular shafts in the diagonals, that on the N with an octagonal pier. The nave ROOF was rebuilt during the restoration of 1957 by *G. Forsyth Lawson.* It has heavy tie-beams whose ends are masked by bold feathery decorations suggestive of wings, which conceal lights. – FONT. Stem with nodding ogee arches supporting the bowl, which has simple panelling. – PULPIT.

With Jacobean panels. – ORGAN. French or Belgian, with
44 elegant and gay C18 decoration, strikingly alien to an English
parish church. The organ comes from the house of Lord
Mayor Beckford, father of Beckford of Fonthill Abbey. He
bought it for £2,000. Lord Pomfret bought it at the Fonthill
Abbey sale and gave it to Towcester. – WALL PAINTING.
Large Pelican – what date? – in an ogee-headed niche in the
s chapel. – STAINED GLASS. Assembled old bits in the s aisle
E window including C15 Sponne arms. – PLATE. Cup and
Paten, 1580; two Cups, 1597; Flagon, 1630; silver-gilt Basin,
1691; Breadholder, 1702; silver-gilt Ewer, c. 1730. – MONU-
MENTS. Archdeacon Sponne, rector 1422–48. Of table type.
On the ground *gisant* or cadaver, on the top effigy, much over-
restored. – Jerome Farmore † 1602 and wife. Small kneeling
figures.

CONGREGATIONAL CHAPEL (formerly Independent Chapel),
Meeting Yard, w of the Town Hall. 1845. Stone, with a brick
pediment. The usual arched windows. The same scheme is
still used in the BAPTIST CHURCH, Watling Street, of 1877,
but the pediment is a little more Baroque, and the red and
yellow brick a little more vociferous.

TOWN HALL and CORN EXCHANGE. By *T. H. Vernon*, 1865.
Italianate with a central tower. Well sited but not worthy of its
site.

POST OFFICE. *See* Perambulation, below.

SPONNE COMPREHENSIVE SCHOOL. Incorporating the
former Secondary Modern, a building of 1914, and the
Grammar School of 1928, linked by additions by the County
Architect, *A. N. Harris*, 1967–9.

TOWCESTER HEALTH CENTRE, Swinneyford Road. By the
County Architect, *John Goff*, 1970–1. A later version of the
one at Daventry. AMBULANCE STATION next door, 1970–1.

POLICE STATION, 263 Watling Street West. 1936–8 by *G. H.
Lewin*, the then county architect. Surprisingly large, and with
its symmetry and its Tudor style looking like a grammar school
of between the two wars.*

WORKHOUSE (former), Brackley Road. 1836 by (*Sir*) *G. G.
Scott*. Ironstone, still Late Classical in composition and details.
Quite unadorned.

TOWN CINEMA, Watling Street East. 1939 by *E. Fancott* (of
Sir John Brown & Henson). Light brick, in the contemporary

---

* For the Roman town, whose wall is visible behind the police station,
see below, p. 435.

style. Built by the first Lord Hesketh as a birthday present to his wife. There is a private family box inside.

PERAMBULATION. All there is to be seen is along WATLING STREET, and with one exception N of the Town Hall. The exception is No. 157 just S of it. Early Georgian. Brown stone, five bays, three storeys, with segment-headed windows and a parapet. Then facing into the little square by the Town Hall on the E side the CHANTRY HOUSE of Archdeacon Sponne, founded in 1447. The wall and the archway and some of the masonry of the house (e.g. the chimneybreast) are original. Its neighbour is the POST OFFICE, red brick with dark blue chequer, of three storeys, dated 1799. The centre projects and has its own quoins and a pediment. Its neighbour, red brick with stuccoed keystones, has been demolished. Opposite, No. 181, a minor piece of timber-framing. No. 185 is of brick, painted, and has a broad doorway with coupled Doric pilasters and a metope frieze. Then LLOYDS BANK and SPONNE HOUSE (formerly the TALBOT HOTEL) of 1707, but with a later porch. Five bays, two storeys, red brick. Central carriage-way and Venetian window above it rising into a broken pediment. Off to the W in PARK STREET a number of minor Georgian houses, especially No. 16 and, opposite, No. 23. The latter is of ironstone, three bays wide, with a one-bay pediment and a pedimented doorway. Back in Watling Street several nice shopfronts, notably No. 201. Opposite a three-bay stuccoed Regency house with a doorway set back behind two Tuscan piers and two Tuscan columns. Again opposite the SARACEN'S HEAD HOTEL, famous from the *Pickwick Papers*. The A5 makes it hard to concentrate on Dickens and the coaching days which were just going when he wrote of them. Fine long ironstone front, seven bays, two storeys. Carriageway in the middle with an arched window over. Nos 160–4, on the E side, is a Late Georgian terrace of three three-storeyed two-bay brick houses.

On the NE side of the town there is the MOTTE of a castle.

LACTODORUM. The site of a named Roman walled town. Of the fortifications bounded on the E by the Tove and extending c. 550 yds either side of Watling Street, only a section behind the police station is readily visible. Foundations, tessellated pavements, 'terra sigillata', Castor ware, and coins of most periods have been found from time to time. Excavations in the NE corner in 1954 revealed that the rampart constructed in the late C2 A.D. overlay a number of earlier houses. The fortifications fell into disrepair in the C4; the first of two post-Roman rebuildings is associated with the construction of Bury Mount in 921.

ROMAN VILLA. At Mileoak Farm, SW of Lactodorum, on the Abthorpe road, is a site first investigated in 1846–8 and re-examined in 1954–6. A W-facing corridor block, measuring 130 by 30 ft, and constructed of wattle and daub on oölite foundations, overlay a Belgic Iron Age settlement marked by rubble flooring and a number of hearths. A group of living rooms to the N were decorated with tessellated floors, a stoke-hole providing heat for an E corridor which may have run under the present road. The Roman settlement was founded in the C1 A.D.

TWYWELL

9070

ST NICHOLAS. Small. Essentially a Norman church. Norman N doorway with tympanum on corbels. In the tympanum diapering in relief (cf. Peterborough Cathedral). Norman S doorway with one order of colonnettes with scalloped capitals. Arch with zigzag, also set at r. angles to the wall surface (cf. Peterborough Cathedral). Big impressive head in the apex.* One Norman N window, one Norman window at the W end of the S aisle (re-set), one Norman chancel window, one Norman window in the tower. Unmoulded tower arch. Of the Norman transepts the blocked arch into the N transept remains, and the many-scalloped E respond and single-stepped arch into the S transept. The S aisle was added in the early C13, and the transept arch thereby altered. The aisle is of two bays and has octagonal piers. W respond with nailhead enrichment. Double-chamfered round arches. In piers and arches alternating blocks of ironstone. Much remodelling c. 1300, i.e. the chancel arch and the chancel windows with Y- and intersected tracery, the arch from the chancel into a former S chapel (now vestry), and the S aisle with Y- and intersected windows (in the E window the middle light is blocked in its lower part for a reredos or an image). In the chancel a most interesting EASTER SEPULCHRE consisting of a low segmental arch on filleted shafts and above it two aumbry doors with a pitched roof like that of a shrine, but in relief and hence only half. There were originally pinnacles at the corners. They stand on

---

* Professor Zarnecki compares this, and the corbels of the N door, with the Norman doorways at Ely Cathedral.

small head-stops. Perp tower top with quatrefoil frieze and
pinnacles. The spire collapsed in 1699. – FONT COVER.
Jacobean, very pretty. – PLATE. Cup, *c.* 1570.

RECTORY, SW of the church and rather big. Dated 1760. Five
bays, three storeys. Centre an unmoulded Venetian window.

MANOR HOUSE, W of the church. Dated 1591, but with a small
pre-Reformation chimney. This consists of two small polygons
of diminishing size. Little gabled smoke openings.

TOLL HOUSE, at the E end of the village. With a semicircular
front. On its r. a HOUSE dated 1663 and still entirely in the
Elizabethan tradition.

UPPER BODDINGTON   4050

ST JOHN BAPTIST. Perp W tower, perhaps of the same date as
the W doorway dated 1629. Inside, an older tower arch. Dec
the slender chancel windows, the S transept S window with
reticulated tracery, and probably the pretty, straight-headed S
and N windows with their small encircled quatrefoils. Four-
bay arcades with octagonal piers and double-chamfered
arches. Two tomb recesses, both of *c.* 1300, that in the N
aisle with a cusped and sub-cusped arch, that in the S transept
with some dog-tooth enrichment. The back wall has the
remains of two pointed-trefoiled blank quadrant arches. –
CHEST. A 'dug-out', iron-bound, on a projecting base with a
quatrefoil frieze. – PLATE. Cup and Cover Paten, 1570;
Breadholder, 1697; Cup, 1750.

(OLD RECTORY, N of the church. Of ironstone. Five bays.
Corner quoins, rusticated doorway, central window with
carved keystone; *c.* 1680. A third storey was added in the early
C19. BB)

UPPER HARLESTONE see HARLESTONE

UPPER STOWE see STOWE-NINE-CHURCHES

UPPER WEEDON see WEEDON

UPTON   7060
1½ m. W of Northampton

ST MICHAEL. Odd Norman windows survive in nave and
chancel. Norman also the N and S doorways and the priest's
doorway, all with shallow-stepped round arches. In the W wall
two small lancets crushed by the W staircase projection of the

tower. The tower was built into the nave in the C14. –
SCREEN. A part re-set in the W wall. – MONUMENTS. Sir
Richard Knightley † 1537 and wife. Made before his death.
Alabaster effigies. Of the panels facing the tomb-chest only
three shield-holding angels remain. – Many tablets, especially
Thomas Samwell Watson Samwell, 1835 by *John Whiting*.
Grecian with mourning female and trophies at the top.

UPTON HALL (now Quinton House School).* The main façade
faces E: an L-shaped front of three storeys, chequered brick
with ironstone dressings. The main portion is seven bays wide.
The central bay, with a pedimented Tuscan doorway, projects slightly, as do the two southern bays. In addition there
are niches dividing the first and second and fourth and fifth
bays of the central five. These contain somewhat cold neo-
classical statues representing the Seasons, of *c.* 1790. The N
wing also has niches, but here they are empty. Rain-water
head with the date 1748 and the initials of Sir Thomas Samwell.
The Samwells bought Upton in 1600 from the Knightleys of
Fawsley, who had owned the house since 1419, and although
most of what we see today is due to the Samwells, the bones
and some of the structure of the Knightley house still survive.
The entrance leads into a wide hall running E–W. On the N
two small sitting rooms, one with a pretty C18 plaster ceiling,
and recesses with garlands below. On the S a tall room rising
through two storeys which is clearly the original great hall
of the early house. The entrance hall thus must be on the site
of the screens passage. Above it is a gallery which looks down
into the hall. The hall (now called the Ballroom) is a splendid
apartment with some of the finest Georgian plasterwork in the
county. Its end walls are decorated with large Rococo medallions with portrait heads of Roman gods and goddesses. In
the long wall is a tall chimneypiece on whose pediment recline
delightful putti holding wheat and grapes on either side of
a benign bust of Ceres. Opposite, a tall niche with an elegant
life-size statue of Apollo, also in stucco. This is signed by
95   *Giuseppe Artari* and dated 1737, and all the work is indeed in
the best manner of the Italian stuccatori. The ceiling, with
Greek key borders, may be later. The gallery at the N end
has a pretty gilded ironwork balustrade. The two doorcases
flanking the fireplace, however, must be later C17 (cf. Webb's
work at Lamport). But the major evidence for the early dating

* This entry is taken from an account of the house specially prepared by
Bruce Bailey.

of the hall is the late medieval roof which survives above the hall ceiling. It is probably reconstructed and has two forms of support alternating: a simple arch-braced construction, and, probably later, a collar with screen-like arcading and curved braces. In the s gable of the hall which survives within the roof-space of the s wing is a blocked four-light window with arched heads and moulded label. To the w another gallery chamber with a fireplace with four-centred head. This sw wing was perhaps added by the Samwells, c. 1600, to the earlier hall.

The rest of the house has been altered at various times. The N front, of two storeys with dormers, is basically c17. Inside is a late c17 staircase. Parts of the NE wing may be older. w of the hall some charming Gothick rooms, e.g. the drawing room with a grey marble Gothick chimneypiece. Finally the s rooms, which date from c. 1810–20.

SAXON BUILDING. W of the church a c6 or c7 rectangular timber building was excavated in 1965.

WADENHOE

0080

ST MICHAEL. Outside the village on a hill above the river Nene, a composition of varied grey blocks. Late Norman w tower, see the bell-openings to the E and a small round-headed window. Others are pointed. At the foot to the N three blank arches, round-pointed-round, with leaf capitals. Later saddleback roof. C13 chancel, see the fenestration and the chancel arch on head corbels – the one a green man, the other the type called in other places the man with a toothache. C13 N arcade of three bays. Quatrefoil piers with nailhead decoration. Double-chamfered arches. Then of c. 1300 the s arcade and s windows. Quatrefoil piers with fillets. One of the capitals and the E respond have big unfinished upright leaves.– FONT. Circular, C13. Top with segmental arches and stiff-leaf foliage under them. Below vertical pairs of flowers and of dog-tooth. – PULPIT. C18. – BENCH ENDS. Perp, simple, with one-light panels. – PLATE. Dish, c. 1726; Cup and Cover Paten, 1755; Flagon, 1776. – MONUMENT. Brooke Bridges † 1702. By E. Stanton (Le Neve). Pilasters and a segmental pediment. Three cherubs' heads at the foot.

At the top of the street to the church a HOUSE with a pediment facing towards the street, and a polygonal end facing N, as if it were a toll house. At the start of the road to Pilton a circular

DOVECOTE. Facing the Green the MANOR HOUSE FARM with dates 1653 and 1670. (Inside two overmantels which look half a century earlier. NMR)

WADENHOE HOUSE. 1657 but now nearly all 1858. The old part seems to have been symmetrical, with two gabled end projections. (Inside two simple C17 overmantels. NMR)

WAKEFIELD LODGE see POTTERSPURY

9090

WAKERLEY

St JOHN BAPTIST. Outside the village on a hill. Excellent Norman chancel arch of the style and date of Castor. The bases of the responds have the same flat zigzag pattern and the capitals the same ornamentation with beaded interlace and figures. On the N respond a siege with a castle and knights on horseback, on the S respond foliage trails with monsters. The arch with roll mouldings and broad zigzag (not a Castor motif!) has been made pointed but was originally no doubt round. The blind arches to the l. and r. were probably reredoses for side altars. Of the Norman church in addition corbel-table and frieze at the SE corner of the nave, re-set lozenge frieze inside the S chapel, and one shafted clerestory window can still be recognized inside. Good W tower, Dec below (see the tower arch and the W window) and Perp above. Tall two-light bell-openings with transom. Quatrefoil frieze below the battlements, tall recessed crocketed spire with two tiers of lucarnes in alternating directions. The aisles are in a transeptal position and only two bays long. The S arcade is C14, the N arcade C15. C14 N porch and N doorway, C15 chancel. – FONT. Late C13 with, on one side, a quatrefoil with leaf and flower motifs, on the second a pointed-trefoiled arch. The other two sides are not visible. – SCULPTURE. In the N chapel a re-set Norman frieze of thin, flat lozenges. – MONUMENT. Richard Cecil, second son of Lord Burghley, 1633. The monument is no doubt made out of an existing Easter Sepulchre. Poor craftsmanship. Tomb-chest. Shallow four-centred arch with thin tracery. Richard Cecil built for himself a large mansion between the church and the river.

BRIDGE. Medieval. Five pointed arches, double-chamfered ribs.

8070

WALGRAVE

St PETER. Late C13 W tower. Bell-openings of two lights with a quatrefoiled circle. Spire with small broaches and two tiers of lucarnes. The aisle windows similar. The church is however mostly of the early C14: see the chancel windows, especially the reticulated E window, and the remarkable two-light 'low-side' window of which the part below the transom has four lights with handsome tracery. See also the S porch and the tall three-bay arcades with piers with four shafts and four small hollows between them – a type which, with different proportions, was going to become standard in the C15. The transeptal Langham Chapel, close to the S porch, is assigned to the C17. (Castellation on the church dated 1633.) – ROOF BOSSES. Exhibited in the chancel. – BENCH ENDS. Two, with poppyheads, re-used to the l. and r. of the showcase. – PLATE. Set, 1671. – MONUMENT. Mountague Lane † 1670. Handsome tablet.

(BAPTIST CHAPEL. 1768. Exceptionally fine interior.)

WALGRAVE HALL. Fragment of a larger house. It continued, according to old illustrations, on the l. with a tower and then a lower wing. The fragment is of ashlar and has a gable on the r. It contained the Hall, now subdivided, but of which the plaster coat of arms of the Langhams with the date 1674 remains, and the handsome staircase with an open well, balusters with Ionic heads with decoration of c. 1630, and openwork newel-posts. Four-light mullioned and transomed windows. Good gatepiers.

RECTORY, E of the church. 1687. Ironstone. Two storeys, five bays, wooden cross-windows.

WAPPENHAM

6040

ST MARY. Chancel arch with stiff-leaf capital on the S respond. The chancel is wide, and its windows have Y-tracery. It may be connected with the foundation of an uncommonly large chantry in the church (warden and five priests) which took place in 1327. The N arcade is C13. Three bays. Circular piers, circular abaci, double-chamfered arches, still round. The S arcade is standard and later (octagonal piers, double-chamfered arches). Early C14 niche set diagonally in the angle between chancel arch and S arcade. Perp E window and Perp W tower. – FONTS. The old one is Norman, circular, with two defaced knob-like heads. The present one is octagonal with close patterns of honeysuckle-like leaves. The most likely date is the 1660s. – PLATE. Paten, 1682; Plate, 1710; Cup and Flagon, 1721. – BRASSES. In the S aisle to Thomas Lovett (of Astwell

Castle) † 1492 and wife, 16 in. figures and to Constance Butler
† 1499, a 1 ft figure. – s of the altar Thomas Lovett † 1542 and
wife, 16 in. figures. – In front of the chancel steps a Knight,
c. 1460, 18 in. – Sir Thomas Billing, Chief Justice, † 1481 and
wife. From Bittelsden Abbey, Buckinghamshire. The bottom
parts are missing. The figures were c. 3 ft 5 in. long (nave
floor).

METHODIST CHAPEL. 1860, but still in the decent, modest
Georgian tradition. With arched windows.

THE MANOR, w of the church. Dated 1704. Six bays, two
storeys. Still mullioned windows, but they are of two lights,
upright and with flat frames. Moulded door surround.

VICARAGE, E of the church. Red brick, three bays, no adorn-
ment, and only remarkable for being *Sir George Gilbert Scott*'s
first building. Built in 1833 for his father.

THE LAURELS. Of c. 1700. Five bays, two storeys, quoins.
Doorway with steep open pediment and an oval in it.

ASTWELL CASTLE. *See* p. 96.

8070

WARKTON

ST EDMUND. Not a specially attractive church, except for the
Perp w tower and – of course – the chancel. The tower has
clasping buttresses, a big doorway with tracery in the spandrels, a quatrefoil frieze above the doorway, a transomed three-
light w window, transomed two-light bell-openings, a top
quatrefoil frieze, battlements and pinnacles. The aisles are all
of the 1868 restoration, except for the late C12 arcades of two
bays (circular pier, square abacus, unmoulded round arches).
Specially typical of the High Victorian restoration the chancel
arch with its flowery capitals. The chancel itself was built
shortly after 1749 to receive four large monuments, two or
three of them only planned. Large arched E window with its
original small glass panes. – COMMUNION RAIL. Of the time
of the chancel; simple. – STAINED GLASS. s aisle w window by
Capronnier, 1875. – PLATE. Paten given in 1683.

MONUMENTS. They are placed in large apsed niches to the
l. and r., two on either side. The first two were filled first. They
contain two of *Roubiliac*'s masterpieces, John Duke of
Montagu, 1752, l.; Mary Duchess of Montagu, 1753, r.*

Duke John's monument, ready in the model in 1749 and in

* It is said that the antiquarian *Martin Folkes* helped to design Duke
John's monument.

stone in 1752, has as its centre a big structure of indeterminate shape somewhat like a Rococo pottery stove. On its ledge lies a large putto-boy, his hands busy hanging up an oval medallion with the profile of the duke. To the r., on the base, stands Charity with two children, her arm stretched up to help him. One of the children is weeping and holding an extinguished torch. To the l., on the ground, that is yet lower down, the Duchess with his coronet and shield of arms. The composition thus has the typical Rococo zigzag movement into space, a scheme equally characteristic of Boucher and of Tiepolo. Behind to the l. and r., projecting from the upper part of the structure, a gun barrel and cannon balls and a big flag and the trumpet of Fame.

Mary Duchess of Montagu, 1753. The niche here has 63 sloping sides with cross-bars. Large urn with two putti draping a garland of flowers over it. Below, the three Fates, three beautiful young women, two seated, the third standing, and again in a zigzag composition into space. The composition is amplified specially piquantly by a little naked boy on the r., on the ground.*

Mary Duchess of Montagu, 1775. Designed by *Robert* 64 *Adam*, the sculpture by *P. M. van Gelder*. There is indeed a marked difference between architecture and sculpture. The architecture is exquisitely elegant and chaste. Coupled Ionic pilasters, coffered apse with bands of guilloche, in the wall panels three small figures in relief. The sculpture in comparison is grosser and obtrudes itself much more than Roubiliac's. Although Roubiliac is Rococo, and Adam Early Neo-Classical, their elegance and sense of delicate *nuance* unite them against the perhaps more virile but also less sensitive handling of van Gelder. In the middle of the stage a neo-classical urn. To the l. stands a big angel in a distorted pointing attitude. To the r. the seated Duchess in despair, with two children, and an old woman who has pulled her big mantle over her head. The group seems to get the worst of both worlds. The figures are still excited, the gestures still flaming, but the illusionism of the group, the acting on a stage, as it were, introduces a *verismo* which the artistry of Roubiliac would have abhorred. Yet Canova e.g. has the same *verismo*.

Elizabeth Duchess of Buccleugh † 1827. By *Campbell*. Centrally placed high plinth. On it a very straight, seated

* The stalls in front of the monument ought to be removed forthwith or replaced by new ones with transparent backs.

matron. Symmetrical figures l. and r., a young woman and a youth with an extinguished torch. How virtuous Campbell and his clients must have felt. Here is rectitude for you, and nobility. The vitality of the C18, however, has dried up.

WARKWORTH

4040

St Mary. Much restored and rebuilt in 1840–1 and 1869 by *Driver*, e.g. the top parts of the tower, the chancel, and the s arcade. Most of the original work is Dec, e.g. the s aisle windows, the s transept E window, the arcades of three bays with octagonal piers, capitals decorated with heads in the cardinal directions, and double-chamfered arches. In the N aisle two tomb recesses and the unusually splendid tomb-chest with the effigy of a knight of *c.* 1350 (Sir John de Lyons?).* Against the tomb-chest three mourners in ogee panels with crocketed tops, and between them coupled panels with shields. At the foot a quatrefoil frieze. – In addition a number of BRASSES, and first the headless and legless demi-figure of Sir John Chetwode † 1412 with praying hands (2 ft 3 in. figure, s transept). Then Lady Chetwode † 1430 (3 ft 8 in., s aisle), John Chetwode † 1420 (3 ft 1 in., N aisle), Margaret Brounyng † 1420 (2 ft 11 in., s transept), William Ludsthorp † 1454 (2 ft 9 in., s transept). Finally, yet another MONUMENT worth looking at is that to Wililam Holman † 1740, signed by *R. Mottley*‡ and purely architectural. Warkworth Castle, a mansion with a big gatehouse and semicircular towers later converted into a spectacular Jacobean house and now alas gone, belonged to the Lyons, then to the Chetwodes, and from 1629 to the Holmans. The house was demolished in 1805. – FONT. Circular, with cusped arches, probably C14. – BENCH ENDS. Mostly with tracery, but one with the Annunciation and one with a group of donors and the inscription Ora pro nobis. – PLATE. Cup, 1570.

WARMINGTON

0090

St Mary. A large, noble, and stylistically uncommonly unified church – built completely between *c.* 1180 and *c.* 1280. The story starts with the ground floor of the w tower, see the round-headed windows and the round-headed staircase door-

---

* Mr L. M. Gotch reminds me that this monument is of clunch.
‡ Information received from Miss Helen Thomas.

way (in the N aisle). To this late C12 stage also belong the 27 capitals of both arcades. They are rather flat, octagonal, with waterleaf, very small scallops, or upright crockety leaves. The piers and arches do not belong to them, or at least not the whole piers. The piers are circular in the S aisle, octagonal in the N aisle. They must have been heightened, as at Rothwell. What sort of arches would originally have belonged to them can be seen next door at Polebrook. The fragment of a N aisle W window shows the narrowness of the original aisles. The C13 added the two porches, both simply rib-vaulted, both with fully shafted entrances and fine inner doorways, and that on the S also with handsome blank arcading (cf. the N transept at Polebrook). The S porch is placed in the middle of the S aisle. Is that a sign of a High Gothic, classic desire for balance? Also C13 the W doorway of the tower. Four orders of colonnettes, trefoiled arch with much dog-tooth, and thin filleted mouldings. Outer arch moulding with alternating big dog-tooth and big flowers. Contemporary tower arch, triple-chamfered. Above the W doorway one-light shafted window with dog-tooth and flowers. Quatrefoiled circular window above this with stiff-leaf on the cusps. Rich two-light bell-openings triple-shafted with shaft-rings and plate tracery and dog-tooth. Shortish spire with low broaches and three tiers of lucarnes projecting rather much, so that the tower from a distance looks almost as if it were disfigured by warts.* The lowest lucarnes have two-light openings under a super-arch, a form of c. 1275.

At about that time a great remodelling of the church began. The arcade piers were heightened and new, finely moulded arches provided. The chancel arch with mouldings of the same character was made, its imposts resting on corbels with rich late stiff-leaf capitals. Above the arcade a vault was decided upon. The vaulting-shafts, so far as they have not been renewed into glorious Victorian foliage, are of the same type as those of the chancel arch. The vault is alas of timber, an acute disappointment. Single-chamfered ribs, quadripartite bays with ridge ribs. Bosses with five mitred bishops or abbots, a priest, a bearded man, grotesques. The clerestory windows are of two lights with typical later C13 bar tracery. The same type of windows in the chancel N side and the N aisle, except for the later E window (which has intersecting tracery). The S aisle

* Yet *Sir G. G. Scott*, who restored the nave in 1876, called the tower 'one of the most perfect of its type', so the Rev. Thomas Finch tells me.

windows are also of the late C13: three stepped lights under one tall arch. There are two windows W of the porch and two, with dog-tooth enrichment, E of it.* In the W wall of the S aisle a three-light Perp window; another on the S side of the chancel. The chancel E window is also Perp of five lights, but has late C13 brackets for images l. and r., that on the l. with a human figure. The chancel was restored in 1865 by *Ferrey*.

FURNISHINGS. FONT. Stem of 1662 with small volutes. – ROOD SCREEN. Perp, the upper parts C19. – PARCLOSE SCREEN to the N aisle. Early Renaissance with ogee-headed openings, but the ogees formed of Renaissance detail. Linenfold panelling side by side with pilasters with sunk panels with light Renaissance foliage. – REREDOS. Part of a screen which, with its rounded trefoils under pointed arches, looks remarkably early. – PULPIT. C15, but over-restored. – BENCH ENDS. High and low alternate. With coarse fleurs-de-lis. – DOOR. In the S aisle. C13 with iron hinges. – SCULPTURE. Beautiful C13 corbel, representing Wrath, one of the deadly sins. She is piercing herself with a sword (chancel E wall). – STAINED GLASS. E window 1876. – (N chancel late C13 grisaille. RM) – PLATE. Chalice with lid dated 1569–70; Flagon, 1736; Plate, 1834. – MONUMENTS. Very big plain tomb-chest (chancel N), *c.* 1500? – Thomas Elmes † 1664. Hanging monument. Inscription surrounded by an oval wreath. Columns l. and r. and open scrolly segmental pediment. – Sarah Cuthbert † 1723. Small tablet with bust rising in an open segmental pediment.

MANOR HOUSE. Jacobean with significant alterations of 1677, e.g. the broad cross-windows, the heavily framed doorway, the oval tablet above, the shape of the balusters of the staircase, and the stone fireplaces with heavy eared surrounds, etc.
EAGLETHORPE HOUSE, ½ m. N. Symmetrical C17 front of three bays with mullioned and transomed windows. Inside a door and wooden door surround said to come from Fotheringhay Castle. The door has linenfold panels, the spandrels of the surround are carved. Note the hawk in the fetterlock of Edward IV.

WATFORD

ST PETER AND ST PAUL. Partly of *c.* 1300 etc., partly Perp. Perp the W tower with the big four-light W window and the

---

* Inside the S aisle two tomb recesses.

tall arch towards the nave, and Perp the chancel fenestration. Five-light E window, big three-light side windows. Of the window details of the earlier period the most interesting is the N chapel E window of five lights with two Y-groups l. and r. and above the middle light a big cinquefoiled circle. Other windows pairs of lancets (s), three stepped lancet lights (s), three-light intersected, uncusped (s) and cusped (N). Of the same time the arcades of three bays. Octagonal piers, double-chamfered arches. Long N chapel opening to the chancel in one bay, and one very richly detailed arch no doubt originally holding an important monument. The N aisle and chapel have in their N wall three more tomb recesses. – PLATE. Set, 1720; Almsdish, c. 1800. – MONUMENTS. Sir George Clerke † 1649. Uncommonly noble, very simple architectural tablet. No Jacobean exuberance left. Two black columns and an open segmental pediment. – George Clerke, probably the one who died in 1689 (to the l. of the former). Corinthian columns and an elongated urn at the top.

WATFORD COURT. The N porch carried a date 1568, now illegible. It has a doorway with a four-centred head and above it a curved two-storeyed oriel on a big corbel. The wings of this N porch are C19. The S front is a combination of a Victorian centre (1854), replacing a similar Jacobean feature with two bay-windows, and three-bay wings of two storeys which are dated 1657 and 1659 and have been attributed to *Webb*. These are of deep brown ironstone and have cross-windows with very pretty small bits of volute and scroll decoration in the ears and above the lintels. Similar bits at the ends of the frieze between the two storeys. The house has been allowed to decay and the interior is now past saving (1972). Inside, an exceedingly fine fireplace of c. 1660, with the typical compact garlands of that date in the wooden overmantel. The wall panelling still in small oblong pieces, not yet the big panels of the late C17. A smaller fireplace of the same time with slender volutes on the first floor. Also inside a former outer doorway of 1627, and of the same time a staircase with flat tapering balusters. Several original Jacobean windows survive, and one Elizabethan one with arched lights.

WEEDON

6050

ST PETER. Norman w tower – see the one w window, the large shafted bell-openings, and the low unmoulded (but pointed) arch towards the nave. The body of the church 1825, except for the chancel, which was rebuilt in 1863 by *E. F. Law*. Interior with thin timber piers with thinner shafts and shallow arched braces to connect them longitudinally and also with the aisle walls. This arrangement is probably also of *c.* 1860. – SCULPTURE. Base of an octagonal shaft with monsters. C14 or C15. – PLATE. Cup, 1649.

The church is cut off from the village by the railway viaduct and from the E by the earth wall of the raised Grand Union Canal.

CONGREGATIONAL CHAPEL. 1792. Three bays, segment-headed windows, and two arched doorways. Pyramid roof.

99 BARRACKS. Begun in 1803 and originally quite remarkably extensive. The group consisted of twelve powder magazines, two barracks for two regiments of the line, and the composition of three pavilions which remains. The original barracks have been pulled down. The site was chosen as being the farthest point from any coast, an engagingly naive idea. The composition with the three pavilions is the royal pavilion built for George III to retire to when the feared invasion came. It consists of three yellow brick buildings, the middle one of five bays and three storeys, the side wings of four bays, one of two storeys, one of three.* The middle building has a three-bay pediment. Greek Doric porches. The ground-floor windows are arched. Also of yellow brick is what must be called the gatehouse of the canal wharf. The wharf is protected from invasion by sea by means of a portcullis. The gatehouse has a cupola. Behind it the wharf itself, flanked by four long ranges of red brick on an ironstone ground floor. Each range has eleven bays with arched ground-floor windows and a central archway with Doric pilasters.

THE PRIORY, Oak Street, Upper Weedon. A fragment of a large house. Buttresses and windows with arched lights to E and W.

THE FIRS, Queen Street, at the W end of Upper Weedon. Dated 1692. Five-bay front of two storeys. Upright two-light mullioned windows. Above the doorway a horizontally placed oval window. The gables banded of ironstone and grey oölite.

WEEDON LOIS

ST MARY. Early Norman evidence the herringbone masonry in the W wall and the lower part of the crossing tower. Cruciform churches tend to be early anyway. The rest C14 to C15.

* The side wings are to be demolished (1972).

Dec N doorway – the N aisle is of 1849 – S porch and S doorway, tomb recess in the S aisle, and ogee-headed PISCINA in
the S aisle. In the chancel one blocked lancet window. Perp
the upper parts of the crossing tower. The arches of the
crossing are identical to the W, N, and S, but differ towards the
chancel, where the responds and the abaci are concave-sided.
Many head-corbels and stops in various places. (Beneath the
E window a Dec ogee arch.*) – FONT. Circular, Norman. At
the top hanging lunettes, beaded and with leaf inside (cf.
Dodford). – PULPIT. 1849. Based on the octagonal font in
Bloxham church, Oxfordshire. Stone, Perp, with ogee-
headed panels. Pretty ogee-headed entrance to the pulpit
through a crossing-pier. – WALL PAINTINGS. Two seated
figures above the E arch of the S aisle. – PLATE. Paten, 1685.
– MONUMENT. In the extension to the churchyard, Edith
Sitwell † 1964. By *Henry Moore*. A large tapering upright
slab. Attached to it a square bronze plaque with two delicate
hands in high relief, signifying Youth and Age.
(VICARAGE. Stone. Built between 1696 and 1704. Altered later.)

WEEKLEY

ST MARY. Externally Perp, but for three items. S doorway of
c. 1200. Two orders of shafts, round arch with roll mouldings,
over-restored. In the N wall of the chancel one early lancet,
now leading into the vestry. Dec W tower with battlements
and a short recessed spire. Two tiers of lucarnes. At the sill-
line of the lower tier a band. Triple-chamfered arch into the
nave. Perp interior. Arcades of three bays with piers of the
familiar section with four shafts and four hollows (cf. Kettering). The chancel arch of the same type. E end by *Blomfield*,
1873. – SCULPTURE. In the E wall of the N aisle fragment of a
Norman slab with e.g. four rosettes. – PLATE. Cup and Paten,
1717. – MONUMENTS. Sir Edward Montagu of Boughton
House, Chief Justice of the King's Bench, † 1557. Recumbent
alabaster effigy. Tomb-chest with a shield in the middle,
flanked by twisted shafts. No indication of the Renaissance
yet. – Sir Edward Montagu † 1602. Six-poster attached to the
wall, with three columns and three pilasters covered with
strapwork. The columns have broad shaft-rings. Tomb-chest

---

* Mrs Kathleen Lewis suggests that this may have been a shrine of St
Lucien. There was a priory belonging to St Lucien Beauvais in the village,
and a mineral well dedicated to St Loys (or Lucien).

with two recumbent effigies. The superstructure coffered on the underside. Top with obelisks and a pierced strapwork centrepiece around the arms. – Sir Edward Montagu † 1644. Noble tablet. Marble inscription flanked by two pairs of columns placed one behind the other. Shield under the simple pediment.

Former MONTAGU HOSPITAL. 1611. For a master and six brethren. Very pretty. Two storeys, widely spaced mullioned windows. Centre with a four-centred doorhead, an entablature on brackets, two obelisks on shells, and a bulbous gable with three obelisks. Large painted sundial. Now a private house (1972).

Former FREE SCHOOL, founded in 1624. Four-centred doorhead and inscription. Mullioned windows. C19 additions.

VICARAGE. In the Tudor style, by *Blomfield*, 1873.

ROMAN SETTLEMENT. *See* Kettering.

WELDON *see* GREAT WELDON

6080

WELFORD

ST MARY. The best thing in the church is the E.E. s arcade, five bays long and built all at one go. The first pier is circular, the second circular with four attached shafts (cf. Rothwell), the third octagonal, the fourth again circular. Real crocket capitals of the French type. Double-chamfered arches. The N aisle and arcade are of 1872 (by *E. F. Law*), and only the arched tomb recess is original. Perp w tower with a tall arch to the nave, clasping buttresses, and battlements. Late Perp s chapel of two bays, taller than the aisle. The details inside are coarse and include very large head corbels on the responds.* – FONT. Octagonal, with pointed-trefoiled arches and in the spandrels quatrefoils with pointed quatrefoils in them – probably late C13. – SCREENS. To the N and s chapels; Jacobean. – BENCH ENDS. Two, re-used for the reader's desk, are inscribed William Lovell. – (REREDOS. 1888. A memorial to the Rev. G. Aycliffe Poole. BB) – PLATE. Silver-gilt Paten, *c.* 1330, the only piece of pre-Reformation plate in Northamptonshire. The hand of God appears on it. – Silver-gilt Cup, 1568; Flagon, 1760. – MONUMENTS. Low tomb-chest with shields and quatrefoils in panels. – (Incised slab to a Civilian and his wife, *c.* 1460, the female effigy effaced.) – (Francis

* The date is *c.* 1510 (BB).

Saunders. Later c16. Mural tablet with small allegorical figures. Brass plate with kneeling figures. There is a similar monument at Harrington. BB)

(CONGREGATIONAL CHAPEL. 1793. Large and square.)

MANOR HOUSE, N of the church. Stone, five bays, two storeys, with a porch carrying a broken pediment on Tuscan columns.

The former GEORGE HOTEL, at the N end of the village (actually in Leicestershire). Brick, embattled, and with an embattled porch. A CANAL WHARF adjoins the building.

Welford is a brick village altogether.

WELLINGBOROUGH

8060

CHURCHES

ALL HALLOWS. Well placed in a churchyard with old trees and away from the traffic of the town. The only Norman survival is the S doorway. The shafts are decorated with zigzag and the arch has a zigzag moulding at r. angles to the wall surface. Otherwise there is much of the late c13 to early c14, and much that is Perp, the latter telling more outside, the former more inside. The W tower is of c. 1250–1300, its lower part in bands of ironstone and grey stone, the upper part grey. W doorway with three orders of shafts. A rose window above it with six arches radiating from a circle. Much-shafted pairs of two-light bell-openings, spire with low broaches and two tiers of lucarnes. Arcades of c. 1300, four bays, octagonal piers, double-hollow-chamfered arches. Dec chancel with a spectacular five-light E window. The lights are ogee-arched, but the top is still a circle with three inscribed cusped trefoils. Up the jambs and the arch little heads and flowers. Dec porches, both two-storeyed, that on the S side vaulted below with a tierceron star and curious details. Perp N and S chapels with stone piers of four-shafts-and-four-hollows section. Perp most windows and the copious battlements. There are several Perp roofs, the best being the panelled one of the S transept with angels and bosses.* – SCREENS. Perp. To both chancel chapels, with broad one-light divisions and much small tracery above the arches. – STALLS. Six, with MISERICORDS. They represent a wood carver, an ale-wife with a customer, a mermaid, an eagle, two lions, a fox, and a goose. – WALL PAINT-

* The church was restored by *E. F. Law* in 1861 (R. Hubbuck).

ING. S transept. Ascension by *Hans Feibusch*, 1952. – STAINED GLASS. E window by *Alexander Gibbs*, 1871. – The church has the best collection of modern stained glass in the county. – S aisle W window by *Evie Hone*, 1955. Excellent, in a Continental Expressionism, with the Lamb, the flames of the Holy Ghost, the ark, the seven-branched candelabrum, loaves and fishes, etc. – N aisle W window by *Patrick Reyntiens*, designed by *John Piper*, 1961. Symbols of the Evangelists above emblems of the prophets. As impressive as the Evie Hone window. Also Expressionist, in brilliant colours. – S chapel W end: another window by *Piper* and *Reyntiens*, 1969. Abstract, quieter in mood, the colours green, red, but mostly blue. – S chapel, second window from E. St Crispin and Crispinian. By *Jean Barillet*, 1962. – W tower rose window. By *Piper*, 1964. – ROYAL ARMS. Stuart, carved wood. – PLATE. All silver-gilt. Cup and Cover Paten, 1564; Cup, Paten, and two Flagons, given by Sir Paul Pindar, 1634; Paten, 1719; Cup bought in Spain, *c.* 1730. – MONUMENTS. Tablet dated 1570. Two tapering atlantes, the tapering pedestals with a vertical band of linked oblongs and ovals (cf. Rushton Hall). Shield with two supporting figures. Pediment at the top. – John Frederick † 1773. Nice, with an urn before an obelisk. By *Nicholas Love*.

ALL SAINTS, Midland Road. 1867–8 by *C. A. Buckeridge* (GR). Enlarged 1890. Large, with an apse, but without a tower. Lancet and Geometrical windows. Low W porch. – STAINED GLASS. By *Kempe*. Apse 1887, S aisle 1893, chancel N 1903. – PLATE. Silver-gilt Cup, Spanish, *c.* 1750; Cup and Paten, 1725.

ST BARNABAS, St Barnabas Street. 1950–4 by *Paul J. J. Panter*. Light brown brick with a square SW tower, block shapes altogether, and square-headed slender windows. Low, passage-like aisles, round-arched openings towards them. Square E end with a small circular window above the altar, crossed by a large cross outside.

ST MARY, Knox Road. *Sir Ninian Comper*'s most complete and, it is said, favourite achievement. The money was given by the Misses Sharman. Begun with the N chapel in 1908 and built gradually, until the nave was reached in 1930. The furnishing is not yet entirely complete now, but it glistens and reveals and conceals to one's heart's delight. The building is severe, the furnishings are full of fantasy and fearless of the mixing of styles. Every detail inside and outside, right down to the iron gates from the street, is by Comper. The external style is Perp, the material ironstone. Severely simple w tower. Nave with clerestory. Two-storeyed N porch with a tall polygonal turret, open in its top stage. It is placed unusually far to the E. The interior has eight bays of tall concave-sided octagonal piers with capitals decorated with lilies. They carry a most flamboyant lierne-vault of plaster with pendants. It was intended to be all blue and gold. At present only the w bay, the E bay, and the part above the rood screen are painted. Of furnishings there is more than one can enumerate; a ROOD SCREEN with gilded and painted Tuscan columns and Gothic loft and rood, a SIDE SCREEN to the N chapel, a SCREEN round the lobby past the porch, the ORGAN CASE above this lobby, the BALDACCHINO over the altar, with gilded Corinthian columns, the gilded FRONTAL, the gilded SCREEN round the font. The FONT CANOPY, blue and gold, with Tuscan columns, spire, and bulgy pinnacles, is by J. S. Comper, 1969. – STAINED GLASS. The N chapel E window is a memorial to Mrs Comper † 1932. Her ashes are in the N chapel. The chancel E window is of 1919–21.

OUR LADY OF THE SACRED HEART, Ranelagh Road. 1885–6 by S. J. Nicholl. The tower was not built. The interior has a strange junction of transepts and chancel chapels. Rose-window at the E end. See p. 518

(CEMETERY. Spiky Gothic chapel of 1857–8 by E. F. Law. BB)

CONGREGATIONAL CHURCH, High Street. By E. Sharman to a plan by Caleb Archer. 1875. Egg-shaped plan with projections. These are gabled, and the windows are pointed, and that does not marry with the curves of the oval. But as a plan it remains interesting. Drew in 1925 called it 'the most successful experiment in free church architecture in this country'.

FRIENDS' MEETING HOUSE, St John's Street. 1819. A delightful little building of ironstone. Four arched windows and a modest porch. Hipped roof.

PUBLIC BUILDINGS

TECHNICAL COLLEGE, N of the church. By the County Architect, A. N. Harris, 1960–8. A group of different heights. The largest building, in plan two linked trapezia, has canted end walls faced with reconstituted ironstone (1964–6). A low curtain-walled range of workshops behind (1960–1).

WELLINGBOROUGH SCHOOL, London Road. By Talbot Brown, 1879–95. Additions of 1908 (Chapel), 1912 (Junior

School), 1934 (Classrooms). More recently, a new Dining Hall has been added, by *David Roberts*, 1962, and Junior School Classrooms (1967), Music School (1971), and Dormitories (1972), all by *Sursham, Tompkins & Partners*. A new Arts Block is planned.

VICTORIA SCHOOLS, Mill Road. 1895, also by *T. Brown*. An early case of a kind of neo-Georgian. Both buildings have cupolas.

TECHNICAL GRAMMAR SCHOOL, Weavers Road. Extensive system-built additions by the County Architect, *John Goff*, 1970–1. The largest block faced with rough ribbed concrete panels. The original buildings are of 1955–7.

COUNTY HIGH SCHOOL, London Road. 1912 by *Sharman & Archer*. Also neo-Georgian, red brick with rounded pedimental gables. Behind, extensions by the County Architect, *A. N. Harris*, 1967. Red brick and concrete.

GRAMMAR SCHOOL, Doddington Road. 1930 by *Talbot Brown & Fisher*. In the same style, with cupola, but in a version clearly of between the two wars. (Extensions by the same firm 1963–5.)

JOHN LEA SECONDARY MODERN SCHOOL, Doddington Road. 1956–7 by the County Architect, *A. N. Harris*. Long curved front with curtain walling. The Hall with a tower separate to the r.

(BREEZEHILL SECONDARY SCHOOL, Gold Street. By the County Architect, *John Goff*, 1965–7 and 1971–2.)

YOUTH CENTRE, Rock Street. A Gothic school of 1873 ingeniously converted by the County Architect, *John Goff*, in 1969–71, with a new interior. Half of the main building consists of a hall, open to the roof, with a movable stage at one end. The other half has an inserted floor, with coffee bar, club room, etc., on the first floor.

PARK HOSPITAL, Irthlingborough Road. The former WORK-HOUSE, with later additions. The original brick building with its cruciform wings is of 1835. Extensions in progress 1971–2 by *A. L. Arschavir* of the Oxford Regional Hospital Board.

See p. 518

TELEPHONE EXCHANGE AND POST OFFICE, Midland Road. Large, but not too obtrusive in a town still full of small buildings. Forceful projecting mullions above a brick-faced ground floor. By *Gotch, Saunders & Surridge*, 1968–71.

STATION. 1857 by *C. H. Driver*. Dark red brick, round-arched windows, and a bargeboarded gable.

PERAMBULATION

We start by the church. The OLD GRAMMAR SCHOOL
(Church Hall) is on the NW of the church facing the church-
yard. It has a date 1617. Mullioned windows. Gables above
the doorway and one dormer. Next door PRIORY COTTAGE
and No. 27, also C17. From the W end of Church Street
HIGH STREET turns NW and SE. To the NW at its end
BROAD GREEN, an attractive triangular green with old trees.
The best buildings are on the N side. From E to W: No. 27
(MANOR HOUSE), a small C17 two-storey house with early
C19 doorcase. Octagonal brick chimneys. Then, set back,
HATTON HALL, mostly C19 Tudor. To be converted into a
hotel, with extensions at the back by *Barker*, *Hammond &*
Cox. In HATTON AVENUE a nice barn dated 1783. Further
on No. 37 Broad Green, C18, then, much grander, HATTON
HOUSE, late C18, of ironstone, five bays and two and a half
storeys. Arched doorway and windows above it. Finally
HOM-I-LEA, late C18 with a good doorcase. In the SE part
of the High Street LEIGHTON HOUSE, early C19, of two
bays and two and a half storeys. Doorcase and window
frames of alternating rustication. The former stables are nicely
neo-classical. Next door the CONSERVATIVE CLUB, by *W.*
Talbot Brown, 1882, aware of the Norman-Shaw revolution,
i.e. with window aprons and two gables plastered and with
incised ornament and inscription. On the other side from the
Conservative Club, No. 29 is C18, with central round-headed
windows.

To the W from the S end of High Street OXFORD STREET.
Nos 61–2 are an early C19 double house of six bays. The two
doorways adjoin and have one rather stretched-out door surround with Tuscan columns and an entablature. Opposite
Nos 61–2, a tall disused SCHOOL of 1859, Gothic, with much
polychrome decoration. Then WEST END HOUSE, Early
Georgian, of five bays and two storeys with segment-headed
windows, and WESTLANDS, late C18 with altered ground
floor. Opposite, No. 18 (WELFARE OFFICE), also late C18,
with several Venetian windows. After that Victorian villas in
their gardens; on the l. KENROYAL with an Italianate tower
(1864).*

SE from the High Street by Silver Street to the MARKET
SQUARE. At the W end of it the CORN EXCHANGE, 1861,

---

* LOTHERSDALE on the N side, *c*. 1824 in the Tudor style, was demolished
in 1971.

with a thoroughly debased but jolly tower,* was replaced by a nondescript supermarket in 1959–60. The area between Market Street, Silver Street, and Church Street is to form Phase I of the town redevelopment. A new LIBRARY is to be built here (work starting 1972). SE from here SHEEP STREET. The HIND HOTEL faces down Market Street. It has three identical gables with windows of the later C17 type which are tripartite and straight-headed but include an arch in the middle light. The porch reaches over the pavement and has coupled fluted Corinthian piers. (A room on the first floor has a fireplace flanked by giant Corinthian pilasters. NMR) The side of the hotel faces BURYSTEAD PLACE, where Nos 2–3 are early C18 (but with imitation-C17 ground-floor windows). At the end of this a TITHE BARN of Croyland Abbey, of ironstone and limestone striped, six bays divided by stepped buttresses, with two cart entrances.‡ To the S is the entrance to CROYLAND ABBEY, a large and rambling house, now derelict and threatened with demolition (1972). It is chiefly Jacobean and Victorian, but the remains of a medieval house are embedded in the W range.

In Sheep Street on the W side a timber-framed, much renovated house with an oversailing upper floor, then the GOLDEN LION, again with a timber-framed oversailing gable, and No. 20, Georgian, with a front chequered in red and yellow brick and with two shallow ground-floor bow-windows. Finally, facing the S end of Sheep Street, SWANSPOOL HOUSE (Wellingborough U.D.C. offices), early C19, rendered, of five bays and two and a half storeys with all the ground-floor windows in blank arches. The two upper middle windows are of the plainest Venetian kind.

WELLINGTON TOWER see FINEDON

5060
WELTON

ST MARTIN. Dec and Perp. Dec the W tower and the N and S doorways. Tall arcades of four bays, octagonal piers, double-chamfered arches. – SCULPTURE. The corbel on the W wall of the nave is supported by a bearded head, probably C12. – PLATE. Patens, c. 1700 and 1809; Flagon, 1814. – MONUMENTS. Many tablets, e.g. Isaac Astley † 1757 by *William*

* The Corn Exchange was by *Bellamy & Hardy* (G. Hamilton).
‡ Damaged by fire in 1972.

Cox, John Clarke † 1816 by *Samuel Cox Jun.* (still with sarcophagus and obelisk), and John Plomer Clarke † 1826 (turned Gothic).

WELTON PLACE. A mid-C18 house of five bays and two storeys with a rusticated Venetian doorway and a rusticated Venetian window above it. The other windows are segment-headed. Three-bay wing of *c.* 1810. (Interiors of the same date, except for the staircase of *c.* 1750 with three balusters for each tread and carved tread-ends.) The archway from the road to the garden (N of the house) must be of the mid C17.

MANOR HOUSE. Mid Georgian. The front has a canted bay-window in the middle and Venetian windows, heavily detailed, to the l. and r. on both floors. Excellent staircase with three balusters to the tread, one columnar, the other two twisted to different patterns. Carved tread-ends. The staircase comes from the Moot Hall at Daventry, built in 1769.

WEST HADDON

6070

ALL SAINTS. Early C13 arcades and S doorway. The arcades have octagonal piers and double-chamfered arches. One has a stiff-leaf capital. In the chancel one 'low-side' lancet. Most of the windows are altered or renewed. Dec W tower. C18 S porch. The medieval S aisle wall with random ironstone and limestone patterning. – FONT. Square, Norman, with well 35 preserved and interesting sculptured scenes on the four sides. They represent the Nativity, the Baptism of Christ, the Entry into Jerusalem, and Christ in Glory between the Eagle of St John and the Angel of St Matthew. The date proposed by Professor Zarnecki is *c.* 1120. Fine timber roof. The principals rest on figures. – COMMUNION RAIL. C17. – STAINED GLASS. S aisle E. By *Pugin*, 1850.* – PLATE. Cup and Cover Paten, 1610.

(BROWNSTONES, next to the church. The former rectory. Dated 1676. Stone front of three bays. Inside, a good staircase with turned balusters, and a chimneypiece said to be made up from an Elizabethan moulded handrail from Holdenby. BB)

ALMSHOUSES, at the W end of the village. Red and blue brick. With porches and a cupola.

(WEST HADDON HALL. Late Georgian. The top storey demolished in 1946. The original entrance was on the S. The present W entrance is C19. GI)

* According to information kindly given me by Mrs Stanton.

5040

WESTON

¾ m. w of Weedon Lois

BAPTIST CHAPEL. 1791. Plain three-bay front with very elongated windows and a pyramid roof.

WESTON HALL. Late C17 with a wing of 1776–7. The front of this to the N has been cemented, gabled, and generally tudorized *c.* 1825–30. The s front is in its original state. Fine fireplace in the drawing room. This comes from Greatworth and must be of *c.* 1740–50. The opening is flanked by cherubs in profile growing out of slender volutes. The staircase is partly of *c.* 1700 (strong twisted balusters), partly of the C18 (slender twisted balusters – two to a tread).

ARMADA HOUSE, opposite. The house was dated 1588. A picturesque gabled and dormered building with mullioned and mullioned and transomed windows.

HOUSE, sw of the chapel. Dated 1694. The windows are mullioned but arranged symmetrically (three bays) and have broad flat frames curving up slightly towards the outer border.

7090

WESTON-BY-WELLAND

ST MARY. 1863–6 'in exact facsimile' (Kelly) of its medieval predecessor. The w tower ashlar, the rest ironstone. Tall pairs of two-light bell-openings with Y-tracery, continuous circular mouldings, i.e. late C13. The other external details Dec. s arcade with quatrefoil piers, N arcade with octagonal piers. Double-chamfered arches. Low tomb recess in the N aisle. – PLATE of 1865 and 1868.

WESTON FAVELL see NORTHAMPTON, p. 348

6060

WHILTON

ST ANDREW. Unbuttressed C13 w tower with upper parts of *c.* 1769. Round-arched bell-openings with Y-tracery. Chancel, higher than the nave, of 1877. The Perp chancel arch however is original. C13 arcades of two bays with circular piers, circular abaci, and double-chamfered arches. The E bays are narrow to connect with the chancel. – PLATE. Set, 1779. – MONUMENT. Tablet to Richard Freeman † 1749 with Ionic pilasters and urn at the top. Rococo cartouche at the foot. A good piece.

OLD RECTORY. Early C19, whitewashed. Five bays with a three-bay pediment and a doorway with broken pediment.

HOME FARMHOUSE. Georgian, of brick, five bays, two storeys.
Several other pleasant houses.

GRAND UNION CANAL. There is a sequence of six locks at
Whilton.

ROMAN SETTLEMENT. *See* Norton.

WHISTON   8060

ST MARY. On a hill, quite on its own, only to be reached on
foot. The church is indeed a monument, built by one man,
Anthony Catesby, and, it seems, within about twenty or thirty
years, and not altered since. The monument to Thomas
Catesby (*see* below) mentions the date 1534 – a last-minute
date, even if it represents the completion of the church. The *See*
early C16 anyway fits the design. The tower must have been *p.*
built first.* It is splendid enough for Somerset. Brown 518
and grey ashlar bands. Friezes of quatrefoils at the base and
below the bell-stage. Buttresses first of the clasping type, then
turning to the set-back type, then developing into pairs of
square pinnacles set diagonally. The bell-openings are pairs
of two lights each with transom. All four are under one hood-
mould with ornamented spandrels. Battlements with tracery
panelling, tall pinnacles, many gargoyles. (At the base of the
tower these are demons and grotesques, higher up they are
angels, some with symbols of the Passion. Enormous water
spouts at the battlement stage: two monkeys to the S and a
bearded woolcomber to the E. BB) Nave and aisles and slightly
projecting chancel. Windows of three, four, and five lights, all
with varieties of the same tracery – monotonous but incisive.
Shallow embattled S porch below the second window.
Attractive interior, airy, with slender piers (four-shafts-four- 31
hollows section), shafts on angel corbels carrying the roof
principals, traceried spandrels, and no clerestory or chancel
arch.‡ Good roofs with moulded and carved beams. – FONT.
Octagonal, Perp, with panelled stem and shields in quatrefoils
on the bowl. – FONT CANOPY. Of oak, with five turned cork-
screw posts supporting a pyramidal top, an unusual design.

---

* Mr Bailey points out that the aisle walls overlap the base corners of the
tower, and that inside, there are buttresses on either side of the tower arch.
There are also other differences between the tower and the body of the
church: the tower is more elaborately ornamented and is of ironstone and
limestone; the body of the church only of limestone.

‡ The quality of all the masonry is very high. Mr Colvin and Mr Bailey
consider that royal masons could have been involved.

Probably mid-c17 (Alec Clifton-Taylor). – BENCHES. Several groups, square-topped with thin buttress-shafts. – COMMUNION RAIL. With turned balusters, early c18? – CANDLESTICKS on the benches. Pretty ironwork, with flowers, probably *c.* 1890. – STAINED GLASS. E window, 1858. (By *O'Connor*. W window by *Mayer* of Munich. BB) – PLATE. Cup, 1570; Paten, c17. – MONUMENTS. Thomas Catesby, erected 1700. Standing monument with two busts on a base showing in relief three kneeling daughters, a small child with a skull, and a baby in swaddling clothes. Ionic columns l. and r. and pediment. – First Lord Boston † 1775. By *Nollekens*. Standing monument. Mourning woman bent over an urn and holding an extinguished torch. Grey obelisk behind. (Both these in the chancel.) – Mary Irby † 1792. With a weeping putto by an urn. Also by *Nollekens* (s aisle). – Second Lord Boston † 1835. By *W. Pitts*. With a relief of the praying family and a rising angel (N aisle).

RECTORY (former), near the church. Tudor, 1852.

MOAT HOUSE (formerly Place House). Oblong buttresses at one corner and some windows with depressed-arched lights.

WHITFIELD

ST JOHN EVANGELIST. By *H. Woodyer*, 1870. In the E.E. style, with a broach spire. Rather bleak N arcade, small N lancet windows connected outside by blank arcading. – STAINED GLASS. By *Morris & Co.*, *c.* 1898–1914. – PLATE. Flagon, 1707; Cup and Paten, 1708; Breadholder, *c.* 1709.

WHITTLEBURY

ST MARY. c13 W tower. The arch towards the nave is pointed and single-stepped. It has dog-tooth decoration in the step and the hood-mould. A nutmeg frieze higher up on the wall. The S porch entrance seems *c.* 1300. Pretty, probably recent, floor of squares made of slates standing on end and placed in alternating directions. The N windows are Late Perp. All the rest is restored beyond redemption. Arcades of three bays with octagonal piers and double-chamfered arches. One capital on the N side must be re-used, as it is late c12. The SW respond is triple-shafted and was probably built in the c13. The chancel mostly of 1878. – STAINED GLASS. Chancel S by *Mayer & Co.* of Munich, 1895; terrible. – MONUMENT. Mrs

Carolette Bradshaw † 1820, by *Chantrey*. Grecian. She is rising gently to heaven.

WHITTLEBURY LODGE. 1865-8 for the Earl of Southampton. By *William Burn*. Damaged by fire and rebuilt in 1871. In the Tudor style, with many gables. Stables with an obtrusive, tall bell-tower.* (FARMHOUSE by *William Wilkinson* of Oxford, 1863-4. A. J. Saint)

SETTLEMENT. Surface features and a few small finds indicative of an Iron Age settlement have been noted on the N edge of Whittlebury Forest, in Old Tun Copse.

ROMAN VILLA, W of the Gullet, beside Watling Street, in the NE corner of the parish. The site was discovered in 1850. Enclosed with a walled courtyard of 150 by 195 ft, with a gate in the centre of the SE side, the bath block, with a mosaic-decorated room, lay in the S corner, adjoining the presumed main building. This lay to the NW, outside the main court-yard. One of the mosaics from this area was given by the Duke of Grafton to Queen Victoria and relaid in a dairy at Windsor. Other finds included painted wall-plaster fragments, 'terra sigillata', and much general domestic refuse.

WICKEN

7030

ST JOHN EVANGELIST. Tall W tower, said to be of 1617. The bell-openings are pairs of lancets. Parapet, pinnacles. The rest of the church of 1758-67, according to an inscription in the N aisle 'designed and built' by *Thomas Prowse*, an amateur and friend of Sanderson Miller. The execution was left, it seems, in the hands of the architect *John Sanderson*.‡ The windows made correctly Gothic in 1897, when transepts were added. Prowse's church is a strange design. Nave and nar-row aisles of the same height, tall quatrefoil piers with two shaft-bands rather than shaft-rings. Capitals with leaves in the French later C13 style. Abaci square with hollows at the angles. The aisles are groin-vaulted, the nave tunnel-vaulted with penetrations or groin-vaulted with disappearing groins. The chancel projects and is gaily fan-vaulted (in plaster) with pendants hanging from openwork ribs. Nave and chancel do not go together, it seems. The nave is a much less pretty but much more serious conception, reminiscent somehow of the work of the Jesuits in the early C17 in the Netherlands and Germany. – FONT. Square, of Purbeck marble, with three

* Demolished 1972.
‡ *See Wicken Church 1758–1958* by C. S. Dickin Moore, p.1.

shallow blank arches to each side. – STAINED GLASS. Chancel N by *Eleanor Brickdale*, 1921. – PLATE. Paten and Flagon, 1721; Cup and Paten, 1770. – MONUMENTS. Charles Hosier and wife, Prowse's parents-in-law, erected 1758. By *Sir Henry Cheere* (BB). Rococo, with an obelisk in front of an open pediment. Urn and many garlands. Extremely pretty. – Mrs Sharp, daughter of Charles Hosier, † 1747. With a standing putto. Pediment at the top. Probably by the same hand as the foregoing.* – John Sharp † 1726. With two seated putti and an obelisk. – John Hosier Sharp † 1734, simpler. – Elizabeth Sharp † 1810. Signed by *J. Bacon Jun.* (BB). Draped urn; relief on the base. Weeping willow by its side.

MANOR FARM. Immediately S of the church. C17. Flat front of three bays with mullioned windows. Formerly the gatehouse to the Manor. It used to have a central archway.

RECTORY, a little further SW. Built in 1703, it is said out of the debris of Lord Spencer's mansion. Seven bays, the first two and last two gabled. Two storeys. Doorway with open segmental pediment. The upper windows all have open segmental pediments ending in small volutes, except for the middle one, which has scrolly double curves. The glazing bars on the ground floor are original.

WICKEN PARK. The present house was a lodge. It was sold in 1716 to Charles Hosier, who enlarged it. It has since been enlarged more. The house of Charles Hosier seems to have been seven bays wide and two and a half storeys high. Very plain. Lower two-bay wings to the garden. To the entrance side they are treated as broad canted bay-windows. Close by an older house, dated 1614, with gables and mullioned windows.

WILBARSTON

8080

ALL SAINTS. Ironstone; much renewed. The E bay of the S arcade has a wide round arch once opening into a transept. It rests on the E side on a respond which may represent a remodelled Norman piece with nook-shafts. In the N arcade it is the W and E responds which are Norman. Upright leaves on the capitals. The W respond must be re-used, if the Norman church indeed had transepts before it had aisles. The priest's doorway has a round arch with a slight chamfer. That also is of before 1200. C13 the rest of the S arcade: circular piers and

* It is identical with the monument by *T. Bastard* in the cloister of Wells Cathedral (BB).

circular abaci; pointed arches with one chamfer and one hollow chamfer. The E pier was adjusted to carry the former transept arch. Hence the two (renewed) detached shafts. The three regular arches of the N arcade with their sunk quadrant mouldings seem to be of *c.* 1300. Late C13 W tower, small. Twin bell-openings with separating shaft. Spire with low broaches. Two tiers of lucarnes. Tower arch with three slight chamfers. Fine late C13 S doorway with a five-cusped arch and fine mouldings. Fine S aisle windows of three lights with a big circle in bar tracery (filled in with Victorian trefoils). Dec the N chapel arch and the REREDOS at the E end of the S aisle, a big cusped and sub-cusped niche with an ogee arch. – PLATE. Cup and Paten, 1570; Breadholder, 1637.

WILBY

8060

ST MARY. A remarkable Dec W tower. It starts square with diagonal buttresses and below the bell-stage turns octagonal. The buttresses develop into diagonally placed pinnacles. There is a quatrefoil frieze and a parapet. The pinnacles connect with the octagon by flying buttresses. The octagon has two-light bell-openings in the cardinal directions. Then there is another quatrefoil frieze, a parapet with pinnacles, and a recessed spire connected again with the pinnacles by short flying buttresses. Two tiers of lucarnes. The W doorway with traceried spandrels and niches l. and r. is a C15 insertion. The small square upper W window with tracery in the form of the so-called four-petalled flower is original. Early C14 S arcade of four bays with octagonal piers and double-hollow-chamfered arches. Tall chancel, rebuilt in 1853, except for the low-side window, which is original work of the C13. – PULPIT. Jacobean, with two tiers of the usual flat, broad arches. – STAINED GLASS. Chancel S. Signed by *A. Lusson* of Paris. – (Nave S. C14 foliage and grisaille. RM)

WILBY HALL. Georgian. Five bays, two storeys, pedimented doorway with Gibbs surround.

WINWICK

6070

ST MICHAEL. A cruciform C13 church to which a Perp W tower was added and whose chancel was replaced by a Victorian one in 1853 (by *E. F. Law*). Of the C13 church the lancet windows and the tomb recesses in the transepts bear witness. The W tower has clasping buttresses and is ashlar-faced. – FONT.

1821 by *Rickman*, the inventor of the terminology of E.E., Dec, and Perp. Panelled stem widening towards the bowl. Angel heads against the underside of the bowl. Octagonal bowl with shields and quatrefoils. – BARREL ORGAN. – PLATE. Flagon, 1660. – MONUMENTS. Sir William Craven † 1707, large architectural tablet, without effigies. Two putti at the top. In front of the altar step, black ledger stone for the same. The stone is known to be by *Edward Stanton*, and so he was probably responsible for the monument as well. – Maria Craven, 1736. Similar architectural tablet, but simpler. Signed by *Samuel Huskisson* of London.

WINWICK MANOR HOUSE. Brick, with vitrified brick diapering, gabled, C16. Only half of the house is preserved. It was originally of half-H shape, with the porch and probably the hall bay projecting in the re-entrant angles. The back doorway is preserved which corresponded to the front porch. The original windows are mullioned and have arched lights. Other windows straightforward mullioned and transomed. The staircase has flat tapering balusters and so goes with the later windows.* In line with the original entrance a GATEWAY in the wall of the front garden. This is a very fine piece of Elizabethan display, tripartite with four Roman Doric columns. In the spaces between the outer columns panels with rosettes and strapwork in simple geometrical forms. In the centre round-headed arch. In the spandrels medallions with figures. The columns carry a metope frieze. In the metopes rosettes and bucrania. Semicircular pediment at the top. The back is treated so roughly that the question has been asked if the gateway was not originally a porch. At r. angles to the house and facing the former front garden the STABLES, also of diapered brick.

WOLLASTON

ST MARY. An odd-looking church, because the tower with its tall spire is a crossing tower and the nave is of 1737. The tower is Dec, with bands of ironstone and grey oölite below, ashlar from the bell-stage upwards. The bell-openings are pairs of two lights. The broaches of the spire are low and have pinnacles standing on them. Three tiers of lucarnes in alternating directions. The arches inside are hollow-chamfered and the

---

* The house was altered by *Morley Horder* c. 1920. A watercolour drawing of c. 1870 shows that the house had already been reduced in size (GI).

capitals are therefore partly concave-sided. In the N transept is a double tomb recess. Nave and aisles are separated
by giant Tuscan columns. The nave ceiling is flat, the aisle
ceilings cove up to it. Externally the nave has three tall round-
arched windows with flat intersected tracery. Broad W front
with an arched doorway and a circular window over. Instead
of the S transept a lobby of 1737. The chancel was re-
gothicized in 1902. – FONT. Baluster stem and heavily
gadrooned bowl. – PULPIT of c. 1737 with marquetry. – Open
PEWS, rather c. 1800 than 1737. – WEST GALLERY with
Roman Doric pilasters. – PLATE. Set, 1773.

WOLLASTON HALL. Built c. 1738. Seven by six bays. One and
a half storeys. Hipped roof. A pretty iron veranda to the S.
(Handsome staircase with plaster ceiling. Earlier cellars.)
STABLES with a three-arched centre, hipped roof, and cupola;
C18. (The house has belonged to the Scott Bader Company
since 1940, and they have built a conference hall, laboratories,
etc. The architects are *Sir John Brown, Henson & Partners*.
The conference hall is a pavilion with a hyperbolic-parabo-
loid ('collapsed-tent') roof. When completed in 1959 it was
the largest in the country. It is of timber, 60 ft square. The
dip is 12 ft. Curtain walling and brick buttressing as a support.)

(WOLLASTON HOUSE. 1856. Said to have been built by *George
Burnham*, a Wellingborough solicitor, for himself. Italianate,
of L-shape, with a tower in the re-entrant angle, and typical
windows of tall arched lights, as e.g. illustrated in Loudon's
Encyclopaedia. Bargeboarded eaves, low-pitched roofs.)

A handsome group of houses to the SE and SW of the church,
especially those at the start of the street called HICKMIRE.

(The VCH mentions a large house of 1657 at the SW end of the
village with a staircase with turned balusters. The Rev. A.
Betteridge draws attention to a disused INDEPENDENT
CHAPEL dated 1752 in a yard off the High Street.)

In the middle of the town, a short distance S of the church,
stands a rather low MOTTE, locally called Beacon Hill.

WOODEND *see* BLAKESLEY

WOODFORD

ST MARY. The interior is one of the standard archaeological
puzzles. The arcades are very long and their elements
ominously various. The history which results is something like

this. A Norman church had its w wall at the e end of the short first bay. It received a N aisle of three bays c. 1200. This has circular piers and capitals with leaf characteristic of that date, circular abaci, and unmoulded round arches. At the same time the then chancel received a N chapel of two bays. The position of the original chancel arch is clear, and the arch from the aisle into the chapel also remains. The arcade details are the same, except that the capitals are moulded and have some nail-head enrichment. After that a w tower was begun w of the Norman nave and connected with it by short pointed arches. The approximate date of the tower can be guessed from its lancet windows, two-light bell-openings with a shaft, trefoil top frieze, shafted pinnacles, and spire, a broach rising behind a parapet with pinnacles and having three tiers of lucarnes. The tower must have been started before 1250 and built into the c14. By then much else had happened. The s aisle had been built, of three regular, much wider, pointed arches. This arrangement shows that it already takes the new tower into consideration. The arcade arches stand on an octagonal pier and a circular pier with an octagonal abacus. The aisle was connected with a new s chapel by an arch with circular piers and circular abaci and an unusual arch moulding with two hollows side by side. The over-restored s aisle doorway belongs to the same time; see the odd leaves on the roll moulding of the trefoiled doorway. The s porch again need not be later. It has a quadripartite rib-vault. In connexion with the s aisle an aisled s transept was begun but soon given up. The first piers, the steep aisle arches, and a springer of an aisle vault can however still be seen. The piers are quatrefoil, and one has a little stiff-leaf in the moulded capital. Of the old chancel there remains, close to its e end on the N side, a large tomb arch of the early c14 with a depressed two-centred arch. On its N side, i.e. at the e end of the N aisle, it cut into, and half destroyed, c13 SEDILIA. The new chancel is in its details of the c19,* except the c13 SEDILIA and PISCINA and the blank arcading opposite. Most of the windows of the church are Perp. – DOOR. In the s aisle, with tracery. – (STAINED GLASS. N chapel. Apostles and prophets of c. 1420. RM) – PLATE. Cup, 1570; Paten, late c17. – MONUMENTS. Two effigies of oak, Knight and Lady, he cross-legged, both very slender, early c14.

* By *James Fowler* of Louth (but the nave was restored by *Slater*) (N. Taylor).

RECTORY. 1820, with a closed-in porch of Tuscan columns.

RECTORY FARM (or Old Manor House), N of the church. The s side has buttresses and a doorway of the C13 or early C14 with continuous mouldings.

(ROUND HOUSE. The inscription says Waterloo Panorama, 1815. This may be unexpected, but the reason is that the Duke of Wellington frequently stayed with the Arbuthnots at Woodford House.*)

(WOODFORD HOUSE. Originally a farmhouse. Bought early in the C19 by Charles Arbuthnot (a close friend of the Duke of Wellington), who demolished the farm buildings to re-erect them ¼ m. SE of the house, which he considerably enlarged. His architect was *Charles Bacon* (who died in 1818) (H. M. Colvin). To the W of the central block he built a commodious stable range and, to the E, a small wing with a billiard room – now the drawing room – and an anteroom, above which are the Duke's bed and dressing rooms. These alterations and additions (according to Mrs Arbuthnot's private journal) were completed by the autumn of 1826. Apparently, therefore, the building programme was spread over thirteen years, as the date above the main doorway is 1813. From the forecourt (on the s side) the house and stables, built of local stone and with low-pitched, deep-eaved roofs, form a delightful group of buildings, with the emphasis on the symmetrical centre block with its regular, typically sashed windows, and flanked by the two recessed but uneven wings on either side of it. The architectural balance of the N elevation has, however, been sadly upset by the protruding billiard room, which was built to the designs of *J. Alfred Gotch* in 1902.)

(WOODFORD RISE. Despite many alterations and additions, this is still a very typical stone-built Northamptonshire house with Collyweston and pantiled roofs and the fine chimney-shafts peculiar to the region. Originally a six-roomed cottage, with direct front to back access, it has gradually acquired the more dignified appearance of a small manor house with a pleasant courtyard and stable range.

The original building is probably C17 and the date-stone of 1729 refers to alterations and additions. These probably include not only the extension of the front by an additional room on the ground and first floors, but also the transformation of the roof space into attic bedrooms with dormer windo s.

* So Mr King kindly tells me, and Mr W. G. Bunning adds that there is a tradition that Wellington found the countryside reminiscent of Waterloo.

Later, the wing at r. angles to the original building was built,
with it forming two sides of the courtyard; the remaining two
sides are defined by the stable block and a garden wall. In the
early C19 a further addition was made to accommodate a new
kitchen and pantry with two rooms above. Finally, in the
1930s, a stone-built dining room was added to the N end of
the main building and the old pantry enlarged. At the same
time the windows along the main SE front, and others overlooking the courtyard, were replaced by stone mullioned
windows, and an ashlar porch took the place of a decaying
wooden one. The fine old oak staircase is said to have come
from the former mansion, now demolished, which stood about
a mile to the NE. In the garage a small Early Dec window.)*

WOODFORD HALSE

5050

ST MARY. Of sandstone. Much restoration in 1878, but
apparently correctly done. N arcade of four bays, circular piers
and octagonal abaci, pointed single-chamfered arches, i.e.
early C13. It is noteworthy that one capital is still of the Late
Norman multi-scalloped type. The S arcade with octagonal
piers and double-chamfered arches is C14 or C15. Externally
much of c. 1300, namely the W tower (cusped Y-tracery in the
W window and bell-openings), the S doorway, and the chancel
(cusped Y and cusped intersected tracery). – FONT. Octagonal
bowl probably of the 1660s. – BENCH ENDS. Some, with
poppy-heads, in chancel and nave. – SCULPTURE. Bottom
part of an image; nave E wall. – PLATE. Cup, 1570; Breadholder, 1688. – MONUMENTS. Effigy of a Lady, stone, early
C14. – Brass to Nicholas Stafford, Vicar, † 1400 (chancel
floor). The figure is 20 in. long. – Mrs Knightley † 1730,
architectural, of variegated marbles. A *Smith* of Warwick
type (*see* Lamport) (BB).

(MANOR HOUSE. Of three bays only. With an elaborately
framed doorway carrying a big segmental pediment. NMR)

HINTON MANOR HOUSE. Late C17, of ironstone, with quoins
and a hipped roof. The SE façade of five bays has georgianized
windows. To the S of it a stable range with mullioned windows.
The SW façade is less regular, but has the original shape and
framing of the windows. They must have had wooden crosses.
Doorway with segmental pediment on brackets.

* Information about the last two houses was kindly given me by Mr W.
Carey Wilson.

(WOODFORD HALSE SOCIAL CLUB, Hinton. Formerly the
Railway Hotel. Large, half-timbered, *c.* 1900. BB)

WOODNEWTON

ST MARY. A cruciform church whose W tower was rebuilt in
the C16. Its arch towards the nave however looks like re-used
material. The double-stepped round (late C12) arch does not
fit the later responds. At the top of the tower battlements and
pinnacles.* The oldest part of the church is the indications of
a nave S wall of before the arcades were built. It appears at the
W end in projections of wall and in the fact that the S transept
N wall is not in line with the S arcade. Late C12 N arch of the
S transept, single-stepped and round. A S aisle was added a
little later, say *c.* 1200–10. Three bays with one round and one
coarse quatrefoil pier, a little nailhead decoration, and, on the
capital of the E respond, a series of human heads. Double-
chamfered arches. To the transept an arch of the same type,
resting on a corbel on the l., on a new or renewed pier on the r.
In the W wall of the aisle traces of a lancet window indicating
that the aisle was formerly narrower. But if that is so, the wall
into the transept must also have been narrower. The respond
seems too thick to assume that. If it was a corbel, as on the
other side, it could have been so. Early C13 also the chancel
S doorway with a zigzag surround to the round-headed opening, the round-headed 'low-side' window to its W, the S
doorway to the aisle, also still round-headed, but with much
dog-tooth, and the materials such as the pointed arch and the
dog-tooth which were used when the porch was remodelled
in 1660. In the late C13 the S aisle was widened and the
transept made part of it. Windows with intersected tracery
(circular mullions) and with (somewhat suspicious) bar tracery
with foiled circles.‡ Perp clerestory. – PLATE. Cup, 1714.

MANOR HOUSE. A most curiously wild composition, as if to
demonstrate how a normal five-bay house of *c.* 1730 can be
made conspicuous. The three-bay centre has three storeys, the
outer bays only one and a half. These outer bays run their
fragmentary pediments up against the middle erection, but in
addition the ground floor of the centre has its own open pedi-

* There is a document recording that 'Newton men' bought battlement
stone 'for their church' from the sale of materials at Fotheringhay in 1573
(M. R. Airs).

‡ The VCH suggests C18 imitation.

ment, and in the open part between the two shanks stands the first-floor centre window. The second-floor window is arched, as are the outer ground-floor windows. The crowning motif is a truncated pediment on which stands the chimneystack.

WOOTTON

7050

St George. The exterior too much renewed to be of interest. The church was restored by *Butterfield* in 1865. In the chancel a C13 lancet and three-light Perp windows. The s and n doorways are of 1300 or thereabouts. The w tower with battlements and pinnacles seems Dec. Two unusually large corbel-heads n and s of the tower arch. C13 arcades of three bays with circular capitals, circular abaci, and double-chamfered arches. – (Font. Expensive. By *G. E. Street*, 1874. BB) – plate. Cup, 1572; Paten, 1828.

Rectory, w of the church. Dated 1630. With mullioned windows and gables.

Workhouse (former), at the corner of the A-road and Water Lane. 1839. Late Classical, of ironstone. One range only. A composition of seventeen bays, with a pedimented higher centre, one-storey connecting links, and end pavilions. Partly demolished (1972).

WOOTTON HALL *see* NORTHAMPTON, p. 354

WOTHORPE

0000

Built early in the C17 for Thomas Cecil, Earl of Exeter, Lord Burghley's eldest son, who died in 1623. It was built for him, so Fuller says in his *Worthies*, 'to retire to while his great house at Burleigh was a sweeping'. Fuller also calls it 'the least of noble houses and the best of lodges'. In ruins since the C18. One of a type of Elizabethan and Jacobean houses which is distinguished by specially compact composition. Barlborough in Derbyshire is probably the nearest relative of Wothorpe. What survives is four corner towers. They are square but have octagonal top storeys and caps. Their windows of one light with the odd square supra-windows with flat volute decoration are curiously reminiscent of Italian Mannerism and completely different from Burghley, or for that matter from Robert Cecil's Hatfield. Between the towers the house projected, i.e. it was cross-shaped with the towers in the re-entrant angles. In the W projection was a big staircase of the same type as Hatfield. The Hall faced N. It was entered in the middle, no longer near one end, as was the medieval and Elizabethan tradition. In front of it was a porch and a courtyard flanked by subsidiary wings. The forecourt was entered by a gateway which survives. It has a curious stepped gable and niches to the l. and r.

(CLARE LODGE. Built c. 1850 by the architect E. Browning for himself. He used some ecclesiastical fragments. H. M. Colvin and NMR)

YARDLEY GOBION 7040

ST LEONARD. 1864 by E. F. Law. Nave and chancel; bellcote at the E end of the nave. Geometrical and Decorated detail.

YARDLEY HASTINGS 8050

ST ANDREW. Short early C13 W tower. Twin nook-shafted bell-openings with separating shaft, the whole under a round arch. The connexion between tower and nave is only a doorway with a slight chamfer. Of the Norman nave wall a little remains W of the arcades, which are of c. 1300. Three bays. Octagonal piers, moulded capitals, double-chamfered arches. The S capitals show a slightly earlier date than the N capitals. The E respond has a corbel with a bust of a man. His gesture is popularly interpreted as toothache, but probably means some obscene challenge. At the E end of the S aisle two brackets for images. The walls of the aisles are of the 1880s. Dec chancel with a straight-headed side window. The westernmost chancel windows with their transom have been of the 'low-side' variety. E window of four lights with reticulated tracery. Much restored SEDILIA with ogee arches. – CHANDELIER. Brass, two tiers, dated 1808.

CONGREGATIONAL CHAPEL. 1813 (Kelly). With four windows and a big pediment. The doorways and upper windows are arranged so that bays one and four carry the main accents.

MANOR HOUSE, immediately N of the church. The remains of the Hall range of the Hastings mansion of c. 1320–40. The N end of the fragment shows on the W side the r. jamb and the springing of the arch which led into the Hall, and on the E side the simpler exit arch. The screens passage must have been to the l. To the r. four doorways, the two middle ones identical and probably leading into the offices; the l. one leads into the cellar, the r. one by a rough wooden stair to the upper storey of the fragment. Lancets and square-headed two-light windows with ogee-headed lights. On the upper floor a fireplace, and in the E wall a garderobe.

OLD RECTORY, at the N end of the village. Dated 1701. Brick front of five bays. Two storeys and basement. Dormers in the roof with steep triangular and with semicircular pediments. Doorway with a broad segmental pediment on brackets.

YARWELL

0090

ST MARY MAGDALENE. Short unbuttressed W tower with small pyramid roof. The tower is largely an C18 remodelling, though the late C13 W window (two lights and a circle; circular mullions) is original. The aisles were both pulled down in 1782.* They dated from the C13. So do the surviving N and S chapels. Circular piers with circular abaci, double-chamfered pointed arches. A little nailhead enrichment in the S arcade and the S chapel arcade. – PLATE. Paten, 1701; Cup, 1786.

STONE HOUSE. In the village street, on the S side. C17, with one canted bay with gable, balanced by a dormer the other side of the entrance. Mullioned windows.

(OLD SULEHAY LODGE, 1¼ m. WNW. C17; gabled, with mullioned windows. NMR)

ROMAN BUILDING. Peel's Quarry, ½ m. W of Wansford, on the S side of the King's Cliffe road, marks the site of a poor structure, perhaps a bailiff's house.

YELVERTOFT

6070

ALL SAINTS. The strange thing about the church is the existence of an outer S aisle. There are thus three arcades in all. They have octagonal piers and double-chamfered arches. The N arcade is of three bays, the other two have four. The N and inner S arcade are Dec, the outer S arcade seems Perp. Added to the inner aisle a one-bay S chapel. The arch towards the chancel on corbels, one with an animal head, the other with leaf. Dec S porch entrance with three orders of ballflower and fleurons and ogee hood-mould. Dec the chancel too, see the (renewed) E window with reticulation and the curiously eroded SEDILIA with nodding ogee arches. The W tower has

* The alterations were made by *Mr Sanderson* (Colvin).

no feature of special interest, except the niche above the W window. Transomed two-light bell-openings with ogee-headed lights. Of special interest, however, is the sudden display of Perp decoration around the chancel N window. Four friezes of quatrefoil etc. below the window, and carried on across the framing buttresses. Their upper parts are moreover panelled. To this display, unaccountable from outside, corresponds a similar display inside, and its centre is the MONUMENT to John Dycson, rector from 1439 to 1445. Effigy of alabaster on a low tomb-chest with many small quatrefoils. Two angels by his pillow. Low segmental arch, panelled back wall. Buttresses l. and r. with tiny niches one above the other. Broad cresting ending in a row of niches. – BENCHES. Broad, unbuttressed ends with very rich tracery. – PLATE. Cup and Paten, 1570; Paten, *c.* 1650. – MONUMENTS. John Dycson, *see* above. – Thomas Plumpin † 1770. By *William Cox Sen.* of Northampton. Very pretty. Also another by the same.

(Six timber-framed houses in the village. Also a SCHOOL, partly of 1792, partly C19. DOE)

GLOSSARY

ABACUS: flat slab on the top of a capital (q.v.).

ABUTMENT: solid masonry placed to resist the lateral pressure of a vault.

ACANTHUS: plant with thick fleshy and scalloped leaves used as part of the decoration of a Corinthian capital (q.v.) and in some types of leaf carving.

ACHIEVEMENT OF ARMS: in heraldry, a complete display of armorial bearings.

ACROTERION: foliage-carved block on the end or top of a classical pediment.

ADDORSED: two human figures, animals, or birds, etc., placed symmetrically so that they turn their backs to each other.

AEDICULE, AEDICULA: framing of a window or door by columns and a pediment (q.v.).

AFFRONTED: two human figures, animals, or birds, etc., placed symmetrically so that they face each other.

AGGER: Latin term for the built-up foundations of Roman roads; also sometimes applied to the banks of hill-forts or other earthworks.

AMBULATORY: semicircular or polygonal aisle enclosing an apse (q.v.).

ANNULET: *see* Shaft-ring.

ANSE DE PANIER: *see* Arch, Basket.

ANTEPENDIUM: covering of the front of an altar, usually by textiles or metalwork.

ANTIS, IN: *see* Portico.

APSE: vaulted semicircular or polygonal end of a chancel or a chapel.

ARABESQUE: light and fanciful surface decoration using combinations of flowing lines, tendrils, etc., interspersed with vases, animals, etc.

ARCADE: range of arches supported on piers or columns, free-standing: or, BLIND ARCADE, the same attached to a wall.

ARCH: round-headed, i.e. semicircular; pointed, i.e. consisting of two curves, each drawn from one centre, and meeting in a point at the top; segmental, i.e. in the form of a segment;

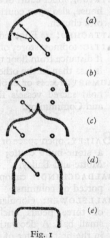

Fig. 1

pointed; four-centred (a Late Medieval form), *see* Fig. 1(*a*); Tudor (also a Late Medieval form), *see* Fig. 1(*b*); Ogee (introduced *c*.1300 and specially popular in the C14), *see* Fig. 1(*c*); Stilted, *see* Fig. 1(*d*); Basket, with lintel connected to the jambs by concave quadrant curves, *see* Fig. 1(*e*) for one example; Diaphragm, a transverse arch with solid spandrels carrying not a vault but a principal beam of a timber roof.

ARCHITRAVE: lowest of the three main parts of the entablature (q.v.) of an order (q.v.) (*see* Fig. 12).

ARCHIVOLT: under-surface of an arch (also called Soffit).

ARRIS: sharp edge at the meeting of two surfaces.

ASHLAR: masonry of large blocks wrought to even faces and square edges.

ATLANTES: male counterparts of caryatids (q.v.).

ATRIUM: inner court of a Roman house, also open court in front of a church.

ATTACHED: *see* Engaged.

ATTIC: topmost storey of a house, if distance from floor to ceiling is less than in the others.

AUMBRY: recess or cupboard to hold sacred vessels for Mass and Communion.

BAILEY: open space or court of a stone-built castle; *see* also Motte-and-Bailey.

BALDACCHINO: canopy supported on columns.

BALLFLOWER: globular flower of three petals enclosing a small ball. A decoration used in the first quarter of the C14.

BALUSTER: small pillar or column of fanciful outline.

BALUSTRADE: series of balusters supporting a handrail or coping (q.v.).

BARBICAN: outwork defending the entrance to a castle.

BARGEBOARDS: projecting decorated boards placed against the incline of the gable of a building and hiding the horizontal roof timbers.

BARROW: *see* Bell, Bowl, Disc, Long, *and* Pond Barrow.

BASILICA: in medieval architecture an aisled church with a clerestory.

BASKET ARCH: *see* Arch (Fig. 1*e*).

BASTION: projection at the angle of a fortification.

BATTER: inclined face of a wall.

BATTLEMENT: parapet with a series of indentations or embrasures with raised portions or merlons between (also called Crenellation).

BAYS: internal compartments of a building; each divided from the other not by solid walls but by divisions only marked in the side walls (columns, pilasters, etc.) or the ceiling (beams, etc.). Also external divisions of a building by fenestration.

BAY-WINDOW: angular or curved projection of a house front with ample fenestration. If curved, also called bow-window: if on an upper floor only, also called oriel or oriel window.

BEAKER FOLK: Late New Stone Age warrior invaders from the Continent who buried their dead in round barrows and introduced the first metal tools and weapons to Britain.

BEAKHEAD: Norman ornamental motif consisting of a row of bird or beast heads with beaks biting usually into a roll moulding.

BELFRY: turret on a roof to hang bells in.

BELGAE: Aristocratic warrior bands who settled in Britain in two main waves in the C1 B.C. In Britain their culture is termed Iron Age C.

BELL BARROW: Early Bronze Age round barrow in which the mound is separated from its encircling ditch by a flat platform or berm (q.v.).

BELLCOTE: framework on a roof to hang bells from.

BERM: level area separating ditch from bank on a hill-fort or barrow.

BILLET FRIEZE: Norman ornamental motif made up of short raised rectangles placed at regular intervals.

BIVALLATE: Of a hill-fort: defended by two concentric banks and ditches.

BLOCK CAPITAL: Romanesque capital cut from a cube by hav-

Fig. 2

ing the lower angles rounded off to the circular shaft below (also called Cushion Capital) (Fig. 2).

BOND, ENGLISH or FLEMISH: see Brickwork.

BOSS: knob or projection usually placed to cover the intersection of ribs in a vault.

BOWL BARROW: round barrow surrounded by a quarry ditch. Introduced in Late Neolithic

times, the form continued until the Saxon period.

BOW-WINDOW: see Bay-Window.

BOX: A small country house, e.g. a shooting box. A convenient term to describe a compact minor dwelling, e.g. a rectory.

BOX PEW: pew with a high wooden enclosure.

BRACES: see Roof.

BRACKET: small supporting piece of stone, etc., to carry a projecting horizontal.

BRESSUMER: beam in a timber-framed building to support the, usually projecting, superstructure.

BRICKWORK: *Header:* brick laid so that the end only appears on the face of the wall. *Stretcher:* brick laid so that the side only appears on the face of the wall. *English Bond:* method of laying bricks so that alternate courses or layers on the face of the wall are composed of headers or stretchers only (Fig. 3*a*). *Flemish Bond:* method of laying

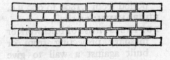

(a)

(b)
Fig. 3

bricks so that alternate headers and stretchers appear in each course on the face of the wall (Fig. 3*b*).

BROACH: see Spire.

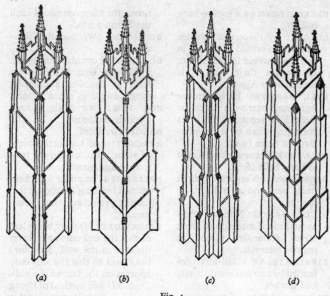

(a)   (b)   (c)   (d)

Fig. 4

BROKEN PEDIMENT: *see* Pediment.

BRONZE AGE: In Britain, the period from *c.*1800 to 600 B.C.

BUCRANIUM: ox skull.

BUTTRESS: mass of brickwork or masonry projecting from or built against a wall to give additional strength. *Angle Buttresses:* two meeting at an angle of 90° at the angle of a building (Fig. 4*a*). *Clasping Buttress:* one which encases the angle (Fig. 4*d*). *Diagonal Buttress:* one placed against the right angle formed by two walls, and more or less equiangular with both (Fig. 4*b*). *Flying Buttress:* arch or half arch transmitting the thrust of a vault or roof from the upper part of a wall to an outer support or buttress. *Setback Buttress:* angle buttress set slightly back from the angle (Fig. 4*c*).

CABLE MOULDING: Norman moulding imitating a twisted cord.

CAIRN: a mound of stones usually covering a burial.

CAMBER: slight rise or upward curve of an otherwise horizontal structure.

CAMPANILE: isolated bell tower.

CANOPY: projection or hood over an altar, pulpit, niche, statue, etc.

CAP: in a windmill the crowning feature.

CAPITAL: head or top part of a column.

CARTOUCHE: tablet with an ornate frame, usually enclosing an inscription.

CARYATID: whole female figure supporting an entablature or other similar member. *Termini Caryatids:* female busts or demi-figures or three-quarter figures supporting an entablature or other similar member and placed at the top of termini pilasters (q.v.). Cf. Atlantes.

CASTELLATED: decorated with battlements.

CELURE: panelled and adorned part of a wagon-roof above the rood or the altar.

CENSER: vessel for the burning of incense.

CENTERING: wooden framework used in arch and vault construction and removed when the mortar has set.

CHALICE: cup used in the Communion service or at Mass. *See also* Recusant Chalice.

CHAMBERED TOMB: burial mound of the New Stone Age having a stone-built chamber and entrance passage covered by an earthen barrow or stone cairn. The form was introduced to Britain from the Mediterranean.

CHAMFER: surface made by cutting across the square angle of a stone block, piece of wood, etc., usually at an angle of 45° to the other two surfaces.

CHANCEL: that part of the E end of a church in which the altar is placed, usually applied to the whole continuation of the nave E of the crossing.

CHANCEL ARCH: arch at the W end of the chancel.

CHANTRY CHAPEL: chapel attached to, or inside, a church, endowed for the saying of Masses for the soul of the founder or some other individual.

CHEVET: French term for the E end of a church (chancel, ambulatory, and radiating chapels).

CHEVRON: Norman moulding forming a zigzag.

CHOIR: that part of the church where divine service is sung.

CIBORIUM: a baldacchino.

CINQUEFOIL: *see* Foil.

CIST: stone-lined or slab-built grave. First appears in Late Neolithic times. It continued to be used in the Early Christian period.

CLAPPER BRIDGE: bridge made of large slabs of stone, some built up to make rough piers and other longer ones laid on top to make the roadway.

CLASSIC: here used to mean the moment of highest achievement of a style.

CLASSICAL: here used as the term for Greek and Roman architecture and any subsequent styles inspired by it.

CLERESTORY: upper storey of the nave walls of a church, pierced by windows.

COADE STONE: artificial (cast) stone made in the late C18 and the early C19 by Coade and Sealy in London.

COB: walling material made of mixed clay and straw.

COFFERING: decorating a ceiling with sunk square or polygonal ornamental panels.

COLLAR-BEAM: *see* Roof.

COLONNADE: range of columns.

COLONNETTE: small column.

COLUMNA ROSTRATA: column decorated with carved prows of ships to celebrate a naval victory.

COMPOSITE: see Order.

CONSOLE: bracket (q.v.) with a compound curved outline.

COPING: capping or covering to a wall.

CORBEL: block of stone projecting from a wall, supporting some feature on its horizontal top surface.

CORBEL TABLE: series of corbels, occurring just below the roof eaves externally or internally, often seen in Norman buildings.

CORINTHIAN: see Order.

CORNICE: in classical architecture the top section of the entablature (q.v.). Also for a projecting decorative feature along the top of a wall, arch, etc.

CORRIDOR VILLA: see Villa.

COUNTERSCARP BANK: small bank on the down-hill or outer side of a hill-fort ditch.

COURTYARD VILLA: see Villa.

COVE, COVING: concave undersurface in the nature of a hollow moulding but on a larger scale.

COVER PATEN: cover to a Communion cup, suitable for use as a paten or plate for the consecrated bread.

CRADLE ROOF: see Wagon roof.

CRENELLATION: see Battlement.

CREST, CRESTING: ornamental finish along the top of a screen, etc.

CRINKLE-CRANKLE WALL: undulating wall.

CROCKET, CROCKETING: decorative features placed on the sloping sides of spires, pinnacles, gables, etc., in Gothic architecture, carved in various leaf shapes and placed at regular intervals.

CROCKET CAPITAL: see Fig. 5. An Early Gothic form.

CROMLECH: word of Celtic origin still occasionally used of single free-standing stones ascribed to the Neolithic or Bronze Age periods.

Fig. 5

CROSSING: space at the intersection of nave, chancel, and transepts.

CROSS-WINDOWS: windows with one mullion and one transom.

CRUCK: big curved beam supporting both walls and roof of a cottage.

CRYPT: underground room usually below the E end of a church.

CUPOLA: small polygonal or circular domed turret crowning a roof.

CURTAIN WALL: connecting wall between the towers of a castle.

CUSHION CAPITAL: see Block Capital.

CUSP: projecting point between the foils in a foiled Gothic arch.

DADO: decorative covering of the lower part of a wall.

DAGGER: tracery motif of the Dec style. It is a lancet shape rounded or pointed at the head, pointed at the foot, and cusped inside (see Fig. 6).

Fig. 6

DAIS: raised platform at one end of a room.

DEC ('DECORATED'): historical division of English Gothic architecture covering the period from c.1290 to c.1350.

DEMI-COLUMNS: columns half sunk into a wall.

DIAPER WORK: surface decoration composed of square or lozenge shapes.

DIAPHRAGM ARCH: see Arch.

DISC BARROW: Bronze Age round barrow with inconspicuous central mound surrounded by bank and ditch.

DOGTOOTH: typical E.E. ornament consisting of a series of four-cornered stars placed diagonally and raised pyramidally (Fig. 7).

Fig. 7

DOMICAL VAULT: see Vault.

DONJON: see Keep.

DORIC: see Order.

DORMER (WINDOW): window placed vertically in the sloping plane of a roof.

DRIPSTONE: see Hood-mould.

DRUM: circular or polygonal vertical wall of a dome or cupola.

E.E. ('EARLY ENGLISH'): historical division of English Gothic architecture roughly covering the C13.

EASTER SEPULCHRE: recess with tomb-chest, usually in the wall of a chancel, the tomb-chest to receive an effigy of Christ for Easter celebrations.

EAVES: underpart of a sloping roof overhanging a wall.

EAVES CORNICE: cornice below the eaves of a roof.

ECHINUS: Convex or projecting moulding supporting the abacus of a Greek Doric capital, sometimes bearing an egg and dart pattern.

EMBATTLED: see Battlement.

EMBRASURE: small opening in the wall or parapet of a fortified building, usually splayed on the inside.

ENCAUSTIC TILES: earthenware glazed and decorated tiles used for paving.

ENGAGED COLUMNS: columns attached to, or partly sunk into, a wall.

ENGLISH BOND: see Brickwork.

ENTABLATURE: in classical architecture the whole of the horizontal members above a column (that is architrave, frieze, and cornice) (see Fig. 12).

ENTASIS: very slight convex deviation from a straight line; used on Greek columns and sometimes on spires to prevent an optical illusion of concavity.

ENTRESOL: see Mezzanine.

EPITAPH: hanging wall monument.

ESCUTCHEON: shield for armorial bearings.

EXEDRA: the apsidal end of a room. See Apse.

FAN-VAULT: see Vault.

FERETORY: place behind the

high altar where the chief shrine of a church is kept.

FESTOON: carved garland of flowers and fruit suspended at both ends.

FILLET: narrow flat band running down a shaft or along a roll moulding.

FINIAL: top of a canopy, gable, pinnacle.

FLAGON: vessel for the wine used in the Communion service.

FLAMBOYANT: properly the latest phase of French Gothic architecture where the window tracery takes on wavy undulating lines.

FLÈCHE: slender wooden spire on the centre of a roof (also called Spirelet).

FLEMISH BOND: see Brickwork.

FLEURON: decorative carved flower or leaf.

FLUSHWORK: decorative use of flint in conjunction with dressed stone so as to form patterns: tracery, initials, etc.

FLUTING: vertical channelling in the shaft of a column.

FLYING BUTTRESS: see Buttress.

FOIL: lobe formed by the cusping (q.v.) of a circle or an arch. Trefoil, quatrefoil, cinquefoil, multifoil, express the number of leaf shapes to be seen.

FOLIATED: carved with leaf shapes.

FOSSE: ditch.

FOUR-CENTRED ARCH: see Arch.

FRATER: refectory or dining hall of a monastery.

FRESCO: wall painting on wet plaster.

FRIEZE: middle division of a classical entablature (q.v.) (see Fig. 12).

FRONTAL: covering for the front of an altar.

GABLE: *Dutch gable:* A gable with curved sides crowned by a pediment, characteristic of c.1630–50 (Fig. 8a). *Shaped gable:* A gable with multi-curved sides characteristic of c.1600–50 (Fig. 8b).

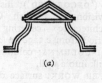

(a)

(b)

Fig. 8

GADROONED: enriched with a series of convex ridges, the opposite of fluting.

GALILEE: chapel or vestibule usually at the W end of a church enclosing the porch. Also called Narthex (q.v.).

GALLERY: in church architecture upper storey above an aisle, opened in arches to the nave. Also called Tribune and often erroneously Triforium (q.v.).

GALLERY GRAVE: chambered tomb (q.v.) in which there is little or no differentiation between the entrance passage and the actual burial chamber(s).

GARDEROBE: lavatory or privy in a medieval building.

GARGOYLE: water spout projecting from the parapet of a wall or tower; carved into a human or animal shape.

GAZEBO: lookout tower or raised

summer house in a picturesque garden.

'GEOMETRICAL': see Tracery.

'GIBBS SURROUND': of a doorway or window. An C18 motif consisting of a surround with alternating larger and smaller blocks of stone, quoin-wise, or intermittent large blocks, sometimes with a narrow raised band connecting them up the verticals and along the face of the arch (Fig. 9).

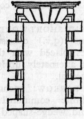

Fig. 9

GROIN: sharp edge at the meeting of two cells of a cross-vault.

GROIN-VAULT: see Vault.

GROTESQUE: fanciful ornamental decoration: see also Arabesque.

HAGIOSCOPE: see Squint.

HALF-TIMBERING: see Timber-Framing.

HALL CHURCH: church in which nave and aisles are of equal height or approximately so.

HAMMERBEAM: see Roof.

HANAP: large metal cup, generally made for domestic use, standing on an elaborate base and stem; with a very ornate cover frequently crowned with a little steeple.

HEADERS: see Brickwork.

HERRINGBONE WORK: brick, stone, or tile construction where the component blocks are laid diagonally instead of flat. Alternate courses lie in opposing directions to make a zigzag pattern up the face of the wall.

HEXASTYLE: having six detached columns.

HILL-FORT: Iron Age earthwork enclosed by a ditch and bank system; in the later part of the period the defences multiplied in size and complexity. They vary from about an acre to over 30 acres in area, and are usually built with careful regard to natural elevations or promontories.

HIPPED ROOF: see Roof.

HOOD-MOULD: projecting moulding above an arch or a lintel to throw off water (also called Dripstone or Label).

ICONOGRAPHY: the science of the subject matter of works of the visual arts.

IMPOST: bracket in a wall, usually formed of mouldings, on which the ends of an arch rest.

INDENT: shape chiselled out in a stone slab to receive a brass.

INGLENOOK: bench or seat built in beside a fireplace, sometimes covered by the chimneybreast, occasionally lit by small windows on each side of the fire.

INTERCOLUMNIATION: the space between columns.

IONIC: see Order (Fig. 12).

IRON AGE: in Britain the period from c. 600 B.C. to the coming of the Romans. The term is also used for those un-Romanized native communities which survived until the Saxon incursions.

JAMB: straight side of an archway, doorway, or window.

KEEL MOULDING: moulding whose outline is in section like that of the keel of a ship.

KEEP: massive tower of a Norman castle.

KEYSTONE: middle stone in an arch or a rib-vault.

KING-POST: see Roof (Fig. 14).

KNEELER: horizontal decorative projection at the base of a gable.

KNOP: a knob-like thickening in the stem of a chalice.

LABEL: see Hood-mould.

LABEL STOP: ornamental boss at the end of a hood-mould (q.v.).

LACED WINDOWS: windows pulled visually together by strips, usually in brick of a different colour, which continue vertically the lines of the vertical parts of the window surrounds. The motif is typical of c. 1720.

LANCET WINDOW: slender pointed-arched window.

LANTERN: in architecture, a small circular or polygonal turret with windows all round crowning a roof (see Cupola) or a dome.

LANTERN CROSS: churchyard cross with lantern-shaped top usually with sculptured representations on the sides of the top.

LEAN-TO ROOF: roof with one slope only, built against a higher wall.

LESENE or PILASTER STRIP: pilaster without base or capital.

LIERNE: see Vault (Fig. 21).

LINENFOLD: Tudor panelling ornamented with a conventional representation of a piece of linen laid in vertical folds. The piece is repeated in each panel.

LINTEL: horizontal beam or stone bridging an opening.

LOGGIA: recessed colonnade (q.v.).

LONG AND SHORT WORK: Saxon quoins (q.v.) consisting of stones placed with the long sides alternately upright and horizontal.

LONG BARROW: unchambered Neolithic communal burial mound, wedge-shaped in plan, with the burial and occasional other structures massed at the broader end, from which the mound itself tapers in height; quarry ditches flank the mound.

LOUVRE: opening, often with lantern (q.v.) over, in the roof of a room to let the smoke from a central hearth escape.

LOWER PALAEOLITHIC: see Palaeolithic.

LOZENGE: diamond shape.

LUCARNE: small opening to let light in.

LUNETTE: tympanum (q.v.) or semicircular opening.

LYCH GATE: wooden gate structure with a roof and open sides placed at the entrance to a churchyard to provide space for the reception of a coffin. The word *lych* is Saxon and means a corpse.

LYNCHET: long terraced strip of soil accumulating on the downward side of prehistoric and medieval fields due to soil creep from continuous ploughing along the contours.

MACHICOLATION: projecting gallery on brackets constructed on the outside of castle towers or walls. The gallery has holes in the floor to drop missiles through.

MAJOLICA: ornamented glazed earthenware.

MANSARD: see Roof.

MATHEMATICAL TILES: Small facing tiles the size of brick headers, applied to timber-framed walls to make them appear brick-built.

MEGALITHIC TOMB: stone-built burial chamber of the New Stone Age covered by an earth or stone mound. The form was introduced to Britain from the Mediterranean area.

MERLON: see Battlement.

MESOLITHIC: 'Middle Stone' Age; the post-glacial period of hunting and fishing communities dating in Britain from c. 8000 B.C. to the arrival of Neolithic communities, with which they must have considerably overlapped.

METOPE: in classical architecture of the Doric order (q.v.) the space in the frieze between the triglyphs (Fig. 12).

MEZZANINE: low storey placed between two higher ones.

MISERERE: see Misericord.

MISERICORD: bracket placed on the underside of a hinged choir stall seat which, when turned up, provided the occupant of the seat with a support during long periods of standing (also called Miserere).

MODILLION: small bracket of which large numbers (modillion frieze) are often placed below a cornice (q.v.) in classical architecture.

MOTTE: steep mound forming the main feature of C11 and C12 castles.

MOTTE-AND-BAILEY: post-Roman and Norman defence system consisting of an earthen mound (the motte) topped with a wooden tower eccentrically placed within a bailey (q.v.), with enclosure ditch and palisade, and with the rare addition of an internal bank.

MOUCHETTE: tracery motif in curvilinear tracery, a curved dagger (q.v.), specially popular in the early C14 (Fig. 10).

Fig. 10

MULLIONS: vertical posts or uprights dividing a window into 'lights'.

MULTIVALLATE: Of a hill-fort: defended by three or more concentric banks and ditches.

MUNTIN: post as a rule moulded and part of a screen.

NAIL-HEAD: E.E. ornamental motif, consisting of small pyramids regularly repeated (Fig. 11).

Fig. 11

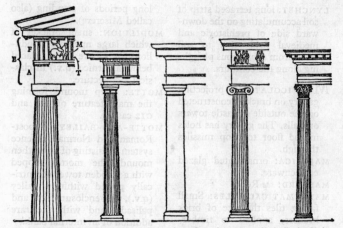

Fig. 12. Orders of Columns (Greek Doric, Roman Doric, Tuscan Doric, Ionic, Corinthian) E, Entablature; C, Cornice; F, Frieze; A, Architrave; M, Metope; T, Triglyph.

NARTHEX: enclosed vestibule or covered porch at the main entrance to a church (*see* Galilee).

NEOLITHIC: 'New Stone' Age, dating in Britain from the appearance from the Continent of the first settled farming communities *c.* 3500 B.C. until the introduction of the Bronze Age.

NEWEL: central post in a circular or winding staircase; also the principal post when a flight of stairs meets a landing.

NOOK-SHAFT: shaft set in the angle of a pier or respond or wall, or the angle of the jamb of a window or doorway.

NUTMEG MOULDING: consisting of a chain of tiny triangles placed obliquely.

OBELISK: lofty pillar of square section tapering at the top and ending pyramidally.

OGEE: *see* Arch (Fig. 1*c*).

ORATORY: small private chapel in a house.

ORDER: (1) *of a doorway or window:* series of concentric steps receding towards the opening; (2) *in classical architecture:* column with base, shaft, capital, and entablature (q.v.) according to one of the following styles: Greek Doric, Roman Doric, Tuscan Doric, Ionic, Corinthian, Composite. The established details are very elaborate, and some specialist architectural work should be consulted for further guidance (*see* Fig. 12).

ORIEL: *see* Bay-Window.

OVERHANG: projection of the upper storey of a house.

OVERSAILING COURSES: series of stone or brick courses, each one projecting beyond the one below it.

OVOLO: convex moulding.

PALAEOLITHIC: 'Old Stone' Age; the first period of human culture, commencing in the

Ice Age and immediately prior to the Mesolithic; the Lower Palaeolithic is the older phase, the Upper Palaeolithic the later.

PALIMPSEST: (1) *of a brass:* where a metal plate has been re-used by turning over and engraving on the back; (2) *of a wall painting:* where one overlaps and partly obscures an earlier one.

PALLADIAN: architecture following the ideas and principles of Andrea Palladio, 1518–80.

PANTILE: tile of curved S-shaped section.

PARAPET: low wall placed to protect any spot where there is a sudden drop, for example on a bridge, quay, hillside, housetop, etc.

PARGETTING: plaster work with patterns and ornaments either in relief or engraved on it.

PARVIS: term wrongly applied to a room over a church porch. These rooms were often used as a schoolroom or as a store room.

PATEN: plate to hold the bread at Communion or Mass.

PATERA: small flat circular or oval ornament in classical architecture.

PEDIMENT: low-pitched gable used in classical, Renaissance, and neo-classical architecture above a portico and above doors, windows, etc. It may be straight-sided or curved segmentally. *Broken Pediment:* one where the centre portion of the base is left open. *Open Pediment:* one where the centre portion of the sloping sides is left out.

PENDANT: boss (q.v.) elongated so that it seems to hang down.

PENDENTIF: concave triangular spandrel used to lead from the angle of two walls to the base of a circular dome. It is constructed as part of the hemisphere over a diameter the size of the diagonal of the basic square (Fig. 13).

Fig. 13

PERP (PERPENDICULAR): historical division of English Gothic architecture covering the period from *c.*1335–50 to *c.*1530.

PIANO NOBILE: principal storey of a house with the reception rooms; usually the first floor.

PIAZZA: open space surrounded by buildings; in C17 and C18 England sometimes used to mean a long colonnade or loggia.

PIER: strong, solid support, frequently square in section or of composite section (compound pier).

PIETRA DURA: ornamental or scenic inlay by means of thin slabs of stone.

PILASTER: shallow pier attached to a wall. *Termini Pilasters:* pilasters with sides tapering downwards.

PILLAR PISCINA: free-standing piscina on a pillar.

PINNACLE: ornamental form crowning a spire, tower, buttress, etc., usually of steep pyramidal, conical, or some similar shape.

PISCINA: basin for washing the Communion or Mass vessels, provided with a drain. Generally set in or against the wall to the s of an altar.

PLAISANCE: summer-house, pleasure house near a mansion.

PLATE TRACERY: *see* Tracery.

PLINTH: projecting base of a wall or column, generally chamfered (q.v.) or moulded at the top.

POND BARROW: rare type of Bronze Age barrow consisting of a circular depression, usually paved, and containing a number of cremation burials.

POPPYHEAD: ornament of leaf and flower type used to decorate the tops of bench- or stall-ends.

PORTCULLIS: gate constructed to rise and fall in vertical grooves; used in gateways of castles.

PORTE COCHÈRE: porch large enough to admit wheeled vehicles.

PORTICO: centre-piece of a house or a church with classical detached or attached columns and a pediment. A portico is called *prostyle* or *in antis* according to whether it projects from or recedes into a building. In a portico *in antis* the columns range with the side walls.

POSTERN: small gateway at the back of a building.

PREDELLA: in an altarpiece the horizontal strip below the main representation, often used for a number of subsidiary representations in a row.

PRESBYTERY: the part of the church lying E of the choir. It is the part where the altar is placed.

PRINCIPAL: *see* Roof (Fig. 14).

PRIORY: monastic house whose head is a prior or prioress, not an abbot or abbess.

PROSTYLE: with free-standing columns in a row.

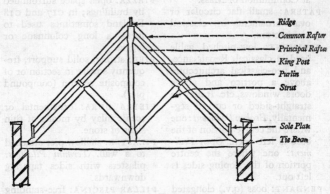

Fig. 14

PULPITUM: stone screen in a major church provided to shut off the choir from the nave and also as a backing for the return choir stalls.

PULVINATED FRIEZE: frieze with a bold convex moulding.

PURLIN: see Roof (Figs. 14, 15).

PUTHOLE or PUTLOCK HOLE: putlocks are the short horizontal timbers on which during construction the boards of scaffolding rest. Putholes or putlock holes are the holes in the wall for putlocks, which often are not filled in after construction is complete.

PUTTO: small naked boy.

QUADRANGLE: inner courtyard in a large building.

QUARRY: in stained-glass work, a small diamond- or square-shaped piece of glass set diagonally.

QUATREFOIL: see Foil.

QUEEN-POSTS: see Roof (Fig. 15).

QUOINS: dressed stones at the angles of a building. Sometimes all the stones are of the same size; more often they are alternately large and small.

RADIATING CHAPELS: chapels projecting radially from an ambulatory or an apse.

RAFTER: see Roof.

RAMPART: stone wall or wall of earth surrounding a castle, fortress, or fortified city.

RAMPART-WALK: path along the inner face of a rampart.

REBATE: continuous rectangular notch cut on an edge.

REBUS: pun, a play on words. The literal translation and illustration of a name for artistic and heraldic purposes (Belton = bell, tun).

RECUSANT CHALICE: chalice made after the Reformation and before Catholic Emancipation for Roman Catholic use.

REEDING: decoration with parallel convex mouldings touching one another.

REFECTORY: dining hall; see Frater.

RENDERING: plastering of an outer wall.

REPOUSSÉ: decoration of metal work by relief designs, formed by beating the metal from the back.

REREDOS: structure behind and above an altar.

RESPOND: half-pier bonded into a wall and carrying one end of an arch.

RETABLE: altarpiece, a picture or piece of carving, standing behind and attached to an altar.

RETICULATION: see Tracery (Fig. 20e).

REVEAL: that part of a jamb (q.v.) which lies between the glass or door and the outer surface of the wall.

RIB-VAULT: see Vault.

ROCOCO: latest phase of the Baroque style, current in most Continental countries between c.1720 and c.1760.

ROLL MOULDING: moulding of semicircular or more than semicircular section.

ROMANESQUE: that style in architecture which was current in the C11 and C12 and preceded the Gothic style (in England often called Norman). (Some scholars extend the use of the term Romanesque back to the C10 or C9.)

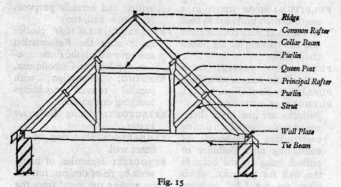

Ridge
Common Rafter
Collar Beam
Purlin
Queen Post
Principal Rafter
Purlin
Strut
Wall Plate
Tie Beam

Fig. 15

ROMANO-BRITISH: A some-
what vague term applied to the
period and cultural features of
Britain affected by the Roman
occupation of the C1–5 A.D.

ROOD: cross or crucifix.

ROOD LOFT: singing gallery on
the top of the rood screen,
often supported by a coving.

ROOD SCREEN: see Screen.

ROOD STAIRS: stairs to give
access to the rood loft.

ROOF: *Single-framed:* if consisting entirely of transverse

members (such as rafters with
or without braces, collars, tie-
beams, king-posts or queen-
posts, etc.) not tied together
longitudinally. *Double-framed:*
if longitudinal members (such
as a ridge beam and purlins)
are employed. As a rule in such
cases the rafters are divided
into stronger principals and
weaker subsidiary rafters.
Hipped: roof with sloped instead of vertical ends. *Mansard:*
roof with a double slope, the

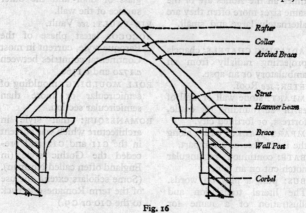

Rafter
Collar
Arched Brace
Strut
Hammerbeam
Brace
Wall Post
Corbel

Fig. 16

lower slope being larger and steeper than the upper. *Saddleback:* tower roof shaped like an ordinary gabled timber roof. The following members have special names: *Rafter:* rooftimber sloping up from the wall plate to the ridge. *Principal:* principal rafter, usually corresponding to the main bay divisions of the nave or chancel below. *Wall Plate:* timber laid longitudinally on the top of a wall. *Purlin:* longitudinal member laid parallel with wall plate and ridge beam some way up the slope of the roof. *Tie-beam:* beam connecting the two slopes of a roof across at its foot, usually at the height of the wall plate, to prevent the roof from spreading. *Collarbeam:* tie-beam applied higher up the slope of the roof. *Strut:* upright timber connecting the tie-beam with the rafter above it. *King-post:* upright timber connecting a tie-beam and collar-beam with the ridge beam. *Queen-posts:* two struts placed symmetrically on a tiebeam or collar-beam. *Braces:* inclined timbers inserted to strengthen others. Usually braces connect a collar-beam with the rafters below or a tiebeam with the wall below. Braces can be straight or curved (also called arched). *Hammerbeam:* beam projecting at right angles, usually from the top of a wall, to carry arched braces or struts and arched braces. (*See* Figs. 14, 15, 16.)

ROSE WINDOW (or WHEEL WINDOW): circular window with patterned tracery arranged to radiate from the centre.

ROTUNDA: building circular in plan.

RUBBLE: building stones, not square or hewn, nor laid in regular courses.

RUSTICATION: *rock-faced* if the surfaces of large blocks of ashlar stone are left rough like rock; *smooth* if the ashlar blocks are smooth and separated by V-joints; *banded* if the separation by V-joints applies only to the horizontals.

SADDLEBACK: *see* Roof.

SALTIRE CROSS: equal-limbed cross placed diagonally.

SANCTUARY: (1) area around the main altar of a church (*see* Presbytery); (2) sacred site consisting of wood or stone uprights enclosed by a circular bank and ditch. Beginning in the Neolithic, they were elaborated in the succeeding Bronze Age. The best known examples are Stonehenge and Avebury.

SARCOPHAGUS: elaborately carved coffin.

SCAGLIOLA: material composed of cement and colouring matter to imitate marble.

SCALLOPED CAPITAL: development of the block capital (q.v.) in which the single semicircular surface is elaborated into a series of truncated cones (Fig. 17).

Fig. 17

SCARP: artificial cutting away of the ground to form a steep slope.

SCREEN: *Parclose screen:* screen separating a chapel from the rest of a church. *Rood screen:* screen below the rood (q.v.), usually at the W end of a chancel.

SCREENS PASSAGE: passage between the entrances to kitchen, buttery, etc., and the screen behind which lies the hall of a medieval house.

SEDILIA: seats for the priests (usually three) on the S side of the chancel of a church.

SEGMENTAL ARCH: *see* Arch.

SET-OFF: *see* Weathering.

SEXPARTITE: *see* Vault.

SGRAFFITO: pattern incised into plaster so as to expose a dark surface underneath.

SHAFT-RING: motif of the C12 and C13 consisting of a ring round a circular pier or a shaft attached to a pier.

SHEILA-NA-GIG: fertility figure, usually with legs wide open.

SILL: lower horizontal part of the frame of a window.

SLATEHANGING: the covering of walls by overlapping rows of slates, on a timber substructure.

SOFFIT: underside of an arch, lintel, etc.

SOLAR: upper living-room of a medieval house.

SOPRAPORTE: painting above the door of a room, usual in the C17 and C18.

SOUNDING BOARD: horizontal board or canopy over a pulpit. Also called Tester.

SPANDREL: triangular surface between one side of an arch, the horizontal drawn from its apex, and the vertical drawn from its springer; also the surface between two arches.

SPERE-TRUSS: roof truss on two free-standing posts to mask the division between screens passage and hall. The screen itself, where a spere-truss exists, was originally movable.

SPIRE: tall pyramidal or conical pointed erection often built on top of a tower, turret, etc. *Broach Spire:* a broach is a sloping half-pyramid of masonry or wood introduced at the base of each of the four oblique faces of a tapering octagonal spire with the object of effecting the transition from the square to the octagon. The *splayed foot spire* is a variation of the broach form found principally in the south-eastern counties. In this form the four cardinal faces are splayed out near their base, to cover the corners, while the oblique (or intermediate) faces taper away to a point. *Needle Spire:* thin spire rising from the centre of a tower roof, well inside the parapet.

SPIRELET: *see* Flèche.

SPLAY: chamfer, usually of the jamb of a window.

SPRINGING: level at which an arch rises from its supports.

SQUINCH: arch or system of concentric arches thrown across the angle between two walls to support a superstructure, for example a dome (Fig. 18).

SQUINT: a hole cut in a wall or through a pier to allow a view of the main altar of a church from places whence it could not otherwise be seen (also called Hagioscope).

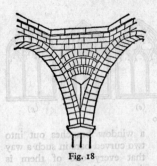

Fig. 18

STALL: carved seat, one of a row, made of wood or stone.

STAUNCHION: upright iron or steel member.

STEEPLE: the tower of a church together with a spire, cupola, etc.

STIFF-LEAF: E.E. type of foliage of many-lobed shapes (Fig. 19).

Fig. 19

STILTED: see Arch.

STOREY-POSTS: the principal posts of a timber-framed wall.

STOUP: vessel for the reception of holy water, usually placed near a door.

STRAINER ARCH: arch inserted across a room to prevent the walls from leaning.

STRAPWORK: C16 decoration consisting of interlaced bands, and forms similar to fretwork or cut and bent leather.

STRETCHER: see Brickwork.

STRING COURSE: projecting horizontal band or moulding set in the surface of a wall.

STRUT: see Roof.

STUCCO: plaster work.

STUDS: the subsidiary vertical timber members of a timber-framed wall.

SWAG: festoon formed by a carved piece of cloth suspended from both ends.

TABERNACLE: richly ornamented niche or free-standing canopy. Usually contains the Holy Sacrament.

TARSIA: inlay in various woods.

TAZZA: shallow bowl on a foot.

TERMINAL FIGURES (TERMS, TERMINI): upper part of a human figure growing out of a pier, pilaster, etc., which tapers towards the base. See also Caryatid, Pilaster.

TERRACOTTA: burnt clay, unglazed.

TESSELLATED PAVEMENT: mosaic flooring, particularly Roman, consisting of small 'tesserae' or cubes of glass, stone, or brick.

TESSERAE: see Tessellated Pavement.

TESTER: see Sounding Board.

TETRASTYLE: having four detached columns.

THREE-DECKER PULPIT: pulpit with Clerk's Stall below and Reading Desk below the Clerk's Stall.

TIE-BEAM: see Roof (Figs. 14, 15).

TIERCERON: see Vault (Fig. 21).

TILEHANGING: see Slatehanging.

TIMBER-FRAMING: method of construction where walls are built of timber framework with the spaces filled in by plaster

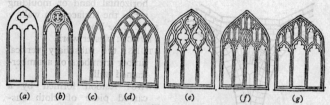

(a)   (b)   (c)   (d)   (e)   (f)   (g)

Fig. 20

or brickwork. Sometimes the timber is covered over with plaster or boarding laid horizontally.

TOMB-CHEST: chest-shaped stone coffin, the most usual medieval form of funeral monument.

TOUCH: soft black marble quarried near Tournai.

TOURELLE: turret corbelled out from the wall.

TRACERY: intersecting ribwork in the upper part of a window, or used decoratively in blank arches, on vaults, etc. *Plate tracery: see* Fig. 20(a). Early form of tracery where decoratively shaped openings are cut through the solid stone infilling in a window head. *Bar tracery:* a form introduced into England *c.*1250. Intersecting ribwork made up of slender shafts, continuing the lines of the mullions of windows up to a decorative mesh in the head of the window. *Geometrical tracery: see* Fig. 20(b). Tracery characteristic of *c.* 1250–1310 consisting chiefly of circles or foiled circles. *Y-tracery: see* Fig. 20(c). Tracery consisting of a mullion which branches into two forming a Y shape; typical of *c.* 1300. *Intersecting tracery: see* Fig. 20(d). Tracery in which each mullion of a window branches out into two curved bars in such a way that every one of them is drawn with the same radius from a different centre. The result is that every light of the window is a lancet and every two, three, four, etc., lights together form a pointed arch. This treatment also is typical of *c.* 1300. *Reticulated tracery: see* Fig. 20(e). Tracery typical of the early C14 consisting entirely of circles drawn at top and bottom into ogee shapes so that a net-like appearance results. *Panel tracery: see* Fig. 20(f) and (g). Perp tracery, which is formed of upright straight-sided panels above lights of a window.

TRANSEPT: transverse portion of a cross-shaped church.

TRANSOM: horizontal bar across the openings of a window.

TRANSVERSE ARCH: *see* Vault.

TRIBUNE: *see* Gallery.

TRICIPUT, SIGNUM TRICIPUT: sign of the Trinity expressed by three faces belonging to one head.

TRIFORIUM: arcaded wall passage or blank arcading facing the nave at the height of the aisle roof and below the clerestory (q.v.) windows. (*See* Gallery.)

TRIGLYPHS: blocks with vertical

grooves separating the metopes (q.v.) in the Doric frieze (Fig. 12).

TROPHY: sculptured group of arms or armour, used as a memorial of victory.

TRUMEAU: stone mullion (q.v.) supporting the tympanum (q.v.) of a wide doorway.

TUMULUS: see Barrow.

TURRET: very small tower, round or polygonal in plan.

TUSCAN: see Order.

TYMPANUM: space between the lintel of a doorway and the arch above it.

UNDERCROFT: vaulted room, sometimes underground, below a church or chapel.

UNIVALLATE: of a hill-fort: defended by a single bank and ditch.

UPPER PALAEOLITHIC: see Palaeolithic.

VAULT: *Barrel-vault:* see Tunnel-vault. *Cross-vault:* see Groin-vault. *Domical vault:* square or polygonal dome rising direct on a square or polygonal bay, the curved surfaces separated by groins (q.v.). *Fan-vault:* late medieval vault where all ribs springing from one springer are of the same length, the same distance from the next, and the same curvature. *Groin-vault* or *Cross-vault:* vault of two tunnel-vaults of identical shape intersecting each other at r. angles. Chiefly Norman and Renaissance. *Lierne:* tertiary rib, that is, rib which does not spring either from one of the main springers or from the central boss. Introduced in the C14, continues to the C16. *Quadripartite vault:* one wherein one bay of vaulting is divided into four parts. *Rib-vault:* vault with diagonal ribs projecting along the groins. *Ridge-rib:* rib along the longitudinal or transverse ridge of a vault. Introduced in the early C13. *Sexpartite vault:* one wherein one bay of quadripartite vaulting is divided into two parts transversely so that each bay of vaulting has six parts. *Tierceron:* secondary rib, that is, rib which issues from one of the main springers or the central boss and leads to a place on a ridge-rib. Introduced in the early C13. *Transverse arch:* arch separating one bay of a vault from the next. *Tunnel-vault* or *Barrel-vault:* vault of semicircular or pointed section. Chiefly Norman and Renaissance. (*See* Fig. 21.)

VAULTING SHAFT: vertical member leading to the springer of a vault.

VENETIAN WINDOW: window with three openings, the central one arched and wider than the outside ones. Current in England chiefly in the C17–18.

VERANDA: open gallery or balcony with a roof on light, usually metal, supports.

VESICA: oval with pointed head and foot.

VESTIBULE: anteroom or entrance hall.

VILLA: (1) according to Gwilt (1842) 'a country house for the residence of opulent persons'; (2) Romano-British country houses cum farms, to which the description given in (1)

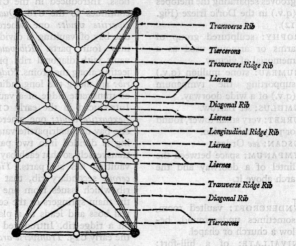

Transverse Rib

Tiercerons

Transverse Ridge Rib

Liernes

Diagonal Rib

Liernes

Longitudinal Ridge Rib

Liernes

Liernes

Transverse Ridge Rib

Diagonal Rib

Tiercerons

Fig. 21

more or less applies. They developed with the growth of urbanization. The basic type is the simple corridor pattern with rooms opening off a single passage; the next stage is the addition of wings. The courtyard villa fills a square plan with subsidiary buildings and an enclosure wall with a gate facing the main corridor block.

VITRIFIED: made similar to glass.

VITRUVIAN OPENING: A door or window which diminishes towards the top, as advocated by Vitruvius, bk. IV, chapter VI.

VOLUTE: spiral scroll, one of the component parts of an Ionic column (*see* Order).

VOUSSOIR: wedge-shaped stone used in arch construction.

WAGON ROOF: roof in which by closely set rafters with arched braces the appearance of the inside of a canvas tilt over a wagon is achieved. Wagon roofs can be panelled or plastered (ceiled) or left uncovered.

WAINSCOT: timber lining to walls.

WALL PLATE: *see* Roof.

WATERLEAF: leaf shape used in later C12 capitals. The waterleaf is a broad, unribbed, tapering leaf curving up towards the angle of the abacus and turned in at the top (Fig. 22).

Fig. 22

WEALDEN HOUSE: timber-framed house with the hall in the centre and wings projecting only slightly and only on the jutting upper floor. The roof, however, runs through without a break between wings and hall, and the eaves of the hall part are therefore exceptionally deep. They are supported by diagonal, usually curved, braces starting from the short inner sides of the overhanging wings and rising parallel with the front wall of the hall towards the centre of the eaves.

WEATHERBOARDING: overlapping horizontal boards, covering a timber-framed wall.

WEATHERING: sloped horizontal surface on sills, buttresses, etc., to throw off water.

WEEPERS: small figures placed in niches along the sides of some medieval tombs (also called Mourners).

WHEEL WINDOW: *see* Rose Window.

INDEX OF PLATES

INDEX OF ARTISTS

INDEX OF PLACES

ADDENDA
(MARCH 1973)

p. 89 [Ashby St Ledgers, St Leodegarius.] Antiquarian MSS. recording the lost glass suggest a date for the nave of *c.* 1470–90 (RM).

p. 95 [Ashton Wold.] The house has been altered recently.

p. 96 [Astrop Park.] (Keeper's lodge, pheasantry, and a cottage, by *W. Wilkinson* of Oxford, 1868. A. Saint)

p. 106 [Blakesley.] (VICARAGE. 1839 by *G. G. Scott.* D. Hansen)

p. 117 [Brackley.] (VICARAGE, near the church, half-timbered (now a school house). By *Charles Buckeridge*, 1868. A. Saint)

p. 123 [Brigstock, St Andrew.] There are restoration drawings of 1867 by *Carpenter & Ingelow.* Restoration was in progress in 1878.

p. 125 [Brixworth, All Saints.] Recent excavations have established that at the w end there were five compartments, extending the full width of the aisles, the centre one forming the porch.

p. 152 [Cogenhoe, St Peter.] The restoration of 1868–9 was by *Buckeridge* (A. Saint).

p. 196 [Earls Barton, All Saints.] There are restoration drawings of 1868 by *Carpenter & Ingelow.* Work was in progress in 1878.

p. 229 [Great Brington, St Mary.] There are early C17 records referring to an inscription in the chancel windows attributing the rebuilding to Sir John Spencer. The N chapel may have been completed by Sir William Spencer, as a window there referred to him, with the date 1526 (RM).

p. 230 [Great Brington, St Mary.] The polygonal bay-window was designed by the then rector, the Rev. *H. Rose* (information from Earl Spencer).

p. 293 [Little Brington.] WASHINGTON HOUSE. Dated 1606. A symmetrical front with three renewed three-light mullioned windows. The house was much repaired after a recent fire. There is no proof that the house was associated with the Washington family. (Information from Earl Spencer.)

p. 309 [Naseby.] (BATTLEFIELD MEMORIAL. A Column with a ball finial. 1936 by *J. A. Gotch*. BB)

p. 316n [Northampton.] Excavations in 1971 between Bearward Street and Silver Street confirmed that there was a pre-Conquest ditch, which was filled in when the town expanded in the C12–13.

p. 349 [Northampton: Weston Favell.] Further S, on the edge of the new Eastern District, will be the WESTON FAVELL DISTRICT CENTRE. This will include a large indoor shopping area, churches, library and health centre, and an upper school complex which will be linked to a Forum incorporating sports hall, swimming pool, conference rooms etc.)

p. 369 [Overstone.] The gateway from Pytchley Hall was destroyed by a car in February 1973.

p. 388 [Rockingham, St Leonard.] (Other stained glass is by *Powell*, 1846. G1)

p. 403 [Sibbertoft.] (The SCHOOL next to the church is of 1846 by *E. F. Law*.)

p. 405 [Southwick Hall.] In the windows of the tower upper floor two fine C14 shields of arms, *in situ* (RM).

p. 419 [Strixton, St John Baptist.] There are restoration drawings of 1869 by *Slater & Carpenter*.

p. 453 [Wellingborough.] (OUR LADY'S R.C. CHURCH AND INFANT SCHOOL, Henshaw Road. By the *Ellis/ Williams Partnership*, 1971–2. A combined church and school. The church is the taller windowless part, with simple toplit interior. The plan is L-shaped, with one arm that can be partitioned off as a school hall. Beyond this are central teaching areas surrounded by partly open classrooms.)

p. 454 [Wellingborough.] (WELLINGBOROUGH MEDICAL CENTRE, Gold Street. By *Aldington & Craig*, under construction 1972–3.)

p. 459 [Whiston, St Mary.] A lost inscription in the glass, recorded by Bridges, also mentions the date 1534, and states that Anthony Catesby, his wife and son 'hanc ecclesiam condiderunt' (RM).

AVON

U.S.\$6.50
CAN.\$8.50

W9-CMZ-959

EAN

ISBN 0-380-78960-4

9 780380 789603

50650

Ray Bradbury

Driving Blind

STORIES

Books by Ray Bradbury

DANDELION WINE
DARK CARNIVAL
DEATH IS A LONELY BUSINESS
FAHRENHEIT 451
THE GOLDEN APPLES OF THE SUN
A GRAVEYARD FOR LUNATICS
GREEN SHADOWS, WHITE WHALE
THE HALLOWEEN TREE
I SING THE BODY ELECTRIC!
THE ILLUSTRATED MAN
KALEIDOSCOPE
LONG AFTER MIDNIGHT
THE MARTIAN CHRONICLES
THE MACHINERIES OF JOY
A MEDICINE FOR MELANCHOLY
THE OCTOBER COUNTRY
QUICKER THAN THE EYE
R IS FOR ROCKET
SOMETHING WICKED THIS WAY COMES
THE STORIES OF RAY BRADBURY
S IS FOR SPACE
THE TOYNBEE CONVECTOR
WHEN ELEPHANTS LAST IN THE DOORYARD BLOOMED
YESTERMORROW
ZEN IN THE ART OF WRITING

Avon Books are available at special quantity discounts for bulk purchases for sales promotions, premiums, fund raising or educational use. Special books, or book excerpts, can also be created to fit specific needs.

For details write or telephone the office of the Director of Special Markets, Avon Books, Inc., Dept. FP, 1350 Avenue of the Americas, New York, New York 10019, 1-800-238-0658.

Ray Bradbury

DRIVING BLIND

STORIES

AVON BOOKS ◆ NEW YORK

AVON BOOKS, INC.
1350 Avenue of the Americas
New York, New York 10019

Collection copyright © 1997 by Ray Bradbury
Inside cover author photo by Tom Victor
Visit our website at **http://www.AvonBooks.com**
Library of Congress Catalog Card Number: 97-4378
ISBN: 0-380-78960-4

First Avon Books Paperback Printing: October 1998
First Avon Books Hardcover Printing: October 1997

AVON TRADEMARK REG. U.S. PAT. OFF. AND IN OTHER COUNTRIES, MARCA REGISTRADA, HECHO EN U.S.A.

Printed in the U.S.A.

WCD 10 9 8 7 6 5 4 3 2 1

With undying love to
the early-arriving granddaughters,
JULIA, CLAIRE, GEORGIA
and MALLORY.

And to
the late-arriving grandsons,
DANIEL, CASEY-RAY, SAMUEL
and THEODORE.

Live forever!

Contents

Night Train to Babylon

J ames Cruesoe was in the club car of a train plummeting out of Chicago, rocking and swaying as if it were drunk, when the conductor, lurching by, glanced at the bar, gave Cruesoe a wink, and lurched on. Cruesoe listened.

Uproars, shouts and cries.

That is the sound, he thought, of sheep in panic, glad to be fleeced, or hang gliders, flung off cliffs with no wings.

He blinked.

For there at the bar, drawn to a blind source of joyous consternation, stood a cluster of men glad for highway robbery, pleased to have wallets and wits purloined.

That is to say: gamblers.

Amateur gamblers, Cruesoe thought, and rose to stagger down the aisle to peer over the shoulders of businessmen behaving like high school juniors in full stampede.

"Hey, watch! The Queen *comes!* She *goes. Presto! Where?"*

"There!" came the cry.

"Gosh," cried the dealer. "Lost my shirt! Again! Queen up, Queen gone! Where?"

He'll let them win twice, Cruesoe thought. Then spring the trap.

"There!" cried all.

"Good gravy!" shouted the unseen gambler. "I'm sunk!"

Cruesoe had to look, he *yearned* to see this agile vaudeville magician.

On tiptoe, he parted a few squirming shoulders, not knowing what to expect.

But there sat a man with no fuzzy caterpillar brows or waxed mustaches. No black hair sprouted from his ears or nostrils. His skull did not poke through his skin. He wore an ordinary dove-gray suit with a dark gray tie tied with a proper knot. His fingernails were clean but unmanicured. Stunning! An ordinary citizen, with the serene look of a chap about to lose at cribbage.

Ah, yes, Cruesoe thought, as the gambler shuffled his cards slowly. That carefulness revealed the imp under the angel's mask. A calliope salesman's ghost lay like a pale epidermis below the man's vest.

"Careful, gents!" He fluttered the cards. "Don't bet too much!"

Challenged, the men shoveled cash into the furnace.

"Whoa! No bets above four bits! Judiciously, sirs!"

The cards leapfrogged as he gazed about, oblivious of his deal.

"Where's my left thumb, my right? Or are there *three thumbs?*"

They laughed. What a jokester!

"Confused, chums? Baffled? Must I lose *again?*"

"Yes!" all babbled.

"Damn," he said, crippling his hands. "'Damn! Where's the Red Queen? Start over!"

"No! The *middle* one! *Flip* it!"

The card was flipped.

"Ohmigod," someone gasped.

"Can't look." The gambler's eyes were shut. "How much did I lose *this* time?"

"Nothing," someone whispered.

"Nothing?" The gambler, aghast, popped open his eyes.

They all stared at a black card.

"Gosh," said the gambler. "I thought you *had* me!"

His fingers spidered to the right, another black card, then to the far left. The Queen!

"Hell," he exhaled, "why's she *there?* Christ, guys, keep your cash!"

"No! No!" A shaking of heads. "You won. You couldn't help it. It was just—"

"Okay. If you insist! Watch out!"

Cruesoe shut his eyes. This, he thought, is the end. From here on they'll lose and bet and lose again. Their fever's up.

"Sorry, gents. Nice try. *There!*"

Cruesoe felt his hands become fists. He was twelve again, a fake mustache glued to his lip and his school chums at a party and the three-card monte laid out. "Watch the Red Queen *vanish!*" And the kids shout and laugh as his hands blurred to win their candy but hand it back to show his love.

"One, two, *three!* Where can she *be?*"

He felt his mouth whisper the old words, but the voice was the voice of this wizard stealing wallets, counting cash on a late-night train.

"Lost again? God, fellas, quit before your wife shoots you! Okay, Ace of spades, King of clubs, Red Queen. You won't see *her* again!"

"No! *There!*"

Cruesoe turned, muttering. *Don't listen! Sit! Drink! Forget your twelfth birthday, your friends. Quick!*

He took one step when:

"That's *three* times lost, pals. I *must* fold my tent and . . ."

"No, no, don't leave *now!* We got to win the damn stuff back. Deal!"

And as if struck, Cruesoe spun about and returned to the madness.

"The Queen was *always* there on the left," he said.

Heads turned.

"'It was there all the *time*," Cruesoe said, louder.

"And who are you, sir?" The gambler raked in the cards, not glancing up.

"A boy magician."

"Christ, a boy magician!" The gambler riffled the deck.

The men backed off.

Cruesoe exhaled. "I know how to do the three-card monte."

"Congratulations."

"I won't cut in, I just wanted these good men—"

There was a muted rumble from the good men.

"—to know *anyone* can win at the three-card monte."

Looking away, the gambler gave the cards a toss.

"Okay, wisenheimer, deal! Gents, your bets. Our friend here takes over. Watch his hands."

Cruesoe trembled with cold. The cards lay waiting.

"Okay, son. Grab on!"

"I can't *do* the trick well, I just know *how* it's *done*."

"Ha!" The gambler stared around. "Hear that, chums? Knows how it *works*, but can't *do. Right?*"

Cruesoe swallowed. "Right. But—"

"But? Does a cripple show an athlete? A dragfoot pace the sprinter? Gents, you want to change horses out here—" He glanced at the window. Lights flashed by. "—halfway to Cincinnati?"

The gents glared and muttered.

"Deal! Show us how you can steal from the poor."

Cruesoe's hands jerked back from the cards as if burnt.

"You prefer not to cheat these idiots in my presence?" the gambler asked.

Clever beast! Hearing themselves so named, the idiots roared assent.

"Can't you see what he's *doing?*" Cruesoe said.

"Yeah, yeah, we see," they babbled. "Even-steven. Lose some, win some. Why don't you go back where you came from?"

Cruesoe glanced out at a darkness rushing into the past, towns vanishing in night.

"Do you, sir," said the Straight-Arrow gambler, "in front of all these men, accuse me of raping their daughters, molesting their wives?"

"No," Cruesoe said, above the uproar. "Just cheating," he whispered, "at cards!"

Bombardments, concussions, eruptions of outrage as the gambler leaned forward.

"Show us, sir, where these cards are inked, marked, or stamped!"

"There *are* no marks, inks, or stamps," Cruesoe said. "It's all prestidigitation."

Jesus! He might as well have cried *Prostitution!*

A dozen eyeballs rolled in their sockets.

Cruesoe fussed with the cards.

"Not marked," he said. "But your hands aren't connected to your wrists or elbows and finally all of it's not connected to . . ."

"To *what*, sir?"

"Your heart," Cruesoe said, dismally.

The gambler smirked. "This, sir, is not a romantic excursion to Niagara Falls."

"Yah!" came the shout.

A great wall of faces confronted him.

"I," Cruesoe said, "am very tired."

He felt himself turn and stagger off, drunk with the sway of the train, left, right, left, right. The conductor saw him coming and punched a drift of confetti out of an already punched ticket.

"Sir," Cruesoe said.

The conductor examined the night fleeing by the window.

"Sir," Cruesoe said. "Look *there*."

The conductor reluctantly fastened his gaze on the mob at the bar, shouting as the cardsharp raised their hopes but to dash them again.

"Sounds like a good time," the conductor said.

"*No*, sir! Those men are being cheated, fleeced, buggywhipped—"

"Wait," said the conductor. "Are they disturbing the peace? Looks more like a birthday party."

Cruesoe shot his gaze down the corridor.

A herd of buffalo humped there, angry at the Fates, eager to be shorn.

"Well?" said the conductor.

"I want that man thrown off the train! Don't you see what he's up to? That trick's in every dime-store magic book!"

The conductor leaned in to smell Cruesoe's breath.

"Do you *know* that gambler, sir? Any of his pals your friends?"

"No, I—" Cruesoe gasped and stopped. "My God, I just realized." He stared at the conductor's bland face.

7

"*You,*" he said, but could not go on.

You are in cohoots, he thought. You share the moola at the end of the line!

"Hold *on,*" said the conductor.

He took out a little black book, licked his fingers, turned pages. "Uh-huh," he said. "Lookit all the biblical/Egyptian names. *Memphis,* Tennessee. *Cairo,* Illinois? Yep! And here's one just ahead. Babylon."

"Where you throw that cheat *off?*"

"No. Someone *else.*"

"You wouldn't do that," Cruesoe said.

"No?" said the conductor.

Cruesoe turned and lurched away. "Damn idiot stupid fool," he muttered. "Keep your smart-ass mouth *shut!*"

"Ready, gentlemen," the insidious cardsharp was shouting. "Annie over. *Flea*-hop! Oh, *no!* The bad-news boy is *back!*"

Jeez, hell, damn, was the general response.

"Who do you think you *are?*" Cruesoe blurted.

"Glad you asked." The gambler settled back, leaving the cards to be stared at by the wolf pack. "Can you guess where I'm going tomorrow?"

"South America," Cruesoe said, "to back a tin-pot dictator."

"Not bad." The sharpster nodded. "Go on."

"Or you are on your way to a small European state where some nut keeps a witch doctor to suck the economy into a Swiss bank."

"The boy's a poet! I have a letter here, from Castro."

8

His gambler's hand touched his heart. "And one from Bothelesa, another from Mandela in South Africa. Which do I choose? Well." The gambler glanced at the rushing storm outside the window. "Choose any pocket, right, left, inside, out." He touched his coat.

"Right," Cruesoe said.

The man shoved his hand in his right coat pocket, pulled out a fresh pack of cards, gave it a toss.

"Open it. That's it. Now riffle and spread. *See* anything?"

"Well . . ."

"Gimme." He took it. "The next monte will be from the deck *you* choose."

Cruesoe shook his head. "That's not how the trick works. It's how you *lay down* and *pick up* the cards. *Any* deck would do."

"Pick!"

Cruesoe picked two tens and a red Queen.

"Okay!" The gambler humped the cards over each other. "Where's the Queen?"

"Middle."

He flipped it over. "Hey, you're good." He smiled.

"You're better. That's the trouble," Cruesoe said.

"Now, see this pile of ten-dollar bills? That's the stake, just put by these gents. You've stopped the game too long. Do you join or be the skeleton at the feast?"

"Skeleton."

"Okay. They're off! There she goes. Queen here, Queen there. Lost! *Where?* You ready to risk all your cash, fellows? Want to pull *out? All* of a single *mind?*"

Fierce whispers.

"*All*," someone said.

"No!" Cruesoe said.

A dozen curses lit the air.

"Smart-ass," said the cardsharp, his voice deadly calm, "do you realize that your static may cause these gentlemen to lose *everything?*"

"No," Cruesoe said. "It's not my static. *Your* hands deal the cards."

Such jeers. Such hoots. "Move! My God, move!"

"Well." With the three cards still under his clean fingers the gambler stared at the rushing storm beyond the window. "You've ruined it. Because of you, their choice is doomed. You and only you have intruded to burst the ambience, the aura, the bubble that enclosed this game. When I turn the card over my friends may hurl you off the train."

"They wouldn't do that," Cruesoe said.

The card was turned over.

With a roar the train pulled away in a downpour of rain and lightning and thunder. Just before the car door slammed, the gambler thrust a fistful of cards out on the sulfurous air and tossed. They took flight: an aviary of bleeding pigeons, to pelt Cruesoe's chest and face.

The club car rattle-banged by, a dozen volcanic faces with fiery eyes crushed close to the windows, fists hammering the glass.

His suitcase stopped tumbling.

The train was gone.

He waited a long while and then slowly bent and began to pick up fifty-two cards. One by one. One by one.

A Queen of hearts. Another Queen. Another Queen of hearts. And one more.

A Queen . . .

Queen.

Lightning struck. If it had hit him, he would never have known.

If MGM Is Killed,
Who Gets the Lion?

"**H**oly Jeez, damn. Christ off the cross!" said Jerry Would.

"Please," said his typist-secretary, pausing to erase a typo in a screenplay, "I have Christian ears."

"Yeah, but my tongue is Bronx, New York," said Would, staring out the window. "Will you just look, take one long fat look at *that!*"

The secretary glanced up and saw what he saw, beyond.

"They're repainting the studio. That's Stage One, isn't it?"

"You're damn right. Stage One, where we built the *Bounty* in '34 and shot the Tara interiors in '39 and Marie Antionette's palace in '34 and now, for God's sake, look what they're doing!"

"Looks like they're changing the number."

"Changing the number, hell, they're wiping it *out!*

No more One. Watch those guys with the plastic over-lays in the alley, holding up the goddamn pieces, trying them for size."

The typist rose and took off her glasses to see better.

"That looks like UGH. What does 'Ugh' mean?"

"Wait till they fit the first letter. See? Is that or is that not an H?"

"H added to UGH. Say, I bet I know the rest. Hughes! And down there on the ground, in small letters, the stencil? 'Aircraft'?"

"Hughes Aircraft, dammit!"

"Since when are we making planes? I know the war's on, but—"

"We're not making any damn planes," Jerry Would cried, turning from the window.

"We're shooting air combat films, then?"

"No, and we're not shooting no damn air films!"

"I don't see . . ."

"Put your damn glasses back on and look. Think! Why would those SOBs be changing the number for a name, hey? What's the big idea? We're not making an aircraft carrier flick and we're not in the business of tacking together P-38s and—Jesus, *now* look!"

A shadow hovered over the building and a shape loomed in the noon California sky.

His secretary shielded her eyes. "I'll be damned," she said.

"You ain't the only one. You wanna tell me what that thing is?"

She squinted again. "A balloon?" she said. "A barrage balloon?"

"You can say that again, but *don't!*"

She shut her mouth, eyed the gray monster in the sky, and sat back down. "How do you want this letter addressed?" she said.

Jerry Would turned on her with a killing aspect. "Who gives a damn about a stupid letter when the world is going to hell? Don't you get the full aspect, the great significance? Why, I ask you, would MGM have to be protected by a barrage—hell, there goes *another!* That makes *two* barrage balloons!"

"*No* reason," she said. "We're not a prime munitions or aircraft target." She typed a few letters and stopped abruptly with a laugh. "I'm slow, right? We *are* a prime bombing target?"

She rose again and came to the window as the stencils were hauled up and the painters started blow-gunning paint on the side of Stage One.

"Yep," she said, softly, "there it is. AIRCRAFT COMPANY. HUGHES. When does he move *in?*"

"What, Howie the nut? Howard the fruitcake? Hughes the billionaire bastard?"

"*That* one, yeah."

"He's going nowhere, he still has his pants glued to an office just three miles away. Think! Add it up. MGM is here, right, two miles from the Pacific coast, two blocks away from where Laurel and Hardy ran their tin lizzie like an accordion between trolley cars in 1928!

And three miles north of us and *also* two miles in from the ocean is—"

He let her fill in the blanks.

"Hughes Aircraft?"

He shut his eyes and laid his brow against the window to let it cool. "Give the lady a five-cent seegar."

"I'll be damned," she breathed with revelatory delight.

"You ain't the only one."

"When the Japs fly over or the subs surface out beyond Culver City, the people painting that building and re-lettering the signs hope that the Japs will think Clark Gable and Spencer Tracy are running around Hughes Aircraft two miles north of here, making pictures. And that MGM, *here*, has Rosie the Riveters and P-38s flying out of that hangar down there all day!"

Jerry Would opened his eyes and examined the evidence below. "I got to admit, a sound stage does look like a hangar. A hangar looks like a sound stage. Put the right labels on them and invite the Japs *in. Banzai!*"

"Brilliant," his secretary exclaimed.

"You're fired," he said.

"What?"

"Take a letter," said Jerry Would, his back turned.

"Another letter?"

"To Mr. Sid Goldfarb."

"But he's right upstairs."

"Take a letter, dammit, to Goldfarb, Sidney. Dear Sid. Strike that. Just Sid. I am damned angry. What the hell is going on? I walk in the office at eight a.m. and it's MGM. I walk out to the commissary at noon and Howard Hughes is pinching the waitresses' behinds. Whose bright idea was this?''

"Just what *I* wondered," his secretary said.

"You're fired," said Jerry Would.

"Go on," she said.

"Dear Sid. Where was I? Oh, yeah. Sid, why weren't we informed that this camouflage would happen? Remember the old joke? We were all hired to watch for icebergs sailing up Culver Boulevard? Relatives of the studio, uncles, cousins? And now the damned iceberg's here. And it wears tennis shoes, a leather jacket, and a mustache over a dirty smile. I been here twelve years, Sidney, and I refuse—aw, hell, finish typing it. Sincerely. No, not sincerely. Angrily yours. Angrily. Where do I sign?''

He tore the letter from the machine and whipped out a pen.

"Now take this upstairs and throw it over the transom."

"Messengers get killed for messages like this."

"Killed is better than fired."

She sat quietly.

"Well?" he said.

"I'm waiting for you to cool down. You may want to tear this letter up, half an hour from now."

"I will not cool down and I will not tear up. Go."

And still she sat, watching his face until the lines faded and the color paled. Then very quietly she folded the letter and tore it across once and tore it across twice and then a third and fourth time. She let the confetti drift into the trash basket as he watched.

"How many times have I fired you today?" he said.

"Just three."

"Four times and you're out. Call Hughes Aircraft."

"I was wondering when you—"

"Don't wonder. Get."

She flipped through the phone book, underlined a number, and glanced up. "Who do you want to talk to?"

"Mr. Tennis Shoes, Mr. Flying Jacket, the billionaire butinsky."

"You really think he ever answers the phone?"

"Try."

She tried and talked while he gnawed his thumbnail and watched them finish putting up and spraying the AIRCRAFT stencil below.

"Hell and damn," she said at last, in total surprise. She held out the phone. "He's *there!* And answered the phone *himself!*"

"You're putting me on!" cried Jerry Would.

She shoved the phone out in the air and shrugged.

He grabbed it. "Hello, who's this? What? Well, say, Howard, I mean Mr. Hughes. Sure. This is MGM Studios. My name? Would. Jerry Would. You *what?* You heard me? You saw *Back to Broadway?* And *Glory Years.* But sure, you once owned RKO Studios, right? Sure, sure. Say, Mr. Hughes, I got a little problem here. I'll make this short and sweet."

He paused and winked at his secretary.

She winked back. The voice on the line spoke nice and soft.

"What?" said Jerry Would. "Something's going on over at *your* place, *too*? So you know why I'm calling, sir. Well, they just put up the aircraft letters and spelled out HUGHES on Stage One. You like that, huh? Looks great. Well, I was wondering, Howard, Mr. Hughes, if you could do me a little favor."

Name it, said the quiet voice a long way off.

"I was thinking if the Japs come with the next tide by air or by sea and no Paul Revere to say which, well, when they see those big letters right outside my window, they're sure going to bomb the hell outta what they think is P-38 country and Hughes territory. A brilliant concept, sir, brilliant. Is *what?* Is everyone here at MGM happy with the ruse? They're not dancing in the streets but they do congratulate you for coming up with such a world-shaking plan. Now here's my point. I gotta lot of work to finish. Six films shooting, two films editing, three films starting. What I need is a nice safe place to work, you got the idea? That's it. Yeah. That's it. You got a nice small corner of one of your hangars that—sure! You're way ahead of me. I should *what?* Yeah, I'll send my secretary over right after lunch with some files. You got a typewriter? I'll leave mine here. Boy, How—Mr. Hughes, you're a peach. Now, tit for tat, if *you* should want to move into *my* office here? Just joking. Okay. Thanks. Thanks. Okay. She'll be there, pronto."

And he hung up.

His secretary sat stolidly, examining him. He looked away, refused to meet her stare. A slow blush moved up his face.

"*You're* fired," she said.

"Take it easy," he said.

She rose, gathered a few papers, hunted for her purse, applied a perfect lipstick mouth, and stood at the door.

"Have Joey and Ralph bring all the stuff in that top file," she said. "That'll do for starters. You coming?"

"In a moment," he said, standing by the window, still not looking at her.

"What if the Japs figure out this comedy, and bomb the *real* Hughes Aircraft instead of this fake one?"

"Some days," sighed Jerry Would, "you can't win for losing."

"Shall I write a letter to Goldfarb to tell him where you're going?"

"Don't write, call. That way there's no evidence."

A shadow loomed. They both looked up at the sky over the studio.

"Hey," he said, softly, "there's another. A *third* balloon."

"How come," she said, "it looks like a producer I used to know?"

"You're—" he said.

But she was gone. The door shut.

Hello, I Must Be Going

Here was a quiet tapping at the door and when Steve Ralphs opened it there stood Henry Grossbock, five foot one inches tall, immaculately dressed, very pale and very perturbed.

"Henry!" Steve Ralphs cried.

"Why do you sound like that?" Henry Grossbock said. "What have I done? Why am I dressed like this? Where am I going?"

"Come in, come in, someone might see you!"

"Why does it matter if someone *sees* me?"

"Come in, for God's sake, don't stand there arguing."

"All right, I'll come in, I have things to talk about anyway. Stand aside. There. I'm in."

Steve Ralphs backed off across the room and waved to a chair. "Sit."

"I don't feel welcome." Henry sat. "You have any strong liquor around this place?"

"I was just thinking that." Steve Ralphs jumped, ran into the kitchen, and a minute later returned with a tray, a bottle of whiskey, two glasses, and some ice. His hands were trembling as he poured the liquor.

"You look shaky," said Henry Grossbock. "What's wrong?"

"Don't you know, can't you *guess?* Here."

Henry took the glass. "You sure poured me a lot."

"You're going to need it. Drink."

They drank and Henry examined his coat front and his sleeves.

"You still haven't told me where I am going," he said, "or have I been there already? I don't usually dress this way except for concerts. When I stand up there before an audience, well, one desires respect. This is very good scotch. Thanks. Well?"

He stared at Steve Ralphs with a steady and penetrating stare.

Steve Ralphs gulped half of his drink and put it down and shut his eyes. "Henry, you've already been to a far place and just come back, for God's sake. And now you'll have to return to that place."

"What place, *what* place, stop the riddles!"

Steve Ralphs opened his eyes and said, "How did you get here? Did you take a bus, hire a taxi, or . . . walk from the graveyard?"

"Bus, taxi, walk? And what's that about a graveyard?"

"Henry, drink the rest of your drink. Henry, you've been in that graveyard for years."

"Don't be silly. What would I be doing *there?* I never applied for any—" Henry stopped and slowly sank back in his chair. "You mean—?"

Steve Ralphs nodded. "Yes, Henry."

"Dead? And in the graveyard? Dead and in the graveyard four years? Why didn't someone *tell* me?"

"It's hard to tell someone who's dead that he *is.*"

"I see, I see." Henry finished his drink and held the glass out for more. Steve Ralphs refilled.

"Dear, dear," said Henry Grossbock, slowly. "My, my. So *that's* why I haven't felt up to snuff lately."

"That's why, Henry. Let me catch up." Steve Ralphs poured more whiskey in his own glass and drank.

"So that's why you looked so peculiar when you opened the door just now—"

"That's why, Henry."

"Sorry. I really didn't mean—"

"Don't get up, Henry. You're here now."

"But under the circumstances—"

"It's all right. I'm under control. And even given the circumstances, you were always my best friend and it's nice, in a way, to see you again."

"Strange. *I* wasn't shocked to see *you.*"

"There's a difference, Henry. I mean, well—"

"You're alive, and I'm not, eh? Yes, I can see that. Hello, I must be going."

"What?"

"Groucho Marx sang a song with that title."

"Oh, yeah. Sure."

23

"Marvelous man. Funny. Is he still around? Did he die, too?"

"I'm afraid so."

"Don't be afraid. I'm not. Don't know why. Just now." Henry Grossbock sat up straight. "To business."

"What business?"

"Told you at the front door. Important. Must tell. I am very upset."

"So was I, but this liquor does wonders. Okay, Henry, shoot."

"The thing is—" Henry Grossbock said, finishing his second drink quickly, "my wife is neglecting me."

"But Henry, it's perfectly natural—"

"Let me finish. She used to come visit constantly. Brought me flowers, put a book nearby once, cried a lot. Every day. Then every other day. Now, never. How do you explain that? Refill, please."

Steve Ralphs tipped the bottle.

"Henry, four years is a long *time*—"

"You can say that again. How about Eternity, there's a *real* vaudeville show."

"You didn't really expect to be entertained, did you?"

"Why not? Evelyn always spoiled me. She changed dresses two or three times a day because she knew I loved it. Haunted bookshops, brought me the latest, read me the oldest, picked my ties, shined my shoes, her women's-lib friends joshed her for *that*. Spoiled. Yes, I expected to have someone fill the time for me."

"That's not how it works, Henry."

Henry Grossbock thought and nodded, solemnly, and sipped his whiskey. "Yes, I guess you're right. But let me name the *biggest* problem."

"What's that?"

"She's stopped crying. She used to cry every night, every day at breakfast, twice in the afternoon, just before supper. Then, lights out, crying."

"She missed you, Henry."

"And now she doesn't?"

"Time heals all wounds, they say."

"I don't want this wound healed. I liked things just the way they were. A good cry at dawn, a half decent cry before tea, a final one at midnight. But it's over. Now I don't feel wanted or needed."

"Think about it the way you had to think about your honeymoon with Evelyn. It had to end sometime."

"Not entirely. There were stray bits of it for the rest of forty years."

"Yes, but you *do* see the resemblance?"

"Honeymoon ended. Life over. I certainly don't much care for the residue." A thought struck Henry Grossbock. He set his glass down, sharply. "Is there someone *else?*"

"Someone . . ."

"*Else!* Has she taken up with—?"

"And what if she has?"

"How *dare* she!"

"Four years, Henry, four years. And no, she hasn't taken up with anyone. She'll remain a widow for the rest of her life."

"That's more like it. I'm glad I came to see you first. Set me straight. So she's still single and—hold on. How come no more tears at midnight, crying at breakfast?"

"You didn't really expect that, did you?"

"But damn, I miss it. A man's got to have *something!*"

"Don't you have any friends over at the—" Steve Ralphs stopped, flushed, refilled his glass, refilled Henry's.

"You were going to say graveyard. Bad lot, those. Layabouts. No conversation."

"You were always a great talker, Henry."

"Yes, yes, that's so, wasn't I? *Aren't* I? And you were my best listener."

"Talk some more, Henry. Get it all out."

"I think I've hit the high points, the important stuff. She's stopped coming by. That's bad. She's stopped crying. That's the very worst. The lubricant that makes—what I have become—worth the long while. I wonder if I showed up, would she cry again?"

"You're *not* going to visit?"

"Don't think I should, eh?"

"Nasty shock. Unforgivable."

"*Who* wouldn't forgive me?"

"Me, Henry. *I* wouldn't."

"Yes, yes. Oh dear. My, my. Good advice from my best friend."

"Best, Henry." Steve Ralphs leaned forward. "You *do* want her to get over you, don't you?"

"No! Yes. No! God, I don't know. Yes, I guess so."

"After all she *has* missed you and cried every day for most of four years."

"Yes." Henry Grossbock nursed his glass. "She *has* put in the time. I suppose I *should* let her off the hook."

"It would be a kindness, Henry."

"I don't *feel* kind, I don't *want* to be kind, but hell, I'll be kind anyhow. I do love the dear girl."

"After all, Henry, she has lots of years ahead."

"True. Damn. Think of it. Men age better but die younger. Women live longer but age badly. Strange arrangement God has made, don't you agree?"

"Why don't you ask Him, now that you're there?"

"Who, God? An upstart like me? Well, well. Ummm." Henry sipped. "Why not? What's she up to? If she's not dashing about in open cars with strange men, *what?*"

"Dancing, Henry. Taking dance lessons. Sculpting. Painting."

"Always wanted to do that, never could. Concert schedules, cocktail parties for possible sponsors, recitals, lectures, travel. She always said *someday.*"

"Someday is here, Henry."

"Took me by surprise, is all. Dancing, you say? Sculpting? Is she any good?"

"A fair dancer. A *very* fine sculptor."

"Bravo. Or is it brav*a?* Yes. Brava. I think I'm glad for that. Yes, I *am* glad. Fills the time. And what do *I* do? Crosswords."

"Crosswords?"

"Dammit, what else is there, considering my circumstances? Fortunately, I recall every single good and bad puzzle ever printed in the *New York Times* or the *Saturday Review*. Crossword. Short nickname, three letters, for Tutankhamen. Tut! Four letters, one of the Great Lakes. *Erie!* Easy, that one. Fourteen letters, old Mediterranean capital. Hell. Constantinople!"

"Five letters. Word for best pal, good friend, fine husband, brilliant violinist."

"Henry?"

"Henry. You." Steve Ralphs smiled, lifted his glass, drank.

"That's my cue to grab my hat and leave. Oh, I didn't bring a hat. Well, well."

Steve Ralphs suddenly swallowed very hard.

"What's this?" said Henry, leaning forward, listening.

"A repressed sob, Henry."

"Good! That's better. Warms the old heart, *that* does. I don't suppose you could—"

"Suppress a few more sobs, once or twice a week for the next year?"

"I hesitate to ask—"

"I'll try, Henry." Another mysterious sound moved up Steve Ralph's throat. He hastened to lid it with whiskey. "Tell you what. I'll call Evelyn, say I'm writing a book about you, need some of your personal books, notes, golf clubs, spectacles, the lot, bring them here, and, well, once a week, anyway, look them over, feel sad. How's *that* sound?"

"That's the ticket, or what are friends for?" Henry

Grossbock beamed. There was color in his cheeks. He drank and stood up.

At the door, Henry turned and peered into Steve Ralph's face.

"Dear me, dear me, are those tears?"

"I think so, Henry."

"Well now, that's more like it. Not Evelyn's of course, and you're not heaving great sobs. But it'll do. Much thanks."

"Don't mention it, Henry."

"Well." Henry opened the door. "See you around."

"Not too soon, Henry."

"Eh? No, of course not. No hurry. Good-bye, friend."

"Oh, good-bye, Henry." Yet another mysterious gulp arose in the younger man's throat.

"Yes, yes." Henry smiled. "Keep that up until I'm down the hall. Well, as Groucho Marx said—"

And he was gone. The door shut.

Turning, slowly, Steve Ralphs walked to the telephone, sat down, and dialed.

After a moment the receiver on the other end clicked and a voice spoke.

Steve Ralphs wiped his eyes with the back of his hand and at last said:

"Evelyn?"

House Divided

Small fifteen-year-old fingers plucked at the buttons on Chris' trousers like a moth drawn to a flame. He heard whispered words in the dark room that meant nothing, and could not be remembered a moment after they were spoken.

Vivian's lips were so fresh that it was unbelievable. Chris had the feeling that this was a dream. This was a pantomime carried out in the dark, which he could not see. Vivian herself had switched out every light. It had started as every evening like it had started. With Chris and his brother Leo climbing upstairs with Vivian and Shirley, their girl cousins. The girls were both blonde and smiling. Leo was sixteen and clumsy. Chris was twelve and knew nothing of such moths darting in the warm pantomime, or that there was a light shining in him he had never known about, that some girl might want. Shirley was ten, going on eleven, but very curious. Vivian was the ringleader; she was fifteen and beginning to see the world's people.

Chris and Leo had arrived in the family car, acting properly grave, since it was such a grave situation. They walked silently behind Mother and Dad into the Johnsons' house on Buttrick Street, where all the other relatives were gathered in a hushed spell of waiting. Uncle Inar sat by the phone, looking at it, his big hands twitching all by themselves, uneasy animals in his lap.

It was like walking into the hospital itself. Uncle Lester was very badly off. They were waiting for news now from the hospital. Lester had been shot in the stomach on a hunting trip and had lingered half-alive for three days now. So they had come tonight to be together, just in case they received the news of their Uncle Lester's passing. All three sisters and Lester's two brothers were there, with their wives and husbands and children.

After a proper interval of hushed speaking, Vivian had very carefully suggested, "Mama, we'll go upstairs and tell ghost stories, so you grown-ups can talk."

"Ghost stories," said Uncle Inar vaguely. "What a thing to tell tonight. Ghost stories."

Vivian's mama agreed. "You can go upstairs if you're quiet. We don't want any racket."

"Yes, ma'am," said Chris and Leo.

They left the room, walking slowly on the edge of their shoes. Nobody noticed their going. They could have been several phantoms passing for all the attention they got.

Upstairs, Vivian's room had a low couch against one wall, a dressing table with pink-folded silk for a skirt, and flower pictures. There was a green leather diary, fabulously inscribed but securely padlocked on the table, freckles of powder on it. The room smelled sweetly soft and nice.

They sat upon the couch, backs lined neatly against the wall, a row of solemn ramrods, and Vivian, like always, told the first ghost story. They turned out all but one lamp, which was very feeble, and she put her voice low in her rounded breasts and whispered it out.

It was that ancient tale about lying abed late one night, with stars cold in the sky, al alone in a big old house when some *thing* starts creeping slowly up the stairs to your room. Some strange and awful visitor from some other world. And as the story advanced, slowly step by step, step by step, your voice got more tense and more whispery and you kept waiting and waiting for that shocking finale.

"*It* crept up to the second step, it stepped up to the third step, it came to the fourth step . . ."

All four of their hearts had churned to this story a thousand times. Now, again, a cold sweat formed on four anticipatory brows. Chris listened, holding Vivian's hand.

"The strange sounds came on to the sixth step, and rustled to the seventh step, and then to the eighth step . . ."

Chris had memorized the story, often, and told it often, but no one could tell it quite like Vivian. She was husking it now, like a witch, eyes half shut, body tensed against the wall.

Chris went over the story in his mind, ahead of her. "Ninth, tenth, and eleventh steps. Twelve, thirteen, fourteen steps. *It* came to the *top* of the stairs . . ."

Vivian went on. "Now it's in the hall at the top of the stairs. Outside the door. Now it's coming inside. Now it's closing the door." A pause. "Now it's walking across your room. Now it's passing the bureau. Now it's over your bed. Now it's standing right over you, right over your head . . ."

A long pause, during which the darkness of the room got darker. Everybody drew in their breath, waiting, waiting.

"*I GOTCHA!*"

Screaming, then giggling, you burst out! You let the black bat crash into the web. You had built the web of tension and horror so completely inside, minute by minute, step by step, around and around, like a very dainty horrible spider weaving, and in that tumultuous climax when I GOTCHA! flew out at you, like a sickening bat, it shattered the web down in trembling apprehension and laughter. You had to laugh to cover up your old old fear. You shrieked and giggled, all four of you. You hollered and shook the couch and held onto each other. Oh that familiar old story! You rocked back and forth, shivering, breathing fast. Funny how it still scared you after the hundredth telling.

The giggling subsided quickly. Footsteps, real ones, were hurrying up the steps to Vivian's room. By the sound of them Chris knew it was Auntie. The door opened.

"Vivian," cried Auntie. "I told you about noise! Don't you have any respect!"

"All right, Mama. We're sorry."

"I'm sorry, Auntie," said Chris, meaning it. "We just forgot ourselves. We got scared."

"Vivian, you keep them quiet," directed Auntie, her scowl softening. "And if I hear you again you'll all come downstairs."

"We'll be good," said Leo, quietly, earnestly.

"Well, all right, then."

"Has the hospital called?" asked Shirley.

"No," said Auntie, her face changing, remembering. "We expect to hear soon."

Auntie went downstairs. It took another five minutes to get back into the spell of storytelling.

"Who'll tell a story now?" asked Shirley.

"Tell another one, Vivian," said Leo. "Tell the one about the butter with the evil fungus in it."

"Oh, I tell that *every* time," said Vivian.

"I'll tell one," said Chris. "A *new* one."

"Swell," said Vivian. "But let's turn out the other light first. It's too light in here."

She bounced up, switched out the last light. She came back through the utter dark and you could smell her coming and feel her beside you, Chris realized. Her hand grabbed his, tightly. "Go on," she said.

"Well . . ." Chris wound his story up on a spool,

getting it ready in his mind. "Well, once upon a time—"

"Oh, we heard *that* one before!" they all laughed. The laughter came back from the unseen wall of the room. Chris cleared his throat and started again.

"Well, once upon a time there was a black castle in the woods—"

He had his audience immediately. A castle was a darn nice thing to start with. It wasn't a bad story he had in mind, and he would have told it all the way through, taking fifteen minutes or more to hang it out on a line in the dark bedroom air. But Vivian's fingers were like an impatient spider inside his palm, and as the story progressed he became more aware of her than of the story people.

"—an old witch lived in this black castle—"

Vivian's lips kissed him on the cheek. It was like all her kisses. It was like kisses before bodies were invented. Bodies are invented around about the age of twelve or thirteen. Before that there are only sweet lips and sweet kisses. There is a sweet something about such kisses you never find again after someone puts a body under your head.

Chris didn't have a body yet. Just his face. And, like every time Vivian had ever kissed him, he responded. After all, it was fun and it was as good as eating and sleeping and playing all kinds of games. Her lips were like a subtle sugar, and nothing else. For the past four years since he was eight, every time he met Vivian and that was usually once every month, because she lived on the far side of town, there would be ghost stories and kisses and subtle sugar.

"—well, this witch in this castle—"

She kissed him on the lips, momentarily crumbling the castle. About ten seconds later he had to build it up again.

"—this witch in this castle had a beautiful young daughter named Helga. Helga lived in a dungeon and was treated very poorly by her evil old mother. She was very pretty and—"

The lips returned. This time for a longer stay.

"Go on with the story," said Leo.

"Yeah, hurry up," said Shirley, perturbed.

"—Ah," said Chris, breaking away a little, his breath a bit funny. "—One day the girl escaped from the dungeon and ran out into the woods, and the witch shouted after her—"

From there on the story got slower and slower, and wandered off in aimless, vague, and blundering directions. Vivian pressed close to him, kissing and breathing on his cheek as he told the halting tale. Then, very slowly, and with an architect's wonderful ability, she began to build his body for him! The Lord said ribs and there were ribs. The Lord said stomach and there was stomach! The Lord said legs and there were legs! The Lord said something else and there was something else!

It was funny finding his body under him so suddenly. For twelve years it had never been there. It was a pendulum under a clock, that body, and now Vivian was setting it in motion, touching, urging, rocking it to and fro, until it swung in dizzy warm arcs under the machinery of the head. The clock was now running. A clock cannot run until the pendulum moves. The clock can be whole, ready, and intact and healthy, but until that pendulum is thrust into motion there is nothing but machinery without use.

"—and the girl ran out into the woods—"

"Hurry up, hurry up, Chris!" criticized Leo.

It was like the story of the thing coming up the stairs, one by one, one by one. This whole evening, here, now, in the dark. But—different.

Vivian's fingers deftly plucked at the belt buckle and drew the metal tongue out, loosening it open.

Now she's at the first button.

Now she's at the second button.

So *like* that old story. But this was a *real* story.

"—so this girl ran into the woods—"

"You said that before, Chris," said Leo.

Now she's at the third button.

Now she's moved down to the fourth button, oh God, and now to the fifth button, and now—

The same words that ended that *other* story, the *very same two words*, but this time shouted passionately, inside, silently, silently, to yourself!

The two words!

The same two words used at the end of the story about the thing coming up the stairs. The same two words at the end!

Chris' voice didn't belong to him anymore:

"—and she ran into something, there was something, there was, well, anyway, this, she . . . well, she tried . . . er, someone chased her . . . or . . . well, she ran, anyway, and she came, down she went and she ran and then, and then, she—"

Vivian moved against him. Her lips sealed up that story inside him and wouldn't let it out. The castle fell thundering for the last time into ruin, in a burst of blazing flame, and there was nothing in the world but this newly invented body of his and the fact that a girl's body is not so much land, like the hills of Wisconsin, pretty to look at. Here was all the beauty and singing and firelight and warmth in the world. Here was the meaning of all change and all movement and all adjustment.

Far away in the dim hushed lands below a phone rang. It was so faint it was like one of those voices crying in a forgotten dungeon. A phone rang and Chris could hear nothing.

It seemed there was a faint, halfhearted criticism from Leo and Shirley, and then a few minutes later, Chris realized that Leo and Shirley were clumsily kissing one another, and nothing else, just clumsily adjusting faces to one another. The room was silent. The stories were told and all of space engulfed the room.

It was so strange. Chris could only lie there and let Vivian tell him all of it with this dark, unbelievable pantomime. You are not told all of your life of things like this, he thought. You are not told at all. Maybe it is too good to tell, too strange and wonderful to give words about.

Footsteps came up the stairs. Very slow, very sad footsteps this time. Very slow and soft.

"Quick!" whispered Vivian. She pulled away, smoothing her dress. Like a blind man, fingerless, Chris fumbled with his belt buckle and buttons. "Quick!" whispered Vivian.

She flicked the light on and the world shocked Chris with its unreality. Blank walls staring, wide and sense-less after the dark; lovely, soft, moving, and secretive dark. And as the footsteps advanced up the stairs, the four of them were once again solemn ramrods against the wall, and Vivian was retelling her story:

"—now he's at the top stair—"

The door opened. Auntie stood there, tears on her face. That was enough in itself to tell, to give the message.

"We just received a call from the hospital," she said. "Your Uncle Lester passed away a few minutes ago."

They sat there.

"You'd better come downstairs," said Auntie.

They arose slowly. Chris felt drunk and unsteady and warm. He waited for Auntie to go out and the others to follow. He came last of all, down into the hushed land of weeping and solemn tightened faces.

As he descended the last step he couldn't help but feel a strange thing moving in his mind. Oh, Uncle Les-ter, they've taken your body away from you, and I've got *mine*, and it isn't fair! Oh, it isn't fair, because this is *so good!*

In a few minutes they would go home. The silent house would hold their weeping a few days, the radio would be snapped off for a week, and laughter would come and be throttled in birth.

He began to cry.

Mother looked at him. Uncle Inar looked at him and some of the others looked at him. Vivian, too. And Leo, so big and solemn standing there.

Chris was crying and everybody looked.

But only Vivian knew that he was crying for joy, a warm good crying of a child who has found treasure buried deep and warm in his very body.

"Oh, Chris," said Mother, and came to comfort him. "There, there."

Grand Theft

Emily Wilkes had her eyes pried open by a peculiar sound at three o'clock in the deep morning, with no moon, and only the stars as witness.

"Rose?" she said.

Her sister, in a separate bed not three feet away, already had her eyes wide, so was not surprised.

"You *hear* it?" she said, spoiling everything.

"I was going to tell *you*," said Emily. "Since you already seem to know, there's no use—"

She stopped and sat up in bed, as did Rose, both pulled by invisible wires. They sat there, two ancient sisters, one eighty, the other eighty-one, both bone-thin and bundles of nerves because they were staring at the ceiling.

Emily Wilkes nodded her head up. "*That* what you heard?"

"Mice in the attic?"

"Sounds bigger'n that. Rats."

"Yes, but it sounds like they're wearing boots and carrying bags."

That did it. Out of bed, they grabbed their wrappers and went downstairs as fast as arthritis would allow. No one wanted to stay underneath whoever wore those boots.

Below they grabbed the banister and stared up, whispering.

"What would anyone do in our attic *this* time of night?"

"Burgling all our old junk?"

"You don't think they'll come down and *attack* us?"

"What, two old fools, with skinny backsides?"

"Thank God, the trapdoor only works one way, and is locked beneath."

They began to edge step by step back up toward the hidden sounds.

"I *know!*" said Rose, suddenly. "In the Chicago papers last week: they're stealing *antique furniture!*"

"Pshaw! We're the only antiques here!"

"Still, there's some up there. A Morris chair, that's old. Some dining room chairs, older, and a cut crystal chandelier."

"From the dime store, 1914. So ugly we couldn't put it out with the trash. Listen."

It was quieter above. On the top floor, they gazed at the ceiling trapdoor and cocked their ears.

"Someone's opening my trunk." Emily clapped her hands to her mouth. "Hear that? The hinges need oiling."

"Why would they open your trunk? Nothing is there."

"Maybe *something* . . ."

Above, in the dark, the trunk lid fell.

"Fool!" whispered Emily.

Someone tiptoed across the attic floor, careful after being clumsy.

"There's a window up there, they're climbing out!"

The two sisters ran to their own bedroom window.

"Unlock the screen, poke your head out!" cried Rose.

"And let them *see* me? No, ma'am!"

They waited and heard a scraping noise and a clatter as something fell on the driveway below.

Gasping, they shoved the screen out to peer down and see a long ladder being toted along the driveway by two shadows. One of the shadows grasped a small white packet in his free hand.

"They stole something!" hissed Emily. "Come!"

Downstairs, they threw the front door wide to see two sets of footprints on the lawn in the dew. A truck, at the curb, pulled away.

Running out, both ladies shaded their eyes to read the vanishing license plate.

"Damnation!" cried Emily. "Did you *see*?"

"A seven and nine, is all. Do we call the police?"

"Not till we know what's *gone*. Shake a leg."

By flashlight on the attic stairs they unlocked the trapdoor and climbed up into darkness.

Emily swept the attic room with the flash as they

stumbled through old suitcases, a child's bike, and that truly ugly chandelier.

"Nothing's gone," said Rose. "Odd-peculiar."

"Maybe. Here's the trunk. Grab on."

As they lifted, the lid sprang back with an exhalation of dust and ancient scent.

"My God, remember *that?* Ben Hur perfume, 1925, came out with the movie!"

"Hush," said Emily. "Oh, hush!"

She poked the flashlight into an empty place in the middle of an old party dress: a sort of crushed pocket, two inches deep, four inches wide, and eight inches long.

"Dear God in heaven!" cried Emily. "They're gone!"

"Gone?"

"My love letters! From 1919 and 1920 and 1921! Wrapped in a pink ribbon, thirty of them. Gone!"

Emily stared down at the coffin-shaped emptiness in the middle of the old party dress. "Why would anyone steal love letters written so far back by someone probably dead to someone, me, good as dead?"

"Emily Bernice!" exclaimed Rose. "Where you been lately? You ever see those TV matinees make you want your mouth washed out with soap? How about the gossip columns in the town gazette? You ever look at the crazy ladies' magazines at the beauty parlor?"

"I try *not* to."

"Next time, look! All those folks got up on the dark side of the bed. Our phone'll ring tomorrow. Whoever stole your letters'll want cash to hand them back, or edit them for some crazed women's book club, or for advice in a lovelorn column. Blackmail. What else? Publicity! Come on!''

"Don't call the police! Oh, Rose, I won't wash my underwear for them or anyone! Is there any grape wine left in the pantry? Rose, move! It's the end of the world!''

Going down, they almost fell.

The next day every time a special-delivery mail truck ran by, Emily would part the parlor curtains and wait for it to stop. It never did.

The day after, when a TV repair van slowed to seek an address, Emily stepped out to fend off any ill-mannered reporters who might nose in. They never nosed.

On the third day, when intuition said there had been time enough for the *Green Town Gazette* to save up its spit and let fly, the spit was not saved or flown.

But . . .

On the fourth day a single letter fell in her mailbox with no mailman in sight. Emily's name on the letter seemed written in lemon juice and scorched to raise the calligraphy.

"Look," Emily whispered, "Emily Bernice *Watriss!* And the two-cent stamp is canceled: June fourth, 1921." She held the letter up to X-ray its mystery. "Whoever stole this four nights ago," she gasped, "is sending it *back* to me! Why?''

"Open it," said Rose. "The outside is sixty-two years old. What's *inside?*''

Emily took a deep breath and slid out the brittle paper with brownish handwriting in a fine flourished Palmer penmanship.

"June fourth, 1921," she read. "And the letter says: My dearest dear Emily—"

Emily let a tear drop from one eye.

"Well, go *on!*" said Rose.

"It's *my* love letter!"

"I know, I know, but we're two old battle-axes now. Nothing can offend us! Gimme that!"

Rose grabbed and turned the letter toward the light. Her voice faded as her eyes squinted along the fine calligraphy from another year:

"My dearest dear Emily: I know not how to pour out all that is in my heart. I have admired you for so many years and yet, when we have danced or shared picnics at the lake, I have been unable to speak. At home I stare at myself in the mirror and hate my cowardice. But now at last I must speak my tenderest thoughts or go mad beyond salvation. I fear to offend, and this small letter will take many hours to rewrite. Dear, dear Emily, know my affection and willingness to share some part of my life near or with you. If you could look upon me with the smallest kindness, I would be overcome with happiness. I have had to stop myself from touching your hand. And the thought of anything more, the merest kiss, shakes me that I even dare to say these words. My intentions are honorable. If you would permit, I would like to speak to your parents. Until that hour and day, I send you my affections and kindest thoughts for your future life and existence."

Rose's voice sounded clearly with these last words . . .

"Signed William Ross Fielding."

Rose glanced at Emily. "William Ross Fielding? Who was *he*, writing to you and madly in love?"

"Oh, God," Emily Bernice Watriss cried, her eyes blind with tears. "I'll be damned if *I* know!"

Day after day the letters arrived, not by mail, but slipped in the box at midnight or dawn to be read aloud by Rose or Emily who took turns wiping their eyes. Day after day the writer from a far year begged Emily's pardon, worried on her future, and signed himself with a flourish and an almost audible sigh, William Ross Fielding.

And each day Emily, eyes shut, said, "Read it again. I *almost* got a face to match the words!"

By week's end, with six ancient letters stacked and crumbling fast, Emily fell into exhaustion and exclaimed, "Stop! Devil take that sinful blackmailer who won't show his face! Burn it!"

"Not yet," said Rose, arriving with no ancient yellowed note, but a spanking bright new envelope, nameless outside, nameless in.

Emily, back from the dead, snatched it and read:

"I am ashamed for assisting all this trouble which now must stop. You can find your mail at 11 South St. James. Forgive."

And no signature.

"I don't understand," Emily said.

"Easy as pie," said Rose. "Whoever's sending your letters back is making affectionate approaches with someone else's notes from when Coolidge was president!"

"My God, Rose, feel my face: red-hot. Why would someone climb a ladder, rob an attic, and run? Why not stand on our lawn and yell?"

"Because," said Rose, quietly, turning the new letter over, "maybe whoever wrote this is just as shy now as William Ross Fielding was way back where you can't remember. Now what?"

"I wonder . . ." Emily stared out the window. ". . . who lives at 11 South St. James."

"Here it is."

They stood in front of it late in the day.

11 South St. James.

"Who's there looking out at us this very minute?" said Emily.

"Not the gent who sent you the confession," said Rose. "He just helped carry the ladder but can't carry the guilt. In there now is the mad fool who's been sending your notes. And if we don't move the whole street'll be a beehive. Shake a leg."

They crossed the porch and rang the bell. The front door drifted wide. An old man, well into his late seventies, stood there, astonished.

"Why, Emily Bernice Watriss," he exclaimed. "Hello!"

"What," said Emily Bernice Watriss, "in hell's name are you *up* to?"

"Right now?" he said. "Tea's ready. Yes?"

They sidled in, perched themselves, ready to run, and watched him pour teakettle water over some orange pekoe leaves.

"Cream or lemon?" he asked.

"Don't cream and lemon me!" Emily said.

"Please."

They took their cups but said nothing and drank none, as he sipped his own and said:

"My friend called to admit he had revealed my address. This whole week has made me incredibly sad."

"How do you think *I* feel?" Emily exclaimed. "You *are* the one, then, who stole my mail and sent it back?"

"I am that one, yes."

"Well then, make your demands!"

"Demands? No, no! Did you fear blackmail? How stupid of me not to guess you might think so. No, no. Are those the letters there?"

"They are!"

"The letter on the top, the first one, dated June fourth, 1921. Would you mind opening it? Just hold it where I can't read it, and let me speak, yes?"

Emily fumbled the letter out on her lap.

"Well?" she said.

"Just this," he said, and shut his eyes and began to recite in a voice they could hardly hear:

"My dearest dear Emily—"

Emily sucked in her breath.

The old man waited, eyes shut, and then repeated the words signed across the inside of his eyelids:

"My dearest dear Emily. I know not how to address you or pour out all that is in my heart—"

Emily let her breath out.

The old man whispered:

"—I have admired you for so many months and years, and yet when I have seen you, when we have danced or shared picnics with your friends at the lake, I had found myself unable to speak—but now at last I must speak my tenderest thoughts or find myself mad beyond salvation—"

Rose took out her handkerchief and applied it to her nose. Emily took out hers and applied it to her eyes.

His voice was soft and then loud and then soft again:

"—and the thought of anything more than that, the merest kiss, shakes me that I dare to put it in words—"

He finished, whispering:

"—until that hour and day, I send you my affections and kindest thoughts for your future life and existence. Signed William Ross Fielding. Now. Second letter."

Emily opened the second letter and held it where he could not see it.

"Dearest dear one," he said. "You have not answered my first letter which means one or several things: you did not receive it, it was kept from you, or you received, destroyed it, or hid it away. If I have offended you, forgive— Everywhere I go, your name is spoken. Young men speak of you. Young women tell rumors that soon you may travel away by ocean liner . . ."

"They did that, in those days," said Emily, almost

to herself. "Young women, sometimes young men, sent off for a year to forget."

"Even if there was nothing *to* forget?" said the old man, reading his own palms spread out on his knees.

"Even that. I have another letter here. Can you tell me what it says?"

She opened it and her eyes grew wet as she read the lines and heard him, head down, speak them quietly, from remembrance.

"Dearest dear, do I dare say it, love of my life? You are leaving tomorrow and will not return until long after Christmas. Your engagement has been announced to someone already in Paris, waiting. I wish you a grand life and a happy one and many children. Forget my name. Forget it? Why, dear girl, you never knew it. Willie or Will? I think you called me that. But there was no last name, really, so nothing to forget. Remember instead my love. Signed W.R.F."

Finished, he sat back and opened his eyes as she folded the letter and placed it with the others in her lap, tears running down her cheeks.

"Why," she asked at last, "did you steal the letters? And use them this way, sixty years later? Who told you where the letters might be? I buried them in that coffin, that trunk, when I sailed to France. I don't think I have looked at them more than once in the past thirty years. Did William Ross Fielding tell you about them?"

"Why, dear girl, haven't you guessed?" said the old man. "My Lord, I *am* William Ross Fielding."

There was an incredibly long silence.

"Let me look at you." Emily leaned forward as he raised his head into the light.

"No," she said. "I wish I could say. Nothing."

"It's an old man's face now," he said. "No matter. When you sailed around the world one way, I went another. I have lived in many countries and done many things, a bachelor traveling. When I heard that you had no children and that your husband died, many years ago, I drifted back to this, my grandparents' house. It has taken all these years to nerve myself to find and send this best part of my life to you."

The two sisters were very still. You could almost hear their hearts beating. The old man said:

"What now?"

"Why," said Emily Bernice Watriss Wilkes slowly, "every day for the next two weeks, send the rest of the letters. One by one."

He looked at her, steadily.

"And then?" he said.

"Oh, God!" she said. "I don't know. Let's see."

"Yes, yes. Indeed. Let's say good-bye."

Opening the front door he almost touched her hand.

"My dear dearest Emily," he said.

"Yes?" She waited.

"What—" he said.

"Yes?" she said.

"What . . ." he said, and swallowed. "What . . . are you . . ."

She waited.

"Doing tonight?" he finished, quickly.

Remember Me?

"**R**emember me? Of course, surely you *do!*"
His hand extended, the stranger waited.

"Why, yes," I said. "You're—"

I stopped and searched around for help. We were in middle-street in Florence, Italy, at high noon. He had been rushing one way, I the other, and almost collided. Now he waited to hear his name off my lips. Panicking, I rummaged my brain which ran on empty.

"You're—" I said again.

He seized my hand as if fearing I might bolt and run. His face was a sunburst. He *knew* me! Shouldn't I return the honor? There's a good dog, he thought, *speak!*

"I'm Harry!" he cried.

"Harry . . . ?"

"Stadler!" he barked with a laugh. "Your butcher!"

"Jesus, of course. Harry, you old son of a bitch!" I pumped his hand with relief.

He almost danced with joy. "*That* son of a bitch, yes! Nine thousand miles from home. No wonder you didn't know me! Hey, we'll get killed out here. I'm at the Grand Hotel. The lobby parquetry floor, amazing! Dinner tonight? Florentine steaks—listen to your butcher, eh? Seven tonight! Yes!"

I opened my mouth to suck and blow out in a great refusal, but—

"Tonight!" he cried.

He spun about and ran, almost plowed under by a bumblebee motorbike. At the far curb he yelled:

"Harry Stadler!"

"Leonard Douglas," I shouted, inanely.

"I know." He waved and vanished in the mob. "I know . . ."

My God! I thought, staring at my massaged and abandoned hand. Who *was* that?

My butcher.

Now I saw him at his counter grinding hamburger, a tiny white toy-boat cap capsizing on his thin blond hair, Germanic, imperturbable, his cheeks all pork sausage as he pounded a steak into submission.

My butcher, *yes!*

"Jesus!" I muttered for the rest of the day. "Christ! What made me accept? Why in hell did he *ask?* We don't even *know* each other, except when he says, That's five bucks sixty, and I say, So long! Hell!"

I rang his hotel room every half hour all afternoon. No answer.

"Will you leave a message, sir?"

"No thanks."

Coward, I thought. Leave a message: sick. Leave a message: died!

I stared at the phone, helpless. Of course I hadn't recognized him. Whoever recognizes anyone away from their counter, desk, car, piano, or wherever someone stands, sits, sells, speaks, provides, or dispenses? The mechanic free of his grease-monkey jumpsuit, the lawyer devoid of his pinstripes and wearing a fiery hibiscus sport shirt, the club woman released from her corset and crammed in an explosive bikini—all, all unfamiliar, strange, easily insulted if unrecognized! We all expect that no matter where we go or dress, we will be instantly recognized. Like disguised MacArthurs we stride ashore in far countries crying: "*I* have returned!"

But does anyone *give* a damn? This butcher, now—minus his cap, without the blood-fingerprinted smock, without the fan whirling above his head to drive off flies, without bright knives, sharp tenterhooks, whirled bologna slicers, mounds of pink flesh or spreads of marbled beef, he was the masked avenger.

Besides, travel had freshened him. Travel does that. Two weeks of luscious foods, rare wines, long sleeps, wondrous architectures and a man wakes ten years younger to hate going home to be old.

Myself? I was at the absolute peak of losing years in gaining miles. My butcher and I had become quasi-teenagers reborn to collide in Florentine traffic to gibber and paw each other's memories.

57

"Damn it to hell!" I jabbed his number on the touch-phone, viciously. Five o'clock: silence. Six: no answer. Seven: the same. Christ!

"Stop!" I yelled out the window.

All of Florence's church bells sounded, sealing my doom.

Bang! Someone slammed a door, on their way out. Me.

When we met at five minutes after seven, we were like two angry lovers who hadn't seen each other for days and now rushed in a turmoil of self-pity toward a supper with killed appetites.

Eat and run, no, eat and flee, was in our faces as we swayed in mid-lobby, at the last moment seized each other's hands. Might we arm-wrestle? From somewhere crept false smiles and tepid laughter.

"Leonard Douglas," he cried, "you old son of a bitch!"

He stopped, red-faced. Butchers, after all, do not swear at old customers!

"I mean," he said, "come *on!*"

He shoved me into the elevator and babbled all the way up to the penthouse restaurant.

"What a coincidence. Middle of the street. Fine food here. Here's our floor. Out!"

We sat to dine.

"Wine for me." The butcher eyed the wine list, like an old friend. "Here's a swell one. 1970, St. Emilion. Yes?"

"Thanks. A very dry vodka martini."

My butcher scowled.

"But," I said, quickly, "I *will* have some wine, of course!"

I ordered salad to start. He scowled again.

"The salad and the martini will ruin your taste for the wine. Beg pardon."

"Well then," I said, hastily, "the salad, *later*."

We ordered our steaks, his rare, mine well-done.

"Sorry," said my butcher, "but you *should* treat your meat more kindly."

"Not like St. Joan, eh?" I said, and laughed.

"That's a good one. Not like St. Joan."

At which moment the wine arrived to be uncorked. I offered my glass quickly and, glad that my martini had been delayed, or might never come, made the next minute easier by sniffing, whirling, and sipping the St. Emilion. My butcher watched, as a cat might watch a rather strange dog.

I swallowed the merest sip, eyes closed, and nodded.

The stranger across the table also sipped and nodded.

A tie.

We stared at the twilight horizon of Florence.

"Well . . ." I said, frantic for conversation ". . . what do you think of Florence's art?"

"Paintings make me nervous," he admitted. "What I *really* like is walking around. Italian women! I'd like to ice-pack and ship them home!"

"Er, yes . . ." I cleared my throat. "But Giotto . . . ?"

"Giotto bores me. Sorry. He's too soon in art history for me. Stick figures. Masaccio's better. Raphael's best. And *Rubens!* I have a butcher's taste for flesh."

"Rubens?"

"Rubens!" Harry Stadler forked some neat little salami slices, popped them in his mouth, and chewed opinions. "Rubens! All bosom and bum, big cumulus clouds of pink flesh, eh? You can feel the heart beating like a kettledrum in a ton of that stuff. Every woman a bed; throw yourself on them, sink from sight. To hell with the boy David, all that cold white marble and no fig leaf! No, no, I like color, life, and meat that covers the bone. You're not *eating!*"

"Watch." I ate my bloody salami and pink bologna and my dead white provolone, wondering if I should ask his opinion of the cold white colorless cheeses of the world.

The headwaiter delivered our steaks.

Stadler's was so rare you could run blood tests on it. Mine resembled a withered black man's head left to smoke and char my plate.

My butcher growled at my burnt offering.

"My God," he cried, "they treated Joan of Arc better than that! Will you puff it or chew it?"

"But yours," I laughed, "is still *breathing!*"

My steak sounded like crunched autumn leaves, every time I chewed.

Stadler, like W. C. Fields, hacked his way through a wall of living flesh, dragging his canoe behind him.

He killed his dinner. I buried mine.

We ate swiftly. All too soon, in a shared panic, we sensed that we must talk once more.

We ate in a terrible silence like an old married couple, angry at lost arguments, the reasons for which were also lost, leaving irritability and muted rage.

We buttered bread to fill the silence. We ordered coffee, which filled more time and at last settled back, watching that other stranger across a snowfield of linen, napery, and silver. Then, abomination of abominations, I heard myself say:

"When we get home, we must have dinner some night to talk about our time here, yes? Florence, the weather, the paintings."

"Yes." He downed his drink. *"No!"*

"What?"

"No," he said, simply. "Let's face it, Leonard, when we were home we had nothing in common. Even here we have nothing except time, distance, and travel to share. We have no talk, no interests. Hell, it's a shame, but there it is. This whole thing was impulsive, for the best, or at the worst, mysterious reasons. You're alone, I'm alone in a strange city at noon, and here tonight. But we're like a couple of grave-diggers who meet and try to shake hands, but their ectoplasm falls right through each other, hmm? We've kidded ourselves all day."

I sat there stunned. I shut my eyes, felt as if I might be angry, then gave a great gusting exhalation.

"You're the most honest man I've ever known."

"I hate being honest and realistic." Then he laughed. "I tried to call you all afternoon."

"I tried to call *you!*"

"I wanted to cancel dinner."

"Me, too!"

"I never got through."

"I missed *you.*"

"My God!"

"Jesus Christ!"

We both began to laugh, threw our heads back, and almost fell from our chairs.

"This is *rich!*"

"It most certainly *is!*" I said, imitating Oliver Hardy's way of speaking.

"God, order another bottle of champagne!"

"Waiter!"

We hardly stopped laughing as the waiter poured the second bottle.

"Well, we have *one* thing in common," said Harry Stadler.

"What's that?"

"This whole cockamamie silly stupid wonderful day, starting at noon, ending here. We'll tell this story to friends the rest of our lives. How I invited you, and you fell in with it not wanting to, and how we both tried to call it off before it started, and how we both came to dinner hating it, and how we blurted it out, silly, silly, and how suddenly—" He stopped. His eyes watered and his voice softened. "How suddenly it wasn't so silly anymore. But okay. Suddenly we liked each other in our foolishness. And if we don't try to make the rest of the evening too long, it won't be so bad, after all."

I tapped my champagne glass to his. The tenderness had reached me, too, along with the stupid and silly.

"We won't ever have any dinners back home."

"No."

"And we don't have to be afraid of long talks about nothing."

"Just the weather for a few seconds, now and then."

"And we won't meet socially."

"Here's to that."

"But suddenly it's a nice night, old Leonard Douglas, customer of mine."

"Here's to Harry Stadler." I raised my glass. "Wherever he goes from here."

"Bless me. Bless you."

We drank and simply sat there for another five minutes, warm and comfortable as old friends who had suddenly found that a long long time ago we had loved the same beautiful librarian who had touched our books and touched our cheeks. But the memory was fading.

"It's going to rain." I arose with my wallet.

Stadler stared until I put the wallet back in my jacket.

"Thanks and good night."

"Thanks to you," he said, "I'm not so lonely now, no matter what."

I gulped the rest of my wine, gasped with pleasure, ruffled Stadler's hair with a quick hand, and ran.

At the door I turned. He saw this and shouted across the room.

"Remember me?"

I pretended to pause, scratch my head, cudgel my memory. Then I pointed at him and cried:

"The butcher!"

He lifted his drink.

"Yes!" he called. "The butcher!"

I hurried downstairs and across the parquetry floor which was too beautiful to walk on, and out into a storm.

I walked in the rain for a long while, face up.

Hell, I thought, I don't feel so lonely *myself!*

Then, soaked through, and laughing, I ducked and ran all the way back to my hotel.

Fee Fie Foe Fum

The postman came melting along the sidewalk in the hot summer sun, his nose dripping, his fingers wet on his full leather pouch. "Let's see. Next house is Barton's. Three letters. One for Thomas Q., one for his wife, Liddy, and one for old Grandma. Is *she* still alive? How they *do* hang on."

He slid the letters in the box and froze.

A lion roared.

He stepped back, eyes wide.

The screen door sang open on its taut spring. "Morning, Ralph."

"Morning, Mrs. Barton. Just heard your pet lion."

"What?"

"Lion. In your kitchen."

She listened. "Oh, *that?* Our Garburator. You know: garbage disposal unit."

"Your husband buy it?"

"Right. You men and your machines. That thing'll eat anything, bones and all."

"Careful. It might eat you."

"No. I'm a lion-tamer." She laughed, and listened. "Hey, it *does* sound like a lion."

"A hungry one. Well, so long."

He drifted off into the hot morning.

Liddy ran upstairs with the letters.

"Grandma?" She tapped on a door. "Letter for you."

The door was silent.

"Grandma? You in there?"

After a long pause, a dry-wicker voice replied, "Yep."

"What're you doing?"

"Ask me no questions, I'll tell you no lies," chanted the old one, hid away.

"You've been in there all morning."

"I might be here all year," snapped Grandma.

Liddy tried the knob. "You've locked the door."

"Well, so I *have!*"

"You coming down to lunch, Grandma?"

"Nope. Nor supper. I won't come down till you throw that damned machine out of the kitchen." Her flinty eye jittered in the keyhole, staring out at her granddaughter.

"You mean the Garburator?" Liddy smiled.

"I heard the postman. He's right. I won't have a lion in *my* house! *Listen!* There's your husband now, *using* it."

Below stairs, the Garburator roared, swallowing garbage, bones and all.

"Liddy!" her husband called. "Liddy, come on down. See it work!"

Liddy spoke to Grandma's keyhole. "Don't you want to watch, Grandma?"

"Nope!"

Footsteps arose behind Liddy. Turning, she found Tom on the top stairs. "Go down and try, Liddy. I got some extra bones from the butcher. It really *chews* them."

She descended toward the kitchen. "It's grisly, but heck, why not?"

Thomas Barton stood neat and alone at Grandma's door and waited a full minute, motionless, a prim smile on his lips. He knocked softly, delicately. "Grandma?" he whispered. No reply. He patted the knob tenderly. "I know you're there, you old ruin. Grandma, you *hear*? Down below. You *hear*? How come your door's locked? Something wrong? What could bother you on such a nice summer day?"

Silence. He moved into the bathroom.

The hall stood empty. From the bath came sounds of water running. Then, Thomas Barton's voice, full and resonant in the tile room, sang:

"Fee fie foe fum
I smell the blood of an Englishmum;
Be she alive or be she dead,
I'll gurrrr-innnnnnd her bones to make my bread!"

In the kitchen, the lion roared.

Grandma smelled like attic furniture, smelled like

dust, smelled like a lemon, and resembled a withered flower. Her firm jaw sagged and her pale gold eyes were flinty bright as she sat in her chair like a hatchet, cleaving the hot noon air, rocking.

She heard Thomas Barton's song.

Her heart grew an ice crystal.

She had heard her grandson-in-law rip open the crate this morning, like a child with an evil Christmas toy. The fierce cracklings and tearings, the cry of triumph, the eager fumbling of his hands over the toothy machine. He had caught Grandma's yellow eagle eye in the hall entry and given her a mighty wink. Bang! She had run to slam her door!

Grandma shivered in her room all day.

Liddy knocked again, concerning lunch, but was scolded away.

Through the simmering afternoon, the Garburator lived gloriously in the kitchen sink. It fed, it ate, it made grinding, smacking noises with hungry mouth and vicious hidden teeth. It whirled, it groaned. It ate pig knuckles, coffee grounds, eggshells, drumsticks. It was an ancient hunger which, unfed, waited, crouched, metal entrail upon metal entrail, little flailing propellers of razor-screw all bright with lust.

Liddy carried supper up on a tray.

"Slide it under the door," shouted Grandma.

"Heavens!" said Liddy. "Open the door long enough for me to poke it in at you."

"Look over your shoulder; anyone *lurking* in the hall?"

"No."

"So!" The door flew wide. Half the corn was spilled being yanked in. She gave Liddy a shove and slammed the door. "That was close!" she cried, holding the rabbit-run in her bosom.

"Grandma, what's got *in* you?"

Grandma watched the knob twist. "No use telling, you wouldn't believe, child. Out of the goodness of my heart I moved you here a year ago. Tom and I always spit at each other. Now he wants me gone, but he won't get *me*, no sir! I know his trick. One day you'll come from the store and I'll be nowhere. You'll ask Tom: What happened to old Grandma? Sweet-smiling, he'll say: Grandma? Just now decided to hike to Illinois! Just packed and *left!* And you won't see Grandma again, Liddy, you know why, you got an inkling?"

"Grandma, that's gibberish. Tom *loves* you!"

"Loves my house, my antiques, my mattress-money, *that's* what he loves dearly! Get away, I'll work this out myself! I'm locked in here till hell burns out."

"What about your canary, Grandma?"

"*You* feed Singing Sam! Buy hamburger for Spottie, he's a happy dog, I can't let him starve. Bring Kitten up on occasion, I can't live without cats. Now, shoo! I'm climbing in bed."

Grandma put herself to bed like a corpse preparing its own coffin. She folded her yellow wax fingers on her ruffly bosom, as her mothlike eyelids winced shut. What to do? What weapon to use against that clockwork mechanic? Liddy? But Liddy was fresh as new-baked bread, her rosy face was excited only by cinnamon buns and raised muffins, she smelled of yeast and warm milk. The only murder Liddy might consider was one where the victim ended on the dinner platter, orange sucked in mouth, cloves in pink hide, silent under the knife. No, you couldn't tell wild truths to Liddy, she'd only laugh and bake another cake.

Grandma sighed a lost sigh.

The small vein in her chicken neck stopped throbbing. Only the fragile bellows of her tiny lungs moved in the room like the ghost of an apprehension, whispering.

Below, in its bright chromed cage, the lion slept.

A week passed.

Only "heading for the bathroom" ran Grandma out of hiding. When Thomas Barton throttled his car she panicked from her bedroom. Her bathroom visits were frantic and explosive. She fell back in bed a few minutes later. Some mornings, Thomas delayed going to his office, purposely, and stood, erect as a numeral one, mathematically clean, working on her door with his eyes, smiling at this delay.

Once in the middle of a summer night, she sneaked down and fed the "lion" a bag of nuts and bolts. She trusted Liddy to turn on the beast at dawn and choke it to death. She lay in bed early, hearing the first stirs and yawns of the two arising people, waiting for the sound of the lion shrieking, choked by bolt, washer, and screw, dying of indigestible parts.

She heard Thomas walk downstairs.

Half an hour later his voice said, "Here's a present for you, Grandma. My lion says: No thanks."

Peeking out, later, she found the nuts and bolts laid in a neat row on her sill.

On the morning of the twelfth day of imprisonment, Grandma dialed her bedroom phone:

"Hello, Tom, that *you*? You at *work*, Tom?"

"This is my office number, *why?*"

"True." She hung up and tiptoed down the hall stairs into the parlor.

Liddy looked up, shocked. "Grandma!"

"Who else?" snapped the old one. "Tom here?"

"You *know* he's working."

"Yes, yes!" Grandma stared unblinkingly about, gumming her porcelain teeth. "Just phoned him. Take ten minutes for him to drive home, don't it?"

"Sometimes half an hour."

"Good." Grandma mourned. "Can't stay in my room. Just had to come down, see you, set awhile, breathe." She pulled a tiny gold watch from her bosom. "In ten minutes, back up I go. I'll phone Tom then, to see if he's still at work. I might come down again, if he is." She opened the front door and called out into the fresh summer day. "Spottie, here, Spot! Kitten, here, Kitt!"

A large white dog, unmarked, appeared, yelping, to be let in, followed by a plump black cat which leaped in her lap when she sat.

"Good pals," Grandma cooed, stroking them. She

lay back, eyes shut, and listened for the song of her wonderful canary in his golden cage in the dining room bay window.

Silence.

Grandma rose and peeked through the dining room door.

It was an instant before she realized what had happened to the cage.

It was empty.

"Singing Sam's gone!" screamed Grandma. She ran to dump the cage upside down. "Gone!"

The cage fell to the floor, just as Liddy appeared. "I thought it was quiet, but didn't know why. I must've left the cage open by mistake—"

"You *sure?* Oh my God, *wait!*"

Grandma closed her eyes and groped her way out to the kitchen. Finding the kitchen sink cool under her fingers, she opened her eyes and looked down.

The Garburator lay gleaming, silent, its mouth wide. At its rim lay a small yellow feather.

Grandma turned on the water.

The Garburator made a chewing, swallowing noise.

Slowly, Grandma clamped both skinny hands over her mouth.

Her room was quiet as a pool; she remained in it like a quiet forest thing, knowing that once out of its shade, she might be set on by a jungle terror. With Singing Sam's disappearance, the horror had made a mushroom growth into hysteria. Liddy had had to fight her away from the sink, where Grandma was trying to bat the gluttonous machine with a hammer. Liddy had forced her upstairs to put ice compresses on her raging brow.

"Singing Sam, he's killed poor Sam!" Grandma had sobbed and wailed. But then the thrashing ceased, firm resolve seeped back. She locked Liddy out again and now there was a cold rage in her, in company with the fear and trembling; to think Tom would *dare* do this to her!

Now she would not open the door far enough to allow even supper in on a tray. She had dinner rattled to a chair outside, and she ate through the door-crack, held open on a safety chain just far enough so you saw her skeleton hand dart out like a bird shadowing the meat and corn, flying off with morsels, flying back for more. "Thanks!" And the swift bird vanished behind the shut door.

"Singing Sam must've flown off, Grandma." Liddy phoned from the drugstore to Grandma's room, because Grandma refused to talk any other way.

"Good *night!*" cried Grandma, and disconnected.

The next day Grandma phoned Thomas again.

"You *there*, Tom?"

"Where *else?*" said Tom.

Grandma ran downstairs.

"Here, Spot, Spottie! Here, Kitten!"

The dog and cat did not answer.

She waited, gripping the door, and then she called for Liddy.

Liddy came.

"Liddy," said Grandma, in a stiff voice, barely audible, not looking at her. "Go look in the Garburator. Lift up the metal piece. Tell me what you see."

Grandma heard Liddy's footsteps far away. A silence.

"What do you see?" cried Grandma, impatient and afraid.

Liddy hesitated. "A piece of white fur—"

"Yes?"

"And—a piece of black fur."

"Stop. No more. Get me an aspirin."

Liddy obeyed. "You and Tom must stop, Grandma. This silly game, I mean. I'll chew him out tonight. It's not funny anymore. I thought if I let you alone, you'd stop raving about some lion. But now it's been a week—"

Grandma said, "Do you really think we'll ever see Spot or Kitten again?"

"They'll be home for supper, hungry as ever," Liddy replied. "It was crude of Tom to stuff that fur in the Garburator. I'll stop it."

"Will you, Liddy?" Grandma walked upstairs as in a trance. "Will you, really?"

Grandma lay planning through the night. This all must end. The dog and cat had not returned for supper, though Liddy laughed and said they would. Grandma

nodded. She and Tom must tie a final knot now. Destroy the machine? But he'd install another, and, between them, put her into an asylum if she didn't stop
babbling. No, a crisis must be forced, on her own
grounds, in her own time and way. How? Liddy must
be tricked from the house. Then Grandma must meet
Thomas, at long last, alone. She was dead tired of his
smiles, worn away by this quick eating and hiding, this
lizard-darting in and out doors. No. She sniffed the
cooling wind at midnight.

"Tomorrow," she decided, "will be a grand day for
a picnic."

"Grandma!"

Liddy's voice through the keyhole. "We're leaving
now. Sure you won't come along?"

"No, child! Enjoy yourselves. It's a fine morning!"

Bright Saturday. Grandma, early, had telephoned
downstairs suggesting her two relatives take ham and
pickle sandwiches out through the green forests. Tom
had assented swiftly. Of course! A picnic! Tom had
laughed and rubbed his hands.

"Good-bye, Grandma!"

The rustle of picnic wickers, the slamming door, the
car purring off into the excellent weather.

"There." Grandma appeared in the living room.
"Now it's just a matter of time. He'll sneak back. I
could tell by his voice; *too* happy! He'll creep in, all
alone, to visit."

She swept the house with a brisk straw broom. She felt she was sweeping out all the numerical bits and pieces of Thomas Barton, cleaning him away. All the tobacco fragments and neat newspapers he had flourished with his morning Brazilian coffee, clean threads from his scrupulous tweed suit, clips from his office supplies, out the door! It was like setting a stage. She ran about raising green shades to allow the summer in, flooding the rooms with bright color. The house was terribly lonely without a dog making noise like a typewriter on the kitchen floor or a cat blowing through it like silk tumbleweed over rose-patterned carpets, or the golden bird throbbing in its golden jail. The only sound now was the soft whisper that Grandma heard as her feverish body burned into old age.

In the center of the kitchen floor she dropped a pan of grease. "Well, look what I did!" she laughed. "Careful. Someone might slip and fall on that!" She did not mop it up, but sat on the far side of the kitchen.

"I'm ready," she announced to the silence.

The sunlight lay on her lap where she cradled a pot of peas. In her hand a paring knife moved to open them. Her fingers tumbled the green pods. Time passed. The kitchen was so quiet you heard the refrigerator humming behind its pressed-tight rubber seals around the door. Grandma smiled a pressed and similar smile and unhinged the pods.

The kitchen door opened and shut quietly.

"Oh!" Grandma dropped her pan.

"Hello, Grandma," said Tom.

On the floor, near the grease spot, the peas were strewn like a broken necklace.

"You're back," said Grandma.

"I'm back," Tom said. "Liddy's in Glendale. I left her to shop. Said I forgot something. Said I'd pick her up in an hour."

They looked at each other.

"I hear you're going East, Grandma," he said.

"That's funny, I heard *you* were," she said.

"All of a sudden you left without a word," he said.

"All of a sudden you packed up and went," she said.

"No, *you*," he said.

"*You*," she said.

He took a step toward the grease spot.

Water which had gathered in the sink was jarred by his moves. It trickled down the Garburator's throat, which gave off a gentle chuckling wet sound.

Tom did not look down as his shoe slipped on the grease.

"Tom." Sunlight flickered on Grandma's paring knife. "What can I *do* for you?"

The postman dropped six letters in the Barton mailbox and listened.

"There's that lion again," he said. "Here comes someone," said the postman. "Singing."

Footsteps neared the door. A voice sang:

"Fee fie foe fum,
I smell the blood of an Englishmun,
Be he alive or be he dead,
I'll grr-innnd his bones to make my bread!"

The door flew wide.
"Morning!" cried Grandma, smiling.
The lion roared.

Driving Blind

"**D**id you see that?"

"See what?"

"Why, hell, look *there!*"

But the big six-passenger 1929 Studebaker was already gone.

One of the men standing in front of Fremley's Hardware had stepped down off the curb to stare after the vehicle.

"That guy was driving with a hood over his head. Like a hangman's hood, black, over his head, driving blind!"

"I saw it, I saw it!" said a boy standing, similarly riven, nearby. The boy was me, Thomas Quincy Riley, better known as Tom or Quint and mighty curious. I ran. "Hey, wait up! Gosh! Driving *blind!*"

I almost caught up with the blind driver at Main and Elm where the Studebaker turned off down Elm followed by a siren. A town policeman on his motorcycle, stunned with the traveling vision, was giving pursuit.

When I reached the car it was double-parked with the officer's boot up on the running board and Willy Crenshaw, the officer, scowling in at the black Hood and someone under the Hood.

"Would you mind taking that thing off?" he said.

"No, but here's my driver's license," said a muffled voice. A hand with the license sailed out the window.

"I want to see your face," said Willy Crenshaw.

"It's right there on the license."

"I want to check and see if the two compare," said Willy Crenshaw.

"The name is Phil Dunlop," said the Hooded voice. "121 Desplaines Street, Gurney. Own the Studebaker Sales at 16 Gurney Avenue. It's all there if you can read."

Willy Crenshaw creased his forehead and inched his eyesight along the words.

"Hey, mister," I said. "This is real neat!"

"Shut up, son." The policeman ground his boot on the running board. "What you *up* to?"

I stood arching my feet, peering over the officer's shoulder as he hesitated to write up a ticket or jail a crook.

"What you *up* to?" Willy Crenshaw repeated.

"Right now," said the Hooded voice, "I'd like a place to stay overnight so I can prowl your town a few days."

Willy Crenshaw leaned forward. "What *kind* of prowling?"

"In this car, as you see, making people sit up and notice."

"They done that," the policeman admitted, looking at the crowd that had accumulated behind Thomas Quincy Riley, me.

"Is it a big crowd, boy?" said the man under the Hood.

I didn't realize he was addressing me, then I quickened up. "Sockdolager!" I said.

"You think if I drove around town twenty-four hours dressed like this, people might listen for one minute and hear what I *say?*"

"All ears," I said.

"There you have it, Officer," said the Hood, staring straight ahead, or what seemed like. "I'll stay on, 'cause the boy says. Boy," said the voice, "you know a good place for me to shave my unseen face and rest my feet?"

"My grandma, she—"

"Sounds good. Boy—"

"Name's Thomas Quincy Riley."

"Call you Quint?"

"How'd you guess?"

"Quint, jump in, show the way. But don't try to peek under my cover-up."

"No, *sir!*"

And I was around the car and in the front seat, my heart pure jackrabbit.

"Excuse us, Officer. Any questions, I'll be sequestered at this child's place."

"Six one nine Washington Street—" I began.

"I know, I know!" cried the officer. "Damnation."

"You'll let me go in this boy's custody?"

"Hell!" The policeman jerked his boot off the running board which let the car bang away.

"Quint?" said the voice under the dark Hood, steering. "What's *my* name?"

"You said—"

"No, no. What do *you* want to call me?"

"Hmm. Mr. Mysterious?"

"Bull's-eye. Where do I turn left, right, right, left, and right again?"

"Well," I said.

And we motored off, me terrified of collisions and Mr. Mysterious, real nice and calm, made a perfect left.

Some people knit because their fingers need preoccupations for their nerves.

Grandma didn't knit, but plucked peas from the pod. We had peas just about most nights in my life. Other nights she plucked lima beans. String beans? She harped on those, too, but they didn't pluck as easy or as neat as peas. Peas were it. As we came up the porch steps, Grandma eyed our arrival and shelled the little greens.

"Grandma," I said. "This is Mr. Mysterious."

"I could *see* that." Grandma nodded and smiled at she knew not what.

"He's wearing a Hood," I said.

"I noticed." Grandma was still unaffected and amiable.

"He needs a room."

"To need, the Bible says, is to have. Can he find his way up? Excuse the question."

"And *board*," I added.

"Beg pardon, how's he going to eat through that *thing*?"

"Hood," I said.

"*Hood?*"

"I can manage," Mr. Mysterious murmured.

"He can manage," I translated.

"That'll be worth watching." Grandma stitched out more green peas. "Sir, do you have a name?"

"I just *told* you," I said.

"So you did." Grandma nodded. "Dinner's at six," she said, "sharp."

The supper table, promptly at six, was loud with roomers and boarders. Grandpa having come home from Goldfield and Silver Creek, Nevada, with neither gold nor silver, and hiding out in the library parlor behind his books, allowed Grandma to room three bachelors and two bachelor ladies upstairs, while three boarders came in from various neighborhoods a few blocks away. It made for a lively breakfast, lunch, and dinner and Grandma made enough from this to keep our ark from sinking. Tonight there was five minutes of uproar concerning politics, three minutes on religion, and then the best talk about the food set before them, just as Mr. Mysterious arrived and everyone shut up. He glided among them, nodding his Hood right and left, and as he sat I yelled:

"Ladies and gentlemen, meet Mr.—"

"Just call me Phil," murmured Mr. Mysterious.

I sat back, somewhat aggrieved.

"Phil," said everyone.

They all stared at him and couldn't tell if he saw their stares through the black velvet. How's he going to eat, hid like that, they thought. Mr. Mysterious picked up a big soup spoon.

"Pass the gravy, please," he whispered.

"Pass the mashed potatoes," he added quietly.

"Pass the peas," he finished.

"Also, Mrs. Grandma . . ." he said. Grandma, in the doorway, smiled. It seemed a nice touch: "Mrs." He said, ". . . please bring me my blue-plate special."

Grandma placed what was indeed a Chinese garden done in blue ceramics but containing what looked to be a dog's dinner. Mr. Mysterious ladled the gravy, the mashed potatoes, and the peas on and mashed and crushed it shapeless as we watched, trying not to bug our eyes.

There was a moment of silence as the voice under the dark Hood said, "Anyone mind if I say grace?"

Nobody would mind.

"O Lord," said the hidden voice, "let us receive those gifts of love that shape and change and move our lives to perfection. May others see in us only what we see in them, perfection and beauty beyond telling. Amen."

"Amen," said all as Mr. M. snuck from his coat a thing to astonish the boarders and amaze the rest.

"That," someone said (me), "is the biggest darn soda fountain straw I ever seen!"

"Quint!" said Grandma.

"Well, it *is!*"

And it was. A soda fountain straw two or three times larger than ordinary which vanished up under the Hood and probed down through the mashed potatoes, peas, and gravy dog's dinner which silently ascended the straw to vanish in an unseen mouth, silent and soundless as cats at mealtime.

Which made the rest of us fall to, self-consciously cutting, chewing, and swallowing so loud we all blushed.

While Mr. Mysterious sucked his liquid victuals up out of sight with not even so much as a purr. From the corners of our eyes we watched the victuals slide silently and invisibly under the Hood until the plate was hound's-tooth clean. And all this done with Mr. M.'s fingers and hands fixed to his knees.

"I—" said Grandma, her gaze on that straw, "hope you liked your dinner, sir."

"Sockdolager," said Mr. Mysterious.

"Ice cream's for dessert," said Grandma. "Mostly melted."

"Melted!" Mr. M. laughed.

*   *   *

It was a fine summer night with three cigars, one cigarette, and assorted knitting on the front porch and enough rocking chairs going somewhere-in-place to make dogs nervous and cats leave.

In the clouds of cigar smoke and a pause in the knitting, Grandpa, who always came out after dark, said:

"If you don't mind my infernal nerve, now that you're settled in, what's *next?*"

Mr. Mysterious, leaning on the front porch rail, looking, we supposed, out at his shiny Studebaker, put a cigarette to his Hood and drew some smoke in, then out without coughing. I stood watching, proudly.

"Well," said Mr. M., "I got several roads to take. See that car out there?"

"It's large and obvious," said Grandpa.

"That is a brand-new class-A Studebaker Eight, got thirty miles on it, which is as far from Gurney to here and a few runaround blocks. My car salesroom is just about big enough to hold three Studebakers and four customers at once. Mostly dairy farmers pass my windows but don't come in. I figured it was time to come to a live-wire place, where if I shouted 'Leap' you might at least hop."

"We're waiting," said Grandpa.

"Would you like a small demonstration of what I pray for and *will* realize?" said the cigarette smoke wafting out through the fabric in syllables. "Someone say 'Go.'"

Lots of cigar smoke came out in an explosion.

"Go!"

"Jump, Quint!"

I reached the Studebaker before him and Mr. Mysterious was no sooner in the front seat than we took off.

"Right and then left and then right, correct, Quint?"

And right, left, right it was to Main Street and us banging away fast.

"Don't laugh so loud, Quint."

"Can't help it! This is *peacherino!*"

"Stop swearing. Anyone following?"

"Three young guys on the sidewalk here. Three old gents off the curb there!"

He slowed. The six following us soon became eight.

"Are we almost at the cigar-store corner where the loudmouths hang out, Quint?"

"You *know* we are."

"Watch this!"

As we passed the cigar store he slowed and choked the gas. The most terrific Fourth of July BANG fired out the exhaust. The cigar-store loudmouths jumped a foot and grabbed their straw hats. Mr. M. gave them another BANG, accelerated, and the eight following soon was a dozen.

"Hot diggity!" cried Mr. Mysterious. "Feel their love, Quint? Feel their *need?* Nothing like a brand-new eight-cylinder super prime A-1 Studebaker to make a man feel like Helen just passed through Troy! I'll stop now that there's folks enough for arguments to possess and fights to keep. *So!*"

We stopped dead-center on Main and Arbogast as the moths collected to our flame.

"Is that a brand-new just-out-of-the-showroom Studebaker?" said our town barber. The fuzz behind my ears knew him well.

"Absolutely spanking brand-new," said Mr. M.

"*I* was here first, *I* get to ask!" cried the mayor's assistant, Mr. Bagadosian.

"Yeah, but *I* got the money!" A third man stepped into the dashboard light. Mr. Bengstrom, the man who owned the graveyard and everyone *in* it.

"Got only *one* Studebaker now," said the sheepish voice under the Hood. "Wish I had more."

That set off a frenzy of remorse and tumult.

"The entire price," said Mr. M. in the midst of the turmoil, "is eight hundred and fifty dollars. The first among you who slaps a fifty-dollar bill or its equivalent in singles, fives, and tens in my hand gets to pink-slip this mythological warship home."

No sooner was Mr. Mysterious' palm out the window than it was plastered with fives, tens, and twenties.

"Quint?"

"Sir?"

"Reach in that cubby and drag out my order forms."

"Yes, *sir!*"

"Bengstrom! Cyril A. Bengstrom!" the undertaker cried so he could be heard.

"Be calm, Mr. Bengstrom. The car is yours. Sign *here.*"

Moments later, Mr. Bengstrom, laughing hysterically, drove off from a sullen mob at Main and Arbogast. He circled us twice to make the abandoned crowd even more depressed then roared off to find a highway and test his craze.

"Don't fret," said the voice under the dark Hood. "I got one last Studebaker prime A-1 vehicle, or maybe two, waiting back in Gurney. Someone drop me there?"

"Me!" said everyone.

"So *that's* the way you function," said Grandpa. *"That's* why you're here."

It was later in the evening with more mosquitoes and fewer knitters and smokers. Another Studebaker, bright red, stood out at the curb. "Wait till they see the sun shine on *this* one," said Mr. Mysterious, laughing gently.

"I have a feeling you'll sell your entire line this week," said Grandpa, "and leave us wanting."

"I'd rather not talk futures and sound uppity, but so it seems."

"Sly fox." Grandpa tamped philosophy in his pipe and puffed it out. "Wearing that sack over your head to focus need and provoke talk."

"It's more than that." Mr. M. sucked, tucking a cigarette through the dark material over his mouth. "More than a trick. More than a come-on. More than a passing fancy."

"What?" said Grandpa.

*   *   *

"What?" I said.

It was midnight and I couldn't sleep.

Neither could Mr. Mysterious. I crept downstairs and found him in the backyard in a wooden summer recliner perhaps studying the fireflies and beyond them the stars, some holding still, others not.

"Hello, Quint!" he said.

"Mr. Mysterious?" I said.

"*Ask* me."

"You wear that Hood even when you *sleep?*"

"All night long every night."

"For most of your life?"

"Almost most."

"Last night you said it's more than a trick, showing off. What *else?*"

"If I didn't tell the roomers and your grandpa, why should I tell you, Quint?" said the Hood with no features resting there in the night.

" 'Cause I want to know."

"That's about the best reason in the world. Sit down, Quint. Aren't the fireflies nice?"

I sat on the wet grass. "Yeah."

"Okay," said Mr. Mysterious, and turned his head under his Hood as if he were staring at me. "Here goes. Ever wonder what's under this Hood, Quint? Ever have the itch to yank it off and see?"

"Nope."

"Why not?"

"That lady in *The Phantom of the Opera* did. Look where it got *her*."

"Then shall I *tell* you what's hidden, son?"

"Only if you want to, sir."

"Funny thing is, I do. This Hood goes back a long way."

"From when you were a kid?"

"Almost. I can't recall if I was born this way or something happened. Car accident. Fire. Or some woman laughing at me which burned just as bad, scarred just as terrible. One way or another we fall off buildings or fall out of bed. When we hit the floor it might as well have been off the roof. It takes a long time healing. Maybe never."

"You mean you don't remember when you put that thing on?"

"Things fade, Quint. I have lived in confusion a long while. This dark stuff has been such a part of me it might just be my living flesh."

"Do—"

"Do what, Quint?"

"Do you sometimes *shave?*"

"No, it's all smooth. You can imagine me two ways, I suppose. It's all nightmare under here, all graveyards, terrible teeth, skulls and wounds that won't heal. Or—"

"Or?"

"Nothing at all. Absolutely nothing. No beard for shaving. No eyebrows. Mostly no nose. Hardly any eyelids, just eyes. Hardly any mouth; a scar. The rest a vacancy, a snowfield, a blank, as if someone had erased

91

me to start over. There. Two ways of guessing. Which do you pick?"

"I can't."

"No."

Mr. Mysterious arose now and stood barefooted on the grass, his Hood pointed at some star constellation.

"You," I said, at last. "You still haven't told what you started tonight to tell Grandpa. You came here not just to sell brand-new Studebakers—but for something else?"

"Ah." He nodded. "Well. I been alone a lot of years. It's no fun over in Gurney, just selling cars and hiding under this velvet sack. So I decided to come out in the open at last and mix with honest-to-goodness people, make friends, maybe get someone to like me or at least put up with me. You understand, Quint?"

"I'm trying."

"What good will all this do, living in Green Town and thriving at your supper table and viewing the tree-tops in my cupola tower room? *Ask*."

"What good?" I asked.

"What I'm hoping for, Quint, what I'm praying for, son, is that if I delve in the river again, wade in the stream, become part of the flow of folks, people, strangers even, some sort of kind attention, friendship, some sort of half-love will begin to melt and change my face. Over six or eight months or a year, to let life shift my mask without lifting it, so that the wax beneath moves and becomes something more than a nightmare at three a.m. or just nothing at dawn. Any of this make sense, Quint?"

"Yeah. I guess."

"For people *do* change us, don't they? I mean you run in and out of this house and your grandpa changes you and your grandpa shapes you with words or a hug or your hair tousled or maybe once a year, a slap where it hurts."

"*Twice.*"

"Twice, then. And the boarders and roomers talk and you listen and that goes in your ears and out your fingers and that's change, too. We're all in the wash, all in the creeks, all in the streams, taking in every morsel of gab, every push from a teacher, every shove from a bully, every look and touch from those strange creatures, for *you* called women. Sustenance. It's all breakfast tea and midnight snacks and you grow on it or you don't grow, laugh or scowl or don't have any features one way or the other, but *you're* out there, melting and freezing, running or holding still. I haven't done that in years. So just this week I got up my courage—knew how to sell cars but didn't know how to put *me* on sale. I'm taking a chance, Quint, that by next year, this face under the Hood will make itself over, shift at noon or twilight, and I'll feel it changing because I'm out wading in the stream again and breathing the fresh air and letting people get at me, taking a chance, not hiding behind the windshield of this or that Studebaker. And at the end of that next year, Quint, I'll take off my Hood forever."

At which point, turned away from me, he made a gesture. I saw the dark velvet in his hand as he dropped it in the grass.

"Do you want to see what's here, Quint?" he asked, quietly.

"No, sir, if you don't mind."

"Why not?"

"I'm scared," I said, and shivered.

"That figures," he said, at last. "I'll just stand here a moment and then hide again."

He took three deep breaths, his back to me, head high, face toward the fireflies and a few constellations. Then the Hood was back in place.

I'm glad, I thought, there's no moon tonight.

Five days and five Studebakers later (one blue, one black, two tans, and one sunset-red) Mr. Mysterious was sitting out in what he said was his final car, a sun-yellow open roadster, so bright it was a canary with its own cage, when I came strolling out, hands in overall pockets, watching the sidewalk for ants or old unused firecrackers. When Mr. M. saw me he moved over and said, "Try the driver's seat."

"Boy! *Can* I?"

I did, and twirled the wheel and honked the horn, just once, so as not to wake any late-sleepers.

" 'Fess up, Quint," said Mr. Mysterious, his Hood pointed out through the windshield.

"Do I look like I need 'fessing'?"

"You're ripe-plumful. Begin."

"I been thinking," I said.

"I could tell by the wrinkles in your face," said Mr. M., gently.

"I been thinking about a year from now, and you."

"That's mighty nice, son. Continue."

"I thought, well, maybe next year if you felt you were cured, under that Hood, that your nose was okay and your eyebrows neat, and your mouth good and your complexion—"

I hesitated. The Hood nodded me on.

"Well, I was thinking if you got up one morning and without even putting your hands up to feel underneath you knew the long waiting was over and you were changed, people and things had changed you, the town, everything, and you were great, just great, no way of *ever* going back to nothing."

"Go on, Quint."

"Well, if that happened, Mr. Mysterious, and you just *knew* you were really great to see forever, why then, Mr. M., you wouldn't *have* to take off your Hood, *would* you?"

"What'd you *say*, son?"

"I said, you wouldn't have to ta—"

"I heard you, Quint, I heard," gasped Mr. M.

There was a long silence. He made some strange sounds, almost like choking, and then he whispered hoarsely, "No, I wouldn't need to take off my Hood."

" 'Cause it wouldn't matter, would it? If you really knew that underneath, everything was okay. Sure?"

95

"Oh, Lord yes, sure."

"And you could wear the Hood for the next hundred years and only you and me would know what's underneath. And we wouldn't tell or care."

"Just you and me. And what would I look like under the Hood, Quint? Sockdolager?"

"Yes, sir."

There was a long silence and Mr. Mysterious' shoulders shook a few times and he made a quiet choking sound and all of a sudden some water dripped off the bottom of his Hood.

I stared at it. "Oh," I said.

"It's all right, Quint," he said, quietly. "It's just tears."

"Gosh."

"It's all right. Happy tears."

Mr. Mysterious got out of the last Studebaker then and touched at his invisible nose and dabbed at the cloth in front of his unseen eyes.

"Quintessential Quint," he said. "No one else like you in the whole world."

"Heck, that goes for *everyone*, don't it?"

"If you say so, Quint."

Then he added:

"Got any last things to upchuck or confess, son?"

"Some silly stuff. What if—?"

I paused and swallowed and could only look ahead through the steering wheel spokes at the naked silver lady on the hood.

"What if, a long time ago, you never *needed* the Hood?"

"You mean never? Never *ever?*"

"Yes, sir. What if a long time ago you only *thought* you needed to hide and put on that stuff with no eye-holes even. What if there was never any accident, or fire, or you weren't born that way, or no lady ever laughed at you, what *then?*"

"You mean I only imagined I had to put on this sackcloth and ashes? And all these years I been walking around thinking there *was* something awful or just nothing, a blank underneath?"

"It just came to me."

There was a long silence.

"And all these years I been walking around not knowing or pretending I had something to hide, for no reason, because my face was there all the time, mouth, cheeks, eyebrows, nose, and didn't need melting down to be fixed?"

"I didn't mean—"

"You *did.*" A final tear fell off the bottom rim of his Hood. "How old are you, Quint?"

"Going on thirteen."

"No. Methuselah."

"He was *real* old. But did he have any jellybeans in his *head?*"

"Like you, Quincy. A marvel of jellybeans."

There was a long silence, then he said:

"Walk around town? Need to flex my legs. Walk?"

We turned right at Central, left at Grand, right again

at Genesee, and stopped in front of the Karcher Hotel, twelve stories, the highest building in Green County or beyond.

"Quint?"

His Hood pointed up along the building while his voice under observed. "Thomas Quincy Riley, you got that *one last thing* look. Spit it out."

I hesitated and said, "Well. Up inside that Hood, is it *really* dark? I mean, there's no radio gadgets or see-back-oscopes or secret holes?"

"Thomas Quincy Riley, you been reading the Johnson Smith & Co. Tricks, Toys, Games and Halloween Catalogue from Racine, Wisconsin."

"Can't help it."

"Well, when I die you'll inherit this sack, wear it, and know darkness."

The head turned and I could almost feel his eyes burn the dark material.

"Right now, I can look through your ribs and see your heart like a flower or a fist, opening, closing, open, shut. You believe that?"

I put my fist on my chest.

"Yes, sir," I said.

"Now."

He turned to point his Hood up along the hotel for twelve stories.

"Know what I been thinking?"

"Sir?"

"Stop calling myself Mr. Mysterious."

"Oh, *no!*"

"Hold on! I've done what I came for. Car sales are runaway. Hallelujah. But look, Quint. Look up and touch. What if I became the Human Fly?"

I gasped. "You mean—"

"Yessireebob. Can't you just see me up six stories and eight and twelve at the top, with my Hood still on, waving down at the crowd?"

"Gee!"

"Glad for your approval." Mr. M. stepped forward and started to climb, reaching for holds, finding, and climbing more. When he was three feet up he said, "What's a good *tall* name for a Human Fly?"

I shut my eyes, then said:

"*High*tower!"

"Hightower, by God! Do we go home to breakfast?"

"Yes, *sir*."

"Mashed bananas, mashed cornflakes, mashed oat-meal—"

"Ice cream!" I added.

"Melted," said the Human Fly and climbed back down.

I Wonder What's Become
of Sally

Somebody started playing the yellow-keyed piano, somebody started singing, and somebody, myself, started thinking. The words of the song were slow, sweet, and sad:

> "I wonder what's become of Sally,
> That old gal of mine."

I hummed it. I remembered some more words:

> "The sunshine's gone from out our alley,
> Ever since the day Sally went away."

"I knew a Sally once," I said.
"You did?" said the bartender, not looking at me.
"Sure," I said. "Very first girlfriend. Like the words

of that song, makes you wonder, whatever happened to her? Where's she tonight? About all you can do is hope she's happy, married, got five kids, and a husband who isn't late more than once a week, and remembers, or doesn't remember, her birthdays, whichever way she likes it most."

"Why don't you look her up?" said the bartender, still not looking at me, shining a glass.

I drank my drink slowly.

> *"Wherever she may go,*
> *Wherever she may be,*
> *If no one wants her now,*
> *Please send her back to me."*

The people around the piano were finishing the song. I listened, eyes shut.

> *"I wonder what's become of Sally,*
> *That old gal of mine."*

The piano stopped. There was a lot of quiet laughter and talk.

I put the empty glass down on the bar and opened my eyes and looked at it for a minute.

"You know," I said to the bartender, "you just gave me an idea . . ."

Where do I start? I thought, outside on the rainy street in a cold wind, night coming on, buses and cars moving by, the world suddenly alive with sound. Or do you start at all, which is it?

I'd had ideas like this before; I got them all the time. On Sunday afternoons if I overslept I woke up thinking I had heard someone crying and found tears on my face and wondered what year it was and sometimes had to go off and find a calendar just to be sure. On those Sundays I felt there was fog outside the house, and had to go open the door to be sure the sun was still slanting across the lawn. It wasn't anything I could control. It just happened while I was half asleep and the old years gathered around and the light changed. Once, on a Sunday like that, I telephoned clear across the United States to an old school chum, Bob Hartmann. He was glad to hear my voice, or said he was, and we talked for half an hour and it was a nice talk, full of promises. But we never got together, as we had planned; next year, when he came to town, I was in a different mood. But that's how those things go, isn't it? Warm and mellow one second, and the next I looked around and I was gone.

But right now, standing on the street outside of Mike's Bar, I held out my hand and added up my fingers: first, my wife was out of town visiting her mother downstate. Second, tonight was Friday, and a whole free weekend ahead. Third, I remembered Sally very well, if no one else did. Fourth, I just wanted somehow to say, Hello, Sally, how are things? Fifth, why didn't I start?

I did.

* * *

I got the phone book and went down the lists. Sally Ames. Ames, Ames. I looked at them all. Of course. She was married. That was the bad thing about women: once married they took aliases, vanishing into the earth, and you were lost.

Well then, her parents, I thought.

They were unlisted. Moved or dead.

What about some of her old friends who were once friends of mine? Joan something-or-other. Bob whatsisname. I drew blanks, and then remembered someone named Tom Welles.

I found Tom in the book and telephoned him.

"Good God, is that you, Charlie?" he cried. "Good grief, come on over. What's new? Lord, it's been years! Why are you—"

I told him what I was calling about.

"Sally? Haven't seen her in years. Hey, I hear you're doing okay, Charlie. Salary in five figures, right? Pretty good for a guy from across the tracks."

There hadn't been any tracks, really; just an invisible line nobody could see but everyone felt.

"Hey, when can we see you, Charlie?"

"Give you a call soon."

"She was a sweet girl, Sally. I've told my wife about her. Those eyes. And hair color that didn't come out of a bottle. And—"

As Tom talked on, a lot of things came back. The way she listened, or pretended to listen, to all my grand talk about the future. It suddenly seemed she had never talked at all. I wouldn't let her. With the sublime dumb ego of a young man I filled up the nights and days with building tomorrows and tearing them down and building them again, just for her. Looking back, I was embarrassed for myself. And then I remembered how her eyes used to take fire and her cheeks flush with my talking, as if everything I said was worth her time and life and blood. But in all the talk, I couldn't remember ever saying I loved her. I should have. I never touched her, save to hold her hand, and never kissed her. That was a sadness now. But I had been afraid that if I ever made one mistake, like kissing, she would dissolve like snow on a summer night, and be gone forever. We went together and talked together, or I talked, rather, for a year. I couldn't remember why we broke up. Suddenly, for no reason, she was gone, around the same time we both left school forever. I shook my head, eyes shut.

"Do you remember, she wanted to be a singer once, she had a swell voice," said Tom. "She—"

"Sure," I said. "It all comes back. So long."

"Wait a minute—" said his voice, being hung back on the receiver hook.

I went back to the old neighborhood and walked around. I went in the grocery stores and asked. I saw a few people who I knew but who didn't remember me. And finally I got a line on her. Yes, she was married. No, they weren't sure of the address. Yes, *his* name was Maretti. Somewhere on that street down that way and over a few blocks, or maybe it was the other way.

I checked the name I the phone book. That should have warned me. No phone.

Then by asking questions at some grocery stores down the line, I finally got the Maretti address. Third apartment, fourth floor, rear, number 407.

"Why are you doing this?" I asked myself, going up the stairs, climbing in the dim light in the smell of old food and dust. "Want to show her how well you've done, is *that* it?

"No," I told myself. "I just want to see Sally, someone from the old days. I want to get around to telling her what I should have told her years ago, that, in my own way, at one time, I loved her. I never told her that. But I was afraid. I'm not afraid now that it doesn't make any difference.

"You're a fool," I said.

"Yes," I said, "but aren't we all."

I had to stop to rest on the third landing. I had a feeling, suddenly, in the thick smell of ancient cooking, in the close, whispering darkness of TVs playing too loud and distant children crying, that I should walk down out of the house before it was too late.

"But you've come this far. Come on," I said. "One more flight."

I went up the last stairs slowly and stood before an unpainted door. Behind it, people moved and children talked. I hesitated. What would I say? Hello, Sally, remember the old days when we went boating in the park and the trees were green and you were as slender as a blade of grass? Remember the time that—well.

I raised my hand.

I knocked on the door.

It opened and a woman answered. I'd say she was about ten years older, maybe fifteen, than me. She was wearing a two-dollar basement dress which didn't fit, and her hair was turning gray. There was a lot of fat in the wrong places, and lines around her tired mouth. I almost said, "I've got the wrong apartment, I'm looking for Sally Maretti." But I didn't say anything. Sally was a good five years younger than me. But this was she, looking out of the door into the dim light. Behind her was a room with a battered lampshade, a linoleum floor, one table, and some old brown overstuffed furniture.

We stood looking at each other across twenty-five years. What could I say? Hello, Sally, I'm back, here I am, prosperous, on the other side of town now, here I am, a good car, home, married, children through school, here I am president of a company, why didn't you marry me and you wouldn't be here? I saw her eyes move to my Masonic ring, to the boutonniere in my lapel, to the clean rim of the new hat in my hand, to my gloves, to my shined shoes, to my Florida-tanned face, to my Bronzini tie. Then her eyes came back to my face. She was waiting for me to do one thing or the other. I did the right thing.

"I beg your pardon," I said. "I'm selling insurance."

"I'm sorry," she said. "We don't need any."

She held the door open for just a moment as if at any moment she might burst open.

"Sorry to have bothered you," I said.

"That's all right," she said.

I looked beyond her shoulder. I had been wrong. There were not five children, but six at the dinner table with the husband, a dark man with a scowl stamped on his brow.

"Close the door!" he said. "There's a draft."

"Good night," I said.

"Good night," she said.

I stepped back and she closed the door, her eyes still on my face.

I turned and went down the street.

I had just stepped off the bottom of the brownstone steps when I heard a voice call out behind me. It was a woman's voice. I kept walking. The voice called again and I slowed, but did not turn. A moment later someone put a hand on my elbow. Only then did I stop and look around.

It was the woman from apartment 407 above, her eyes almost wild, her mouth gasping, on the point of tears.

"I'm sorry," she said, and almost pulled back but then gathered herself to say, "This is crazy. You don't happen to be, I know you're not, you aren't Charlie McGraw, *are* you?"

I hesitated while her eyes searched my face, looking for some halfway familiar feature among all the oldness.

My silence made her uneasy. "No, I didn't really think you were," she said.

"I'm sorry," I said. "Who was he?"

"Oh, God," she said, eyes down, stifling something like a laugh. "I don't know. Maybe a boyfriend, a long time ago."

I took her hand and held it for a moment. "I wish I were," I said. "We should have had a lot to talk about."

"Too much, maybe." A single tear fell from her cheek. She backed off. "Well, you can't have everything."

"No," I said, and gave her back her hand, gently.

My gentleness provoked her to a last question.

"You're *sure* you're not Charlie?"

"Charlie must've been a nice fellow."

"The best," she said.

"Well," I said, at last. "So long."

"No," she said. "Good-bye." She spun about and ran to the steps and ran up the steps so quickly that she almost tripped. At the top she whirled suddenly, her eyes brimmed, and lifted her hand to wave. I tried not to wave back but my hand went up.

I stood rooted to the sidewalk for a full half minute before I could make myself move. Jesus, I thought, every love affair I ever had I ruined.

I got back to the bar near closing time. The pianist, for some obscure reason, hating to go home was probably it, was still there.

Taking a double shot of brandy and working on a beer, I said,

"Whatever you do, don't play that piece about

wherever she may go, wherever she may be, if no one wants her now, please send her back to me . . ."

"What song is that?" said the pianist, hands on the keys.

"Something," I said. "Something about . . . what was her name? Oh, yeah. Sally."

Nothing Changes

There is this truly wonderful bookstore by the ocean where you can hear the tide under the pier, shaking the shop, the books on the shelves, and you.

The shop is dark and has a tin roof above the ten thousand books from which you blow dust in order to turn pages.

And it is not just the tide below but the tide above that I love when storm rains shatter that tin roof, banging it like orchestras of machine-gun-cymbal-and-drum. Whenever it is a dark midnight at noon, if not in my soul, like Ishmael, I head for the storm beneath and the storm above, tambourining the tin and knocking silverfish off forgotten authors, row on row. With my smile for a flashlight, I linger all day.

Pure hyperventilation in storms, I arrived one noon at White Whale Books, where I walked, slowly, to the entrance. My anxious taxi driver pursued with his umbrella. I held him off. "Please," I said. "I *want* to get wet!"

"Nut!" cried the cabbie and left.

Gloriously damp, I ducked inside, shook myself like a dog, and froze, eyes shut, hearing the rain bang that high tin roof.

"Which way?" I said to the darkness.

Intuition said left.

I turned and found, in the tintinnabulation of downpour (what a great word: tintinnabulation!) stacks of shelves of old high school annuals which I usually avoid like funerals.

For bookshops are, by their nature, graveyards where old elephants drop their bones.

Uneasily, then, I prowled the high school yearbooks to read the spines: Burlington, Vermont, Orange, New Jersey, Roswell, New Mexico, big sandwiches of memorabilia from fifty states. I did not touch my own godforsaken yearbook, which lay buried with its scribbled time-capsule insults from the Great Depression: "Get lost, sappo. Jim." "Have a great life, you should live so long. Sam." "To a fine writer, lousy lover. Fay."

I blew the dust off Remington High, Pennsylvania, to thumb through scores of baseball, basketball, football braves no longer brave.

1912.

I scanned ten dozen bright faces.

You, you, and you, I thought. Was your life good? Did you marry well? Did your kids like you? Was there a great first love and another later? How, how did it *go*?

Too many flowers here from too many biers. All those eager eyes staring above their wondrous smiles.

I almost shut the book but . . .

My finger stayed on the pictures of the 1912 graduating class, with World War I not yet, unimagined and unknown, when I blinked at one snapshot and gasped:

"My God! Charles! Old Charlie *Nesbitt!*"

Yes! Framed there in a far year, with his freckles, roostercomb hair, big ears, flared nostrils, and corncob teeth. Charles Woodley Nesbitt!

"Charlie!" I cried.

The rain buckshot the tin roof above. The cold blew down my neck.

"Charlie," I whispered. "What're you doing *here?*"

I carried the book out to a better light, heart thumping, and stared.

The name under the picture was Reynolds. Winton Reynolds.

Destined for Harvard
Wants to make a million.
Likes golf.

But the *picture?*

"*Charlie*, dammit!"

Charlie Nesbitt was god-awful homely, a tennis pro, top gymnast, speed swimmer, girl collector. How come? Did those ears, teeth, and nostrils make girls swarm? To *be* like him, we would have signed up for lessons.

And now here he was on a wrong page of an old

book in a lost year with his berserk smile and crazed ears.

Could there once have been *two* Charlie Nesbitts alive? Identical twins, separated at birth? Hell. *My* Charlie was born in 1920, same as me. Wait!

I dodged back in the stacks to grab my 1938 yearbook and riffle the graduate photos until I found:

Wants to be a golf pro.
Heads for Princeton.
Hopes to be rich.

Charles Woodley Nesbitt.

The same goofy teeth, ears, and multitudinous freckles!

I placed the two annuals to study these seeming "twins."

Seemed? No! *Absolutely* the *same!*

Rain drummed the high tin roof.

"Hell, Charlie, hell, Winton!"

I carried the books up front where Mr. Lemley, as old as his books, peered at me over his Ben Franklin specs.

"Found *those*, did you? Take 'em. Free."

"Mr. Lemley, look . . ."

I showed him the pictures and the names.

"I'll be damned." He snorted. "Same family? Brothers? Naw. Same fella, though. How'd you find this?"

"Just did."

"Give me the collywobbles. Coincidence. One in a million births, right?"

"Yeah." I turned the pages back and forth, over and over. "But what if all the faces in *all* the annuals in all the towns in all the states, hell, what if they *all look* alike!

"What'd I just *say?*" I cried, hearing myself.

What if *all* the faces in all the annuals were the *same!*

"Outta the way!" I shouted.

Tearing up the cabbage patch is how Mr. Lemley told it later. If the God of Vengeance and Terror was Shiva with many arms, I was a small but louder god, with a dozen hands seizing books, cursing at revelations, frights, and elations, alone, as witness to a big parade marching nowhere, with separate bands and different choirs in towns strewn across a blind world. From time to time as I leaped through the stacks, Mr. Lemley brought coffee and whispered: "Rest up."

"You don't understand!" I cried.

"No, I don't. How *old* are you?"

"Forty-nine!"

"Act like a nine-year-old running up the aisle at a bad movie, peeing."

"Good advice!" I ran and came back.

Mr. Lemley checked the linoleum for wet spots. "Continue."

I seized more annuals:

"Ella, there's Ella *again.* Tom, there's Tom who looks like Joe, and Frank, a dead ringer for Ralph. Ringer, hell, spittin' *image!* And Helen who's a twin to Cora!

And Ed and Phil and Morris to fit Roger and Alan and Pat. Christ!"

I had two dozen books butterflied, some torn in my haste. "I'll pay, Mr. Lemley, I'll *pay!*"

In the mist of the storm-fever I stopped on page 47 of the Cheyenne 1911 *Book of High School Remembrances.*

For there was the sap, the simpleton, the ignoramus, the shy wimp, the lost soul.

His name, in that lost year?

DOUGLAS DRISCOLL.

His message to the future?

Admired as a thespian.
Will soon join the unemployed.
Headed for literary distinction.

Poor fool, lost dreamer, final achiever.

Douglas Driscoll, Cheyenne, 1911.

Me.

My eyes streaming tears, I bumped my way out of the twilight stacks to show my melancholy gift to Mr. Lemley.

"Gosh." He touched the picture. "That *can't* be someone named Driscoll.

"That's got to be," he said, *"you."*

"Yes, sir."

"Damn," he said, softly. "You *know* this boy?"

"No."

"Got any relatives in . . . Wyoming?"

"No, sir."

"How'd you come on this?"

"Wild hunch."

"Yeah, you really tore up the tundra." He studied my identical twin, half a century ago. "What will you do? Look this fella *up*?"

"If graveyards count for looking."

"It *is* a long time back. How about his kids, or *grand*kids?"

"What would I tell them? They wouldn't necessarily look like him anyway."

"Hell," said Mr. Lemley. "If one kid looks like you, 1911, why not someone *close*. Twenty years ago, or, hot damn, *this* year?"

"Repeat that!" I cried.

"*This* year?"

"You *got* some? *This* year's yearbooks?"

"God, I dunno. Hey, why are you *doing* this?"

"You ever feel," I shouted, "you're on the verge of a bombshell annihilating discovery?"

"Swimming once I found a big chunk of something awful. Ambergris! I thought. Sell it to a perfume factory for thousands! I ran to show the damned stuff to the lifeguard. Ambergris? Horseflies! I flung it back in the sea. *That* kind of annihilating discovery?"

"Maybe. Genealogies. Genetics."

"From what year?"

"Lincoln," I said. "Washington, Henry the Eighth. God, I feel as if I found all Creation, some obvious truth that's been sitting right in front of us forever and we didn't see. This could change history!"

"Or spoil it," said Mr. Lemley. "You sure you ain't been drinking back there in the stacks? Don't stand there. Go!"

"One side or a leg-off," I said.

I read and tossed, tossed and read, but there were no really new annuals. Phone calls and airmail was the answer.

"Jeez Christopher," observed Mr. Lemley. "Can you afford to *do* that?"

"I'll die if I don't."

"And die if you do. Closing time. Lights out."

The annuals streamed in during the week before graduations all across the country.

I stayed up two nights, sleepless, riffling, Xeroxing pages, tallying lists, twinning pasteups of ten dozen new faces against ten dozen old.

Christ, I thought, you damn stupid blind idiot on a runaway train. How do you steer? Where the hell is it going? And, oh God, *why?*

I had no answers. Gone mad, I mailed and phoned, sent and got back, like a blind man in a closet sorting clothes, trying inanities, discarding reason.

The mail was an avalanche.

It could not be, and yet it was. All biological rules? Out the window. The history of flesh was what? Darwinian "Sport." Genetic accidents that birthed new species. Derailed genes which spun the world afresh. But what if there were freak/sport replays? What if Nature hiccuped, and its needle jumped *back?* Then, having lost its genetic mind, wouldn't it clone generation after generation of Williamses, Browns, and Smiths? Not related by family, no. But mindless rebirths, blind matter trapped in a mirror maze? Impossible.

Yet there it was. Dozens of faces repeated in hundreds of faces across the world! Twin upon twin, *in excelsis*. And where did that leave room for new flesh, a history of progress and survival?

Shut up, I thought, and drink your gin.

The cascade of high school annuals continued.

I flipped their pages like decks of cards until, at last . . .

There it was.

Its arrival blew a hole in my stomach.

There was a name on page 124 of the Roswell High annual, published this week and just arrived. The name was:

William Clark Henderson.

I stared at his picture and saw:

Me.

Alive and graduating this week!

The other me.

An exact replica of every eyelash, eyebrow, small pore and large, ear fuzz and nostril hair.

Me. Myself. I.

No! I thought. I looked again. *Yes!*

I jumped. I ran.

Lugging a folder of pictures, I flew to Roswell and, sweating, grabbed a cab to reach Roswell High at twelve noon straight up.

The graduation procession had begun. I panicked. But then as the young men and women passed an immense calmness touched me. Destiny and Providence whispered as my gaze wandered over two hundred young faces in line and at some late-arriving wild smiles, manic with joy now that the long haul was over.

And still the young moved on their way to good or unborn wars, bad marriages, fine or awful employments.

And there *he* was. William Clark Henderson.

The other me.

As he walked, laughing, with a pretty dark-haired girl, I traced my own profile in my high school annual long ago. I saw the soft line under his chin, the unshaven cheeks, the unfocused half-blind eyes that would never understand life but hide out in libraries, duck behind typewriters.

As he passed, he glanced up and froze.

I almost waved, but stopped for he could not make himself move.

He staggered as if struck in the chest. His face grew pale as he groped toward me and gasped.

"Dad! What're you doing *here?*"

I felt my heart stop.

"You *can't* be here!" the young man cried, tears brimming his eyes. "You're *dead!* Died two years ago! Can't be. What? How?"

"No." I said at last. "I'm not . . ."

"Dad!" He seized my arms. "Oh, God! God!"

"Don't!" I said. "Not me!"

"Then *who?*" he pleaded and crushed his head against my chest. "What's going *on?* Christ!"

"Please." I broke his grip. "They're *waiting!*"

He fell back. "I don't understand," he said, the tears flowing.

"*I* don't understand," I said.

He lurched forward. I raised my hand swiftly. "No. Don't."

"Will you," he mourned, "be here . . . *after?*"

"Yes," I said, agonized. "No. I don't *know.*"

"At least *watch,*" he said.

I was silent.

"Please," he said.

At last I nodded and saw color in his face.

"What's going *on?*" he asked again, bewildered.

They say that drowning victims' lives flash through their heads. Here, with William Clark Henderson frozen in the processional, my thoughts, sunk in revelations, sought answers, found none. Were there families worldwide with similar thoughts, plans, dreams locked in mirror-image flesh? Was there a genetic plot to seize the future? Would a day dawn when these unseen, unrecognized fathers, brothers, nephews, cousins rose as rulers? Or was this just God's ghost and spirit, his Providence, his unfathomable Will? Were we all identical seeds hurled forth in wide broadcasts so as not to collide?

Were we then in some broad and incalculable fashion, brother to wolves, birds, and antelope, all inked, spotted, colored the same, year on year and generation on generation back as far as minds could see? To what purpose? To economize on genes and chromosomes? Why? Would the faces of this Family, grown apart, vanish by 2001? Or would the replicas increase to envelop all cousined flesh? Or was it just a miracle of mere existence, misunderstood by two stunned fools shouting across blind generations on a summer's graduation day?

All this, all this exploded light dark, light dark across my gaze.

"What's going on?" the other me repeated.

For the line of young men and women was almost gone, quitting a scene where two idiots raved with two similar voices.

I said something, quietly, which he could not hear. When this is done, I thought, I must tear up the pictures, burn the notes. To continue this way, with old annuals, lost faces: *madness!* Trash it all, I thought. *Now.*

The young man's mouth trembled. I read his lips.

"*What* did you just say?" he asked.

"Nothing changes," I whispered.

Then, louder:

"Nothing changes!"

I waited to hear Kipling's words to that song of great sadness: "*Lord God of old, be with us yet. Lest we forget.*"

Lest we forget.

When I saw the diploma go into the hands of William Clark Henderson—

I backed off, weeping, and ran.

That Old Dog Lying
in the Dust

They say that Mexicali has changed. They say it has many people and more lights and the nights are not so long there anymore and the days are better.

But I will not go see.

For I remember Mexicali when it was small and alone and like an old dog lying out in the dust in the middle of the road. And if you drove up and honked it just lay there and twitched its tail and smiled with its rusty brown eyes.

But most of all I remember a lost-and-gone one-ring Mexican circus.

In the late summer of 1945, with the war ending beyond the world somewhere, and tires and gas rationed, a friend called to ask if I would like to ramble down past the Salton Sea to Calexico.

We headed south in a beat-up Model A which steamed and seeped brown rust-water when we stopped in the late hot afternoon to skinny-dip in the cool irrigation canals that make the desert green along the Mexican border. That night we drove across into Mexico and ate cold watermelon in one of those palm-fringed outdoor stands where whole families gather happy and loud and spitting black seeds.

We strolled the unlit border town, barefoot, treading the soft brown talcum dust of its unpaved summer roads.

The warm dust blew us around a corner. The little one-ring Mexican circus lay there: an old tent full of moth holes and half-sewn wounds, propped up from within by an ancient set of dinosaur bones.

Two bands played.

One was a Victrola which hissed "*La Cucaracha*" from two black funeral horns buried high in the trees.

The second band was mortal flesh. It consisted of a bass-drummer who slammed his drum as if killing his wife, a tuba player sunk and crushed in brass coils, a trumpeter with a pint of sour saliva in his horn, and a trap-drummer whose effervescent palsy enabled him to gunshot everyone: musicians quick or musicians dead. Their mouth-to-mouth breathing brought forth "*La Raspa*."

To both calamities, my friend and I crossed the warm night-wind street, a thousand crickets frolicking at our pants cuffs.

The ticket-seller raved into his wet microphone. Volcanoes of clowns, camels, trapeze acrobats waited just inside to fall upon us! Think!

We thought. In a mob of young, old, well-dressed, poor, we hustled to buy tickets. At the entrance a tiny lady with great white piano-teeth fried tacos and tore tickets. Under her faded shawl, starlight spangled. I knew that soon she would shed her moth wings to become a butterfly, eh? She saw my face guess this. She laughed. She tore a taco in half, handed it to me, laughed again.

Pretending nonchalance, I ate my ticket.

Inside was a single ring around which were tiered three hundred slat-board seats cleverly built to kill the spines of plain meadow-beast folk like us. Down circling the ring stood two dozen rickety tables and chairs where sat the town aristocrats in their licorice-dark suits with black ties. There also sat their proper wives and uncomfortable children, all meticulous, all quiet as behooves the owners of the town cigar store, the town store that sells liquor, or the best car mechanic in Mexicali.

The show was to start at eight p.m. or as soon as the tent was full; by rare luck, the tent was full by eight-thirty. The extravaganzas lit their fuses. A whistle shrieked. The musicians, outside, flung down their instruments and ran.

They reappeared, some in coveralls to haul rope, others as clowns to bounce across the ring.

The ticket-seller lurched in, bringing with him the Victrola which he banged onto a band platform near the ring. In a great shower of sparks and minor explosions, he plugged it in, looked around, shrugged, spun a record, poised the needle. We could have either a live band or live acrobats and trapeze artists. We chose the latter.

The huge circus began—small.

Now a sword-swallower choked on a sword, sprayed kerosene in a gout of flame, and wandered out to applause from five small girls.

Three clowns knocked each other across the ring and bounded off to aching silence.

Then, thank God, the little woman leaped into the ring.

I knew those spangles. I sat up swiftly. I knew those vast teeth, those quick brown eyes.

It was the taco-seller!

But now she was—

The beer-keg juggler!

She rolled flat on her back. She shouted. The sword-swallower tossed a red-white-green keg. She caught it deftly with her white ballet-slippered feet. She spun it, as a John Philip Sousa record beat hell out of the tent canvas with a big brass swatter. The tiny lady kicked the whirling keg twenty feet up. By the time it fell to crush her, she was gone, running.

"Hey! *Ándale! Vamanos!* Ah!"

Out beyond in the dusting night I could see the colossal grand parade corseting itself together, girding its gouty loins. A small mob of men was leaning against what looked like an irritable camel out by the watermelon stands. I thought I heard the camel curse. I knew I saw its lips move with obscene belches. Were they or were they not slipping a stomach belt on the beast? *Did* it have multiple hernias?

But now one of the sweating rope-haulers jumped on the bandstand, crammed a red fez on his head, mouthed the trombone in a great wail. A new record trumpeted like a herd of elephants.

The great parade dusted in, led and followed by ten million crickets who had nothing else to do.

First in the parade was a donkey led by a fourteen-year-old boy in blue overalls with an Arabian Nights turban over his eyes. Then six dogs ran in, barking. I suspected that the dogs, like the crickets, had gotten tired of the nearest street corner and came every night to volunteer their services. There they were, anyway, dashing about, watching from the corners of their eyes to see if we saw them. We did. That drove them wild. They cavorted and yipped and danced until their tongues hung out their mouths like bright red ties.

This, for the first time, stirred the audience. As one, we burst into shouts and applause. The dogs went mad. They bit their tails on the way out.

Next came an old horse with a champanzee on his back, picking his nose and showing results to all. More applause from the children.

And then, the grandest part of the sultan's vast parade.

The camel.

It was a high-society camel.

Which is to say that while it was patched at the seams, needled and glued together with bits of yellow

127

thread and old hemp, with floppy turrets, torn flanks, and bleeding gums, it nevertheless had one of those looks which say, I smell bad but you smell worse. That mask of utter disdain which only rich old women and dying dromedaries share.

My heart leaped.

Riding on the back of this beast, in charge of tinsel, was the tiny woman who had taken tickets, sold tacos, juggled beer kegs, and was now—

Queen of Sheba.

Flashing her lighthouse-smile to all, she waved a salute as she rode between the coming-and-going tides of camel-humps, jolting.

I shouted.

For, half 'round the ring, the camel, seized with an earthquake of arthritis, collapsed.

It fell as if its tendons were chopped.

With a ridiculous leer, with a grimace that begged our pardon, the camel crashed like a wall of canvas and dung.

It knocked one of the ringside tables flat. Beer bottles shattered amidst one elegant funeral-director husband, his hysterical wife, and two sons made joyous by this event which they would tell about for the rest of their lives.

The tiny lady with the big teeth, waving bravely, smiling her own pardon, went down with the ship of the desert.

Somehow she retained her seat. Somehow she was not rolled on or crushed. Pretending that nothing whatsoever was wrong, she continued to wave and smile as the various rope-haulers, trombone players, and trapeze artists, half-in half-out of their new-old disguises, ran to butt, kick, pummel, and spit on the eye-rolling beast. Meanwhile the rest of the parade circled the ring, making a wide detour around this point of collapse.

Getting the camel put back together this leg here, that joint there, and the neck, so! was like putting up an Arab tent in a hurricane. No sooner had these sweating architects established one leg and nailed it to the earth, than another leg creaked and broke apart.

The camel's humps flopped in opposite directions, wildly. The little woman stayed bravely sidesaddle. The phonograph brass-band pulsed, and at last the camel was reassembled; the great homely jigsaw of bad breath and Band-Aid–covered pelt reared up to shamble, walking wounded, drunk and disorderly, threatening to crack yet other tables flat, one last time around the ring.

The tiny lady way up there on the smelly dune of beast waved a final time. The audience cheered. The parade limped out. The trombone player rushed over to the platform to shut the fanfare off.

I found that I was standing, my mouth open and aching, my lungs raw with shouts of encouragement I had not heard myself give. I saw that there were dozens of others, like myself, who had been caught up in the despair of the woman and the embarrassment of the camel. Now we all sat down, giving each other quick proud looks, glad for happy endings. The band shuffled back in, wearing gold epaulettes on their work-coveralls. They struck a brass note.

"The Great Lucretia! The Butterfly of Berlin!" cried the ringmaster, appearing for the first time by the very proper tables, his trumpet hidden behind his back. "Lucretia!"

Lucretia danced out.

But of course it was not just Lucretia who danced, but tiny Melba and Roxanne and Ramona Gonzales. With many hats, many costumes, she ran with the same vast piano smile. Oh, Lucretia, Lucretia, I thought.

O woman who rides camels that fail, O woman who juggles kegs and rips tacos—

O woman, I added, who tomorrow will drive one of those flimsy tin locust-scourge trucks across the Mexican desert toward some lonely town inhabited by 200 dogs, 400 cats, 1,000 candles, and 200 forty-watt bulbs, plus 400 people. And of those 400 people, 300 will be old women and old men, 80 will be children and 20 young women waiting for young men who will never come back from across the desert where they have vanished toward San Luis Potosí, Juárez, and sea-bottoms dry and empty and baked to salt. And here comes the circus, packed in a few grasshopper-plague cars, flicking, rattling, jouncing over the pothole roads, squashing tarantulas to strawberry phlegm, crushing slow dogs to tarpaulin papier-mâché shapes left to flake at high noon on an empty turnpike, and the circus, not looking back, gone.

And this small woman, I thought, why, she is almost the whole thing. If *she* ever dies . . .

Ta-ta! said the orchestra, calling me back from reveries of dust and sun.

A silver buckle flew down out of the tent sky on a fishing line. It had come to fish for—*her!*

She attached the silver buckle to her smile.

"Oh my God, look!" said my friend. "She . . . she's going to—*fly!*"

The tiny woman with the biceps of a truck driver and the legs of a six-day bike-rider jumped.

God, on his long fishing line, drew her whizzing into the brown flapping-tent sky.

The music soared with her.

Applause shattered the air.

"How high would you say she is?" whispered my friend.

I would not answer. Twenty feet, maybe twenty-five.

But somehow, with this tent and these people and this night, it seemed a hundred.

And then, the tent began to die. Or rather the Smile began to collapse the tent.

Which is to say, the teeth of the tiny woman attached to the silver buckle pulling one way, toward the center of the earth, caused all the tent-poles to groan. Wire hummed. The canvas boomed like a drum.

The audience gasped and stared.

The Butterfly spun and whirled in her bright unfurled cocoon.

But the ancient tent gave up. Like a hairy mammoth despairing of his bones, the tent leaned, wishing to roll over and sleep.

The men holding to the rope, which had yanked the Smile, the Teeth, and Head, the Body of the brave little muscled woman fifteen and then twenty feet into the air, these men now also gazed up in terror. The poles would crush, the canvas smother their insignificant lives. Their eyes flicked to the ringmaster who snapped his whip and cried "Higher!" as if there was somewhere yet to go. She was almost to the top of the tent now and all the poles were vibrating, shaking, leaning. The orchestra brassed out a single note as if to summon an evil wind. The wind came. Outside in the night, a very dry Santa Ana indeed arrived, picked up the skirts of the tent, let the night peer under, blew a vast whiff of hot oven air in on us with dust and crickets, and fled.

The tent boomed its canvas. The crowd shivered.

"Higher!" cried the ringmaster, bravely. "*Finale!* The Great Lucretia!" Then he hissed in an explosive aside: "Lucy, *vamanos!*" Which translates to: "God sleeps, Lucy. Down!"

But she gave an impatient shake, twist, ripple of her entire muscled Mickey Rooney body. She shed her wings. She became an angry hornet cutting swathes. She spun faster, divesting herself of silks. The band played "Dance of the Seven Veils." She whipped off layer on layer of red, blue, white, green! With a series of amazing metamorphoses she spellbound our uplifted eyes.

"*Madre de Dios*, Lucretia!" cried the ringmaster.

For the canvas heaved, exhaled. The tent skeleton groaned. The angle-pullers, the rope-haulers shut their eyes, moaning, afraid to see that insanity in the air.

Lucy-Lucretia snapped both hands. Zap! A Mexican flag, an American flag sprang from nowhere into her fingers. Crick!

The band, seeing this, played the Mexican national anthem (four bars), and ended with Francis Scott Key (two).

The audience clapped, yelled! With luck, that midget dynamo would be down on the earth instead of the tent down on our heads! *Olé!*

The three ropemen let her drop.

She fell a full ten feet before they remembered she had no net. They seized the smoking rope again. You could smell their burning skin. Devil's fire leaped from their palms. They laughed with pain.

The little toy lady hit the sawdust, her smile still attached to the buckle. She reached up, unplucked the rope, and stood waving the two bright flags at the gone-mad crowd.

The tent, relieved of 110 pounds of mighty muscle, sighed. Through the many moth holes in the gray-brown canvas skin, I saw a thousand stars twinkling in celebration. The circus was to live for yet another day.

Pursued by a tidal wave of applause, the Smile and the tiny lady who owned it ran along the sawdust shore, gone.

Now: the finale.

Now, an act which would put out our lives, blow out our souls, destroy our sanity by its beauty, terror, weight, power, and imagination!

So said a rope-hauler over the lilyhorns!

The rope-hauler waved his trumpet. The band fell in a heap of super-induced affection upon a triumphal march.

The lion-tamer, in a banging cloud of pistol-fire, bounded into the ring.

He wore a white African hunter's helmet, a Clyde Beatty blouse and puttees, and Frank Buck boots.

He cracked a black whip. He fired his pistol to wake us up. The air was filled with an immense bloom of scent.

But under the shadow of his white helmet, and behind his fierce new mustache, I saw the face of the ticket-seller out front an hour ago, and the eyes of the ringmaster.

Another pistol crack. Ta!

The round lion-tamer's cage, hidden until now under a bright tarpaulin toward the rear of the tent, was revealed as its brilliant cover was yanked off.

The ring-attendants came trudging in, pulling a crate inside which we could smell a single lion. This they pushed up to the far side of the cage. Doors were opened. The lion-tamer leaped into the main cage, slammed the door, and fired his weapon at the open door of the lion's shadowy crate.

"Leo! *Ándale!*" cried the tamer.

The audience leaned forward.

But . . . no Leo.

He was asleep somewhere in that small portable crate.

"Leo! *Vamanos! Ándale!* Presto!" The tamer snapped in through the small crate door with his whip, like someone turning meat on a tired spit.

A big fluff of yellow mane rolled over with an irritable mumble.

"Gah!" The pistol was next fired into the deaf old lion's ear.

There was a most deliciously satisfying roar.

The audience beamed and settled back.

Leo suddenly manifested in the crate door. He blinked into the damned light. And he was—

The oldest lion I have ever seen.

It was a beast come forth from a retirement farm in the Dublin Zoo on a bleak day in December. So wrinkled was his face, it was a smashed window, and his gold was old gold left out in the long rains and beginning to run.

The lion needed glasses, this we could guess from his furious blinking and squinting. Some of his teeth had fallen out in his breakfast gruel only that morning. His ribs could be seen under his mangy pelt which had the look of a welcome mat trampled on by a billion lion-tamers' feet.

There was no more outrage in him. He was angered out. There was only one thing to do. Fire his pistol into the beast's left nostril—bang!

"Leo."

Roar! went the lion. Ah! said the audience. The drummer stirred up a storm on his snare drum.

The lion took a step. The tamer took a step. Suspense!

Then a dreadful thing . . .

The lion opened his mouth and yawned.

Then an even more dreadful thing . . .

A small boy, no more than three years old, somehow freed from his mother's clutch, left the elite table at the edge of the ring and toddled forward across the sawdust toward the monstrous iron cage. Cries filled the tent: No, no! But before anyone could move, the small boy plunged laughing forward and seized the bars.

No! came the gasp.

But worse still, the little boy shook not just two bars, but the *entire* cage.

With the littlest move of his tiny pink-brown fists, the boy threatened to topple the whole jungle edifice.

No! cried everyone silently, leaning forward, gesticulating at the boy with fingers and eyebrows.

The lion-tamer, with his whip and pistol upraised, sweated, waited.

The lion exhaled through his fangless mouth, eyes shut.

The small boy gave the bars a last rattling shake of terrible Doom.

Just as his father, in one swift run, scooped him up, half hid him under his Sunday coat, and retreated to the nearest formal table.

Bang! The audience exhaled, collapsed in relief, the lion roared, circled round after its own tail, and leaped upon a flake-painted pedestal, there to rear up on its hind feet.

By now, the shaken cage had stopped trembling.

Bang! The tamer fired into that vast yellow-sun face. The lion blazed a real scream of anguish and leaped! The tamer ran pell-mell. The lion raced. The tamer reached the cage door, with the lion not one pace behind. The audience shrieked. The tamer flung the door wide, spun, fired, bang, bang! then out, clang! and the door locked safe, he whipped his toupee off, flung his pistol to earth, cracked his whip, and smiled a smile that swallowed us all!

Roar! That's what the crowd did. On its feet, it imitated the lion-beast. Roar!

The show was over.

The two bands were playing outside in the watermelon-eating dust-blowing cricket-jumping night and the audience was going out and my friend and I sat for a long while until we were almost alone in the moth-eaten tent through which the stars moved yet new bright constellations into place and would continue to move their small strange fires during the night. The tent flapped its wings in a hot wind of ancient applause. We went out with the last of the crowd in silence.

We looked back in at the empty ring, at the high line at the tent-top where the silver buckle waited to be attached to the Smile.

I felt a taco in my hand and looked up. There before me was the tiny lady who rode disorganized camels, juggled kegs, tore tickets, and changed from moth to butterfly each night in the small sky. Her Smile was near, her eyes searched to find the cynic in me, and found but a friend. We both had hold of opposite ends of one taco. At last she let go. With my gift, I went.

Nearby, the phonograph hissed *"La Galondrina."* And there stood the lion-tamer, perspiration falling from his brow to make a suit of lights where it touched his khaki shirt. Lips pressed to his horn, eyes shut, he did not see me pass.

Under dusty trees, we turned a corner, and the circus was gone.

All night the wind blew warm up out of Mexico, taking the dry land with it. All night the crickets rained on our bungalow windowpanes.

We drove north. For weeks after, I beat the hot dust out of my clothes and picked the dead crickets out of my typewriter and luggage.

And still nights, twenty-nine years later, I hear that one-ring circus playing its two bands, one real, one hiccuping on records, a long way off on a warm Santa Ana wind, and I wake and sit up in bed, alone, and it is not there.

Someone in the Rain

Everything was almost the same. Now that the luggage was brought into the echoing damp cottage, with the raindrops still shining on it, and he had drawn the canvas over the car which was still warm and smelling of the drive two hundred miles north into Wisconsin from Chicago, he had time to think. First of all, he had been very lucky to get this same cabin, the one he and his brother Skip and his folks had rented twenty years ago, in 1927. It sounded just the same, there was the empty echo of your voice and your feet. Now, for some unaccountable reason, he was walking about barefoot, because it felt good, perhaps. He closed his eyes as he sat on the bed and listened to the rain on the thin roof. You had to take a lot of things into account. First of all, the trees were larger. You looked out of your streaming car window in the rain and you saw the Lake Lawn sign looming up and something was different and it was only now, as he heard the wind outside, that he realized what the real change was. The trees, of course. Twenty years of growing lush and high. The grass, too; if you wanted to get particular, it was the same grass, perhaps, he had lain in that long time ago, after the jump in the lake, his swimsuit still cold around his loins and around his thin small chest. He wondered, idly, if the latrine still smelled the way it did: of brass and disinfectant and old shuffling fumbling men and soap.

The rain stopped. It tapped occasionally on the house from the washing trees above, and the sky was the color and had the feel and expectancy of gunpowder. Now and again it cracked down the middle, all light; and then the crack was mended.

Linda was over in the ladies' rest room, which was just a run between the bushes and the trees and the small white cottages, a run through puddles now, he supposed, and bushes that shook like startled dogs when you passed, showering you with a fresh burst of cool and odorous rain. It was good that she was gone for awhile. He wanted to look for certain things. First there was the initial he had carved on the windowsill fifteen years ago on their last trip up for the late summer of 1932. It was a thing he would never have done with anyone about, but now, alone, he walked to the window and ran his hand over the surface. It was perfectly smooth.

Well then, he thought, it must have been another window. No. It was this room. And this cottage, no doubt of it. He felt a sudden resentment at the carpenter who had come in here some time ago and smoothed and sandpapered surfaces and taken away the immortality he had promised himself that rainy night when, locked into the house by the storm, he had busied himself with the careful initialing. Then he had said to himself, People will come by, years from now, and see this.

He rubbed his hand on the empty sill.

Linda arrived through the front door. "Oh, what a place," she cried, and she was almost soaked, her blonde hair was full of rain, and her face was wet. She looked at him with half an accusation. "So this is Wonderland. When did they build it? You'd think each house would have a toilet, but oh no! It's just a stone's throw to the toilet, where I spent two minutes trying to find the light switch, and five minutes after that batting off a big moth while I tried to wash up!"

A large moth. He straightened up and smiled. "Here." He gave her a towel. "Dry off. You'll be all right."

"I ran into a bush, look at my dress, drenched. God." She submerged into the towel, talking.

"I've got to go over to the men's room myself," he said, looking out the door, smiling at a thing that had come into his mind. "I'll be back."

"If you're not back in ten minutes, I'll send the Coast Guard—"

The door banged.

He walked very slowly, taking deep breaths. He just let the rain fall on him and he felt the wind tugging at the cuffs of his pants. That cottage there was where

Marion, his cousin, had stayed with her mother and father. God, how many nights had they crept off to the woods and sat on damp grass to tell ghost stories while looking at the lake. And get so scared that Marion would want to hold hands and then maybe kiss, just those small innocent kisses of ten- and eleven-year-old cousins, only touches, only gestures against loneliness. He could smell her now, Marion, the way she was before the nicotine got to her and the bottled perfumes got to her. She hadn't been his cousin, really now, for ten years or so, never really, since growing up. The really natural creature had been back here somewhere. Oh, Marion was mature now, and so was he to a certain degree. But all the same, the smell of maturity wasn't quite as pleasant.

He reached the men's washroom, and Christ, it wasn't changed a bit.

The moth was waiting for him.

It was a big soft fluttery white ghost of a moth, batting and whispering against the single filament bulb. It had been there twenty years, sighing and beating in the moist night air of the rest room, waiting for him to come back. He remembered his first encounter with it. He had been only eight and the moth had come at him like a powdery phantom, dusting down its horrible wings, screaming silently at him.

He had run, shrieking, out of the latrine, across the dark August grass, into his cottage. And, rather than go back to the latrine, he watered himself free of his bursting pain behind the cottage. After that, he had been sure to go to the toilet many times during the day, so he would not have to go back to the latrine to face the powdering terror.

Now he looked at the Moth.

"Hello," he said. "Been waiting long?"

It was a silly thing to say, but it was good being silly. He didn't like the look on Linda's face. He knew that the more excuses he could make in the next day or so to be out of her sight, the better for himself. He would save money on cigarettes by not being too near her. He would be very solicitous. "What if I run up for a bottle of whiskey, darling?" "Darling, I'm going down to the boat dock to pick up some bait." "Darling, Sam wants me to golf this afternoon." Linda didn't keep well in this kind of weather. There was something a little sour about her already.

The moth beat gently at his face. "You're pretty damned big," he said, suddenly feeling a return of the cool chill to his spine, where it had used to be. He hadn't been afraid in years, now he let himself be just a little, enjoyably, afraid of the white, whispering moth. It tinkled against the light bulb. He washed up, and for the hell of it looked into a booth to see if there was some of that mysterious writing he had once read as a boy. Magic words then, incomprehensible, strange. Now—nothing. "I know what you mean, now," he said. "Words. Limericks. All the magic gone."

Somehow, he caught himself in the mirror, the blurred, fuzzy mirror, and his face was disappointed. All the words had not turned out to be half as grand as he had conjured them to seem. Once they had been golden pronouncements of mystery. Now they were vulgar, short, shocks against accumulated taste.

He lingered to finish out a cigarette, not wanting quite yet to return to Linda.

When he entered the cottage, Linda looked at his shirt.

"That's your good shirt, and why didn't you put on your coat, it's all wet."

"I'll be all right," he said.

"You'll catch cold," she said. She was unpacking some things on the bed. "Boy, the bed's hard," she said.

"I used to sleep the sleep of the innocent on it," he said.

"Frankly," she said, "I'm getting old. When they put out a bed made of whipped cream, I'm bait."

"Lie down for awhile," he suggested. "We've got three hours before dinner—"

"How long will this rain go on?" she said.

"I don't know, probably just today, and then tomorrow, everything green. Boy, does it smell good after a rain."

But he was lying. Sometimes it rained for a week. And he hadn't minded it. He had run down to the gray choppy lake in the needling rain, while the sky over him, like a great gray crock overturned and storming, from time to time took on a crackle glaze of electric blue. Then the thunder knocked him off his feet. And he had swum in the lake, his head out, the lake feeling warm and comfortable, just because the air was filled with cold needles and he looked out at the pavilion where people danced nights, and the hotels with the warm long dim corridors hushed and quiet with running porters, and he looked at the cottage under the August thunder, him in the lake, paddling dog-fashion, the air like winter above. And he never wanted to come out of the lake, he wanted only to remain suspended in the warm water, until he turned purple with enjoyment.

Linda lay down on the bed. "God, what a mattress," she said.

He lay down beside her, not touching her.

The rain started again, gently, upon the cottage. It was as dark as night, but a very special feeling, because you knew it was four in the afternoon, though black, and the sun was above all the blackness, oh, very special.

At six o'clock, Linda painted a fresh mouth on. "Well, I hope the food's good," she said. It was still raining, a thumping, pounding, never-ending drop of storm upon the house. "What do we do this evening?" she wanted to know.

"Dance? There's a pavilion, cost a million dollars, built in 1929 just before the crash," he said, tying his tie. And again he was out of the room, in thought, and under the raining trees, eighteen years ago. Him and Marion and Skip, running in their rustling slickers, making a noise like cellophane, with the rain patting them all over, their faces greased with it, past the playground and the slides, along the posted road, and to the pavilion. Children were not allowed inside. They had stood outside with their faces pressed to the screen, watching the people inside, buying drinks, laughing, sitting at the tables, getting up and going out to dance on the dance floor to music that was muted and enclosed. Marion had stood there, enchanted, the light on her face. "Someday," she had said, "I'm going to be inside, and dance."

They had stood, with the rain touching around them, in the dark wet night, the rain dripping from the eaves of the pavilion. And the music had played "I Found My Love in Avalon" and things like "In Old Monterrey."

Then, after half an hour of the rain seeping into their shoes, and their noses chilling, and rain slipping into their raincoat collars, they had turned from the warm pavilion light and walked off, silently, the music fading, down the road back to their cabins.

Someone knocked on the front door. "Sam!" called a voice. "Hey, you two! Ready? Time for dinner!"

They let Sam in. "'How do we get up to the hotel?" asked Linda. "Walk?" She looked at the rain outside the door.

"Why not," said her husband. "It'd be fun. God, we never do anything anymore, you know what I mean, we never walk anywhere, if we have to go anyplace past a block we get in the car. Hell, let's put on our raincoats and march up, eh, Sam?"

"Okay with me, how about you, Linda?" cried Sam.

"Oh, walk?" she complained. "All that way? And in this rain?"

"Come off it," the husband said. "What's a little rain."

"All right," she said.

There was a rustling as they got into raincoats. He laughed a lot and whacked her on the backside and helped her buckle it up tight. "I smell like a rubber walrus," she said. And then they were out in the lane of green trees, slipping on the squelching grass, in the lane, sinking their rubbered feet into sludge mud furrows where cars came splashing by, whining in the thick wet dark.

"Oh, boy, this is swell!" he shouted.

"Not so fast," she said.

The wind blew, bending the trees, and by the look of it, it would last a week. The hotel was up the hill and they walked now, with less laughing, though he tried starting it again. It was after Linda slipped and fell that nobody said a thing, though Sam, when helping her up, tried to make a joke.

"If nobody minds, I'm hitching a ride," she said.

"Oh, be a sport," he said.

She thumbed the next car going up the hill. When the car stopped, the man in it shouted, "You all want a ride to the hotel?" But he walked on without saying a word, so Sam had to follow.

"That wasn't polite," said Sam.

Lightning stood on the sky, like a naked and newborn tree.

*　　*　　*

Supper was warm, but not of much taste, the coffee was thin and unpalatable and there were not many people in the dining room. It had that end-of-the-season feel, as if everybody had taken their clothes out of storage for the last time, tomorrow the world was ending, the lights would go out, and it was no use trying too hard to please anybody. The lights seemed dim, there was too much forced talk and bad cigar smoke.

"My feet are soaked," said Linda.

They went down to the pavilion at eight o'clock, and it was big and empty and echoing, with an empty bandstand, which filled slowly until at nine o'clock there were a lot of people seated at the tables, and the orchestra, a nine-piece band (hadn't it been a twenty-piece band in 1929, wondered the husband), broke into a medley of old tunes.

His cigarettes tasted damp, his suit was moist, his shoes were sopping, but he said nothing. When the orchestra played its third number, he asked Linda out on the floor. There were about seven couples out there, in the rainbow changing lights, in the vast echoing emptiness. His socks squeaked water as he walked, they were very cold.

He held Linda and they danced to "I Found My Love in Avalon," just because he had telephoned earlier to have it played. They moved quietly around the floor, not speaking.

"My feet are soaking wet," said Linda, finally.

He held on to her and kept moving. The place was

dim and dark and cool and the windows were washed with fresh rain still pouring.

"After this dance," said Linda, "we'll go to the cabin."

He didn't say yes or no.

He looked across the shining floor, to the empty tables, with a few couples spotted here and there, beyond them, to the watery windows. As he moved Linda across the floor, nearer to the window, he squinted, and there they were.

Outside the window, a few child faces, peering in. One or two. Perhaps three. The light on their faces. The light shining in their eyes. Just for a minute or so.

He said something.

"What'd you say?" asked Linda.

"I said I wish I were outside the window now, looking in," he said. She looked at him. The music was ending. When he looked at the window again, the faces were gone.

Madame et
Monsieur Shill

It was while shuttling his eye down the menu posted in a nineteenth-century silver frame outside Le Restaurant Fondue that Andre Hall felt the merest touch at his elbow.

"Sir," said a man's voice, "you look to be hungry."

Andre turned irritably.

"What makes you think—?" he began, but the older man interrupted, politely.

"It was the way you leaned in to read the menu. I am Monsieur Sault, the proprietor of this restaurant. I know the symptoms."

"My God," said Andre. "*That* made you come out?"

"Yes!" The older man examined Andre's coat, the worn cuffs, the too-often-cleaned lapels and said, "*Are* you hungry?"

"Do I sing for my supper?"

"No, no! *Regardez* the window."

Andrew turned and gasped, shot through the heart.

For in the window sat the most beautiful young woman, bent to ladle her soup to a most *delicious* mouth. Bent, as if in prayer, she seemed not to notice their tracing her profile, her mellow cheeks, her violet eyes, her ears as delicate as seashells.

Andre had never dined on a woman's fingers, but now the urge overwhelmed him as he fought to breathe.

"All you must do," whispered the proprietor, "is sit in that window with the lovely creature and eat and drink during the next hour. And return another night to dine with the same lovely vision."

"Why?" said Andre.

"*Regardez.*" The old man turned Andre's head so he might gaze at himself in the window's reflection.

"What do you see?"

"A hungry art student. Myself! And . . . not bad-looking?"

"Ah hah! Good. Come!"

And the young man was pulled through the door to sit at the table while the beautiful young woman laughed.

"What?" he cried, as champagne was poured. "What's so funny?"

"You," the beauty smiled. "Hasn't he said why we're here? Behold, our audience."

She pointed her champagne glass at the window where people now lingered outside.

"Who are they?" he protested. "And *what* do they see?"

"The actors." She sipped her champagne. "The beautiful people. Us. My fine eyes, nose, fine mouth, and *look* at you. Eyes, nose, mouth, *all* fine. Drink!"

The proprietor's shadow moved between them. "Do you know the magician's theater where a volunteer who is the magician's assistant *pretends* innocence to secretly help the sorcerer, eh? And the *name* of such assistants? *Shill.* So, seated with a proper wine and your audience beyond the window, I now dub thee . . ."

He paused.

"Shill. Madame *et* Monsieur . . . Shill."

And indeed as the lovely creature across from Andre raised her glass, in the twilight hour beyond the window, passersby hesitated and were pleasured by the incredible beauty and a man as handsome as she was lovely.

With a murmuring and shadowing the couples, lured by more than menus, filled the tables and more candles were lit and more champagne poured as Andre and his love, fascinated with each other's immortal faces, devoured their meal without seeing it.

So the last plates were cleared, the last wine tasted, the last candles extinguished. They sat, staring at one another, until the proprietor, in the shadows, raised his hands.

Applause.

"Tomorrow night," he said. "*Encore?*"

*   *   *

Encore and another after that and still another followed with their arrivals and departures, but always they met in silence to cause the room's temperature to change. People entering from the cool night found summer on this hearth where he fed on her warmth.

And it was in the midst of the sixteenth night that Andre felt a ventriloquist's ghost in his throat move his mouth to say:

"I love you."

"Don't!" she said. "People are watching!"

"They've been watching for weeks. They see two lovers."

"Lovers? No. We're not!"

"Yes! Come back to my room or let me come to *yours!*"

"That would spoil it! This is perfect *now.*"

"Being with you would be perfect."

"Sit! Look at all the people we make happy. Consider Monsieur Sault, whose future we assure. Think: before you arrived last month, what were your plans for next year? Drink the wine. They say it's excellent."

"Because they *say* it's excellent?"

"Careful. The people outside might read lips and leave. Give me your hand. *Gently!* Eat. Smile. Nod your head. There. Better?"

"I love you."

"Stop or I'll go!"

"Where?"

"Somewhere!" She smiled her false smile for the

people beyond the window. "Where working conditions are better."

"Am *I* a bad working condition?"

"You endanger us. See, Monsieur Sault glares! Be still. Pour the wine. Yes?"

"Yes," he said at last.

And so it went for another week until he burst out and said, "Marry me!"

She snatched her hand from his. "No!" Then, because a couple had paused at their window, she laughed.

"Don't you love me a little bit?" he pleaded.

"Why should I? There were no promises."

"Marry me!"

"Monsieur Sault!" she cried. "The check!"

"But there has never *been* a check!"

"Tonight," she said, "there *is*."

The next night she vanished.

"You," cried Monsieur Sault. "You fiend! Look what you've done!"

Inside the window there was no beautiful young woman: the last night of spring, the first night of summer.

"My business is ruined!" cried the old man. "Why couldn't you have shut your mouth and eaten your pâté or drunk a second bottle and stuck the cork in your teeth?"

"I told the truth as I felt it. She'll come back!"

"So? Read *this*!"

Andre took the note the old man gave him and read: *Farewell*.

"Farewell." Tears leaked from Andre's eyes. "Where's she gone?"

"God knows. We never knew her real name or address. Come!"

Andre followed up through a labyrinth of stairs to the roof. There, swaying as if he might pitch headlong down, Monsieur Sault pointed across the twilight city.

"What do you see?"

"Paris. Thousands of buildings."

"And?"

"Thousands of restaurants?"

"Do you truly know how many there are between here, the *Tour Eiffel*, and there, Notre-Dame? Twenty thousand restaurants. Twenty thousand hiding places for our nameless wonder. Would you find her? Search!"

"All twenty thousand restaurants?"

"Bring her and you'll be my son and partner. Come without her and I will kill you. Escape!"

Andre escaped. He ran to climb the hill to the white splendor of Sacré-Coeur and looked out at the lights of Paris drowned in the blue and gold colors of a vanished sun.

"Twenty thousand hiding places," he murmured.

And went down in search.

In the Latin Quarter across the Seine from Notre-Dame you could wander past forty restaurants in a single block, twenty on each side, some with windows where beauties might sit by candlelight, some with tables and laughing people in the open.

"No, no," Andre muttered. "Too much!" And veered off down an alley that ended at the Boulevard St. Michel where brasseries, *tabacs*, and restaurants swarmed with tourists; where Renoir women spoke wine as they drank, spoke food as they ate, and ignored this strange, haunted, searching young man as he passed.

My God, Andre thought. Must I cross and recross Paris from the Trocadero to Montmartre to Montparnasse, to find a single small theater-café window where candlelight reveals a woman so beautiful that all appetites bud, all joys, culinary and amorous, conjoin?

Madness!

What if I miss that one window, that illumination, that face?

Insane! What if in my confusion I revisit alleys already searched! A map! I must cross out where I've been.

So each night at sundown with the shades of violet and purple and magenta flooding the narrow alleys he set out with bright maps that darkened as he left. Once on the Boulevard de Grenelle he shouted his taxi to a halt and leaped out, furious. The taxi had gone too fast; a dozen cafés had flashed by unseen.

Then suddenly, in despair, he said:

"Honfleur? Deuville? Lyon?"

"What if," he continued, "she is *not* in Paris but

has fled to Cannes or Bordeaux with their thousands of restaurants! My God!"

That night he woke at three a.m. as a list of names passed through his head. Elizabeth. Michelle. Arielle. Which name to speak if at last he found her? Celia? Helene? Diana? Beth?

Exhausted, he slept.

And so the weeks passed into months and in the fourth month he shouted at his mirror:

"Stop! If you haven't found her special 'theater' this week, burn your maps! No more names or streets at midnight or dawn! Yes!"

His image, in silence, turned away.

On the ninety-seventh night of his search, Andre was moving along the Quai Voltaire when he was suddenly seized by a storm of emotion so powerful it shook his bones and knocked his heart. Voices that he heard but did not hear made him stagger toward an intersection, where he froze.

Across the narrow street under a bower of trembling leaves, there was a small audience staring at a brass-framed menu, and the window beyond. Andre stepped, as in a trance, to stand behind the people.

"Impossible," whispered Andre.

For in the candlelit window sat the most beautiful woman, the most beautiful love of his life. And across from her sat an amazingly handsome man. They were lifting glasses and drinking champagne.

Am I outside or in? Andre wondered. Is that me in there, as before, and in love? *What?*

He could only swallow his heart as, for an instant, the gaze of the beautiful young woman passed over him like a shadow and did not return. Instead she smiled at her friend across the candlelit table. Stunned, Andre found the entryway and stepped in to move and stand close by the couple who whispered and laughed quietly.

She was more beautiful than in all the nights he had imagined her multitudinous names. Her travels across Paris had colored her cheeks and brightened her incredible eyes. Even her laughter was made rich by a passage of time.

Outside the restaurant window, a new audience watched as Andre said:

"Excuse."

The beautiful young woman and the handsome man looked up. There was no remembrance in her eyes, nor did her lips smile.

"Madame *et* Monsieur Shill?" Andre asked, numbly.

They held hands and nodded.

"Yes?" they said.

And finished the wine.

The Mirror

Good Lord, there must be a thousand ways to tell of these two ladies. When they were girls, in yellow dresses, they could stand and comb their hair looking at each other. If life was a great Swiss clock, then these were the sprightliest cuckoos that ever jumped out of two doors at once, announcing the exact same time, each of them, not a second lost between. They blinked as if one cord was pulled by a great magician hidden behind the scenes. They wore the same shoes, tilted their heads in the same direction, and trailed their hands like white ribbons on the air as they floated by. Two bottles of cool milk, two new Lincoln pennies were never more the same. Whenever they entered the school proms the dancers halted as if someone had suddenly removed all of the air from the ballroom; everyone gasped.

"The twins," everyone said. Not a name was mentioned. What matter if their name was Wycherly; the parts were interchangeable, you didn't love one, you loved a corporative enterprise. The twins, the twins, how they floated down the great river of years, like two daisies tossed upon the waters.

"They'll marry the kings of the world," people said.

But they sat upon their porch for twenty years, they were as much a part of the park as the swans, you saw their faces uplifted and thrust forward like winter ghosts in the dark night of the film theater.

Oh, once there'd been men, or a man in their life. The word "life" is suggested because a plural noun would not do justice to their oneness. A man had tipped his hat to them here or there, only to have the hat returned to him as he was floated to the door. "Twins is what we're looking for!" you could hear the older sister saying across the twilight lawns. "We've two of everything in the house, beds, shoes, sun-chairs, dark glasses; and now how wonderful if we could find twins like ourselves, for only twins would understand what it is to be an individual and a mirror reflection—"

The older sister. Born nine minutes before the younger, and the divine right of elegant queens in her veins. "Sister do this, sister do that, sister do the other thing!"

"I'm the mirror," said Julia, the youngest, at the age of twenty-nine. "Oh, I've always known. Coral, everything went to her, the sense, the tongue, the mind, the coloring . . ."

"Alike as two vanilla cones, both of you."

"No, you don't see what I see. My pores are larger

and my skin redder and my elbows are rough. Coral says sandpaper is talcum by comparison. No, she's the person, and I only stand here and act out what she is and what she does, like a mirror, but always knowing I'm not real, I'm only so many waves of light, an optical illusion. Anyone who hit me with a rock would have seven years bad luck."

"Both of you will be married come spring, no doubt, no doubt *of* it!"

"Coral maybe, not me. I'll just go along to talk evenings when Coral has a headache and make the tea, that's a natural-born gift I have, making tea."

In 1934 there was a man, the town remembers, and not with Coral at all, but with the younger Julia.

"It was like a siren, the night Julia brought her young man home. I thought the tannery had gone down in flames. Came out on my front porch half-dressed with shock. And there was Coral on the front porch making a spell on the young man across half the lawn, and asking the earth to swallow her, and Julia hidden inside the screen door, and the young man just standing there with his hat on the wet grass. The next morning I saw Julia sneak out and grab it and run in. After that, didn't see the twins for, well, a week, and after that, there they were, sailing like boats again, down the sidewalk, the two of them, but after that I always knew which was Julia—yes, you could tell every year after that which was Julia by looking in her face."

Only last week they turned forty, the old and the young Wycherly. There must have been something about that day which broke a harp-thread so quick and so loud you could hear the clear sound of it across town.

On that morning, Julia Wycherly awoke and did not comb her hair. At breakfast the oldest one looked in her faithful mirror and said, "What's the matter with your comb?"

"Comb?"

"Your hair, your hair, it's a bird's nest." The older put her delicate porcelain hands to her own coiffure which was like gold spun and molded to her regal head, not a plait ajar, not a strand afloat, not so much as a fleck of lint or a fragment of microscopic flesh in sight. She was so clean she smelled of alcohol burning in a brass bowl. "Here, let me fix it." But Julia rose and left the room.

That afternoon another thread broke.

Julia went downtown alone.

People on the street did not recognize her. After all, you do not recognize one of a pair when for forty years you've seen only the two, like a couple of dainty shoes promenading in the downtown store-window reflections. People everywhere gave that little move of the head which meant they expected to shift their gaze from one image to its painstaking duplicate.

"Who's there?" asked the druggist, as if he'd been wakened at midnight and was peering out the door. "I mean, is that you, Coral, or Julia? Is Julia or Coral sick, Julia? I mean—damn it!" He talked in a loud voice as if a phone connection was giving him trouble. "Well?"

"This is—" The younger twin had to stop and feel herself, and see herself in the gleaming side of the apothecary vat which held green mint-colored juice in it. "This is Julia," she said, as if returning the call. "And I want, I want—"

"Is Coral dead, my God, how horrible, how terrible!" cried the druggist. "You poor child!"

"Oh, no, she's home. I want, I want—" She moistened her lips and put out a hand like vapor on the air. "I want some red tint for my hair, the color of carrots or tomatoes, I guess, the color of wine, yes, wine; I think I'd like that better. Wine."

"Two packages, of course."

"What, what?"

"Two packages of tint. One for each of you?"

Julia looked as if she might fly off, so much milkweed, and then she said, "No. Only one package. It's for me. It's for Julia. It's for Julia all by herself."

"Julia!" screamed Coral at the front door as Julia came up the walk. "Where've you been? Running off, I thought you'd been killed by a car, or kidnapped or some horrible thing! Good God!" The older sister stopped and fell back against the side of the porch rail. "Your hair, your lovely golden hair, thirty-nine inches it was, one for every year almost, one for every year." She stared at the woman who waltzed and curtsied and turned on the front lawn sidewalk, her eyes closed. "Julia, Julia, Julia!" she shrieked.

"It's the color of wine," said Julia. "And oh my it *has* gone to my head!"

"Julia, the sun, you went without your hat, and no lunch, you ate no lunch, it stands to reason. Here, let me help you in. We'll go to the bathroom and wash out that terrible color. A clown for the circus, that's what you are!"

"I'm Julia," said the younger sister. "I'm Julia, and look—" She snatched open a parcel she carried beneath her arm. She held up a dress as bright as the grass of summer, green to complement her hair, green like the trees and green like the eyes of every cat on back to the pharaohs.

"You know I can't wear green," said Coral. "Wasting our heritage money, buying dresses like that."

"One dress."

"One dress?"

"One, one, one," said Julia quietly, smiling. "One." She went in to put it on, standing in the hall. "And one pair of new shoes."

"With open toes! How ridiculous!"

"You can buy a pair just like them if you want."

"I will *not!*"

"And a dress like this."

"Ha!"

"And now," said Julia, "it's time for tea, we're due at the Applemans', remember? Come along."

"You're not serious!"

"Tea is so nice, and it's a lovely day."

"Not until you rinse your hair!"

"No, no, and I might even let it grow out, in the next six months, all gray."

"Shh, the neighbors," cried Coral, then, lower: "Your hair's not gray."

"Yes, gray as a mouse, and I'll let it grow out, we've been coloring it for years."

"Only to bring out the natural highlights, the highlights!"

They went off to tea together.

Things went quickly after that: after one explosion, another, another, another, a string, a bunch of ladyfinger firecracker explosions. Julia bought floppy flowered hats, Julia wore perfume, Julia got fat, Julia turned gray, Julia went out alone nights, pulling on her gloves like a workman approaching a fascinating job at the foundry.

And Coral?

"I'm nervous," said Coral. "Nervous, nervous, nervous. Look at her stockings, all runs. Look at her smeared lipstick, and us always neat as pins, look at her cheeks, no powder over the freckles, and her hair all dirty snow; nervous, nervous, nervous, oh, I'm nervous.

"Julia," she said at last, "the time's come. I won't be seen with you anymore.

"Julia," she said, a month later, "I've got my bags packed. I've taken room and board at Mrs. Appleman's, where you can call me if you need me. Oh, you'll call, you'll come sniveling, alone, and it'll be a long night of talking to get me home."

And Coral sailed away like a great white skiff across the sea of summer afternoon.

There was a thundershower next week. The largest single bolt of green-bolt lightning jumped around in the sky, picked its spot, and rammed itself feet-first into the center of the town, shaking birds from their nests in insane confettis, launching three children into the world two weeks ahead of time, and short-circuiting a hundred conversations by women in storm-darkened homes in mid-gallop on their way through sin and torment and domestic melodrama. This thunderbolt which jumped back up at the sky in a billion fragments was nothing to the following morning's item in the paper which said that Henry Crummitt (the man with his arm around the shoulder of the cigar-store wooden Indian) was marrying one Julia Wycherly on that self-same day.

"Someone marry Julia!"

And Coral sat down to gasp and laugh and then gasp again at the incredible lie.

"What? With her ragged seams and her dirty linens, and her awful white hair and her unplucked brows and her shoes run over? Julia? Someone take Julia to the license bureau? Oh, oh!"

But just to satisfy her humor which veered wildly between comedy and sheer slapstick which was not funny at all, she went round to the little church that afternoon and was startled to see the rice in the air and the handful of people all shouting and laughing, and there, coming out of the church, was Henry Crummitt and linked to his arm . . .

A woman with a trim figure, a woman dressed in taste, with golden hair beautifully combed, not a fleck of lint or a scrap of dandruff visible, a woman with neat stocking seams and well-delineated lipstick and powder on her cheeks like the first cool fall of snow at the beginning of a lovely winter.

And as they passed, the younger sister glanced over and saw her older sister there. She stopped. Everyone stopped. Everyone waited. Everyone held their breaths.

The younger sister took one step, took two steps forward and peered into the face of this other woman in the crowd. Then, as if she were making up in a mirror, she adjusted her veil, smoothed her lipstick, and refurbished her powder, delicately, carefully, and with no trace of hurry. Then, to this mirror she said, or it was reliably passed on she said:

"I'm Julia; who are *you?*"

And after that there was so much rice nobody saw anything until the cars had driven off.

End of Summer

One. *Two.* Hattie's lips counted the long, slow strokes of the high town clock as she lay quietly on her bed. The streets were asleep under the courthouse clock, which seemed like a white moon rising, round and full, the light from it freezing all of the town in late summer time. Her heart raced.

She rose swiftly to look down on the empty avenues, the dark and silent lawns. Below, the porch swing creaked ever so little in the wind.

She saw the long, dark rush of her hair in the mirror as she unknotted the tight schoolteacher's bun and let it fall loose to her shoulders. Wouldn't her pupils be surprised, she thought; so long, so black, so glossy. Not too bad for a woman of thirty-five. From the closet, her hands trembling, she dug out hidden parcels. Lipstick, rouge, eyebrow pencil, nail polish. A pale blue negligee, like a breath of vapor. Pulling off her cotton nightgown, she stepped on in, hard, even while she drew the negligee over her head.

She touched her ears with perfume, used the lipstick on her nervous mouth, penciled her eyebrows, and hurriedly painted her nails.

She was ready.

She let herself out into the hall of the sleeping house. She glanced fearfully at three white doors. If they sprang open now, then what? She balanced between the walls, waiting.

The door stayed shut.

She stuck her tongue out at one door, then at the other two.

She drifted down the noiseless stairs onto the moonlit porch and then into the quiet street.

The smell of a September night was everywhere. Underfoot, the concrete breathed warmth up along her thin white legs.

"I've always wanted to do this." She plucked a blood rose for her black hair and stood a moment smiling at the shaded windows of her house. "You don't know what I'm doing," she whispered. She swirled her negligee.

Down the aisle of trees, past glowing street lamps, her bare feet were soundless. She saw every bush and fence and wondered, "Why didn't I think of this a long time ago?" She paused in the wet grass just to feel how it was, cool and prickly.

The patrolman, Mr. Waltzer, was wandering down Glen Bay Street, singing in a low, sad tenor. As he passed, Hattie circled a tree and stood staring at his broad back as he walked on, still singing.

When she reached the courthouse, the only noise was the sound of her bare toes on the rusty fire escape. At the top of the flight, on a ledge under the shining silver clock face, she held out her hands.

There lay the sleeping town!

A thousand roofs glittered with snow that had fallen from the moon.

She shook her fists and made faces at the town. She flicked her negligee skirt contemptuously at the far houses. She danced and laughed silently, then stopped to snap her fingers in all four directions.

A minute later, eyes bright, she was racing on the soft lawns of the town.

She came to the house of whispers.

She paused by a certain window and heard a man's voice and a woman's voice in the secret room.

Hattie leaned against the house and listened to whispering, whispering. It was like hearing two tiny moths fluttering gently inside on the window screen. There was a soft, remote laughter.

Hattie put her hand to the screen above, her face the face of one at a shrine. Perspiration shone on her lips.

"What was that?" cried a voice inside.

Like mist, Hattie whirled and vanished.

When she stopped running she was by another house window.

A man stood in the brightly lighted bathroom, perhaps the only lighted room in the town, shaving carefully around his yawning mouth. He had black hair and blue eyes and was twenty-seven years old and every morning carried to his job in the railyards a lunch bucket packed with ham sandwiches. He wiped his face with a towel and the light went out.

Hattie waited behind the great oak in the yard, all film, all spiderweb. She heard the front door click, his footsteps down the walk, the clank of his lunch pail. From the odors of tobacco and fresh soap, she knew, without looking, that he was passing.

Whistling between his teeth, he walked down the street toward the ravine. She followed from tree to tree, a white veil behind an elm, a moon shadow behind an oak. Once, he whirled about. Just in time she hid from sight. She waited, heart pounding. Silence. Then, his footsteps walking on.

He was whistling the song "June Night."

The high arc light on the edge of the ravine cast his shadow directly beneath him. She was not two yards away, behind an ancient chestnut tree.

He stopped but did not turn. He sniffed the air.

the night wind blew her perfume over the ravine, as she had planned it.

She did not move. It was not her turn to act now. She simply stood pressing against the tree, exhausted with the shaking of her heart.

It seemed an hour before he moved. She could hear the dew breaking gently under the pressure of his shoes. The warm odor of tobacco and fresh soap came nearer.

He touched one of her wrists. She did not open her eyes. He did not speak.

Somewhere, the courthouse clock sounded the time as three in the morning.

His mouth fitted over hers very gently and easily.

Then his mouth was at her ear and she was held to the tree by him. He whispered. So *she* was the one who'd looked in his windows the last three nights! He kissed her neck. She, *she* had followed him, unseen, last night! He stared at her. The shadows of the trees fell soft and numerous all about, on her lips, on her cheeks, on her brow, and only her eyes were visible, gleaming and alive. She was lovely, did she know that? He had thought he was being haunted. His laughter was no more than a faint whisper in his mouth. He looked at her and made a move of his hand to his pocket. He drew forth a match, to strike, to hold by her face, to see, but she took his hand and held it and the unlit match. After a moment, he let the matchstick drop into the wet grass. "It doesn't matter," he said.

She did not look up at him. Silently he took her arm and began to walk.

Looking at her pale feet, she went with him to the edge of the cool ravine and down to the silent flow of the stream, to the moss banks and the willows.

He hesitated. She almost looked up to see if he was still there. They had come into the light, and she kept her head turned away so that he saw only the blowing darkness of her hair and the whiteness of her arms.

He said, "You don't have to come any further, you know. Which house did you come from? You can run back to wherever it is. But if you run, don't ever come back; I won't want to see you again. I couldn't take any more of this, night after night. Now's your chance. Run, if you want!"

Summer night breathed off her, warm and quiet.

Her answer was to lift her hand to him.

Next morning, as Hattie walked downstairs, she found Grandma, Aunt Maude, and Cousin Jacob with cold cereal in their tight mouths, not liking it when Hattie pulled up her chair. Hattie wore a grim, high-necked dress, with a long skirt. Her hair was a knotted, hard bun behind her ears, her face was scrubbed pale, clean of color in the cheeks and lips. Her painted eyebrows and eyelashes were gone. Her fingernails were plain.

"You're late, Hattie," they all said, as if an agreement had been made to say it when she sat down.

"I know." She did not move in her chair.

"Better not eat much," said Aunt Maude. "It's eight-thirty. You should've been at school. What'll the superintendent say? Fine example for a teacher to set her pupils."

The three stared at her.

Hattie was smiling.

"You haven't been late in twelve years, Hattie," said Aunt Maude.

Hattie did not move, but continued smiling.

"You'd better go," they said.

Hattie walked to the hall to take down her green umbrella and pinned on her ribboned flat straw hat.

They watched her. She opened the front door and looked back at them for a long moment, as if about to speak, her cheeks flushed. They leaned toward her. She smiled and ran out, slamming the door.

Thunder in the Morning

At first it was like a storm, far away, a touch of thunder, a kind of wind and a stirring. The streets had been emptied by the courthouse clock. People had looked at the great white clock face hours ago, folded their newspapers, got up from the porch swings, hooked themselves into their summer night houses, put out the lights, and settled into cool beds. All this the clock had done, just standing above the courthouse green. Now there was not a thing on the street. Overhead street lights, casting down illumination, made shines upon the asphalt. On occasion a leaf would break loose from a tree and clatter down. The night was so dark you could not see the stars. Why this was so there was no way of telling. Except that everyone's eyes were closed and that way no stars were seen, that's how dark the night was. Oh, here and there, behind a window screen, if one peered into a dark room, one might see a red point of light, nothing else; some man

179

sitting up to feed his insomnia with nicotine, rocking in a slow rocker in the dark room. You might hear a small cough or someone turn under the sheets. But on the street there was not even a policeman swinging along with his club pointed to the earth in one hand.

From far away the small thunder began. First it was far across town. You could hear it across the ravine, going along the street over there, three blocks away across the deep blackness. It took a direction, it made square cuts, this sound of thunder, then it crossed over the ravine on the Washington Street bridge, under the owl light, and turned a corner and—there it was, at the head of the street!

And with a whiskering, brushing, sucking noise down the street between the houses and trees came the thundering metal cleaning machine of Mr. Britt. It was a tornado, funneling, driving, whispering, murmuring, feeling of the street ahead of it with big whirl-around brushes like sewer lids with rotary brushes under them, spinning, with a big rolling-pin brush turning under all the scattered trivia of the world's men, the ticket stubs from that show at the Elite tonight, and the wrapper from a chewing gum stick that now rested on top of a bureau in one of the houses, a small chewed cannonball of tasteless elasticity, and the candy wrapper from a bar now hidden and folded into the small accordion innards of a boy high in a cupola house in a magic room. All these things, streetcar trransfers to Chessman Park, to Live Oak Mortuary, to North Chicago, to Zion City, giveaway handbills on hairdos at that new chromium shop on Central. All these were whiskered up by the immense moving mustache of the machine, and on top of the machine, like a great god, in his leather-metal saddle, sat Mr. Roland Britt, age thirty-seven, the strange age between yesterday and tomorrow, and he, in his way, was a duplicate of the machine upon which he rode, with his proud hands on the steering wheel. He had a little curly mustache over his mouth, and little curly hairs that seemed to rotate upon his scalp under the passing lamps, and a little sucking nose that was continually astonished with the world, sucking it all in and blowing it out the astonished mouth. And he had hands that were always taking things and never giving at all. He and the machine, very much the same. They hadn't begun that way. Britt had never *started* to be like the machine. But after you rode it awhile it got up through your rump and spread through your system until your digestion roiled and your heart spun like a small pink top in you. But, on the other hand, neither had the machine intended being like Britt. Machines change also, and become like their masters, in imperceptible ways.

The machine was gentler than it used to be under an Irishman named Reilly. They sailed down the midnight streets together, through little streams of water ahead of them to dampen the trivia before combing it into its gullet. It was like a whale, with a mouth full of bristle, swimming in the moonlight seas, slaking in ticket minnows and gum-wrapper minnows, feeding and feeding in the silvery school of confetti that lived in the shallows of the asphalt river. Mr. Britt felt like a Greek god, even with his concave chest, bringing gentle April showers with him with the sprinklers, cleansing the world of dropped sin.

Halfway up Elm Road, whiskers bristling, great mustache hungrily eating of the street, Mr. Britt, in a fit of sport, swerved his great storm machine from one side of the street to the other, just so he could suck up a rat.

"Got him!"

Mr. Britt had seen the large running gray thing, leprous and horrible, skittering across under a lamp flare. Whisk! And the foul rodent was now inside the machine, being digested by smothering tides of paper and autumn leaf.

He went on down the lonely rivers of night, bringing and taking his storm with him, leaving fresh-whisked and wetted marks behind him.

"Me and my magical broomstick," he thought. "Me a male witch riding under the autumn moon. A good witch. The good witch of the East; wasn't that it, from the old Oz book when I was six with whooping cough in bed?"

He passed over innumerable hopscotch squares which had been made by children drunk with happiness, they were so crooked. He sucked up red playbills and yellow pencils and dimes and sometimes quarters.

"What was that?"

He turned upon his seat and looked behind.

The street was empty. Dark trees whirled past,

swishing down branches to tap his brow, swiftly, swiftly. But in the midst of the stiff thunder he had thought he heard a cry for help, a kind of violent screaming.

He looked in all directions.

"No, nothing."

He rode on upon the whirl-away brooms.

"What!"

This time he almost fell from his saddle the cry was so apparent. He looked at the trees to see if some man might be up one, yelling. He looked at the pale street-lights, all bleached out with so many years of shining. He looked at the asphalt, still warm from the heat of the day. The cry came again.

They were on the edge of the ravine. Mr. Britt stopped his machine. The bristles still spun about. He stopped one rotary broom, then the other. The silence was very loud.

"Get me out of here!"

Mr. Britt stared back at the big metal storage tank of the machine.

There was a man inside the machine.

"What did you say?" It was a ridiculous thing to ask, but Mr. Britt asked it.

"Get me out of here, help, help!" said the man inside the machine.

"What happened?" asked Mr. Britt, staring.

"You picked me up in your machine!" cried the man.

"I what?"

"You fool; don't stand there talking, let me out, I'll suffocate to death!"

"But you couldn't possibly have gotten into the machine," said Mr. Britt. He stood first on one foot, then on another. He was very cold, suddenly. "A thing as big as a man couldn't fit in up through the vent, and anyway, the whiskers would have prevented you from behind taken in, and anyway I don't remember seeing you. When did this happen?"

There was a silence from the machine.

"When did this happen?" demanded Mr. Britt.

Still no answer. Mr. Britt tried to think back. The streets had been entirely empty. There had been nothing but leaves and gum-wrappers. There had been no man, anywhere. Mr. Britt was a thoroughly clear-eyed man. He wouldn't miss a pedestrian if one fell.

Still the machine remained strangely silent. "Are you there?" said Mr. Britt.

"I'm here," said the man inside, reluctantly. "And I'm suffocating."

"Answer me, when did you get inside the machine?" said Britt.

"A while ago," said the man.

"Why didn't you scream out then?"

"I was knocked unconscious," said the man, but there was a quality to his voice, a hesitation, a vagueness, a slowness. The man was lying. It came to Mr. Britt as a shock. "Open up the top," said the inside man. "For God's sake, don't stand there like a fool talking, of all the ridiculous inanities, a street cleaner at midnight talking to a man inside his machine, what would people think." He paused to cough violently and spit and sputter. "I'm choking to death, do you want to go up for manslaughter?"

But Mr. Britt was not listening. He was down on his knees looking at the metal equipment, at the brushes under the machine. No, it was quite impossible. That opening was only a foot across, under there, no man could possibly be poked up into it. And anyway he hadn't been going fast. And anyway the rotary brushes would have bounced a man ahead of the machine. And anyway, he hadn't *seen* a man!

He got to his feet. He noticed for the first time that the top of his forehead was all perspiration. He wiped it off. His hands were trembling. He could hardly stand up.

"Open up, and I'll give you a hundred dollars," said the man inside the machine.

"Why should you be bribing me to let you out?" said Mr. Britt. "When it is only natural that I should let you out *free*, after all, if I picked you up I should let you out, shouldn't I? And yet, all of a sudden, you start offering me money, as if I didn't *intend* to let you out, as if you knew that I might know a reason for *not* letting you out. Why is that?"

"I'm dying," coughed the man, "and you debate. God, God, man!" There was a fierce wrestling and a pounding inside. "This place in here is full of dirt and leaves and paper. I can't *move!*"

Mr. Britt stood there. "It is *not possible*," he said,

clearly and firmly, at last, "that a man could be in my machine. I know my machine. You do not belong in there. I did not ask you to be in there. It is your responsibility."

"Bend closer . . ."

"What?"

"Listen!"

He put his ear to the warm metal.

"I am here," whispered the high voice, the sweet high fading voice. "I am in here and I wear no clothes."

"What!"

He felt his hands jerk, his fingers twitch in on themselves. He felt his eyes squeeze up almost to blind him.

"I am in here and I have no clothes," said the voice. And after a long while, "Don't you want to see me? Don't you? Don't you want to see me? I'm in here now. I'm waiting . . ."

He stood by the side of the great machine for a full ten seconds. The echo of his breathing jumped off the metal a foot from his face.

"Did you hear what I said?" whispered the voice.

He nodded.

"Well then, open the lid. Let me out. It's late. Late at night. Everyone asleep. Dark. We'll be alone . . ."

He listened to his heart beating.

"Well?" said the voice.

He swallowed.

"What are you waiting for?" said the voice, lasciviously.

The sweat rolled down his face.

There was no answer. The fierce breathing that had been in the machine for a while now suddenly stopped. The thrashing stopped.

Mr. Britt leaned forward, put his ear to the machine.

He could hear nothing now but a kind of soft inner squeaking under the lid. And a sound like one hand, cut off from the body perhaps, moving, struggling by itself. It sounded like a small thing moving.

"I climbed in to sleep," said the man.

"Oh, now you *are* lying," said Mr. Britt.

He climbed up on his silent machine and sat in the leather saddle. He put his foot down to start the motor.

"What are you doing?" the voice shouted from under the lid suddenly. There was a dull stir. There was a sound as of a large body again. The heavy breathing returned. It was so sudden it made Mr. Britt almost fall from his perch. He looked back at the lid.

"No, no, I won't let you out," he said.

"Why?" cried the failing voice.

"Because," said Mr. Britt, "I have my work to do." He started the machine and the whisking thunder of the brushes and the roar of the motor drowned out the screams and shouts of the captured man. Looking ahead, eyes wet, hands hard on the wheel, Mr. Britt took his machine brooming down the silent avenues of the night town, for five minutes, ten minutes, half an hour, an hour, two hours more, sweeping and scouring and never stopping, sucking in tickets and combs and dropped soup-can labels.

At four in the morning, three hours later, he drew

up before the vast rubbish heap that slid down the hill in a strange avalanche to the dark ravine. He backed the machine up to the edge of the avalanche and for a moment cut the motor.

There was not the slightest sound from inside the machine.

He waited, but there was nothing but the beat of his heart in his wrists.

He flipped a lever. The entire cargo of branches and dust and paper and tickets and labels and leaves fell back and piled in a neat pile upon the edge of the ravine. He waited until everything had slid out upon the ground. Then he flipped the lever, slamming the lid shut, looked back once at the silent mound of rubbish, and drove off down the street.

He lived only three houses from the ravine. He drove his machine up before his house, parked, and went in to bed. He lay in the quiet room, not able to sleep, from time to time getting up and going to look out the window at the ravine. Once he put his hand on the doorknob, half opened the door, shut it, and went back to bed. But he could not sleep.

It was only at seven in the morning as he was brewing some coffee, when he heard the sound, that he knew any relief. It was the sound of young Jim Smith, the thirteen-year-old boy, who lived across the ravine. Young Jim came whistling down the street, on his way to the lake to fish. Every morning he came along in mists, whistling, and always he stopped to rummage through the rubbish left by Mr. Britt to seek dimes and quarters and orange bottle caps to pin to his shirtfront. Mr. Britt moved the window curtains aside to peer out into the early dawn mists to see little Jim Smith walk jauntily by carrying a fish pole over one shoulder, and on the end of the line at the top of the fish pole, swinging back and forth like a gray pendulum in the mists, was a dead rat.

Mr. Britt drank his coffee, crept back in bed, and slept the sleep of the victorious and innocent.

The Highest Branch on the Tree

I often remember his name, Harry Hands, a most unfortunate name for a fourteen-year-old boy in ninth grade in junior high in 1934, or in any other year, come to think of it. We all spelled it 'Hairy' and pronounced it with similar emphasis. Harry Hands pretended not to notice and became more arrogant and smart-ass, looking down his nose at us dumb peasants, as he called us. We didn't see at the time that it was our harassment that made him pretend at arrogance and display wits that he probably only half had. So it went with Hands and his incredible moniker Hairy.

The second memory is often of his pants up a tree. That has stayed with me for a lifetime. I have never for a month forgotten. I can't very well say I recalled his pants up a tree every day, that would not be true. But at least twelve times a year I would see Harry in full flight and us ninth graders after him, myself in the lead, and his pants in the air flung up to the highest branch and everyone laughing there on the school grounds and a teacher leaning out a window and ordering one of us, why not me, to climb and bring those pants down.

"Don't bother," Harry Hands said, blushing there, revealed in his boxer BVD underwear. "They're mine. *I'll* get 'em."

And Harry Hands climbed up, almost fell, and reached his pants but did not put them on, just clutched to the bole of the tree and when we all gathered below the tree, knocking each other's elbows and pointing up and laughing, simply looked down at us with the strangest grin and . . .

Peed.

That's right.

Took aim and peed.

There was a mob flight of indignant teenagers, off away, but no one came back to climb up and drag him down, for when we started to come back, wiping our faces and shoulders with handkerchiefs, Harry yelled down:

"I had *three* glasses of orange juice for lunch!"

So we knew he was still loaded and we all stood thirty feet back from the tree yelling euphemisms instead of epithets, the way our folks had taught us. After all, it was another time, another age, and the rules were observed.

Harry Hands did not put on his pants up there nor did he come down even though the principal came out and ordered him to leave and we backed off and heard the principal shouting up at Harry that the way was clear now and he could come down. But Harry Hands shook his head: no *way*. And the principal stood under the tree and we yelled to him to watch out, Harry Hands was armed and dangerous and hearing this the principal backed off, hastily.

Well, the long and short of it was, Harry Hands never came down, that is, we didn't see him do it, and we all got bored and went home.

Someone later said he came down at sunset or midnight, with no one around to see.

The next day, the tree was empty and Harry Hands was gone forever.

He never came back. He didn't even come back to protest to the principal, nor did his parents come or write a letter to lodge a complaint. We didn't know where Harry Hands lived, and the school wouldn't tell us, so we couldn't go find him, perhaps with the faintest notion that maybe we should apologize and ask him back. We knew he wouldn't come, anyway. What we had done was so horrendous, it could never be forgiven. As the days passed and Harry Hands didn't show, most of us lay in bed at night and wondered how *we* would feel if someone had "pantsed" us and threw our pants to the highest branch of some tree in front of God and everyone. It caused a lot of unexpected bed tossing and pillow punching, I don't mind saying. And most of us didn't look up at that tree for more than a few seconds before turning away.

Did any of us ever sweat over the dire consequences? Did we perspire on the obvious that perhaps he might have fallen just at midnight, to be harvested as broken bones at dawn? Or did we imagine he might have lurched himself out in a high-jump of doom, with the same shattered consequence? Did we think his father might lose his job or his mother take to drink? We wrestled none of these or if we did, shut our traps to preserve our silent guilt. Thunder, as you know, occurs when lightning sucks back up its track and lets two handsful of white-hot air applaud. Harry Hands, whose parents were never seen, withdrew to a bang of thunder that only we ninth-grade second-rate criminals heard while waiting for sleep, which never came, to arrive.

It was a bad end to a good year and we all went off to high school and a few years later, going by the schoolyard, I saw that the tree had got some sort of disease and had been cut down, which was a relief. I didn't want some future generation to be surprised at the ghost shape of a pair of pants up there, hurled by a mob of apes.

But I run ahead of my story.

Why, you ask, why did we do that to Harry Hands? Was he some sort of super-villain who deserved our Christian persecution, a dumb sort of semi-crucifixion to appall the neighbors and ruin school history so that in the annals of time people would say, "1934, wasn't that the year that—" And fill in the blanks with Look, ma, no pants, no Hands.

What, in sum, was H.H.'s crime sublime?

It's a familiar case. Happens every year, every school, everywhere at one time or another. Except our case was more spectacular.

Harry Hands was smarter than anyone else in the whole school.

That was the first crime.

His second crime, worse than the first, was he didn't do a better job of hiding it.

It reminds me of an actor friend who a few years ago drove up to the front of my house in a brand-new super-powered XKE twelve-cylinder Jaguar and yelled at me, "Eat your heart out!"

Well, Harry Hands, in effect, had arrived at our school from somewhere back East—hadn't we all?—and flaunted his IQ from the first hour of day one. Through every class from just after breakfast to just before lunch to last afternoon bell his arm was permanently up, you could have raised a flag on it, and his voice was demanding to be heard and damn if he wasn't right when the teacher gave him the nod. A lot of collective bile was manufactured that day under all our tongues. The miracle was we didn't rip his clothes off on that first day. We delayed because it was reported that in gym he had put on the boxing gloves and bloodied three or four noses before our coach told everyone to run out and do six laps around the block to lance our boils.

And, Jesus off the cross and running rings around us, wouldn't you know as we made the fifth lap, panting, tasting blood, here came Harry Hands, fresh as a potted daisy, jogging along, nice and easy, passing us and adding another lap to prove he was tireless.

By the end of the second day he had no friends. No one even *tried* to be one. It was hinted that if anyone took up with this Hands guy, we would beat the tar out of them next time we did laps and were out of sight of our coach.

So Harry Hands came and went alone, with a look of the insufferable book reader and, worse, book rememberer, he forgot nothing and would offer data if someone paused, stuttered, or broke wind.

Did Harry Hands see his crucifixion coming? If he did, he smiled at the prospect. He was always smiling and laughing and being a good chum, although no one smiled or laughed back. We took our homework home. He did it in class in the last five minutes of the hour and then sat there, mightily pleased with his intellectual strengths, moistening his vocal chords for the next recitation.

Fade out. Fade in.

We all went away to life.

After about forty years it got so I only thought about Harry Hands once every two years instead of once every two months. It was in the middle of a sidewalk in downtown Chicago where I walked when I had two hours between trains, on my way to New York, that I met this stranger coming toward me, unrecognizable, and he had almost passed when he froze in midstride and half turned to me and said:

"Spaulding?" he said. "*Douglas* Spaulding?"

It was my turn to freeze and I mean I turned cold, for I had this ungodly feeling I was confronted by a ghost. A whole flock of geese ran over my grave. I cocked my head and eyed the stranger. He was dressed in a beautifully tailored blue-black suit with a silk shirt and a reticent tie. His hair was dark and moderately gray at the temples and he smelled of a mild cologne. He held out a well-manicured hand.

"Harry Hinds," he said.

"I don't think . . ." I said.

"You *are* Douglas Spaulding, aren't you?"

"Yes, but—"

"Berendo Junior High School, class of summer 1935, though *I* never graduated."

"Harry," I said and stopped, his last name a stone in my mouth.

"Use to be Hands. Harry Hands. Changed it to Hinds, late spring 1935—"

Jut after you climbed down, I thought.

The wind blew around one of those Chicago corners.

I smelled pee.

I glanced to left and right. No horses in sight. No dogs.

Only Harry Hinds, aka Harry Hands waiting for me to open up.

I took his fingers as if they contained electric shocks, shook them quickly, pulled back.

"My goodness," he said. "Am I still poison?"

"No, but—"

"You look well," he said quickly. "Look as if you've had a good life. That's nice."

"You, too," I said, trying not to look at his expensively manicured nails and brightly polished shoes.

"I can't complain," he said, easily. "Where are you headed?"

"The Art Institute. I'm between trains. I have almost two hours' layover and always go to the museum to look at that big Seurat."

"It is big, isn't it, and beautiful. Mind if I come partway?"

"No, no. Please, join up."

We walked and he said, "It's on the way to my office, anyway, so we'll have to talk fast. Give me your resume, for old times' sake?"

We walked and I told. Not much for there wasn't much to detail. Fair life as a writer, nicely established, no international fame but a few fans across country and enough income to raise a family. "That's it," I said. "In a nutshell. End of resume."

"Congratulations," he said and seemed to mean it, nodding. "Well done."

"What about you?" I said.

"Well," he said, reluctantly. It was the only time in all the years, then and now, I ever saw him hesitate. He was looking sidewise at a building facade which seemed to make him nervous. I glanced over and saw:

HARRY HINDS AND ASSOCIATES

FIFTH AND SIXTH FLOORS

Harry caught my gaze and coughed. "It's nothing. I didn't mean to bring you here. Just passing—"

"My God," I said. "That's quite a building. Do you own the whole thing?'

"Own it, built it," he admitted, brightening somewhat, leaning toward the old young Harry of forty years back. "Not bad, eh?"

"Not bad at all," I said, gasping.

"Well, I'd better let you get on to the Seurat," he said, and shook my hand. "But hold on. Why not? Duck inside for just sixty seconds. Then I'll let you run. Yes?"

"Why not," I said, and he took my elbow and steered me, opening the door ahead of me and bowing a nod and leading me out into the center of a spacious marble lobby, an area some sixty feet high and eighty or ninety feet across, in the center of which was an arboretum with dense jungle foliage below and a buckshot scattering of exotic birds, but with only one singular dramatic piece in the middle.

It was a single tree of some forty or fifty feet in height, but it was hard to tell what kind of tree it was, maple, oak, chestnut, what? because there were no leaves on the tree. It was not even an autumn tree with the proper yellow and red and orange leaves. It was a barren winter tree that reached for a stark sky with empty twigs and branches.

"Ain't she a beaut?" said Harry Hinds, staring up.

"Well," I said.

"Remember when old Cap Trotter, our gym coach, used to make us go out and run around the block six or seven times to teach us manners—"

"I don't recall—"

"Yes, you do," said Harry Hinds, easily, looking at the interior sky. "Well, do you know what I used to do?"

"Beat us. Pull ahead and make the six laps. Win and not breathe hard. I remember now."

"No, you don't." Harry studied the glass roof seventy feet above. "I never ran the laps. After the first two I hid behind a parked car, waited for the last lap to come around, then jumped out and beat the *hell* out of all of you."

"So *that's* how you did it?" I said.

"The secret of my success," he said. "I've been jumping from behind cars on the last lap for years."

"God damn," I whispered.

"Yeah," he said, and studied the cornices of the interior court.

We stood there for a long moment, like the pilgrims at Lourdes waiting for the daily miracle. If it happened, I was not aware. But Harry Hinds was. He pointed with his nose and eyebrows up, up along that huge tree and said, "See anything up there?"

I looked and shook my head. "Nope."

"You *sure*?" said Harry.

I looked again and shook my head.

"The highest branch on the tree?" said Harry.

"Nothing," I said.

"Funny." Harry Hinds snorted faintly. "How come I see it clearly?"

I did not ask what it was he was seeing.

I looked up at the bare tree in the middle of an arboretum in the center of the lobby of the Harold Hinds Foresight Corporation.

Did I expect to see the phantom outlines of a pair of pants way up there on the highest branch?

I did.

But there was nothing there. Only a high branch and no clothing.

Harry Hinds watched me looking at the tree and read my thought.

"Thanks," he said, quietly.

"What?" I said.

"Thanks to you, to all of you, for what you did," he said.

"What'd we do?" I lied.

"You know," he said, quietly. "And thanks. Come on."

And before I could protest, he led the way to the men's and raised his brows, nodding, did I need to go? I did.

Standing at the porcelains, unzipped, Harry looked down as he watered the daisies.

"You know," he smiled, "there isn't a day in my life, when I do this, that I don't remember that day forty years ago and me up the tree and you down

below and me peeing on all of you. Not a day passes
I don't remember. You, them, and peeing."

Standing there, I froze and did nothing.

Harry finished, zipped up, and stood remembering.

"Happiest day of my life," he said.

A Woman Is a
Fast-Moving Picnic

The subject was women, by the singles and in the mobs.

The place was Heeber Finn's not-always-open but always-talking pub in the town of Kilcock, if you'll forgive the implication, in the county of Kildare, out along the River Liffey somewhat north and certainly beyond the reach of Dublin.

And in the pub, if only half full of men but bursting with talk, the subject was indeed women. They had exhausted all other subjects, hounds, horses, foxes, beers as against the hard stuff, lunatic mother-in-laws out of the bin and into your lives, and now the chat had arrived back to women in the pure state: unavailable. Or if available, fully dressed.

Each man echoed the other and the next agreed with the first.

"The dreadful fact is," said Finn, to keep the converse aroar, "there is no single plot of land in all Ireland which is firm or dry enough to lie down with purpose and arise with joy."

"You've touched the bull's-eye and pierced the target," said Timulty, the local postmaster, in for a quick one, there being only ten people waiting at the postoffice. "There's no acre off the road, out of sight of the priest or out of mind of the wife, where physical education can be pursued without critical attention."

"The land is all bog," Nolan nailed it, "and no relief."

"There's no place to cavort," said Riordan, simply.

"Ah, that's been said a thousand times this night," protested Finn. "The thing is, what do we *do* about it?"

"If someone would only stop the rain and fire the priests," suggested Nolan.

"That'll be the day," cried all, and emptied their drinks.

"It reminds me of that Hoolihan tragedy," said Finn, refilling each glass. "Is that remembered?"

"*Say* it, Finn."

"Well, Hoolihan wandered this woman who was no Madonna, but neither was she last year's potatoes, and they passed a likely turf which seemed more flatland than swamp and Hoolihan said, Trot on out on that bog. If it holds, I'll follow. Well, she trotted out and turns around and—*sinks!* Never laid a hand on her. Before he could shout: No! she was gone!"

"The truth is," Nolan obtruded, "Hoolihan threw her a rope. But she slung it round her neck instead of her waist and all but strangled in the pulling out. But I like your version best, Finn. Anyways, they made a song of it!"

And here Nolan began, but everyone put in to finish the verse:

"The sinking of Molly in old Kelly's bog
Is writ in the Lord Mayor's roll call and a log
Poor Molly went there with the Hoolihan boy
And sank out of sight with one last shriek of joy.
He took her out there for what do you suppose?

And was busy at ridding the lass of her clothes,
But no sooner deprived of each last seam and stitch
Than she wallowed and sank and was lost in the ditch.
The ducks they all gaggled and even the hog
Wept Christian salt-tears for Moll sunk in the bog—"

"It goes on from there," said Nolan. "Needless to say the Hoolihan boy was distraught. When you're thinking one thing and another occurs, it fair turns the mind. He's feared to cross a brick road since without testing for quicksand. Shall I go on?"

"No use," cried Doone, suddenly, no more than four foot ten inches high but terrible fast plummeting out of theaters ahead of the national anthem, the local Anthem Sprinter, as everyone knows. Now, on tiptoe, he boxed the air around the pub and voiced his protest. "What's the use of all this palaver the last thousand nights when it's time to act? Even if there was a sudden flood of femininity in the provinces with no lint on them and their seams straight, what would we *do* with them?"

"True," admitted Finn. "God in Ireland just tempts man but to disown him."

"God's griefs and torments," added Riordan. "I haven't even wrestled Adam's old friend Eve late nights in the last row of the Gayety Cinema!"

"The Gayety Cinema?" cried Nolan in dread remorse. "Gah! I crept through the dark there once and found me a lass who seemed a salmon frolicking upstream. When the lights came on, I saw I had taken communion with a troll from the Liffey bridge. I ran to commit suicide with drink. To hell with the Gayety and all men who prowl there with dreams and slink forth with nightmare!"

"Which leaves only the bogs for criminal relief and drowned in the bargain. Doone," said Finn, "do you have a plan, you with that big mouth in the tiny body?"

"I have!" said Doone, not standing still, sketching the air with his fists and fingers as he danced to his own tune. "You must admit that the various bogs are the one place the Church puts no dainty toe. But also a place where a girl, representing the needy, and out of her mind, might test her will to defy the sinkage. For it's true, one grand plunge if you're not careful and no place to put her tombstone. Now hear this!"

Doone stopped so all might lean at him, eyes wide, and ears acock.

"What we need is a military strategist, a genius for

scientific research, in order to recreate the Universe and undo the maid. One word says it all. Me!"

"You!" cried all, as if struck in a collective stomach.

"I have the hammer," said Doone. "Will you hand me the nails?"

"Hang the picture," said Finn, "and fix it straight."

"I came here tonight with Victory in mind," said Doone, having slept late till noon and gone back to bed at three to adjust the sights and rearrange our future. "Now, as we waste our tongues and ruin our nervous complexions, the moon is about to rise and the empty lands and hungry bogs await. Outside this pub, in boneyards of handlebars and spokes, lie our bikes. In a grand inquest, should we not bike on out to peg and string the bogs for once and all, full of brave blood and booze, to make a permanent chart, map the hostile and innocent-looking flats, test the sinkages, and come back with the sure knowledge that behind Dooley's farm is a field in which if you do not move fast, you sink at the rate of two or three inches per minute? Then beyond, Leary's pasture in which his own cows have the devil's time grazing quick enough to survive the unsteady turf and live on the road. *Would that not be a good thing to know* for the rest of our lives so we can shun it and move to more substantial grounds?"

"My God," said all in admiration. "It *would!*"

"Then what are we waiting for?" Doone ran to the door. "Finish your drinks and mount your bikes. Do we live in ignorance or at last play in the fields, as it 'twere, of the Lord?"

"The fields!" The men drank.

"Of the Lord!" they finished, plummeting Doone out the door.

"Time!" cried Finn, since the pub was empty. "Time!"

No sooner on the road, with coattails flying as if heaven lay ahead and Lucifer behind, than Doone pointed now here, now there with his surveyor's nose:

"There's Flaherty's. Terrible quick. You're out of sight, a foot a minute and no one the wiser if they look the other way."

"Why, Christ himself," said someone in the sweating biking mob, "might not make it across!"

"He'd be the first and last and no one between!" Finn admitted, catching up with the team.

"Where are you taking us, Doone?" gasped Nolan.

"You'll see soon enough!" Doone churned his sprockets.

"And when we *get* there," asked Riordan, suddenly struck with the notion, "in the penultimate or final sinkage tests *who* will be the woman?"

"True!" gasped all, as Doone veered the path and sparked his wheels, "there's only *us*."

"Never fear!" said Doone. "One of us will *pretend* to be the poor put-upon maid, maiden, courtesan—"

"Hoor of Babylon?" volunteered Finn.

"And who would that be?"

"You're looking at his backside!" cried Doone, all elusive speed. "*Me!*"

"You!"

That almost swerved them into multiple collisions. But Doone, fearing this, cried, "And more surprises, if all goes well. Now, by God, *on* with the brakes. We're here!"

It had been raining, but since it rained all the while, no one had noticed. Now the rain cleared away like a theater curtain, to reveal:

Brannagan's off-the-road-and-into-the-woods pasture, which started in mist, to be lost in fog.

"Brannagan's!" Everyone braked to a stillness.

"Does it not have an air of the mysterious?" whispered Doone.

"It does," someone murmured.

"Do you *dare* me to be brave?"

"*Do* that," was the vote.

"But are you *serious*, Doone?"

"Jesus," said Doone. "It'll be no test for judgments and sinkage tests if someone for starters doesn't do more than jog about the territory like mindless bulls. There must be *two* people making tracks, beyond. Me, playing the woman for sure. And some volunteer amongst you."

The men inched back on their bike-seats.

"Ah, you and your scientific logic will be the death of brewing and the burial of gin," said Finn.

"But Doone, your verisimilitude, if there is such a word. It'll be hard for us to conjure you up as a female."

"Why not," offered Riordan, "go fetch a real lass here? A gal from the nunnery—"

"Nunnery!" cried all, shocked.

"Or one of the wives?" said Doone.

"Wives?" cried all, in worse shock.

And they would have driven him like a spike into the earth, had they not realized he was yanking their legs to steer them crooked.

"Enough!" Finn interjected. "Do we have pencils and paper at hand to align the sums and recall the burial sinks, plot on plot?"

The men muttered.

No one had thought to bring pencil and paper.

"Ah, hell," groused Riordan. "We'll recall the numerals, back at the pub. Out with you, Doone. In time, a volunteer, playing the male counterpart, will follow."

"Out it is!" Doone threw down his bike, doused his throat with gargle, and trotted, elbows in a grand rhythm, over the endlessly waiting and terribly damp boneyard of sexual beasts.

"This is the silliest damn thing we ever tried," said Nolan, tears in his eyes for fear of never seeing Doone again.

"But what a *hero*!" reasoned Finn. "For would we dare come here with a real crazed female if we did not know the logistics of tug and pull, devastation or survival, love-at-last as against another night of being strangled by our underwear?"

"Aw, put a sock in it!" shouted Doone, far out now, beyond rescue. "Here I go!"

"*Further* out, Doone!" suggested Nolan.

"Cripes!" cried Doone. "First you say it's a silly damn thing we do, then you instruct me to the land mines! I'm furthering by fits and starts."

Then suddenly Doone shrieked. "It's an elevator I'm in! I'm going *down!*"

He gesticulated wildly for balance.

"Off with your coat!" Finn yelled.

"What?"

"Eliminate the handicaps, man!"

"What?"

"Tear off your *cap!*"

"My cap? Nitwit! What good would *that* do?"

"Your pants then! Your shoes! You must pretend to get ready for the Grand Affair, with or without rain."

Doone kept his cap on but yanked his shoes and belabored his coat.

"The *test*, Doone!" Nolan shouted. "If you do not writhe to remove your shoelaces and untie your tie, we will not know just how fast a maid in the undressing or a man at his mating dance will slide from view. Now we must find is there or is there *not* time for a consummation devoutly to be wished?"

"Consummation—devoutly—damn!" cried Doone.

And grousing epithets and firing nouns to smoke the air, Doone danced about, flinging off his coat and then his shirt and tie and was on his way to a dropping of the pants and the rising of the moon when a thunderous voice from Heaven or an echo from the mount banged the air like a great anvil somehow fallen to earth.

"What goes *on* there?" the voice thundered.

They froze, a riot iced by sin.

Doone froze, an art statue on its way to potato deeps.

All *time* froze and again the pile-driver voice was lifted and plunged to crack their ears. The moon fled behind a fog.

"Just what in hell is going *on* here?" thundered the voice of Kingdom Come and the Last Judgment.

A dozen heads spun on a dozen necks.

For Father O'Malley stood on a rise in the road, his bike clenched in his vengeful fists, so it looked like his skinny sister, straddled and lost.

For a third time, Father O'Malley tossed the bolt and split the air. "You and you and you! What are you *up* to?"

"It's not so much up as down to my smalls," piped Doone in a wee piccolo voice, and added, meekly, "Father—"

"Out, out!" shouted the priest, waving one arm like a scythe. "Away!" he blathered. "Go, go, go. Damn, damn, damn."

And he harvested the men with maniac gesticulations and eruptions of lava enough to lay a village and bury a blight.

"Out of my sight. Away, the mangy lot of you! Go search your souls, and get your asses to confession six Sundays running and ten years beyond. It's lucky 'twas me came on this calamity and not the Bishop, me and not the sweet morsel nuns from just beyond Meynooth, me and not the child innocents from yonder school. Doone, pull up your socks!"

"They're pulled!" said Doone.

"For one last time, out!" And the men might have scattered but they held to their bikes in deliriums of terror and could only listen.

"Will you tell me now," intoned the priest, one eye shut to take aim, the other wide to fix the target, "what, what in hell are you *up* to?"

"Drowning, your lordship, your honor, your reverence."

And this Doone almost did.

Until the monsignor was gone, that is.

When he heard the holy bike ricket away over the hill, Doone still stood like a chopfallen Lazarus to survey his possible ruination.

But at last he called across the boggy field with a strange frail but growing-more-triumphant-by-the-minute voice:

"Is he gone?"

"He is, Doone," said Finn.

"Then look upon me," said Doone.

All looked, then stared, then gaped their mouths.

"You are not *sinking*," gasped Nolan.

"You have not *sunk*," added Riordan.

"I have *not!*" Doone stomped his foot as if to test, then, secure, he lowered his voice for fear that the priest, though gone, might catch the echo.

"And why not?" he asked the heavens.

"*Why*, Doone?" was the chorus.

"Because I distilled the rumors and cadged the notions that once on a time, a hundred years back, on this very spot once stood—"

He paused for the drama, then finished the act:

"A church!"

"A church?"

"Good Roman rock on uncertain Irish soil! The beauty of it distilled faith. But the weight of it sank its cornerstone. *The priests fled and left* the structure, altar and all, so it's on that firm foundation that Doone, your sprinter, holds still. I stand *above* ground!"

"It's a revelation you've made!" Finn exclaimed.

"I have! And it is here we shall conjugate our verbs and revive our faith in women in all futures, near and far," announced Doone, way out there on the rainy moss. "But just in case .."

"In case?"

Doone waved over beyond them.

The men, straddling their bikes, turned.

And on a rise, unseen heretofore, but now half revealed to the sight, some hundred feet away, there appeared two women, not transfigured rose gardens, no, but their homely glances somehow turned fine by night and circumstance.

Short women they were. Not Irish-short but circus-short, carnival-size.

"Midgets!" exclaimed Finn.

"From the vaudeville in Dublin last week!" admitted Doone, out in the bog. "And both weighing half again less than me, should the church roof below suddenly lose its architectural roots and douse the bunch!"

Doone whistled and waved. The tiny maids, the little women, came on the run.

When they reached Doone and did not vanish, Doone called to the mob, "Will you give up your bikes and join the dance?"

There was a mass movement.

"Hold it!" cried Doone. "One at a time. We don't want to meet back at the pub at midnight—"

"And find someone *missing?*" asked Finn.

Virgin Resusitas

She sounded crazy with joy on the phone. I had to calm her down.

"Helen," I said, "take it easy. What's going on?"

"The greatest news. You must come over, now, right now."

"This is Thursday, Helen. I don't usually see you on Thursdays. Tuesdays were always it."

"It can't wait, it's too wonderful."

"Can't you tell me over the phone?"

"It's too personal. I hate saying personal things on the phone. Are you *that* busy?"

"No, I just finished up some letters."

"Well then, come and celebrate with me."

"This had better be good," I said.

"Wait till you hear. Run."

I hung up slowly and walked slowly to put on my coat and reach for my courage. There was a feeling of doom waiting outside my door. I plowed through it, made it to my car, and drove through a self-imposed silence, with an occasional curse, to Helen's apartment across town. I hesitated at knocking on her door, but it sprang open, surprising me. The look on Helen's face was so wild I thought she had come off her hinges.

"Don't just stand there," she cried. "Come in."

"It's not Tuesday, Helen."

"And never will be *again!*" she laughed.

My stomach turned to lead. I let her pull me by the elbow, lead me in, sit me down, then she whirled through the room finding wine and filling glasses. She held one out to me. I only stared at it.

"Drink," she said.

"I have a feeling it won't do any good."

"Look at me! *I'm* drinking! It's a celebration!"

"Every time you've ever used that word, part of the continent falls off into space. Here goes. What am I celebrating?"

I sipped and she touched my glass, indicating I should finish it so it could be refilled.

"Sit down, Helen. You make me nervous standing there."

"Well." She finished her glass and refilled both and sat down with a great exhalation of joy. "You'll never guess."

"I'm trying hard not to."

"Hold on to your hat. I've joined the Church."

"You—what church?" I stammered.

"Good grief! There's only *one!*"

"You have a lot of Mormon friends, and a few Lutherans on the side . . ."

"My God," she cried. "Catholic, of course."

"Since when have you liked Catholics? I thought you were raised in an Orange family, family from Cork, *laughed* at the Pope!"

"Silly. That was then, this is now. I am certified."

"Give me that bottle." I downed my second wine and refilled and shook my head. "Now, give me that again. Slowly."

"I've just come from Father Reilly's down the street."

"who—?"

"He's the head priest at St. Ignatius. He's been preparing me, you know, instruction, the last month or so."

I fell back in my chair and peered into my empty glass. "Is *that* why I didn't see you last week?"

She nodded vigorously, beaming.

"Or the week before or the week before *that?*"

Again a wild nodding agreement, plus a burst of laughter.

"This Father Kelly—"

"Reilly."

"Reilly, Father. Where did you meet him?"

"I didn't exactly meet him." She glanced at the ceiling. I looked up to see what was there. She saw me looking and glanced back down.

"Well, bumped into him, then," I inquired.

"I—well, hell. I made an *appointment*."

"A fallen-away-long-time-ago Cork-energized *Baptist* maid?"

"Don't get in an uproar."

"This is not an uproar. It's a former lover trying to comprehend . . ."

"You're *not* a former lover!"

She reached out to touch my shoulder. I looked at her hand and it fell away.

"What am I, then? An *almost* former?"

"Don't *say* that."

"Maybe I should let *you* say it. I can see it in your mouth."

She licked her lips as if to erase the look.

"How long ago did you meet, bump, make an appointment with Reilly?"

"*Father* Reilly. I dunno."

"Yes, you do. An appointment like that is a day that will live in infamy, or that's how I see it."

"Don't jump to conclusions."

"No jumps. Just hopping mad. Or *will* be if you don't come clean."

"Is this supposed to be my second confession of the day?" She blinked.

"My God," I said, feeling an invisible stomach punch. "So that's it! You came plunging out of the confessional an hour ago and the first person you called with the lunatic news—"

"I didn't *plunge* out!"

"No, I suppose not. How long were you cooped up in there?"

"Not long."

"*How* long?"

"Half an hour. An hour."

"Is Reilly, Father Reilly taking a nap now? He *must*. How many dozen years of sin did you unload? Did he slip a word in edgewise? Was God mentioned?"

"Don't joke."

"Did that *sound* like a joke? So you trapped him for an hour, did you? I bet he's chugalugging the altar wine right now."

"Stop it!" she cried, and there were tears in her eyes. "I call you with good news and you spoil it."

"How long ago did you make this appointment with Reilly, *Father*, that is? Your first appointment, for instruction. It must take weeks or months. He does most of the talking, right, at the start?"

"Most."

"I'd just like to know the date is all. Is that asking too much?"

"January fifteenth, a Tuesday. Four o'clock."

I figured swiftly, sending my mind back. "Ah, yes," I said, and closed my eyes.

"Ah, yes, what?" She leaned forward.

"That was the last Tuesday, the final time you asked me to marry you."

"Was it?"

"Asked me to leave my wife and kids and marry you, yes."

"I don't recall."

"Yes, you do. And you recall my answer. No. Just

like the dozen other times. No. So you picked up the phone and called Reilly."

"It wasn't all that quick."

"No? Did you wait half an hour, forty-five minutes?"

She lowered her eyes. "An hour, maybe two."

"Let's say an hour and a half, split the difference, and he had the time and you went over. A glad hand for the Baptist. Jesus, Mary, and Moses. Give me that."

I grabbed the wine back and did away with my third glass.

"Shoot," I said, looking up at her.

"That's all," she said, simply.

"You mean you brought me all the way over here just to tell me you are a practicing Catholic and have unloaded fifteen years of accumulated guilt?"

"Well—"

"I'm waiting for the other shoe to drop."

"Shoe?"

"That glass slipper I slipped on your foot three years back, the one that fit so perfectly. When it drops it'll break. I'll be on my feet till midnight picking up the pieces."

"You're not going to cry, are you?" She leaned forward, peering into my face.

"Yes, no. I haven't decided. If I did, would you put me over your shoulder, like you always do, and burp me? You always did that and made me well. Now what?"

"You said it all."

"How come I thought I was waiting for you to say it? Say it."

"The priest said—"

"I don't want to hear what the priest said. Don't blame him. What do *you* say?"

"The priest said," she went on, as if not hearing me, "since I am now a member of his flock, that from now on I mustn't have anything to do with married men."

"What about *un*married men, what did he say about those?"

"We only talked 'married.' "

"Now we've almost got it. What you are saying is that . . ." I figured swiftly, counting back. "Is that the Tuesday before the Tuesday before last was our last tossing-the-blanket pillow fight?"

"I guess so," she said, miserably.

"You *guess* so?"

"Yes," she said.

"And I'm not to see you again?"

"We can have lunch—"

"Lunch, after all those midnight banquets and delicatessen-appetite-inducing brunches and made-in-heaven snacks?"

"Don't exaggerate."

"Exaggerate? Hell, I've lived inside a tornado for three incredible years and never touched ground. There wasn't a hair of my body that didn't throw sparks if you touched me. I no sooner got out your door with the sun going down every Tuesday than I wanted to charge back in and rip the paper off the walls, crying

your name. Exaggerate? Exaggerate! Call the mad-
house. Rent me a room!"

"You'll get over it," she said, lamely.

"Around about next July, maybe August. By Halloween I'll be a basket case . . . So from now on, Helen,
you'll be seeing this Reilly, this father, this priest?"

"I don't like you putting it that way."

"He'll be instructing you every Tuesday afternoon,
right as rain, on the nose? Well, will he or *won't* he?"

"Yes."

"My God!" I got up and walked around, talking to
the walls. "What a plot for a book, a movie, a TV sit-
com. Woman, lacking courage, no guts, figures amazingly clever way to ditch her boyfriend. Can't just say,
Out, go, be gone. No. Can't say, It's over, it was nice
but it's over. No, sir. So she takes instruction and gets
religion and uses the religion to call a halt and regain
her virginity."

"That's not the way it was."

"You mean to say you just happened to get religion
and once you were inoculated it suddenly struck you
to call the Goodwill to come get me?"

"I never—"

"Yes, you did. And it's a perfect out. There's no
way around it. I'm trapped. My hands are tied. If I
forced you to love me now, you'd be sinning against
Reilly's good advice. Lord, what a situation!"

I sat down again.

"Did you mention my name?"

"Not your *name*, no . . ."

"But you did talk about me, right? Hours and hours?"

"Ten minutes, maybe fifteen."

"How I was good at this and that and you couldn't bear to live without me?"

"I'm living without you now and free as a bird!"

"I can tell by that fake laugh."

"It's not fake. You just don't want to *hear* it."

"Continue."

"What?"

"Go on with your grocery list."

"That's all."

She laced and unlaced her fingers.

"Well, one other thing . . ."

"What?"

She took out a tissue and blew her nose.

"Every time we made love, it hurt."

"What?" I cried, stunned.

"It did," she said, not looking at me. "From the start. Always."

"You mean to say," I gasped, "that every time we took a trip to the moon on gossamer wings, it was *painful?*"

"Yes."

"And all those shouts and cries of joy were cover-ups for your discomfort?"

"Yes."

"All those *years*, all those *hours*, why didn't you *tell* me?"

"I didn't want to make you unhappy."

"Good God!" I cried.

And then, "I don't believe you."

"It's true."

"I don't believe you," I said, fighting to control my breath. "It was too wonderful, it was too great, it was—no, no, you couldn't have lied each time, every time." I stopped and stared at her. "You're making this up to tie it in with this Father Reilly thing. That's it, isn't it?"

"Honest to God—"

"Watch it. You're certified now! That's *blasphemy!*"

"Just *'honest'* then. No lie."

I lapsed back into hot confusion.

There was a long silence.

"We could still have lunch," she said. "Someday."

"No thanks. I couldn't stand it. To see you and have to sit across from you and not touch, oh, Lord! Where's my hat? Was I *wearing* one?"

I put my hand on the doorknob.

"Where are you going?" she cried.

I shook my head, eyes shut. "I don't know. Yes, I do. To join the Unitarian Church!"

"What?"

"Unitarians. *You* know."

"But you can't do *that!*"

"Why?"

"Because—"

"Because?"

"They never mention God or Jesus. They're embarrassed if you talk about them."

"Right."

"Which means, when I see you *I* wouldn't be able to mention God or Jesus."

"Right."

"You *wouldn't* join them!"

"No? You made the first move. Now it's mine. Checkmate."

I turned the doorknob and said:

"I'll call you next Tuesday, a last time. But if I do, don't ask me to marry you."

"Don't call," she said.

"Oh, love that I still dearly love," I said, "good-bye."

I went out and shut the door. Quietly.

Mr. Pale

"He's a very sick man."

"Where is he?"

"Up above on Deck C. I got him to bed."

The doctor sighed. "I came on this trip for a vacation. All right, all right. Excuse me," he said to his wife. He followed the private up through the ramps of the spaceship and the ship, in the few minutes while he did this, pushed itself on in red and yellow fire across space, a thousand miles a second.

"Here we are," said the orderly.

The doctor turned in at the portway and saw the man lying on the bunk, and the man was tall and his flesh was sewed tight to his skull. The man was sick, and his lips fluted back in pain from his large, discolored teeth. His eyes were shadowed cups from which flickers of light peered, and his body was as thin as a skeleton. The color of his hands was that of snow. The doctor pulled up a magnetic chair and took the sick man's wrist.

"What seems to be the trouble?"

The sick man didn't speak for a moment, but only licked a colorless tongue over his sharp lips.

"I'm dying," he said, at last, and seemed to laugh.

"Nonsense, we'll fix you up, Mr. . . .?"

"Pale, to fit my complexion. Pale will do."

"Mr. Pale." This wrist was the coldest wrist he had ever touched in his life. It was like the hand of a body you pick up and tag in the hospital morgue. The pulse was gone from the cold wrist already. If it was there at all, it was so faint that the doctor's own fingertips, pulsing, covered it.

"It's bad, isn't it?" asked Mr. Pale.

The doctor said nothing but probed the bared chest of the dying man with his silver stethoscope.

There was a faint far clamor, a sigh, a musing upon distant things, heard in the stethoscope. It seemed almost to be a regretful wailing, a muted screaming of a million voices, instead of a heartbeat, a dark wind blowing in a dark space and the chest cold and the sound cold to the doctor's ears and to his own heart, which gave pause in hearing it.

"I was right, wasn't I?" said Mr. Pale.

The doctor nodded. "Perhaps you can tell me . . ."

"What caused it?" Mr. Pale closed his eyes smilingly over his colorlessness. "I haven't any food. I'm starving."

"We can fix that."

"No, no, you don't understand," whispered the man. "I barely made it to this rocket in time to get aboard. Oh, I was really healthy there for awhile, a few minutes ago."

The doctor turned to the orderly. "Delirious."

"No," said Mr. Pale, "no."

"What's going on here?" said a voice, and the captain stepped into the room. "Hello, who's this? I don't recall . . ."

"I'll save you the trouble," said Mr. Pale. "I'm not on the passenger list. I just came aboard."

"You couldn't have. We're ten million miles away from Earth."

Mr. Pale sighed. "I almost didn't make it. It took all my energy to catch you. If you'd been a little farther out . . ."

"A stowaway, pure and simple," said the captain. "And drunk, too, no doubt."

"A very sick man," said the doctor. "He can't be moved. I'll make a thorough examination . . ."

"You'll find nothing," said Mr. Pale, faintly, lying white and long and alone in the cot, "except I'm in need of food."

"We'll see about that," said the doctor, rolling up his sleeves.

An hour passed. The doctor sat back down on his magnetic chair. He was perspiring. "You're right. There's nothing wrong with you, except you're starved. How could you do this to yourself in a rich civilization like ours?"

"Oh, you'd be surprised," said the cold, thin, white man. His voice was a little breeze blowing ice through the room. "They took all my food away an hour or so ago. It was my own fault. You'll understand in a few minutes now. You see, I'm very very old. Some say a million years, some say a billion. I've lost count. I've been too busy to count."

Mad, thought the doctor, utterly mad.

Mr. Pale smiled weakly as if he had heard this thought. He shook his tired head and the dark pits of his eyes flickered. "No, no. No, no. Old, very old. And foolish. Earth was mine. I owned it. I kept it for myself. It nurtured me, even as I nurtured it. I lived well there, for a billion years, I lived high. And now here I am, in the name of all that's darkest, dying too. I never thought I could die. I never thought I could be killed, like everyone else. And now *I* know what the fear is, what it will be like to die. After a billion years I know, and it is frightening, for what will the universe be without me?"

"Just rest easily, now, we'll fix you up."

"No, no. No, no, there's nothing you can do. I overplayed my hand. I lived as I pleased. I started wars and stopped wars. But this time I went too far, and committed suicide, yes, I did. Go to the port there and look out." Mr. Pale was trembling, the trembling moved in his fingers and his lips. "Look out. Tell me what you see."

"Earth. The planet Earth, behind us."

"Wait just a moment, then," said Mr. Pale.

The doctor waited.

"Now," said Mr. Pale, softly. "It should happen about *now*."

A blind fire filled the sky.

The doctor cried out. "My God, my God, this is terrible!"

"What do you see?"

"Earth! It's caught fire. It's burning!"

"Yes," said Mr. Pale.

The fire crowded the universe with a dripping blue yellow flare. Earth blew itself into a thousand pieces and fell away into sparks and nothingness.

"Did you see?" said Mr. Pale.

"My God, my God." The doctor staggered and fell against the port, clawing at his heart and his face. He began to cry like a child.

"You see," said Mr. Pale, "what a fool I was. Too far. I went too far. I thought, What a feast. What a banquet. And now, and now, it's over."

The doctor slid down and sat on the floor, weeping. The ship moved in space. Down the corridors, faintly, you could hear running feet and stunned voices, and much weeping.

The sick man lay on his cot, saying nothing, shaking his head slowly back and forth, swallowing convulsively. After five minutes of trembling and weeping, the doctor gathered himself and crawled and then got to his feet and sat on the chair and looked at Mr. Pale who lay gaunt and long there, almost phosphorescent, and from the dying man came a thick smell of something very old and chilled and dead.

"Now do you see?" said Mr. Pale. "I didn't want it this way."

"Shut up."

"I wanted it to go on for another billion years, the high life, the picking and choosing. Oh, I was king."

"You're mad!"

"Everyone feared me. And now *I'm* afraid. For there's no one left to die. A handful on this ship. A few thousand left on Mars. That's why I'm trying to get there, to Mars, where I can live, if I make it. For in order for me to live, to be talked about, to have an existence, others must be alive to die, and when all the living ones are dead and no one is left to die, then Mr. Pale himself must die, and he most assuredly does not want that. For you see, life is a rare thing in the universe. Only Earth lived, and only I lived there because of the living men. But now I'm so weak, so weak. I can't move. You must help me."

"Mad, mad!"

"It's another two days to Mars," said Mr. Pale, thinking it through, his hands collapsed at his sides. "In that time you must feed me. I can't move or I would tend myself. Oh, an hour ago, I had great power, think of the power I took from so much and so many dying at once. But the effort of reaching this ship dispersed the power, and the power is self-limiting. For now I have no reason to live, except you, and your wife, and the twenty other passengers and crew, and those few on Mars. My incentive, you see, weakens, weakens . . ." His voice trailed off into a sigh. And then, after swallowing, he went on, "Have you wondered, Doctor, why the death rate on Mars in the six months since you established bases there has been nil? I can't be everywhere. I was born on Earth on the same day as life was born. And I've waited all these years to move on out into the star system. I should have gone months ago, but I put it off, and now, I'm sorry. What a fool, what a greedy fool."

The doctor stood up, stiffening and pulling back. He clawed at the wall. "You're out of your head."

"Am I? Look out the port again at what's left of Earth."

"I won't listen to you."

"You must help me. You must decide quickly. I want the captain. He must come to me first. A transfusion, you might call it. And then the various passengers, one by one, just to keep me on the edge, to keep me alive. And then, of course, perhaps even you, or your wife. You don't want to live forever, do you? That's what would happen if you let me die."

"You're raving."

"Do you dare believe I am raving? Can you take that chance? If I die, all of you would be immortal. That's what man's always wanted, isn't it? To live forever. But I tell you, it would be insanity, one day like another, and think of the immense burden of memory! Think! Consider."

The doctor stood across the room with his back to the wall, in shadow.

Mr. Pale whispered, "Better take me up on this. Bet-

235

ter die when you have the chance than live on for a million billion years. Believe me. I *know.* I'm almost glad to die. Almost, but not quite. Self-preservation. Well?"

The doctor was at the door. "I don't believe you."

"Don't go," murmured Mr. Pale. "You'll regret it."

"You're lying."

"Don't let me die . . ." The voice was so far away now, the lips barely moved. "Please don't let me die. You need me. All life needs me to make life worthwhile, to give it value, to give it contrast. Don't . . ."

Mr. Pale was thinner and smaller and now the flesh seemed to melt faster. "No," he sighed. "No . . ." said the wind behind the hard yellowed teeth. "Please . . ." The deep-socketed eyes fixed themselves in a stare at the ceiling.

The doctor crashed out the door and slammed it and bolted it tight. He lay against it, weeping again, and through the ship he could see the people standing in groups staring back at the empty space where Earth had been. He heard cursing and wailing. He walked unsteadily and in great unreality for an hour through the ship's corridors until he reached the captain.

"Captain, no one is to enter that room where the dying man is. He has a plague. Incurable. Quite insane. He'll be dead within the hour. Have the room welded shut."

"What?" said the captain. "Oh, yes, yes. I'll attend to it. I will. Did you see? See Earth go?"

"I saw it."

They walked numbly away from each other. The doctor sat down beside his wife who did not recognize him for a moment until he put his arm around her.

"Don't cry," he said. "Don't cry. Please don't cry."

Her shoulders shook. He held her very tightly, his eyes clenched in on the trembling in his own body. They sat this way for several hours.

"Don't cry," he said. "Think of something else. Forget Earth. Think about Mars, think about the future."

They sat back in their seats with vacant faces. He lit a cigarette and could not taste it, and passed it to her and lit another for himself. "How would you like to be married to me for another ten million years?" he asked.

"Oh, I'd like that," she cried out, turning to him and seizing his arm in her own, fiercely wrapping it to her. "I'd like that very much!"

"*Would* you?" he said.

That Bird That Comes
Out of the Clock

"You remember people by the things they do," said Mrs. Coles, "rather than by how their face looks or what their tongues say, while they're doing what they do. Now, if you ask me, this new woman across the street and down two houses, Kit Random, that her name? She is, to put it mildly, a woman of action."

Everybody on the porch looked.

There was Kit Random with a flower in her hand, in the garden. There she was drawing the shade in the upstairs window. There fanning herself in the cool dark doorway of her front porch. There making mosquito-delicate etchings under a lemon-colored hurricane lamp at night. There throwing clay on a potter's wheel early mornings, singing in a loud clear-water voice. There shoving dozens of ashtrays into a kiln she had built of bricks. And again you saw her baking pies for God knows who in her empty house and setting them to cool in windowsills so men on the far side of the street crossed over, noses lifted, passing. Then, when the sun set, she swung in a great hairy hemp swing she had tied to the vast oak in her backyard. About nine at night, carrying a crank phonograph like the white Victrola dog in her hands, she'd come out, crank up the machine, put on a record, and swing in the giant child's swing, being a poor butterfly or a red red robin hop hop hopping along.

"Yes," said Mrs. Tiece. "She's either a very shrewd woman up to her feminine tricks or—" And here she debated a moment. "She's that little bird that comes out of the clock . . . that little bird that comes out of the clock . . ."

All along the street, women tapped their heads with knowing forefingers and looked over her fence, like women peering over a cliff, ready to scream at how high up they were, but all they saw was the nine o'clock backyard, as dim as a cavern full of sprouting leaves, starred with flowers, the phonograph hissing and clearing its throat before launching itself down the grooves of "June Night" or "Poor Butterfly." And there, with the regularity of an unseen, but nevertheless ticking pendulum, back and forth, one arm up to cushion her pink little pillow of cheek, sighing quietly to herself, was Kit Random, swinging in her swing, in rhythm to the things the phonograph said were poor about the butterfly or nice about the June night.

"Where's she from?"

"No one knows."

"What's she doing here?"

"No one knows."

"How long's she going to stay?"

"Go ask *her!*"

The facts were simple enough. The house had been unrented for a year, and then it was rented. One April afternoon a large moving van drove up and two men ran in and out, like Keystone Cops, the nearest thing to collision, but always skidding around each other with a fast-action routine of clocks, lamps, chairs, tables, and urns. In what seemed a minute they had driven away. The house was left alone, unoccupied. Mrs. Coles had walked by it four times and peered in, and only seen that the moving men had hung the pictures, spread the rugs, adjusted the furniture, and made everything womanly and neat before they had come running out to go away. There was the nest, waiting for the bird.

And promptly at seven o'clock, just after supper, when everyone could see her, up drove Kit Random in a yellow taxicab, and moved into the waiting house, alone.

"Where's Mr. Random?" asked everyone.

"There isn't any."

"Divorced, that's what she is, divorced. Or maybe her husband dead. A widow, that's better. Poor thing."

But there was Kit Random smiling at every window and every porch, on her way to buy T-bone steaks, tomato soup, and dishwater soap, not looking tired, not looking sad, not looking alone, but looking as if a company of clowns lived with her by day, and a handsome film gentleman with a waxed mustache by night.

"But no one ever comes *near* her place. At first I thought, well . . ." Mrs. Coles hesitated. "A woman living alone. Oh, *you* know. But there hasn't even been an iceman close. So there's only one thing to figure: as someone said, she's that bird that comes out of the clock. Four times an hour," she added.

At that very moment, Miss Kit Random called to the ladies, now her voice up in the soft green trees, now up in the blue sky on the opposite side of the yard. "Ladies?"

Their heads twisted. Their ears prickled.

"Ladies," called Miss Kit Random, in flight. "I've come to get me a man. That's *it*, ladies!"

All the ladies backed off to their houses.

It was the next afternoon that they found Mr. Tiece over in Miss Kit Random's front yard playing marbles. Mrs. Tiece put up with it for about two minutes and thirty-five seconds and then came across the street, almost on roller skates.

"Well, what're we *doing*?" she demanded of the two hunched-down figures.

"Just a moment." A marble spun bright under Henry Tiece's thumb. Other marbles spat against each other and clacked away.

"Looks like you won," said Kit Random. "You're darned good at mibs, Hank."

"It's been years." Mr. Tiece glanced uneasily at his

wife's ankle. She had veins like runners of light blue ink on her legs. It looked like the map of Illinois. Desplaines River here, Mississippi there. He scanned up as far as Rock Island when his wife said:

"Isn't it a little strange playing marbles?"

"Strange *thing?*" Mr. Tiece dusted himself off. "I *won!*"

"What you going to do with them marbles?"

"It's not what I *do* with them, it's victory that *counts.*"

Mrs. Tiece glared at them as if they were toadstools. "Thanks for giving Henry a game."

"Anytime, Clara, anytime," said Kit Random.

"I'll just leave these with you." Henry handed over the marbles hastily. "No room at my place."

"I want you to cut the grass," said Mrs. Tiece.

He and Mrs. Tiece sort of walked across the street, he not looking at her, she keeping up so he walked faster, she increasing her pace, he increasing his until they almost leaped up the porch steps. He ran to the door first, she tailed after. The door-slam was such that birds abandoned their nests three houses down.

The next incident occurred exactly an hour later. Mr. Tiece was out mowing the lawn, his eyes fixed to the rotating machine and each of one hundred clover blossoms, all with tiny heads like Mrs. Tiece. He cut furiously east, west, north, south, perspiring and wiping his brow as Mrs. Tiece shouted, "Don't miss the outer drive! And down the middle, you missed a ridge. Watch that stone, you'll ruin the cutter!"

Exactly at two o'clock two trucks drove up in front of Miss Kit Random's house and a couple of laborers began tossing dirt out of Miss Random's lawn. By four o'clock they poured a solid sheet of cement all over Miss Random's yard.

At five o'clock, the truck drove off, taking Miss Kit Random's lawn with it, at which point Miss Kit Random waved over to Mr. Tiece. "Won't have to mow this lawn again for a couple years I guess!" She laughed.

Mr. Tiece started to laugh back when he sensed someone hidden inside the dark screen door. Mr. Tiece ducked inside. This time, with the door-slam, two potted geraniums fell off the porch rail.

"The nerve of that woman."

"Did it on purpose."

"Trying to make us look like slave drivers. Putting cement over her lawn. Giving Mr. Tiece ideas. Well, we're not cementing *our* lawn, he'll cut it every week, or my name isn't Clara Moon Tiece!"

The three ladies snorted over their knitting.

"Seems like some sort of plot to me," said Mrs. Coles. "Look at her backyard, a jungle, nothing in its right place."

"Tell us about the marble game again, Clara."

"Good grief. There he was down on his knees, both laughing. I—wait a minute. You *hear* something?"

It was twilight, just after supper, and the three

women on Mrs. Coles' porch right next door. "That Clock Woman's out in her backyard again, laughing."

"Swinging in her swing?"

"Listen. Shh!"

"I haven't done this in *years!*" a man's voice laughed. "Always wanted to, but folks think you're crazy! Hey!"

"Who's that?" cried Mrs. Coles.

The three women clapped their hands to their thumping chests and lurched to the far end of the porch, panicked excursioners on a sinking ship.

"Here you go!" cried Kit Random, giving a push.

And there in her backyard going up in the green leaves one way, then down and swooping up on the other, in the twilight air was a laughing man.

"Don't that sound a bit like your Mr. Coles?" one of the ladies wondered.

"The idea!"

"Oh, Fanny."

"The *idea!*"

"Oh, Fanny, go to sleep," said Mr. Coles in bed. The room was warm and dark. She sat like a great lump of ice cream glowing in the dim room at eleven o'clock.

"Ought to be run out of town."

"Oh, for God's sake." He punched his pillow. "It was just a backyard swing, haven't swung in years. Big damn swing, plenty hefty to ride a man. You left me to finish the dishes so you could go out and blather with those hens, I went to toss out the garbage and there she was swinging in the swing and I said how nice it looked and she said did I want to try? So, by God, I just climbed over to pump myself up for a ride."

"And cackling like an idiot rooster."

"Not cackling, damn it, but laughing. I wasn't pinching her behind, was I?" He punched his pillow twice more and rolled over.

In his sleep she heard him mumble, "Best damn swing I ever swung," which set her off into a new fit of weeping.

It remained only for Mr. Clements to jump off the cliff the next afternoon. Mrs. Clements found him blowing bubbles on Miss Kit Random's back garden wall, discussing the formation, clarity, and coloration of same with her. Her phonograph was warbling an old tune from World War I sung by the Knickerbocker Quartet titled "The Worst Is Yet to Come." Mrs. Clements acted out the song's words by grabbing Mr. Clements by the ear and lugging him off.

"That woman's yard," said Mrs. Coles, Mrs. Clements, and Mrs. Tiece, "is, as of this hour, day, and minute, forbidden territory."

"Yes, dear," said Mr. Coles, Mr. Clements, and Mr. Tiece.

"You are not to say good morning or good night, Nurse, to her," said Mrs. Coles, Mrs. Clements, and Mrs. Tiece.

"Of course not, dear," said the husbands behind their newspapers.

"You *hear* me?"

"Yes, sweetheart," came the chorus.

From then on Mr. Coles, Mr. Clements, and Mr. Tiece could be seen mowing lawns, fixing lights, trimming hedges, painting doors, cleaning windows, washing dishes, digging bulbs, watering trees, fertilizing flowers, rushing to work, rushing back, bending, flexing, running, pausing, reaching, busy at a thousand and one tasks with a thousand and one perspirations.

Whereas in Kit Random's clocks had stopped, flowers died or went insane with abundance. Doorknobs fell off if you tapped them, trees shed their leaves in mid-summer for lack of water; paint flaked from doors, and the electric light-system, burnt out, was replaced with candles rammed in wine jugs: a paradise of neglect, a beautiful chaos.

Somewhere along the line Mrs. Coles, Mrs. Clements and Mrs. Tiece were stunned at the pure unadulterated nerve of Kit Random shoving notes in their mailboxes during the night, inviting them to come by at four next day for poisoned tea.

They absolutely refused.

And *went*.

Kit Random poured them all the orange pekoe which was her favorite and then sat back, smiling.

"It was nice of you ladies to come," she said.

The ladies nodded grimly.

"There's a lot for us to talk about," she added.

The ladies waited stone-cold, leaning toward the door.

"I feel you don't understand me at all," said Kit Random. "I feel I must explain everything."

They waited.

"I'm a maiden lady with a private income."

"Looks *suspiciously* private to me," observed Mrs. Tiece.

"Suspiciously," echoed Mrs. Cole.

Mrs. Clements was about to toss her teabag in the cup when Kit Random uncorked a laugh.

"I can see no matter what I say you'll add sugar lumps and stir your spoons so loud I can't be heard."

"Try us," said Mrs. Tiece.

Kit Random reached over to pick up a shiny brass tube and twist it.

"What's *that?*" asked all three at once and then covered their mouths as if embarrassed not one of them had said anything original.

"One of them toy kaleidoscopes." Kit Random shut one eye to squint through the odd-colored shards. "Right now I'm examining your gizzards. Know what I *find?*"

"How could we possibly care?" cried Mrs. Clements. The others nodded at her snappy retort.

"I see a solid potato." Kit Random fixed the device to X-ray Mrs. Tiece, then moved to the others. "A rutabaga and a nice round turnip. No innards, stomach, spleen, or heart. I've listened. No pulse, just solid flesh, fit to burst your corsets. And your tongues? Not connected to your cerebral cortex . . ."

"Our cerebral *what?*" cried Mrs. Tiece, offended.

"*Cortex*. Not as off-color as it sounds. And I've made a brave decision. Don't get up."

The three women squirmed in their chairs and Kit Random said:

"I'm going to take your husbands, one by one. I'm going to, in the words of the old song, steal their hearts away. Or what's there if you left any on the plate. I've decided that flimsy-whimsy as I am, I'll be a darn sight better midnight or high-noon companion than all of you in a bunch. Don't speak, don't leave. I'm almost done. There's nothing you can do to stop me. Oh, yes, one thing. Love these fine men. But I don't think it crossed your minds, it's so long ago. Look at their faces. See how they crush their straw hats down hard over their ears and grind their teeth in their sleep. Heck, I can hear it way over *here!* And make fists when they walk, with no one to hit. So stand back, don't even try to interfere. And how will I do it? With cribbage and dead man's poker, and miniature golf in my garden, I'll pull flowers to sink par-three holes. Then there's blackjack, dominoes, checkers, chess, beer and ice cream, hot dogs noons, hamburgers midnights, phonograph moonlight dancing, fresh beds, clean linens, singing in the shower allowed, litter all week, clean up on Sundays, grow a mustache or beard, go barefoot at croquet. When the beer stops, gin stays. Hold on! Sit!"

Kit Random lectured on:

"I can see what you think, you got faces like sieves. No, I'm not the Hoor of Babylon, nor the Tart from Le Petit Trianon, which, incidentally, is *not* a movie-house.

I am a traveling Jungle Gym, first cousin to a sideshow, never a beauty, almost a freak. But one day years back, I decided not to make *one* man sad but a *handful* happy! I found I was trying to win all the time, which is an error beyond most women's imagination. If you make a man lose all the time, hell, he'll go play golf or handball and lose *right*. At least he can add it *up!* So I started out, two years in Placerville, three in Tallahassee and Kankakee until I ran out of steam or my rolling stock rusted. What was my great secret? Not playing Parcheesi, or Uncle Wiggily says jump back three hops to the henhouse, no. It was *losing*. Don't you *see?* I learned how to cheat and lose. Men *like* that. They know what you're up to, sure, but pretend not to notice and the more you lose the more they love. Next thing you know you got 'em bound head and foot with just plain old self-destruction pinochle or I'm-dead-send-flowers hopscotch. You can get a man to jump rope if you convince him he's the greatest jumper since the Indian rope trick. So you go on losing and find you've won all along as the men tip their hat to you at breakfast, put down the stock-market quotes and *talk!*

"Stop fidgeting! I'm almost out of gas. Will you get your halfway loved ones back? Mebbe. Mebbe not. A year from now I'll check to see if you've watched and learned from my show-and-tell. I'll give you the loan of those lost but now found souls and once a year after that bus back through to see if you're losing proper in order to learn to laugh. Meanwhile, there's nothing you can do, starting this very second. Now, consider I've just fired off a gun. Go home. Bake pies. Make meatballs. But it won't work. The pies will fall flat and the meatballs? Dead on arrival. Because you arm-wrestle them to the table and spoil men's appetites. And don't lock your doors. Let the poor beasts run. Like you've excused."

"We've just begun to fight!" cried all three and then, confused at their echoes, almost fell down the porch stairs.

Well, that was the true end. There was no war, not even a battle or half a skirmish. Every time the ladies glanced around they found empty rooms and quietly shut on tiptoes front doors.

But what really scalded the cat and killed the dog was when three strange men showed up half-seen in the twilight one late afternoon and caused the wives to pull back, double-lock their doors, and peer through their lace curtains.

"Okay, open up!" the three men cried.

And hearing voices from today's breakfast, the wives unlocked the doors to squint out.

"Henry Tiece?"

"Robert Joe Clements, what—?"

"William Ralph Cole, is that *you*?"

"Who the hell do you *think* it is!"

Their wives stood back to watch the almost hairless wonders pass.

"My God," said Mrs. Tiece.

"What?" said Mrs. Clements.

"What have you done to your hair?"

"Nothing," said all three husbands. "*She* did."

The wives circled their relatives by marriage.

"I didn't recognize you," gasped Mrs. Tiece.

"You weren't *supposed* to!"

And so said all the rest.

Adding, "How you *like* it?"

"It's not the man I married," they said.

"Damn tootin'!"

And at last, almost in chorus, though in separate houses:

"You going to change your *name* to fit the *haircut?*"

The last night of the month, Mr. Tiece was found in his upper-stairs bedroom packing a grip. Mrs. Tiece clutched a doorknob and held on. "Where you going?"

"Business."

"Where?"

"A ways."

"Going to be gone long?"

"Hard to say," he said, packing a shirt.

"Two days?" she asked.

"Maybe."

"Three days?"

"Where's my blue necktie? The one with the white mice on it."

"I never did like that necktie."

"Would you mind finding the blue necktie with the white mice on it for me?"

She found it.

"Thank you." He knotted it, watching himself in the

mirror. He brushed his hair and grimaced to see if he had brushed his teeth.

"*Four* days?" she asked.

"In all probability," he said.

"A *week* then?" She smiled wildly.

"You can almost bet on it," he said, examining his fingernails.

"Eat good meals now, not just quick sandwiches."

"I promise."

"Get plenty of sleep!"

"I'll get plenty of sleep."

"And be sure to phone every night. Have you got your stomach pills with you?"

"Won't need the stomach pills."

"You've *always* needed the stomach pills." She ran to fetch them. "Now, you just take these stomach pills."

He took and put them in his pocket. He picked up his two suitcases.

"And be sure and call me every night," she said.

He went downstairs with her after.

"And don't sit in any draughts."

He kissed her on the brow, opened the front door, went out, shut the door.

At almost the same instant, so it couldn't have been coincidence, Mr. Cole and Mr. Clements plunged, blind with life, off their front porches, risking broken legs or ankles to be free, and raced out to mid-street where they all but collided with Mr. Tiece.

They glanced at each other's faces and luggage and in reverberative echoes cried:

"Where're you going?"

"What's *that?*"

"My suitcase."

"My valise."

"My overnight case!"

"Do you realize this is the first time we've met in the middle of the street since Halloween twenty years ago?"

"Hell, this *is* Halloween!"

"Yeah! For what? Trick or treat?"

"Let's go see!"

And unerringly, with no chart, map, or menu, they turned with military abruptness and headlong sparked Kit Random's yardwide cement with their heels.

In the next week the sounds that abounded in Kit Random's abode might as well have been a saloon bowling alley. In just a handful of days, three various husbands visited at nine, ten, then ten after midnight, all with smiles like fake celluloid teeth hammered in place. The various wives checked their breaths for liquid sustenance but inhaled only tart doses of medicinal mint; the men wisely gargled mid-street before charging up to confront their fortress Europas.

As for the disdained and affronted wives, what culinary battlements did they rear up? What counterattacks ensued? And if small battles, or skirmishes, were fought, did victories follow?

The problem was that the husbands backing off and then headlong racing off let all of the hot air out of their houses. Only cold air remained, with three ladies delivered out of ice floes, refrigerated in their corsets, stony of glance and smile that in delivering victuals to the table caused frost to gather on the silverware. Hot roast beef became tough icebox leftovers two minutes from the oven. As the husbands glanced sheepishly up from their now more infrequent meals, they were greeted with displays of glass eyes like those in the optician's downtown window at midnight, and smiles that echoed fine porcelain when they opened and shut to let out what should have been laughter but was pure death rattle.

And then at last a night came when three dinners were laid on three tables by candlelight and no one came home and the candles snuffed out all by themselves, while across the way the sound of horseshoes clanking the stake or, if you really listened close, taffy being pulled, or Al Jolson singing, "Hard-hearted Hannah, the vamp of Savannah, I don't mean New Orleans," made the three wives count the cutlery, sharpen the knives, and drink Lydia Pinkham's Female Remedy long before the sun was over the yardarm.

But the last straw that broke the camel herd was the men ducking through a whirlaround garden sprinkler one untimely hot autumn night and, seeing their wives in a nearby window, they yelled, "Come on *in*, the water's *fine!*"

All three ladies gave the window a grand slam.

Which knocked *five* flowerpots off rails, skedaddled six cats, and had ten dogs howling at no-moon-in-the-sky halfway to dawn.

A Brief Afterword

In a long life I have never had a driver's license nor have I learned to drive. But some while back one night I dreamed that I was motoring along a country road with my inspirational Greek muse. She occupied the driver's seat while I occupied the passenger's place with a second, student's, wheel.

I could not help but notice that she was driving, serenely, with a clean white blindfold over her eyes, while her hands barely touched the steering wheel.

And as she drove she whispered notions, concepts, ideas, immense truths, fabulous lies, which I hastened to jot down.

A time finally came, however, when, curious, I reached over and nabbed the edge of her blindfold to peer beneath.

Her eyes, like the eyes of an ancient statue, were rounded pure white marble. Sightless, they stared at the road ahead, which caused me, in panic, to seize *my* wheel and almost run us off the road.

"No, no," she whispered. "Trust me. I know the way."

"But I don't," I cried.

"It's all right," she whispered. "You don't need to know. If you must touch the wheel, remember Hamlet's advice, 'Use all gently.' Close your eyes. Now, quietly, reach out."

I did. *She* did. "There, *see?*" she whispered. "We're almost there."

We arrived. And all of the tales in this new book were finished and done.

"Night Train to Babylon" is an almost true story; I was nearly tossed off a train some years ago for interfering with a three-card monte scam. After that, I shut my mouth.

"That Old Dog Lying in the Dust" is an absolutely accurate detailing of an encounter I had with a Mexican border-town one-ring circus when I was twenty-four years old. A dear-sad evening I will remember to the end of my life.

"Nothing Changes" was triggered when one afternoon in the twilight stacks of Acres of Books in Long Beach I came upon a series of 1905 high school annuals in which (impossible) the faces of my own 1938 school chums seemed to appear again and again. Rushing from the stacks, I wrote the story.

"If MGM Is Killed, Who Gets the Lion?" is another variation on an amusing reality. During World War II MGM was camouflaged as the Hughes Aircraft Company, while the Hughes Aircraft Company was disguised as MGM. How could I *not* describe the comedy?

Finally, "Driving Blind" is a remembrance of my acquaintance with a Human Fly who climbed building facades when I was twelve. You don't find heroes like that by the dozen.

As you can see, when the Muse speaks, I shut my eyes and listen. In Paris once, I touch-typed in a dark room, no lights, and wrote 150 pages of a novel in seventeen nights without seeing what I put down. If that isn't Driving Blind, what is?

Ray Bradbury
Los Angeles
April 8, 1997

Copyright Notices